D1555041

Praise for *Defense Budgeting for a Safer World*

"This collection is an important call to better marshal the national strength that sustains strategy. It is an urgent book by a distinguished group of nonpartisan contributors."

—**Henry Kissinger**, former secretary of state and national security advisor

"The United States' transition to great-power competition not only has shown us the complex and intricate relationship between all national components of power, including economics, politics, and the military, but also challenges us to deploy those components effectively and simultaneously. While our adversaries continue to shore up their capabilities to engage in destructive behaviors, the US continues to face challenges with passing a strong defense budget on time, securing the defense industrial base, and spurring innovation. *Defense Budgeting for a Safer World* offers a unique concentration of expert analysis to discuss how the United States can project power at any time and deter threats through a strong defense budget. A deep understanding and passion for the global economy, history, and armed forces are what we need to solve some of the most important security issues, and that is precisely what is offered in these pages."

—**US Representative Jimmy Panetta** (D-CA), member of the House Armed Services Committee, Budget Committee, and Ways and Means Committee

"Modern warfare demands modern, agile defense budgeting. This collection brilliantly tackles the challenge, highlighting important reforms that would revitalize America's defense industrial base, enhance lethality, and thereby strengthen deterrence. Written by the experts who know the system best, this book should be on the shelf or in the hand of every legislator and policymaker charged with preventing war in the near term and winning our new cold war with Communist China over the long term."

—**US Representative Mike Gallagher** (R-WI), chair of the House Armed Services Subcommittee on Cyber, IT, and Innovation and the Select Committee on US-China Strategic Competition, and member of the House Intelligence Committee

"There is broad agreement throughout government, think tanks, and industry that the defense budget and the process for developing and executing it are badly broken. Described for years as inflexible, ponderous, resistant to innovation, unpredictable, sclerotic, dysfunctional, misaligned, and more, the current budgeting process is viewed by many as endangering the US ability to deter or deal with growing threats—including, above all, China and Russia. *Defense Budgeting for a Safer World: The Experts Speak* provides an extraordinary and comprehensive road map for the reforms needed to address critical shortcomings in budgeting for the most important and expensive part of the federal government. Defining current and future threats, this volume starkly hammers home the reality that failure to reform the defense budgeting process truly undermines our military capabilities and imperils the nation. It offers a realistic menu of specific proposals to address the challenges. This book is a must-read for members of Congress, leaders of the executive branch, and all who care about our national security."

—**Robert M. Gates**, former secretary of defense (2006–11) and director of central intelligence (1991–93)

"A timely and exceptional collection of essays by key civilian and military leaders and thinkers on the major contemporary security challenges facing the United States and how to address them. *Defense Budgeting for a Safer World* is a tremendous source of invaluable insights, assessments, and policy proposals, and an extraordinary contribution to the most significant debates of the day."

—**General David Petraeus**, US Army (Ret.), former commander of the surge in Iraq, US Central Command, and NATO/US forces in Afghanistan, and former director of the CIA

"These are dangerous times, with the nation's values, interests, and security threatened around the globe and its economic well-being threatened by an unsustainable federal budget outlook. At the intersection lies the defense budget and America's military. Boskin, Rader, and Sridhar have assembled essays from an impressive group of experts that navigate a complex terrain that contains threat assessment, strategy, capabilities and technologies, personnel, and budgeting. *Defense Budgeting for a Safer World* is the ideal book for this moment in history."

—**Douglas Holtz-Eakin**, former director, Congressional Budget Office

DEFENSE BUDGETING
FOR A SAFER WORLD

 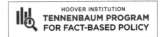

The Hoover Institution gratefully acknowledges Michael and Suzanne Tennenbaum for their endowment support of the Tennenbaum Program for Fact-Based Policy, this publication, and the conference on which it is based.

DEFENSE BUDGETING FOR A SAFER WORLD

The Experts Speak

EDITED BY Michael J. Boskin, John N. Rader, and Kiran Sridhar

With contributions from

General Keith Alexander
Michael J. Boskin
Captain Corey Braddock
Michael Brown
David S. C. Chu
James M. Cunningham
Commander Bart D'Angelo
Mackenzie Eaglen
Eric Fanning
Joseph H. Felter
Michèle Flournoy
Vishaal "V8" Hariprasad
Lieutenant Colonel James M. Harrington
Tim Kane
Christopher Kirchhoff
Ellen Lord
Oriana Skylar Mastro
Secretary Jim Mattis
Elaine McCusker

Michael McFaul
H.R. McMaster
Casey "Waldo" Miller
Admiral Mike Mullen
David L. Norquist
Michael O'Hanlon
Secretary Leon Panetta
John N. Rader
Secretary Condoleezza Rice
Admiral Gary Roughead
Nadia Schadlow
Jacquelyn Schneider
Raj Shah
Kiran Sridhar
Mac Thornberry
Mark R. Wilson
Roger Zakheim
Amy Zegart

HOOVER INSTITUTION PRESS
STANFORD UNIVERSITY | STANFORD, CALIFORNIA

hoover.org

Hoover Institution Press Publication No. 733

Hoover Institution at Leland Stanford Junior University, Stanford, California 94305-6003

First printing 2023
Simultaneous first paperback printing 2023
29 28 27 26 25 24 23   7 6 5 4 3 2 1

Manufactured in the United States of America
Printed on acid-free, archival-quality paper

Library of Congress Cataloging-in-Publication Data
Names: Rethinking Defense Budgeting (Conference) (2023 : Hoover Institution on War, Revolution, and Peace), author. | Boskin, Michael J., editor. | Rader, John N., editor. | Sridhar, Kiran, editor.
Title: Defense budgeting for a safer world : the experts speak / edited by Michael J. Boskin, John N. Rader, and Kiran Sridhar.
Other titles: Hoover Institution Press publication ; 733.
Description: Stanford, California : Hoover Institution Press, Stanford University, 2023. | Series: Hoover Institution Press publication ; no. 733 | Papers and presentations originally presented at the conference, Rethinking Defense Budgeting, held January 19, 2023 at the Hoover Institution. | Includes bibliographical references and index. | Summary: "Renowned experts on national security and the defense budget share ideas, perspectives, and solutions for budget reform to ensure its adequacy and flexibility for the current complex geopolitical environment"— Provided by publisher.
Identifiers: LCCN 2023028098 (print) | LCCN 2023028099 (ebook) | ISBN 9780817925949 (cloth) | ISBN 9780817925956 (paperback) | ISBN 9780817925963 (epub) | ISBN 9780817925987 (pdf)
Subjects: LCSH: National security—United States—Congresses. | United States—Armed Forces—Appropriations and expenditures—Congresses. | United States—Military policy—Congresses. | LCGFT: Conference papers and proceedings.
Classification: LCC UA23 .R4585 (print) | LCC UA23 (ebook) | DDC 355/.033573—dc23/eng/20230724
LC record available at https://lccn.loc.gov/2023028098
LC ebook record available at https://lccn.loc.gov/2023028099

Contents

Part 2: National Security Strategy

Part 3: Technology, Innovation, Procurement

Part 4: Personnel and Talent Recruitment and Retention

Part 5: Reform Recommendations and Budget Implications

Part 6: The View from Congress: National Security and the Budget

Foreword

America's role in protecting its interests and values in world affairs depends heavily on the combined excellence of its military, diplomatic, and intelligence capabilities. Together with its allies, America has been and can continue to be formidable in defending freedom and fostering prosperity and peace. Still, our ability to deter aggression and, if necessary, to defeat it requires—more than any other capability—a strong military and the willingness to deploy it. And the foundation on which that military capability is built is the defense budget. It supplies the resources to recruit, train, and equip our people in uniform; the weapons systems they need to defend us; and the ability to maintain a modern and technologically sophisticated defense industrial base that can sustain our armed forces.

The Hoover Institution's Defense Budget Working Group has collected a remarkable array of experts with deep knowledge and experience in the military, academe, think tanks, and private firms to analyze and interpret strengths, weaknesses, and options for reform in the defense budget and budgeting process. They have served as important military and civilian leaders of the highest rank and include prominent scholars who focus on these vital issues.

Democracies have typically underinvested in the military in peacetime. But given Russia's attack on Ukraine in 2022, China's growing assertiveness toward Taiwan and in the South China Sea, Iran's closing in on nuclear weapons capability, North Korea's ballistic missiles and nuclear programs, and the continuing threat of terrorism, the complexity and challenges facing the US military (as well as intelligence and diplomatic capabilities) are the greatest they have been since the end of the Cold War.

Defense Budgeting for a Safer World: The Experts Speak provides important perspectives on each of the key issues needed to understand the defense budget and determine important funding and procedural reforms to strengthen military capabilities. The authors and participants examine these reforms to improve the budget's adequacy, predictability, flexibility, and accountability, helping achieve a greater return on taxpayers' investment in military funding, as well as greater national security. The experts provide information, insights, ideas, and solutions on threats, strategy, procurement and innovation, personnel, reform proposals, and the view from Congress, which provides the funding and authorities that create the capabilities.

From its founding, the Hoover Institution has applied its world-renowned assets and programs—its fellowship of scholars, its Library & Archives, and the conferences it convenes—toward dealing with the issues of war and peace. I'm delighted to add this landmark volume to Hoover's contributions, and I commend it to all who wish to learn more about these issues, which are so vital to America's and the world's future.

Condoleezza Rice
Tad and Dianne Taube Director
Thomas and Barbara Stephenson Senior Fellow on Public Policy

Preface

The defense budget provides the resources and authorities for the nation's military to deter aggression and, if necessary, defeat aggressors. Its adequacy and composition reflect America's priorities in dealing with threats to our national security. Those threats are growing in potential severity and spreading throughout the world. Yet the defense budget has experienced wild fluctuations in recent years, from sequester starvation to sizable increases of uncertain duration. Worse yet, it has often been subject to significant delays beyond the start of the fiscal year.

Shortly before the COVID-19 lockdowns, a small group at the Hoover Institution began discussions about bringing together leading experts from the military, government, academe, and think tanks to debate and discuss ways to improve defense budgeting. The idea was to assemble leaders with backgrounds in national security, economics, budgeting, diplomacy, politics, and history, to share their ideas and perspectives. The topics to be covered included each of the major interrelated areas necessary to understand the strengths, weaknesses, challenges, and opportunities involved in reforming the defense budget, and not just within the context of the budget itself but also among the myriad processes that produce it. The goal was to better enable a more effective national security.

So the informal Hoover Institution working group on defense budget reform, under the auspices of Hoover's National Security Task Force, began a series of meetings at Hoover and in Washington, in person and via videoconferencing, with several dozen leading experts, to broaden and deepen our understanding of how the defense budget, budget process, and Pentagon operations affect preparedness and the ability to execute in the field. The National Security Task Force had been established with late former secretary of state George P. Shultz and Admiral (Ret.) James O. Ellis Jr. as cochairs.

The traditional formal name for Hoover is the Hoover Institution on War, Revolution and Peace, so it is not surprising that from its inception it has placed a high priority on national security studies and archival materials. For example, every year, Hoover brings together high-potential midcareer national security affairs fellows from every US military service plus the State Department to spend a year at Hoover, each working on an important project in between command postings. These fellows interact extensively with Hoover scholars in economics, international relations, political science, and other areas, as well as those directly concerned with national security. And Hoover scholars have always included former—and sometimes future—leaders from the military and diplomatic arenas.

In fact, shortly after World War II, President Harry S. Truman called on former president Herbert Hoover to lead a commission on the organization of the executive branch to suggest reforms, including for the Pentagon, as the nation and federal government transitioned from a wartime to peacetime posture. The commission's members included Dean Acheson and James Forrestal. The Hoover Commission recommendations, strongly endorsed by President Truman in a message to Congress, to grant "an adequate measure of authority and flexibility" and that the "ability of department heads to carry out their responsibilities not be impaired by numerous detailed statutory regulations" echo to this day.

A quarter century later, David Packard became deputy secretary of defense and, among other tasks, worked on streamlining the Pentagon with better business practices. Then under secretary of defense William J. Perry (later secretary of defense) spearheaded the use of advanced technologies for precision weaponry that would offset superior numbers of conventional weapons among US adversaries (e.g., Soviet tanks). In recent years, Hoover scholars have included multiple former secretaries of state, secretaries of defense, national security advisors, top military brass, and many who have served and continue to serve in other positions, each of whom has contributed enormously to Hoover's intellectual vitality. Many were also participants in the conference, "Rethinking Defense Budgeting," held at Hoover on January 19, 2023, where the papers and presentations collected in this volume were originally presented.

Defense Budgeting for a Safer World: The Experts Speak is the result of that collaboration. It brings together in one place analysis of, and ideas to strengthen, the nation's ability to deal with: the threats to our national security; a comprehensive national security strategy to guide it; military procurement, technology, and innovation; personnel, talent acquisition, and management; and reform options and recommendations and the politics of defense budgeting as viewed from Congress.

There are many opportunities and options for reform to strengthen the security of the United States and the world by combining efficiency actions, realignment of priorities, and greater flexibility with the additional spending necessary to do the job. Whether the nation has the political will to seize the best of them with the urgency required remains an open question. In the face of an ever-more dangerous world, our national security in the coming years depends on doing so. We hope the papers and presentations by leading experts in this volume will serve as a valuable resource in that effort.

Michael J. Boskin
John N. Rader
Kiran Sridhar
Stanford, California, 2023

Acknowledgments

A book such as this does not get into print—and a conference such as the one these papers and presentations reflect does not occur, let alone run smoothly—without the diligence of many talented people. We owe a debt of gratitude and would like to especially acknowledge the participants in the conference whose papers, presentations, and discussions are included in this volume. Each approached their role with seriousness and candor and contributed to a spirited and insightful series of panel discussions. Each also graciously spent time advising us as we planned the conference content. That the people who have been among the leaders responsible for our nation's security on the one hand, and its scholarly evaluation on the other, invested so much time and effort in this project was more than ample recompense for our work in bringing them together. Special thanks go to Hoover senior fellow John Cogan, who helped us conceptualize this effort from the beginning and was a valuable guiding hand throughout. The idea for and development of this project trace back to discussions between the late George P. Shultz and virtually all of those contributing to this book, as well as several cohorts of Hoover's national security affairs fellows and many others, among them Bill Perry, Brad Carson, Ash Carter, Jimmy Panetta, Colin Powell, Jim Ellis, Bill Inglee, and James M. Cunningham, each of whom generously shared their time, experience, knowledge, and insights.

This project benefited from the research assistance of two Hoover Institution student fellows, James Burns and Trenton Hicks, who ably combed through reams of Pentagon, Office of Management and Budget, and Congressional Budget Office data to help us tell a cogent story about the Department of Defense budget—and necessary reforms.

The staff at Hoover covered every detail of the conference and publication, from facilities and catering to sound, high-quality large-screen videoconferencing connectivity, substantive note-taking, audiovisual recording, transcription, copyediting, and book production, all superbly. Included in alphabetical order are: Barbara Arellano, Andrew Engle, Darin Evans, David Fedor, Lynette Garcia, Danica Michels Hodge, Claire Jaqua, Alison Law, Omar Marte, Jessica Martinez, LeAnn Racoma, Janet Smith, Aries Vitug, and Bill Walton. We would also like to thank Gayle Ronan for her superb copyediting expertise and Howie Severson for the engaging cover design.

Our deepest gratitude goes to Michael J. Boskin's executive, administrative, and research assistants, respectively, Kelli Nicholas, Jennie Tomasino, and Garrett Te Kolste, who helped ensure the conference and this volume proceeded on schedule and, limited only by academic norms and budget, with style.

Abbreviations

AI	artificial intelligence
AVF	all-volunteer force
CBO	Congressional Budget Office
CR	continuing resolution
CT	counterterrorism
DIB	Defense Innovation Board
DIUx	Defense Innovation Unit Experimental (later known as DIU)
DoD	Department of Defense
GAO	Government Accountability Office
HIMARS	high-mobility artillery rocket system
JADC2	Joint All-Domain Command and Control
NDAA	National Defense Authorization Act
NDS	National Defense Strategy
NSS	National Security Strategy
OCO	offensive cyber operations
OMB	Office of Management and Budget
OSD	Office of the Secretary of Defense
OTA	Other Transaction Authority
PLA	People's Liberation Army
PPBE	planning, programming, budgeting, and execution
PRC	People's Republic of China
QRMC	Quadrennial Review of Military Compensation
WTO	World Trade Organization

Introduction

Michael J. Boskin, John N. Rader, and Kiran Sridhar

The belief that the world has become increasingly dangerous has been a staple in national security circles for some time. Russia's invasion of Ukraine spread awareness of this harsh reality to the broader public. Adding Chinese president Xi Jinping's increasing assertiveness, especially toward Taiwan but also far beyond; continued terrorist threats from multiple corners; North Korea's nuclear weapons and ballistic missile tests; Iran's coming ever closer to acquiring nuclear-weapon capability and continued sponsoring of terrorism; risks in the cyber and space domains; and of course the potential of an "unknown unknown" military conflict leaves America's geopolitical strategy and military preparedness stretched and challenged.

The foundation of America's ability to deter aggression and, if necessary, defeat aggressors is the strength of our military, combined with high-quality intelligence and diplomatic capabilities and alliances. Military capability rests on the nation's defense budget, which provides the resources and authorities necessary to protect national security. The navy cannot send ships it does not have to keep sea-lanes open. The army cannot deploy troops it has been unable to recruit, train, and equip. Ditto for the capacity of the air force, marines, coast guard, space force, and, if necessary, the Reserves and National Guard. And for each and all the services, in cooperation with the private sector, rapidly developing and deploying technology and recapitalizing and equipping with surge capacity have become urgent priorities. As former chairman of the Joint Chiefs and secretary of state Colin Powell summarized, "Show me your budget, and I'll show you your strategy."

Simultaneously, adversaries have been strengthening their military capabilities, often with sophisticated technology and directly focused on potential conflict with the United States. Thus, threats evaluation and strategy must be based on this unfortunate reality, with a healthy dose of humility, when forecasting where, how, when, and with whom conflict may arise. The essays, panel presentations, and discussions in this volume, featuring contributions from many of the nation's leading experts, address these concerns.

The volume brings together and interweaves the main contemporary topics in national security budgeting. These include the geopolitical, military, and fiscal context for defense budget reforms; the threats the nation faces and might face; the strategies necessary to enable effective actions to deal with those threats; and the technology, recapitalization, and innovation challenges the services face and the opportunities for better harnessing new technologies. Also covered are personnel strengths and weaknesses, from recruiting to training and retaining the active-duty force; to the best mix of active-duty and reserve personnel and private contractors, including highly technical talent. There are also overviews of reform possibilities and the checkered history of previous reform attempts and a discussion of the politics of enacting defense budgets that are adequate, flexible, and incentivized enough to do the job without the undue burden of non-core-mission spending that crowds out mission-critical imperatives.

We have encountered many people who believe they need to know more about national security and defense budgeting but seek help in cobbling together a comprehensive view from disparate places and sources. In a poll jointly coordinated last year by the Hoover Institution's Tennenbaum Program for Fact-Based Policy and YouGov, respondents ranked national security and the defense budget as among the five most important public policy topics (out of the fifteen surveyed) about which they would most value more objective information.

We hope bringing these commentaries and analyses from leading experts together in one place can serve that purpose, adding to the significant individual insights and independent value that each brings. Their collective wisdom should prove valuable not just to those in the national security community and those interacting with it directly but also to those who would benefit from deeper knowledge on these issues in dealing with the economy, the budget, politics, and international relations as citizens and voters.

Setting the stage for the intensive discussions ahead, we lead off by laying out the geopolitical, military, and fiscal context for efforts to reform the defense budget. The wide military capability gap over potential adversaries the United States has enjoyed for decades is narrowing. While partly due to the underinvestment in America's military and defense industrial base, this situation is mostly due to our adversaries' increasing capabilities and sophistication. In short, while America retains the world's strongest military, other nations have been gaining ground. And while they are targeting specific theaters, we as a country must remain alert to several simultaneously. So we must deter, and if necessary defeat, not just their current greatly improved capabilities but where those capabilities will be in future years. And we must do so while also facing a trifecta of fiscal issues—the large and growing national debt, the predictable insolvency of the Social Security and Medicare trust funds over the next nine or ten years, and the dilemma that budgetary pressure will create for making the necessary investments in defense. But we note some reasons for cautious optimism on rightsizing the budget's adequacy, flexibility, and accountability.

On threats, Oriana Skylar Mastro focuses on what the United States can and should do to successfully deter China from invading Taiwan. She warns that because China has failed to convince Taiwan to willingly unify with the People's Republic of China, it has enlarged, modernized, and upgraded its military to take the island by force. While invading Taiwan likely exceeds current People's Liberation Army capabilities, by 2027 it may be able to take the island and defeat US intervention. She recommends in-theater bases of operation, purchasing significantly more long-range precision-guided munitions to attrite Chinese forces, expanding military sales to regional allies, and improving joint operations capabilities.

Leading intelligence expert Amy Zegart examines the adaptation challenges facing US intelligence agencies. She focuses on the crucial question: How much does money matter? Despite record spending, US intelligence agencies are losing their relative advantage. When budget scarcity and budget abundance both lead to the same suboptimal outcomes, more systemic problems exist, which she labels "organizational pathologies." Intelligence agencies' structures, cultures, and incentives persist as the silent but deadly killers of innovation in the defense space. After reviewing the most significant challenges facing the intelligence community, she recommends the creation of a new and dedicated open-source intelligence agency.

Joseph H. Felter captures the activities and threats posed by jihadist groups such as al-Qaeda, ISIS, and state-sponsored organizations, then suggests guiding principles for future counterterrorism policies, and finally identifies the strategy, policies, and resources necessary to address the danger. He argues for a better understanding of threats and US current counterterrorism capabilities and limitations, combined with deeper coordination with allies.

General Keith Alexander warns that the worst national security threat our nation faces today is having Russia and China working together, becoming powerful enough to challenge the world order and accomplish their respective goals in their spheres of influence. He urges the United States to develop a more robust strategy—showcasing US cyber capabilities—to confront China's and Russia's objectives, which could counter their next moves, as well as Iran's. He warns of Russia's continued antagonism unless the United States more energetically thwarts its hostile actions. At the same time, he predicts that China will continue to grow its military with the end goal of taking Taiwan in Xi Jinping's lifetime. He ends by recommending that our partners and allies, especially Japan, play a larger role alongside the United States as these threats continue to grow and predicts that public-private partnerships will be the future for cybersecurity.

Admiral Gary Roughead encourages the United States to look longer term and more broadly in its strategic planning and to better assess US power, presence, and influence in reshaping Eurasia as we counter the moves from Russia and China, as well as Iran and Turkey. He implores a focus on replenishing our military, both in equipment and personnel, and laments that development efforts around the world, historically US led, are being replaced by China and its Belt and Road Initiative. He is encouraged by Japan's adoption of new national security and defense strategies, as well as its commitment to spending more on national defense. This changing landscape, with its rising threats, requires coordinated action by allies and partners around the world working together with the United States.

Ambassador Michael McFaul asserts that the United States would benefit from a holistic approach to threat assessment, supported by an adequate national security budget. He highlights the intelligence community's excellent work in predicting the Russian invasion of Ukraine but also points out that the West underestimated Ukraine's strength relative to Russia. The United States should improve its ability to assess threats, including the capabilities, intentions, will to fight, and command-and-control effectiveness of our adversaries. He recommends that US intelligence agencies utilize more open-source intelligence in future assessments.

On strategy, Michael O'Hanlon argues that the current geostrategic situation is as complex as any the United States has ever faced, but he cautions against overreacting. He frames grand strategy around a return to great-power competition and agrees with national security leaders that China is America's "pacing challenge." Rightsizing the China threat includes the ability to deter

China from attacking Taiwan. As for Russia, its influence and ambitions in key parts of Europe extend well beyond Ukraine. But he sees little likelihood of having to confront both Russia and China militarily at the same time and places a high priority on protecting Eastern Europe with US and NATO military deployments and the ability to fend off a Chinese amphibious assault effectively. In short, the system of treaty-based alliances and forward-based military forces can continue to keep the peace among the great powers.

Nadia Schadlow explains how, in most domains, American power has gone from virtually uncontested to contested over the last three decades. Although its defense budget is the largest in the world, America's relative advantages are declining. She analyzes four main challenges: resetting US strategic forces; rightsizing and integrating US and allies' conventional forces; restoring the US defense industrial base; and preserving freedom of action in space. For each, she describes the shift from Cold War times, highlights current Department of Defense (DoD) and private-sector imperatives and solutions, and examines their defense budget implications.

Admiral Mike Mullen argues that now is the most dangerous time since the 1962 Cuban Missile Crisis. Russia and China really are together, and Russia's invasion of Ukraine has fundamentally changed the global security structure. Despite legitimate criticisms of the acquisition system, the weapons we have provided to Ukraine have performed quite well. Vladimir Putin will keep going, so we need more US troops in Eastern Europe. The US-China relationship is at its lowest point since 1972. We need to avoid drifting into war, and the best way to do that is to create more capability, including logistics, and support, particularly among Japan, Australia, and South Korea. To sustain domestic support for these necessary actions, we need to educate the American people that they are relevant to our security and economic prosperity. The importance of Taiwan Semiconductor to America's and China's economies provides some deterrent effect against a potential skirmish on the island, but it is critical that we learn how to think from the Chinese perspective to understand how to deter and help Taiwan defend itself from an amphibious assault. On the budget, the problem is less about the topline number than where those funds are allocated. The relevant committees of Congress need to help the Pentagon move away from its tendency to divvy up changes in resources roughly equally among the services.

H.R. McMaster argues that the biggest strategic challenge is that we don't know *how* to think about a future war. For example, the choice whether to fight two wars simultaneously will be imposed upon us—we won't get to pick. It is important to integrate all elements of national power—military, diplomatic, and economic—to deter an adversary. But without military forces forward positioned at scale for sufficient duration to ensure a potential enemy cannot accomplish its objectives at an acceptable cost, such an adversary will not be deterred. Arguments that the next war will be "fast, cheap, efficient, and waged from standoff range," he maintains, haven't been the case in Afghanistan, Iraq, or Ukraine. War is an extension of politics; people fight for the same reasons they have for thousands of years: fear, honor, and interest. War is uncertain and a contest of wills; enemies will adapt, so we too must learn to adapt. National leadership must explain the rationale and develop and sustain will. The ability to implement solutions in the necessary time frame is paramount and requires a size of force, currently too small, to be rightsized, along with its readiness and capabilities.

On technology, innovation, and procurement, Jacquelyn Schneider draws lessons from history, explaining how unmanned systems were adopted by the military. Contrary to popular belief that militaries adopt the most potent or effective technologies, she concludes that "human beliefs, organizational preferences, exogenous shocks, and domestic political processes ultimately determine winners and losers."

James M. Cunningham explains how the Pentagon has taken a procurement holiday of more than three decades since the Reagan administration's defense buildup in the 1980s. He details how this disinvestment has caused a dangerous readiness crisis—precisely when our adversaries have grown increasingly bellicose and capable. He questions whether we can afford to wait for "promised game-changing technology [that remains] years away from maturity," particularly when the "window of maximum danger" lies within the next five years.

Christopher Kirchhoff recounts the Pentagon's checkered history of adapting to technologically advanced warfare. While organizations like the Defense Innovation Unit have successfully procured close to $50 billion of goods and services from start-ups, the DoD at large has been reluctant to embrace commercial technology. "The stalling of the innovation agenda," he warns, "may spell a future strategic surprise for the United States."

Michael Brown asserts that our sclerotic defense procurement system is a national security threat in and of itself, because it precludes the Pentagon from adopting innovative technologies at the necessary speed and with sufficient agility. He advocates for the Defense Department to implement a "hedge strategy," where it more rapidly procures lots of smaller complements to major weapons systems. He also proposes a fast-follower strategy for acquiring commercial technology.

Michèle Flournoy focuses on the "realistic" "near-term" changes the military should adopt to deter China from invading Taiwan over the next five years. She proposes marrying legacy systems and new technologies to achieve the best outcomes. The Pentagon needs to put more emphasis on protecting Taiwan, and senior DoD executives should be focused on preventing China from going to war in the Taiwan Strait, just as many in the building are now focused on supporting Ukraine's resistance.

Eric Fanning argues that improving the procurement process will require the collaboration of Congress, the defense industrial base, and the DoD. Congress will need to get back to regular order and pass budgets on time to send predictable demand signals to defense contractors. The defense industrial base—comprising companies from $100 billion defense primes to fledgling start-ups—must collaborate to meet the department's most pressing needs. And finally, bureaucrats in the Pentagon will need to take risks, which they often are not conditioned or incentivized to do.

Raj Shah suggests that to get better military outcomes, the "best software engineers" should be working on the military's problems. A quarter to a third of spending on platforms is devoted to software. He sanguinely notes that the Russian invasion of Ukraine and the reemergence of great-power competition have caused a sea change in sentiment in Silicon Valley. Many of the nation's top technical minds now want to leverage their talent to help defend the nation.

In a moderated discussion, Secretary Condoleezza Rice, Secretary Jim Mattis, and Secretary Leon Panetta assess national security and the defense budget and the fundamental issues in which they are embedded. Both Mattis and Panetta highlight the incredible capabilities and dedication of those in the military and intelligence communities. And they lament the decline in the sense of duty to the nation among the broader population, with Panetta calling for two years of national service for young adults. Rice raises the nature of the threats democracies face, the role of allies in protecting our—and their—national security, the need to move more nimbly on technology, and the fusion of intelligence, diplomacy, and the military. Panetta emphasizes that we need to better understand how our allies and adversaries think about their own security challenges.

Both Panetta and Mattis detail the damage done to national security from the dysfunctional budget process, e.g., continuing resolutions that cause delay and create confusion. Panetta believes significant procurement efficiencies, efforts to reduce duplication and bloated bureaucracy, and greater funding to modernize core functions must be applied to dealing with the full set of budget issues, with "everything on the table." Mattis had three main goals as secretary of defense: to make the military more lethal so our diplomats were listened to; to reform business practices; and to expand the number of allies and deepen trust and cooperation with them. On that score, he recalls Winston Churchill's famous dictum: "There is only one thing worse than fighting with allies, and that is fighting without them."

On personnel, David S. C. Chu, former under secretary of defense for personnel, shines a light on how vast the Pentagon's workforce truly is. In addition to the 1.3 million active-duty soldiers, 1 million reservists, and 800,000 civilians, many more work as contractors. The Pentagon needs to better optimize the "best mix of personnel communities—active, reserve, federal civilian, and contractor—to provide the capabilities needed," he argues. And he imparts lessons to future personnel reformers from efforts of the past—both those that succeeded and those that failed.

Vishaal "V8" Hariprasad and Casey "Waldo" Miller note that while members of cyber armed forces earn a fraction of the pay they would in private-sector cyber roles, many still enjoy the work, because they are able to complete missions that would not be possible outside of the military. But several reforms would enable better recruitment and retention. Squadron-level commanders should be entrusted with making hiring and firing decisions on their own; the services need to do a better job of providing bonuses to highly skilled workers; and those with a particular passion for cyber operations should be placed on a dedicated "technical track."

Tim Kane observes that since the establishment of the all-volunteer force, the US military does not "look like America," because enlistees surpass average Americans on a number of measures. He is therefore opposed to a relaxation in military standards. But he suggests that antiquated compensation and retirement structures, which hinder the military from retaining personnel, should be reformed. Finally, he advocates for continued US troop deployments overseas, which he says ultimately save the Pentagon money by deterring conflict.

Mackenzie Eaglen notes that many defense personnel are performing "non-core" functions. The focus of the military should be on "things that the Defense Department can do that only it's expected to do": deter and, if necessary, fight and win. Money could be saved by eliminating jobs that fall outside of this scope. She also suggests linking the size of the civilian workforce in the DoD to that of the active-duty force. The number of civilians, she argues, should not "bulge when active duty gets squeezed."

On reform possibilities, Eaglen notes that DoD has been undergoing constant reforms for decades but has not achieved enough lasting results. Removing barriers is more important than adding new layers of manpower or organization, so slashing calcified procedures, regulations, and bureaucracy is essential. She recommends a two-year budget deal for defense and non-defense discretionary spending to offer clarity and certainty to the Pentagon and contractors to plan and allocate resources more efficiently. A topline defense budget growing by inflation plus 3 percent would more rapidly support the national defense strategy. More reprogramming and carryover authority would provide greater agility and flexibility. And she proposes a solution to debilitating continuing resolutions: sequestering congressional paychecks until appropriations are passed.

Elaine McCusker highlights three weaknesses in defense budgeting: it is burdened with too many programs that do *not* produce military capability; it is not structured to meet needs at the necessary speed; and it falls short of meeting important management and oversight responsibilities. She identifies $109 billion in annual spending not directly related to military needs, including items related to domestic, environmental, and social policy, as well as indirect costs of supporting the all-volunteer force, such as community services and family housing. Continuing resolutions (CRs) extending more than 1,600 days since 2010 have taken a heavy toll; the fall 2022 CR cost DoD $17 billion in buying power, as well as the lost time. She suggests that consideration be given to moving defense-related entitlements to a separate budget.

Mark R. Wilson provides a revealing history of US defense budget reforms, successful and not. Four goals have dominated: coherence, adequacy, stability, and agility. Most of today's budgeting elements were put in place in the 1950s through the 1970s, so major reform seems overdue, and suggestions will come from the current PPBE Commission. But given the endurance of the old system, modest reforms are more likely. As late as 1970, the defense authorization bill was about ten pages and passed with little debate on a voice vote. A decade later, it contained hundreds of line items; now, it is thousands. Repeated attempts to move to multiyear budgeting and to consolidate the authorization and appropriations committees have gone nowhere, despite influential support. Modest procedural workarounds providing more flexibility in funding outside the budget and special acquisition authorities within it have helped reduce the constraints.

Roger Zakheim notes that the United States has not committed to a substantial multiyear military rebuilding since the Reagan era, nearly four decades ago. Reforms and efficiencies, while important, will not be enough, he argues. Considerably more funding is necessary and urgent for a robust strategy that seeks to deter adversaries on multiple fronts. Rebuilding today's force must be done simultaneously with investing in future modernization, so targeting defense spending of up to 5 percent of GDP, a level last reached (indeed, exceeded) in the Reagan buildup, is necessary, and six priority areas are identified. He notes that the results of the Reagan National Defense Survey conducted after the 2022 election revealed that majorities of both parties support increased defense spending.

Admiral Gary Roughead emphasizes the perception problems of the defense budget. The topline is large, and much of the public wonders why it isn't sufficient for DoD to do what it needs to get done. Pulling out the investment account from the total budget would more closely align with how people think about budgets. He also thinks that the DoD should embrace commercial technology because the DoD no longer is—contrary to the beliefs of many of its leaders—the center of the technology universe. Roughead agrees with Admiral Mike Mullen that there is huge overhead on the civilian force. But equally important is how onerous it has become for people in the private sector—for example, those with substantial experience in running businesses—to come in and out of the military. Also baleful is the fact that promising officers risk seeing their careers stall if they work in the acquisition or budgeting systems as opposed to taking battlefield commands. The system incentivizes people to move around for promotion purposes even if they leave a program before milestones are achieved, something the private sector wouldn't do. Vital military technology, from the Manhattan Project to the Nuclear Navy, transformed warfare by "betting on horses," not on processes. The industrial-base workforce requires trade skills, such as those of welders and electricians, but our society has not incentivized people to train for skills despite the substantial pay involved.

Ellen Lord analyzes three vital budgeting reform issues, the first of which is the problem of overall communications to the general public to help them understand that the benefits they enjoy from our economic strength are tightly interwoven with our national security. This theme resurfaces in many of the presentations, including Mac Thornberry's outlining how Congress makes defense budget decisions; Admiral Mullen's expressions of concern that after fifty years of the all-volunteer force, there is a risk that the military is too separated from the general public; and Secretary Panetta's call for broadening requirements for national service. Lord emphasizes that public awareness is not only important for general understanding but also for the choices citizens make to study, work in, or otherwise become involved in national security. Second, regarding technology, she observes that decades ago, most critical technology was developed by the government and rolled out for commercial use. Now most of it is commercially developed. Congress has put some reforms in place, but too often they have not been followed through on and translated into policy, implementation guidance, and workforce training. Third, she spoke about the importance of close cooperation with our allies, who want to develop capabilities in order to compete against our major common adversaries.

David L. Norquist shares how, in his time as under secretary (controller) and CFO of defense, he implemented a key reform: the first DoD audit. A defense strategy in excess of funding creates vulnerabilities, and an audit can help identify such cases. For example, it could find supplies a service did not know it had because it hasn't been logged into the system. Senior leaders that once viewed audits as a waste of money and time now view them as central to running the department. Norquist describes methods he used to get the DoD to embrace audits including: asking lots of questions; scouting for obstacles; having schedules and plans and being a champion for the change; paying attention to incentives; and understanding that the transition likely will outlast you, so it's worthwhile if the next administration continues it. He also stresses the importance of the defense industrial base as part of national security planning, a point also emphasized by many others.

On the view from Congress, former House Armed Services Committee chairman Mac Thornberry, who authored bipartisan National Defense Authorization Act (NDAA) legislation, reflects on his experience in that role and lessons learned for laying out the "art of the possible" in future defense budget levels and reforms. It's the money and where it goes that make the difference, and under the US Constitution, it's Congress that spends the money. So you will not be able to implement a strategy without Congress having a role. There are four key issues: how much we spend; what we spend it on; the process used to spend it; and the time it takes, especially given the pace at which technology and our adversaries are moving. While waiting for the PPBE Commission to recommend broad reform, there is interest in Congress for greater budget flexibility *if* matched with greater transparency. For acquisition reform, another commission that can get down into the details of what regulations and laws need to be changed would be useful. Thornberry responds to specific questions, ranging from the best avenues for greater flexibility, advance appropriations, a separate capital budget, the growth of the NDAA to thousands of pages, the difficulty of recruiting highly skilled talent, and many other issues.

The perspectives, concerns, ideas, and solutions offered by these leading experts form a comprehensive, readily accessible overview of the major interrelated issues in defense budgeting upon which America's national security and the prospects for a safer world depend. On some issues, there is a range of disagreement—for example, on the time frame within which China might attempt a military takeover of Taiwan, or the need to expand active-duty personnel and weapons systems, by how much, and for which services.

But on most issues, there is general widespread, if importantly nuanced, agreement among these experts, most of whom have served in key leadership positions, encompassing administrations of both major political parties. They agree that the geopolitical environment is increasingly dangerous and complex; that adversaries are devoting ever-greater resources to closing the military gap with the United States in their respective theaters of interest, as we must contend with multiple adversaries in multiple theaters; that it is important to better coordinate with allies; that greater adequacy, flexibility, and accountability are needed in the defense budget; that strengthening the defense industrial base while investing in modernization to replace aging systems and equipment is urgent; that we can and should better integrate commercial technology, more rapidly, in the acquisition process; that more flexible incentive-based reforms are necessary to more readily recruit, train, promote, and retain human resources, including those with advanced technical and business skills; that there is considerable opportunity for reforms to lead to efficiencies and to reductions of non-DoD-core-mission spending to help free up resources to complement necessary topline funding; and that there is a vital need to better educate the public on the role that its investment of tax dollars in the defense budget plays in enabling the military, along with intelligence and diplomacy, to keep America safe, free, and prosperous.

1

The Geopolitical, Military, and Fiscal Context for Defense Budget Reform

Michael J. Boskin, John N. Rader, and Kiran Sridhar

If history is any guide, democracies usually underinvest in their militaries during peacetime. Maintaining and improving defense capability seems like an expensive luxury to many voters, who have other priorities that press on their government's budget. A famous example was the British public and government. Both ignored Winston Churchill's admonitions about Great Britain's poor preparation for Germany's assault in World War II, given the speed and magnitude of the German buildup and the Nazi Party's intentions for using it. Such underinvestment too often requires an expensive—in treasure and lives—and rapid reversal.

A government's budget is a statement of its national priorities. And its defense budget—its level and composition—is the foundation on which its capability to deter aggression and, if necessary, to defeat the aggressors rests. Unfortunately, America confronts many active and potential adversaries across the globe to which our military (and relatedly, intelligence and diplomacy) must be prepared to respond. What is unpredictable is knowing which aggressors to respond to and when.

As former defense secretary (and CIA director) Bob Gates summarized, "When it comes to predicting future conflicts, what kind of fights they will be, and what will be needed, we need a lot more humility."[1]

Even more daunting, plans are often mugged by the reality of battle. As the famous late-nineteenth-century German military strategist Moltke the Elder declared, "No plan survives contact with the enemy."

The views expressed in this chapter are solely those of the individual authors and do not necessarily reflect the views of any organization with which they are, or have been, affiliated.

Thus, a robust national security strategy that covers the main contingencies, embodies great adaptability, and envisions sufficient and flexible capabilities to respond to emerging threats is key to national security. But that strategy must be matched with sufficient budgetary resources and authorization capabilities.

Budgets poorly matched to strategic imperatives are not just penny-wise and pound-foolish but dangerous. In light of the multiple threats the nation faces, three huge, interrelated risks necessitate defense budget and budgeting reforms. The next section of this chapter describes each: America's military capabilities relative to a robust strategy to deal with the threats, the growing military capabilities and intentions of adversaries, and a fiscal trilemma that will increasingly make it difficult to respond appropriately. We then discuss some basic principles that ought to guide defense budget reform to maximize capability: adequacy; consistency and predictability; flexibility; incentive compatibility; and accountability, all of which we illustrate with a few examples. We conclude with some reasons for cautious optimism amid the daunting budgetary and readiness challenges America faces.

These concerns, issues, ideas, and solutions are developed and debated far more fully by the prominent experts in the chapters and panel discussions that follow. Their knowledge and experience on each subject (save perhaps the overall fiscal picture in which it is embedded) is well beyond our own. Indeed, in large measure, what we know derives from reading their work and from discussions with them and others.

The Interplay of Three Large Risks to National Security

America's national security is facing a trifecta of rapidly growing risks. Given the time frames involved, if these are not urgently addressed, the nation's security and geopolitical influence may be significantly harmed—or worse. Defense budget reforms can play a vital role in enhancing security in light of these and other risks, known and unknown. At the highest level, the three interrelated risks are the following:

1. America's Military Readiness Relative to Security Threats

While America still has the strongest military in the world, its capabilities have been stretched and are not aligned and resourced closely enough to a national security strategy that has identified pressing threats from all corners of the world.[2] The causes are many, including, for example, the long wars in Afghanistan and Iraq and a two-decade-long focus on global counterterrorism following the 9/11 attacks. To some extent, these concerns inevitably shifted focus and resources away from adversaries such as Russia and China.

Combined with the haphazard funding of Defense Department needs, the result has been a damaging delay in recapitalizing and modernizing aging weapons systems, developing and exploiting new technology (including commercial technology), and a stop-and-go uncertainty that has compromised a range of defense programs, from training to weapons procurement. In fact, the National Transportation Safety Board has blamed fatal navy ship collisions on insufficient training. Every sequester, which sharply reduces the defense budget, or continuing resolution (CR), which funds the Pentagon at the same nominal levels as the previous year, adds cumulatively to limits or delays in funding. While harmful enough in the short term, such fiscal instability permeates through capability and readiness for years. For example, by imposing uncertainty on future procurement spending, CRs send unpredictable demand signals to current and potential contractors. Defense firms become less able to risk making large investments in developing, expanding, and speeding capacity, for example, by adding more production lines or producing next-generation technology. Combined with supply chain constraints and globalization, this unpredictability has atrophied the defense industrial base, creating a major challenge to rapidly expanding capability.

Indeed, a primary culprit for the Pentagon's shrinking relative competitive advantage is that the US military has not been sufficiently recapitalized or modernized since the 1980s, when acquisition spending crested at nearly 3 percent of GDP. By 1995, it had fallen to 1 percent of GDP, where it currently sits (see fig. 1.1). This lack of acquisition funding has baleful consequences. The military's fleet is shrinking—even as the United States faces threats from more actors and may have to fight wars in multiple distant theaters simultaneously. The US Navy, for instance, is projected to lose one submarine every two years from now until 2040, and in 2022 it came close to a trough that would have been below previous requirements.[3] And the equipment that remains is increasingly unreliable. The average US Air Force fighter jet is twenty-eight years old, and only 70 percent of in-service aircraft are considered "mission capable."[4]

Procurement is not a binary, either-or choice between lots of smaller weapons—built rapidly with low-cost available commercial technology—and new generations of exquisite systems such as the F-35 stealth fighter and B-21 stealth bomber that require large expenditures and long time frames to bring online. A strategy that simultaneously combines both is necessary,

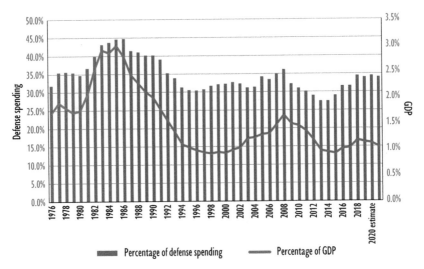

Figure 1.1 Acquisition Spending, 1976–2020

Source: Office of Management and Budget (OMB), Historical Tables, Table 5.1, "Budget Authority by Function and Subfunction: 1976–2028," and Table 10.1, "Gross Domestic Product and Deflators Used in the Historical Tables: 1940–2025."

especially because of the different time frames. We are not going to quickly build a lot of new advanced submarines and surface ships that may be useful in deterring and, if necessary, responding to a Chinese invasion of Taiwan in this decade. But we can improve how quickly we deploy many distributed antiship weapons in the meantime.

The defense budget must be reformed and enhanced for the military to meet its challenges successfully. The Pentagon needs resources to recapitalize its force as necessary and to invest in the equipment, technology, and personnel required by contemporary and likely future warfare simultaneously. Thankfully, Washington—and increasingly the public at large—is beginning to awake from its post–Cold War stupor. Over 76 percent of Americans polled in the 2022 Reagan National Defense Survey support increasing spending on the military.[5] That may drop off some when how to pay for it is considered, but it's a promising base. So, too, is a YouGov poll conducted for Hoover's Tennenbaum Program for Fact-Based Policy, which revealed that among fifteen public policy issues, national security and the defense budget were among the few that respondents said they would most benefit from learning more about.[6]

But more money alone will not solve the US military's challenges. Defense budgeting must become more closely linked with strategy to allocate spending more judiciously. Reforms must reduce the oppressive micromanagement imposed by thousands of line items, too many "colors of money," and a slow-moving bureaucracy. As former under secretary of defense for policy Michèle Flournoy states, "Bureaucratic inertia has prevented new capabilities and practices from being adopted with speed and at scale."[7] That limits the effective and efficient use of appropriated defense dollars and necessitates partial workarounds. Budgets should be predictable and consistent so that defense leaders can make the requisite long-term investments to build new capabilities. It would also be wise to hedge our bets and invest in a variety of capabilities, mainly because of our military and political leaders' checkered history of predicting the future of warfare and sufficiently funding preparation. And policy makers should demand accountability and transparency: the Pentagon must be an effective steward of taxpayer dollars and convince the public that it is spending its money wisely.

2. Increasingly Sophisticated Adversaries

While America has been disinvesting in the military, its adversaries have not stood still. Russia's invasion of Ukraine highlighted the danger of Vladimir Putin's long-expressed desire to build a modern-day version of the Russian Empire. It's a desire that has long been implicit in his pronouncements, for instance, that the breakup of the Soviet Union was the greatest disaster of the twentieth century—thus worse than World War II, in which twenty million Russians died. And it was expressed in his seizure of part of Georgia and all of Crimea. The invasion made his plans explicit enough to rally the United States, its NATO allies, and public opinion behind supporting Ukraine's unexpectedly strong resistance effort. The equally unexpected initial weakness of the Russian military was revealing. However long that conflict lasts and however it ultimately ends, it would be foolish to conclude that it is the end of Russian expansionism. Even more dangerous are Russia's large nuclear arsenal and Putin's periodic threats to use it. It doesn't take much imagination to conjure up a scenario where the United States is involved in a China-Taiwan conflict and Putin—or a successor—sees it as an opportune time to seize more territory, even in the extreme, from the Baltics, which would require NATO to invoke Article 5, the commitment that an attack on one is an attack on all. The apparent "without limits" cooperation between Putin and Xi Jinping, which has thus far seen little Chinese military support for the Ukraine invasion, might at some point make it strategically advantageous for China to help enable a second front for the United States and its allies.

But even more important has been the rapid emergence of China as a major world military power and the world's second-largest economy. The current administration's National Security Strategy (NSS) rightly focuses on China as the military's pacing challenge.

For several decades, the predominant view had been that economic reform and liberalization, begun in the late 1970s by Deng Xiaoping, Mao Zedong's successor, would ultimately lead to political liberalization. Nobody believed China would become a mixed capitalist democracy like Canada in short order, but when the Berlin Wall fell and the Soviet Union broke apart, this view gained credence, particularly among intellectuals and some political leaders. Milton Friedman, Lee Kuan Yew, Bill Clinton, and many others propounded the view that economic liberalization would lead to political liberalization. This view and the prospect of low-cost supply chains and a large pool of Chinese middle-class consumers rapidly becoming richer encouraged America and other wealthy democracies to allow Beijing to join the World Trade Organization in 2001. The result was that China's GDP quadrupled in a historically unprecedented decade and a half as its economy became intricately interlinked with the advanced economies as the world's factory. China's economic growth created the biggest reduction in abject poverty in human history, but it also allowed the resources to fund a huge military buildup and assert China's interests more aggressively in global affairs.

Indeed, since 2000, China's inflation-adjusted military spending has swelled by roughly 700 percent, according to estimates from the Stockholm International Peace Research Institute.[8] Much of that funding has been devoted to countering the United States in a potential war in East and South Asia. China has invested in sophisticated long-range weapons, mines, submarines, and, more recently, potent cyber and jamming capabilities to neutralize US military platforms. And now, unclassified war games simulating a Chinese invasion of Taiwan conducted by the Center for Strategic and International Studies conclude that the Pentagon would likely suffer massive losses were it to intervene in the conflict—dozens of ships, hundreds of aircraft, and tens of thousands of troops.[9] To be sure, doubts remain about the capabilities of the People's Liberation Army (PLA) to carry out an invasion, given its limited battle experience and the logistic challenges of an amphibious assault. However, counting on its weakness is not a sensible strategy.

President Xi Jinping has consolidated power more tightly than any leader since Mao. He has crushed hope for political reform, extending the reach of the Chinese Communist Party deeply into Chinese people's lives. His plan for China's "national rejuvenation" is for it to become the world's largest economy and a world-class military power that could reunite Taiwan, as the Communist Party Constitution calls for, by force if necessary. According to the former head of the US Indo-Pacific Command, Admiral Philip Davidson, that could perhaps happen as soon as 2027, the one hundredth anniversary of the founding of the PLA.[10] And, in contravention of international law, China is building military bases on new islands constructed in disputed territory in the South China Sea, thereby threatening shipping lanes affecting over one-third of all global seaborne trade.

Of course, hopefully, conflict with China can be avoided and deterred, and perhaps other tensions over trade, intellectual property theft, and the like can also be resolved without even larger economic disruption. Only time will tell.

Unfortunately, the possibilities the nation's security agencies must prepare for extend beyond China and Russia. A likely nuclear Iran, a belligerent North Korea with nuclear weapons and ballistic missiles, and terrorist threats in many parts of the world demand continued attention and resources. Each actor could potentially see openings to advance its designs were the United States to become engaged in other hostilities. Of course, other regional tensions could flare up as well. And that's only what we know today.

As former national security advisor General H.R. McMaster put it a while back: "We have a perfect record in predicting future wars . . . and that record is 0 percent." That is not an isolated interpretation. Former chairman of the Joint Chiefs of Staff Mike Mullen acknowledged that "we're pretty lousy at predicting where we'll go. We're pretty lousy at predicting the kind of warfare we'll be in."[11] Former secretary of defense General Jim Mattis echoed these sentiments: "I have never fought anywhere I expected to in all my years."[12]

3. America's Fiscal Trilemma

The ability and willingness to fund the budgets necessary for our military (and complementary intelligence and diplomatic agencies) to execute strategy and confront enemies are compromised by three large, looming, and interrelated fiscal crises.

The first is that recently we have amassed more publicly held national debt, relative to GDP, than at any point since the immediate aftermath of World War II. The situation is markedly worse than in 2010 when Mullen

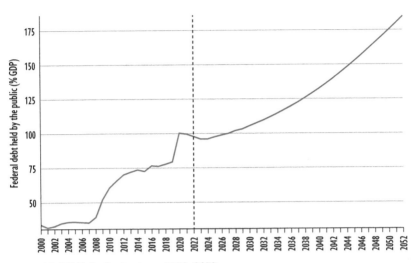

Figure 1.2 US Debt Projections, 2000–2052

Source: Data from Congressional Budget Office (CBO), *The 2022 Long-Term Budget Outlook* (July 2022), CBO publication 57971.

prophetically pronounced that "the most significant threat to our national security is our debt."[13] At the time, the national debt stood at 65 percent of GDP. It is now close to 100 percent of GDP and is expected to grow rapidly in the coming decades (see fig. 1.2), driven primarily by the growth of unfunded entitlement spending (see fig. 1.3). When the nation's first Treasury secretary, Alexander Hamilton, argued the new federal government should assume the debilitating Revolutionary War debt of the states, he claimed such debt should be viewed as "the price of Liberty." Now it mostly funds growing entitlement benefits.

Concern over deficits and debt is neither an idle nor a distant challenge for the defense budget. The nation's debt will likely constrain defense budgets this decade, when the Pentagon faces emboldened adversaries and acute recapitalization needs. It is already a concern for next year's budget and is potentially at risk in any "budget deal" to resolve a likely political impasse, e.g., over the debt limit or appropriations. House Republicans plan to try to return discretionary spending, the less than one-third of the budget that is annually appropriated (see fig. 1.4), to FY2022 levels, unadjusted for inflation. Commentators have calculated that such a move could cost the defense budget $75 billion. While several prominent House Republican leaders have unambiguously stated that defense will not be cut, they have stated that

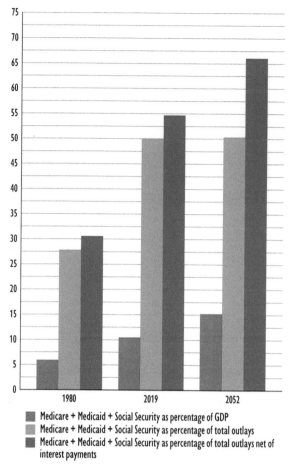

Figure 1.3 US Entitlement Spending Projections: 1980, 2019, and 2052
Source: CBO, 2022 Long-Term Budget Outlook.

reforms will be necessary. Speaker of the House Kevin McCarthy has tried to thread the needle, stating in essence that defense is on the table because we should go after wasteful spending anywhere and everywhere. So the optimist may sense an opportunity to advance beneficial reforms; the pessimist, however, worries that defense capabilities will be curtailed.

To combat the worst inflation in forty years, the Federal Reserve has already raised its target interest rate to 4.5 percent from close to zero, where it had been for most of the past fourteen years. The rise in interest rates on both newly issued debt and existing debt as it matures and is rolled over greatly

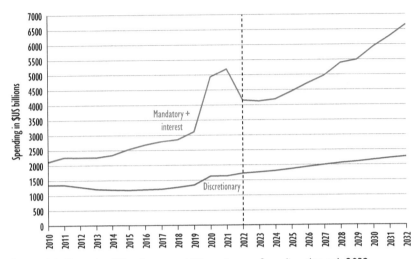

Figure 1.4 Growth of Mandatory and Discretionary Spending through 2032

Source: CBO, *The Budget and Economic Outlook: 2022 to 2032* (May 2022), CBO publication 57950.

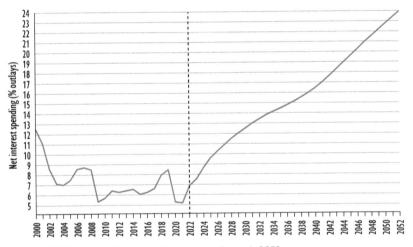

Figure 1.5 US Interest Spending Projections through 2052

Source: CBO, *2022 Long-Term Budget Outlook.*

exacerbates the deficit and debt outlook (see fig. 1.5). The cost of the debt that had been "hidden" by artificially low interest rates has now been exposed, along with the foolish notion that the debt is costless.

While nobody can be sure what level of debt over what period will cause a major economic or financial disruption, the recent inflation surge, for which large deficit-financed spending is a prime culprit, should serve as a reminder of the risks. Hoping to kick the proverbial can down the road is becoming increasingly risky.

There are clearly several political and budgetary risks to defense spending. First, as the history below will show, the last time there was a political impasse over the debt limit with a Republican House and a Democrat president, the result was the 2011 Budget Control Act, which imposed damaging sequester caps on the defense budget. Second, even past the short-run challenge, there is a risk that a major multiyear overhaul of the federal budget designed to at least stabilize the debt could result in damaging cuts to defense.

Consider the proposals outlined by the Congressional Budget Office (CBO) in its influential *Options for Reducing the Deficit, 2023 to 2032* report released in December 2022. The report contained three alternatives for downsizing the force and saving at least $1 trillion (see table 1.1 and fig. 1.6). It concludes that the force is still primarily wedded to the 2017 NSS, which emphasized that "deterring military aggression relied heavily on the threat of the rapid defeat of enemy forces by US combat forces . . . to strike with sufficient speed and firepower and to maneuver forces in a way that would overwhelm an enemy's military." In contrast, the 2021 interim NSS and full 2022 NSS emphasized "an integrated approach . . . placing less importance on the threat of using US combat forces and more on the threat of broad-based punitive actions by the United States and its international partners."[14] The CBO shows three alternative ways to align a smaller force to the 2022 integrated deterrence strategy, with large cuts for the services across unit types.

The second challenge is the impending exhaustion of the Hospital Insurance Trust Fund (Medicare Part A), the Social Security Trust Fund, and the (smaller) Highway Trust Fund, all of which are projected to be exhausted within the next decade.

To get a sense of the potential economic disruption and political turmoil, the year of exhaustion would trigger a 45 percent reduction (from the elevated levels of the recent infrastructure bill) from the highway fund, an 8 percent reduction in spending from the hospital insurance fund, and a 23 percent reduction in spending on social security retirement benefits. There will be intense budget battles over how to forestall these cuts, especially any reduction involving popular Social Security and Medicare benefits. The back-and-forth over spending and taxes that has characterized America's fiscal politics for over forty years is likely to grow more intense, not just over topline numbers but over the composition of spending and tax rates. These specific issues

Table 1.1 CBO Options for Reducing the Department of Defense's Annual Budget (in $US billions)

Change in Spending	2023	2024	2025	2026	2027	2028	2029	2030	2031	2032	Total 2023–2027	2023–2032
Budget authority	0	−64	−90	−105	−132	−138	−142	−146	−150	−154	−391	−1,121
Outlays	0	−37	−68	−88	−112	−126	−133	−139	−144	−148	−305	−995

This option would take effect in October 2023.

The estimated outlay savings reflect the Congressional Budget Office's assessment of how quickly total funding provided to the Department of Defense is spent and do not reflect the details of any particular alternative.

Source: CBO, Options for Reducing the Deficit, 2023 to 2032—Volume I: Larger Reductions, CBO publication 58164, 60.

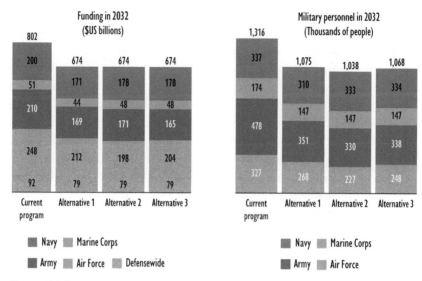

Figure 1.6 Budgetary and Military Effects of Three Alternatives to Reduce the Defense Budget

Source: CBO, *Options for Reducing the Deficit, 2023 to 2032.*

will potentially trigger action overall and also on the defense budget. Thus, we should act on defense budget reforms with urgency, ahead of these other budget deadlines.

The third challenge is the likelihood that the current and impending fiscal pressures will lead to even worse and more costly inconsistencies in defense appropriations than the checkered history of the past dozen years. The recent past has been characterized by more lengthy CRs, sequesters, spending caps and cuts, and reversals that have degraded the ability of the military and the contractor ecosystem to plan efficiently and effectively.

Recent fiscal history, which we describe for potential insights into possible future political budgeting, is not reassuring, except for the large defense buildup under President Ronald Reagan that helped win the Cold War. The difficulty in controlling domestic spending and large supply-side tax reductions that strengthened economic growth but did not fully pay for themselves contributed to large budget deficits. In 1985, Congress passed the Gramm-Rudman-Hollings legislation, which required the president's budget to forecast declining deficits over several years until the budget was balanced. It likely did produce some restraint—due more to moral suasion than to enforcement rules, which were absent.

A still large (at the time) deficit led to the 1990 Budget Enforcement Act, designed to achieve $500 billion in deficit reduction over five years. It capped discretionary spending and imposed a pay-as-you-go ("PAYGO") rule that required spending increases or tax cuts to be offset—in effect, a "marginal" balanced budget rule. President George H. W. Bush, facing large Democratic majorities in the House and Senate, finally agreed to it but only if it contained a provision that walled off defense spending from cuts for three years in the immediate aftermath of the fall of the Berlin Wall and concomitant calls for large reductions in defense spending. But its modest tax hikes following candidate Bush's "Read My Lips: No New Taxes" pledge split the Republican Party and contributed to his reelection defeat, a message that reverberates politically to this day. Drawing lessons from his electoral defeat, most Republicans are now stridently opposed to all tax rate increases. Only higher revenue achieved through tax reform, similar to President Reagan's landmark 1986 tax reform, which lowers tax rates while broadening the base, achieving stronger economic growth, receives support from many Republicans.

There was a significant Clinton-era defense drawdown as a percentage of GDP (see fig. 1.7). The reduction in defense spending and the strong economy led to balanced budgets following agreements between the president and the Republican-controlled Congress. But it didn't last long. To get the large increases in security spending he deemed necessary, especially after the 9/11 attacks, President George W. Bush agreed to large, nondefense spending hikes as well, a pattern that has permeated spending deals since.

As the deficit and debt grew, aggravated by the financial crisis and great recession, President Barack Obama appointed the bipartisan Simpson-Bowles Commission to propose ways to put the country on a more sustainable fiscal path. Their recommendations included sensible steps to slow the growth of entitlement spending and a tax code with lower rates on a broader base, the two main proposals of serious economists and intellectual leaders in both parties since the 1970s. Democrats would get more tax revenue, and Republicans would get slower spending growth. We will never know if the reforms could have passed, because President Obama walked away from his own commission's recommendations.

Various groups of House and Senate members banded together to offer proposals. House Speaker John Boehner thought he had a deal with the president, but it fell through despite Boehner agreeing to some modest tax hikes. Finally, a deal was struck that was supposed to limit discretionary spending to

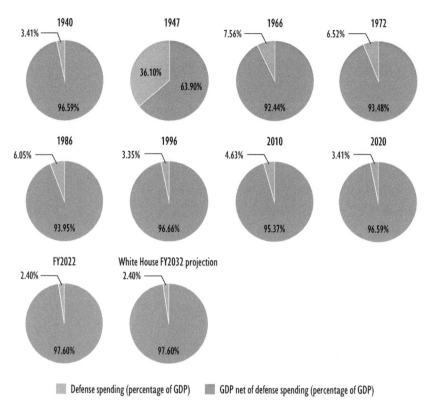

Figure 1.7 US Defense Spending as a Percentage of GDP since World War II

Sources: OMB, Historical Tables, Table 3.1, "Budget Authority by Function and Subfunction: 1940–2028"; and The White House, Budget of the US Government Fiscal Year 2022, Table S-5, "Proposed Budget by Category as a Percent of GDP."

lower predetermined levels. If no specific agreement on details was reached, it would impose mandatory cuts in defense and nondefense discretionary spending via sequester. The belief (hope) was that Republicans couldn't tolerate defense cuts and Democrats couldn't tolerate nondefense cuts, so a deal would be reached. Unfortunately, it didn't work, and the sequester went into effect.

The result for the military was the quite damaging Budget Control Act of 2011 (BCA). We calculate that inflation-adjusted defense spending in each subsequent year was over $100 billion less than in 2010 (see fig. 1.8); by 2022, the cumulative total budget shortfall had reached $1.7 trillion and was projected to worsen under the Future Years Defense Program (FYDP). Removing

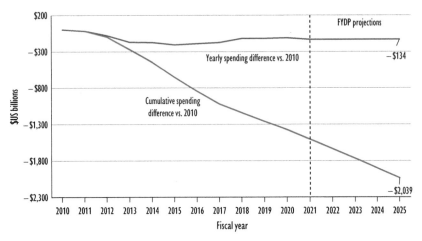

Figure 1.8 Since 2010, Total Defense Spending, Including Base and OCO, Has Never Recovered

Sources: Authors' calculations from DoD, Office of the Under Secretary of Defense (Comptroller), *National Defense Budget Estimates (Green Book)* for the years shown.

Overseas Contingency Operations (OCOs) funding fully, or adjusting that amount by removing the share that was for enduring operations, real dollars to the Pentagon still fell considerably.[15] Some of the pressure—if not all uncertainty—was relieved by workarounds that supplemented the regular appropriations, e.g., continuing OCOs.

But Democrats have continued to insist that large nondefense discretionary spending hikes be tied to major increases in military spending and that any cuts be made pari passu. President Donald Trump, with a Republican House and Senate, secured large defense funding increases, but the military could not make up for years of inadequate spending. And there was considerable uncertainty over how long higher spending would last.

Most recently, President Joe Biden, with Democrats controlling the House and Senate, in his budget has projected ten years of declining constant-dollar defense spending amid huge increases in nondefense spending. But in each of the past two years, a bipartisan majority led by the Armed Services and Appropriations Committees approved omnibus bills that added considerable defense spending to the president's budget request.

We take this brief tour through a simplified fiscal history to suggest that if history is any guide, future defense spending will likely be challenged in amount and consistency, perhaps abruptly, in the context of almost certain future political budget struggles having little to do with national security. We thus conclude that reforming defense budgeting to get more out of every defense dollar and complementing more dollars as politically possible while achieving closer alignment with the strategy that threats necessitate is vital and urgent.

Principles for Reform

Many reform principles have been suggested by previously appointed commissions, other stakeholders, and thought leaders as cornerstones of an effective and strategically coherent budgeting process. These include Pentagon reforms but also reforms in congressional and executive branch processes as well. We focus on the five we believe to be most important.

Principle 1: Adequacy

We need a budget that is robust and adequate enough to provide the Department of Defense (DoD) with the resources it needs to deter or fight threats. Given budget pressures and political polarization, absent outright conflict, we cannot rely on the vastly larger funding scale reached in the Reagan years of 6 percent of GDP. But while *adequate* does mean considerably larger funding, it must be provided alongside reforms that enable the Pentagon to get more bang for the defense buck. How can that be achieved?

Principle 2: Predictability and Consistency

The budget needs to be predictable and consistent enough to better enable the development of new capabilities over time while funding current readiness. It took Admiral Hyman G. Rickover, even when given a wide berth, seven years to commission the first nuclear-powered submarine, the USS *Nautilus*. Yet defense has been subject to CRs in nine of the last ten years, including 218 days in 2018. As Admiral Michael Gilday, the former chief of naval operations, warned, CRs only provide enough resources to invest in current programs and don't even account for inflation, preventing the military from investing enough in the new and innovative capabilities necessary to sustain its competitive edge. Nor do CRs allow either the DoD or the defense industrial base to plan and deliver efficiently. Increased use of multiyear funding would help ameliorate this self-inflicted damage.

Principle 3: Flexibility

America also faces a complicated threat landscape, with escalating competition from China and Russia, perpetual challenges from North Korea, Iran, and other rogue nations, and a profusion of nonstate terrorist attackers who've proven nimble at recruitment and have often transmuted after defeats. The capabilities required to thwart each adversary are different. Given the country's checkered history of anticipating and planning for future conflicts, a flexible budget is needed, one that hedges by investing in multiple capabilities to serve the military's needs and enabling the United States to react quickly to changes in the threat environment. And, as several of the following chapters argue, the DoD planning, programming, budgeting, and execution (PPBE) process must be reformed to provide, and Congress must authorize, greater flexibility and speed to reprogram funding for other use cases and to spend appropriated dollars across multiple fiscal years.

Principle 4: Incentive Compatibility

More funding consistency and flexibility may be necessary but could prove insufficient if budgeting fails to consider incentives within and outside the Pentagon. The DoD has more than 1.3 million active-duty personnel and even more reservists and civilians. Recruitment, retention, skills enhancement, and promotion reforms must account for the incentives of those potentially affected. Past reforms have sometimes failed to incentivize intended behavior. For example, program officers underutilize authorities, including the Commercial Solutions Opening program, which speeds up procurement of innovative technologies, and the Cyber Excepted Service, a group of technologically skilled civilians eligible to earn higher salaries. Indeed, even as secretaries of defense have trumpeted the need for the department to procure more innovative technologies, acquisition officers are not sufficiently judged by—nor promoted for—purchasing cutting-edge products and services from the array of private firms producing them. The Pentagon must better understand and utilize incentives for personnel, contractors, and services to use its budgetary resources effectively. It is often difficult for high performers to rise quickly and for underperformers to be weeded out. Better-designed incentives could also help the services, which have struggled to enlist at target levels, a problem made more acute in a strong labor market.

Principle 5: Accountability

The Pentagon is accountable to Congress and, therefore, ultimately to the American voter. Its budget is neither sufficiently transparent nor accountable. While it has made considerable progress, the DoD just failed its fifth consecutive audit, struggling to account for 61 percent of its assets.[16] Reforms that increase accountability and transparency, without jeopardizing security where possible, will likely be necessary to help build the political support to protect, let alone increase, the defense budget.

General Recommendations

Our analysis leads to several conclusions, most importantly that the level of resources and the inflexible budgeting authorities the DoD has today fall far short of what is necessary to support a strategy relevant to today's threats. Of course, given the country's long-standing appropriate civilian oversight of the military embodied in the president as commander in chief and Congress as authorizer and appropriator, the military must do its best to deal with changing political priorities and decisions. The Pentagon hews to the budget it receives but, hopefully, constructively influences. It could be helped considerably in achieving its mission if reforms along the following lines were implemented:

1. Far greater use of multiyear appropriations.
2. Streamlining the PPBE process to enable the DoD to purchase more quickly and to acquire more commercially available technology.
3. Greater and simpler reprogramming authorities across programs and even services, if necessary.
4. Much broader categories of programs and colors of money.
5. Repurposing at least a major portion of Pentagon spending that does not advance the DoD's core mission, with some transitioned to other relevant agencies and some shifted to the DoD's core mission capabilities. At the very least, non-core-mission spending should be displayed separately in the budget to enhance the public's understanding and build support for what's needed for national security.

Conclusion

We are cautiously optimistic that at least some considerable progress can be made despite the challenges mentioned above and the associated risks. Politicians and the public increasingly recognize the threats made real by Putin's war on Ukraine and China's military buildup and assertiveness. This is why there was a bipartisan agreement in Congress to increase the Pentagon's budget over the last two years. Polling suggests greater interest in national security and the defense budget and support for increased defense spending.

America's allies in different theaters also increasingly recognize that they face more threats. NATO allies are raising their defense spending. Japan plans to double its military budget, and our allies are collaborating more closely with us on common defense efforts.

Commissions, including the 2017 National Defense Strategy Commission, are clearly laying out the threats the country faces. And the PPBE Commission will recommend reforms to the sixty-year-old internal Pentagon system, which, as structured, is ill suited to procure innovative technology, certainly at the speed necessary.

Also encouraging is the increased interest from private technology companies—large and small—in working with the DoD. Indeed, one of the most important contributions to Ukraine's defenses has been Starlink, Elon Musk's satellite system, helping to keep command and control up and running. That could be an advantage for America, as well, deterring an adversary from thinking it could quickly degrade America's command-and-control system in the event of hostilities.

And the growing number of veterans in Congress, whose attractiveness to voters for their experience, problem solving, and mission-completion orientation, will serve the nation well in future defense budget reform debates.

Notes

1. Robert M. Gates, *Duty: Memoirs of a Secretary at War* (New York: Alfred A. Knopf, 2014), 590.

2. The White House, "National Security Strategy," October 2022.

3. Megan Eckstein, "US Navy Avoided a 2022 'Trough' in Submarine Fleet Size, but Industry Challenges Threaten Future Growth," *Defense News*, January 3, 2022.

4. Rachel S. Cohen and Stephen Losey, "US Air Force Fleet's Mission-Capable Rates Are Stagnating. Here's the Plan to Change That," *Air Force Times*, February 14, 2022.

5. Reagan National Defense Survey, Reagan Foundation, 2022.

6. Hoover Institution, "The Hoover Institution's Tennenbaum Program for Fact-Based Policy Rolls Out Initial Research Projects," press release, October 11, 2022.

7. Michèle Flournoy, "America's Military Risks Losing Its Edge," *Foreign Affairs* 100, no. 3 (May/June 2021).

8. Dr. Nan Tian and Fei Su, "A New Estimate of China's Military Expenditure," Stockholm International Peace Research Institute, January 2021.

9. Mark F. Cancian, Matthew Cancian, and Eric Heginbotham, "The First Battle of the Next War: Wargaming a Chinese Invasion of Taiwan," Center for Strategic and International Studies, January 9, 2023.

10. Mallory Shelbourne, "Davidson: China Could Try to Take Control of Taiwan in 'Next Six Years,'" *USNI News*, March 9, 2021.

11. Quoted in Micah Zenko, "100% Right 0% of the Time: Why the US Military Can't Predict the Next War," *Foreign Policy*, October 16, 2012.

12. Quoted in Col. Gary "GI" Wilson (ret.), Lt. Col. William A. Woods (ret.), and Col. Michael D. Wyly (ret.), "Send In the Marines? Reconsider Force Design 2030 Beforehand," *Defense News*, August 4, 2022.

13. CNN Wire Staff, "Mullen: Debt Is Top National Security Threat," CNN, August 27, 2010.

14. Congressional Budget Office, "Reduce the Department of Defense's Annual Budget," in *Options for Reducing the Deficit, 2023 to 2032—Volume 1: Larger Reductions*, December 7, 2022, https://www.cbo.gov/budget-options/58632.

15. The BCA expired in 2021, and OCOs as a separate category were not extended in the 2022 National Defense Authorization Act. See note with figure 1.8, and CBO, *Funding for Overseas Contingency Operations and Its Impact on Defense Spending*, October 2018.

16. Jim Garamone, "DOD Makes Audit Progress, but Much More Needs to Happen, Official Says," US Department of Defense, November 16, 2022.

Part 1

National Security Threats

2

The Military Challenge of the People's Republic of China

Oriana Skylar Mastro

Over the past twenty-five years, the People's Republic of China (PRC) has heavily invested in modernizing its military, the People's Liberation Army (PLA). Thanks to a 740 percent increase in its budget, top-leadership attention, strategic emulation, and innovation, the PLA now presents a formidable challenge to the US-led international order, the security of US allies and partners, and the United States itself.[1] The increase in resources and effort has resulted in more frequent, sophisticated, and multifaceted PLA presence and activities in the region and beyond, undermining faith in the US's willingness to live up to its defense commitments. Additionally, PLA's anti-access/area denial capabilities instill doubt in capitals around the world that the United States has the necessary military capacity to fight and win a war against China.

In this chapter, I lay out Chinese activities and capabilities with respect to a Taiwan contingency as well as US challenges in countering (and thus deterring) China. The last section presents a series of recommendations to mitigate US defense challenges in deterring China from attempting a fait accompli.

The New Strategy of Peaceful Reunification

For the past twenty-five years, China has tried to strengthen economic, social, and cultural ties with the people of Taiwan to convince them to unify with the PRC. The strategy has failed; today, only 4 to 7 percent of the people of Taiwan are willing to consider unification with the PRC.[2] The PRC's 2005 Anti-Secession Law clarifies that available options include armed reunification, a path currently under open and vigorous debate within Chinese strategic circles. Chinese leaders continue to use the language of peaceful

The views expressed in this chapter are solely those of the individual author and do not necessarily reflect the views of any organization with which they are, or have been, affiliated.

reunification officially, but the terms of the strategy have changed to "peaceful reunification backed by significant military force," according to my conversations with party officials. In other words, as the PLA prepares for armed unification, it is also increasing its belligerent rhetoric and military activities in the vicinity of Taiwan to show Taiwan that it does not stand a chance in a war with the PRC and thus should capitulate without a fight.

The PLA uses constant air and naval sorties to harass Taiwan's military and slowly wear at their systems. From January 1 to July 31, 2022, the PLA averaged more than four daily incursions into Taiwan's southwestern air defense identification zone (ADIZ). In the two months following House Speaker Nancy Pelosi's August 2–3, 2022, visit to Taipei, the PLA flew more than 1,200 sorties near Taiwan's skies, with 40 percent of those entering the island's ADIZ.[3] In just a one-month period in late 2022, Taiwan's Ministry of National Defense reported one hundred instances of the People's Liberation Army Navy (PLAN) vessels sailing in the waters around Taiwan.[4]

China has also been conducting military exercises of greater sophistication and scope, partly as a show of force. In August 2022, in response to Pelosi's visit, the PLA launched a series of live-fire drills, antisubmarine practices, and raid rehearsals, imposing a de facto blockade on the island. China's Foreign Minister Wang Yi condemned the United States for disrupting peace in the Taiwan Strait and obstructing the reunification of China.[5] Demonstrating Beijing's ample capability to disrupt Taiwan's economy, the exercises included multiarmed joint sea assaults, land strikes, and air superiority operations, and involved as many as fifty ships, eleven conventional missiles launched across the Median Line, and more than one hundred fighter aircraft.[6] For its part, Taipei initiated military exercises off of its East Coast city of Hualien and condemned China's "continuous military provocations."[7] The Chinese Communist Party (CCP) subsequently released a white paper on the Taiwan question, reaffirming China's aggressive stance toward Taiwan and insistence on national reunification.[8]

All these activities display the sophistication and confidence of the Chinese armed forces but also their mere mass. China currently has the largest navy in the world, with 340 ships consisting of aircraft carriers, cruisers, destroyers, frigates, corvettes, submarines, and amphibious assault ships. By 2025, the PLAN is expected to expand to a fleet of four hundred, replacing its previous generations of platforms, most notably with major surface combatants. Major developments include the 7,500-ton Luyang III guided-missile Type 052D(L) destroyers and the 13,000-ton Type 55 Renhai-class guided-missile cruisers; twenty-five of the former and at least five of the latter are currently in commission.[9] The destroyers could be useful in blockading Taiwan, while the large size of the fleet itself could be deployed to keep the United States and its allies at bay during a Taiwan contingency.[10] The Chinese Air Force is also developing a new strategic stealth bomber called the Xian H-20, which is anticipated to be operational within the next decade. The H-20, likely possessing a range of at least 8,500 km and having both conventional and nuclear capabilities, will join the J-20 fighters, Y-20 airlifters, and Z-20 helicopters in the PLA Air Force's "20" series of new aircraft.[11]

Chinese military improvements are especially concerning, given China's increasingly strident rhetoric over Taiwan. In his New Year's Day speech in 2019, Xi Jinping warned Taiwan that unification is the ultimate goal of any talks over its future and any efforts by the island to assert full independence would be met with armed force.[12] At the celebration of the centennial of the CCP in 2021, Xi delivered a speech emphasizing the inevitability of China's "national rejuvenation" and deemed China's "complete reunification" to be "a historic mission and an unshakable commitment" of the CCP.[13] This goal was further emphasized in subsequent speeches, most recently at the Twentieth National Congress of the CCP in October 2022. It seems that Xi demands concrete progress toward reunification, and he might soon be confident he has the military power for a full amphibious assault to seize Taiwan by force.

Despite this military modernization, invading Taiwan would still represent an immense challenge to the PLA due to the demands that modern, complex operations place on a military's logistical and command-and-control capabilities. Indeed, in November 2022, US chairman of the Joint Chiefs of Staff General Mark Milley assessed that a near-term Chinese attempt to invade Taiwan would result in a "debacle" for the Chinese military.[14] Russia's difficulties in its invasion of Ukraine have also shown how difficult complex offensive operations are, and an amphibious landing would be much more difficult than Russia's overland operations.

First, an amphibious invasion of Taiwan would present an immense logistical challenge to the PLA, and Chinese analysts know it. PLA sources estimate that China would need 3,000 military trains, 1 million vehicles, and over 2,100 aircraft to pull off an invasion. It would require 30 million tons of combat matériel and over 50 million tons of oil.[15] The PLA has made efforts to reform its logistics capabilities, most notably with the 2016 establishment of the Joint Logistics Support Force, but PLA analysts still assess themselves to be severely lacking in areas critical for an operation on the scale of a cross-strait invasion.[16]

Successful joint operations also require effective command-and-control (C2) structures capable of orchestrating disparate military branches to achieve a particular goal. To subdue Taiwan, China would need the PLA Rocket Force to pummel Taiwan's defenses, the PLA Navy to cordon off Taiwan's merchant and military shipping in a blockade, and other naval forces to escort PLA Army and PLAN Marine Corps units to the landing beaches. All the while, the PLA Air Force would need to maintain air superiority over the region, and the PLA Strategic Support Force would need to use its extensive intelligence, surveillance, and reconnaissance (ISR) capabilities to watch for signs of American intervention.

But the takeaway is not that the complexity of joint operations or that Russia's difficulties in Ukraine imply that China won't (or can't) invade Taiwan. The takeaway is that China knows logistics, precision-guided munitions, and adequate C2 structures are integral to modern warfare. For decades, Chinese military leadership has issued a host of sayings, such as Hu Jintao's "Two Incompatibles" and Xi Jinping's "Two Inabilities" and "Five Incapables," all of which point out severe PLA deficiencies.[17] China's lagging logistical and C2 capabilities might preclude invasion now, but after a few more years of increasingly realistic exercises and ongoing reform efforts, the PLA may have the ability to take Taiwan by 2027.

Deterring China over Taiwan: The Attractiveness of a Fait Accompli

In addition to projecting power over the Taiwan Strait, China's military modernization has focused on the ability to prevent a decisive US response, referred to as its anti-access/area denial (A2/AD) strategy. Anti-access refers to the ability to prevent an opposing force from entering an area of operations. Here China has developed capabilities that can slow down the deployment of opposing forces into the theater, prevent US forces from operating in certain areas (like the first island chain—the "barrier" extending from Japan, past Taiwan and the Philippines, to maritime and peninsular Southeast Asia), or compel US forces to operate from distances farther from the conflict than operationally ideal. Chinese strategists recognize that antisatellite operations on communication satellites or cyberattacks on the opponent's command-and-control system would disrupt how the US deploys and operates its forces.[18]

The objective of area denial, on the other hand, is not prevention but disruption—to compel the desired behavior by imposing severe costs on the enemy's freedom of action once it has gained access. Chinese integrated air defenses, antiship cruise and ballistic missiles, maritime bombers, missile- and torpedo-carrying submarines, and fast patrol boats are all designed to inflict prohibitively high costs on any country that dares to operate within the first island chain near the China mainland.[19] Chinese capabilities could force US navy vessels to operate well beyond the first island chain and the US air force to operate at higher altitudes. Both would limit the United States' ability to effectively target PLA units, whether on the mainland, in transit across the strait, or in Taiwan itself. In short, China's increasingly capable layered air defenses, as well as its fighter, ship, and missile assets, could target US bases and assets in the region, hampering operations.

The main vulnerabilities the United States experiences in its military power in Asia stem from the fact that it is not a resident power in Asia and thus is attempting to project power across vast distances. The emerging US way of war exhibits several dependencies that China's A2/AD strategy targets. First and foremost, the United States relies on other countries for base access, while China can rely on home bases. This is problematic for several reasons. The number of bases the United States has access to in the first island chain has atrophied since the end of the Cold War, while China has infinite possibilities for basing options on its massive soil. In practice, the result is that the United States has one air base, Kadena Air Base in Okinawa, within combat range of Taiwan, while China has thirty-nine.[20] Each air base can only support so many aircraft (Kadena can house about eighty aircraft, only fifty-four of which are fighters. And even here, the US Air Force has also started to pull many of these aging aircraft out of the base, replacing them only with a temporary unit of more modern F-22s), which translates into China being able to generate far more sorties than the United States.[21]

But the biggest issue is that the United States may not be able to get any aircraft into the sky; all US forward bases in South Korea and Japan, including Okinawa, are highly vulnerable to Chinese attack, most likely with ballistic missiles and ground- or air-launched land-attack cruise missiles. China's missile-launch capabilities in the region are staggering. A 2016 RAND report estimated that air force bases in Japan and South Korea, including Kadena, could see thousands of Chinese missiles launched at them, and even Andersen Air Force Base on Guam is within striking range of hundreds of Chinese missiles launched from bombers and fighters. Specifically, the J-20, deployed in

2017, greatly increased China's ability to strike regional air bases, logistical facilities, and other ground-based infrastructure.[22] Similarly, Chinese H-6 bombers have undergone several refits enabling them to strike targets as far as Guam.[23]

China has long been aware of the vulnerability of the US bases in the Asia Pacific region and Washington's potential efforts to strengthen its bases.[24] Media cite the 2008 RAND simulation that thirty-four Chinese missiles could damage 75 percent of the aircraft in Kadena and call attention to Washington's efforts to build up forces beyond the range of Chinese missiles.[25] The *People's Daily Online* and *China News* republished the *Global Times* report on a 2014 *National Interest* article that argued Washington's Asian military bases were the US Army's greatest weakness, due to China's increasing missile capabilities.[26] The articles specifically mentioned that the Yokosuka and Sasebo naval bases in Japan would become targets for Chinese missiles, leaving US maritime strike forces in the region isolated.

While the degree of damage depends on China's strategy, the impact on the United States' ability to operate in the region after an attack would be severely limited. US bases could be closed for more than six weeks, with almost all aircraft damaged or destroyed.[27] The range of China's destructive capability is only increasing. Indeed, China's cruise and ballistic missile programs, the heart of its long-range precision strike capability, are the most advanced and active in the world; China has deployed thousands of cruise missiles, six hundred short-range ballistic missiles (SRBMs), and more than five hundred medium-range ballistic missiles (MRBMs) capable of conducting precision strikes against land targets and naval vessels out to the first island chain.[28] China's MRBMs can extend PLA's range to 1,000–2,000 kilometers, and new intermediate-range ballistic missiles (IRBMs), including the DF-26, of which China has approximately 250, extend operational ranges to 3,000 km. These are capable of precision attacks on Guam and US carrier battle groups operating beyond the first island chain, in the Indian Ocean, or in the South China Sea.[29]

According to the Pentagon's annual reports to Congress, China's ICBM (intercontinental ballistic missile) count grew from 45 to 300 missiles between 2010 and 2022; IRBMs grew from 20 to 250; MRBMs grew from 115 to 500. Land-attack cruise missiles and SRBMs actually decreased during this time; however, this might be due to China's replacing aging systems with newer, more sophisticated variants.[30] China's missiles have improved dramatically in terms of quality as well as quantity. For instance, the DF-16, which only entered service in 2015, is nearly six times more accurate than the DF-15.[31]

In addition to its forward bases, the United States also projects power into the region from out-of-area locations. A classic example is the aircraft carrier—five of which are assigned to the Indo-Pacific region, with two home-ported in San Diego, two home-ported in Washington State, and only one ported in the region, in Yokosuka, Japan. Aircraft carriers work to project power by geographically unlocking air superiority, allowing air forces to operate even without nearby airbases. The spillover effects of air superiority, or even competitiveness in the air, are many. For instance, during World War II, American aircraft carriers enabled success in critical naval battles, provided air support to make possible amphibious landings, and were able to protect shipping lanes despite the vastness of the Pacific Ocean and incidents being far away from American airbases. The 2022 film *Top Gun: Maverick* shows how the carrier can be used for deep-strike operations. In the movie, the pilots take off and return to a carrier off the coast of an unnamed hostile country without any concern for the carrier's safety. This makes sense, as most countries lack the ability to target a moving ship at sea from their shores, especially one as heavily defended as a carrier.

But this is not the case with China. The PLA has terminally guided anti-ship ballistic missile systems, most notably the DF-21D, that reportedly can engage adversary surface ships up to 1,000 nautical miles (nm) from the PRC coast, cued by increasingly sophisticated surveillance and attack networks, holding at risk Tokyo, Manila, Pusan, and targets throughout the South China Sea. With a combination of ballistic missiles, supersonic cruise missiles, rocket torpedoes, and rocket-propelled sea mines laid by submarines, China can destroy or render operationally ineffective all the aircraft carrier strike groups that the United States has in the Indo-Pacific region without levying comparable forces. US commanders are now reluctant to send carriers into a conflict, making it difficult for the United States to establish air superiority.[32]

Even if US aircraft manage to get in the air despite the threat to aircraft carriers and regional bases, they are still threatened by a robust Chinese air defense system. Any air defense system encompasses two main functions: first, warning systems, including radar networks and other scanners; and second, air defense capabilities, including surface-to-air missiles (SAMs) and fighter deployments. Chinese radar systems are strategically placed to overlap and are on the artificial islands it built in the South China Sea, extending China's early-warning range further into the Pacific.[33] In terms of SAMs,

China has continuously increased its deployments of long-range advanced missiles, deploying the HQ-9, the HQ-9B, and the Russian-built SA-10 and SA-20 missiles. All Chinese SAM missiles currently in use can intercept aircraft and also cruise missiles. The overlapping defenses increase the chance of kill and make their system more robust.[34]

Indeed, such capabilities will make it difficult for the United States to surmount Chinese air defenses with its usual set of tools (e.g., jamming, standoff, and stealth weapons) in the case of a Taiwan contingency. China's Integrated Air Defense System (IADS) is sophisticated enough to prevent the United States' fourth-generation, nonstealth aircraft from operating over and near the Chinese mainland. As former senior intelligence officer Lonnie Henley told Congress, by denying the United States the ability to conduct air operations over the Taiwan Strait, largely thanks to its IADS, China could maintain a blockade of the island and continue launching its planes to strike targets on Taiwan or US Navy ships indefinitely.[35] Although the United States would do better in conflicts surrounding more remote areas such as the Spratly Islands, Chinese capabilities such as advanced SAM systems and defensive combat air patrols could still stave off an easy defeat.[36] In both scenarios, the US would have to rely on fifth-generation stealth technology and standoff weapons to strike Chinese targets on the mainland, but China is also making progress with the HQ-19.[37] Although it is unclear whether Chinese air defense could maintain a constant track on advanced US stealth aircraft, the United States would be forced to operate at higher altitudes and disable or destroy antiaircraft capabilities with long-range missiles before being able to establish regional air superiority.[38]

Because the United States would largely be projecting power from outside the first island chain—from places like Guam, Hawaii, or even the continental United States—its military also relies on many "enablers," or augmented capabilities that directly impact mission accomplishment. These are assets that main platforms or units need to engage in operations. These enablers also create vulnerabilities that China can exploit to hurt the US's ability to project power. For example, bombers and fighters need aerial refueling to engage in long-range operations, and thus they need tankers to carry and provide the fuel. But tankers are vulnerable to being shot down by Chinese surface-based defenses and fighters. Thus, China would compel the United States to refuel farther away from the conflict zone, reducing the amount of combat time fighters and bombers have (since they are flying farther and farther to get more fuel).[39]

Another obvious example of an enabler is the increasing US reliance on cyber capabilities. Between the Gulf War in 1991 and the Iraq War in 2003, US commanders gained access to forty-two times as much bandwidth and information flow. That number continues to increase, especially as more processes become automated and operation units become accustomed to an informational surplus.[40]

Chinese analysts quickly became aware of the US dependence on space-based assets and services for commanding deployed troops, passing ISR data and enabling precision targeting and engagement.[41] Conducting network attacks, blinding, dazzling, or even destroying satellites with a kinetic kill vehicle like an antisatellite missile could stymie deployed US military forces by disrupting communications and denying information vital for determining the location and the movement of forces.[42] To paraphrase an authoritative Chinese military source, cyber operations can be used to disseminate false information, simulate various combat operations of the troops to mislead the enemy into wrong decisions, disrupt the enemy's information obtainment, paralyze the enemy's command-and-control systems, or access the enemy's internet system and cause information destruction.[43] Indeed, Chinese sources describe deterrence in outer space as "the first choice of future deterrence" since space is not limited by politics or geography and could "project the power of deterrence to every corner on the surface of the earth."[44]

Given these realities, Chinese experts have advised that the PLA should emphasize military-civil fusion and develop offensive and defensive cyber capabilities that target enemy vulnerabilities.[45] As a result of this top leadership focus, China evolved from "a position of relative backwardness in electronics in the 1990s" to "conducting large-scale cyber operations abroad, aiming to acquire intellectual property, achieve political influence, carry out state-on-state espionage and position capabilities for disruptive effect in case of future conflict."[46] China is now among the top five leading source countries for denial-of-service and web application–based global cyberattacks.[47]

China has also proactively exploited the absence of established norms in space to put forth its own that would constrain the United States and cater to its strengths. For example, China's Prevention of the Placement of Weapons in Outer Space, the Threat or Use of Force against Outer Space Objects (PPWT) proposal would limit offensive weapons in space but does little to restrain antisatellite weaponry.[48] The United States, which sees little to gain in an agreement that would limit its offensive capabilities while leaving China and Russia's antisatellite missiles untouched, continues to oppose the

PPWT.[49] China has also pushed for incorporating concepts such as "cyber sovereignty" through the United Nations and its own Digital Silk Road initiative. The term means that states are free to regulate their information technology industries in ways they see fit, justifying China's stringent censorship of its internet.[50]

Recommendations

The following recommendations are based on three main assessments about how to deter a war across the Taiwan Strait. First, cost imposition is less impactful than deterrence by denial.[51] Second, there is no indication that Xi Jinping needs to take Taiwan by 2027 to secure a new term. Third, Chinese power is not in for a hard fall, making it now or never.[52] In other words, China can be deterred. Below are some options for achieving this—none of which are easy, and all of which are far from guaranteed.

More Access, Basing, and Overflight

The US military's force posture needs to be completely overhauled. Given the difficulty of adequately defending its bases and assets against Chinese attack, the best strategy is dispersal, redundancy, and resilience. In other words, if the United States cannot defend against a Chinese attack, at the very least it has to ensure such attacks do not render the combat force ineffective. One way of achieving this goal is to operate from more locations. Negotiating access agreements and signaling to China that countries will support US military operations in case of a contingency should be a top priority for the State Department. Countries in the region are reluctant to get involved, but in practice they are choosing China when they choose neutrality, because that is all China needs to win. Access, basing, and overflight (ABO) will be most forthcoming if it is clear that China is the aggressor and Beijing is unable to take Taiwan quickly. US leaders should avoid political maneuvering that does not improve the operational situation and must ensure the country can respond quickly and with minimal warning if China launches an attack on Taiwan.[53]

More Mass on Targets

More locations from which to operate will mitigate the problem of Chinese attacks but will be insufficient to deny China the capability to take Taiwan. Doing so would require the United States to hit Chinese ships as they make the one-hundred-mile voyage to Taiwan's shores.

Even if by some miracle the United States' power projection system survived an initial Chinese attack and the majority of its forces were within targeting range of the Taiwan Strait, the United States does not have the type and number of precision-guided munitions necessary to attrit enough Chinese ships to put the operation's success at risk. A 2021 report, written before the Russia-Ukraine war, warned Congress that the services were buying low quantities of these weapons despite the high demand that any conflict would place on US stockpiles.[54] For instance, in its April 2022 procurement request, the US Air Force requested fewer than two hundred long-range antiship missiles (LRASMs), while the navy requested fewer than 450.[55] When asked by reporters why the air force prioritized long-range standoff weapons designed to hit fixed, rather than surface, targets, an official replied that the service was not focused on hitting naval targets.[56] The United States also fields the Harpoon antiship missile, the Maritime Strike Tomahawk, the Naval Strike Missile, and the ground-based high-mobility artillery rocket system (HIMARS, capable of firing antiship missiles). But here too, the United States is not buying enough. The lone exception might be the HIMARS, of which the US Army hopes to procure five hundred by 2028, just barely in time for when the risk of invasion may begin to rise dramatically.[57]

Consider the LRASM a useful example of the deficiency in US procurement plans. Capable of being launched from air or ship and with a range of over three hundred kilometers, the LRASM represents one of the best options for striking Chinese naval and logistics vessels in a cross-strait invasion. PLA analyses estimate that China would need between 550 and 700 logistics ships to transport men and matériel across the Taiwan Strait.[58] Open-source reports suggest that China could pull from nearly two thousand civilian ships currently suited for mobilization.[59] Under a best-case scenario—in which all of the US Air Force's LRASMs and bomber fleets survive an initial Chinese missile strike, each LRASM evades China's impressive antiair defenses, and each missile scores a killing blow against its target—the air force's paltry 179 LRASMs would barely put a dent in this logistics fleet (not to mention its navy's surface combatants); likewise for the navy, which would only bring another 450 missiles to the fight. Adjust these overly optimistic conditions by assuming that half of the LRASMs survive a first strike and that only half of those missiles find a home, and you are left with 157 missiles on target. As one report notes, with only 179 missiles, the air force could only fly *nine* B-52 sorties or *seven* B-1 sorties.[60] With each LRASM costing around $4 million, buying five times as many missiles over the next five years would cost the United States about $13 billion, representing just 1.5 percent of the amount Congress granted the military for 2023 alone.[61]

The US defense industry cannot support the type, amount, and pace of production needed. The United States also faces a backlog of nearly $19 billion in weapons meant for Taiwan, including hundreds of Stingers, Javelins, and Paladin guided artillery. The COVID-19 pandemic and related staffing shortages have led to much of this sclerosis.[62] The crisis in Ukraine and tensions over the Taiwan Strait highlight the long-standing problem that the United States does not have the surge production needed. Part of the problem is that the Department of Defense (DoD) does not provide the demand to justify these companies' keeping their production lines online or at least ready to be scaled quickly. For instance, because the Pentagon has not ordered Stingers since 2003, only a few foreign buyers kept Raytheon's Stinger production lines operational.[63]

Some experts view the US Navy's fleet of fifty-three fast-attack submarines, consisting of submarines in the Seawolf, Los Angeles, and Virginia classes, as a comparative advantage over China. PLA antisubmarine warfare capabilities are considered poor, while US submarines are world class.[64] But however poor China's antisubmarine warfare capabilities are, these boats would be operating in a very tight environment in the Taiwan Strait and would have to face the combined might of China's surface fleet, submarines, and airborne antisubmarine warfare assets. Procurement and maintenance problems exist here, too. According to the navy, less than one-third of US attack submarines have completed maintenance on time over the past decade, and navy officials have expressed concern over how stressed US submarine shipyards have become.[65]

The United States needs to develop frameworks for better coordination and cooperation between the defense industry and the government. Operation Warp Speed (OWS), the interagency initiative that led to the rapid development, approval, and distribution of COVID-19 vaccines, could serve as an example. Defense procurement experts should study this program and determine how DoD might apply OWS's successes to its research, development, and procurement efforts.[66] Governments must often step in as providers of public goods when the market does not have the incentives necessary to motivate private companies to produce or provide a good or service. It might not make economic sense to train personnel and build production lines that are ultimately underutilized, but the need for a surge capacity in times of war makes sense strategically. The US government should explore options for a reserve force to produce defense equipment.

Moreover, the civil-military partnership needs to be revitalized. In the 1960s, the DoD funded about half of the country's entire research and development budget; today, that number is just 10 percent. While this may allow the Pentagon to piggyback off technology funded and developed by private corporations, it does lessen the military's ability to guide the nation's overall research and development effort.[67]

Leveraging Partners

Most US efforts in foreign military sales, joint training, and exercises are designed to build partner capacity. The United States, the principal weapons supplier for Taiwan, has been busy helping Taipei adopt its "Overall Defense Concept" (ODC), or what some experts call the "Porcupine Strategy." The ODC sees Taiwan relying on high numbers of low-cost weapons such as mines, missiles, and mobile artillery systems, rather than expensive, flashy platforms such as fighter jets and submarines.[68]

Apart from Taiwan, the United States is helping countries across the region prepare for conflict with China. The AUKUS deal will provide Australia with nuclear fast-attack submarines, while Japan plans to buy Tomahawk missiles from the United States to bolster its long-range counterstrike capability.[69] The Biden administration recently sold Indonesia $14 billion in F-15 fighter jets, which would certainly help Indonesia contest Chinese air supremacy over the South China Sea. And the Pentagon has made clear that the Philippines' human rights issues will not impede arms sales in the future, which should become more relevant considering the new president, Ferdinand Marcos Jr., is seen as much more hawkish on China than his predecessor.[70]

Nowhere is building partnership capacity more important than in Taiwan's building its own self-defense. Over the past two administrations, the United States has sold Taiwan over $20 billion in arms. These include deals for cutting-edge F-16V fighter jets, radar arrays, Harpoon antiship missiles, and Patriot missile defense systems.[71] The United States has also quietly deployed special operations units to Taiwan to train its troops.[72]

But these actions alone do not present enough of a credible threat to Beijing. The mechanism through which this deters China is that Taiwan needs to show it can hold off long enough to allow the United States to come to its aid; then, other countries need to show the willingness to directly support US military operations.

In prioritizing US allyship, Japan is positioned to play the most pivotal role. It boasts the third-largest economy in the world and the second-largest population in Northeast Asia. And despite the limitations imposed by its constitution, the Japanese Maritime Self-Defense Force (JMSDF) is one of the best navies in Asia. It boasts more than fifty surface combatants, including eight Aegis-equipped guided missile destroyers and four helicopter carriers, two of which were converted into aircraft carriers capable of fielding advanced F-35B fighters.[73] The JMSDF also fields twenty-one diesel-electric attack submarines and has commissioned two of a planned twenty-two Mogami-class multirole frigates.[74] The JMSDF's five major bases at Yokosuka, Sasebo, Kure, Maizuru, and Ōminato also provide JMSDF and US Navy ships with in-theater ports for repair and replenishment.[75] The US Navy's only permanently forward-deployed aircraft carrier, the USS *Ronald Reagan*, is home-ported at Yokosuka. In short, Japan's size, geography, and naval might could prove decisive in a US-China conflict.

But the role of allies and partners is not relegated only to military roles. Much ink has been spilled about the enormous economic costs Beijing would face from a coordinated, US-led sanctions regime.[76] But the bottom line is that there are few indications that many countries would be willing to endure the pain of implementing such a regime, especially if China took Taiwan quickly with limited casualties.[77] The United States needs to work now to brainstorm potential sanctions packages that would be enough to set back Chinese economic growth by a significant margin. US and allied sanctions on Russia have brought that country's GDP down by about 3.5 percent, so any sanctions package would need to far exceed that figure—and Washington must also convince countries to communicate their willingness to implement such measures if there is a Chinese use of force.[78]

Conclusion

The issue is not that China *has* surpassed the United States in military power; it has not. The issue is that, given current trends, China will meet or outmatch US regional capabilities in the next five to ten years. China will soon have a modern military capable of conducting joint operations, such as those necessary to deny access to the South China Sea, retake islands, or force reunification with Taiwan. If, in the meantime, the US military does not improve and strengthen its force posture in Asia, improve its resiliency, and increase its ability to deny China these objectives forcibly, then Chinese leaders may decide it is worth the risk to use force. This is how we end up in a war with

China—not because we are overly provocative or push back too much, but because we do not do enough to maintain deterrence in the region, and China gains the confidence to jettison a cautious approach.

Military capabilities are not the best answer, but they are the easiest. Upgrading political relationships can be even more challenging, especially given the latent threat of China lurking in the background. We need to ask Indo-Pacific countries what would be necessary to get their support and a closer military relationship—and be open-minded about what such relationships may require.

To balance against the Soviet Union during the Cold War, we had the strategic mindset and political will to look beyond China's political system, normalize relations, and move that relationship forward. We need that degree of strategic thinking and political will; adhering to the same policies but expecting different outcomes will not change current trends in East Asia. We need to think differently, whether in creating a reserve force for the defense industry, coordinating economic sanctions ahead of time, or managing capability gaps with strategic agility. For example, since the United States might receive an unambiguous warning of an invasion, we should communicate to China (and the world) that the amassing of a certain quantity of troops and ships will be taken as a sign of an impending assault. None of these recommendations is easy, but deterring a war is always less painful than fighting one. For the sake of peace and security in Asia, experimentation is worth the risk.

Notes

The author would like to thank Thomas Causey for his expert research assistance.

1. Amrita Jash, "China's 2022 Defense Budget: Behind the Numbers," Jamestown Foundation, *China Brief* 22, no. 8 (April 29, 2022).

2. Election Study Center, "Taiwan Independence vs. Unification with the Mainland (1994/12~2022/12)," National Chengchi University, January 13, 2023, https://esc.nccu.edu.tw/PageDoc/Detail?fid=7801&id=6963.

3. Adrian Ang U-Jin and Olli Pekka Suorsa, "The 'New Normal' in PLA Incursions into Taiwan's ADIZ," *The Diplomat*, September 27, 2022.

4. "Military News Overview," Taiwan Military News Agency, accessed December 22, 2022, https://mna.gpwb.gov.tw/news/overview.

5. "Wang Yi Made a Speech Regarding the US's Violation of China's Sovereignty [王毅就美方侵犯中国主权发表谈话]," *People's Daily* [人民日报], August 4, 2022, http://paper.people.com.cn/rmrb/html/2022-08/04/nw.D110000renmrb_20220804_4-03.htm.

6. Brad Lendon, "China Fires Missiles Near Taiwan in Live-Fire Drills as PLA Encircles Island," *CNN*, August 4, 2022; Alastair Gale and Nancy A. Youssef, "China's

Military Exercises Showcase Modern Fighting Force Preparing for Possible War in the Taiwan Strait," *Wall Street Journal*, August 8, 2022. The Median Line runs through the middle of the Taiwan Strait. While Taiwan uses it, the PRC has never recognized it and disputes the line's legitimacy.

7. Johnson Lai, "Taiwan, China Hold Opposing Military Drills amid Tensions," AP News, August 17, 2022.

8. "Taiwan Issue and China's Reunification 1993," Information Office of the State Council of the People's Republic of China, https://www.mfa.gov.cn/ce/cejp/chn/zt /twwt/t62660.htm.

9. Sam LaGrone, "Pentagon: Chinese Navy to Expand to 400 Ships by 2025, Growth Focused on Surface Combatants," *USNI News*, November 29, 2022.

10. Gabriel Dominguez, "As China's Navy Grows Even Larger, So Does the Threat to Taiwan," *Japan Times*, August 25, 2022.

11. Kris Osborn, "Doomsday or Dud? China's H-20 Stealth Bomber Looks to Rival B-21," *National Interest*, August 13, 2022.

12. Chris Buckley and Chris Horton, "Xi Jinping Warns Taiwan That Unification Is the Goal and Force Is an Option," *New York Times*, January 1, 2019.

13. David Sacks, "What Xi Jinping's Major Speech Means for Taiwan," Council on Foreign Relations, July 6, 2021.

14. "Secretary Austin and General Milley News Conference," C-SPAN, November 16, 2022, https://www.c-span.org/video/?524313-1/defense-secretary-missile -landed-poland-ukraine.

15. Operational Logistics Support [作战后勤保障], All Army Logistics Academic Research Center [全军后勤学术研究中心], February 2017, cited in Kevin McCauley, "China Maritime Report No. 22: Logistics Support for a Cross-Strait Invasion: The View from Beijing," China Maritime Studies Institute, July 2022, https://digital -commons.usnwc.edu/cmsi-maritime-reports/22.

16. LeighAnn Luce and Erin Richter, "Handling Logistics in a Reformed PLA: The Long March toward Joint Logistics," in *Chairman Xi Remakes the PLA: Assessing Chinese Military Reforms*, ed. Phillip C. Saunders, Arthur S. Ding, Andrew Scobell, Andrew N. D. Yang, and Joel Wuthnow (Washington, DC: National Defense University Press, 2018), 257–92; McCauley, "Logistics Support for a Cross-Strait Invasion," 32–33.

17. Dennis J. Blasko, "The Chinese Military Speaks to Itself, Revealing Doubts," *War on the Rocks*, February 18, 2019.

18. Yu Jixun [于际训], *The Science of Second Artillery Campaigns* [第二炮兵战役学] (Beijing: Liberation Army Press [解放军出版社], 2004), 341; Huang Zhicheng [黄志澄], "Thinking and Knowledge about Space War [关于太空战的认知与思考]," *Aerospace International* [国际太空], no. 6 (2003): 10–15; Wang Jijian [王积建], "Perspective on Adjustments to US Space Strategy: Moving from Space Support to Space Control [透视美国太空战略的调整：从太空支援走向太空控制]," *World Military* [环球军事], no. 4 (2006): 44–47.

19. "The China Syndrome," *The Economist*, June 9, 2012.

20. Eric Heginbotham et al., *The US-China Military Scorecard: Forces, Geography, and the Evolving Balance of Power, 1996–2017* (Santa Monica, CA: RAND, 2015).

21. "18th Wing," United States 5th Air Force, undated, accessed December 5, 2022, https://www.5af.pacaf.af.mil/About-Us/Fact-Sheets/Display/Article/1483 830/18th-wing; Stephen Losey, "F-22s Arrive at Kadena, as Aging F-15s Prepare to Depart," *Defense News*, November 7, 2022.

22. Timothy R. Heath, Kristen Gunness, and Cortez A. Cooper III, "The PLA and China's Rejuvenation: National Security and Military Strategies, Deterrence Concepts, and Combat Capabilities" (Washington, DC: RAND Corporation, 2016), 38–39. Cited in China Power Team, "Does China's J-20 Rival Other Stealth Fighters?" *China Power*, February 23, 2018.

23. US Department of Defense (DoD), *Military and Security Developments Involving the People's Republic of China 2022: Annual Report to Congress*, November 29, 2022, 81–82.

24. "The Five Chinese Weapons That the US Army Is Most Afraid Of: DF-21D Is the First [美军最害怕的5款中国武器 DF-21D导弹居首]," China Military Website [中国军网], May 8, 2014, http://www.81.cn/bqtd/2014-05/08/content _5895795.htm.

25. "Hong Kong Media Hypothetical Sino-US Conflict: Asia-Pacific Bases Will Be the Achilles Heel of the United States [港媒假想中美冲突：亚太基地将是美国致命弱点]," *China News* [中新网], March 4, 2016, https://www.chinanews.com.cn /m/mil/2016/03-04/7783387.shtml.

26. "American Media: Chinese Missiles Make America's Asia-Pacific Military Bases into the Fatal Fall of the US Army [美媒：中国导弹令美亚太军事基地太为美军致命伤]," *People's Daily Online* [人民网], May 20, 2014, http://military.people .com.cn/n/2014/0520/c1011-25039554.html.

27. In a RAND simulation of an attack on Kadena, 36 Chinese missiles closed the runways for four days, scaling up to 43 days of closure if 274 missiles were to be used. The study also noted that the DF-21C-class missile could carry hundreds of submunitions, blanketing hundreds of square feet so that every aircraft parked in the area would have a high probability of being damaged. With just 108 missiles, China could shut down the airfield for a week and, with high probability of success, destroy every single fighter on the base. See Heginbotham et al., *US-China Military Scorecard*, 60.

28. DoD, *Military and Security Developments Involving the People's Republic of China 2021: Annual Report to Congress*, November 3, 2021, 167; Jin Yu, ed. *The Science of Second Artillery Campaigns* [*Dierpaobing zhanyixue*] (Beijing: People's Liberation Army Press, 2004), 82–86.

29. DoD, *Military and Security Developments 2022*, 167.

30. DoD, *Military and Security Developments Involving the People's Republic of China 2010: Annual Report to Congress*, undated [2010], 66, http://www.andrewerickson .com/wp-content/uploads/2015/11/DoD_China-Report_2010.pdf; DoD, *Military and Security Developments 2022*, 167.

31. David Webb, "Dong Feng-16 (CSS-11)," Missile Defense Advocacy Online, February 2017; "DF-15," Missile Threat CSIS, August 5, 2021.

32. In 2013, the PLA tested the DF-21D against a stationary, ground-based target about the size of a US aircraft carrier. In 2020, China fired the DF-21D and its intermediate-range counterpart, the DF-26, at a moving target in the South China Sea. However, it remains unclear whether the test was successful. See DoD, *Military and Security Developments 2022*, 65.

33. "A Constructive Year for Chinese Base Building," Asia Maritime Transparency Initiative, December 14, 2017; DoD, *Military and Security Developments 2022*, vii.

34. DoD, *Military and Security Developments 2022*, viii; Heginbotham et al., *US-China Military Scorecard*, 170.

35. US-China Economic and Security Review Commission, *Hearing on Cross-Strait Deterrence*, February 18, 2021, testimony by Lonnie Henley, "PLA Operational Concepts and Centers of Gravity in a Taiwan Conflict."

36. Heginbotham et al., *US-China Military Scorecard*, 130–31.

37. Heginbotham et al., *US-China Military Scorecard*, 130.

38. Kris Osborn, "Could the US Military Gain Air Supremacy in a War with China?" *National Interest*, November 8, 2021.

39. Timothy A. Walton and Bryan Clark, "Resilient Aerial Refueling: Safeguarding the US Military's Global Reach," Hudson Institute, November 2021, 29.

40. David Talbot, "How Technology Failed in Iraq," *MIT Technology Review*, November 1, 2004.

41. Wei Chengxi [魏晨曦], "Space War and Its Operational Environment [太空战及其作战环境]," *Aerospace China* [中国航天], no. 10 (2001): 40; Zhang Yuliang [张玉良] et al., eds., *The Science of Campaigns* [战役学] (Beijing: Guofang Daxue Chubanshe [国防大学出版社], 2006), 87.

42. Interestingly, these acknowledgments often come in the form of translating and publishing Western analysts' perspectives on Chinese capabilities; see Xin Lian [信莲], "American Media: PLA Space Capabilities Might Overtake the US Military [美媒: 解放军空天战力或 "逆袭" 美军]," *China Daily* [中国日报网], April 23, 2014, http://world.chinadaily.com.cn/2014-04/23/content_17456442 .htm; and "American Media: The Contest in Space Is the Next 'Great-Power Competition' [美媒: 太空之争，下一场中美 "大国竞赛"]," *Xinhuanet* [新华网], January 31, 2021, http://www.xinhuanet.com/mil/2021-01/31/c_1211004592.htm.

43. Yu, *Second Artillery Campaigns*, 341.

44. Zhang Yan [张岩], *Theory of Strategic Deterrence* [战略威慑论] (Beijing: Social Sciences Literature Press [社会科学文献出版社], 2018), 97–98.

45. Long Kun [龙坤] and Zhu Qichao [朱启超], "Algorithmic Warfare: Concept, Characteristics and Implications [算法战争" 的概念、特点与影响]," *National Defense Science & Technology* [国防科技] 38, no. 6 (2017): 41.

46. Brad D. Williams, "US 'Retains Clear Superiority' in Cyber; China Rising: IISS Study," *Breaking Defense*, June 28, 2021; International Institute for Strategic Studies, "Cyber Capabilities and National Power: A Net Assessment," June 28, 2021.

47. Omer Yoachimik and Vivek Ganti, "DDoS Attack Trends for Q4 2021," *Cloud-flare Blog*, January 10, 2022. In its 2021 annual report, cybersecurity firm CrowdStrike found that Chinese state-affiliated hacker groups were responsible for 67 percent of intrusions in the year leading up to June 2021; see "Nowhere to Hide: 2021 Threat Hunting Report," CrowdStrike, June 2021. As further evidence that its cyber strategy is about exploiting US vulnerabilities, China has not invested the same into its own cyber defenses, which remain weak, and its cyber-resilience policies for its critical national infrastructure are only in the initial stages; see Williams, "US 'Retains Clear Superiority.'"

48. Ministry of Foreign Affairs of the People's Republic of China, "China and Russia Jointly Submitted the Draft Treaty on PPWT to the Conference on Disarmament," February 2, 2008; Bradley Bowman and Jared Thompson, "Russia and China Seek to Tie America's Hands in Space," *Foreign Policy*, March 31, 2021.

49. Todd Harrison, "International Perspectives on Space Weapons," Center for Strategic and International Studies, Aerospace Security Project, May 2020; Almudena Azcárate Ortega, "Placement of Weapons in Outer Space: The Dichotomy between Word and Deed," *Lawfare*, January 28, 2021.

50. Ministry of Foreign Affairs of the People's Republic of China, "Remarks at the Opening Ceremony of the Second World Internet Conference (by Xi Jinping)," December 16, 2015, https://www.fmprc.gov.cn/eng/wjdt_665385/zyjh_665391 /201512/t20151224_678467.html.

51. Oriana Skylar Mastro, "Deterrence in the Indo-Pacific," National Bureau of Asian Research, *Asia Policy* 17, no. 4 (October 2022): 8–18.

52. For evidence of Xi's political motivation, see Mattathias Schwartz, "Why China Doesn't Actually Want to Invade Taiwan," *Insider*, November 12, 2022; and Derek Grossman, "Xi Jinping Is Not Looking to Go to War over Taiwan Anytime Soon," *NIKKEI Asia*, November 16, 2022. For a counter to the peaking China argument, see Oriana Skylar Mastro and Derek Scissors, "China Hasn't Reached the Peak of Its Power: Why Beijing Can Afford to Bide Its Time," *Foreign Affairs*, August 22, 2022.

53. Oriana Skylar Mastro, "Biden Says We've Got Taiwan's Back, but Do We?" *New York Times*, May 27, 2022.

54. John Hoehn, "Precision-Guided Munitions: Background and Issues for Congress," Congressional Research Service R45996, June 11, 2021.

55. DoD, "Department of Defense Fiscal Year (FY) 2023 Budget Estimates—Air Force, Missile Procurement," Department of the Air Force (April 2022) 1–31, 43, https://www.saffm.hq.af.mil/Portals/84/documents/FY23/PROCUREMENT _/FY23%20Air%20Force%20Missile%20Procurement.pdf?ver=QeRLpOSY7 vcLmsKbr3C-Qw%3d%3d; DoD, "Department of Defense Fiscal Year (FY) 2023 Budget Estimates—Navy, Weapons Procurement," Department of the Navy (April 2022), 1–121, 227, https://www.secnav.navy.mil/fmc/fmb/Documents/23pres/WPN _Book.pdf.

56. John A. Tirpak, "As Air Force Ramps Up JASSM, Work Begins on Its Replacement," *Air & Space Forces Magazine*, August 5, 2021 (also cited in Robert Haddick,

"Defeat China's Navy, Defeat China's War Plan," *War on the Rocks*, September 21, 2022).

57. For HIMARS, see Joe Saballa, "US Army Seeking 500 New HIMARS by 2028," *Defense Post*, September 14, 2022.

58. Li Peng [李鹏], Sun Hao [孙浩], and Liu Enyang [刘思阳], "Study on Joint Projection Command for Theater Command [战区联合投送指挥研究]," *Journal of Military Transportation University* [军事交通学院学报] 21, no. 5 (May 2019): 1–5, quoted in McCauley, "Logistics Support for a Cross-Strait Invasion," 6.

59. "Hu Xiubin: 'Four Insufficients' Present in the Construction of China's Maritime Strategic Projection Reserve Forces [胡修斌: 我国海上战略投送后备力量建设存在 "四个不足"]," China National Radio [央广网], March 9, 2017, quoted in Conor M. Kennedy, "Getting There: Chinese Military and Civilian Sealift in a Cross-Strait Invasion," in *Crossing the Strait: China's Military Prepares for War with Taiwan*, ed. Joel Wuthnow, Derek Grossman, Phillip C. Saunders, Andrew Scobell, and Andrew N. D. Yang (Washington, DC: National Defense University Press, 2022), 223–52.

60. Stacie Pettyjohn and Hannah Dennis, "Precision and Posture: Defense Spending Trends and the FY23 Budget Request," Center for a New American Security, November 2022, 10.

61. DoD, "Program Acquisition Cost by Weapon System (FY 2021)," Department of Defense Comptroller, May 2021, 5–11, https://assets1.cbsnewsstatic.com/i /cbslocal/wp-content/uploads/sites/15909806/2021/08/fy2021_Weapons.pdf; Patricia Zengerle, "US Senate Passes Record $858 Billion Defense Act, Sending Bill to Biden," Reuters, December 15, 2022.

62. Doug Cameron, "Defense Companies Hurt by Staffing Shortages amid Growing Weapons Demand," *Wall Street Journal*, July 30, 2022.

63. Joe Gould and Bryant Harris, "As Raytheon Struggles to Replenish Stinger Missiles, Lawmaker Pushes Defense Production Act," *Defense News*, April 26, 2022.

64. Lyle Goldstein, "China Is Improving Its Anti-submarine Warfare Capabilities," *National Interest*, November 28, 2021.

65. Sam LaGrone, "NAVSEA: Navy 'Struggling' to Get Attack Subs Out of Repairs on Time as Demand Increases," *USNI News*, September 21, 2022; Andrew Greene, "US Admiral Issues Blunt Warning on Building Australian Submarines in Overstretched Shipyards," ABC Australia, September 1, 2022.

66. David Adler, "Inside Operation Warp Speed: A New Model for Industrial Policy," *American Affairs* 5, no. 2 (Summer 2021): 3–32.

67. Paul Scharre and Ainikki Riikonen, "Defense Technology Strategy," Center for a New American Security, November 17, 2020.

68. Lee Hsi-min and Eric Lee, "Taiwan's Overall Defense Concept, Explained," *The Diplomat*, November 3, 2020.

69. "AUKUS Reshapes the Strategic Landscape of the Indo-Pacific," *The Economist*, September 25, 2021; Michelle Ye Hee Lee and Ellen Nakashima, "Japan to Buy

Tomahawk Missiles in Defense Buildup amid Fears of War," *Washington Post*, December 12, 2022.

70. Nick Aspinwall, "US to Sell Philippines Arms despite No Human Rights Reforms," *Nikkei Asia*, February 24, 2021.

71. "US Arms Sales to Taiwan," Forum on the Arms Trade, accessed December 21, 2022, https://www.forumarmstrade.org/ustaiwan.html.

72. Gordon Lubold, "US Troops Have Been Deployed in Taiwan for at Least a Year," *Wall Street Journal*, October 8, 2021.

73. International Institute for Strategic Studies, *The Military Balance: The Annual Assessment of Global Military Capabilities and Defence Economics* (London: International Institute for Strategic Studies, February 2020), 279–83, cited in Toshi Yoshihara, *Dragon against the Sun: Chinese Views of Japanese Seapower*, Center for Strategic and Budgetary Assessments, 2020.

74. Tim Fish, "Japan Countering China's Naval Build-Up with Modern Fleet," *USNI News*, April 11, 2022; "Japan Adds Two Ships to Its Fleet of Aegis-Equipped Destroyers," *Japan Times*, November 21, 2022.

75. International Institute for Strategic Studies, *The Military Balance: The Annual Assessment of Global Military Capabilities and Defence Economics* (London: International Institute for Strategic Studies, February 2020), 277.

76. Jude Blanchette and Gerard DiPippo, "'Reunification' with Taiwan through Force Would Be a Pyrrhic Victory for China," Center for Strategic and International Studies, November 2022.

77. Oriana Skylar Mastro and Derek Scissors, "Beijing Is Used to Learning from Russian Failures," *Foreign Policy*, April 18, 2022.

78. Boris Grozovski, "Russia's Economy at the End of 2022: Deeper Troubles," Wilson Center, November 23, 2022.

3

I Spy a Problem

Transforming US Intelligence Agencies for the Technological Age

Amy Zegart

This paper examines the adaptation challenges of US intelligence agencies today with an eye toward a crucial question: How much does money matter? The short answer is that nobody really knows, but it's probably less than we think. The US Intelligence Community (IC) failed to adapt to the rising terrorist threat in the 1990s, when intelligence budgets were cut dramatically after the Cold War, and the IC is also struggling to adapt to the technological age today, when intelligence budgets have never been higher. When budget scarcity and abundance lead to the same suboptimal outcome, something more systematic is likely at work. Its name is organizational pathologies. To be sure, higher spending certainly can help shift intelligence priorities and deliver new capabilities. And reduced spending can hurt. But I find that organizational features of intelligence agencies are often silent but deadly killers of innovation. Agency structures, cultures, and career incentives critically shape what is valued, what gets done, and how well. Unless these organizational features are aligned more rapidly with the threat landscape, intelligence agencies will struggle to deliver timely insights to policy makers no matter how much funding they have.

The first section of this chapter issues a cautionary note about the difficulties of analyzing the relationship between intelligence spending and

The views expressed in this chapter are solely those of the individual author and do not necessarily reflect the views of any organization with which they are, or have been, affiliated.

An earlier version of this paper appeared in *Foreign Affairs*. See Amy B. Zegart, "Open Secrets: Ukraine and the Next Intelligence Revolution," *Foreign Affairs* 102, no. 1 (December 20, 2022; January/February 2023): 54–71.

performance outcomes, offers a broad overview of declassified intelligence budgets over time, and examines how organizational weaknesses were the root cause of intelligence failures leading to 9/11. The second section examines how in a range of policy areas—from health care and K–12 education to defense—greater spending is not producing better results. I then turn to intelligence, arguing that despite record spending, US spy agencies are losing their relative advantage today. Thanks to the rise of emerging technologies and the explosion of data, intelligence isn't just for superpower spy agencies anymore. The third section concludes with what can be done, starting with the creation of a new dedicated open-source intelligence agency.

Breadcrumbs and Budgets

At the outset, it's worth underscoring that studying anything in intelligence is tricky business, because the public record is so incomplete. It's hard to identify the causal factors that lead to success or failure when failures are often public but successes are often secret.

The impact of budgeting decisions is especially challenging. Intelligence spending is so highly classified that until 2007, with rare exceptions, even the topline total intelligence budget remained secret.[1] As a result, for years, expert analysts have estimated intelligence spending over time based on breadcrumbs of data from declassified reports and remarks by government officials.[2]

Since 2007, total intelligence spending in two major categories has been released annually. These are the National Intelligence Program (NIP), which covers programs, projects, and activities of the IC, and the Military Intelligence Program (MIP), which covers intelligence activities of military departments and agencies in the Defense Department that support tactical US military operations. In FY2022, the NIP was $65.7 billion, and the MIP was $24.1 billion, for a total intelligence budget of $89.8 billion.[3] Yet even this aggregate figure is incomplete. It excludes other specific intelligence-gathering programs in cabinet departments and agencies (such as Homeland Security) as well as military programs that include intelligence but have a different primary purpose—such as the MQ-9 Reaper unmanned aerial strike platform.[4]

More importantly, declassified intelligence budgets do not provide meaningful data to assess whether the eighteen agencies of the US Intelligence Community are deploying their resources against the right priorities, particularly as the threat landscape changes. How much does the US government spend by intelligence agency, activity, or capability? How much is spent on understanding and countering nation-state actors like China and Russia versus transnational terrorists, the proliferation of weapons of mass destruction, or cyber threats? Is the IC dedicating sufficient resources to attracting and retaining the right STEM talent? We don't know. There are, of course, good national security reasons for not making this kind of information publicly available. My point is that analyzing the efficiency or effectiveness of intelligence spending from the outside is an exercise in speculation. Humility is in order.

Here's what we do know: In broad-brush terms, spending for US intelligence increased significantly during the Cold War, declined by approximately 20 percent during the 1990s, and skyrocketed after 9/11. Figure 3.1 is an

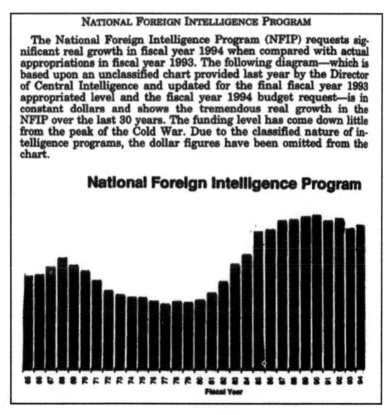

Figure 3.1 Intelligence Spending, 1965–94 (in 1994 constant US dollars)

Source: From H.R. Rep. No. 103-254, Department of Defense Appropriations Act, 1994, to accompany H.R. 3116, reproduced in Michael E. DeVine, "Intelligence Community Spending: Trends and Issues," Congressional Research Service Report R44381, updated June 18, 2018.

unclassified chart released by a 1994 House report showing spending trends from 1965 to 1994 (note all actual numbers were omitted). The House report describes Cold War spending as experiencing "tremendous real growth" over thirty years.

The Soviet Union's collapse in 1991 brought dramatic reductions to intelligence and defense budgets, which lawmakers dubbed the "peace dividend." Some, including Senator Daniel Patrick Moynihan, argued that the CIA should be abolished, because it was no longer needed. According to former director of national intelligence James R. Clapper, in the 1990s, the IC experienced a 23 percent budget reduction, creating a "damaging downward spiral."[5] Director of Central Intelligence George Tenet told the 9/11 Commission that during the 1990s, the entire IC lost 25 percent of its workforce, the CIA suffered a 16 percent workforce decline, and the agency's budget declined by 18 percent in real terms. "This loss of manpower was devastating," noted Tenet, "particularly in our two most manpower intensive activities: all-source analysis and human source collection. By the mid-1990s, recruitment of new CIA analysts and case officers had come to a virtual halt. NSA [National Security Agency] was hiring no new technologists during the greatest information technology change in our lifetimes."[6] The real picture was even worse than these numbers suggest, because personnel reductions were made through voluntary attrition rather than targeted cuts to retain top talent, weed out poor performers, or ensure key skill sets and geographic and functional areas were well covered.[7]

Declining budgets undoubtedly made it difficult for the IC to adapt to the rising terrorist threat in the years before the September 11, 2001, terrorist attacks. Yet evidence suggests there's much more to the story than shrinking resources. I find that the roots of the failure to prevent 9/11 lay in broader, deeper organizational weaknesses in US intelligence agencies that had surprisingly little to do with funding. Throughout the 1990s, even as America's spy agencies warned of the growing terrorist danger, they remained stuck in their Cold War posture, operating with organizational structures, cultures, and career incentives that offered little chance of stopping al-Qaeda from committing the worst terrorist attack in American history. My five-year examination of thousands of pages of declassified documents and interviews with seventy-five current and former intelligence and government officials found that the CIA and FBI had twenty-three opportunities to penetrate and possibly stop the 9/11 plot. Organizational weaknesses led to failure every time.[8] Below are thumbnails of two such lost opportunities.

The CIA's Watchlisting Failure

The 9/11 Commission and the Congressional Joint Inquiry both suggest that perhaps the best chance to stop the 9/11 attacks involved the travel of two al-Qaeda operatives named Khalid al-Mihdhar and Nawaf al-Hazmi. Both men were part of the team that crashed American Airlines Flight 77 into the Pentagon.

They first tripped the wire in January 2000, when they attended a secret al-Qaeda meeting in Malaysia. The CIA was watching. The agency got a photograph of al-Mihdhar, learned his full name, obtained his passport number, and uncovered that he held a multiple-entry US visa. By March 2000, CIA officials identified al-Hazmi as having attended the same meeting, learned his full name, and discovered he had already entered the United States. Between fifty and sixty CIA officials had access to this information about al-Mihdhar and al-Hazmi. And yet nobody put these two men on the State Department's watchlist denying them entry into the United States or notified the FBI for the next year and a half.[9] Why?

The simplest answer is that the CIA had never been in the habit of watchlisting suspected al-Qaeda terrorists before. For more than forty years, the agency and the rest of the IC had operated with Cold War priorities, procedures, and thinking, all of which had little need to ensure dangerous foreign terrorists stayed out of the United States. Before 9/11, there was a watchlisting program in name but not in practice: there was no formal training, no clear process, and no priority placed on it.[10] As one CIA officer told congressional investigators after 9/11, he believed it was "not incumbent" even on the CIA's special Osama bin Laden unit to place people like al-Mihdhar on the State Department's watchlist.[11]

The FBI's Failed Search for Two al-Qaeda Operatives

On August 23, 2001, just nineteen days before 9/11, the CIA finally told the FBI that al-Mihdhar and al-Hazmi were probably in the United States and needed to be found. The FBI responded by putting the search for these two suspected terrorists at the bottom of the priority list and handing it to the C-team. The "nationwide" hunt was the focus of just one of the bureau's fifty-six US field offices. It was designated "routine," the lowest level of priority. And it was assigned to a junior agent who had just finished his rookie year and had never led this kind of investigation before.[12]

Here too, organizational pathologies, not individual screwups, were to blame. The bureau dedicated just one office to what should have been a nationwide search, because the FBI had always been a decentralized organization where each field office operated largely autonomously—and that's how all cases were handled. Putting one office on each case made sense for catching criminals after the fact and tailoring priorities to local law enforcement needs. It was a poor organizational setup for collecting and coordinating intelligence about future national security threats to the nation as a whole. Culture explains why finding al-Mihdhar and al-Hazmi went to the bottom of the pile. Although the FBI's own strategic plan declared counterterrorism its number one priority in 1998 and resolved to improve its domestic intelligence capabilities, the bureau was first and foremost a law enforcement organization with a culture that prized catching perpetrators of past crimes far more than gathering intelligence to stop a possible future tragedy.[13] In fact, a Justice Department investigation found that before 9/11, intelligence analysis was considered so unimportant, the vast majority of FBI analysts were rated unqualified to do their jobs.[14] Promotion incentives reflected this culture. Handing the search to a junior agent wasn't a mistake; it was how things were supposed to work. Convictions made careers, so finding two potential terrorists who hadn't yet committed a crime and might never do anything illegal went to one of the office's least experienced investigators, because it was one of the least desirable jobs.[15] In short, the bureau's decentralized structure guaranteed that the alarm would be sounded only in one place. Its law enforcement culture ensured the alarm would be muffled by criminal cases and priorities. And incentives promised that someone with the least experience and expertise would be answering the call.

We now know that Khalid al-Mihdhar and Nawaf al-Hazmi should not have been hard to find. For months before the attack, they hid in plain sight in San Diego, using their true names on everything from rental agreements and credit cards to a California ID card and the telephone directory. They even contacted several targets of FBI counterterrorism investigations, at one point living with an FBI informant—all unknown to the FBI. The two al-Qaeda operatives didn't need secret identities or clever schemes to succeed. They just needed the CIA and the FBI to operate as usual.[16]

In short, while declining intelligence budgets in the 1990s certainly reduced the CIA's workforce and forced intelligence leaders to tackle a new problem set with fewer resources, the roots of failure on 9/11 appear to go deeper. Consider the counterfactual: If the CIA and FBI had unlimited resources in the run-up to 9/11, would they have succeeded in watchlisting and finding Khalid al-Mihdhar and Nawaf al-Hazmi before it was too late?

More Money, More Problems

Twenty years later, intelligence agencies now face a much more favorable budgetary environment, and yet they are struggling again to adapt to a shifting geopolitical landscape—driven this time by emerging technologies that are disrupting every facet of the intelligence enterprise. Despite record spending over the past two decades, intelligence agencies are losing their relative advantage.

The US intelligence budget has increased dramatically since 9/11, jumping from an estimated $60.37 billion in FY2001 to $89.8 billion in FY2022 in constant 2022 dollars—an increase of 49 percent over twenty years (see fig. 3.2).[17] Although budgets dipped in the period of 2010 to 2015, the broader historical pattern is growth. Indeed, the Congressional Research Service estimates that intelligence spending quadrupled from 1980 to 2010 in real terms.[18]

In policy areas, from health care to K–12 education to defense, increased government spending has not translated into better results. A 2021 study compared eleven of the world's richest countries and found that the United States spent the highest percentage of GDP on health care yet ranked last in affordability, access, and outcomes, including infant mortality and life expectancy at age sixty.[19] Economist Eric Hanushek has found that US K–12 education spending per pupil quadrupled from 1960 to 2017 in constant dollars. Yet student scores on national tests estimating achievement across subjects remained flat. American student performance on international tests also

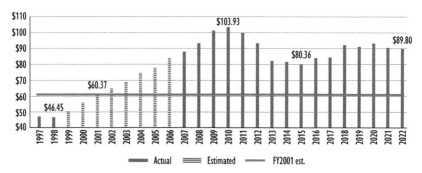

Figure 3.2 **Total Intelligence Community Budget (constant $US billions)**

Sources: Data for 1997 and 1998 from Steven Aftergood, "CIA Discloses FY1998 Intelligence Budget Total" (accessed December 7, 2022); data for 2007 to 2022 from Office of the Director of National Intelligence, "US Intelligence Community Budget." See endnote 17 of this chapter for an explanation of the author's analysis for 1999–2006.

remains persistently poor, and racial and income gaps have persisted.[20] And if the air force is any guide, bigger defense budgets have also not translated into better military readiness. While air force budgets have fluctuated since the 1980s, the number of air force aircraft, personnel, and other measures of end strength have all gradually declined.[21] In 2021, House Armed Services Committee chair Adam Smith publicly called the F-35 Joint Strike Fighter—a fifth-generation fighter jet riddled with technical deficiencies, which was the most expensive weapons program in history and ten years behind schedule— a "rathole."[22] The United States is estimated to spend more than the following nine countries in terms of defense budgets combined, and yet China's relative defense advantages are growing.[23] In short, American taxpayers seem to be getting less bang for their buck across various policy areas.

Increased intelligence spending after 9/11 produced arguably better outcomes than in these other policy areas, enabling the US to prosecute the War on Terror and defend the homeland to great effect. Changes included creating the National Counterterrorism Center and the Office of the Director of National Intelligence, an expanded drone program, and tighter integration between intelligence and military counterterrorism operations. As a result of these and other measures, the United States has not suffered another major catastrophic terrorist attack on American soil.

However, the dramatic infusion of counterterrorism funding also ended up hard-wiring the bureaucracy to fight the last war. Great-power competition, not transnational terrorism, now tops the threat list. And as I discuss more below, emerging technologies are transforming both the future and how intelligence agencies go about understanding it. This is a moment of reckoning for American spy agencies. And it reveals the paradox of plenty: surging budgets led to wide-scale changes, but by the time US intelligence agencies mastered the al-Qaeda problem, al-Qaeda wasn't the problem anymore.

The Tech Moment of Reckoning for Intelligence

Never before has the world stood at the cusp of so many technologies transforming so much so fast. Internet connectivity has transformed global commerce and supercharged global politics, fueling protests like the Arab Spring and Hong Kong's Umbrella Movement, empowering a new wave of government techno-surveillance led by Beijing, and enabling massive Russian deception operations to influence elections and undermine democracies from within. It's easy to forget how rapidly the internet has developed and how revolutionary it's been. In the early 1990s, less than 1 percent of the global population was online. Now nearly two-thirds of the world is connected to the internet.[24] In the last three years alone, more than a billion people have come online.[25]

Artificial intelligence (AI) is also disrupting nearly every industry and changing how wars are fought—automating everything from logistics to cyber defenses to unmanned fighter jets that can overwhelm defenses with swarms and maneuver faster and better than human pilots. Some estimate that AI could eliminate up to 40 percent of jobs worldwide in the next fifteen years.[26] Russian president Vladimir Putin has declared that whoever leads AI development "will become the ruler of the world," and China has made no secret of its plans to lead the world in AI by 2030.[27] AI has been likened to electricity: a foundational technology that affects everything.

Technology is also revolutionizing the ability of humans to detect events unfolding on Earth from space. Commercial satellite capabilities now offer eyes in the sky for anyone who wants them. The number of satellite launches more than doubled between 2016 and 2018.[28] Today, more than five thousand satellites are orbiting Earth, and the Paris-based firm Euroconsult estimates that seventeen thousand satellites will be launched in the next decade.[29] While US spy satellites have more sophisticated sensing capabilities, commercial satellites are rapidly improving.[30] Some have resolutions so sharp they can detect manhole covers, signs, and even road conditions from space.[31] Others can detect radio frequency emissions, observe dynamic activities like vehicle movement and nuclear cooling plumes, and operate at night, in cloudy weather, or through dense vegetation and camouflage. Constellations of small satellites are offering something new: faster revisit rates over the same location multiple times a day so that changes can be detected over shorter periods. In 1960, when a US CORONA spy satellite successfully delivered images of the Soviet Union for the first time, the CIA's deputy director for science and technology, Albert "Bud" Wheelon, remarked, "It was as if an enormous floodlight had been turned on in a darkened warehouse."[32] Commercial satellites are turning that occasional floodlight into a continuously running video.

That's not all. Advances in quantum computing could eventually unlock the encryption protecting nearly all the world's data. Synthetic biology enables scientists to engineer living organisms with the potential for revolutionary improvements in food production, medicine, data storage, and weapons of war.

Perhaps most important from an American national security perspective is that nearly all of today's emerging technologies are invented outside the government, made available to the world, and have widespread applications for commerce and conflict. That's new.

In the Cold War, breakthroughs like the internet and GPS were invented by US government agencies and later commercialized by the private sector. Few technologies were inherently dual use, which meant they could be classified at birth and restricted forever to keep them out of enemy hands. Nuclear technology, for example, was born secret and stayed that way, limiting the proliferation of the world's most dangerous weapons.

Now the script has flipped. Technological innovations are more likely to be developed in the private sector, where they are funded by foreign investors, developed by a multinational workforce, and sold to global customers. Today's technologies are born open, not classified, and are widely available, not easily restricted. AI, for example, has become so widespread and simple to use that high school students with no coding background can make deepfakes—AI-generated fake videos that look and sound real. Already, deepfakes impersonating former US ambassador to Russia Michael McFaul have been used to dupe Ukrainian officials and undermine the Ukrainian war effort, prompting McFaul to tweet, "WARNING. Someone using the phone number +1 (202) 7549885 is impersonating me. If you connect on a video platform with this number, you will see an AI-generated 'deep fake' that looks and talks like me. It is not me. This is a new Russian weapon of war. Be careful."[33]

This reversal gives private-sector leaders new power and national security officials new challenges. American social media platforms now find themselves on the front lines of information warfare, deciding what's real and what's fake, what speech is allowed, and what is suppressed. Start-up founders are inventing capabilities that can be used by enemies they can't foresee with consequences they can't control. As the war in Ukraine rages on and greatpower competition with China intensifies, companies and investors have to weigh their economic interests against the national interest in new ways. Meanwhile, US intelligence agencies are struggling to adopt critical new technologies from the outside and move at the speed of invention instead of the pace of bureaucracy. Increasingly, private-sector leaders have responsibilities they don't want, and government leaders want capabilities they don't have. Power isn't just shifting abroad. Power is shifting at home.

All these forces unleashed by emerging technologies create a moment of reckoning for America's intelligence agencies. If we think of intelligence as a competitive contest for insight, then the challenges arising from emerging technologies become more clear. They fall into five core categories—the "five mores."

More Threats, Speed, Data, Customers, and Competitors

The first challenge is more threats. Today's threat landscape has never been more crowded, complicated, or fast moving. After spending nearly half a century countering the Soviet Union and two decades fighting terrorists, US leaders now confront a diverse multitude of dangers that place demands on intelligence, including transnational threats like pandemics and climate change; great-power competition with Russia and China; terrorism and other threats arising from weak and failed states; and cyberattacks that steal, spy, disrupt, destroy, and deceive at stunning speeds and scale.

The list isn't just longer. Thanks to technology, it's harder. Cyber threats operate in ways that make them far more consequential than they appear and far more vexing to understand, detect, and defeat than the threats of yesteryear. Cyberspace is not just another military battleground like air, land, and sea, where the old tools and rules apply.

For centuries, power and geography have been the mainstays of security. Countries with the most powerful militaries and the blessings of geography—like the two vast oceans separating the US from the world's dangerous neighborhoods—were more protected. Not anymore. In cyberspace, power brings vulnerability, because the most powerful countries tend to be digitally reliant. And there's no such thing as good geography online; anybody can inflict damage from anywhere.

The character of war is different, too. Physical warfare tends to involve big moves that generate big consequences. But cyberwarfare is a bleed-every-minute affair where small attacks add up to devastating damage before you know it. China has stolen its way to technological advantage one hack at a time, in what FBI Director Christopher Wray has called one of the greatest transfers of wealth in human history, and "the biggest long-term threat to our economic and national security."[34]

Russia's interference in the 2016 US presidential election showed that cyberattacks can hack minds, not just machines, polarizing societies and undermining democracies from within at speed and scale. Russia wrote the playbook on using American tech companies to turn Americans against one another. Today, China doesn't need it. The popular social media app TikTok is owned by Chinese firm ByteDance and has quickly amassed more than a billion users, including an estimated 135 million in the US. That's 40 percent of the US population.[35] Alarm bells are ringing. Democrats and Republicans are worried that TikTok could enable the Chinese government to vacuum all sorts of data about Americans and launch massive influence campaigns that serve Beijing's interest under the guise of giving American consumers what they want. In a world of information warfare, where weapons don't even look like weapons, it's fair to say the threat landscape isn't what it used to be.

Second, technological advances are generating the need for more speed in intelligence. Intelligence must be timely to be useful, delivering information when policy makers need it—before a missile launches, a summit convenes, or the National Security Council makes a decision.

Timeliness has always been important, but the speed of relevance is accelerating. In the 1962 Cuban Missile Crisis, President John F. Kennedy famously had thirteen days to pore through intelligence and consider his policy options in secret after U-2 surveillance photographs revealed Soviet nuclear installations in Cuba. On September 11, 2001, President George W. Bush had less than thirteen hours from the time the first hijacked plane crashed into the World Trade Center to review intelligence about who was responsible and announce America's response to the world. Today, the time for presidents to consider intelligence before making major policy decisions may be closer to thirteen minutes or thirteen seconds, or it could already be too late, because cyber breaches are often discovered long after the damage is done. In December 2020, for example, cybersecurity firm FireEye detected a massive breach of the software firm SolarWinds. Like a bad horror movie, when officials rushed to survey the damage, they discovered that hackers from Russia's elite foreign espionage service had been inside the house for a very long time—penetrating US nuclear labs, the departments of Defense, State, and Homeland Security, and much of the Fortune 500 more than a year before anyone found them.[36]

Now breaking events and hot takes are flowing directly into the hands of policy makers with the touch of a button, putting greater pressure on intelligence agencies to speed up or get left behind. But moving too fast also carries risks. It takes time to vet source credibility, tap expert knowledge across fields, and consider alternative explanations. Without careful intelligence analysis, leaders may make premature or even dangerous decisions. The potential consequences of rash action became evident in December 2016, when a news story reported that Israel's former defense minister threatened a nuclear attack against Pakistan if Islamabad deployed troops to Syria. Pakistan's defense minister, Khawaja Muhammad Asif, quickly rattled his own nuclear saber, tweeting, "Israeli def min threatens nuclear retaliation presuming pak role in Syria against Daesh. Israel forgets Pakistan is a Nuclear state too, AH."[37] The original story, including the Israeli threat, had been fabricated, but the tweet apparently went out before it was verified. Satisfying policy makers' need for speed while carefully collecting, vetting, and assessing intelligence has always been a delicate balance, but it's getting harder to strike.[38]

The third challenge is data. The volume of data available online has grown so vast that it's hard to fathom. According to the World Economic Forum, in 2019, internet users posted 500 million tweets, sent 294 billion emails, and posted 350 million photos on Facebook every day.[39] Google answers several billion queries a day.[40] Every second, the internet transmits about 1 petabyte of data—the equivalent of binge-watching movies nonstop for over three years.[41] Data accumulation shows no sign of slowing. Some estimate that the amount of Earth's data doubles every twenty-four months.

American intelligence agencies are struggling to keep up. Already, they are collecting far more information than humans can analyze effectively. In 2020, one soldier deployed to the Middle East was so concerned about the crushing flow of classified intelligence emails he was receiving that he decided to count them. He received ten thousand emails in 120 days. And that's just the classified information.

Fourth, who needs intelligence to protect American lives and interests is changing radically, too. Until now, intelligence agencies produced classified reports for people with security clearances who read them in secured facilities with guards outside. Increasingly, however, important decision makers live worlds apart from Washington, making consequential policy choices in boardrooms and living rooms, not just the White House Situation Room. Voters need intelligence about foreign election interference and influence campaigns. Big tech companies like Microsoft and Google need intelligence about cyber threats to and through their systems. Most of America's critical infrastructure, from energy companies to financial services firms, is in private-sector hands. They can't go it alone in cyberspace, either. And because cyber threats don't stop at the border, American security increasingly depends on sharing intelligence faster and better with allies and partners.

Serving a broader array of customers requires producing unclassified products and engaging with the outside world. For agencies used to operating in secret, this is an unnatural act. Important efforts are underway. In the fall of 2022, the CIA launched a podcast called *The Langley Files*. Its aim:

demystifying the agency and educating the American public. "At CIA, there are truths we can share and stories we can tell," each podcast begins.

There are now public service videos from intelligence agencies about foreign threats to US elections. The National Geospatial-Intelligence Agency has launched a project called Tearline, a collaboration with think tanks, universities, and nonprofits to create unclassified reports about climate change, Russian troop movements, human rights issues, and more. Public-private partnerships in cybersecurity used to be a one-way street where NSA and the FBI asked companies for information but rarely provided any. Those days have changed. In 2021, NSA began issuing joint cyber advisories with the FBI and the Department of Homeland Security's Cybersecurity and Infrastructure Security Agency detailing major cyber threats, exposing the entities behind them, and explaining how to shore up defenses against them. In October 2022, these agencies even released the technical details of the top-twenty vulnerabilities exploited by the Chinese government to hack into US and allied networks, along with detailed instructions about how to defend against them.[42] The US government is now also issuing advisories with foreign intelligence partners.

The success of this public-facing strategy has been on full display in Ukraine. It helped the United States warn the world about Russia's invasion and rally the West behind a fast response. It continues to frustrate Moscow. Most recently, after Washington revealed intelligence indicating that senior Russian military leaders were discussing using tactical nuclear weapons in Ukraine, Chinese president Xi Jinping issued a rare public warning against the "use of, or threats to use, nuclear weapons."[43] Xi's trumpeted "no limits" relationship with Putin suddenly had limits after all.[44]

The fifth challenge for intelligence agencies in the technological age is more competition. It used to be that government spy agencies were the only organizations capable of launching satellites, collecting information at scale, and analyzing global threats. Not anymore.

The explosion of online open-source information, commercial satellite capabilities, and automated analytics like AI enables all sorts of individuals and organizations worldwide to collect, analyze, and disseminate intelligence—often better and faster than governments can.

In the past several years, the amateur investigators of Bellingcat, which describes itself as "an intelligence agency for the people," have identified the Russian hit team that tried to assassinate a former Russian military officer named Sergei Skripal, living in the United Kingdom, and located supporters of ISIS in Europe.[45] It also proved that Russians were behind the shootdown of Malaysia Airlines Flight 17 over Ukraine.[46]

Bellingcat is not the only civilian intelligence initiative. When the Iranian government claimed a small fire had broken out in an industrial shed under construction in 2020, two American researchers working independently and using only their computers and the internet proved that Tehran was lying—within hours. David Albright and Fabian Hinz quickly found that the building was actually a nuclear centrifuge assembly facility at Natanz, Iran's main uranium enrichment site.[47] The damage was so extensive that the fire may well have been caused by an explosion, raising the possibility of sabotage. In 2021, nuclear sleuths at the James Martin Center for Nonproliferation Studies in California used commercial satellite imagery to discover more than two hundred new intercontinental ballistic missile silos in China, a finding that could signal historic increases in China's nuclear arsenal.[48]

And in the past year, Russia's war in Ukraine has given rise to an array of experts wielding unclassified information to track daily events and offer longer-term analysis online, from the Twitter feeds of former US officials to the Institute for the Study of War, which even features an interactive map. At Stanford University, there are now open-source intelligence courses for undergraduates, and a major volunteer effort has produced a series of reports compiling and confirming human rights atrocities in Ukraine for the United Nations. The Stanford student team, led by former army and open-source imagery analyst Allison Puccioni, used commercial satellite thermal and electro-optical imaging, TikTok videos posted online, geolocation tools, and more. "Today, anyone and everyone can access reasonably credible first-hand reports of attacks leveled against Ukraine," says Puccioni. "These pictures or videos are informative in and of themselves. But when cross-checked against other forms of freely or cheaply available information like satellite imagery, they can be triangulated to calculate location and time-stamp of the event, creating something akin to the synthesized, multisourced insight of conventional classified intelligence."[49]

Open-Source Intelligence Is Having a Moment

For American intelligence agencies, open-source intelligence brings significant new opportunities as well as risks. On the positive side, citizen sleuths offer more eyes and ears around the world, scanning for developments and dangers as they arise. The wisdom of the crowd can be a powerful tool, especially for piecing together tiny bits of information. Open-source information can be shared easily within government agencies, across them, and with the public, all without revealing sensitive sources or methods. As 9/11 showed, the barriers to sharing classified information are often too high, and the costs can be tragic.

But features are also flaws. Open-source intelligence is open to everyone, everywhere, regardless of their motives, national loyalties, or capabilities. Citizen sleuths don't have to answer to anyone or train anywhere. The line between the wisdom of crowds and the danger of mobs is thin, and small bits of information can deceive in big ways. After a 2013 terrorist attack on the Boston Marathon killed three people and wounded more than 260 others, Reddit users jumped into action. Posting pet theories, unconfirmed chatter on police scanners, and other crowdsourced tidbits of information, amateur investigators fingered two "suspects," and the mainstream media publicized the findings. Both turned out to be innocent.[50]

These weaknesses can create serious headaches for governments. When errors go viral, intelligence agencies have to burn time and divert resources fact-checking the work of others and reassuring policy makers about the job they were doing already and the assessments they had made before. Accurate open-source discoveries can cause problems, too. Findings, for example, can force leaders into corners instead of keeping things secret to make room for compromise and graceful exits in crises. To diffuse the Cuban Missile Crisis, for example, Kennedy agreed to secretly remove US nuclear weapons from Turkey if the Soviets took their missiles out of Cuba. Had satellite imagery been publicly available, Kennedy might have been too worried about the domestic political backlash to make a deal.

The Future of Intelligence: It's the Organization, Stupid

American intelligence leaders know that their success in the twenty-first century hinges on adapting to a world of more threats, more speed, more data, more customers, and more competitors. They have been working hard to get there—launching organizational reforms, technology innovation programs, and new hiring initiatives to recruit top science and engineering talent. But the challenges are hard, efforts have been piecemeal, and progress remains slow.[51] The rate of progress is especially concerning given that the challenges are well known, the stakes are high, and intelligence weaknesses have been festering for years. Multiple reports and articles have found that intelligence agencies are not keeping pace with technological developments.[52]

If I'm right, then Washington cannot address its present intelligence challenges by throwing more money at existing agencies. Instead, developing US intelligence capabilities for the tech age requires building something new: a dedicated, open-source intelligence agency focused on combing through unclassified data and discerning what it means.

Creating a nineteenth intelligence agency may seem duplicative and unnecessary, but it is essential. Despite Washington's best efforts, open-source intelligence has always been a second-class citizen in the US intelligence community, because it cannot overcome existing organizational structures, cultures, and incentives. Open-source intelligence has no agency with the budget, hiring power, or seat at the table to champion it. As long as open-source intelligence remains embedded in secret agencies that value secret information above all, it will languish. A culture of secrecy will continue to strangle the adoption of cutting-edge technology tools from the commercial sector. Agencies will struggle to attract and retain desperately needed talent to help them understand and use new technologies. And efforts to harness the power of open-source intelligence collectors and analysts outside government will fall short.

A new open-source intelligence agency would bring innovation, not just information, to the US intelligence community by providing fertile soil for the growth of far-reaching changes in human capital, technology adoption, and collaboration with the burgeoning open-source intelligence ecosystem. Such an agency would be a powerful lever for attracting the workforce of tomorrow. Because it deals with unclassified information, the agency could recruit top scientists and engineers to work right away without requiring them to wait months or years for security clearances. Locating open-source agency offices in technology hubs where engineers already live and want to stay—such as Austin, San Francisco, and Seattle—would make it easier for talent to flow in and out of government. The result could be a corps of tech-savvy officials who rotate between public service and the private sector, acting as ambassadors between both worlds. They would increase the intelligence community's presence and prestige in technology circles while bringing a continuous stream of fresh tech ideas back inside.

By working with unclassified material, the open-source agency could also help the intelligence community do a better and faster job of adopting new collection and analysis technologies. The open-source agency could test new inventions and, if they proved effective, pass them along to agencies that work with secrets. The agency would also be ideally positioned to engage with leading open-source intelligence organizations and individuals outside the government. These partnerships could help US intelligence agencies outsource more of their work to responsible nongovernmental collectors and analysts, freeing up intelligence officials to focus their capabilities and clandestine collection efforts on missions that nobody else can do.

And there will still be many such missions. After all, even the best open-source intelligence has limits. Satellite imagery can reveal new Chinese missile silos but not what Chinese leaders intend to do with them. Identifying objects or tracking movements online is important, but generating insight requires more. Secret methods remain uniquely suited to understanding what foreign leaders know, believe, and desire. There is no open-source substitute for getting human spies inside a foreign leader's inner circle or penetrating an adversary's communications system to uncover what that adversary is saying and writing. Analysts with clearances will also always be essential for assessing what classified discoveries mean, how credible they are, and how they fit with other unclassified findings.

If history is any guide, the agencies, processes, and cultures that got us here will not get us there. The country faces a dangerous new era that includes great-power competition, a renewed war in Europe, ongoing terrorist attacks, and fast-changing cyberattacks. New technologies are driving these threats and determining who will be able to understand and chart the future. To succeed, the US Intelligence Community must adapt to a more open, technological world.

Notes

1. Office of the Director of National Intelligence (ODNI), "US Intelligence Community Budget," https://www.dni.gov/index.php/what-we-do/ic-budget (accessed December 7, 2022); director of Central Intelligence George Tenet released the FY1997 and FY1998 total intelligence budgets after Steven Aftergood from the Federation of American Scientists filed a Freedom of Information Act lawsuit, but Tenet then reversed course in FY1999. Subsequent toplines remained classified until 2007 when Congress mandated that the director of national intelligence disclose "the aggregate amount of funds appropriated by Congress" for the National Intelligence Program in Section 601 of the Implementing Recommendations of the 9/11 Commission Act (Public Law 110-53). Freedom of Information Act requests have produced some agency-level budget justification documents, but these are heavily redacted. See also Steven Aftergood, "CIA Discloses FY1998 Intelligence Budget Total," press release, Federation of American Scientists, March 20, 1998; Brian

Clampitt, "US Intelligence Budget Request Revealed," *Harvard National Security Journal*, February 23, 2011; "Intelligence Budget Data," Federation of American Scientists, https://irp.fas.org/budget (accessed December 7, 2022).

2. Marshall C. Erwin and Amy Belasco, "Intelligence Spending and Appropriations: Issues for Congress," Congressional Research Service Report R42061, September 18, 2013, 5.

3. ODNI, "US Intelligence Community Budget."

4. Anne Daugherty Miles, Michael E. DeVine, and Sofia Plagakis, "Intelligence Community Spending Trends," Congressional Research Service Report R44381, Version 16, updated January 9, 2023, 1–2.

5. James R. Clapper, "Current and Projected National Security Threats to the United States," Senate Select Committee on Intelligence, March 12, 2013, 9, https://www.intelligence.senate.gov/sites/default/files/hearings/11389.pdf.

6. Hon. George Tenet, "Written Statement for the Record, National Commission on Terrorist Attacks Upon the United States," submitted testimony for the eighth public hearing of the 9/11 Commission, March 24, 2004, 24, https://9-11commission.gov/hearings/hearing8/tenet_statement.pdf.

7. Amy B. Zegart, *Spying Blind: The CIA, the FBI, and the Origins of 9/11* (Princeton, NJ: Princeton University Press, 2007), 3, 73–74; Aspin-Brown Commission Final Report, "Chapter 9: The Need to 'Right-Size' and Rebuild the Community," March 1, 1996, 96–97.

8. Zegart, *Spying Blind*, 12.

9. Office of Inspector General, *OIG Report on CIA Accountability with Respect to the 9/11 Attacks*, June 2005, declassified August 2007, xiv, https://irp.fas.org/cia/product/oig-911.pdf.

10. Zegart, *Spying Blind*, 2.

11. Quoted in Eleanor Hill, "The Intelligence Community's Knowledge of the September 11 Hijackers Prior to September 11, 2001," statement before the House Permanent Select Committee on Intelligence and the Senate Select Committee on Intelligence Joint Inquiry, 107th Cong., 2d Sess., September 20, 2002, 8.

12. Zegart, *Spying Blind*, 156–57.

13. Federal Bureau of Investigation, *Draft FBI Strategic Plan: 1998-2003: Keeping Terrorism Safe*, unclassified version, May 8, 1998.

14. *Joint Inquiry into Intelligence Community Activities before and after the Terrorist Attacks of September 11, 2001*, report of the Senate Select Committee on Intelligence and the House Permanent Select Committee on Intelligence, S. Rep. No. 107-351, H.R. Rep. No. 107-792, 107th Cong., 2d Sess., December 2002, 340.

15. Zegart, *Spying Blind*, 156–68.

16. Zegart, *Spying Blind*, 156–68.

17. FY2001 intelligence spending in nominal terms is estimated at $37.60 billion, based on the Congressional Research Service's 2013 report "Intelligence Spending and Appropriations: Issues for Congress" (Erwin and Belasco). This figure was then

inflation adjusted to $60.37 billion in 2022 dollars, using the Bureau of Labor Statistics' CPI Inflation Calculator, https://www.bls.gov/data/inflation_calculator.htm. Estimates for intelligence spending from 1999 through 2006 assume equal yearly increases between the unclassified 1998 and 2007 budgets and were also inflation adjusted using the Bureau of Labor Statistics' CPI Inflation Calculator. See Erwin and Belasco, "Intelligence Spending," 4–5; for FY2022, see ODNI, "US Intelligence Community Budget."

18. Erwin and Belasco, "Intelligence Spending," 5.

19. Eric C. Schneider, Arnav Shah, Michelle M. Doty, Roosa Tikkanen, Katharine Fields, and Reginald D. Williams II, "Mirror, Mirror 2021: Reflecting Poorly: Health Care in the US Compared to Other High-Income Countries," The Commonwealth Fund, August 2021. The eleven countries examined in the study were: Australia, Canada, France, Germany, the Netherlands, New Zealand, Norway, Sweden, Switzerland, the United Kingdom, and the United States. Health outcomes are a product of many causes, including underlying social and economic conditions. The study uses measures that focus more on outcomes likely to be affected by health care, such as life expectancy at age sixty rather than life expectancy at birth.

20. Eric A. Hanushek, "The Fall of Educational Productivity and Policy Paralysis," in The Not-So-Great Society, ed. Lindsay M. Burke and Jonathan Butcher (Washington, DC: Heritage Foundation, 2019), 45–51; Dana Goldstein, "'It Just Isn't Working': PISA Test Scores Cast Doubt on US Education Efforts," New York Times, December 3, 2019.

21. Todd Harrison, "The Air Force of the Future: A Comparison of Alternative Force Structures," Center for Strategic and International Studies, October 29, 2019.

22. Valerie Insinna, "Watchdog Group Finds F-35 Sustainment Costs Could Be Headed Off Affordability Cliff," Defense News, July 7, 2021; Sébastien Roblin, "The Air Force Admits the F-35 Fighter Jet Costs Too Much. So It Wants to Spend Even More," NBC News, March 7, 2021; Government Accountability Office, "F-35 Joint Strike Fighter: Cost Growth and Schedule Delays Continue," Report 22-105943, April 7, 2022; Aaron Gregg, "Powerful Lawmaker Calls F-35 Fighter Jet a 'Rathole,' Suggests Pentagon Should Cut Its Losses," Washington Post, March 5, 2021.

23. "US Defense Spending Compared to Other Countries," Peter G. Peterson Foundation, May 11, 2022; Anthony H. Cordesman, with the assistance of Grace Hwang, Chinese Strategy and Military Forces in 2021: A Graphic Net Assessment, revised August 3, 2021, 83–86; US Department of Defense, Military and Security Developments Involving the People's Republic of China 2022: Annual Report to Congress, November 29, 2022.

24. "Individuals Using the Internet," International Telecommunication Union (ITU), United Nations, 2022, https://www.itu.int/en/ITU-D/Statistics/Pages/stat/default.aspx; Kelsey Campbell-Dollaghan, "Why One of World's Most Remote Places Has the Fastest Internet," Gizmodo, April 1, 2014; "Help with Internet and Social Media in an Authentic Bedouin Camp in Wadi Rum, Jordan," Workaway.info, updated January 2023, https://www.workaway.info/en/host/458895548546.

25. "Individuals Using the Internet."

26. Kai-Fu Lee, "Facial and Emotional Recognition; How One Man Is Advancing Artificial Intelligence," *60 Minutes*, interview by Scott Pelley, January 13, 2019.

27. James Vincent, "Putin Says the Nation That Leads AI 'Will Be the Ruler of the World,'" *The Verge*, September 4, 2017; Paul Mozur, "Beijing Wants AI to Be Made in China by 2030," *New York Times*, July 20, 2017.

28. Daniel R. Coats, "Worldwide Threat Assessment of the US Intelligence Community," Senate Select Committee on Intelligence, January 29, 2019, 17.

29. Alan Burkitt-Gray, "'Fourfold Increase' in Satellites over the Next 10 Years to 17,000," Capacity Media, December 10, 2021; The following section uses data from the Union of Concerned Scientists, which maintains one of the most comprehensive databases of active satellites. Data available at Union of Concerned Scientists, UCS Satellite Database, updated May 1, 2022, https://www.ucsusa.org/resources /satellite-database.

30. Union of Concerned Scientists, UCS Satellite Database.

31. Chris Gormeller, "Introducing 15 cm HD: The Highest Clarity from Commercial Satellite Imagery," Maxar Technologies, November 12, 2020.

32. Quoted in Philip Taubman, *Secret Empire: Eisenhower, the CIA, and the Hidden Story of America's Space Espionage* (New York: Simon & Schuster, 2003), 35.

33. Sami Quadri, "Former US Ambassador Says Russia Is Using 'Deepfakes to Impersonate Him,'" *Evening Standard*, October 1, 2022.

34. For greatest transfer of wealth, see Russell Flannery, "China Theft of US Information, IP One of Largest Wealth Transfers in History: FBI Chief," *Forbes*, July 7, 2020; for biggest long-term threat, see Christopher Wray, "Director's Remarks to Business Leaders in London," July 6, 2022, https://www.fbi.gov/news/speeches /directors-remarks-to-business-leaders-in-london-070622 (accessed March 10, 2023).

35. Lily Hay Newman, "It's Time to Get Real about TikTok's Risks," *Wired*, September 6, 2022.

36. Natasha Bertrand and Eric Wolff, "Nuclear Weapons Agency Breached amid Cyber Onslaught," *Politico*, December 17, 2020; Jon Porter, "White House Now Says 100 Companies Hit by SolarWinds Hack, but More May Be Impacted," *The Verge*, February 18, 2021; Dina Temple-Raston, "A 'Worst Nightmare' Cyberattack: The Untold Story of the SolarWinds Hack," *NPR*, April 17, 2021.

37. "Fake News Sets Off Twitter Confrontation between Pakistan and Israel," *CBS News*, December 25, 2016.

38. Chu Wang, "Twitter Diplomacy: Preventing Twitter Wars from Escalating to Real Wars," Belfer Center for Science and International Affairs, Harvard University, May 20, 2019; "Twitter Is the Prime Social Media Network for World Leaders," PR Newswire, May 31, 2017.

39. Jeff Jardins, "How Much Data Is Generated Each Day?" World Economic Forum, April 17, 2019.

40. Internet Live Stats, https://www.internetlivestats.com/one-second/#traffic -band (accessed December 7, 2022).

41. Tim Fisher, "Terabytes, Gigabytes, and Petabytes: How Big Are They?" *Lifewire*, January 1, 2021; Pranshu Verma, "This Chip Transmits an Internet's Worth of Data Every Second," *Washington Post*, October 27, 2022.

42. Cybersecurity Advisory, "Top CVEs Actively Exploited by People's Republic of China State-Sponsored Cyber Actors," white paper, October 6, 2022.

43. Stuart Lau, "China's Xi Warns Putin Not to Use Nuclear Arms in Ukraine," *Politico*, November 4, 2022.

44. Chris Buckley and Steven Lee Meyers, "In Beijing, Olympic Spectacle and Global Power Games," *New York Times*, February 4, 2022.

45. Eliot Higgins, "How Bellingcat Uncovered Russia's Secret Network of Assassins," *Wired*, April 2, 2021; Narjas Zatat, "Isis Supporters in Europe Are Accidentally Revealing Their Locations on Social Media," *Indy100*, May 22, 2016.

46. Will Croxton, "How Bellingcat Tracked a Russian Missile System in Ukraine," *60 Minutes Overtime*, February 23, 2020.

47. Jon Gambrell, "Analysts: Fire at Iran Nuclear Site Hit Centrifuge Facility," *Washington Post*, July 2, 2020.

48. Joby Warrick, "China Is Building More than 100 New Missile Silos in Its Western Desert, Analysts Say," *Washington Post*, June 30, 2021; Editorial Board, "More Missile Silos Have Been Found in China. That's an Ominous Sign," *Washington Post*, July 30, 2021.

49. Author interview, October 31, 2022.

50. Alexis C. Madrigal, "#BostonBombing: The Anatomy of a Misinformation Disaster," *The Atlantic*, April 19, 2013; Jay Caspian Kang, "Should Reddit Be Blamed for the Spreading of a Smear?" *New York Times*, July 25, 2013; Chris Wade, "The Reddit Reckoning," *Slate*, April 15, 2014.

51. Kelley M. Sayler, "Artificial Intelligence and National Security," Congressional Research Service Report R45178, November 10, 2020, 10.

52. Amy Zegart and Michael Morell, "Spies, Lies, and Algorithms: Why US Intelligence Must Adapt or Fail," *Foreign Affairs*, May/June 2019; "Maintaining the Intelligence Edge: A Report of the CSIS Technology and Intelligence Task Force," Center for Strategic and International Studies, January 2021; Elizabeth Leyne and Yvette Nonte, "Is the Intelligence Community Staying Ahead of the Digital Curve?" Harvard Belfer Center Report, August 2021.

4

Terrorism and Counterterrorism in an Era of Great-Power Competition

Joseph H. Felter

Hours after the last US military forces withdrew from Afghanistan on September 1, 2021, President Joe Biden reassured a conflict-weary public in an address from the White House, "My fellow Americans, the war in Afghanistan is now over." Later in this same White House address, the president emphasized:

> The world is changing. We're engaged in a serious competition with China. We're dealing with the challenges on multiple fronts with Russia. We're confronted with cyberattacks and nuclear proliferation.
>
> We have to shore up America's competitive[ness] to meet these new challenges in the competition for the 21st century. And we can do both: fight terrorism and take on new threats that are here now and will continue to be here in the future.[1]

But what will it require in terms of policies and resources to "do both"—compete effectively with strategic rivals like China and Russia while concurrently maintaining the vigilance and commitment required to defend the homeland against ever-present terrorist threats and prevent another catastrophic 9/11–magnitude attack or worse? America will rightfully continue to assume its global leadership role in meeting the challenges of this century's evolving international security environment. And we can expect to be continuously targeted by terrorist groups in some part because of this. The

The views expressed in this chapter are solely those of the individual author and do not necessarily reflect the views of any organization with which they are, or have been, affiliated.

National Commission on Terrorism published a report the year prior to the 9/11 attacks on America's preparedness and role in dealing with terrorism, concluding:

> Terrorists attack American targets more often than those of any other country. America's pre-eminent role in the world guarantees that this will continue to be the case, and the threat of attacks creating massive casualties is growing. If the United States is to protect itself, if it is to remain a world leader, this nation must develop and continuously refine sound counterterrorism policies appropriate to the rapidly changing world around us.[2]

This statement was made at a time of anticipated transition for US national security priorities. It was understood that defeating and deterring terrorist threats required sustained US commitment and resources; however, it was clear to policy makers even at the turn of this century that defending America's vital and important interests would require a shift to the Asia Pacific region and a focus on balancing against the People's Republic of China.[3]

The terrorist attacks on September 11, 2001, provided shocking validation of the commission's warning from the previous year—that the United States "must develop and continuously refine sound counterterrorism policies." Yet this focus on terrorism meant that the prescient policy prescriptions calling for a shift in emphasis to more effectively engaging and balancing against China—developed in the early months of the Bush administration and continued during the Obama administration—were eclipsed by America's overwhelming response to the 9/11 attacks.

America's subsequent and near-singular focus on interdicting and defending against the terrorist threats responsible for the 9/11 attacks derailed intended efforts to shift policy emphasis to balancing China and engagement in the Asia Pacific. In hindsight, most policy analysts would agree that, even with the possibility of catastrophic terrorist attacks on the US homeland, the pendulum for US policy and budget priorities shifted too far toward addressing the threat of terrorism and away from anticipating and addressing the pacing threat of China and its aggressive actions in the Indo-Pacific region and beyond.

The United States arguably faces the reverse challenge today. There is broad bipartisan consensus that China poses an existential threat to the United States and its allies. Far more ambiguous—across the political spectrum—is the assessment of the nature, sources, and degree of the current and expected future threats of terrorism to the United States. In a largely zero-sum fiscal budget environment, we should expect resourcing strategic competition with China and Russia to tap funds formerly devoted to counterterrorism activities. But how far is too far? What are "sound counterterrorism" policies, and what portion of the Department of Defense (DoD) budget should focus on executing these policies?

Two essential truths provided in the 2000 National Commission on Terrorism report cited here have enduring policy relevance today. First, as a global leader on the world stage, America will be the target of terrorist attacks now and in the future. A wide array of terrorist actors will continue to maintain the capabilities and intent to attack America, its allies, and interests around the world. These terrorist actors represent a number of ideological and geopolitical perspectives, including violent jihadists such as al-Qaeda and the Islamic State, but also threats from state-sponsored terrorism such as Iranian-backed proxies in Iraq, Yemen, Lebanon, and Syria. Second, effective counterterrorism policies and allocating the resources necessary to implement them require continuous and dynamic assessment based on the evolving nature of the threats as well as competing threats to our national security and important interests.

In the two decades following the 9/11 attacks, US counterterrorism (CT) policies were developed and implemented with comparatively fewer constraints, either in terms of the underlying powers granted to CT programs or their financial cost, stemming from the national trauma that the attacks inflicted, as well as the belief that these policies would be effective at mitigating the terrorist threat. But this era, where prosecuting the Global War on Terrorism was America's main effort and received the highest budgeting priorities, has ended. Successfully achieving national CT objectives, even as they are further reduced, will require US defense, intelligence, and law enforcement agencies to be pragmatic and disciplined in discerning and identifying which capabilities and activities to sustain, which to refine, and which to abandon.

Road Map

In this paper, I identify a set of guiding principles to assist policy makers and defense officials in the dynamic process of developing and refining our national CT policies and budgeting priorities. In order to successfully navigate and defend US interests in an era of diffuse threats and increasingly constrained

resources, US CT policy decisions should be guided by three general principles: (1) an accurate assessment of the nature, degree, and sources of the
threat; (2) a rigorous understanding of US CT capabilities and limitations;
and (3) a pragmatic assessment of where CT investments can yield the largest
returns. I discuss and provide context for each of these categories and offer
specific recommendations for executing effective and efficient US counterterrorism policy in this era of great-power competition (GPC).

Note: Addressing the threat of domestic terrorism, specifically that posed
by racially or ethnically motivated violent extremists, antigovernment or
antiauthority violent extremists, or militia-violent extremists, is an increasingly pressing challenge facing US CT practitioners and policy makers.[4] This
paper limits its scope to focus on foreign terrorist threats to the US, namely
jihadist and state-sponsored terror groups, which fall within the jurisdiction
of the DoD.

Contemporary Threats from International Terrorist Groups

Although the United States invested in counterterrorism and engaged in
CT actions before September 11, 2001, it was only after that point that CT
became the top US national security priority, consuming a significant portion
of the budgets of a wide array of US government agencies, including the DoD.
However, the threat from international terrorism has changed markedly since
September 11 in ways that must be recognized to appropriately calibrate our
counterterrorism resources to deter and defend against terrorist threats from
abroad. I highlight three prominent international terrorist threats and briefly
describe how the threats from these groups have changed over time and how
these changes have important implications for our CT strategy and resources
going forward.

Al-Qaeda and Affiliated Groups

It took only nineteen terrorists trained and resourced by al-Qaeda to execute
the deadly 9/11 terrorist attacks.[5] At the time, al-Qaeda enjoyed sanctuary in
Taliban-controlled Afghanistan and largely existed as a centralized bureaucratic structure.[6] The ensuing Global War on Terror initiated by the Bush
administration decimated the group's leadership and forced al-Qaeda to alter
how it organized itself.[7] Eventually, the group transformed into more of a constellation of allied and affiliated groups, in which al-Qaeda was the center and
exercised some efforts at control over the associated groups.[8] These groups
eventually came to carry out more of the operational activities than the core

al-Qaeda group did, as it became much more of the ideological rather than the operational hub of a networked global jihadist umbrella.

Following the death of Osama bin Laden, al-Qaeda's founder and long-time leader, in May 2011 during a US Special Operations Forces raid of his hideout in Abbottabad, Pakistan, al-Qaeda's center group struggled to remain relevant.[9] The elimination of Bin Laden's successor, Ayman al-Zawahiri, in July 2022 further marginalized the group. But even as its role in planning and executing terrorist attacks has diminished, and continues to diminish, al-Qaeda still inspires and maintains the allegiance of a number of its affiliated groups around the world. This includes the Somalia-based al-Shabaab, Hurras al-Din in Syria, al-Qaeda in the Arabian Peninsula, al-Qaeda in the Islamic Maghreb, Jama'a Nusrat ul-Islam wa al-Muslimin' in Mali, and a nascent but growing group on the Indian subcontinent known as al-Qaeda in the Indian Subcontinent (AQIS). A 2018 estimate put the size of the total network of al-Qaeda at between thirty thousand and forty thousand fighters, but these numbers are hard to verify.[10] The START (National Consortium for the Study of Terrorism and Responses to Terrorism) 2022 Global Terrorism Database indicates that al-Qaeda and its affiliated groups listed here carried out 360 operations in 2020, with the vast majority taking place on the African continent.[11]

Indeed, Africa remains the most exposed region to jihadist violence, with Nigeria and Libya host to terrorist threats that have the potential to severely destabilize regional governments and wreak significant and costly damage to state and economic capacity. Boko Haram's activities in Northern Nigeria, Cameroon, Chad, Mali, and Niger have elicited international condemnation, and French special forces have been deployed to support building up nascent foreign internal defense capabilities.[12] Analysts agree that it is essential for global security and American interests that global terrorism does not metastasize even further in Africa, where it has the potential to devastate fragile paths toward economic development for millions and trigger bloody, inter-ethnic conflict on a scale unseen since the 1990s.[13]

Islamic State

The group that currently calls itself the Islamic State was, in an earlier era, al-Qaeda's main affiliate in Iraq. Eventually, as the Syrian civil war heated up, so too did tensions between the group then known as ISIS or ISIL and al-Qaeda. Eventually, the participants in this intragroup jihadi conflict deemed reconciliation impossible and split up. The Islamic State then became the most prominent and violent force in Iraq and Syria.[14] Eventually, the Islamic State counted upward of sixty thousand members and held de facto control over forty-one thousand square miles, comprising nearly half of Iraq's territory and a third of Syria's.[15] As the group grew, it called for pledges of allegiance from other jihadi groups around the world, eventually collecting pledges from groups from Algeria to East Asia.

From that high-water mark, the Islamic State has seen its formal territorial control shrink, but it maintains a robust group of affiliates. Again, this is especially the case in Africa, which has seen significant operational activity among the group's several affiliates, including Central Africa Province, Democratic Republic of the Congo, Greater Sahara, Somalia, and West Africa Province.[16] In mid-2022, it was reported that over half of all Islamic State's global provinces and half of its claimed operations were in Africa.[17] Beyond Africa, Islamic State Khorasan Province (ISIS-K) continues its attacks, seeking to undermine whoever the government is in Afghanistan. In August 2021, ISIS-K carried out a suicide bombing amid the chaotic US withdrawal from Afghanistan, killing nearly two hundred, including thirteen US military members.[18] The following year, in August 2022, ISIS-K carried out a suicide bombing targeting a school, killing as many as fifty-two people, mainly young women. Although the number cannot be verified, in its magazines, the group has claimed more than eight hundred attacks for all affiliated organizations through November 2022.[19]

State-Sponsored Terrorism

Perhaps the most glaring example of the potential danger of terrorist organizations aided by a state sponsor comes from Iran and the constellation of actors supported by the regime operating all over the globe. Ever since the fall of the shah in 1979, Iran and the United States have long been adversaries on the global stage. Over time, this antagonism resulted in Iran providing support directly to groups such as Badr Organization, Fatemiyoun Division, Hezbollah, and Kata'ib Hezbollah, for a variety of terrorism and insurgent activities against the United States in Lebanon, Iraq, and Syria.[20]

Although it is more difficult to get a sense of the overall operational activity of Iran's proxy network, several anecdotes are useful in illustrating the network's efforts. For example, in an incident on September 11, 2021, an Iranian proxy allegedly flew two drones filled with explosives toward coalition forces at Erbil International Airport to "remind the Americans of the September 11 attacks in our own way."[21] More broadly, an examination of Iranian support to proxies in Syria found that Iran was seeking to insert itself by providing military support to proxies and also through the provision of social services, logistical help, and ideological guidance.[22] Finally, the US Department of Justice released indictments against Iranian agents attempting to develop a plot against senior US officials, including former secretary of state Michael Pompeo and former national security advisor John Bolton.[23] While these plots might arguably not be considered cases of terrorism, they highlight Iran's potential threat when it chooses to exert itself to advance its foreign policy interests.

Understanding the Threat

The brief overviews of three current international terrorist threats highlighted above indicate that, despite the significant activity, none of these groups, especially al-Qaeda and the Islamic State, look today as they did at their inception or even at the moment of their most prominent attacks. Al-Qaeda, its affiliated groups, and the Islamic State have largely decentralized in response to counterterrorism pressure. Moreover, a large number of leadership losses in these groups and networks have deprived them of strategic continuity and forced them to focus on short-term survival rather than achieving their long-term goals.

But this does not suggest that threats from international terrorist groups are now nor will remain insignificant—quite the contrary. According to a yearly analysis of the trajectory of prominent al-Qaeda and Islamic State entities, none of the thirteen were "weakening" in 2021. There was a slight improvement in 2022, with two of the fourteen in the "weakening" category.[24] An accurate understanding of the threat suggests that the United States—and the world—cannot choose to be done with counterterrorism, no matter how important and resource intensive it becomes to compete with strategic rivals Russia and China.

Succinctly, international terrorist groups possess the desire to strike the United States and its allies, as well as the capabilities to do so. The National Counterterrorism Center describes the al-Qaeda threat aptly: "Al-Qaeda and its affiliates in South Asia, Africa, and the Middle East remain a resilient organization committed to conducting attacks in the United States and against American interests abroad."[25] The former commander of US CENTCOM, General Kenneth McKenzie, made a statement about the Islamic State in 2020 that offers excellent and enduring guidance to keep in mind when assessing the anticipated threats from international terrorist groups, "This threat is not going away. There's never going to be a time, I believe, when either ISIS or whatever follows ISIS is going to be completely absent from the global stage."[26] Continued CT pressure will be critical to keeping these groups, especially their external operations capabilities, at bay. But this pressure can be challenging to generate in a resource-constrained environment, despite the impressive CT capabilities the United States has developed over the past twenty years.

Capabilities and Limitations of US Counterterrorism Strategy

An array of international terrorist groups maintain the strength and intent to threaten US interests overseas and at home, and this threat is enduring. Developing and continuously refining effective and efficient US CT strategies and policies in this era where priorities have shifted to resourcing competition with our strategic rivals will require a disciplined focus on exploiting the greatest strengths of America's CT capabilities and mitigating our weaknesses. As our strategies evolve, we will expect to ask those implementing CT policy and executing operations to "do the same with less," i.e., protect the homeland and defend vital and important interests against the threat of terrorism with fewer relative resources than were provided in the previous two decades.

And this is happening now. DoD and Intelligence Community partners focused on CT are experiencing drastic cuts to their budget and reductions in personnel assigned.[27] DoD budget proposals over the past several years have seen the near elimination of overseas contingency operations funding, a separate line item that provided significant support for US military operations in Iraq, Afghanistan, and the southern Philippines, among other regions of operational importance where our forces conducted or supported CT missions. Our defense budgets are also shifting away from acquiring weapons and platforms optimized for interdicting terrorist and insurgent threats and instead moving toward procuring the systems and equipment needed to prepare and prevail in a conflict with other states.[28]

Over-the-Horizon Counterterrorism—a Viable Way Ahead or Oxymoron?

President Biden announced our new "over-the-horizon" counterterrorism strategy hours after the departure of the last American military forces from Afghanistan. This approach "without boots on the ground" entailed interdicting terrorist targets through intelligence-informed drone strikes launched from secure locations outside conflict zones.[29] The strategy's efficacy received validation by the targeted killing of al-Qaeda's leader, Ayman al-Zawahiri, on July 31, 2022, in a drone strike at the residential home where he was staying in downtown Kabul. The strike resulted from careful and dedicated intelligence work by US agencies on the lookout for the return of top al-Qaeda figures to Afghanistan.[30]

The US intelligence officials and other professionals responsible for the Zawahiri strike deserve significant praise for the successful outcome of this strike. But most experts agree that the conditions that led to the successful targeting and discriminate interdiction of Zawahiri will be extremely difficult, if not impossible, to reproduce against other terrorist targets.[31] Importantly, the strategic aims of over-the-horizon counterterrorism are arguably ill-defined. Lethal interdiction and attrition of high-value terrorist targets are more accurately viewed as an effective counterterrorism *tactic*—not a strategy in itself—and can be successfully employed only if sufficient intelligence and targeting data are available.

In developing a more cost-effective and efficient CT strategy, US policy makers must avoid conflating measures of performance—the attrition of terrorists through kinetic actions—with measures of effectiveness—protecting the US homeland and our allies and partners from costly terrorist attacks. America's current CT strategy relies heavily on over-the-horizon CT and can point to examples of successful performance across the Middle East, East Africa, and Central Asia. Policy makers are obliged to develop viable and sustainable counterterrorism strategies that reflect current and anticipated budget realities, ensuring they have clearly defined goals and objectives and focus on effectively and efficiently achieving priority strategic ends.[32] A lack of coherence in our strategy is perhaps the biggest current limitation to our ability to carry out effective, efficient, and sustained counterterrorism operations and activities.

Biggest "No Bang" for the Buck: Optimize Returns on CT Investment

The total costs of funding counterterrorism efforts over the last two decades have been significant. US aggregate counterterrorism spending—measured from the aftermath of the 9/11 attacks through the end of 2017, when the Trump administration's National Security Strategy, marking a strategic shift to great-power competition, was released—is estimated to have exceeded $2.8 trillion. This is a sixteenfold increase over combined CT

spending in the year prior to 9/11, amounting to 15 percent of the $18 tril-
lion of total discretionary spending for that period. This figure includes a
broad range of CT-related efforts, including government spending on homeland security, the wars in Afghanistan, Iraq, and Syria, and other international counterterrorism activities and programs. US CT spending peaked
in 2008 at $260 billion—22 percent of total discretionary spending—and
fell to $175 billion in 2017, which was 14 percent of discretionary spending
that year.[33]

The DoD has shouldered a significant portion of the CT budgetary burden
throughout this period. In 2008, at the height of spending on CT, the DoD
expended over 30 percent of the total defense budget toward CT-related
activities and requirements—this amounted to $206.7 billion allocated
toward CT and $479.2 billion toward non-CT-related expenditures. In 2017,
the DoD spent 17.6 percent of the defense budget on activities considered
CT related for a total of $96 billion, compared to $549.9 billion on non-
CT-related defense spending that year.[34] Since 9/11, the average US defense
spending on CT as a percentage of its total budget is estimated to be nearly
20 percent.[35]

How much lower can the DoD budget for CT-related activities go without incurring unacceptable risks is difficult to determine and will be judged
in hindsight, e.g., did the United States suffer a catastrophic attack from an
international terrorist group? Resourcing the formal shift in US-stated strategic priorities to great-power competition and identifying the inevitable
trade-offs required to do so going forward will not be easy. The persistence of
threats to the United States from international terrorism and the decreasing
resources available for combating these threats demand that CT investments
target opportunities where they will have the greatest impact at the least cost.
Several areas where the United States can achieve cost-effective returns on
its CT investments and recommendations on opportunities to do so are provided below.

Strengthening Counterterrorism Partnerships

The 2018 National Defense Strategy identified strengthening alliances and
building new partnerships as one of DoD's three major lines of effort.[36] This
emphasis on leveraging America's comparative advantage of its dense network
of alliances and partnerships is reflected in the 2022 National Defense Strategy
(NDS), which also emphasizes, "Mutually-beneficial Alliances and partnerships are an enduring strength for the United States, and are critical to achieving

our objectives."[37] The advantages and opportunities afforded by these relationships can be translated to develop and sustain effective counterterrorism with reduced unilateral US actions or the forward presence of troops.

One representative example of the cost-effectiveness of the partnership approach to counterterrorism comes from Kenya. On September 21, 2013, four members of the Somali militant group al-Shabaab entered the Westgate Shopping Mall in Nairobi, Kenya, with assault rifles and grenades. When the incident was over, seventy-one people were dead, including the perpetrators, in an attack covered in local and international media for days. Several years later, in January 2019, al-Shabaab carried out another attack in a Nairobi hotel that left nearly two dozen dead. In the wake of this tragedy and recognizing the continuing threat al-Shabaab posed to Kenyan citizens, the Kenyan and US governments formed the first Joint Terrorism Task Force outside the United States. This initiative, designed to provide Kenyan investigators with access to and training in more advanced law enforcement techniques to combat al-Shabaab, was credited by the Kenyan government for playing a role in reducing the level of terrorist activity in the country. This approach, in which the US provides training and logistical assistance to partners but does not take the lead, can be replicated elsewhere and potentially deliver the type of cost-effective returns necessary to make it a viable and sustainable option in a resource-constrained environment.

Increasing the role and contribution of our allies and partners in interdicting and defending against international terrorist groups with global reach can be achieved by changing policies and without major increases to the defense budget, which is perhaps the most cost-effective and efficient approach for enhancing US CT policy now and going forward. Every additional CT mission, role, and activity shouldered by our allies and partners can translate into reducing the financial burden formerly carried by the United States. Beyond this direct cost reduction, decreasing US presence and activities abroad generally undercuts the narratives of international terrorist groups like al-Qaeda and ISIS that point to US overseas interventions as a direct and deliberate threat to Islam.

An effective way to bolster the role of CT partnerships in executing US counterterrorism strategy, for example, is expanding information and intelligence sharing beyond the "Five Eyes" countries (Australia, Canada, New Zealand, the United Kingdom, and the United States) and empowering key partners with greater access to US information and intelligence without compromising sensitive sources and methods. Several countries across the

Indo-Pacific region, in particular, can play a greater role in executing a mutually beneficial counterterrorism strategy through closer cooperation with the
United States. Treaty allies like Japan and even South Korea have the potential to play a much more prominent and impactful role in regional CT with
greater information sharing and access to intelligence—all of which could be
provided with a limited security risk.

Beyond our formal allies, CT cooperation with many of our key partners
can and should also be increased. India, for example, is designated as a major
defense partner of the United States with a range of defense-enabling agreements that can facilitate secure communications, intelligence sharing, geo-
spatial information sharing, and technology transfer.[38] India borders and is
close to the sanctuaries of some of the most dangerous international terrorist groups. It also shares interests in CT cooperation with the United States,
which are far from fully exploited. Indonesia is another prime example of a
US partner with vast potential for increased CT cooperation that can be more
fully realized by developing closer and more interoperable defense and intelligence relationships. This would require changes in policies and restrictions,
not increases in spending.[39]

Know Your Enemy—Why and How They Operate

Terrorist attacks can be viewed as symptoms of even more sinister underlying causes. Cost-effective CT policies should strive to target the root causes
of attacks directed or inspired by international terrorist groups. I have argued
that the actual center of gravity of the violent movements that sustain Islamic
extremist terrorist groups like al-Qaeda and ISIS can be understood as "the
ideas of radical Jihadist thought."[40] These ideas—not necessarily the individual leaders themselves—can insulate and protect jihadist groups against
external pressure and enable jihadist movements to spread even when the
leaders of these groups are killed or captured. Ultimately, "it is not possible
to capture, kill, or incarcerate ideas."[41] When developing and executing cost-
effective policies to address international terrorist threats, al-Qaeda, ISIS, and
other jihadist terrorist groups should not be viewed strictly in terms of the
organizational charts and bureaucratic hierarchies used to describe a more
conventional military enemy. Doing so will emphasize more kinetic CT strategies and policies, which we know from experience are expensive and can
have limited efficacy.[42]

During the darkest days of the US intervention in Iraq, researchers at West
Point's Combating Terrorism Center published seminal work concluding,

"The key to defeating the jihadi movement is identifying its strengths and weaknesses so that the former may be countered or co-opted and the latter exploited. . . . The people who know these strengths and weaknesses best are the jihadis themselves; one just needs to know where (and how) to look for their insights."[43] Terrorist groups have ideological and organizational vulnerabilities that can be exploited using information that is available online or otherwise is "hiding in plain sight." Responsibly releasing this material and making it available to the public can put terrorists on the defensive and is relatively cost-free for the DoD to initiate. And the DoD literally has terabytes of data available on the types of information that can make terrorists vulnerable if made public.[44]

Cost-effective CT policies will fund efforts to better access and exploit information gleaned from terrorists themselves in order to help discredit and delegitimize the hostile ideology driving jihadist-inspired terrorism and to exploit internal weaknesses and fractures within these terrorist organizations. Some specific activities that effective and efficient CT policy could support include (1) establishing programs that translate and analyze influential jihadi strategic texts and other communications; (2) exploiting the divisions and critical vulnerabilities identified by the terrorists themselves through their written and intercepted communications; and (3) taking advantage of opportunities to better leverage diverse communities of expertise on jihadist thinking.[45]

Technology

International terrorist organizations like al-Qaeda and ISIS, despite their desire for a return to a medieval-era caliphate, are not made up of non–technologically savvy individuals plotting the return of society back to the days before computers and cell phones. Far from this, today's terrorists are internet-savvy and dedicated users of social media, drones, and other advanced technologies. This reliance by terrorist groups on technology, however, can be a significant weakness, especially given the advantage that governments have in expertise, access to technology, and resources. For example, when it declared itself a caliphate in 2014, the Islamic State wielded one of the most potent propaganda production and publication infrastructures for any terrorist group, with the ability to regularly produce compelling photo reports, videos, and newsletters. Yet, the very technology upon which the group was relying also made it vulnerable to efforts in cyberspace to undermine its efficacy and increase risks to operational security.

Operation Glowing Symphony, discussed publicly for the first time in 2019, is an example of technology-enabled CT and the type that effective and efficient CT policy should fully support and exploit. This operation saw analysts and cyber specialists from US Cyber Command and the National Security Agency hack into accounts held by key Islamic State media figures, lock them out of their accounts, obtain intelligence information, and make the distribution of propaganda from central servers difficult or impossible.[46] This "no boots on the ground" operation was highly effective and executed with limited risks and costs.

Cost-effective US CT efforts will exploit the vulnerabilities terrorist use of technology creates and better leverage the advantages of US access to advanced technologies in developing and implementing counterterrorism responses. Significantly, most technological advances that have the potential to enhance our CT capabilities originate in the commercial technology base—not in government labs or by major defense primes. A number of forward-leaning initiatives by the DoD exist to facilitate the development, adoption, and deployment of technologies critical to our national security, such as those initiated by the Defense Innovation Unit and the recently established Office of Strategic Capital.[47] Technologies that empower more cost-effective and efficient CT applications must remain a priority for these efforts.

"Dual-Use" Policies Supporting Counterterrorism
and Great-Power Competition

Counterterrorism and great-power competition are not necessarily mutually exclusive, and funding them is not zero-sum relative to the two policy priorities. The capabilities developed over twenty years of intense CT operations can be repurposed to support activities supporting GPC objectives and priorities as well. Some of the most cost-effective and efficient investments in counterterrorism in this era of great-power competition support both CT and GPC interests and objectives. For example, international military training and exercises will sometimes be more palatable and supportable for US partners if they are designed as counterterrorism cooperation and avoid the optics of being geared toward other security threats that might subject these partners to an expected backlash from China. Former state counterterrorism coordinator Nathan Sales sums up positive externalities of partner CT cooperation as having the ability to "cement relationships with existing and potential partners" and "serving as a reminder of the rewards of cooperation."[48]

Cost-effective CT policy will seek to include CT cooperation and activities with the added upside benefit of strengthening bilateral and multilateral relationships and interoperability, which will be critical in supporting GPC objectives.

A compelling example of a past investment justified by its CT efficacy but also significantly supporting broader GPC objectives and priorities was the limited US military and contractor presence maintained in Afghanistan in the year prior to the abrupt US departure in August 2021. Consider the operational and deterrent value in the GPC context of preventing the total collapse of even a highly flawed, elected Afghan government and maintaining a de facto US and NATO base like Bagram Airfield in a country bordering China, Iran, Pakistan, and three former Soviet republics now on Russia's southern flank. In his post–US withdrawal address, President Biden claimed, "And there's nothing China or Russia would rather have, would want more in this competition, than the United States to be bogged down another decade in Afghanistan."[49] In this era of competition and strategic rivalry among great powers, China, Russia, Iran, and others more likely applauded the departure of US troops from Afghanistan. US strategy and policies must avoid such debacles going forward. The return on investment of a relatively modest commitment of troops—less than 7 percent of the size of the New York Police Department in the case of US forces deployed to Afghanistan in 2021—far exceeded the costs of maintaining them, especially when viewed in terms of its efficacy in supporting both CT and GPC priorities.[50]

Final Thoughts

The opportunity costs of sustaining the level of spending and the strategic priority placed on counterterrorism by the US in the two decades since the 9/11 attacks have been significant. In the context of competition with strategic rivals like China, the United States arguably lost considerable ground measured across a range of indicators, from degrading our edge in critical technologies to ceding strategic influence in areas like the South China Sea. Prevailing in this century's strategic competition demands significant investment and will remain a major focus for defense budgeting, requiring compromise across competing national security priorities. As our political leaders and policy makers assess the threats to US interests that will inform the trade-offs and calculated risks taken in our CT policies and budgets going forward, however, it is important they remember that the threat to the United

States from international terrorism is determined by the real capabilities and intentions of these groups and not by best-case scenarios and untested assumptions made by well-intended government officials obliged to allocate resources to fund national security priorities as determined by our senior political leadership.[51]

America must maintain a disciplined commitment to investing in sufficient CT capabilities despite competing threats and budget priorities. No president or political leader can unilaterally declare that our war against the terrorist threats responsible for catastrophic events like the 9/11 attacks is over—our enemies get a vote. But neither can any president or political leader afford to misappropriate excessive funding in a largely zero-sum budget environment to threats posed by terrorism to the detriment of responding to major geopolitical challenges facing the United States.

Combating terrorism is an extraordinarily challenging endeavor, even when it is a national priority and is resourced accordingly. The threat from international terrorism is enduring, and budgets available to the DoD to address these threats are dwindling. Sun Tzu warns that "to defend everywhere is to defend nowhere." Decisions on where and how to defend against international terrorist threats and to what level are as much art as science. Difficult compromises lie ahead in determining the appropriate allocation of resources to defend against terrorist threats concurrent with prevailing in the competition with strategic rivals and addressing other threats to the United States' vital and important interests.

Notes

1. The White House, "Remarks by President Biden on the End of the War in Afghanistan," Briefing Room speech, August 31, 2021.

2. National Commission on Terrorism (Bremer Commission), "The Changing Threat of International Terrorism," August 2, 2000.

3. The administration of George W. Bush initiated a reorientation of US strategy toward the Asia Pacific region. See Nina Silov, "The Pivot before the Pivot: US Strategy to Preserve the Power Balance in Asia," *International Security*, Spring 2016.

4. The White House, "National Strategy for Countering Domestic Terrorism," June 15, 2021.

5. Commission on Terrorist Attacks Upon the United States, *The 9/11 Commission Report: Final Report of the National Commission on Terrorist Attacks Upon the United States*, US Government, July 22, 2004.

6. Bruce Hoffman, "The Changing Face of Al Qaeda and the Global War on Terrorism," *Studies in Conflict and Terrorism* 27, no. 6 (November–December 2004): 549–60.

7. Jacob Shapiro, *The Terrorist Dilemma* (Princeton, NJ: Princeton University Press, 2013).

8. Barak Mendelsohn, *The Al-Qaeda Franchise: The Expansion of Al-Qaeda and Its Consequences* (New York: Oxford University Press, 2016).

9. Nelly Lahoud, Stuart Caudill, Liam Collins, Gabriel Koehler-Derrick, Don Rassler, and Muhammad al-'Ubaydi, *Letters from Abbottabad: Bin Ladin Sidelined?* (West Point, NY: Combating Terrorism Center, 2012), available at the Defense Technical Information Center, https://apps.dtic.mil/sti/citations/ADA560875.

10. Bruce Hoffman, "Al-Qaeda's Resurrection," Council on Foreign Relations, March 6, 2018.

11. START (National Consortium for the Study of Terrorism and Responses to Terrorism), Global Terrorism Database 1970–2020 [data file], accessed January 10, 2023, https://www.start.umd.edu/gtd.

12. Stephen Burgess, "Military Intervention in Africa: French and US Approaches Compared," *US Air Force Journal of European, Middle Eastern, and African Affairs* 1, no. 1 (Spring 2019): 69–89.

13. Zachary Devlin-Foltz, "Africa's Fragile States: Empowering Extremists, Exporting Terrorism," Africa Center for Strategic Studies, August 30, 2010; United Nations, "Fragile Democratic Gains at Risk in Central Africa as Violence by Armed Groups Escalates," *UN News*, June 7, 2021.

14. Muhammad al-'Ubaydi, Nelly Lahoud, Daniel Milton, and Bryan Price, *The Group That Calls Itself a State: Understanding the Evolution and Challenges of the Islamic State* (West Point, NY: Combating Terrorism Center, 2014).

15. Daniel Milton, *Structure of a State: Captured Documents and the Islamic State's Organizational Structure* (West Point, NY: Combating Terrorism Center, 2021).

16. Jacob Zenn, "ISIS in Africa: The Caliphate's Next Frontier," Newlines Institute for Strategy and Policy, May 26, 2020.

17. Jason Warner, Paolo Caruso, and Chris Keller, "The Islamic State's 'African Turn': Why the African Continent Is Showing Outsized Importance for IS," *FMSO's Foreign Perspectives Brief*, Foreign Military Studies Office, November 2022, https://community.apan.org/wg/tradoc-g2/fmso/m/fmso-monographs/427985.

18. Lara Seligman, Alexander Ward, Andrew Desiderio, Daniel Lippman, and Paul McLeary, "13 US Troops Killed in ISIS Attacks on Kabul Airport," *Politico*, August 26, 2021.

19. This number is based on a dataset of Islamic State operational claims compiled by Muhammad al-'Ubaydi of the Madison Policy Forum and made available to researchers at the West Point Combating Terrorism Center with permission.

20. Joseph Felter and Brian Fishman, *Iranian Strategy in Iraq: Politics and "Other Means"* (West Point, NY: Combating Terrorism Center, 2008); Matthew Levitt, "Iran's Support for Terrorism in the Middle East," testimony before the US Senate, Committee on Foreign Relations, Subcommittee on Near Eastern and South and Central Asian Affairs, July 25, 2012; Ashley Lane, "Iran's Islamist Proxies in the Middle East," Wilson Center, December 5, 2022.

21. Michael Knights, Crispin Smith, and Hamdi Malik, "Iran's Proxies in Iraq Undertake the World's Only Terrorist Attack Commemorating 9/11," Washington Institute for Near East Policy, September 14, 2021.

22. Nakissa Jahanbani and Suzanne Weedon Levy, *Iran Entangled: Iran and Hezbollah's Support to Proxies Operating in Syria* (West Point, NY: Combating Terrorism Center, 2022).

23. Matthew Levitt, "Contending with IRGC Plots," *Lawfare*, August 16, 2022.

24. Katherine Zimmerman and Kate Chesnutt, "The State of al Qaeda and ISIS around the World," American Enterprise Institute, September 8, 2022.

25. The National Counterterrorism Center published documents further admonishing, "The group has advanced a number of unsuccessful plots in the past several years, including against the United States and Europe. This highlights [al-Qaeda's] ability to continue some attack preparations while under sustained counterterrorism pressure and suggests it may be plotting additional attacks against the United States at home or overseas." See the National Counterterrorism Center, https://www.dni .gov/index.php/nctc-home.

26. "CENTCOM and the Shifting Sands of the Middle East: A Conversation with CENTCOM Commander Gen. Kenneth F. McKenzie Jr.," Middle East Institute, event transcript, June 10, 2020, https://www.mei.edu/events/centcom-and-shifting -sands-middle-east-conversation-centcom-commander-gen-kenneth-f-mckenzie.

27. Intelligence community official with direct knowledge of budget and personnel reductions; phone conversation with the author, December 27, 2023.

28. Office of the Under Secretary of Defense (Comptroller) / Chief Financial Officer, *Defense Budget Overview: United States Department of Defense Fiscal Year 2023 Budget Request* (Arlington, VA: Department of Defense, 2022); Marcus Weisgerber, "Biden's $773B Request for Pentagon Stays Focused on China," *Defense One*, March 7, 2022; David Welna, "Defense Budget Shifts Military's Focus from Terrorism to China and Russia," NPR.org, August 5, 2018.

29. The White House, "Remarks by President Biden," August 31, 2021.

30. Matt Murphy, "Ayman al-Zawahiri: How US Spies Found Al-Qaeda's Top Man in Kabul," BBC.co.uk, August 2, 2022.

31. "Experts React: Al-Qaeda Chief Ayman Al-Zawahiri Is Dead. What's Next for US Counterterrorism?" Atlantic Council, August 1, 2022.

32. Andy Forney, "Drone Strikes Forever: The Problems with Over-the-Horizon Counterterrorism and a Better Way Forward," Modern War Institute at West Point, October 28, 2022.

33. Stimson Study Group on Counterterrorism Spending (Amy Belasco, Mackenzie Eaglen, Luke Hartig, Tina Jonas, Mike McCord, and John Mueller), "Counterterrorism Spending: Protecting America While Promoting Efficiencies and Accountability," *Conventional Arms*, May 2018, https://www.stimson.org/2018 /counterterrorism-spending-protecting-america-while-promoting-efficiencies-and -accountability.

34. Stimson Study Group, "Counterterrorism Spending."

35. This rough estimate is based on the data provided by the Stimson Study Group in "Counterterrorism Spending," with more recent years based on author estimates using similar base data sources currently available.

36. US Department of Defense (DoD), "Summary of the 2018 National Defense Strategy of the United States of America: Sharpening the American Military's Competitive Edge," https://dod.defense.gov/Portals/1/Documents/pubs/2018 -National-Defense-Strategy-Summary.pdf.

37. DoD, "Fact Sheet: 2022 National Defense Strategy," https://media.defense .gov/2022/Mar/28/2002964702/-1/-1/1/NDS-FACT-SHEET.PDF.

38. US Department of State, Bureau of Political-Military Affairs, "US Security Cooperation with India," January 20, 2021, https://www.state.gov/u-s-security-co operation-with-india.

39. Author discussion with current Indonesian defense minister Prabowo Subianto in Jakarta, December 10, 2022; and with Indonesian TNI chief (defense chief), December 12, 2022. Both expressed interest in expanding CT cooperation in the region.

40. Joseph Felter, "The Internet: A Portal to Violent Islamist Extremism," testimony before the US Senate Committee on Homeland Security and Governmental Affairs, May 3, 2007, https://www.hsgac.senate.gov/imo/media/doc/050307Felter.pdf.

41. Felter, "The Internet."

42. Felter, "The Internet."

43. Jarret Brachman and William McCants, Stealing Al-Qaeda's Playbook (West Point, NY: Combating Terrorism Center, February 2006).

44. For example, the Combating Terrorism Center at West Point has, since 2005, used material from inside terrorist organizations to showcase the weaknesses of these groups.

45. James J. F. Forest, Jarret Brachman, and Joseph Felter, Harmony and Dishar-mony: Exploiting Al-Qa'ida's Organizational Vulnerabilities (West Point, NY: Combat-ing Terrorism Center, February 14, 2006).

46. National Security Archive, "Joint Task Force ARES and Operation GLOWING SYMPHONY: Cyber Command's Internet War against ISIL," August 13, 2018.

47. Defense Innovation Unit and activities described at https://www.diu.mil; Department of Defense Office of Strategic Capital at https://www.cto.mil/osc.

48. Nathan Sales, "Counterterrorism and Great-Power Competition," Atlantic Council, September 7, 2021.

49. The White House, "Remarks by President Biden on the End of the War in Afghanistan," August 31, 2021.

50. Joseph Felter, "The Enemy Gets a Vote: The Forever War and Future War after Afghanistan," The Hill, August 30, 2022.

51. Felter, "The Enemy Gets a Vote."

National Security Threats

With General Keith Alexander, Admiral Gary Roughead,
and Michael McFaul, Moderated by Commander Bart D'Angelo

COMMANDER BART D'ANGELO: Let's start with General Keith Alexander.

GENERAL KEITH ALEXANDER: The papers were great. I want to talk about two issues: cybersecurity and then the growing national threats that we see in the future. I was in Admiral Mike Mullen's office in 2007. He asked me to come down there because some submarine popped up in the middle of one of the fleets. Admiral Mullen asked, why didn't we give him insight into it? We had a discussion, and the answer was we can't predict the future without seeing it, but we can understand the adversaries' intent and future options with cyber. Admiral Mullen was clearly impressed and intrigued by the discussion. He asked, how many people would we need from the navy. And I said, about a thousand people.

And that became the foundation for US Cyber Command. I bring that up because it was the thought that cyber would be an element of national power. Two thousand eight was actually when we started cyber command because of the attack on the Defense Department by Russia trying to exploit our military in Afghanistan through the use of compromised thumb drives. This event was called Buckshot Yankee. And that started us down the road of establishing cyber command. General Jim Mattis was at CENTCOM [US Central Command] and came up to NSA [National Security Agency] to be briefed on a classified program we were running in cyber to support his command. We had a chance to show them what a real cyber operation looks like. Not ones that you read about in the paper, about some four-hundred-pound

guy sitting on a bed hacking. This was sixty-four people in a focused operation going after a target that everybody said was impossible. There were
three things they said were impossible to do. We had this young lady who
talked really fast, and just watching her talk to General Mattis at the time was
amazing.

And what they did is they solved three problems that everybody said you
couldn't do. You can't do this, you can't do this, you can't do this. They did
each one of those, and we did the same thing on other adversaries. And what
that really led us to understand is that we didn't think about cyber as an element of national power. Today in Ukraine and over the time since General
Mattis was secretary, what happened during the elections, and what cyber
command was able to do is just a small portion of what can happen with
cyber. The fact that you can go in and do things to the critical infrastructure
of a nation, to their defense department, to their communications, is so mis-
understood by almost everyone, how bad that can really be, that we really
need to rethink how do we now delve and weave cyber operations into our
national security strategy.

Because I think it's coming with AI, with all the advances, and it's good to
have Raj [Shah] and Mike [Brown] here, because you guys see this from your
roles at DIU [Defense Innovation Unit], but the part that's missing is often
people who are in cyber operations are thinking about doing one thing, end-
point or a SIEM [security information and event management tool]. Oh no, I
do firewalls. What we're talking about is not looking at those things. Those are
tools. It's like a rifle and a bullet. We're talking about what's the strategy that
follows the national strategy in accomplishing missions and goals, because
cyber is clearly playing a part in that right now in Ukraine. We've had US and
European forces helping Ukraine since the beginning, actually a few months
ahead of that. And that intelligence information and those actions led to
many of the things that were given by the US to Europe saying, "Here's what's
going to happen, A, B, C, and D."

And they nailed every one of those. That's from good intelligence, that's
from good operations, and it has some tremendous opportunities for the
future. We don't think about it like that. And I think that's something that
I just put on the table because it is going to change at a significant rate in
the near future. With everything that's going on in these networks, it's changing. Everybody has a computer and a phone. Everybody's connected. We see
all these things going on, and our adversaries are connected even when they
don't believe they're connected. *So this is going to be the first phase of the next*

battle. China has that in its doctrine. When they take on a technologically superior adversary, the US, they're going to start with cyber.

And they have more people than we do. So when you think about it, that's a problem. Our adversaries are going to attack us first in cyber. We need to respond faster than we would with missile defense, and we need to be prepared to do that.

Russia made a mistake, a big mistake, going into Ukraine. You can just walk all the way through it. So how does this end? Well, if I were to just predict it, my boss was down and saying, "Okay, what's going to happen?" I'd say it doesn't look good for Putin, doesn't look good. And who would take his place? Nikolai Patrushev, Alexander Bortnikov. One of those two guys is probably in the lead. And they're both just as bad.

So the issue that we're going to face is, I think, Putin is clinging onto office right now. Going after Crimea and giving Ukraine more capability is absolutely in our best interest. If you think about where Russia sits, the worst thing that our nation can have happen to it is to have Russia and China together and powerful enough to accomplish the goals they want. We would not be able to stop it. There would go Taiwan. There would go parts of Eastern Europe, and we couldn't stop it. So we have an opportunity now to stop it by breaking off Russia. I think as a strategic goal, if you could make Russia neutral or maybe even an ally, it would change the whole equation with China. Think about that. Think about what could happen. So all of a sudden [opposition leader Alexei] Navalny takes on a whole new meaning.

What if he were running Russia? What would that mean for us? By going after Crimea, letting Ukraine go after Crimea would really put intense pressure on Putin, and I'm not sure he could make it. H.R. [McMaster] and others can jump in on that. I don't think that'll happen. With respect to China and Oriana [Skylar Mastro]'s paper on China, I think there are a couple things to consider regarding Xi Jinping. His life growing up was influenced by Japan. They were humiliated by the Japanese. He talks about that. He says that will never happen again. His first and ongoing interest is in having a military that will ensure that will never happen again. And the second is the unification of Taiwan. He wants both of those to happen in his lifetime. And it's interesting. He is driven, in my opinion, to make those happen.

I think taking China on head-to-head would be really tough for us, especially if Russia were on their side. This would be really tough. I think we have to look at that landscape and say China, Russia, and I'd put Iran over here because that's going to have a part in it. What do we do about those three, and how do we help change that landscape? And interestingly, we have the time now to impact what's going on in Ukraine, to actually help shift that whole future to a much more favorable position for our country and for the world. Because now, Xi Jinping is going to look out, "Okay, sanctions really work. Russia collapsed. I don't want that to happen. Maybe I take a little bit more time, and we can go to a more peaceful solution." Iran, I just put Iran in because they're an outlier. The Supreme Leader was reportedly going to die last September. He didn't do that; he missed that event. But the guy who potentially would take over is Ebrahim Raisi, the guy who helped execute ten thousand people in 1988 because those people were against the revolution.

Raisi is a hard-liner. And remember, Iran went after our financial sector in 2012, after going after Saudi Aramco and others with distributed denial of service attacks. And they threatened to do that with wiper viruses in 2014. If that had happened, it would've shut down the global financial system, and they would have nothing to lose, because they were under sanctions. So you have those three countries that we should be thinking about in a macro strategy of how we are going to handle these threats in the future. I believe cyber is something that can actually help push and maneuver our national strategy in a favorable way.

And so I'm very thankful for all the work that you all did in helping us set that up. I think that's part of our future. I'll leave you this one thought. Ninety-plus percent of cyber is in civilian hands. The government can't see it. If you want to protect the country, we need a radar system for cyber where the government can see attacks on it in an anonymized way, in such a way that we can defend the nation from an attack, because it's going to come and we need to be ready. And so that public-private partnership is the future for cybersecurity. Thank you.

D'ANGELO: Over to Admiral Gary Roughead.

ADMIRAL GARY ROUGHEAD: Keith, you're wonderful. We haven't seen one another in about three or four years, and he just set me up beautifully. So I can't wait to start, but I'm going to step back a little bit and then drill down into some more specific things that I think will echo what Oriana has written. But my view is as we look longer term and more broadly, we really need to take a look at ourselves and assess our power, presence, and influence in reshaping Eurasia, which I think is what Keith is talking about. And the players in that reshaping are going to be the four world empires, China, Persia

[Iran], Ottoman, and Russia. And so, how will all that play out? How do we want to posture ourselves? And it's more than just the military dimension, because as we think about access and influence, what people in the region like to see of the United States is our military, the development that we can provide them, and the change in their lives. And then the other is markets. Our military has, many have said here, significantly diminished over time.

With respect to development, we're getting our butts kicked by China primarily, largely because of our hesitancy toward risk-taking and for insisting on very high US content that prohibits us from engaging in cooperative efforts with other countries. And then in markets, we are just not there, particularly in the Pacific. Our absence in TTP, now CPTTP [Comprehensive and Progressive Agreement for Trans-Pacific Partnership], is resounding. We can hold up the IPEF [Indo-Pacific Economic Framework for Prosperity], a lot of good stuff in IPEF, but on my recent visits to the region, they'll say good things about it, but it's not access to our market.

And so that influence and presence and power that we have in this new reshaping area, I think, is going to be a bit of a challenge. And we need to think about that as well. In that reshaping, the potential for conflict is in the East, Middle, and West. We're already in a conflict in the West, and I know Mike McFaul will go on about that. We've taken our eye off the middle. But that still has great potential to disrupt. And we've created a bit of a vacuum there. And that takes me to the East, and we can talk about Taiwan, but a conflict there is a conflict in the East Asian littoral.

Why? Because China is going to play the East China Sea, the immediate area around Taiwan and the South China Sea, as one theater. As has been said, all the discussion about when the invasion of Taiwan is going to take place, I think, is extraordinarily unhelpful. One guy knows when that could happen, and that's Xi Jinping. The other dimension is that we keep focusing on an invasion, but the ability to squeeze, coerce, and use cyber to really disrupt the Taiwan public is significant, and that will not be lost on China. The other thing I think that we need to focus on significantly is we're not fighting in Ukraine. We're supplying Ukraine. We're supplying them with weapons, with information, and with moral support.

We need to think about supplying Taiwan. And we are so inadequately prepared to do that, it's almost embarrassing. The geography, we need to issue maps to those who want to talk about Taiwan so that they have an appreciation for the distances. Yokohama is roughly two thousand miles from Taiwan, Singapore about the same, Guam is about the same. It's almost seven thousand miles from Long Beach to Taiwan.

And the distance that we're supplying Ukraine, I think it's 428 miles by road from Warsaw to Kyiv. So we're just unaware of what this vast area would be. US flag shipping constitutes 6 percent of the global fleet. The last mobilization we did for the ready force that would be in the front lines to provide supplies had just a 41 percent readiness rate. And if we don't think that China is going to lean on shipping companies and flag countries with regard to what they move with their lines, we're badly mistaken. I think it is something that we need to plan for. But in the area, we don't have the tanking, nor do we have the logistics support for the rapid turnaround of rearming, because there are a lot of weapons that would be used that can't be armed at sea. So we need to think deeply about that.

I would offer some cautions as well about China. Almost every conference you go to where you talk about the Taiwan conflict, someone points out that China hasn't been to war in decades. China hasn't been bloodied. China's entire military, as Oriana said, is designed for one thing, and that's the East Asian littoral. It is focused on that. They trained to do that. And oh, by the way, when it comes to capital losses, we haven't been bloodied in decades. We are going to have another *Moskva* [Russian Navy cruiser] in the East Asian littoral. It's as simple as that.

The other thing I would say, as part of that, we need to think about what the operational command structure is going to be in that very disrupted space. What we have now was put in place essentially after World War II. It's not ready for this fight in East Asia, and yet we're completely locked into that. One of the points that was raised was the role of allies. Love the allies, they're hugely important. But I think we have to be realistic, particularly as it comes to the European allies. Absolutely essential politically, absolutely essential economically, for any type of sanctions that we want to play. But when it comes to fighting in East Asia, it's not an option, and we have to be realistic about that. Canada wanted to show their support, so they were going to move more frigates to the Pacific. They have five frigates in the Pacific. They have seven more left to move. That's it. That's the size of their major combatant naval force. And the newest one is twenty-seven years old. Germany has eleven combatants, and yet they would like to be in the Eastern Pacific or in the Western Pacific. And the Royal Navy is now down to eighteen. And so my point there is I think that as we look at where these potential conflicts are, the allies really need to stick to their geographic knitting. In the case of Europe, it's Europe, the Mediterranean, and the Middle East, and that brings us to the Pacific. And it's Japan, Japan, and Japan. We should be encouraged by their new security and defense strategy and by their commitment for more money. That's going to take some time to kick in.

They need to be brought into Five Eyes [the intelligence network of the United States, United Kingdom, Canada, New Zealand, and Australia]. They should become a Six Eyes partner. I got some of the issues that we may have with that. We should get away from AUKUS [the trilateral security agreement of Australia, the United Kingdom, and the United States]. It should become JAUKUS, and [we should] get Japan in that group, because they can bring real technical capability to the problem. And we have to appreciate their public as well, as Oriana touched on.

Post-Ukraine, public opinion in Japan went way up. But when you start shutting down highways in Japan to move logistics from Yokohama to Yokosuka, or Atsugi, when you start flying more out of the airfield, that's going to change the equation. So we have to understand that problem. We have to work with Japan in that regard and begin to think about the predicament that they're in because, as they say, they're on the nuclear fault line. They have China, Russia, and North Korea that they have to worry about at the same time. So, we really need to think anew about Japan, upgrade that level of alliance and really get skin in the game with codevelopment and coinvestment on some common systems. So I'll end on that note. Thank you.

MICHAEL MCFAUL: I read these excellent papers. If you haven't read them yet, please do so. I read them through a very particular lens—thinking about what are the lessons from Ukraine that we could learn from these papers regarding the way we assess threats and deal with threats.

I've got eight points and eight minutes, and I've got my stopwatch running here. I'm going to finish in time. I want to start, though, with a giant caveat. We're doing these assessments regarding the war in Ukraine only after one year of conflict. It's as if we're assessing the outcome of World War II in 1940. I just want to emphasize that I don't know how this war's going to end.

So with that caveat, I want to run through eight points that I think are lessons building on Oriana's paper and Joe [Felter], right at the end, building on your paper. And focuses on Amy [Zegart]'s as well.

Number one, the US intelligence community did a fantastic job of predicting the invasion. Fantastic. And then they declassified their analysis to warn the world that it was coming. That was brilliant. But then they did a less-than-fantastic job of assessing the balance of military power between Russia and Ukraine. We abandoned our embassy in Kyiv because we feared Russian soldiers would be in downtown Kyiv in a matter of days or weeks. In the run-up to Putin's invasion of Ukraine, I was in many discussions with military experts, both in and outside of the US government. Very few people thought that the Ukrainians' armed forces would be successful in defending Kyiv and then going on the counteroffensive so successfully last fall. As we're building budgets for threat assessments, I think this failure in intelligence must compel us to ask: How did we get the measurement of power—the assessment of the balance of power between Ukraine and Russia at the start of the war—so wrong?

I think this a big challenge for first, the intelligence community, and second, for the broader national security community, including us here today. On the intelligence community, I would speculate—reflecting on Amy's paper—there was the decline in spending in the nineties on threat assessments in the post-Communist world, and then a shifting of resources after September 11, 2001, to other priorities. Our expertise on Russia declined. But even more dramatically, we lost our depth of expertise on what I would call the periphery of the Russian Empire or the Soviet Empire.

When I was a student here at Stanford, I was paid by the US government to learn Polish during the Cold War, because we wanted expertise on the non-Russian, non-Soviet parts of the empire. We're not doing that as much now. It was noticeable to me when I served in the government almost a decade ago; I am guessing those trends hadn't changed much until the Russian invasion of Ukraine last year. My guess is that we have more Pashto speakers than Ukrainian speakers in the US government today. We've got to change that, and I think that's part of why we got it so wrong.

Who's the leading expert in the United States government or in academia, for that matter, on Ukraine? Go through your list in your head right now. There are some, but not many. (Stanford, by the way, should establish an endowed chair in Ukrainian studies.) Who are the leading experts on the Ukrainian military in or outside government? Have you noticed that a lot of the commentators and writers on the Ukrainian military are actually specialists on the Russian military? In the multitude of conversations and discussions in which I participated in the run-up to the war, I was impressed with the depth of knowledge our expert community had on the Russian army but struck by how little we knew about the Ukrainian military. We need to change that.

Second, related to that, I think we have a problem in threat assessment, and Oriana and I have had this discussion for years, including in Taiwan just a few months ago. We count things that we can see—soldiers, tanks, planes, drones, military spending, etc. We are not very good at counting will to fight, preparedness, doctrine, strategy, software, etc. If you look at the assessments of capabilities of the Russian military before February 24, 2022, it was one of the top three armies in the world. I'm writing a book about lessons from the Cold War for how to deal with China and Russia right now. Our failures in threat assessment from Russia before the beginning of this war remind me a lot of the threat assessments we had in the 1970s about the Soviets, because we could count certain things but couldn't see other things.

Third, we rightly spend a lot of time measuring capabilities and intentions of threatening states, reading Putin's mind, assessing his beliefs and wants, and tracking his instruments of influence abroad. I am an eager student, not an expert on China, but it seems to me that Chinese experts give similar attention to trying to assess the intentions and capabilities of Xi Jinping and the Chinese Communist Party. We rightly want to know what they are seeking to do in other countries. We spend less attention on measuring the actual impact of Russian or Chinese actions in target countries. We need more deep analysis of impact, not just intentions. We often assume that the target countries don't have a say, right? There's just so little agency assigned to the countries being targeted in our threat assessments. Obviously, that was a big mistake regarding Putin's intentions in Ukraine.

In Africa, we can count Chinese spending on BRI [Belt and Road Initiative], but what actual effect are these investments having on regime type or foreign policy orientation of the recipient countries? China today is spending outrageous amounts of money on [foreign-language news channel] CGTN and other media outlets targeted at audiences around the world. Are these programs having the desired effect? Just counting up the budgets for the media outlets doesn't answer the question about impact. I used to live in Washington and used to get the *China Daily* insert in the *Washington Post*. Did that have any effect in terms of preferences of *Washington Post* readers?

These are empirical questions. They are hard to answer both for the US intelligence community and the academic community. But to develop better threat assessments, we cannot just look at the intensions and capabilities of competitor states but must also look at impact.

Fourth, open-source intelligence. I love what Amy's writing about. I think we have to focus a lot more on that. I don't want to tuck it back into the government. I think some more hybrid model is the right model. I would like to see it as much more of a fusion model than inside the government. There is not enough connectivity between those outside of government and those working inside US intelligence. There is so much more "intel" now on social media that does not require security clearances to read and assess. The role that TikTok and Twitter are playing regarding the Russian war in Ukraine is unprecedented. (The explosion of disinformation on these platforms and others is also unprecedented.) By the way, it would be a national security catastrophe if Twitter collapsed. We should think about that.

Fifth, Russia's invasion of Ukraine has underscored that old-fashioned weapons like long fires and tanks still matter. I've been to a hundred conferences on cyber threats since I got out of the government eight years ago. I have never been to a conference on Howitzers. I want a conference on Howitzers. I want a conference on HIMARS. I want a conference on 155 millimeters versus 152, because it turns out that Howitzers still matter in warfare in the twenty-first century. All the cyber weapons and all the drones matter too. But better threat assessments in the future require us to get back to the basics of conventional warfare.

Sixth and related, the Russian war in Ukraine should teach us a lot about our defense industrial base, as well as the defense industrial base of other countries. Ours is strained right now with the war in Ukraine. We have given less attention to making these older, less sophisticated weapons. And now we are running out of them. Oriana and I were in Taiwan last summer. I was shocked to learn how some weapons that were promised years ago to the Taiwanese have not been sent yet. We've got to fix that problem, and maybe one of the ways we fix it is through joint ventures and coproduction. The Ukrainians want this for the future. Maybe it's another model that we should think about moving forward.

Seventh, deterrence enhancement. This is an echo of what Oriana has been discussing. We need to very soberly admit that deterrence in Europe against Putin failed. We didn't want this war. Deterrence failed. So we should figure out why it failed and then make sure it doesn't fail with respect to China and Taiwan. And when doing so, we must remember an obvious fact: deterrence only works ahead of time. It does no good after the fact. In the US, we had a big debate about sanctions before the war. I advocated spelling out our plans for sanctions in as much detail as possible before Putin invaded as a way of shaping his calculus. The US government had a different view. They worried, with good reason perhaps, that any discussion of sanctions before the war started would only fuel division within the coalition of countries implementing sanctions. I still think that was a giant mistake. But it's a debate we should be having now about China and Taiwan.

Could announcing the sanctions we intend to impose on the PRC [People's Republic of China] if Xi invaded Taiwan help to deter that threat? I don't know. But we should be having that discussion now, not later, not after the war has started.

Finally, I think we need a holistic approach to threat assessment but also to the national security budget. I want everything to be all together. In part because I want to hide in that budget things that I think are critical that we are not doing well—for instance, public diplomacy. The ideological struggle that Joe wrote about, we're losing that inside Russia. We're losing it in the Global South. Too many countries don't agree with our framing of Russia's war in Ukraine as a war of imperialism and annexation. We have to up our game. We have to understand that this ideological contest with both Russia and China is central to our national security. In a newly imagined national security budget, I also want to see funds for Ukrainian reconstruction. Like what we did in Europe after World War II, reconstruction in Ukraine after this war is over is such a vital thing for our national security, and yet we are not framing it for this war, and therefore I worry that Ukraine could win the war but lose the peace. What we need is a giant NDAA [National Defense Authorization Act] that includes all these things that I'm talking about so that we can begin to reconceptualize public diplomacy, economic development, and support for democracy abroad as vital components of our national security. Someday, we could have one budget for defense, development, democracy, and diplomacy.

D'ANGELO: Questions? Comments?

ERIC FANNING: Oriana—or anyone else—you talked about how it doesn't matter if it doesn't have an operational impact. The Chinese are just focused on capabilities. What are they thinking about economic aspects in terms of their decision calculus?

ORIANA SKYLAR MASTRO: The economic stuff would be more effective than the military stuff. The problem is it's even harder and so far from where it needs to be. So, of the many discussions that Mike and I have, and other people have, comparing the situation with Ukraine and the situation with China, yes, it was very impressive how everyone came together to sanction Russia, but China did not learn the lessons you think they learned from that. Specifically, because I asked this of the Japanese, and they said, "We're going to be firm," and I replied, "What are you telling the Chinese?"

When I asked senior cabinet members, they got so flustered, red in the face, and said, "Well, our relationship is very important." And so the bottom line is yes, a lot of countries are sanctioning Russia, but when I've been in the region, and I've asked government officials, "What are you going to do if China attacks Taiwan?" senior people say, "Well, our trade with China is more≈than our trade with the United States."

So I think China expects, right now, token sanctions for three to five years. They've tried to sanction-proof their economy by focusing on ten critical industries, getting overland oil pipelines from Russia. And so it's not that they don't care about the economic costs. This goes to the point that General Alexander made. Xi Jinping is driven, but he's completely deterrable. I like to say this war is inevitable, but we can delay it forever.

And so if all the US allies got together and said, "China, if you attack Taiwan, we will no longer trade with you." I don't mean we won't buy this one thing or that thing but we're going to completely cut off trade, that is far too high of a cost for China. Xi Jinping is not going to want to risk the rejuvenation of the Chinese nation, but it's my understanding that we are nowhere close to getting that type of coordination and agreement.

And I'll just say, I think Mike made this last point about signaling. I've read a lot of Chinese writings analyzing the war, and one of the interesting things is they talk about the failure of US deterrence and they talk about how the United States economically responded in unpredictable ways. And then they have these indirect pleas that are, "Hey, anyone in the United States, if we're wrong about our assessment about how this is going to look after we attack Taiwan, maybe the United States should make that clear at some point." But we haven't done that at this point.

JACQUELYN SCHNEIDER: So I really was struck by your comments, Gary, and I want to ask a question that I think may be helpful as we go through the rest of the day. And I'm struck when we think about Ukraine. One of the large differences with Taiwan is the difficulty of replenishment, and we don't have Poland right on the border to bring weapons through.

And so I was interested, especially from the navy side and the navy background, how do we build a navy that's not only able to fight in a Taiwan scenario but also able to support and defend the logistical chains that are going to have to occur. And then, is it even possible to bring weapons in on a side of the island that's not in the midst of the fray?

So I was interested; we've talked a lot in public about how big a navy needs to be and what it needs to include. The navy doesn't generally like to think about itself as convoys, but what could that look like for the future navy?

ROUGHEAD: And I think one of the realistic things that needs to be faced is what timeline are you looking at? Because if you want to build a navy that could sustain protected sea-lanes across the Pacific, I'll be dead by the time it even starts. But I think that you could do some realignment, which is politically hard domestically. Some of us have tried to move assets from one port to another. You just get killed politically, domestically, but I think that has to be part of the drill.

I think the other dimension is to rapidly acquire, as cheaply as you can, some more lift, strategic lift. We now should be engaged with foreign shipping companies and other countries that have flag shipping on some commitments for being able to move things. I think pre-positioning, particularly in Japan, is going to be important as well as in Guam.

But I really think getting some heavy lift in place to do what I call keeping the lights on in Taiwan is needed because the squeeze would come on food and fuel, and we need to have some reliable conveyors to take that in. So short term, acquire what you can, arrange what you can, and then have plans to be able to sustain from Japan.

The other thing I would say is the concept about the places, not bases, within the first island chain. We've been working on those for thirty years, and we're no closer. Xi Jinping was there in the Philippines last week, and he dumped $23 billion into the economy. How's that decision going to come out when we go in and say, "Hey, we'd like to have some more access."

That's why we talk about markets and development because that's what can sway people over to our side, and we're not playing that game.

MASTRO: If I can just add a quick operational point of things I do not understand about why we're not doing them in the naval service, and maybe Admiral Roughead can explain it to me. The first thing is submarines are so critical to this fight. I think they're the most critical asset and most of our submarines have to go all the way back to Guam or Hawaii, as they don't replenish in Japan. I've asked people at USFJ [US Forces Japan] why this is the case. There's some speculation about nuclear power, but then our aircraft carriers are allowed in Japan. Torpedoes are conventional. Whatever it is, we absolutely need to do all of that stuff in Japan. I mean the Japanese subs take two to three days to get to the Taiwan area. We take three weeks.

The second thing is the importance of Kadena [Air Base, Okinawa, Japan] and the combat radius of Taiwan because my assumption was, given what Admiral Roughead had said about the vulnerabilities of tankers, that we would not be trying to do significant air-to-air refueling if we were operating from Kadena. I have recently learned that that is not our operational plan, which doesn't make a lot of sense to me.

The whole benefit of Kadena is you don't have to do that. So I get the benefit of having more time on target if you do air-to-air refueling but given the vulnerabilities, we should probably rethink that. And then we need, it's not only in Japan, I think the Southwest Islands we need to start building those up significantly, even farther south, closer to Taiwan even than Kadena. We need new bases there.

And the last thing about places, not bases, a friend of mine recently showed me a picture of an F-22 landing on a dirt road. They have recently been allowed to start exercising in that way. Our assets are very expensive. I get it. It's like me just this morning wearing a new pair of my Jimmy Choo boots, and then my kids spilled their whole cereal all over them, so, "Why do I even try to have nice things?" So I get it. We don't want to ruin these assets, but we need to be much more flexible in how we're operating.

And the amount of time I spent on duty researching where we could put air-conditioned facilities for things like wartime and posture, I was like, okay, we might not have that.

MICHAEL J. BOSKIN: A couple of quick points that span the entire panel, Gary, Oriana, Keith, and others. If I was stepping back and I was Xi Jinping or the military leadership, and I had this vision of invading and so if they don't capitulate, I'd want to be doing a lot of things that weaken their will and disrupt them in advance, way in advance of an invasion.

And it seems to me the most obvious one—maybe not to you, you all know a lot more about this than me—would be a massive cyberattack on the Hsinchu Science Park [that would] shut down Taiwan Semiconductor and really wreck their economy. In the short run, it would destroy a large fraction of their exports, a large fraction, half the world's advanced chips if they could keep it closed for a period of time.

So Keith and Oriana, are they capable of doing that? Would we have the political will to respond to that, short of an explicit invasion? I mean, how do we start thinking about things like that if they're relevant? If you think I'm off base, just say so.

ALEXANDER: China will attack Taiwan with cyber and they would attack government and significant commercial companies as you stated. Hopefully, Taiwan Semiconductor is isolated from the internet. But there is always a way to get in and do destructive things. You can see what happened to Iran and others. Such an attack would have a global impact and would probably do as much harm to China economically and politically as anyone else.

I do think you bring up a key point. Russia, what they're doing in cyber, and what they end up with. If Putin wins, China is going to be more emboldened. Putin can't win, and it goes back to some of the comments. So we have to stop that, take that off the table, make Russia pay a price that would be unacceptable. I think that's the greatest deterrence for China.

And what they see going on right now in cyber, they're all over the Russian attackers. China is seeing what's going on. They know somebody out there is really good at what they're doing, and they're having success, and it's the US and Europe combined. So I think the Chinese would be very careful about doing something at that level because we could hit back. That's a national security decision.

MASTRO: So if I can just add, China has already won that battle over weakening the will of the people of Taiwan, at least from their perspective. I mean 74 percent of the people of Taiwan think China would never attack them. In our discussions when we were in Taiwan in August, the biggest concern was the lack of willingness to fight. In our discussions with senior people in the semiconductor industry, I directly asked. They said, "There are forty people who are critical to this industry." And so I said, "Does the United States need to get these people out before China attacks?"

And to a person, they all kind of wave, and they're like, "Well, I've been to China a lot, it's not so bad." So maybe I read a lot from the US perspective based on our experiences in Afghanistan and Iraq, we're like, "Okay, there's going to be this huge opposition in Taiwan, and so China's not going to want to take Taiwan because sure, they can get Taiwan, but it'll be a pyrrhic victory because then they'll be fighting for decades."

I mean, they have more people in camps in Xinjiang than there are young men in Taiwan. They are very concerned about the PLA [People's Liberation Army]'s ability to land on the island. Internal repression, they spend more on that than they do on their military.

So I think, obviously, we need to enhance the ability of Taiwan to hold off, mainly so the United States can get there. But there is no scenario. I think we should all be clear, there is no scenario in which Taiwan can defend itself without direct US involvement.

And I'll just say really quickly about Russia because I have finished a two-and-a-half-year project on China/Russia military relations. They are very clearly preparing not to fight together, not to fight simultaneously, but for Russia to serve as support, indirectly maybe in equipment, as a strategic rear, energy. Things that will make it harder for us to coerce. Even the Russians might do some air patrols that limit our freedom of maneuver, which look purely defensive so Russia can say they're defending the Far East.

So it's going to complicate what we can do even if their two sides are not fighting together in any direct way. And I do think Xi Jinping's watching what happens there but it's not a direct comparison of, they did bad, so we're going to do bad, or they were punished, or we're not punished.

In a lot of cases, "That's very interesting information that is irrelevant to us," is how they see it.

ROUGHEAD: We fixate on semiconductors, but the other business linkages in Taiwan to the mainland in so many different sectors come into play as well, and they have a voice, and I think that would be hugely important.

And then my point about Japan's location. Russia, just by pressing airspace with the Japanese having to respond to that, dilutes the effort down to the south. So we really need to think of the position that Japan would be in and how that would dilute any support that we would get from them for legitimate reasons.

MCFAUL: So, one quick three-part comment. One on just thinking about the lessons, right? We're talking about supply lines. I would just remind everybody before Russia invaded Ukraine, everybody assessed that they had a giant advantage. They didn't have to go through sea. The country they were invading was right on their border. Why did that not give them the advantage we assessed before?

Second, I would say the same thing about missiles, by the way. Lots of discussion about the asymmetry there, and yet they're barely farther along than ten months of fighting, and all those missiles being lobbed in have not achieved the military objectives I think we had assessed. Why is that?

And then third, on the sanctions piece, and I'm not an expert on trade with China, but I would just say three things. One, in February, January, and in the lead-up, we had exactly the same discussion. Europe is dependent on oil and gas. They'll never do these things. Guess what? As of this month, Europe is using more American gas than Russian gas. Nobody predicted that eleven months ago.

Number two, thousands of companies have voluntarily left Russia. Not because of sanctions but because they just decided it was not in their public interest to be there, and they left billions and billions of dollars in Russia. They just left, ExxonMobil being the biggest one. And I just wonder if we're not underestimating.

If China invades Taiwan, with the American public, the political debate we have about China right now, is it really going to be feasible to say, "Well, we've just got to keep doing business as usual." We need to think about what the political moment will feel like if there's a war in Asia. I would like us to front-load that, just like we should have front-loaded HIMARS and Javelins. We should front-load that debate about sanctions but I think we should be careful. It's one thing when it's before the war. After the war, I think it's going to be a lot harder to say, "Well, we're just going to continue to trade with China."

MASTRO: Can I just highlight? China has to know that, and it has to happen before the war if it's going to contribute to deterrence.

MACKENZIE EAGLEN: I want to reinforce Admiral Roughead's point, which reinforces a point Oriana made. So why does geography matter? It's why mass

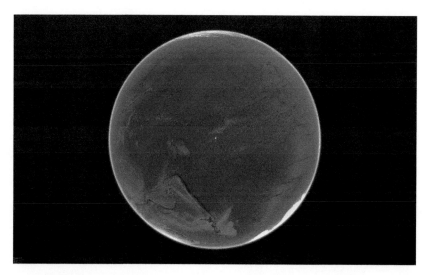

Source: Google Earth

matters. So this is a view of the Earth with just a pin in the center of the Pacific Ocean. I think pictures speak a thousand words, and it is just something I saw on Twitter and it has stuck with me ever since, to just give you a sense of the sheer distance that we're talking about in terms of the Pacific Ocean.

BOSKIN: All of us have taken flights to Asia and Europe and realize the difference. Four-movie flights from the Bay Area.

Part 2

National Security Strategy

5

The International Environment and Threat Backdrop

Michael O'Hanlon

Today's global situation is undoubtedly as complex as any the United States has ever faced. A rising China, revanchist and violent Russia, nuclear-armed North Korea (to say nothing of Pakistan and India, and possibly other nuclear proliferators in the future), nuclear-desirous Iran, the ongoing threat of terrorism—together with twenty-first-century transnational threats including cyber dangers, pandemics, advanced biological pathogens, and climate change—and it all makes for a geostrategic witches' brew.[1] The ongoing war in Ukraine is a serious threat not only to the people and sovereignty of Ukraine but indeed to the broader region and the world.

That said, we would do well not to overreact. The current period remains an era without a great-power war. There is a very high probability this will remain the case if the United States and its allies stay vigilant and resolute but also calm and restrained.

The essence of American grand strategy since the end of World War II— the maintenance of strong and credible military alliances with most of the world's major democratic and industrial powers, backed by the forward deployment or stationing of US combat forces on the territories of geographically exposed American allies, and American conventional and nuclear power writ large—remains a very good construct for maximizing the odds of successful deterrence.[2] Strong bipartisan consensus for an $858 billion US national defense budget this year, exceeding peak levels of the Cold War in inflation-adjusted terms, also bodes well. So do recent bipartisan decisions to strengthen America's technological and industrial foundations in key sectors at home.

The views expressed in this chapter are solely those of the individual author and do not necessarily reflect the views of any organization with which they are, or have been, affiliated.

It is an honor to be participating in this timely Stanford project with the likes of H.R. McMaster and General Jim Mattis, two friends and heroes of mine (there will undoubtedly be others in the conference about whom I would say the same!). They did much to construct a National Security Strategy (NSS) and a National Defense Strategy (NDS) early in the Trump era that can stand the test of time and guide us wisely into the difficult world of the 2020s. The Biden administration has benefited greatly from these documents. In its own strategies, it has sought to build on the 2017 NSS and 2018 NDS rather than to change them fundamentally, as a number of its officials have told me in public and in private. Despite the polemics of partisan politics in the contemporary United States, we have a rather strong underpinning for national consensus on key security issues of the day. In particular, the framing of a grand strategy around the concept of the return of great-power competition is compelling. Indeed, I believe the Trump team of McMaster, Mattis, and others was more correct than its successor in emphasizing Russia and China equally—the Biden team may go somewhat too far in prioritizing the People's Republic of China (PRC) at a time when Russia is killing tens of thousands in the heart of Eurasia. Former chairman of the Joint Chiefs General Joseph Dunford was also right to emphasize a "four-plus-one" threat framework lest we forget about North Korea, Iran, and terrorism—though in the interest of keeping this paper reasonably short, I will not dwell on the latter three concerns here.

Yet, if I had one additional word of counsel for the United States today, it would be to avoid demonizing China, even as we focus squarely and correctly on addressing its capabilities and its ambitions. We are at risk of overhyping the China threat. I agree with 80 to 90 percent of our policies that focus on addressing that threat, but the last 10 to 20 percent (notionally speaking) may be on the verge of going too far. Much of the rest of this paper is written, accordingly, as a provocation. It is not my own effort to mimic the worldwide threat assessments that the directors of national intelligence or defense intelligence agencies produce each winter. Instead, this is an interpretative essay about what we are getting right and what we perhaps are not in what is quickly becoming a new collective wisdom in the United States about the nature of the China threat in particular.

General Strategic Considerations

For some, the rise of China poses an inordinate risk to global order. Graham Allison, a brilliant Harvard strategist and historian, has coined the phrase

"Thucydides trap" to underscore the risks when a rising power challenges an existing and established rival (though in his era, it was a rising partial democracy, Athens, that increasingly challenged an existing "hegemon," Sparta). In the specific case of China, we face an autocratic regime brimming with confidence, a strong desire to bring Taiwan back under its rule, and substantial ambitions in the Western Pacific, broader Middle East, and beyond. China wields the world's largest manufacturing base, second-largest economy by traditional exchange-rate measures, largest economy when adjusted for purchasing power parity, and impressive technological capabilities in the crucial digital and cyber sectors. It now has the world's second largest population (India's exceeds China's by a whisker)—though that is a mixed blessing, given that its working-age population has already peaked in size. Demographics will largely work against China in the decades to come.

Allison is right to warn in general terms about what such big changes have meant historically. But there is so much that is different about today's world. To repeat, there exists a preponderance of democracies forming the core of the modern US-led alliance system, along with strong and standing and often forward-deployed or forward-stationed American military forces to undergird those alliances, nuclear deterrence, and some aspects of globalization. Combined, these features give considerable reason for hope that past patterns in great-power relations can be changed. Arguably, since 1945, they already have been, despite the partial backsliding in recent years.[3]

The Biden administration's NSS prioritizes China as the "most consequential strategic competitor" of the United States, and its NDS designates the PRC as America's "pacing challenge." These are reasonable terms. They have led the Biden team, like the Trump team before it, to increase defense spending, emphasize military innovation and modernization within the defense budget, seek to address national vulnerabilities in cyber and space and infrastructural domains, prioritize the Pacific region in national security terms, and undertake a number of key initiatives to that same end with major allies and partners. All of this is to the good. None of it was easy or automatic. None is guaranteed to endure unless we stay appropriately vigilant.

There is vigorous debate in the United States over whether Beijing might see a window of opportunity to attack Taiwan by the late 2020s. The former head of US Indo-Pacific Command, Admiral Philip Davidson, has warned of that possibility.[4] Secretary of State Tony Blinken concluded by October 2022 that China had become "determined to pursue reunification on a much faster timeline."[5] Xi Jinping has told his military to be fully modernized and ready for all contingencies by 2027.[6] Some strategists also believe that, in light of its demographic decline and other internal challenges that could get much worse by the 2030s, China may perceive itself to have a relatively narrow window of opportunity to take Taiwan in the late 2020s or so.[7] It is true that China faces long-term economic and environmental challenges that are quite significant.[8]

But on the latter point, I see little evidence that Chinese leaders lack confidence in their country's long-term future. And as for Xi's promulgation of a 2027 deadline for modernization, his language may be mostly hortatory. The idea that any military can ever complete a full modernization program by a certain date is never quite plausible; military innovation is continuous in the real world.[9] Thus, some scholars, while hardly downplaying the China threat, tend to view it as a more general and lasting problem as opposed to an acute challenge in a given window of time.[10] I lean toward this latter interpretation myself, largely because China is in the business of issuing various kinds of five-year, ten-year, and other plans—not all of which can be linked to specific and secret and binding military plans for the future. Notably, Beijing's Made in China 2025 plan, promulgated back in 2015, calls for China to be a leader in ten high-tech sectors, including a number of technology sectors such as robotics, with major military relevance by the year 2025; other plans focus on 2030 or 2035, or aspire to major changes by the one hundredth anniversary of Chinese Communist Party rule in China in 2049.[11]

What about the Russia threat? We must not lose sight of that challenge—as General McMaster and Secretary Mattis rightly underscored in their 2017 and 2018 documents. It is Russia, after all, that is laying waste to cities in Europe and issuing nuclear threats against the West even as these words are written; it is Vladimir Putin who seems to have a pathological hatred of all things Ukrainian, especially its (admirable) leader Volodymyr Zelensky, and a contempt for the idea that there even should be such a thing as an independent Ukrainian nation.[12] Ironically, Putin's aggressions against Ukraine may have done more to unify and cohere its people and stoke their sense of distinctiveness as well as nationalism than anything else in their history.[13] And Putin continues to act on these sentiments, with little evidence that what is left of Russian democracy can exert any meaningful checks and balances on his behavior. Putin has also spent two decades building up resentment against the West—over NATO and EU expansion, the Kosovo war, American support for "colored revolutions" in Ukraine and Georgia in the early 2000s, American support for some of Putin's political opponents at home, and what Putin sees as unilateralist American blundering from Iraq to Afghanistan and Libya after 9/11.

Putin has spent recent years in Russia further marginalizing his internal critics and weakening, if not ending his country's democracy.[14] Alas, the history of leaders like Putin around the world hardly suggests that he will likely leave office soon—or that he will be replaced by a more democratic and benign political system once gone.[15]

Some have described Russia as a regional power with nuclear weapons, or a giant gas station, or some other such derogatory term. Although it is true that Russia's GDP is comparable to that of a midlevel Western European power and that its scientific and technology capacity has atrophied (even before the sanctions of 2022), it is hardly to be trifled with.[16] It is the world's top nuclear weapons state, the world's largest country, the world's most geographically exposed and yet geographically menacing country (those two attributes being flip sides of the same coin), and a proud nation with a strong sense of national identity and global purpose. It has four times the population of Iraq or Afghanistan (or Ukraine). Moreover, in its near abroad, it is highly motivated and reasonably powerful—a combination that Kathryn Stoner convincingly argues gives it considerable power and influence in some key parts of Europe.[17]

All that said, I believe we have most of the makings of a successful Russia policy today. Supporting Ukraine strongly in its war effort, sustaining sanctions on Russia, and fortifying NATO's eastern flank provide the raw ingredients for a successful Russia policy in the months and years to come—provided we stay focused, vigilant, and united.

It will be entirely fair game if a GOP-majority House of Representatives asks for more accountability and more answers to tough questions about the endgame for the Ukraine war as it considers future Biden administration requests for aid for Ukraine. But such questioning must not actually interrupt the flow of crucial assistance or smack of irresoluteness on our collective part. Provided we get that balance right and think creatively about that endgame in Ukraine, I believe our Russia policy can succeed. Thus, I will spend more time below on China, where we do not yet have the paradigm quite right, in my judgment.

Rightsizing the China Threat

Whatever the most relevant time frame, and even in light of the importance of staying focused on the challenges posed by China's rise, I believe it is crucial that we keep our strategic composure and sense of perspective on the nature of the problem. America is capable of groupthink, as we arguably saw, for example, in the Vietnam War and in the prelude to the Iraq invasion of

2003. We need to avoid the temptation to unify so strongly around the China threat paradigm that we unwittingly increase the risks of confrontation our-selves—perhaps by goading Taiwan toward provocative action, or overreact-ing to a crisis in the South China Sea or East China Sea.

Consider the nature of the PRC's foreign policy. It is certainly concerning. China has, for example, been assertive and threatening in the South China Sea and East China Sea (and along its Himalayan border with India). However, while assertive, sometimes imprudent, and occasionally downright aggres-sive, China's behavior in the Western Pacific has generally stopped short of belligerence or the lethal use of force. We are dealing with a country that has not gone to war since 1979. That fact should count for something.

Even on law of the sea matters, where China's behavior is unsettling, there is nuance in the situation. Even India does not share Washington's view about so-called freedom of navigation operations. Delhi believes that any country wishing to traverse not just the territorial seas but, in fact, the exclusive eco-nomic zones (generally extending out two hundred nautical miles from the coastline) of another nation should request permission for such a transit in advance.[18] China, of course, agrees.

The United States should continue to operate its naval forces freely in the South China Sea. But it should not, to my mind, be too surprised that China finds such operations off-putting.[19] The broader debate should also bear in mind that, by Washington's reckoning, dozens of countries commit infractions of customary law and the UN Convention on the Law of the Sea. However, the fact that the United States itself has not ratified the latter puts it on shaky legal ground with regard to this whole subject. According to the Department of Defense (DoD), in 2021, American allies Italy, Japan, South Korea, and Costa Rica were among the perpetrators![20] To be sure, China's assertiveness puts it in a separate category from most others.[21] But the existence of a dis-agreement between Washington and Beijing over maritime rights does not itself prove that China seeks to overturn the rules-based order. More accu-rately, I believe it is trying to modify that order to suit its own interests.

Ongoing commitment to forward presence in international airways and sea-lanes, combined with institutional vehicles like the Quad (with Japan, India, and Australia) as well as the new AUKUS arrangement (with Canberra and London)—and the continued refinement of "integrated deterrence" as an instrument of US and allied security policy that promises economic pun-ishment and military realignments in response to low-grade Chinese aggres-sion—provide reasons to think that most of China's broader impulses and ambitions can be mitigated.[22] I do not see integrated deterrence as an alternative to robust military capabilities or a means of cutting the defense budget. Rather, it provides a more credible type of deterrent for scenarios that either do not rise to the level of seriousness where direct and lethal military response would be appropriate or that challenge US and allied military capabilities to the point where a military response may not be successful.

Then there is Taiwan. It may represent the most dangerous flashpoint in the US-China relationship, with China viewing the island of twenty-three million as integral to its own territory and the United States seeing Taiwan as a valuable democratic partner (and with some others viewing America's commitment to Taiwan as a canary in the coal mine on its broader commitment to Asian allies in the face of China's rise).

Deterring China from attacking Taiwan, however, *should* be a doable strategic task—provided that Taiwan itself does not force the issue of independence. An attempt to invade and conquer Taiwan would be a huge strategic roll of the dice by Beijing, with a high probability of failure. Taipei as well as Washington have options to make its prospects even less likely in the coming years, with the right kinds of military modernizations that put sensors and antiship missiles in survivable locations on shore and on survivable platforms like the XQ-58A unmanned aircraft, which can be launched like a rocket and recovered by parachute.[23] These are the best ways to more confidently deter an invasion attempt. A Chinese blockade might have better prospects of tactical military success if the goal is to squeeze Taiwan into submission economically. But a blockade is also a much more indirect and uncertain form of military coercion than an invasion. It also carries, just like the invasion scenario, considerable escalation risks of its own.[24]

So I say "yes" to deterring Chinese attacks, especially on Taiwan. We must stay focused intently on military modernization efforts across the board. Focusing on China as a pacing challenge—our most consequential strategic competitor—in military and technological terms is wise.

But in some other ways, we may go too far. Take, for example, the Biden administration's highly inflammatory use of the term "genocide" to describe China's treatment of its Uyghur population in Xinjiang province, as witnessed in the US 2022 NSS and other pronouncements.[25] Secretary of State Mike Pompeo had accused China of the same heinous crime in the latter weeks of the Trump administration. I would submit that this is not the right term—and words matter in such domains. Beijing does commit severe repression against the Uyghurs. It should be held accountable for that repression. A recent UN

Human Rights Council investigative report chose the correct language, determining that China has been committing "serious human rights violations" in its August 2022 report on the subject, unlike the US Department of State under both Secretary Pompeo and Secretary Blinken.[26] But diluting a culture and even curtailing some reproductive rights, however morally and politically objectionable, do not constitute genocide. That latter term has a clear and palpable historical and political meaning that conjures up images of gas chambers and mass butchery. Whatever the lawyers may be able to argue, what China does in Xinjiang is terrible, but it is not genocide.

It is also increasingly common to hear China described, at least by national security hawks, as an adversary or enemy. This approach risks creating a self-fulfilling prophecy, convincing us that a military showdown is at some point inevitable when that mindset could increase the risks of a crisis escalating. It could also lead us, wittingly or unwittingly, to support Taiwan's aspirations for independence more than prudence should dictate.

As McMaster's excellent *The Atlantic* article of a few years ago underscored, there is too much swagger in Xi's inner circle.[27] Yet there do also seem to be checks and balances and restraint. Notably, to date, Beijing appears not to have sent any weaponry to Russia during the Ukraine war, despite Putin's requests that China do so.[28] Yet the Pentagon's 2022 Annual Report to Congress on China does not acknowledge this crucial limitation in China-Russia cooperation.[29] We risk taking it for granted or overlooking it when, in fact, this lack of coordination is a very important and desirable reality.

China's military budget, while robust, remains at less than 2 percent of its GDP—the level considered a *minimal* acceptable effort, on burden-sharing terms, within the NATO alliance. Of course, NATO is a defensive alliance, and China's recent actions are often too assertive. The point is not that China is unthreatening—only that by most metrics, it is not engaged in blatant arms racing either.

China's ambitions to build perhaps 1,500 nuclear warheads, around five times what it has contented itself with in the past, may be regrettable. But a superpower like the United States, with five thousand warheads of its own, should not be surprised that a rising superpower like the PRC desires to have one-third that total itself. China's decision to pursue a nuclear buildup may be regrettable—and may complicate American strategy—but it is not, in and of itself, reckless.[30]

The Pentagon also harps on the fact that, by ship count, China now has the world's largest navy. It generally fails to note, however, that because US ships are typically much bigger, America's naval tonnage exceeds China's by a ratio of about two to one.[31] Neither metric is adequate as a way of understanding the military balance or predicting combat outcomes; both, and others as well, need to be considered in any serious net assessment.

Rather than pit China as already an adversary, as some prominent American voices have done, it is better to view it as a rival and competitor—but one that we should try to steer back toward the rules-based international order with a long-term goal of fostering cooperation. As Asia expert and former George W. Bush administration senior official Mike Green has convincingly written, when describing the overall grand strategy toward China of Japan, South Korea, and Australia, while advocating that Washington think similarly:

> All three major allies seek to work with Beijing on issues of concern from a position of strength backed by closer alignment with the United States and other like-minded countries in the region. Put another way, US allies in Asia still hope for some version of the strategy that US presidents from Richard Nixon to Obama pursued in the region: a combination of balancing and engaging China, but with a longer-term aim of integrating the country under rules favorable to the advanced industrial democracies. The idea is to compete with China, but with a clear end state in mind.[32]

Conclusion: Russia and China Together

What about the possibility of *both* Russia and China confronting the West militarily at the same time? It is indeed prudent to consider the possibility.[33] Militarily, it is crucial that we not allow either to achieve faits accomplis quickly as a result of teaming together; that would tempt deterrence failure. Hence the importance of protecting Eastern Europe with forward US and NATO military deployments and ensuring that Taiwan, with or even without American and allied help, has the ability to fend off a Chinese amphibious assault effectively.

But I do not see much evidence about a true anti-American axis emerging in Moscow or Beijing. Again, the latter has chosen *not* to provide weaponry to the former during the Ukraine war. A chief goal of US national security policy should be to keep things that way—avoiding policies that would unnecessarily drive Russia and China closer together. I also believe that the difficulty of deterring Russia from attacking NATO territory in Europe is moderate at most; proper forward stationing of defense assets in eastern alliance member states should be up to the task, given the limitations on Russia's military capabilities as well as the impressive strength and cohesion of the NATO alliance. It is largely for this reason that I do not think American combat forces need to be sized and structured for a possible war against both China and Russia at once. However, my relatively sanguine assessment depends on an outcome to the current Ukraine war that seeks to offer some way for Russia eventually to rejoin the international community in good standing. Notably, Ukraine should not, in my view, be brought into NATO; alternative security structures are needed instead.[34]

Similar logic applies to the Korean peninsula, where the US presence is already correctly sized and situated. As such, the United States does not need a true two-war capability—a standard it has often struggled to meet in the past, even when it attempted to achieve it.[35] And the 2022 NDS is correct not to set that overly ambitious standard for sizing American military forces.

Thus, in my view, the 2022 NDS of the Biden administration is correct to focus on fighting only a single adversary at a time. To wit, it says, "Building on the 2018 NDS [National Defense Strategy, under Secretary of Defense Jim Mattis], the *2022 NDS Force Planning Construct* sizes and shapes the Joint Force to simultaneously defend the homeland; maintain strategic deterrence; and deter and, if necessary, prevail in conflict."[36]

In some ways, this sentence understates the capabilities of the strategy. Even in the event of war against Russia or China, forward-stationed forces in the other theater will likely remain in position—providing a measure of capability. Because any attack against them (say, against US forces stationed in Poland, the Baltic states, or Romania) would almost inevitably lead to American retaliation—if not immediately, then eventually—some degree of deterrence would likely remain. That is also true, thankfully, on the Korean peninsula.

Our system of treaty-based alliances and forward-based military forces has helped keep the great-power peace for seventy-seven years through thick and thin. There is good reason to believe it can do so in the future as well, even in today's troubling and complex threat environment.

Notes

1. On the challenges of deterrence in a world of multiple regional nuclear powers, see Vipin Narang, *Nuclear Strategy in the Modern Era: Regional Powers and International Conflict* (Princeton, NJ: Princeton University Press, 2014).

2. Michael O'Hanlon, *The Art of War in an Age of Peace: US Grand Strategy and Resolute Restraint* (New Haven, CT: Yale University Press, 2021), 1–50.

3. Graham Allison, "The Thucydides Trap," and David K. Richards, "Thucydides Dethroned: Historical Differences That Weaken the Peloponnesian Analogy," in *The Next Great War?* ed. Richard N. Rosecrance and Steven E. Miller (Cambridge, MA: MIT Press, 2015), 73–90.

4. Adela Suliman, "China Could Invade Taiwan in the Next 6 Years, Assume Global Leadership Role, US Admiral Warns," NBC News, last modified March 10, 2021.

5. Ellen Francis, "China Plans to Seize Taiwan on 'Much Faster Timeline,' Blinken Says," *Washington Post,* last modified October 18, 2022.

6. Kevin Rudd, *The Avoidable War: The Dangers of a Catastrophic Conflict between the US and Xi Jinping's China* (New York: PublicAffairs, 2022), 159; CBS Evening News, "Putin Can Be 'Dangerous and Reckless': CIA Director Discusses Russian President's Path Forward," last modified October 3, 2022.

7. Hal Brands and Michael Beckley, *Danger Zone: The Coming Conflict with China* (New York: W. W. Norton and Co., 2022).

8. David Dollar, "China's Economy Is Slowing Down," *Milken Institute Review,* July 25, 2022.

9. M. Taylor Fravel, *Active Defense: China's Military Strategy Since 1949* (Princeton, NJ: Princeton University Press, 2019).

10. Aaron L. Friedberg, *Getting China Wrong* (Cambridge: Polity, 2022), 117–57; Scott L. Kastner, "The Taiwan Issue in US-China Relations: Sliding into a Security Dilemma?" in *After Engagement: Dilemmas in US-China Security Relations,* ed. Jacques deLisle and Avery Goldstein (Washington, DC: Brookings Institution Press, 2021), 244–51; "The Pulse of the Indo-Pacific with Former Assistant Secretary of Defense Randy Schriver," Heritage Foundation, August 2, 2021, video interview, 41:33, https://www.youtube.com/watch?v=t3zy1XStwGQ.

11. Christian Brose, *The Kill Chain: How Emerging Technologies Threaten America's Military Dominance* (New York: Hachette Books, 2020), 90.

12. Serhii Plokhy, *The Gates of Europe: A History of Ukraine,* rev. ed. (New York: Basic Books, 2021); Vladimir Putin, "Article by Vladimir Putin 'On the Historical Unity of Russians and Ukrainians,'" Kremlin, Moscow, July 12, 2021, http://en .kremlin.ru/events/president/news/66181.

13. Steven Pifer, "Mr. Putin: Turning Neighbor into Adversary," Brookings Institution, November 1, 2017.

14. Fiona Hill and Clifford G. Gaddy, *Mr. Putin: Operative in the Kremlin,* new and expanded edition (Washington, DC: Brookings Institution, 2015); "Putin's War in Ukraine: A Conversation with Fiona Hill and Angela Stent," Brookings Institution, September 19, 2022.

15. Andrea Kendall-Taylor and Erica Frantz, "After Putin: Lessons from Autocratic Leadership Transitions," *Washington Quarterly* 45, no. 1 (Spring 2022): 79–96; see also Timothy Snyder, *The Road to Unfreedom: Russia, Europe, America* (New York: Tim Duggan Books, 2018).

16. William J. Burns, *The Back Channel: A Memoir of American Diplomacy and the Case for Its Renewal* (New York: Random House, 2019).

17. Kathryn E. Stoner, *Russia Resurrected: Its Power and Purpose in a New Global Order* (Oxford: Oxford University Press, 2021), 31–68; see also Jeffrey Mankoff, "Russia in the Era of Great Power Competition," *Washington Quarterly* 44, no. 3 (Fall 2021): 107–25.

18. Rahul Roy-Chaudhury and Kate Sullivan de Estrada, "India and US FONOPs: Oceans Apart," *Survival* 64, no. 1 (February/March 2022): 131–56; Bruce D. Jones, *To Rule the Waves: How Control of the World's Oceans Determines the Fate of the Superpowers*, paperback edition (New York: Simon & Schuster, 2023).

19. For an insightful discussion of this issue, albeit within a novel in the new security-studies school of "useful fiction," see Elliot Ackerman and Admiral James Stavridis, *2034: A Novel of the Next World War* (New York: Penguin Press, 2021), 2.

20. US Department of Defense (DoD), "Annual Freedom of Navigation Report to Congress, 2021," Department of Defense, April 1, 2022.

21. Lynn Kuok, "How China's Actions in the South China Sea Undermine the Rule of Law," in *Global China: Assessing China's Growing Role in the World*, ed. Tarun Chhabra, Rush Doshi, Ryan Hass, and Emilie Kimball (Washington, DC: Brookings Institution, 2021), 75–85.

22. Michael E. O'Hanlon, Melanie W. Sisson, and Caitlin Talmadge, "Managing the Risks of US-China War: Implementing a Strategy of Integrated Deterrence," Brookings Institution, September 2022.

23. Christian Brose, *The Kill Chain: Defending America in the Future of High-Tech Warfare* (New York: Hachette Books, 2020, updated March 2022), 142, 236.

24. Ryan Hass, *Stronger: Adapting America's China Strategy in an Age of Competitive Interdependence* (New Haven, CT: Yale University Press, 2021), 134–42.

25. Joseph Biden, "National Security Strategy," The White House, October 2022.

26. Office of the High Commissioner for Human Rights, "OHCHR Assessment of Human Rights Concerns in the Xinjiang Uyghur Autonomous Region, People's Republic of China," August 2022, 43.

27. H.R. McMaster, "How China Sees the World and How We Should See China," *The Atlantic*, May 2020.

28. Jorge L. Ortiz and John Bacon, "No Indications China Is Helping Russia, Biden Says; Schools Close in Russian Border Area: Updates," *USA Today*, September 18, 2022.

29. DoD, "Military and Security Developments Involving the People's Republic of China: 2022 Annual Report to Congress," 143.

30. Karoun Demirjian, "Pentagon Warns of China's Plans for Dominance in Taiwan and Beyond," *Washington Post*, November 29, 2022.

31. Michael E. O'Hanlon and James Steinberg, *A Glass Half Full?: Rebalance, Reassurance, and Resolve in the US-China Strategic Relationship* (Washington, DC: Brookings Institution, 2017), 27.

32. Michael J. Green, "The Real China Hands: What Washington Can Learn from Its Asian Allies," *Foreign Affairs* 101, no. 6 (November/December 2022): 100.

33. Thomas G. Mahnken, "Could America Win a New World War?: What It Would Take to Defeat Both China and Russia," *Foreign Affairs*, October 27, 2022; Jessica Brandt and Zack Cooper, "Sino-Russian Splits: Divergences in Autocratic Coercion," *Washington Quarterly* 45, no. 3 (Fall 2022): 23–46.

34. Lise Howard and Michael O'Hanlon, "What Should Eurasian Security Look Like after the Russia-Ukraine War?" *The Hill*, December 26, 2022.

35. Robert P. Haffa Jr., *The Half War: Planning US Rapid Deployment Forces to Meet a Limited Contingency, 1960–1983* (Boulder, CO: Westview Press, 1984).

36. Lloyd J. Austin III, "2022 National Defense Strategy of the United States of America," US Department of Defense, October 2022, 17.

6

America's Operational Imperatives

Some Budgetary Considerations

Nadia Schadlow

Introduction

Following the collapse of the Soviet Union over forty years ago, national security planners expressed optimism. The United States was "the only nation with the military to influence events globally" and Washington was "heartened and encouraged" that the "hammer and sickle no longer flies over Moscow."[1] President George H. W. Bush would observe that we had "entered a remarkable stage in our relationship with the Soviet Union," allowing us to "narrow our differences and seize this historic opportunity to help create lasting peace."[2] Today, in startling contrast, threats abound, gloom predominates, and America's economic, political, and military strength, and resolve, are in question. Russia's invasion of Ukraine and China's looming threat to Taiwan underscore this transformation.

In the post–Cold War period, Pax Americana and the concurrent period of Western ascendency undergirded a relative peace that was founded on liberal values, democratic governance, and free markets. The predominant views through the 1990s and 2000s were that nations were drawing together around Western values, particularly political and economic liberalization. This direction of progress seemed inevitable, and US military and economic strength overmatched any potential rival.

America's power relative to other powers was at its apex. The economy had grown robustly from the reforms of the Reagan revolution. The Reagan military buildup modernized and equipped all the armed services and broke new

The views expressed in this chapter are solely those of the individual author and do not necessarily reflect the views of any organization with which they are, or have been, affiliated.

ground with the Strategic Defense Initiative and other programs. Russia was mired in a deep economic depression, its military in shambles. Communist China, still reeling from the Tiananmen Square demonstrations, had not yet fully opened up its economy, and its military still adhered to antiquated doctrines of the people's war. Iran was emerging from the catastrophic, decade-long war with Iraq. North Korea was experiencing a famine. The major powers of Europe were consumed with the creation of the European Union, while Germany dealt with the assimilation of East Germany. India, for its part, was on the verge of an economic crisis.

The 1992 National Military Strategy explained that the US would now move away from threat analysis as a basis for planning, since there were no significant threats facing the United States. It observed that "we can still point to a North Korea, a weakened Iraq, and perhaps even a hostile Iran," and there may be "one or two added to such a list without straining credulity" but the real threat was "the threat of the unknown."[3] As one military analyst later observed, "a strategy oriented on a potential enemy was out."[4]

The 1993 Defense Department's Bottom-Up Review set the foundation for major cuts in the US defense budget.[5] Defense Secretary Les Aspin explained that the Department of Defense (DoD) would reduce its combat forces and make related cuts in "support forces, the massive and costly infrastructure of bases, centralized maintenance and supply facilities—all of which were built up during the Cold War." Total active-duty personnel declined from 1.6 million to 1.4 million. The "bottom line of the Bottom-Up Review," he said, "was that most elements of the force will be smaller."[6] The budget cuts that took place were known as the "peace dividend" and persisted throughout the Clinton administration.

The hope during this period was that China could become a responsible stakeholder in the international system.[7] The United States welcomed the "rise of a stable, peaceful, and prosperous China" and hoped that constructive relations could deliver benefits around the world.[8] This view was the basis for China's entry into the World Trade Organization (WTO). While there were some concerns about China's growing military investments, the Pentagon explained that the People's Liberation Army (PLA) had a large but somewhat obsolete force: its "emergent cyber capabilities were rudimentary; its use of information technology was well behind the curve; and its nominal space capabilities were based on outdated technologies for the day."[9] Fundamentally, US defense experts viewed China as a regional, not global, power and argued that its military modernization goals were "to create a force sufficient to defend against any regional opponent, maintain the credibility of territorial claims, protect national interests, maintain internal security, deter any moves by Taiwan toward *de jure* independence, and deter aggression."[10]

Today, as evident in the National Security Strategies of the Trump and Biden administrations, leaders of both political parties accept that we have entered a new era of great-power competition. Moscow continues its attempts to conquer Ukraine; it projects military power into the Middle East and conducts hybrid aggression around the world. Beijing has pursued a breathtaking decades-long military buildup, founded on economic growth catalyzed by access to export markets when it was granted ascension to the WTO. It continues to make illegal claims to sovereignty over the South China Sea, has sought to create a chain of civilian and military maritime facilities across the Indo-Pacific region, and appears to be preparing to coerce Taiwan into unification on China's terms. In addition, Russia and China have proclaimed a partnership with "no limits," designed to challenge the US-led international order and to discredit the idea of universal democratic values. Iran, working through proxies in Iraq, Syria, Lebanon, and Yemen, seeks to dominate the region through the so-called Axis of Resistance and is once again approaching the status of a nuclear threshold state.

The unipolar moment enjoyed by the United States lapsed within two decades, with American power going from uncontested to contested in virtually all military domains. Across the traditional domains of warfare—land, sea, and air—the United States could no longer operate freely. The spread of technologies and the development of new weapons systems, from precision-guided munitions to unmanned autonomous vehicles, meant that America's ability to find and hold targets at risk; supply and safeguard its forces abroad; freely navigate the seas and control sea lines of communication; and protect its homeland had now diminished, significantly. In the critical regions of Eurasia, rival powers sought to create anti-access/area denial zones—areas where US power projection assets would be under threat of ballistic missiles, airpower, and other systems. Due to the proliferation of accurate and extremely fast (even hypersonic) weapons systems, the ability of US aircraft, ships, and troops to get to where they needed to go, on our terms, was gone. With these developments, much of what had given the US military overmatch against its rivals was gone.[11]

While the US defense budget remained the largest in the world, America's relative advantages were declining. US goals and commitments remained the same, including keeping threats away from the homeland, preserving favorable military balances in key regions, and preserving access to global commons of the sea, air, cyber, and space.[12] As rivals recovered and threats rose, resources were stretched thin. It has already been several years since the National Defense Panel pointed out that US military superiority had "eroded to a dangerous degree."[13]

Perhaps one of the biggest shifts in this period has been technology—both as a driver of change and as a domain of competition itself. As the Cold War ended, the internet had barely made a dent in the world. In 1992, less than 1 percent of the world was using the internet, while today that figure is closer to 60 percent.[14] In recent years, US leadership in emerging technologies has been increasingly challenged, primarily by China.[15] Technology is at the heart of a long-term, systemic competition between open, democratic societies and closed, authoritarian systems to shape the future of the international rules-based order.[16] New technological developments will emerge from multiple countries with less warning. This will put increasingly sophisticated capabilities in the hands of small groups and individuals, as well as nation-states.[17]

The United States now faces a formidable pacing threat in China, which under President Xi Jinping's rule continues to pursue military modernization with the goal of developing a world-class military by 2049 that is capable of fighting and winning global wars. In 2020, the Pentagon's annual report on China noted that the PLA's goal is to become "equal to—or in some cases superior to—the US military, or that of any other great power that the People's Republic of China (PRC) views as a threat."[18] The DoD report adds that "the PRC has marshaled the resources, technology, and political will" to do so.[19] It is widely accepted that China's goal is to achieve leadership in key technology fields by 2030—particularly those it sees as critical to its military and economic future, such as biotechnology, advanced computing, and artificial intelligence (AI).

In the broadest sense, the world seems to be fragmenting politically, economically, militarily, and technologically. Globalization is, to a degree, being replaced by regionalization, with countries around the world—from the Middle East to Southeast Asia—seeking opportunities to hedge against the broader US-China systemic rivalry. The United States and China are locked into competition over two different political and economic systems.

This highly contested world is creating a range of operational challenges for the Defense Department, which in turn have budget implications. The purpose of this paper is to describe four of these, which the United States must address if we are to preserve deterrence and to ensure that if deterrence fails, the United States can prevail militarily to protect the safety and security of the American people well into the future.

These challenges are (1) resetting US strategic forces for the second nuclear age; (2) rightsizing and integrating US and allied conventional forces; (3) restoring the US defense industrial base to support a protracted war; and (4) preserving freedom of action in space. All will require a combination of new investments, weapons systems, processes, and force employment concepts that must come together. And undergirding all of these challenges is the cross-cutting need to integrate the software required to upgrade these domains and to protect our ability to operate in cyberspace, which links many of these challenges. Failures in these foundational areas will undercut our chances of success.

There are, of course, more than four challenges facing the department. But these are starting points in considering the range of budgetary pressures in the future. Moreover, they may offer a different way of thinking about how to evaluate the defense budget.

The five categories depicted in figure 6.1 have been in existence for decades.[20] The key strategic question, however, is how these categories of

 The Department of Defense spent $718 billion in 2021 on a broad range of military activities

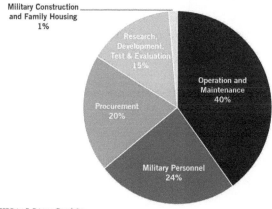

Note: The "Other" category, which accounted for about 0.2 percent of DoD spending in FY2021, is presented in this chart as part of the Operation and Maintenance category.
Source: Peter G. Peterson Foundation, from data provided by the Office of Management and Budget, *Public Budget Database, Budget of the United States Government: Fiscal Year 2023*, March 2022.

spending come together to shape and advance progress on the operational problems that the Defense Department faces. That is a much harder number to assess, but it is an approach that might give us better insights into the degree to which the United States is actually prepared to deter adversaries and, if necessary, to fight and win.

Nuclear Operational Challenges
The Shift

In fall 2022, two former senior Pentagon officials testified before Congress that the United States faces the most "complex configuration of questions about nuclear weapons that it has ever faced since the onset of the nuclear age."[21] The United States now faces a world with three major nuclear powers, along with lesser but rising nuclear powers; qualitative changes in nuclear weapons themselves; challenges related to defending against ballistic missiles and new types of missiles such as hypersonics; and the destabilizing implications of AI and other software on nuclear command-and-control infrastructure.

The years following the Cold War were dominated by a focus on Russia's nuclear arsenal, an arms control regime centered on Washington and Moscow, and a commitment to maintaining the US strategic nuclear triad. Every Nuclear Posture Review since the early 1990s affirmed the importance of doing so, arguing that a mix of delivery systems, each with different characteristics and attributes, would enhance strategic stability by ensuring that no adversary could conduct a successful first strike and thereby eliminate the United States' ability to respond to a nuclear attack.[22] This led to unilateral reductions in US-deployed nuclear weapons.

Today, although Russia is bound by New START, it has refused to allow on-site inspections since the onset of the COVID-19 pandemic. It violated the terms of the INF Treaty by testing weapons with a prohibited range. It has maintained a robust capability at the tactical nuclear level as part of its doctrine to "escalate to de-escalate," which implies that such weapons might be employed to coerce opponents in a conventional conflict.

Regarding China, the US intelligence community has warned that Beijing is pursuing the "most rapid expansion and platform diversification of its nuclear arsenal in its history."[23] China's nuclear buildup puts it on a trajectory to become a nuclear peer of the United States in *qualitative* and *quantitative* terms by 2030.[24] Some experts believe that China has adopted a strategy of limited nuclear first use whereby China could use the threat of nuclear weapons to achieve its objectives, such as deterring a US intervention or coercing Taiwan. Overall, China seems poised to shift from a minimum deterrence posture to one that suggests a more coercive nuclear strategy.[25]

The nuclear arsenals of other countries are also growing. India and Pakistan are both credible nuclear powers with nearly identically sized arsenals.[26] A 2021 RAND study projected that North Korea could have around two hundred nuclear weapons stockpiled by 2027.[27] And Iran's ability to enrich uranium at high enough levels to produce a nuclear weapon is now measured in months.[28]

DoD Imperatives

Given these developments, US nuclear strategy, force structures, and doctrine—all of which assumed a bipolar nuclear order—must be rethought. Similarly, the US nuclear modernization program must be revisited in light of new circumstances. All of these shifts have serious implications for a deterrence construct that has kept nuclear peace for over half a century—and have significant budget implications as well. Four particular challenges stand out.

First, it must address qualitative issues by continuing to modernize US nuclear delivery systems and weapons to ensure they remain effective, safe, and reliable. While there is bipartisan support thus far for this mission, it must be sustained. As the head of US Strategic Command put it, he is working with "submarines built in the 80s and 90s, an air launch cruise missile built in the 80s, intercontinental ballistic missiles built in the 70s, a bomber built in the 60s, and part of our nuclear command and control that predates the internet."[29]

Second, the department must ensure that the US nuclear force structure is adequate to deter two peer competitors *simultaneously*, as well as countries such as Iran and North Korea. With this larger pool of competitors, the number of considerations required to maintain deterrence increases.[30] Already this new dynamic is challenging Washington.[31] As one expert put it, when you "move this into a three-party problem, it is a completely different set of effects, dynamics, that needs lots of work to understand."[32] Deterrence is not just based on the existence of nuclear forces but also on the ability to hold at-risk assets most valued by an enemy.[33] In today's world, there are more of these assets to consider.

Third, the US must maintain a credible missile defense posture. Over a decade ago, the Obama administration's missile defense review outlined the need for a more ambitious approach toward Europe and other regions so that the United States and its allies could defend against short-, medium-, and intermediate-range missiles, as well as against missiles that could threaten the US homeland.[34] These challenges have intensified. Today, in addition to ballistic missiles, the US must be able to defend against ballistic missiles with maneuvering reentry vehicles and hypersonic systems that give adversaries the ability to hold forces at risk from hundreds, even thousands, of miles away, with flight times that are measured in minutes. Hypersonic missiles, in particular, create significant defense challenges due to their speed and maneuverability, making them ideal first-strike weapons. Defenses will need to explore new approaches to these weapons, such as the ability to detect and destroy missiles in the boost phase as well as the use of directed energy weapons for interception, which in turn will require additional resources.[35]

Finally, AI and machine learning will impact nuclear arsenals and command-and-control infrastructure, adding to the challenges presented by the nuclear domain. While AI could offer commanders improved situational awareness, it could also increase instability.[36] For instance, in cases of multilateral nuclear deterrence, a state may perceive that an adversary's investment in AI, even non-nuclear-related, could give that adversary the ability to threaten the state's future second-strike capability.[37] As one expert put it, the question is less "whether nuclear-armed states will adopt AI technology into the nuclear enterprise, but rather by whom, when, and to what degree."

In FY2021, the Congressional Budget Office (CBO) estimated that plans for nuclear forces based on DoD and Department of Energy budget requests would cost a total of $634 billion over the 2021–2030 period, *provided those plans did not change or experience any cost growth or schedule delays*.[38] My emphasis is added to illustrate that key caveat. Given that in the past, actual costs were close to 30 percent higher than originally predicted, this trend will likely continue into the future. Moreover, these CBO estimates do *not* include several categories of costs that are critical to the nuclear domain as well, such as the DoD's overhead and support costs; the costs of dismantling retired nuclear weapons and environmental cleanups; the costs of antiproliferation efforts; and perhaps most importantly, the costs of developing and maintaining active defenses against other countries' nuclear weapons.[39]

Operational Challenge: Integrating Coalitions Better
The Shift

US policy makers consistently herald the strength of America's alliances. The Biden administration's 2022 National Security Strategy reaffirmed that America's "alliances and partnerships around the world are our most important strategic asset" and are indispensable to peace and stability. Yet the ability of the United States and its allies and partners to fight together in highly contested environments in a fully *integrated* manner remains open to question. Working with allies means that the United States can present adversaries with multiple dilemmas. The proximity of allies to key theaters allows for the forward staging of US equipment or better intelligence collection, and of course, such alignments are helpful politically as well.[40] But forward positioning and political unity are quite different from operating together on a battlefield.

The complexity of regional security environments and proliferation of military capabilities, however, make it impossible for the United States to deter or, if required, fight and win alone. The United States does not have or cannot amass capabilities at scale without partners. For example, in the East China Sea, Japan brings significant air defense capabilities.[41] The South Korean Marine Corps is the second largest in the world.[42] As retired US Forces in Europe Commander LTG Ben Hodges put it, "We have no choice but to be in multinational task forces because the United States doesn't have enough capacity to do all that is required."[43]

America's decisive victory in the Gulf War in 1991 created expectations of continued US military dominance; many believed that the United States could shoulder the burden of stability for the world. At the time, two former Defense Department officials observed that "the United States and its allies currently have no strategic understanding that common interests should be defended jointly" and that "current US defense strategy, plans, and preparations are essentially unilateral."[44]

The Defense Department's 1993 Bottom-Up Review did not mention burden sharing and referred to allied capabilities almost as an afterthought. Over a decade later, the 2005 National Defense Strategy assumed that the United States would have no global peer competitor and remain unmatched in military capabilities.[45] In the last year of the Bush (forty-three) administration, the 2008 National Defense Strategy focused on a global struggle against violent extremist ideologies. The focus was on "certain low-risk missions such as peacekeeping and humanitarian assistance."[46] There was no premium placed on integrating higher-end capabilities with allies and partners.

Even as the Obama administration affirmed that the United States would "defend the territorial integrity of every single Ally," the reality was that the United States would likely have trouble fulfilling that pledge.[47] Several war games conducted around that time found that NATO would not be able to defend the territory of the Baltic states in the face of aggression by Russia.[48] The challenges have only grown more complex over the past decade, particularly as China continues to modernize its military and develop its power projection capabilities.

DoD Challenges

The strategic advantages to be gained through coalition operations depend on the ability to operate in a truly integrated manner with high-end capabilities. This will require additional resources, focused attention, and a commitment to reducing stubborn obstacles. Improvements in the ability to fight together are needed across at least five key areas.

First, significant communications challenges exist at the tactical, operational, and strategic levels. At the company and battalion levels, for example, radios must be able to operate inside challenging cyber or electronic warfare environments. At the operational and strategic levels, allies must share a common operating picture (COP) and improve their command-and-control architectures amidst diverse devices and operating systems.[49] In Asia, in particular, US alliances lack the type of structures that NATO has to support integrated command and control and to drive multilateral operations.[50] As a former US military attaché to Japan observed, "Until the US III MEF commander and the local Japanese commander have the same COP on a screen somewhere, any talk of a secure alliance is just a lot of talk."[51] Another retired US military officer explained, "better digital integration is critical."[52]

Second, high-end combined warfare requires that allies integrate their digital fires. The radar of one country needs to be able to relay targeting information to the fire direction center and then onto weapons systems tasked with strike or counter-fire missions. "If you can't do that in a very short amount of time, then you're never going to be able to strike back at who's shooting at you," observed now-retired US Army General Ben Hodges.[53] In artillery or rocket exchanges in Europe, the United States and its allies must shoot back at adversary missile launchers before they can move. This creates a situation in which US forces might track enemy fires using radar systems in one country, relay information to a command post in a second country, and fire back with weapons systems in a third country. This "kill chain" might require three minutes to execute, and it must be connected by secure networks.

Third, the United States must reduce the byzantine bureaucracy of Foreign Military Sales (FMS) that prevents the timely provision of equipment, weapons, and services to its partners. The backlog of FMS orders is immense. In one of the most important theaters in the world, Taiwan, equipment delays are so great that they threaten the ability to execute operational plans to defend the island. There is a three-year backlog in the delivery of $14.2 billion worth of military equipment, including everything from F-16 fighters to the components needed for Patriot missile systems.[54] Sales of the F-16s were approved in 2019 but Taipei does not expect delivery until 2026.[55] The DoD has blamed the backlog on COVID-19, but delays like these have been problematic for years all around the world, and they create budget inefficiencies as well as a mismatch between appropriated funds and actual security outcomes.[56]

Related to these FMS problems are outdated laws—such as the International Traffic in Arms Regulations—that prevent Washington from sharing information with key allies such as Australia and the United Kingdom. Without updates to these laws, for example, Australia cannot service US-made helicopters and naval fighter jets or even receive bolts for US-made aircraft that are flown by the Australian military.[57] As several experts put it, these outdated laws are "unintentionally handing a technological and military advantage to adversaries."[58] And as the US struggles with streamlining its FMS processes, China has become the fourth largest global arms exporter.[59]

Finally, integration will become even harder as the United States comes to depend upon AI to fight what Alex Karp has called "algorithmic warfare."[60] Uneven adoption of AI across coalitions could threaten interoperability.[61] Not all states will develop military applications of AI at the same rate, and many will be sensitive to sharing information, which means even more difficulty coordinating.[62]

Addressing these deficiencies will have budgetary implications. Too many allies and partners have taken a holiday from defense training and procurement, or worse, even effectively disarmed during the post–Cold War period. If we are to deter today's revisionist great powers, US allies and partners must rearm. However, it is essential that they do so in a war that enables integrated combined operations. This means the United States must work with them to agree on how we will fight—we need an agreed concept of operations in each theater and sub-theater—and then must build forces that can communicate and operate seamlessly together. We have not been in this business for decades. We must step up to the task, and it will require new expenditures across our alliances.

Preserving Freedom of Action in Space

The US built a glass house before the invention of stones. . . . The shifting of space from a benign environment to being a warfighting environment requires different capabilities.[63]

The Shift

Since the United States launched satellites to track and monitor nuclear missiles during the Cold War, it has relied on its space infrastructure to protect its national security. For much of the post–Cold War period, the United States was optimistic that it would enjoy advantages in space capabilities across all mission areas; the DoD believed that these advantages would be maintained by "staying at least one technology generation ahead of any foreign or commercial space power."[64] Space was populated by only a handful of countries, home to relatively few satellites, and largely free from threats.[65] Looking back at that period, Air Force Secretary Frank Kendall observed that it was a time when the United States could "put up expensive systems in space and not worry about them."[66]

Close to ninety countries now have space programs. Some US experts believe that China will overtake the US as the dominant space power by 2032.[67] The space domain is now a critical commercial as well as a warfighting domain. And it's highly contested.

Secure and sustained access to space is essential to US military operations at all levels. Space-based assets provide units on the ground with intelligence, surveillance, and reconnaissance capabilities; satellites are the basis for networked communications across the joint force and are central to concepts such as Joint All-Domain Command and Control.[68] In the strategic realm, our nuclear command-and-control infrastructure depends upon space.

Commercially, space plays a critical role in the US economy. In 2019, the space sector accounted for some $366 billion in revenue.[69] Technologies such as satellite communications and precision navigation and timing play central roles in health care, transportation, communications, energy grids, financial systems, and more. Companies such as SpaceX and Blue Origin have driven down the costs of space launches and developed new technologies and products, but these developments have also led to more congestion and orbital debris.[70] In addition, as the DoD increases its work with private-sector actors in conflict contingencies (as in Ukraine), these interactions will complicate deterrence and military planning.

China and Russia have also dramatically expanded their capabilities in space. Both countries aim to exploit the US reliance on space-based systems.[71] Each has its own space force and is "integrating space scenarios into their military exercises."[72] Both are modernizing and increasing capabilities in nearly all major space categories, including satellite communications, remote sensing, and navigation-related technologies.[73] In the period between 2015 and 2018, China and Russia increased their combined satellite fleets by more than 200 percent.[74] China has also conducted several counterspace capability demonstrations, including the test of a hypersonic glide vehicle.

DoD Challenges

Given that space plays a central role in US economic and national security, the Defense Department must maintain and upgrade its capabilities in at least four primary mission areas. These missions and the required capabilities are interrelated; there are certainly different ways to categorize them, but this is one approach. All have defense budgetary implications.

First, the DoD must be able to provide situational awareness to track activities in space and to warn against incoming ballistic missile and hypersonic threats. Absent timely and reliable missile warnings, Washington risks having only minutes to respond to a crisis. Since the Cold War, the United States has relied on a constellation of satellites in geostationary orbit—about twenty-two thousand miles above the Earth's surface—to warn of a nuclear attack. Two key developments have made this mission much harder. One is that China and Russia now have the ability to threaten these geostationary satellites; another is that both are developing hypersonic weapons that are much harder to track than ballistic missiles. The DoD is pursuing two simultaneous approaches to address these new threats. It is replacing the existing constellation of geostationary and polar-orbiting satellites ("the last of their kind," said the director of the Space Development Agency) and also developing a resilient, layered system of satellites in low Earth orbit and medium Earth orbit.[75] The simultaneous pursuit of these systems will cost billions but offer significant increases in hypersonic missile tracking capabilities.[76]

A second key mission for the DoD is to ensure that its assets in space, and related ground-based infrastructure, are survivable. There are four broad types of counterspace weapons, including kinetic and nonkinetic ones.[77] They have different effects, vary in how easy they are to detect and attribute, and differ in terms of the technology and resources needed to develop and field them.[78] So the US must be able to protect against kinetic threats as well as nonkinetic threats such as radio frequency interference (jamming, spoofing) and cyberattacks.

Third, since space is a warfighting domain, the United States must be able to conduct offensive as well as defensive operations. Offensive counterspace operations include the ability to "negate an adversary's use of space capabilities, reducing the effectiveness of adversary forces in all domains."[79] Increased investments to respond to counterspace capabilities are required by the 2023 NDAA.[80]

Finally, the DoD has overall responsibility for a space infrastructure that provides reliable services to all aspects of American life. These include next-generation GPS, internet infrastructures, and assets related to imaging, tracking, and cellular services. In the near future, the DoD will oversee the replacement of current GPS satellites. Not only is this complex in and of itself, but it means that all weapons systems that rely on GPS will need to be updated so that they can "talk" to the new navigation system.[81]

The new space force, numbering some eighteen thousand, is charged with recruiting and training personnel and applying new acquisition tools to acquire needed space systems.[82] The DoD's 2023 budget includes $24.5 billion for the US Space Force and the Space Development Agency—about $5 billion more than what Congress enacted in 2022.[83] This is likely to continue to grow. While the objectives are sound, it will take years to rectify the problems. For over a decade, most of the DoD's major space programs have experienced significant cost and schedule increases, with major programs routinely late by three to nine years and over cost.[84]

Upgrading the Defense Industrial Base
The Shift

During the Cold War, the strength of the US industrial base was not in question. It was considered a source of long-term strategic advantage for the United States. It produced the bombers and missiles on which nuclear deterrence rested and armed the US military with world-class weapons and reliable guided munitions that were cheap enough to be employed in large numbers.[85]

With the dissolution of the USSR and the absence of a peer competitor, the concept of "rapid decisive operations" emerged, leading to the view that wars would be short and that the United States could coerce or defeat the enemy "without a lengthy campaign."[86] Underlying this view was a certainty about war. H.R. McMaster, a colonel at the time, criticized the belief that the US could achieve "near certainty" in war and warned that this type of thinking could lead to bad planning assumptions.[87] By assuming that wars would be short, the United States avoided planning for protracted wars.[88]

The collapse of the Soviet Union also increased pressures to reduce the defense budget and led to the reallocation of a large portion of the budget from national security to other national needs.[89] At the time, the CBO acknowledged that cuts could result in job losses from six hundred thousand to 1.4 million jobs and that industries "readily identified with defense" would suffer.[90] These developments led to the consolidation of defense firms, setting the foundation for the situation today. The government took a hands-off approach to the industrial base, leading to supplier monopolies or duopolies, which in turn began to erode competition.[91] Over time, the DoD became reliant on a smaller number of contractors for critical defense capabilities. Over the last three decades, the number of suppliers in major weapons system categories has declined substantially: tactical missile suppliers declined from thirteen to three, fixed-wing aircraft suppliers declined from eight to three, and 90 percent of missiles come from three sources.[92]

Other trends also contributed to the erosion of the Defense Innovation Board (DIB). These included decisions about manufacturing based on efficiencies over security; an increasingly onerous regulatory environment that, for example, made it hard, if not impossible, for US firms to mine for critical minerals in the United States; and the consistent underfunding of procurement, which led to undersourcing capacity and the recapitalization of legacy systems.[93]

The weaknesses of the defense industrial base came to a head with Russia's attack on Ukraine. As the United States and other NATO allies supplied Ukraine with Javelins and other comparable man-portable missile systems, concerns grew about whether the United States itself had sufficient long-range, precision-strike munitions for even a short conflict, much less a drawn-out one.[94]

DoD Challenges

There are differences between producing and sustaining "advanced weapon systems" and munitions like Javelins, but the five areas discussed below are relevant to a range of weapons systems.[95] They are not in order of priority.

First, the Pentagon needs to increase suppliers, which will only happen if well-known procurement problems are addressed. It has recently called for more competition, arguing that it is an important indicator of the ability to deliver products and key technologies. The DoD has noted that insufficient competition may leave gaps and result in higher costs since firms can "leverage their market position to charge more and raise barriers for new entrants." But over the past decade, despite new initiatives, it remains very difficult for new entrants. In fact, there have been drops in new entrants of vendors to the DoD.[96] Small businesses actually receiving contract awards plummeted 43 percent from 2011 to 2022.[97]

Second, while the DoD continues to call attention to the problem of supply chain security—in areas from advanced batteries to microchips—a shift in these supply chains could take decades.[98] Many obstacles to relocating manufacturing remain—from the lack of situational awareness on highly complex supply chains (the GAO estimated that the US industrial base consisted of over two hundred thousand companies) to bureaucratic and regulatory obstacles that can add years to meaningful shifts.[99]

Third, maintenance delays have a direct impact on combat capabilities, since aircraft or ships are not available when needed. If the purpose of the DIB is to supply the military with equipment, this counts. One report found that from 2015 to 2019, maintenance delays on aircraft carrier and submarine repairs meant that vessels were not available for operations for close to eight thousand days—that's about twenty years![100] As one retired senior officer put it, it's "the equivalent of losing half an aircraft carrier and three submarines each year."[101] Last year, the GAO noted that the budgetary cost of the backlog of navy restoration and modernization projects increased by over $1.6 billion in the last five years.[102] In addition, the average age of capital equipment continues to increase, and half the equipment is already past its expected service life. The navy's effort to address some of these deficiencies, the Shipyard Infrastructure Optimization Plan, is estimated to cost $21 billion and will take some twenty years to implement. Even if the cost is acceptable, the time period is not. Similar stories abound across the services.

Further complicating maintenance problems is the need to upgrade to advanced manufacturing. As one retired admiral put it, while we need to improve existing physical infrastructure, we also need to take the "opportunity to build the digital infrastructure required to accelerate our readiness advantage."[103] While this may save money over the long term, in the shorter term, capital costs will be high.[104]

Fourth, conceptually, the DoD needs to consider stockpiling as a strategic necessity, since it provides strategic depth. This means it must increase its procurements of systems and weapons to build these stockpiles. Multiyear contracts are central to this effort.[105] Not only are there deterrent benefits, since adversaries can see preparations, but there are cost benefits as well. Multiyear contracts reduce weapons costs significantly.[106] Yet, every time the Pentagon wants to contract for longer than one year, it needs specific approval from the appropriations committees—even with the current need for sustained purchases of munitions for Ukraine, no multiyear procurements were approved in the tranches of aid passed by Congress since the start of the war.[107]

These problems are compounded when it comes to our allies and partners, all of whom must make qualitative and quantitative overhauls of their munitions stockpiles. A former top official at the German defense ministry stated that no NATO country other than the US has sufficient stockpiles or the industrial capacity to create the necessary reserves to fight a major artillery war.[108] The Royal United Services Institute found that at the height of the fighting in the Donbas area in Ukraine, Russia was using "more ammunition in two days than the entire stock of the British military."[109] This crisis extends to Japan and Australia as well. It's a good sign that the US and Japan are holding talks on stockpiles, but the timeline matters, and as discussed previously, the current process for FMS could take years of negotiation before production can even begin.[110]

The United States does not seek to fight a protracted war. But as defense scholar Andrew Krepinevich explains, the "best way to avoid these costs is to demonstrate to great-power rivals that the United States is capable of prevailing in a protracted conflict."[111] This in turn requires the capabilities to produce and deliver weapons systems and equipment to military forces. Yet well before China was designated a pacing threat and before the war in Europe, experts across the defense enterprise have been sounding warnings about everything from critical mineral vulnerabilities to manufacturing facilities that dated from World War II. Over twenty-five years ago, DoD leaders expressed concerns that due to reductions in procurement, the DoD would lose a "particular supplier or a particular capability."[112] Fifteen years ago, the 2006 Defense Science Board report argued that the DoD must develop a National Security Industrial Vision, and several external studies highlighted problems as well.[113]

Problems exist at all layers: the experts needed to produce weapons systems; the material components of these systems; the factories needed to assemble them; and the companies willing and able to produce them. The problem is now glaring and could very well decide the fate of Ukraine. While it has garnered welcome and high-level Pentagon attention, the roots of the situation are much deeper and will take more investments, and more than a few years, to fix.

Cross-Cutting Challenges

The battlegrounds tell the story of a larger paradox of a techno-economic superpower suffering from strategically significant technological vulnerabilities.[114]

Improvements across the four operational areas discussed in this paper will depend significantly on the sustained adoption of software upgrades. Software resides in virtually every piece of electronic, from weapons systems to business systems.[115] As one defense tech investor observed, software is taking over the battlefield: autonomous systems, networked weapons, and cyber weapons are all powered by software.[116] Without modernized software, the United States will not be able to derive tactical, operational, and strategic advantages, which could lead to failure in war. As noted in the 2018 National Defense Strategy, the United States needs to be able to "deliver performance at the speed of relevance."[117] Processes for software acquisitions are very different from those for traditional acquisitions, and current DoD processes are "not responsive to need."[118] Thus, the latent power of the US technology ecosystem is not currently being harnessed for national purposes.[119]

Yet software is integral to America's architecture in space, and problems can disrupt the entire ecosystem.[120] Software-dependent capabilities include satellite command and control, early detection and tracking of objects' orbits, GPS signals, and radio communication for military forces. One 2019 GAO study found that four major DoD space programs all faced challenges in using commercial software: they had used outdated software tools and had "limited knowledge" of newer software developments.[121] These programs ended up costing up to three times original estimates and had been in development for periods ranging from "five to over twenty years." As reliance on unmanned systems increases, which in turn depends on space-based assets *and* the integration of AI, these problems will become more pressing.[122]

The US nuclear arsenal also relies heavily on software. As the vice chairman of the Joint Chiefs of Staff explained, "the common thread for all missile defense systems is, can I see the threat coming at me. . . . The big piece is not shooters but sensors."[123] Fundamentally, sensors depend on software. The nuclear enterprise is rife with cybersecurity risks, and the National Nuclear Security Administration continues to struggle with this problem.[124]

Alarmingly, a 2016 GAO study found that the DoD still utilized a legacy system, which relied on eight-inch floppy disks to operate its nuclear forces.[125] Delays in modernizing the Columbia-class nuclear submarine were related to integrating a new "design software tool."[126] Similarly, the air force's long-range standoff weapon, designed to penetrate air defense systems and deliver a nuclear payload, had not acquired the most up-to-date software and as a result, its guidance and control system was approaching maturity.[127]

Software also affects virtually all levels of US and allied integrated operations, from communications to the coordination of direct fires. The war in Ukraine has made the need to develop and field an integrated battle management command-and-control system even more pressing.[128]

Some of these software integration problems are due to the DoD's fundamental ambivalence about whether it is a "consumer" or a "creator" of software.[129] Defense analysts Bryan Clark and Dan Patt have described how at times, the DoD focuses on procuring externally developed software faster. But in other cases, it aims to develop its internal expertise. Yet to fully benefit from the extraordinary advances in software by the private sector, the DoD will need to embrace its primary role as a consumer, not a creator. It must begin to think of commercial suppliers as partners or retailers and not as contractors.[130]

Conclusions

It is perhaps trite to observe how much has changed since America's relatively unmatched power during the post–Cold War period and, in particular, the loss of its relative power since that time. This paper has sought to describe just some of the sweeping changes over the past two decades, particularly those in the military and economic realms. These developments have created challenges for the defense enterprise, requiring both the development of new or refined operational concepts and additional or reallocated resources.

Yet reaffirming the scope of how the world has changed and its impacts on American power remains important if only to highlight how much of our defense infrastructure and the processes that undergird the department have *not* actually changed. Indeed, much of it remains stubbornly archaic, which is crippling America's ability to respond to new threats. The Biden administration's 2022 National Security Strategy is correct in noting that the next ten years will be the "decisive decade," one which will determine "our competitive position long into the future." I am not sure we have ten years. To buy us some time, there are three considerations that will affect the ability of policy makers to develop and implement the operational concepts required to meet new and emerging threats. All are relevant to the much broader range of challenges the DoD faces.

First, policy makers must ask why so many past efforts to address longstanding problems have failed. Very few new officials are "present at the creation." Virtually every challenge discussed in this paper has been recommended for over a decade, if not more. Unless defense officials begin their initiatives by identifying the underlying obstacles to change and actually spend the bureaucratic capital required to reduce those obstacles, new effects are unlikely. The stakes for addressing these persistent obstacles are high. They will continue to impact the ability of the United States to field new capabilities such as hypersonics. For instance, at a recent meeting with top DoD leaders, CEOs of defense firms expressed concerns about supply chain constraints, acquisition barriers, budget instability, and access to test facilities.[131]

Second, policy makers need to consider the implications of the limited flexibility in the defense budget. In a sense, the budget is a microcosm of the characteristics of the entitlement programs John Cogan describes in his recent book, *The High Cost of Good Intentions*.[132] As one defense budget expert observed, between two-thirds and three-quarters of the budget is essentially fixed, even before the changes needed to address new threats.[133] In practice, this means few "flexible dollars" to address new requirements. And it is projected that with an inflation rate of 7 to 8 percent, the DoD would lose $100 billion of purchasing power in the next five years.[134]

Third, we might consider better ways to assess how existing categories of defense spending—categories that have been fixed for some forty years—actually come together to address operational challenges that the DoD needs to address. It is difficult to assess how the resources within each category combine to address an operational challenge since most require the integration of many types of capabilities. For instance, to develop advanced manufacturing in our defense industrial base requires investments in AI, plant facilities, and in people. These "inputs" draw from different spending categories. That is a much harder number to assess, but it is an approach that might give us better insights into the degree to which the United States is actually prepared to deter adversaries and, if necessary, to fight and win.

Notes

1. US Department of Defense (DoD), "National Military Strategy of the United States," January 1, 1992.

2. George H. W. Bush, "Remarks at the Aspen Institute Symposium in Aspen, Colorado," American Presidency Project, August 2, 1990.

3. DoD, "National Military Strategy," 3.

4. Col. Michael W. Pietrucha, "Essay: Capability-Based Planning and the Death of Military Strategy," *USNI News*, August 5, 2015.

5. Les Aspin, "The Bottom-Up Review: Forces for a New Era," prepared remarks delivered at Georgetown University, September 2, 1993, distributed by the Department of Defense on September 1, 1993.

6. Aspin, "Bottom-Up Review," 5.

7. Robert Zoellick, "Whither China? From Membership to Responsibility," remarks to the National Committee on US-China Relations, New York, September 21, 2005.

8. "National Security Strategy," The White House, February 2015, 24.

9. Office of the Secretary of Defense (OSD), "Military and Security Developments Involving the People's Republic of China 2020: Annual Report to Congress," i.

10. OSD, "Annual Report on the Military Power of the People's Republic of China," Department of Defense, September 5, 2000, https://apps.dtic.mil/sti/pdfs/ADA381499.pdf.

11. Nadia Schadlow, "The End of American Illusion," *Foreign Affairs*, August 11, 2020.

12. *Alternative Approaches to Defense Strategy and Force Structure*, hearing before the Committee on Armed Services, US Senate, 114th Cong. (2015), statement by Andrew F. Krepinevich, President, Center for Strategic and Budgetary Assessments (CSBA), available at https://csbaonline.org/uploads/documents/Andrew-Krepinevich-Defense-Strategy-Written-Statement-10-28-2015.pdf.

13. National Defense Strategy Commission, "Providing for the Common Defense: The Assessments and Recommendations of the National Defense Strategy Commission," United States Institute of Peace, November 13, 2018.

14. World Bank, "Individuals Using the Internet (% of Population)," data for 1991–2020, World Bank, 2021, https://data.worldbank.org/indicator/IT.NET.USER.ZS?end=2020&start=1991&view=chart.

15. Office of the Director of National Intelligence (ODNI), "Annual Threat Assessment of the US Intelligence Community," April 9, 2021, 20.

16. Special Competitive Studies Project (SCSP), "Mid-Decade Challenges to National Competitiveness," September 2022, 98.

17. ODNI, "Annual Threat Assessment," 20.

18. OSD, "Military and Security Developments," i.

19. OSD, "Military and Security Developments," i.

20. "Budget Basics: National Defense," Peter G. Peterson Foundation, June 1, 2022.

21. *To Receive Testimony on United States Nuclear Strategy and Policy*, Hearing Before the Committee on Armed Services, US Senate, 117th Cong. (2022), joint

statement by Eric S. Edelman, Counselor, CSBA, and Franklin C. Miller, Principal, The Scowcroft Group.

22. Frank G. Klotz and Alexandra T. Evans, "Modernizing the US Nuclear Triad: The Rationale for a New Intercontinental Ballistic Missile," RAND Corporation, January 3, 2022.

23. ODNI, "Annual Threat Assessment."

24. US-China Economic and Security Review Commission, "2021 Report to Congress," November 2021.

25. Jennifer Bradley, "China's Strategic Ambitions: A Strategy to Address China's Nuclear Breakout," National Institute for Public Policy, August 17, 2022.

26. Ashley J. Tellis, "The Nuclear Arsenals of China, India, and Pakistan Are Growing," *The Economist*, August 11, 2022. India currently possesses around 160 nuclear warheads, with Pakistan possessing around 165 nuclear warheads.

27. Bruce W. Bennett, Kang Choi, Myong-Hyun Go, Bruce E. Bechtol Jr., Jiyoung Park, Bruce Klingner, and Du-Hyeogn Cha, "Countering the Risks of North Korean Nuclear Weapons," RAND Corporation, April 12, 2021.

28. David E. Sanger and William J. Broad, "Iran Nears an Atomic Milestone," *New York Times*, September 13, 2021. According to an April 2021 State Department report, Iran's expansion of uranium enrichment activities allows it to "enrich more uranium more quickly and to higher levels" and has enough weapons-grade HEU for one nuclear weapon. See Peter Huessy, "Iran Accelerates Nuclear Activities under the Guise of Energy Research," Hudson Institute, September 22, 2022.

29. US Strategic Command and US Space Command, "US Strategic Command and US Space Command SASC Testimony," March 9, 2022.

30. Keith B. Payne, "Multilateral Deterrence: What's New and Why It Matters," National Institute for Public Policy Information Series, no. 522 (May 16, 2022).

31. Keith B. Payne and David J. Trachtenberg, "Deterrence in the Emerging Threat Environment: What Is Different and Why It Matters," National Institute for Public Policy Occasional Paper 2, no. 8 (August 2022).

32. US Strategic Command and US Space Command, "SASC Testimony."

33. John R. Harvey, Franklin C. Miller, Keith B. Payne, Bradley H. Roberts, and Robert M. Soofer, "Assessing the Biden 2022 Nuclear Posture Review," *RealClear Defense*, November 16, 2022.

34. US Department of Defense, "Ballistic Missile Defense Review Report," February 2010.

35. For a good overview of the difficulties presented by hypersonics, see Center for Strategic and International Studies (CSIS), "Complex Air Defense: Countering the Hypersonic Missile Threat," February 9, 2022.

36. James Johnson, "AI, Autonomy, and the Risk of Nuclear War," *War on the Rocks*, July 29, 2022.

37. Vincent Boulanin, Lora Saalman, Petr Topychkanov, Fei Su, and Moa Peldán Carlsson, *Artificial Intelligence, Strategic Stability and Nuclear Risk*, Stockholm International Peace Research Institute, June 2020.

38. Congressional Budget Office (CBO), "Projected Costs of US Nuclear Forces, 2021 to 2030," May 24, 2021.

39. The Congressional Budget Office estimated the ten-year costs of missile defense as part of its report "Costs of Implementing Recommendations of the 2019 Missile Defense Review," CBO Publication 56949, January 13, 2021.

40. Hal Brands and Peter Feaver, "What Are America's Alliances Good For?" US Army War College, *Parameters* 47, no. 2 (Summer 2017): 15–30.

41. Jeffrey W. Hornung, "Japan's Potential Contributions in an East China Sea Contingency," RAND Corporation, December 14, 2020.

42. Oriana Skylar Mastro and Sungmin Cho, "How South Korea Can Contribute to the Defense of Taiwan," *Washington Quarterly* 45, no. 3 (2022): 109–29.

43. Former US Europe Commander Army LTG Ben Hodges in an interview with the author, December 2022.

44. David C. Gompert and Richard L. Kugler, "Rebuilding the Team: How to Get Allies to Do More in Defense of Common Interests," RAND Corporation Issue Paper, January 1, 1996.

45. Donald Rumsfeld, "The National Defense Strategy of the United States of America," US Department of Defense, March 2005.

46. Robert Gates, "The National Defense Strategy of the United States of America," US Department of Defense, June 2008.

47. Barack Obama, "Remarks by President Obama to the People of Estonia," The White House, September 3, 2014.

48. David A. Shlapak and Michael Johnson, "Reinforcing Deterrence on NATO's Eastern Flank: Wargaming the Defense of the Baltics," RAND Corporation, January 29, 2016.

49. The SCSP Defense Panel report discusses the need for Joint All-Domain Command and Control architectures. See SCSP, "Mid-Decade Challenges," 142–43. It also notes that gaps in capabilities across US and allies' forces also make combined operations more difficult.

50. Grant Newsham, "Is Japan Ready for War? Not Yet," One Korea Network, August 25, 2022.

51. Author's conversation with Lieutenant General Wallace "Chip" Gregson, USMC (Ret.). He served as the commander of III Marine Expeditionary Force (2001–03), and later as the commander of Marine Corps Forces Pacific.

52. Hodges interview.

53. Sydney J. Freedberg Jr., "General: US Forces in Europe Missing Three Key Capabilities," Atlantic Council, *NATOSource* (blog), September 25, 2015.

54. Bryant Harris, "Taiwan Is Buying US Weapons, but Washington Isn't Delivering Them," *DefenseNews*, August 25, 2022.

55. Harris, "Taiwan Is Buying."

56. For placing the blame on COVID, see Bryant Harris, "Document Reveals $14 Billion Backlog of US Defense Transfers to Taiwan," *DefenseNews*, April 14, 2022.

57. James Carouso, Thomas Schieffer, Jeffrey Bleich, John Berry, and Arthur Culvahouse, "ITAR Should End for Australia," Center for Strategic and International Studies, December 7, 2022.

58. Carouso et al., "ITAR Should End."

59. For more on this and the discussion of "value arms," see Vasabjit Banerjee and Benjamin Tkach, "The Coming Chinese Weapons Boom," *Foreign Affairs*, October 11, 2022.

60. David Ignatius, "Opinion | How the Algorithm Tipped the Balance in Ukraine," *Washington Post*, December 19, 2022.

61. National Security Commission on Artificial Intelligence, "Final Report," 2021; see chapter 3. Also see Erik Lin-Greenberg, "Allies and Artificial Intelligence: Obstacles to Operations and Decision-Making," *Texas National Security Review*, March 5, 2020.

62. Lin-Greenberg, "Allies and Artificial Intelligence."

63. Zack Cooper and Thomas G. Roberts, "Deterrence in the Last Sanctuary," *RealClear Defense*, January 2, 2018.

64. US Department of Defense, "Quadrennial Defense Review Report," February 6, 2006.

65. There was, however, growing concern among experts. In 2007, members of the Allard Commission argued that without "significant improvements in the leadership and management of national security space programs, US space preeminence will erode 'to the extent that space ceases to provide a competitive national security advantage.'" *Hearings before the Committee on Armed Services, US Senate, on S. 1390 (Department of Defense Authorization for Appropriations for Fiscal Year 2010) Part 7: Strategic Forces*, 111th Cong., 1st Sess. (2009), testimony of Cristina T. Chaplain, Director, Acquisition and Sourcing Management, Government Accountability Office.

66. Sandra Erwin, "Biden's 2023 Defense Budget Adds Billions for US Space Force," *SpaceNews*, March 28, 2022.

67. Defense Innovation Unit, "DOD and New Space New Mexico Conclude 4th Annual Space Conference to Advance Prosperity, Sustainability, and US Space Leadership," press release, June 9, 2022.

68. US Department of Defense, "Summary of the Joint All-Domain Command & Control (JADC2) Strategy," March 2022.

69. Matthew Weinzierl and Mehak Sarang, "The Commercial Space Age Is Here," *Harvard Business Review*, February 12, 2021.

70. This growth of orbital objects will drive a need for more satellite tracking—commercial and government—to help distinguish threats from nonthreats, and to prevent collisions.

71. Defense Intelligence Agency (DIA), "Challenges to Security in Space," 2022.

72. DIA, "Challenges to Security in Space," v.

73. DIA, "Challenges," iii.

74. DIA, "Challenges," iii.

75. This is called the Next-Generation Overhead Persistent Infrared System.

76. Theresa Hitchens, "Space Force Phasing Out Missile Warning from GEO, Will Focus on Lower Orbits," *Breaking Defense*, September 21, 2022.

77. Tyler Way, "Counterspace Weapons 101," Aerospace Security Project, Center for Strategic and International Studies, October 28, 2019.

78. Way, "Counterspace Weapons 101."

79. Daniel Pereira, "Space Security and Offensive and Defensive Counterspace Capabilities," *OODA Loop*, April 21, 2022.

80. US Senate Committee on Armed Services, "Summary of the Fiscal Year 2023 National Defense Authorization Act." The NDAA requires a strategy for the protection of DoD satellites.

81. US Government Accountability Office (GAO), "Space Acquisitions: Changing Environment Presents Continuing Challenges and Opportunities for DOD," GAO-22-105900, April 6, 2022.

82. GAO, "Space Acquisitions."

83. Erwin, "Biden's 2023 Defense Budget."

84. US Government Accountability Office, "Challenges Facing DOD as It Changes Approaches to Space Acquisitions," GAO-16-471T, March 9, 2016. See also GAO, "Space Acquisitions."

85. Barry Watts, "The US Defense Industrial Base: Past, Present and Future," Center for Strategic and Budgetary Assessments, October 15, 2008.

86. Chairman of the Joint Chiefs of Staff, "Joint Vision 2020. America's Military—Preparing for Tomorrow," *Joint Force Quarterly* (Summer 2000): 57–76.

87. Herbert R. McMaster, "Crack in the Foundation: Defense Transformation and the Underlying Assumption of Dominant Knowledge in Future War," US Army War College Research Project, April 7, 2003, available at the Defense Technical Information Center, https://apps.dtic.mil/sti/citations/ADA416172.

88. Note that the implications of protracted war are much larger than the issues addressed in this paper. For instance, there are broader economic and social implications of protracted war. Andrew K. Krepinevich Jr. discusses this in "Protracted Great-Power War: A Preliminary Assessment," Center for a New American Security (CNAS) Defense Program, February 2020.

89. Congressional Budget Office (CBO), "The Economic Effects of Reduced Defense Spending," February 1992.

90. CBO, "Economic Effects," 23–25.

91. Watts, "US Defense Industrial Base."

92. Office of the Under Secretary of Defense for Acquisition and Sustainment, "State of Competition within the Defense Industrial Base," Department of Defense, February 2022.

93. Mackenzie Eaglen, "Defense Budget Peaks in 2019, Underfunding the National Defense Strategy," American Enterprise Institute Report, May 17, 2018. Mackenzie Eaglen has written consistently on this point, and she's right.

94. Mark F. Cancian, "Is the United States Running Out of Weapons to Send to Ukraine?" Center for Strategic and International Studies, September 16, 2022. See also Maiya Clark, "Rapidly Depleting Munitions Stockpiles Point to Necessary Changes in Policy," Heritage Foundation Issue Brief no. 5300, December 20, 2022.

95. This discussion also does not cover measures to protect the DIB, like the Committee on Foreign Investment in the United States, or efforts to ensure that capital that supports key companies is "clean" or trusted.

96. US Government Accountability Office, "Actions Needed to Implement and Monitor DOD's Small Business Strategy," GAO-22-104621, October 2021.

97. Yasmin Tadjdeh, "Special Report: Pentagon Struggles to Attract New Entrants into Industrial Base," *National Defense*, February 4, 2022.

98. The White House, "Building Resilient Supply Chains, Revitalizing American Manufacturing, and Fostering Broad-Based Growth: 100-Day Reviews under Executive Order 14017," a report, June 2021.

99. US Government Accountability Office, "Defense Industrial Base: DOD Should Take Actions to Strengthen Its Risk Mitigation Approach," GAO-22-104154, July 2022.

100. US Government Accountability Office (GAO), "Naval Shipyards: Ongoing Challenges Could Jeopardize Navy's Ability to Improve Shipyards," GAO-22-105993, May 10, 2022.

101. James Foggo, "Navy Shipyard Optimization Must Include a Digital Backbone," *Breaking Defense*, January 6, 2023.

102. GAO, "Naval Shipyards."

103. Foggo, "Navy Shipyard Optimization."

104. McKinsey on the manufacturing industry found that leveraging digital technology drove 15 to 50 percent value gains in cost reduction and efficiency; see Ewelina Gregolinska, Rehana Khanam, Frédéric Lefort, and Prashanth Parthasarathy, "Capturing the True Value of Industry 4.0," McKinsey & Company, April 13, 2022. Note that the need for advanced approaches is not new. Over a decade ago, defense experts associated with the National Academy of Sciences urged the DoD to adopt more modern manufacturing approaches to reduce costs and sustain weapons systems more efficiently.

105. Ronald O'Rourke, "Multiyear Procurement (MYP) and Block Buy Contracting in Defense Acquisition: Background and Issues for Congress," Congressional Research Service Report R41909, updated December 21, 2022.

106. Mackenzie Eaglen and Bill Greenwalt, "Multiyear Contracts Could Solve Plenty of Pentagon Problems," *DefenseNews*, September 28, 2022.

107. Eaglen and Greenwalt, "Multiyear Contracts."

108. Bojan Pancevski, "Europe Is Rushing Arms to Ukraine but Running Out of Ammo," *Wall Street Journal*, December 22, 2022.

109. Pancevski, "Europe Is Rushing Arms."

110. Clark, "Rapidly Depleting Munitions Stockpiles."

111. Krepinevich, "Protracted Great-Power War," 1.

112. Under Secretary of Defense for Acquisition and Technology, "A DoD Handbook: Assessing Defense Industrial Capabilities," US Department of Defense, April 1996.

113. Watts, "US Defense Industrial Base." The Watts report is one example of an excellent study—done fifteen years ago. The DoD's Defense Industrial Base assessments have been done since the early 1990s and cite many of the problems we are still discussing today.

114. SCSP, "Mid-Decade Challenges," 20.

115. Office of the Secretary of Defense (Acquisition & Sustainment) Industrial Policy, "Fiscal Year 2020 Industrial Capabilities: Report to Congress," US Department of Defense, January 2021, https://apps.dtic.mil/sti/trecms/pdf/AD 1121517.pdf.

116. Trae Stephens, "Rebooting the Arsenal of Democracy," *War on the Rocks*, June 6, 2022.

117. Jim Mattis, "Summary of the 2018 National Defense Strategy," US Department of Defense, January 2018, 10.

118. Mattis, "2018 National Defense Strategy," 10.

119. SCSP, "Mid-Decade Challenges," 43.

120. US Government Accountability Office (GAO), "DOD Space Acquisitions: Including Users Early and Often in Software Development Could Benefit Programs," GAO-19-136, March 2019.

121. GAO, "DOD Space Acquisitions."

122. US Government Accountability Office, "Artificial Intelligence: Status of Developing and Acquiring Capabilities for Weapon Systems," GAO-22-104765, February 2022.

123. John Grady, "Hyten: US 'Not in a Very Good Position' Due to Chinese and Russian Missile Capabilities," *USNI News*, February 24, 2021.

124. US Government Accountability Office, "Nuclear Weapons Cybersecurity: NNSA Should Fully Implement Foundational Cybersecurity Risk Management Practices," GAO-22-104195, September 2022. It is important to note that in 2019, this system, the Strategic Automated Command and Control System (SACCS), was updated to no longer utilize floppy disks; however, it did take the DoD three years from the publishing of the 2016 GAO study to replace technology from the 1970s. See Liam Stack, "Update Complete: US Nuclear Weapons No Longer Need Floppy Disks," *New York Times*, October 24, 2019.

125. US Government Accountability Office, "Information Technology: Federal Agencies Need to Address Aging Legacy Systems," GAO-16-468, May 2016.

126. US Government Accountability Office (GAO), "Nuclear Triad: DOD and DOE Face Challenges Mitigating Risks to US Deterrence Efforts," GAO-21-210, May 2021.

127. GAO, "Nuclear Triad."

128. Carl Rehberg, "Integrated Air and Missile Defense: Early Lessons from the Russia-Ukraine War," Center for Strategic and Budgetary Assessments, June 10, 2022.

129. Bryan Clark and Dan Patt, "Exploiting the Fast-Follower Advantage," Hudson Institute, November 23, 2022.

130. Clark and Patt, "Fast-Follower Advantage," 47.

131. Courtney Albon and Joe Gould, "Top Pentagon Officials Met with Industry Executives about Hypersonics. What Comes Next?," *DefenseNews*, February 6, 2022.

132. John F. Cogan, *The High Cost of Good Intentions* (Stanford, CA: Stanford University Press, 2017).

133. Mackenzie Eaglen, "The Paradox of Scarcity in a Defense Budget of Largesse," American Enterprise Institute Report, July 18, 2022. This can be attributed to prepaid bills and utilities, inflation, and locked-in operations and maintenance expenses.

134. Peter Bacon, Eric Chewning, Chris Daehnick, Jess Harrington, and Nikola Popovic, "The $773 Billion Question: Inflation's Impact on Defense Spending," McKinsey & Company, March 28, 2022.

National Security Strategy

With Michael O'Hanlon, Admiral Mike Mullen, and H.R. McMaster,
Moderated by Lieutenant Colonel James M. Harrington

LIEUTENANT COLONEL JAMES M. HARRINGTON: Let's start with Michael O'Hanlon.

MICHAEL O'HANLON: I'm mostly aboard with what we've heard this morning, but I'm worried about the broader debate going too far on talking about the US-China relationship in adversarial terms. I don't want to push them closer to Russia. I don't want to push our allies away from us because they think we're too locked in for a looming fight. But I agree with basically everything I've heard on the defense preparation side. And so, in that sense, I'll leave it there on the threat question.

But I wanted to talk about force sizing and how that relates to the overall purpose of the conference because it's a crucial point and it's actually very interesting. I'm delighted that H.R. [McMaster] is lined up to come in the discussion soon after me, after Admiral [Mike] Mullen, and with Secretary [Jim] Mattis here. I'm aware that in the last two national defense strategies of 2018 and 2022, we really did not talk that specifically or explicitly about force sizing as a function of which scenarios we are getting ready for or the operational plans that we're preparing. And that is probably a good idea for a lot of reasons, but I think it's worth just being explicit in this group about what the construct was. As best I understand it, and this is all at an unclassified level, but if you go back to some of the statements that people made in testimony or General [David] Goldfein made when he was chief of staff of the Air Force to explain the force sizing that's behind the 2018 National Defense Strategy and the 2022 National Defense Strategy, essentially what they said, and I hope people will correct me if I've got it wrong, is we want to protect the homeland. We all know our military is not fundamentally sized and structured for that purpose, but there are still some requirements in missile and air defense and so forth. That's one.

Maintain a strong nuclear deterrent while we're doing other things around the world with conventional forces. That's two. And again, that's a specific part of the force structure, but it's crucial. Defeat Russia or China. Deter North Korea and Iran and maintain momentum simultaneously in the fight against transnational violent extremism or global terrorism.

So it's those five things, but it's very interesting. The simultaneity question is, to my mind, not extremely explicitly considered, discussed, or clarified. I know Secretary Mattis, Lt. General McMaster, and others were writing your strategies in 2017 and early 2018, just as you were also working your tail off the rest of your time to make sure we didn't go to war against North Korea when we probably came closer to war against North Korea than at any time since at least the 1970s, maybe the 1950s. So there is an irony in the fact that we were trying to prioritize Russia and China, and we still are, and yet the more plausible fight at that moment was probably North Korea. And I'm not disagreeing with anything. I'm just noting the irony. This is sort of an ongoing tension in US force planning that we always come up with somewhat contrived, artificial, and inaccurate ways of considering the simultaneity question because we can't know the future, and what we're primarily trying to do is to maximize deterrence.

But it still strikes me there is this tension. I have only one modest suggestion about what the importance of this is for our future force planning and budgeting that I'll finish in just a second. But I do want to just again go over the five bases for force planning and invite anybody, including Chairman [Mac] Thornberry and others who have had a central hand in this, to disagree with me if they think I've got it wrong. But again, I'm quoting General Goldfein and some others who have gone public: defend the homeland, maintain nuclear deterrence, defeat Russia or China, deter Iran and North Korea and presumably also Russia and China, whichever one you're not worried about fighting at that moment, and then finally maintain momentum in the counterterrorism struggle. That is sort of four missions at the same time because, with North Korea and Iran, we say we're deterring the other ones. We're either doing things, fighting, or maintaining a very viable capability to defend the homeland and maintain nuclear deterrence.

I think that's probably the right way to think about force sizing. Interestingly, it doesn't lead to any big changes in the force structure. Maybe that's why people settled on it to some extent because they didn't really want the focus to be on changing the force structure. And today's conversation has not been primarily about changing the force structure. It has been about logistics, basing, survivability, space, C4ISR [command, control, communications, computers, intelligence, surveillance, and reconnaissance], and targeting. I think those are the more important areas of emphasis. But if you talk too much about the simultaneity question and the scenarios, you probably wind up driving the force requirements upward from a 1.35 million active-duty force, from a 300-ship navy, from a 312-squadron air force. In fact, we have heard the navy and the air force both say they want a substantially bigger force structure. The navy still wants 355 ships. Now they're starting to add to that number with unmanned vessels.

The air force under General Goldfein said they wanted to go to 386 squadrons from 312 because I think General Goldfein realized the navy did better at finding a single metric that people could rally around and understand, so he wanted to get into that conversation, too. But we actually haven't made that much progress toward growing the navy or the air force. I'm not sure we should, but to the extent we have these goals, those are still sort of the goals on record, expanding each of those services by roughly 20 percent in terms of force structure. So my advice and my bottom line are I think growing the force structures in those ways would probably not be the best use of our resources. We should focus on the agenda that has been talked about today, C4ISR, survivability, logistics, basing, allied interoperability, command and control, and cyber and intelligence.

But we should remind our potentially skeptical fellow Americans when they wonder why we're clamoring for such big defense budgets that actually, as a community, most of us are not asking for a bigger military; 1.35 million is small by historical standards and by international standards. What we're really having a debate about is quality resilience, lethality, survivability, and deployability in this contested environment.

So I guess I'm concluding on the point partly to think about our role in the debate, this conference, and this community. And I think one thing we should bear in mind when we ask Americans pretty soon to sustain a trillion-dollar defense budget because we're pretty close to that, and we'll get there soon, is in the context of debt limit showdowns and other concerns about the deficit and the fiscal situation that you spoke so eloquently about this morning,

Kiran [Sridhar]. We should remind people we're actually not asking, for the most part, for a bigger military.

Some of you would probably want one, and some of the specific things we've asked for today about supply vessels might add a few tens of thousands here or a couple of thousand there. But for the most part, we're talking about improving quality, lethality, survivability, and resilience, and those are crucial. We are not actually talking about being able to fight and win multiple wars at the same time because that is not the force planning construct that is behind either of the last two national defense strategies, and not enough people understand that. Thanks.

HARRINGTON: Next is the former chairman of the Joint Chiefs, Admiral Mike Mullen.

ADMIRAL MIKE MULLEN: Thank you, James. One of the questions that is part of this panel is: Are we positioned for two MRCs [major regional conflicts]? That really gets to Michael [O'Hanlon]'s discussion. We are not positioned for that. When we were positioned for that in the nineties, we weren't really positioned for that, either. Those of us who went through those plans back then, basically, you could do one and hold on the other, whether it was Korea or Russia in Europe. So we have a long way to go, and even at 355 and 386 ships, it's going to take us a long time to get there. In fact, having been involved in building the number of ships for the navy for quite some time, we were well on our way in the early 2000s to a navy of about 220 ships. I mean, we were taking them out incredibly fast, and it was an in-depth analysis over a fairly extensive period of time, done by a number of CNOs [chiefs of naval operations] that at least started to put a floor on that and allowed us to start to build and hold what we have, which has been about the best that we can do.

We can't get to two simultaneous MRCs in the near term in any way. I guess one of the questions is whether we need to do that for the long term.

In terms of the strategic environment, my own view is Russia and China are together. I have feared them being together for the last twenty years. They're together. The idea that we could start to break them apart, I think, is fool's gold at this point. It isn't going to happen, and we have to, at least from a planning standpoint, make that assumption. Right now, Xi Jinping is pretty close to making a decision to help Putin with weapons, which is sort of a big leap from the standpoint of what's going on in Ukraine and what he hasn't done up to this point, just to give you one indication. I think February 24,

2022 [the day Russia invaded Ukraine], changed the national security struc-ture globally for about as far as I can see into the future, and all planning needs to essentially emanate from that.

My own personal view is I think it's the most dangerous time since 1962. Focused on Russia, Ukraine, China, and Taiwan, Gary [Roughead] men-tioned Turkey. I just never want to count them out. I've sat with [Turkish president Recep Tayyip] Erdoğan. Erdoğan is messianic. There are few people I've been with in my life where you look at them and sit with them, and you can kind of see to the back of their head. He is one, and he is going to play for a long time.

There isn't a European I've spoken with who doesn't think that Russia and Ukraine aren't existential to the continent. We are in a war on the continent, which has been something we have feared forever on the continent for centu-ries, not just in recent times.

One of the things I hope we don't get and that we don't lose, despite the criticisms that we have of the acquisition system and the weapons systems that we develop, is when you look at the performance of these systems in Ukraine right now; the HIMARS piece, I'll just use that one. It has been pretty extraordinary. They were not easy to develop, fund, and create, but they have performed magnificently, and we should not completely criticize a system that has produced that. My own view is Putin is undaunted. I don't know how long it's going to go. I didn't know at the beginning, and I have no idea how long it's going to last. He is going to stay. He will see it through and be alive to see it through until whatever version of it ends. We need to plan on that accordingly. Clearly, we're going to have more US forces in Europe and in Eastern Europe, and we need to do that.

Putin has a historical view. Gary mentioned the empires. I think that's really important. We are particularly lousy at history. And Michael said this early, we shouldn't just be talking to ourselves. We need to educate the American people on history. We need to educate ourselves on history in these parts of the world that are relevant to the security challenges and, quite frankly, the economic challenges that we have globally.

I actually took a trip to Taiwan. I'm not unfamiliar with the Western Pacific. I spent a lot of my life there, but I took a trip to Taiwan with a bipartisan del-egation in March. It's the first time I'd been there since I was a junior officer in 1970.

And what I learned in a very, very brief visit there was pretty extraordinary in terms of the detail of what is really going on in that country. I will say in the four years that I was chairman, I spent not one minute on Taiwan. And so this is all in many ways for the national security apparatus new because none of us did that because we had a war in Iraq and Afghanistan, and we had a pretty significant terrorism threat. That has shifted now. So we are learning as we go, and I think the point has been made. It's a big ocean out there. It always has been. Those of us who have operated out there know that, and that the logistics issue is absolutely vital.

Taiwan is extraordinarily complex, as actually were Iraq and Afghanistan, about which we knew very little before we went in. We need to learn more. More specifically, when I was there, 75 percent were for democracy. It's twenty-four million people. It's a thriving population. It's well led politically, although they do have politics. And the president just left as the head of the party, put in the heir apparent, if you will, who is the vice president, who has already said, "We need a trade agreement, and we need strategic clarity." That was his introduction to me when I met him.

I'm a little more confident that TSMC [Taiwan Semiconductor Manufacturing Company] can provide a deterrent to both sides because if they tank, our economy tanks, China's economy tanks, and the global economy tanks, and I think that has huge deterrent potential with respect to Xi Jinping and the whole idea of trying to understand how he's thinking and that Chinese perspective is absolutely critical.

The Chinese-US relationship is at the worst point it has been since 1972. The whole idea of the Bali meeting was to try to put a floor under it. And then, at least, that is the claim. Whether it happens or not or whether it actually continues to move in the wrong direction is an open question. We don't have an embassy in Taiwan, but we've got a group at AIT [American Institute in Taiwan] that's four hundred strong. It's bigger than I don't know how many embassies, but it's a big outfit that knows a lot. How do you extract from that their level of knowledge about what's going on?

The FMS [Foreign Military Sales] system: How do you get them ready? I mean, anybody that has worked with the FMS system and you come to me and say, "Now we're going to take care of Taiwan with FMS." It's a broken system. It has been broken for decades, and they have never been prioritized. Unless Secretary Lloyd Austin has it on his desk and checks on it once a month to start to move the FMS system in a way that helps them, it is not going to provide them with the capability. The will to fight in Ukraine has been instructive. That is certainly not new in history. But will the Taiwanese actually have that as well? I think that's an open question. What I worry about is we're drifting into war. Tensions are so high, and we're both accusing each other of coercing each other.

To balance that, you have to move up the ladder again and create more capability and create more support. And what's the trip wire? When Xi Jinping, who I actually do believe doesn't have the desire to go in now, but when Xi Jinping believes Taiwan is going to be independent, he's going to go in. There is not a Chinese leader that wouldn't do that if he thinks that's the declaration. And that's something that we have to, I think, continue to support.

The allies piece. As I listened to this with Jim [Mattis] and H.R. and Gary here, who were colleagues of mine back in the day, we should remember that when I left the job in 2011, there were forty-nine countries with troops in Afghanistan. That's a lot of political will. That's a lot of support. I'm not arguing one way or another on Afghanistan. The point is allies will come in, and you'd be amazed at how they figure out how to fight despite the high-level interoperability challenges. They have been actually remarkably good. You don't want to wait until that point to have it happen. But the political support, the economic support, particularly in that part of the world with Japan and Australia and South Korea and those kinds of things are going to be very, very important.

Just a couple of things from the US perspective. One is Taiwan. And I haven't even heard this phrase. Is Taiwan a vital national interest? And that's an open question as far as I'm concerned. We certainly haven't made it that way. And if we're going to go to war, and this is the Iraq piece for me, I believe the American people have to make this decision. The American people can't find Taiwan on a map right now, just as they couldn't find Afghanistan before we went there. It is up to the political leadership to basically make the case that it is or it isn't and not then just, "Okay, we've decided to go. We'll throw the military in here, and we'll see how that goes." That's an absolutely key question.

Just a couple of other thoughts about the budget, and I know that's what we're talking about. One of the most ancient and antiquated rules is that we'll just divide this up to one-third, one-third, one-third to each service. And that has killed us over the long term. How do you change that? The services all argued for that as well. The only place that can change is from the Hill. And the only group that can change that is the two committees. So we don't have the right people in the room, quite frankly, to have this discussion. With

Chairman Thornberry here, that's one. But I have found in my career, if you don't get the appropriators on board, you are having a conversation with nobody. And they are the ones that have to make this happen.

It isn't going to happen from the building. It has got to happen from the Hill, and they need to be partners in this and work over time. That construct of one-third, one-third, one-third could change.

The space force is new, almost as new as the Taiwan problem, quite frankly. And so, how do we energize support and have them make a difference in terms of the assets that we now know are there? Ten years ago, you couldn't talk about weaponizing space. Now it's weaponized. It has been weaponized. And so, how do we counter that with this brand-new national force while the other services also try to survive?

Keith [Alexander] talked about being with me in whenever that was; 2006 or 2007. I looked at the Iran war plan in 2006. This was in the navy. I sat with my cyber guy. It wasn't cyber at the time, I think it was C4ISR or something, and we started to talk about the war. I said, "So tell me how this starts." And this three-star who was working for me looked at me, and he said, "CNO, this has already started. The fight is already on, as far as I'm concerned. It's on in cyber. It's on in info. It's on in economics. It's how do you transition or how do you never go kinetic in all of this?" And I think the deterrence piece is critical, and I asked the question in 2005, "Okay, what are we doing? The wall is down."

I hate the term "peace dividend." It hurt us badly, and it was widely used. The wall is down. What does deterrence look like in the twenty-first century? I don't think we know. There can be a lot of work done and should be done to get that to the uniform leaders on what it means now. Some of you, I'm sure, have looked at Taiwan, the CSIS [Center for Strategic and International Studies] thing, the war game that they ran. One of the things, and Gary mentioned this, we haven't been bloodied in a long time at sea. But one of the things that was so underestimated and underresourced wasn't just logistics in Iraq and Afghanistan, it was medical. Nobody knows where the money is in medical. There is no uniform that's in charge of it. And when you talk about the thousands of casualties that are going to happen in that fight, that's not something you can make up overnight. And it gets short shrift in every discussion.

When I've seen jointness work, sadly, is when people are dying. All barriers come down. The sense of urgency that's associated with jointness as we fight together while fighting with our coalition allies, that sense of urgency is right. The challenge is how do you create a sense of urgency without people dying? The programs, the leadership, they make the changes before people are actually dying because all the barriers come down. And that sense of urgency is what we need to do now with respect to this budget. I have, for a long time, over the last decade, said the Pentagon has got enough money. It's a matter of where it is and how are we allocating it. I am now no longer there. That $858 billion [Pentagon topline budget] isn't going to be enough to do what we need to do within the system that we have. Can we dig it out and make it more efficient?

Absolutely. But we don't have a lot of time right now with where we are in the world. So that sense of urgency and this effort, Mike, that you put on, I think, is hugely important.

Lastly, on intel, listen, and it was mentioned, but I thought what [Jacob "Jake"] Sullivan did, and I'm sure it was Jake, I thought his breaking out that intel before Ukraine was an act of God, quite frankly, if you've ever been on the inside to try to get intel to give up any intel, make it public, and declassify it. The question is, how do we do that in the future? What does that mean with respect to China? Right now, should we be doing some of that very specifically? And I just want to give him and whoever did it, but I think Jake was obviously the one that made it happen, an awful lot of credit because it made a huge difference in the calculations, specifically with respect to Russia. Thanks.

HARRINGTON: Over to former national security advisor H.R. McMaster. Looking forward to your opening remarks.

H.R. MCMASTER: Thank you, James. And thank you for authoring the two great papers, Nadia [Schadlow] and Michael [O'Hanlon]. I think what they do is help us think more clearly about the challenges we're facing and challenge the assumptions that we might be buying into. Just to answer the questions here that were posed to the panel, what is the most important of many challenges facing the US? It is that we don't know *how* to think about a future war. We don't think clearly about the problem of future war. Should the military be prepared to wage conflict in two contingencies simultaneously? I think yes. Right? Because we're not going to get to pick. I mean, we might want to win, hold, win. We might want to deal with only one thing at a time. But I think what we're seeing is the interconnected nature of the threats that we're facing today.

And we could maybe talk more about that and the really very high potential, I think, for horizontal escalation of conflicts. Do deterrents have to be from the military, or can principal adversaries be deterred by economic and diplomatic tools? I think the answer is that hard power matters, okay? And I think we've seen this in Ukraine.

Certainly, it's important to integrate all elements of national power to have a deterrent effect. But without the military instrument, without military forces forward positioned who are capable of operating at sufficient scale and for ample duration to ensure that that enemy fails or cannot accomplish his objectives at an acceptable cost, you're not going to deter. We've seen that with Ukraine clearly.

And then finally, what capabilities does the US military need in order to deter conflict in the twenty-first century?

And what I'd like to do to answer that is to propose a framework for thinking and learning about future armed conflict. And then, what are our gaps and opportunities that we can act on in the defense budget to build a military capable of deterring and, if necessary, fighting and winning a war?

So, first of all, why don't we think clearly about future war? I think its because we tend to stress change over continuity. The historian Carl Becker said that memory of the past and anticipation of the future should walk hand in hand in a happy way. And we can convince ourselves that mainly because of technological advances that the next war is going to be fundamentally different from all those that have gone before it. Some argue that the next war will be fast, cheap, efficient, and waged from standoff range. And so, as we see in Ukraine and as we have seen in our own experiences in Iraq and Afghanistan, that's not the case.

[Halford] Mackinder and [Nicholas] Spykman would recognize this world today from a geostrategic perspective as we face two major powers, revisionist and revanchist powers, on the Eurasian land mass. So how can we maybe think more clearly about future war?

I think we have to study war and warfare in the way Michael Howard suggested, in width, in depth, and in context to look at conflict over time, so we identify those continuities, human continuities in the nature of war. What were those qualitative elements of Russian combat power or lack thereof that many analysts missed before the war?

So in width and in depth, look at what's going on in Ukraine. Look at our experiences in Iraq and Afghanistan. Look at the 2006 Israeli fight in southern Lebanon. So the tidy outlines of war dissolve, and you recognize the complex causality of outcomes in war and the full range of combat capabilities you need to succeed in combat. And then in context, obviously, to recognize that war is really waged to overachieving political outcomes. Russia has a political outcome in mind. The Taliban had a political outcome in mind in Afghanistan, and we kept saying that there was no military solution in Afghanistan, but hey, the Taliban came up with one, and it was tied to their overall political aim. So pay attention to those continuities in the nature of war.

Consider war and defense strategy in width, depth, and context, and make sure that the idealized vision of future war is consistent with continuities in the nature of war. We can learn from when we got it wrong in terms of thinking about future war. And Secretary Mattis was, I think, the lead dissident in our joint force in the 1990s when the orthodoxy of the revolution in military affairs and catchphrases like rapid, decisive operations were all the rage, right? Who's going to be against that? Are you for ponderous indecisive operations? And all this stuff looked great on PowerPoint slides, and it was completely disconnected from the nature of war and continuities in the nature of war. And we forgot what Nadia reminded us of with her book, that the consolidation of gains to get to sustainable political outcomes, that's never been an optional phase of war. But we want it to take the George Costanza approach to war and just leave on a high note, right?

Well, we wound up in Afghanistan and Iraq for a hell of a lot longer than we thought we were going to be there. So I think we have to ensure that we are considering both the continuities and changes in the character of warfare and continuities in the nature of war. And what are those continuities? I think there are four of them. And these should be almost evaluation criteria for national security strategy and national defense strategy. Okay, war's an extension of politics. It's like the GEICO commercial: "Everybody knows that," right? [Carl von] Clausewitz said that. But again, what that means is that there has to be a consolidation of gains. War is human. People fight for the same reasons Thucydides identified 2,500 years ago: fear, honor, and interest. And we see how those reasons are driving the will to fight among Ukrainians and have hindered Russia's real ability to fight because there isn't that rationale, that emotional drive to fight in Ukraine.

And then, of course, war is uncertain. War is uncertain because of the interaction of opposites, as Clausewitz would have said it, but it's uncertain because you're interacting with an enemy, multiple enemies. But we also have to recognize that we're interacting with potential enemies in between conflicts. So when we develop a future force capability based on stealth, for example, or some other kind of capability, we have to recognize that our future enemies get to develop countermeasures. There's never been a silver bullet in war—the machine gun, the tank, the antitank missiles, the submarine and the sonar, the bomber, the radar. And so in the nineties, remember, everybody talked about leap-ahead capabilities. When somebody starts talking about leap ahead, you should leap out the window, because what that means is they're setting us up for vulnerabilities. We're not engaged in developing the range of capabilities that joint forces need to play what is essentially the game of rock, paper, scissors, which is joint warfare.

If you don't have one of those three components, if you can't operate together with a range of capabilities, some of them older, some of them newer, then you're not going to be able to seize, retain the initiative, and fight and win in war. And finally, war is a contest of wills, and this gets to Admiral Mullen's point. It has a lot to do with national leadership explaining the rationale for the war. But that also gets to the human dimension of conflict and the need to sustain will and [create] cohesive, confident, and tough, resilient teams, which I think we might be losing focus on, too. We could talk about this as well from a range of perspectives. So the first thing I think we have to do is to think more clearly about future work.

So how can we do that? How can we drive that thinking and tie it to the budgeting process? First, it's through the defense planning scenarios, which are terrible. I haven't seen them for a number of years, but I bet they're still terrible. And some of the problems with them is they lend themselves to just being a targeting exercise. They don't take into consideration these continuities in the nature of war. I mean we target the enemy with our weapons and munition systems, and then we just call it a day and look at the ledger. How we did, do we have enough systems in place? And then also the scenarios don't account for simultaneity and for the geographic range that a conflict may take on. I think it's worth pointing out the Chinese have a base on the south side of the Bab al-Mandeb [Strait]. The Iranians have proxy forces on the north side of the Bab al-Mandeb.

And do you think that Iran would not take advantage of US preoccupation with the conflict with China to maybe do what it wanted to do in the Strait of Hormuz, for example, or what they did in the eighties? So I think that the defense planning scenarios don't allow for that kind of simultaneity, which gets to one of the questions posed here. And I think we have to recognize that our enemies, potential enemies, and adversaries now will at least take advantage of our preoccupation in one area to pursue their interests at our expense in another. And so the defense planning scenarios, make them not targeting exercises, make them consistent with the nature of war. The second part thing we can do to think more clearly is to lay a strong conceptual foundation for joint warfare. Often these concepts, Joint Vision 2010, Joint Vision 2020, look at those documents. They're, in retrospect, silly documents.

And why were they silly? They were silly because they didn't recognize that there are two fundamental ways to fight wars, asymmetrically and stupidly. This is Conrad Crane's observation, and what our enemies have done, potential enemies have done, in this time when we were pursuing the revolution of military affairs or whatever offset we're on now, is not to develop those same capabilities but to find ways to take apart what they saw as the differential advantages we were trying to achieve in the development of the future joint force. So the interactive nature, again with potential enemies, must be considered when prioritizing defense capabilities.

The third recommendation is to establish a framework for learning. I think what the Department of Defense should do is what the joint force did years ago. And I think Secretary Mattis might have pioneered this at Joint Forces Command, to reinvigorate the joint warfighting challenges, bring those back, and I think we ought to just limit them to twenty first-order challenges. For example, how to sustain freedom of movement and action for the joint force at the end of extended and contested lines of communication.

Just pose that question: How to maintain a high degree of situational understanding against elusive and capable enemy forces in restricted and complex terrain? Just ask the questions. Then we can work on those problems, those challenges together across the joint force, and we can develop integrated interim solutions. We're never going to solve these problems forever because potential enemies will adapt as well.

Interim solutions to those challenges combine multiple technologies. As we know, there's no silver-bullet technology. Any military innovation is based on a combination of several technologies along with new doctrine on how to employ those technologies combined with training and leader development. And so the framework for learning that the warfighting challenges provide allows us to assess how well are we doing in the joint force in coming up with an interim solution to each challenge. Who's lagging behind? What do we need to accelerate? And I think that then you can begin to see and audit the budget back to what you're trying to achieve in terms of your warfighting capability. So, third, bring back a framework for learning in a focused, sustained, and collaborative manner.

And finally, what we're going to hear more about today is we have to be able to implement. We have to be able to implement these solutions. Our presenters have already alluded to the major impediments to innovating within the cycle of technology and fielding these capabilities as rapidly as we can.

To close, as we look at our ability to deter and fight and win, we obviously have to look at the range of capabilities we need to develop and field the force. But we also should consider the capacity and the size of the force. I think the armed forces are too small. I mean, we have a problem now already with recruiting to make them larger, but I think that's also a leadership issue in terms of asking young Americans to volunteer and helping to bring in the most talented of our young people. And the capacity actually matters a lot. We can talk more about that, but I do think that the assumption on which we've been developing forces has been that we can trade off capacity for more and more exquisite, expensive, and fewer weapons systems.

Mackenzie [Eaglen]'s done an amazing job on this. Her paper ought to be read by everybody. And then, of course, it's readiness as well as capabilities and capacity. You can look good on paper. You could look good in the May Day parade if you're the Russian army. But it turns out they can't fight competently. They can't sustain themselves, they're not well trained, they're not disciplined, they don't have leaders in place. So anyway, I think as we look at the budget, audit the budget, the way to audit it is to get back to the capabilities we need, those interim solutions, and to look at the range of funding lines, a whole bunch of them will be relevant to that particular interim solution, to that challenge that we have to overcome. And then you can really evaluate the degree to which you're adequately invested to ensure the force has the capabilities, capacity, and readiness level necessary to deter conflict and then, if necessary, to fight and win.

HARRINGTON: Questions? Comments?

ROGER ZAKHEIM: Thank you, I really enjoyed this discussion of the papers. Because time is limited, my comments may come across as glib and provocative, but that's only because of the limitation in time. Wish I had more time to develop them.

First, Michael, I'm glad you pointed out the force planning construct and the continuity between the defense strategies of the Trump and Biden administrations. One area where I disagree, and I think it follows what H.R. just spoke about, is our force is too small. It is unable to carry out what the strategy calls for, full stop. It simply can't do it. The simultaneity issue is actually focusing on an important decision that Trump's strategy made, which was we're not going to get into at all. I'm talking about today's force measured against the win one and hold another and deter today and prevail tomorrow. We're not even close, and it's getting worse, as H.R. pointed out.

So all these other things that have been discussed are additive to the force that we have today or to the strategy we have today. And even this, we have this huge gap between the force and the strategy that we talk about later that is not being addressed, actually getting worse with an army down to 450,000, less than three hundred ships, and the other numbers with respect to the air force and just the three services. So it's truly a hot mess.

Second, on the point about Ukraine and deterrence by disclosure. Admiral, I just don't see it. I mean, the measure for deterrence is whether the tanks do or do not roll in, and they rolled in. So I just have difficulty seeing how that ultimately helped or addressed the primary function of deterrence, which is preventing someone from going to armed conflict. The Russians did.

Last point, Admiral, I was pleased to hear the shift in your thinking, unfortunately, because the security environment has deteriorated so much. But I think we should all agree here today that it is no longer a national security imperative to make reductions to our deficit through cutting national defense. Let's just all agree. Now the politicians may decide that we have to cut defense. I'm hopeful that the great people at this conference will work hard to prevent that from happening. But the notion that people around this table could advocate that our national security is enhanced by taking defense dollars to reduce the deficit is of a different day and is absolutely not what anyone who's looking at the national security landscape should be advocating or be okay with. And no doubt they'll be elected officials who will try to make that argument, and we should hold them to account for that. Thanks.

HARRINGTON: Any of the panel members want to address the comments?

NADIA SCHADLOW: I just want to echo Roger's point about the US use of intelligence in the war. Initially, I thought it would be heretical to question the impact of the release of it. Now I feel better about doing so. It has been pointed out very consistently by the administration that the release of intelligence was very, very important. But I don't completely understand. There were maybe some operational implications of that release, maybe we were able to move satellites as a result and do certain things in different ways, and it might have bolstered, a little bit, the political will of the allies to get them to take Russian actions seriously. But the operational implications of the release of the intelligence are still unclear to me for the reasons Roger pointed out. It did not deter Russia.

MCMASTER: I think just to defend Admiral Mullen, I think what the intelligence release did do is it took away Putin's narrative that this was a war of NATO aggression. But I think the point that Nadia makes is really important, and it's relevant, too: hard power matters. And if you look at the withdrawal of our forces out of the Black Sea, that was a mistake. We did that because we thought we had to maybe allay Putin's security concerns. We listed all the things we weren't going to do and all the things we weren't going to provide the Ukrainians. Ambiguity in adversaries' calculation of the decision-making process is a good thing for deterrence. And I think we removed a lot of that ambiguity for Putin and, in many ways, in retrospect, essentially inadvertently green-lighted the war.

But the reason I think this is worth talking about just for a moment is it is relevant to deter China as well, vis-à-vis Taiwan. And this is why I'm not a huge fan of removing strategic ambiguity. I think Admiral Mullen said, for example, the American people are going to have a say in that through their representatives in Congress. So even if we were to say now, hey, a hundred percent we're going to defend Taiwan, is that really true? It depends on the circumstances and the American people's will. So anyway, I think ambiguity is a good thing in terms of deterrence. We didn't have that in February of last year.

MULLEN: Just briefly, I mean your comments with respect to the two MRC pieces or the win one and hold on the other. But part of that, and this goes back obviously decades for me to when that was a clear focus in the nineties of what we're supposed to do, and then you sort of fast-forward to this, and the forces are too small, and you look at production lines which are gone, you look at munitions we can't get, you look at how we stopped at some level. Even our own munition stocks right now are in trouble.

And there's an underlying piece, and this is what I think has to change and this is up to the political leadership, I think. There's an underlying piece to me that says, are we really serious about thinking we're going to go to war, or are we just building what we think we might use? Which isn't enough to have a deterrent effect, quite frankly. And I'm not arguing deterrence was great. Clearly, deterrence to Putin, who's a tough nut to figure out, didn't work. It needs to work, in my view. It needs to work with Xi. We need to create the strategic ambiguity. We need to create doubt in his mind for as long as he can look into the future that today's not the right day and do an awful lot in that regard. And I don't think we are doing that in any way, shape, or form.

And then the other comments, the revolution in military affairs, leap-ahead technology, transformation, those are deadly words in terms of getting to the future, and you've got to get to the future. Clearly, we need to develop those capabilities, but everybody runs to those pots of money because people put money in it, and money does drive how the building works in that regard, and the services work, and you don't end up with capabilities.

And then lastly, back to the American people, I believe in the system. I believe we need to go to war if the American people think we should go to war. One of the things that I learned, or what I've argued for Roger, is we need to not increase the revolution in military affairs. I want the strength of the army, which went from 485,000 to 585,000 down to 450,000. And it's natural for the services to always want more force structure. That's how we react. My reaction actually coming out of Iraq and Afghanistan was the opposite for the army. We need to decrease the size of the army to about, I don't know what the number is, 350,000, and this has nothing to do with money. So that the next time we go to war, the president has to convince the American people we're going to go to war and that we'll have to call up a half a million kids to go to war. These wars last longer than three months or six months, they seem to go ten years at a crack.

And thus there's a discussion at every dinner table in the country with an eighteen-year-old son or daughter about is this something we want to do? And that the president and the political leadership bring the American people to the decision, which then goes to Congress to say, yes, we should do that. We haven't done this since World War II. It's that serious. It is the most important decision any president can make. So I'm looking to create that output. And I don't know another way to do that except decrease the size of the army and then require a draft for whatever it's going to take to fight. Because we can put a hundred thousand somewhere for a year, but we can't relieve them. You'll need the draft. There's a host of issues associated with this from a readiness standpoint, from a guard standpoint, I get all that. But quite frankly, how do we motivate the political leadership to get the American people to say yes, this is right for our future. And Taiwan's right in the center of that discussion as far as I'm concerned.

McMaster: I'll just say this quickly, you can't build a capable land force overnight. I mean you just can't do it. So that's why I think the capacity issue is also relevant to whether or not you're going to win that war. And it's also relevant to how many casualties you're going to take. And you can't develop an NCO [noncommissioned officer] in a year. I mean, you can't do it. So I just think that the army, for example, I'm sure it also applies to other services, finds it's much easier to maintain the level of force than it is to build it up quickly. But I'm going to turn it over to James, I'm giving control back to you.

O'Hanlon: Well, just one quick point by me. I think that, by the way, Jim Mattis, you also didn't like the term "effects-based operations" (EBO), if I remember correctly. So thank you for all you did on that as well as many other debates.

McMaster: That saying was, just say no to EBO.

O'Hanlon: Sounds right. On Roger's point, I'm picking up in this discussion, I think, and maybe broadening it for the purpose of the conference, that we probably don't have enough force structure to guarantee a win against China in a Taiwan blockade scenario in particular. However, I'm not sure what force structure does guarantee that win. And so I'm more interested in the kind of improvements to supply infrastructure survivability, C4ISR, etc., than we've been talking about, especially in Panel 1. But it's a good debate.

My point is I think the debate now is between people who think we have a very small but just barely big enough military and those who think we probably do need to push it up a bit. There is really not, to sort of go with the spirit of your earlier comment, a way to see a good, solid analytical case for going much smaller. And we just saw, actually, a good example of an attempt, but even that attempt is designed partly to maybe buy other things, and it's not enough of a radical cut in the army budget. So I think on that general point, I agree with you.

Michael J. Boskin: My point that we are trying to make in our paper is closely related but with a little bit more nuance. Which is I think that the economics and the budget pressure, and political pressure of the budget are going to be a big push against a major increase in the defense budget. I think we need it. I think the force structure is too small, but if you want to see one example of what's going on in that regard, the CBO [Congressional Budget Office] last month put out a report saying the force structure is much larger than we need for the 2022 strategy. And they have three alternatives for how to reduce the force structure service by service and unit type by unit type. Mostly double-digit and sometimes large decreases to be consistent with the 2022 strategy.

So just be aware that that's out there from the side I live in and the people I talk to, and I totally agree, there's not a single person in this room I haven't learned a lot from by reading, by talking, etc. And I think the case is very strong that the force structure is, at best, barely adequate and probably needs to increase.

But the other thing we're going to have to do is make a stronger case to the public and reassure Americans that their dollars will be used effectively and efficiently. And the basic thing that [House Speaker Kevin] McCarthy said the other day, well, we can always go after waste. Of course, there's some waste. Maybe some joker even put it in one of the five thousand line items in the budget. I remember what [former US Representative] David Stockman once wrote in the budget about foreign military sales. He said these are loans, which we do not expect to get paid back. He actually said that in the budget. I'm probably one of fifty people that read that. So, in any event, I just think being aware of that environment is going to be vital, but it's going to be a very, very big push against the political pressures in the budget.

MULLEN: Michael, can I just make one quick point? I'm just dying to do this. Can we get off the audit issue? And I'm not talking about the audit that H.R. was talking about. I started this with [Roger's] dad in, like 2001. This became a political cudgel to beat the Pentagon to death. If you want to find out how many contractors we have, make us do that, whatever the categories are. But to sign us up with the SEC [the Securities and Exchange Commission, which oversees the audit in the private sector], and I've spent a little time with them as well in the private sector and public company world. There is no guaranteed answer there as well. Make us tell you what you want. But given the amount of money, time, effort, and people since 2001, I think, or 2002, that we have spent trying to figure out how to audit the Pentagon would buy a lot of capability.

BOSKIN: Fair point.

Part 3

Technology, Innovation, Procurement

7

Investing in Emerging Technologies
Lessons from Unmanned Systems

Jacquelyn Schneider

It is impossible to separate technology from military power. For thousands of years, the states best able to invent and adopt technologies have found advantages on the battlefield: whether it be the longbow, the *trace italienne*, or the steam engine. However, picking the right technologies and deciding which ones to invest in and how much to allocate for these systems is a complicated set of guesses, a process fraught with uncertainty. This uncertainty is particularly acute when it comes to emerging technologies, in which decision makers must balance educated guesses about the impact of technology with their feasibility—ultimately trading off priorities between known technologies and the promise of future technologies. The states best able to predict the future of technology on the battlefield and make the right investments are ultimately the strategic winners.[1]

Despite the complexity and uncertainty of these decisions, too often, technology is treated as a simple variable; greater investment in technology leads to better outcomes on the battlefield.[2] Therefore, the competition for military power becomes about capacity (in fact, many political scientists use economic capacity and GDP as proxy variables to predict the most capable militaries)—the states that invest in the right technology with the greatest resources generate the greatest military power. And yet, it is often not the case that capacity determines who "wins" the race to master emerging technology or even that greater innovation occurs within the militaries with the largest budgets. Instead, how militaries decide to invest, adopt, and integrate

The views expressed in this chapter are solely those of the individual author and do not necessarily reflect the views of any organization with which they are, or have been, affiliated.

military technologies is just as important as any state's inherent capacity to produce military technologies. Therefore, technology is not a simple binary variable but a messy process in which intervening variables, such as human beliefs, organizational preferences, exogenous shocks, and domestic political processes, ultimately determine winners and losers.

Understanding how human interaction with emerging technology influences military effectiveness is pivotal for militaries as they set out to deter and defeat their adversaries. It is also a pressing issue for the US military, facing a daunting peer competitor in China and staring down a revisionist Russia in Ukraine. The Department of Defense (DoD) must make decisions about investments in a series of emerging technologies: cyberspace, offensive space capabilities, hypersonic missiles, artificial intelligence, quantum computing—a growing list of technological buzzwords that vie with one another and traditional platforms for priority within a budget increasingly crowded with competing requirements.

In this piece, I look at one large and heterogeneous group of technologies, unmanned systems, as a case study to glean lessons learned about how the DoD responds to emerging technologies. What lessons might we learn from the decisions made over the last fifty to one hundred years? Are there patterns, or best practices, that may help us better build budgets for today and in the future? Finally, I use these lessons and best practices from a case study of unmanned systems and apply them to current challenges with cybersecurity, space, missiles, and software.

Unmanned Systems—Lessons and Best Practices

Over the last century, the acquisition of unmanned systems reveals a series of lessons about investments in emerging technologies.[3] While capacity and technological development have been important to which technologies ultimately succeeded, these were often secondary factors behind organizational identities, beliefs, policy entrepreneurs, and exogenous shocks to the system.

Masks of War: The Role of Service Identity in Technological Investments

First, perhaps the greatest determinant of when and why some unmanned technologies have succeeded while others have failed is how the technology interacts with organizational incentives: namely, armed service identities. This is not a new phenomenon. Famously, Carl Builder's 1989 study on American military strategy, *The Masks of War*, identifies distinct service-based personalities within each military branch that define their attitudes toward technology.[4] The navy's focus on tradition and independent command at sea leads to decisions prioritizing the navy as an institution. As the only service operating air, sea, and land forces, the navy has the most subcultures and also views itself as the service least reliant on joint escapades, making it the most traditional service institution—focused among all the services.

As the newest command, the air force is insecure about its independence and therefore advocates a doctrine that emphasizes strategic airpower and prioritizes technology over the individual service member. As Builder writes, the air force "sees itself as the embodiment of an idea, a concept of warfare, a strategy made possible and sustained by modern technology. The bond is not an institution but the love of flying machines and flight."[5] In contrast, the army is focused on personnel and has "roots in the citizenry," making it a late adopter of technology and an advocate for personnel-heavy doctrine over the technology-focused efforts of the air force.[6]

Builder focuses on US service culture to explain DoD weapons and doctrine choices but also discusses subcultural identities that derive from operational specialties. For instance, in the air force, fighter pilots once bandied for influence against bomber pilots, and more recently, pilots of unmanned systems have subdivided into a culture distinct from that of other manned fighter and bomber platforms. The navy has an even more codified set of organizational identities than the air force, with three specialties organized as separate personnel and manning structures: surface warfare officers, submariners, and aircrew. Previous work suggests that specialties that face replacement by emerging technologies may be less likely to adopt them and may actively fight back against the proliferation of these systems through budget choices, doctrine development, and personnel choices.[7] However, the strength of these occupational specialties in the ultimate trajectories of emerging technologies is tempered (or magnified) by competition within the service between occupational identities. When an occupational identity is dominant and therefore not in competition, it will be more likely to affect unmanned trajectories— either by its support, its apathy, or its resistance to unmanned systems.

In exploring investments in unmanned systems, service and occupational identities have been the primary predictors for which technologies ultimately succeeded. It required significant external intervention—a war, Congress, or influential policy entrepreneurs—to overcome these identities. When the unmanned system threatened the service's identity, it was more likely to fail. When the unmanned system didn't have an advocate within the service, it was more likely to stagnate. Joint endeavors, often foisted by Congress in a top-down attempt to streamline or consolidate investment, were almost always unable to gain enough support from within services to survive over multiple budget years.

In contrast, technological innovation was spurred when Congress pitted services against one another to develop platforms. In particular, as the newest service, the air force's consummate need to validate its existence meant that when pitted against another service for control over an unmanned system or mission, the air force was willing to adopt the technology even if it countered its core service identity. For example, Theodore von Kármán (a prominent rocket scientist during World War II and colleague of Hap Arnold, the first general of the air force) explained how the air force wrested control over ballistic missiles, explaining, "We used the term 'pilotless aircraft' to cover all types of missiles, so as to prevent the project from falling into the hands of the army."[8] Decades later, the air force's desire to control missions also led it to invest in and adopt remotely piloted aircraft at a far greater level than any of the other services—despite the power of the fighter pilot identity.

While service identities led to different unmanned technology trajectories within each service, in general, it created an incentive across services to focus on manned platforms, which services prized as core to their identity, over unmanned munitions and support equipment like bombs, missiles, communications, or intelligence assets, and finally over unmanned platforms. For example, despite early successes, the torpedo met significant resistance from the capital-ship navy, which viewed the torpedo as a threat to its traditional structures. As Katherine Epstein recounts in her exploration of torpedo development within the United States, "The result was a race for range between guns and torpedoes that raised the possibility that the entire system of tactics built around capital ships armed primarily with big guns would give way to one built around smaller vessels primarily armed with torpedoes."[9] Decades later, the navy continued its resistance to munitions that threatened operational identities, developing cruise missiles as a last resort to fend off ballistic missiles, which were incongruous with their platform of choice—the aircraft carrier. It wasn't until Admiral Hyman G. Rickover, who led the development of nuclear-powered submarines, saw the ballistic missile as a way to preserve and promote the submarine that ballistic missiles were embraced within the navy budget (this also led to the innovation of liquid over solid propellants).

And while the air force's uneasy embrace of ballistic missiles has already been alluded to, the air force also put up a spirited resistance to cruise missiles in the 1970s, concerned that the munitions would decrease the chance that their new bomber, the B-1, would be funded. This resistance continued beyond missiles and into space, where the navigation satellites of the global positioning system were almost cut multiple times as the air force questioned the prioritization of space-based precision over pilot-directed laser-guided bombs. Finally, the army's Future Integrated Combat System—which promised to link together lightly armored vehicles with drones and other support equipment—famously failed in part because the army was more focused on the vehicles of the system and underfunded the network technology required to link the platforms together.

The Power of Narratives, Beliefs, and Policy Entrepreneurs

In many cases, the only reason that unmanned technologies have survived organizational incentives and service identity bias was that they became part of a larger narrative. Narratives about the future of technology and beliefs about how technology might impact the future battlefield have been key to convincing both service chiefs and Congress to preserve investments in technologies that might otherwise have been cut. In particular, two core belief narratives have dominated US defense discussions about technological investment in the last fifty years. The first belief, technological determinism, is that technology exists within a linear understanding of history in which technology punctuates equilibrium to create revolutionary advances in military effectiveness. Unmanned systems are a part of that linear progression as a component of the most recent information technology revolution.[10] According to these beliefs, technology is the primary agent of change. It is, therefore, the responsibility of the United States to harness the power of unmanned technologies to leapfrog adversaries by creating campaigns of speed, situational awareness, and decisive advantage.

The second set of beliefs—derived primarily from the US experience in Vietnam and midgrade officers who dominated US defense thinking post–Cold War—is about casualty aversion and force protection. It holds both that the US public is casualty intolerant and that its opinion is important for the military to achieve strategic success.[11] Public opinion about the loss of troops constrains decision makers and influences the choice of military tools on the battlefield. By removing US personnel from the battlefield, unmanned technologies provide a technological solution to the constraints decision makers believe are imposed by the American public's casualty intolerance. These beliefs interface with identities created by military service and occupation specialties that shape investments in and the adoption of unmanned technologies based on beliefs about how unmanned systems support or threaten service and operational cultures.[12]

Beliefs become more influential to policy when they are championed by an enterprising individual, particularly one with power within the services—for example, the navy's Admiral Rickover pushing for ballistic missile submarines, the air force's General Curtis LeMay advocating for strategic bombers, General Bernard Schriever energizing the air force's ballistic missile development, or the army's General Donn Starry creating the Corps-86 acquisition program to implement AirLand Battle. Occasionally there are individuals outside the services who can build powerful narratives and create networks of influence that circumvent service identity to influence technology investment choices from the outside in—Senator John McCain famously pushed the navy and other services to evaluate their own biases, and President Dwight Eisenhower played an outsize role in shaping the strategic arsenal of the United States after World War II.

These two dominant narratives that drove technological investments post–Cold War involved individuals who had outsize effects on narratives about technological development. The first type of policy entrepreneurs were those officers like former chair of the Joint Chiefs of Staff Colin Powell—junior or midgrade officers during Vietnam—whose lessons learned about public support and casualty aversion shaped doctrine and technologies focused on force protection. These officers, generally from inside the army and to some extent the air force, influenced decisions about technology investments across the services that focused on range, precision, and situational awareness to decrease the risk to American personnel. A second group of policy entrepreneurs, led by the Office of Net Assessment's Andy Marshall, leaned on civilian scholars, policy leaders, and networks of rising military officers to propagate a theory of revolutions in military affairs. This internal group of military leader entrepreneurs, combined with the outside push of civilian policy entrepreneurs, led to sometimes conjoined narratives about technology to protect the force and create overwhelming technological victories. Together, these individuals created the crucial impetus by which beliefs about unmanned technology translated into policy and acquisition choices that could overcome status-quo biases for service identity.[13]

From the Outside In, the Exogenous Push and Pull on Technological Investments

So far, most of these lessons have been learned by looking at defense technology processes from the inside. However, outside catalysts play a key role in shaping the trajectory of technology. Perhaps most unsurprisingly, wars drive innovation. They provide both an impetus and increased funding for technology, serving as immediate proving grounds for technology that might otherwise be favored (or rejected) by services.

This has happened time and time again for unmanned systems. For example, torpedoes—which showed early promise—languished after World War I.[14] Faced with declining defense budgets, the navy moved the systems to the bottom of their priority list, behind the new aircraft, submarines, and carriers the service was clamoring for. When World War II began, the navy was left with "a tiny dribble of beautifully crafted torpedoes, barely less erratic than their World War I forefathers, produced by an organization corpulent, sluggish, and not so much consciously resistant to change as physically and emotionally unable to."[15] Only World War II forced the navy to restart its torpedo development and introduce the far more capable Mark 24 and 28 torpedoes.

Similarly, Vietnam drove tactical unmanned investments like unmanned aircraft and autonomous munitions, which were ignored under the peacetime dominance of the Strategic Air Command. More recently, 9/11 led to the armed remotely piloted aircraft, a phenomenon that has dominated unmanned system investments in the last two decades. As then secretary of the air force James Roche recounted, there was a lot of resistance to arming the Predator before 9/11, but then "two buildings fell over," and suddenly arming the Predator didn't seem nearly as risky or revolutionary as it had previously.[16]

In some cases, it wasn't just war that provided an exogenous shock to technology. While much of the Cold War was dominated by service identity and organizational competition, Sputnik and the nuclear threat created impetuses for investments in emerging technologies that might have otherwise failed. Despite early studies post–World War II into the feasibility of space reconnaissance and even a 1954 RAND report that called for a "satellite reconnaissance vehicle" as a "vital strategic interest to the United States," satellite development remained a low priority for both the air force and the navy until the exogenous Sputnik shock in 1957.[17] At the time, the navy had a Vanguard satellite program in development, but the program had been kept secret and given a tight budget, ostensibly so it wouldn't compete with investments in ballistic missiles.[18] It also didn't help that then secretary of defense Charles Wilson didn't believe in satellites and showed open ambivalence to the Soviet efforts. All that changed when the Soviets launched Sputnik into orbit, which riveted US onlookers and caused the national security community to worry about a missile gap with implications for intelligence and nuclear stability.[19] The Sputnik moment also created a window of opportunity for the air force's General Schriever. After Sputnik, the Atlas missile program and its descendant, the Titan, sprinted forward technologically as congressional and executive branch pushes to respond to the Soviet lead in space ensured a solid budget allocation.[20]

Congress, and to some extent, the executive branch, play important external catalyst (and confining/shaping) roles for technological development. While Congress is often derided for retaining weapons that support industries within their representative districts, it often plays an important role in saving technology that would otherwise not be funded by the services. Congress and various presidential administrations, for example, can be credited for saving most of the ballistic and cruise missile technology that now exists in the US arsenal. It took civilian intervention, first from President Eisenhower's famous Project Solarium and then from senior civilians in air force research and development, to create a new protected entity within the air force focused solely on developing ballistic missiles.[21] Similarly, the air force's resistance to cruise missiles was largely the byproduct of the service's support for the B-1, a low-altitude, high-speed bomber designed to negate the increasing lethality of Soviet surface-to-air missiles and fighter interceptors. But with new missiles that were far more precise, had much greater ranges, and could evade air defense systems sometimes with better success than manned alternatives, the air force struggled to convince Congress or the executive branch that the US needed a new manned bomber.[22] In fact, President Jimmy Carter almost nixed the B-1 entirely, preferring a new "cruise-missile carrier" over the air force's manned bomber proposal.[23]

Congress and the executive branch also play an important role in influencing budget cycles, which serve as critical junctures for technological trajectories. Investments in research and development made in big-budget years create a path dependency for technologies during subsequent lean years. This can lead to suboptimal technological trajectories. Emerging technologies are more likely to be cut by the services during lean budget years, making outside intervention more important to saving technologies that are not otherwise preferred by the services. It also may leave the military with a glut of technology that isn't optimized for the current context. For example, the massive influx of defense spending during the Reagan years led to innovations in precision munitions but drawdowns in unmanned platforms, while post–9/11 conflicts inflated investment in remotely controlled unmanned platforms over long-range missiles or systems that may be useful in conflicts featuring more capable air defense systems (such as with China or even Russia).

Finally, the unmanned case suggests that the defense industrial base rarely innovates alone. There are very few cases of successful technological innovation started by the defense industrial base without a requirement from the Department of Defense. Instead, the tale of unmanned technologies is replete with examples of civilian innovations that fail to find customers within the military until a large exogenous shock forces the military to revisit (and sometimes resurrect) these technologies. This, understandably, decreases incentives for companies to produce technology that is not already explicitly requested by the DoD. The Predator is a rare exception; General Atomics invested in the system largely without a DoD push—a strategy that only succeeded because of the exogenous shock of 9/11.

Conclusion: Implications for Other Technologies

Investment in unmanned systems over time reveals a few lessons about the process of how emerging technology succeeds and fails. First, the status quo for technologies is that they will succeed or fail based on how well they fit into a service's identity. To negate these biases, it is important to have the services compete against one another when necessary. Also, leaning on Congress and the executive branch can exert important top-down pressure when processes stagnate. Narratives, especially those propagated by successful policy entrepreneurs, can help overcome service biases. But perhaps the biggest implication of this research is that a general self-awareness within the DoD of when technologies might inadvertently be set up to fail because they don't have organizations or individuals to spearhead them in the budget process could lead to better acquisition and development processes for emerging technology. There are also more specific implications for other emerging technologies.

First, this study suggests that cyber technologies—especially those developed for defending the nation—will need a champion to ensure their priority within defense budgets. Services are optimized to develop cyber technologies that benefit their core identities, and yet the primary cyber force tasked with defending the nation is the Cyber National Mission Force (CNMF), a joint organization subordinate to a joint functional command, cyber command.[24] Previous lessons from unmanned systems would suggest that carving out a joint organization to spearhead and defend the nation's mission (ransomware, defending elections, combating intellectual property theft, etc.) would be an uphill battle doomed to fail—fighting the services both for top talent to man billets and for control of cyber acquisition budgets. Indeed, for the last decade, the services have dominated this fight, allocating personnel to their missions first while almost all of the cyber acquisition budget passed straight through cyber command to the service cyber elements. Leading up to 2022, cyber command had budget oversight of only $600 million of an overall DoD $40 billion cyber/information technology budget (and even that small percentage was a significant increase from the $75 million cyber command was given authority over in 2018).[25]

But cyber command, led by the charismatic army general Paul Nakasone, has waged a persistent and successful battle to influence legislation to protect the CNMF and cyber command. Cyber command has not only been given authority (starting in 2024) for full budget control of the cyber/IT portfolio, but it has also elevated the CNMF to a subunified command, securing billets and budgets for the joint organization. How has cyber command been able to do this? First, cyber command crafted a narrative about its role, its mission's uniqueness compared to those of the services, and the need for greater authorities and budgets. In an effort colloquially known as persistent engagement, "Cyber Command published its strategic vision before the Trump National Defense Strategy or Defense Cyberspace Strategy."[26] Doing so preempted the cyber narratives in the DoD and NSC strategies and propagated the idea of a more forward-leaning and independent cyber command through academics, editorials, and professional military education.[27] This narrative benefited from the charisma of General Nakasone, who retained command of cyber command and the National Security Agency even while there was a revolving door of cyber leaders within the White House and in the position of secretary of defense. This campaign also benefited from a small pool of cyber leaders, many of whom served under Nakasone or cyber command before rotating to lead service cyber elements. By promoting within the cyber command instead of from more traditional service hierarchies, cyber command retained influence within service cyber elements. Cyber command also began a public-facing effort to advertise previously covert efforts, creating a new Twitter account to disseminate malware in real time, partnering with the (also charismatic) Chris Krebs at the Department of Homeland Security, and serving as a public face for a successful campaign to defend the US elections against Russian and foreign interference. The congressionally mandated Cyberspace Solarium Commission also protected the Cyber National Mission Force, recommending and then spearheading the legislation that ensured the force would remain funded and increasingly protected from the services. Of course, all these factors were helped by the services' relative disinterest in cyber versus more traditional missions, which allowed for cyber command to play a larger role in cyber budgets and control.

Related, and perhaps even more complicated, are investments in information technology and Joint All-Domain Command and Control (JADC2). The information technology structure of the military is already divided into armed service segments (the air force owns its network and data, etc.)—a phenomenon that makes basic information technology (and cybersecurity) upgrades difficult to implement across the DoD information technology network. It also leads the services to make very different decisions about applications, software development, and basic information technology practices. This creates complications for enterprise-wide initiatives through the Defense Information Systems Agency (DISA) and a natural jockeying between DISA and the armed service information technology organizations. It also means that JADC2—an effort to combine these networks to communicate and share data seamlessly across the services—will be extremely difficult to implement. Joint organizations and initiatives are notoriously challenging, and the services' natural inclination to invest in platforms over infrastructure means that the ambitious information technology program faces multiple obstacles. However, lessons from the unmanned case about interservice competition suggest that Congress may incentivize the services to work together or prioritize information technology funding by threatening to allow one service to run the entire JADC2 program. Pitting, for example, the air force's Advanced Battle Management System against the navy's Project Overmatch may create an impetus for innovation where the status quo default is for stagnation.

The introduction of the US Space Force complicates the role of service identity in investments in emerging technology. The power of service identities means there is a natural inclination for armed services, especially one that is new and concerned about its survival in the future, to push for technologies that create a novel role in space. While the space force is still developing its identity, the focus on offensive weaponry, warriors, and armed competition in space could lead to more investments in space-focused missions (e.g., space-based early warning, space weapons, etc.) over investments in intelligence, communications, and support for terrestrial missions. This was a large concern for President Eisenhower, who was apprehensive that service biases would harm space investments and needlessly cause a space race with Russia. To counteract these biases, Eisenhower placed almost all space capabilities under a civilian organization, the National Reconnaissance Office. In the seventy years since, some would argue that Eisenhower's decision has underemphasized space capabilities in the defense budget and that the creation of the space force only corrects this imbalance. Further, by creating an armed service that must compete for resources, the new structure may lead to innovations in processes and personnel that lead to better acquisition and adoption of emerging technologies (as some would argue the marines have exemplified). For space, the challenge will be surviving as an organization separate from the air force without leaning on identity biases that lead to less effective uses of emerging technology.

This research also has implications for the future of US conventional missile capabilities. Why hasn't the United States invested as much into hypersonic missiles as it probably should have? Why does the United States not have a larger, more sophisticated arsenal of conventional strike surface-to-surface (or even ship-to-ship or ship-to-shore) missiles? Part of the reason why the nation has fallen behind states such as North Korea and Iran in conventional strike options, and China in hypersonic missile options, is a product of context and the US-Soviet relationship in particular. Arms control agreements between the United States and the USSR limited much of the conventional strike arsenal; even cruise missiles (which were not explicitly a part of strategic arms control agreements) were used as part of a negotiating tactic for the United States trying to limit nuclear arsenals. Organizational interests also handicapped the US conventional strike development. The army abdicated its stake in long-range missiles completely by the 1980s to the air force, which was happy to commandeer the mission from the army but also was not interested in investing in missiles that didn't fit into the nuclear mission of Strategic Air Command, nor the conventional campaigns fought by Tactical Air Command. Meanwhile, the navy (like the air force) lost interest in conventional strike missions that might threaten the bread-and-butter aircraft of aircraft carriers, while submarines, generally focused on strategic strike missions, were underprioritized as a conventional missile strike option. Even though missiles were a core part of technological narratives coming out of the DoD after the Cold War, these organizational and contextual complications meant that the focus was on missiles as munitions that could be carried by existing platforms like aircraft and destroyers. Even when leaders recognized the need for emerging technologies like hypersonic missiles, there were few service imperatives to invest in systems that didn't fall neatly into organizational niches and threatened the role of favored platforms.

Finally, this work reminds us that technology does not exist without human intervention. We cannot simply invest more in technology and expect it will lead to victory on the battlefield. Instead, how technology shapes the winners and losers in war is a result of the process by which organizations, individuals, and beliefs create and use that technology in the first place. For the US military, what this means for preparing for a future conflict with China or sustaining support to Ukraine against Russia, is that the United States cannot just increase defense budgets and expect that it will assure a technological edge. Instead, the US military must focus as much on reforming the process of developing, acquiring, and implementing new technology as it does on fighting for larger budgets. A large part of this fight will be in reexamining the power of the armed services. It has been decades since the Goldwater-Nichols Act, the last major initiative to temper the role of service identity in defense budgets, and an evaluation of the success of these reforms is past due. Instead of building new services, the DoD should evaluate whether the current structure and power of the current division of services are best for military effectiveness. This will be a tall order that will require a Congress and executive branch willing to make difficult reforms at a time when civil-military relations are already strained. It will require new policy entrepreneurs from within and above the services, able to build compelling narratives for new weapons and concepts of operation.

Hopefully, the United States can do this without the push of war, because it is unclear that, if left to the status quo, the nation will be able to compete or win against an adversary on the level of China. In many of the emerging technologies that now dominate the discussion about future warfare—hypersonics, artificial intelligence, offensive space capabilities—China looks to be an early leader.

Meanwhile, after decades of conflict against terrorists and insurgents, the United States has an inventory of weapons ill-suited for the high-tech, primarily naval and air fighting in the Pacific. Can we reform our processes to regain the technological edge? Can we pivot our technological investments even in the face of economic uncertainty? The United States may only have a short time to answer these questions.

Notes

1. Jacquelyn Schneider, "Does Technology Win Wars? The US Military Needs Low-Cost Innovation—Not Big-Ticket Boondoggles," *Foreign Affairs*, March 3, 2023.

2. While this paper will focus on the importance of making the right technological investments, it in no way assumes that technology itself can overcome nonmaterial differences between militaries, such as will, professionalism, or tactical innovation.

3. Jacquelyn Schneider and Julia Macdonald, *The Hand behind Unmanned Technologies* (Oxford: Oxford University Press, forthcoming); Jacquelyn Schneider and Julia Macdonald, "Looking Back to Look Forward: Autonomy, Military Revolutions, and the Importance of Cost," *Journal of Strategic Studies*, last revised December 30, 2022, https://ssrn.com/abstract=4001007 or http://dx.doi.org/10.2139/ssrn.4001007.

4. Carl H. Builder, *The Masks of War: American Military Styles in Strategy and Analysis* (Baltimore: Johns Hopkins University Press, 1989).

5. Builder, *Masks of War*, 32.

6. Builder, *Masks of War*, 19.

7. Armin Granulo, Christoph Fuchs, and Stefano Puntoni, "Psychological Reactions to Human versus Robotic Job Replacement," *Nature Human Behaviour* 3, no. 10 (2019): 1062–69.

8. Timothy P. Schultz, *The Problem with Pilots: How Physicians, Engineers, and Airpower Enthusiasts Redefined Flight* (Baltimore: Johns Hopkins University Press, 2018), 118.

9. Katherine C. Epstein, *Torpedo: Inventing the Military-Industrial Complex in the United States and Great Britain* (Cambridge, MA: Harvard University Press, 2014), 10.

10. Clifford J. Rogers, ed., *The Military Revolution Debate: Readings on the Military Transformation of Early Modern Europe* (Boulder, CO: Westview Press, 1995); Steven Metz, *Strategy and the Revolution in Military Affairs: From Theory to Policy* (Darby, PA: Diane Publishing, 1995); Geoffrey Parker, *The Military Revolution: Military Innovation and the Rise of the West, 1500–1800* (Cambridge: Cambridge University Press, 1996); David Parrott, *The Business of War: Military Enterprise and Military Revolution in Early Modern Europe* (Cambridge: Cambridge University Press, 2012); Colin S. Gray, *Strategy for Chaos: Revolutions in Military Affairs and the Evidence of History* (London: Frank Cass, 2002); Steven Metz and James Kievit, *Strategy and the Revolution in Military Affairs: From Theory to Policy* (Carlisle, PA: Strategic Studies Institute, 1995); Wim A. Smit, John Grin, and Lev Voronkov, *Military Technological Innovation and Stability in a Changing World: Politically Assessing and Influencing Weapon Innovation and Military Research and Development* (Amsterdam: VU University Press, 1992); Max Boot, *War Made New: Technology, Warfare, and the Course of History, 1500 to Today* (New York: Penguin, 2006); Allan R. Millett and Williamson Murray, eds., *Military Effectiveness*, vol. 2, *The Interwar Period* (Cambridge: Cambridge University Press, 2010); Michael O'Hanlon, *Technological Change and the Future of Warfare* (Washington, DC: Brookings Institution, 2000); Alvin Toffler and Heidi Toffler, *War and Anti-war: Survival at the Dawn of the 21st Century* (Boston: Little, Brown & Co., 1993); Jon Lindsay, *Information Technology and Military Power* (Ithaca, NY: Cornell University Press, 2020).

11. John E. Mueller, *War, Presidents and Public Opinion* (New York: Wiley, 1973); Scott Gartner, "The Multiple Effects of Casualties on Public Support for War: An Experimental Approach," *American Political Science Review* 102, no. 1 (February 2008): 95–106; Jonathan D. Caverley, *Democratic Militarism: Voting, Wealth, and War* (New York: Cambridge University Press, 2014).

12. Builder, *Masks of War*; Jacob Neufeld, George M. Watson Jr., and David Chenoweth, eds., *Technology and the Air Force: A Retrospective Assessment* (Washington, DC: Air Force History and Museums Program, US Air Force, 1997).

13. Barry Posen, *The Sources of Military Doctrine: France, Britain, and Germany between the World Wars* (Ithaca, NY: Cornell University Press, 1986); Stephen P. Rosen, *Winning the Next War: Innovation and the Modern Military* (Ithaca, NY: Cornell University Press, 1994).

14. Epstein, *Torpedo*, 10.

15. Robert Gannon, *Hellions of the Deep: The Development of American Torpedoes in World War II* (University Park, PA: Penn State University Press, 1996), 33.

16. James Roche in discussion with the author, April 2020.

17. Robert Guerriero, *Space-Based Reconnaissance: From a Strategic Past to a Tactical Future* (Huntsville, AL: Army Space and Missile Defense Command, 2002).

18. Curtis Peebles, *High Frontier: The United States Air Force and the Military Space Program* (Darby, PA: Diane Publishing, 1997), 8.

19. Greg Thielmann, "Looking Back: The Missile Gap Myth and Its Progeny," *Arms Control Today* 41, no. 4 (May 2011): 44.

20. David K. Stumpf, *Minuteman: A Technical History of the Missile That Defined American Nuclear Warfare* (Fayetteville: University of Arkansas Press, 2021).

21. Stumpf, *Minuteman*; G. Harry Stine, *ICBM: The Making of the Weapon That Changed the World* (London: Orion Books, 1991).

22. Michael E. Brown, *Flying Blind: The Politics of the US Strategic Bomber Program* (Ithaca, NY: Cornell University Press, 1992); Robert J. Art and Stephen E. Ockenden, "The Domestic Politics of Cruise Missile Development, 1970–1980," in *Cruise Missiles: Technology, Strategy, Politics*, ed. Richard K. Betts (Washington, DC: Brookings Institution, 1981), 359–413.

23. Brown, *Flying Blind*, 123.

24. US Cyber Command Combined Action Group, "Beyond the Build: How the Component Commands Support the US Cyber Command Vision," *NDU Press*, January 1, 2016, https://ndupress.ndu.edu/Media/News/News-Article-View/Article/643106/beyond-the-build-how-the-component-commands-support-the-us-cyber-command-vision.

25. Mark Pomerleau, "Cyber Command Prepares to Gain Significant Budget Control," *FedScoop*, March 14, 2022, https://www.fedscoop.com/cyber-command-budget-control-preparations-pom.

26. Jacquelyn G. Schneider, "Persistent Engagement: Foundation, Evolution and Evaluation of a Strategy," *Lawfare*, May 10, 2019, https://www.lawfareblog.com/persistent-engagement-foundation-evolution-and-evaluation-strategy.

27. Michael P. Fischerkeller, Emily O. Goldman, and Richard J. Harknett, *Cyber Persistence Theory: Redefining National Security in Cyberspace* (Oxford: Oxford University Press, 2022); Paul M. Nakasone, "A Cyber Force for Persistent Operations," *Joint Force Quarterly* 92, no. 1 (First Quarter 2019): 10–14; Jacquelyn G. Schneider, Emily O. Goldman, Michael Warner, Paul M. Nakasone, Chris C. Demchak, Nancy A. Norton, Joshua Rovner et al., *Ten Years In: Implementing Strategic Approaches to Cyberspace* (Newport, RI: US Naval War College Press, 2020).

8

Our Military Debt Crisis
Preserving America's Strategic Solvency

James M. Cunningham

For thirty years, the United States has deferred the recapitalization and modernization of its armed forces. It did so first under the pretense of peace in the 1990s, then because the demands of the wars in Iraq and Afghanistan predominated, and finally, in the name of politics and so-called fiscal responsibility. America borrowed against its strategic future. It decreased the size and force structure of its military, slashed defense and especially defense procurement funding, canceled dozens of weapons programs, cut planned procurement of others, and put off much-needed recapitalization of the force.

Along the way, warning signs appeared: the hollow force of the late 1990s exposed by two wars in the Middle East, the readiness crisis of the 2010s that claimed lives and undercut America's standing, and the rapid expansion of China's People's Liberation Army (PLA). Yet the requirements of the moment continually superseded the long-term solvency of the American defense enterprise. The modernization debt grew larger.

Now the Chinese Communist Party has come to collect the debt. Confronted with a war in Ukraine and the perilous ambitions of Xi Jinping, America must rapidly recapitalize its fighting force and modernize its military capabilities. Doing so will cost extra because we have not done so for three decades. Doing so will be hard because we must move quickly to win what the Biden administration has called "the decisive decade."[1] And doing so will require us to overcome the temptation to believe that technology alone can save us.

The views expressed in this chapter are solely those of the individual author and do not necessarily reflect the views of any organization with which they are, or have been, affiliated.

However, serious questions remain about our nation's ability to meet the moment. External and internal pressures squeeze the defense budget. Mandatory spending commitments, particularly on social security, Medicare, Medicaid, and other health-care programs, as well as interest payments on the national debt, consume an increasing portion of every federal dollar. Within the defense budget, fixed costs, including personnel pay, health care, and the costs of operating and maintaining the force, constrain funding for modernization.

The following pages recount the making of the modernization debt and the decisions that brought the nation to this point. They then summarize the recapitalization and modernization priorities and identify two limiting factors of note: the tyranny of time and the limitations of the defense industrial base. Finally, they synthesize the pressures constraining future defense spending and close by questioning what the United States can do to preserve its strategic solvency.

The budgetary pressures will not abate. The threat of the Chinese Communist Party will not miraculously dissipate. The need to modernize the military's capabilities will not go away. The debt must be paid—the question is how.

Peace Dividends and War Spending: The Making of the Modernization Debt

The tale of America's strategic insolvency begins following the collapse of the Soviet Union. At the time, the United States saw fit to begin shrinking the US military and to take what has been called a procurement holiday. The cuts went into place swiftly. By 1996, the defense budget was slashed by more than $94 billion, adjusted for inflation.

The procurement budget paid the highest price. It shrunk by more than 45 percent in those first years, and new weapons acquisitions stalled.[2] No fighter aircraft, for example, were acquired in the mid-1990s, and no new army platforms entered service. As the decade progressed, some spending was restored but not enough. A Congressional Budget Office study in 1999 predicted it would cost $90 billion per year "to replace equipment as it wears out or becomes obsolete." Only $49 billion was budgeted for that purpose.[3]

Although the post–Cold War cuts were based on the promise of peace, service members continued to operate around the world, placing great pressure on already aging equipment. Aircraft crews, for example, encountered shortages of spare parts, so maintainers had to cannibalize them from other aircraft—a practice we will see later. And army warrant officers complained about the difficulty of maintaining equipment that had surpassed twenty years in operation.[4] After one decade of deferred modernization, the cracks began to show.

A new millennium brought a new administration but not a renewed interest in recapitalization. While defense spending increased substantially, most of the new dollars went to waging the wars in Iraq and Afghanistan. The hard fighting of the wars and the adverse environmental conditions in which they were waged wore out old equipment and drove up the costs of keeping it in action. Operation and maintenance budgets (O&M) climbed by over 75 percent.

Acquisition budgets also rose but did not translate into a meaningful modernization of the force. From 1991 to 2006, the United States acquired, on average, just 6 major ships, 68 fighter and attack aircraft, and 334 tanks, artillery, and armored vehicles per year. Compare this to the average annual procurement rates in the final fifteen years of the Cold War: 19 ships, 349 fighter and attack aircraft, and 2,083 tanks, artillery, and armored vehicles. The procurement holiday continued well into the 2000s.

There are two principal reasons. First, immediate wartime needs, such as mine-resistant ambush-protected vehicles and defenses against improvised explosive devices, trumped longer-term interests.[5] Second, dozens of the long-term modernization priorities at the time amounted to nothing. Mackenzie Eaglen of the American Enterprise Institute estimates that $81 billion was spent on canceled programs from FY2002 to FY2012, which led to a combined $400 billion in deferred modernization spending.[6] Among these canceled programs was the army's Future Combat Systems, which envisioned new brigades comprising a system of manned and unmanned weapons systems. It consumed over $22 billion and was canceled in 2009, leaving the army without a plan or a program of record to begin replacing its aging tanks and armored personnel carriers.

As Eaglen points out, the long-term losses of this period go beyond these sunken costs. The decision to acquire only 187 F-22 fighter jets, rather than the planned 750, for example, left the air force undersupplied on air superiority capabilities and substantially drove up the program's costs. Tens of billions of dollars were spent to develop cutting-edge weapons. Some programs never saw the light of day. Some did, but in numbers far short of what was required. As a result, in the words of famed defense analyst Andrew Krepinevich, "the

US military can be said to have experienced a 'hollow buildup'" during the first decade of the twenty-first century.[7]

The debt grew deeper with the passage of the Budget Control Act of 2011 (BCA). After the cancellation and truncation of more than two dozen modernization programs, the BCA placed strict spending limits on defense and domestic discretionary accounts. As originally conceived, it would have excised almost $1 trillion from the Obama administration's defense plan. Fortunately, those caps were amended repeatedly to lessen the impact, but serious damage was done. In 2013, the sequestration mechanism went into effect and immediately slashed defense spending, inciting a force-wide readiness crisis that persisted for years. All told, over $550 billion in expected defense resources were lost from 2012 through 2019 thanks to this act.[8]

Recurring congressional fights over appropriations compounded the problem. How could the US military plan beyond the immediate horizon if it didn't know how much money it would have on hand or when that money would be appropriated? How could commanders organize training without an annual budget for their units? Suffering from both budget cuts and total unpredictability about when funding would come through and at what level, the military found itself fighting a losing action.

It is hard to overstate the damage of these cuts and this instability. As already alluded to, they triggered a devastating readiness crisis. The army struggled to field more than three ready brigade combat teams at any given point. The navy ran its fleet and sailors ragged with eight- and even ten-month deployments, which ultimately contributed to the deadly collisions of the USS *John S. McCain* and the USS *Fitzgerald*. Air force pilots regularly received insufficient training, and at least half of the air force's major aircraft have not reached combat readiness status since 2011.[9] Across the services, equipment and training shortages led to an uptick in training accidents and mishaps. Talk of a hollow force returned.

Modernization suffered as well. Between fiscal years 2012 and 2017, the Pentagon's modernization budget—defined as procurement plus research and development—was cut by $200 billion, compared to what had been planned before the BCA. The number of major acquisition programs fell accordingly from ninety-seven to seventy-eight.[10] Planned procurements of high-priority capabilities, like F-35 Joint Strike Fighters, decreased. The US military lived through another lost decade.

Setting aside questions about the strategic wisdom of these actions, the fact remains: the United States deferred the modernization of the fighting force

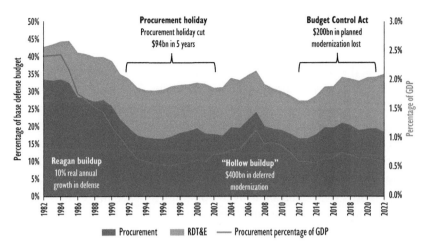

Figure 8.1 The Making of the Modernization Debt

Sources: DoD, Office of the Under Secretary of Defense (Comptroller), *National Defense Budget Estimates for FY 2022* (Green Book), accessed December 2022, available at https://comptroller .defense.gov/Budget-Materials/Budget2022; and Office of Management and Budget, Historical Tables, Table 5.1, "Budget Authority by Function and Subfunction: 1976–2028," accessed December 2022, available at https://www.whitehouse.gov/omb/budget/historical-tables.

for a generation. First, we took a holiday from history and building a military, resulting in nearly $100 billion in procurement cuts in five years. Next, we fought two long wars without fully paying for them, deferring $400 billion in modernization. Finally, we sacrificed the current and future readiness of the fighting force to politics, scrapping $200 billion in planned modernization investments (see fig. 8.1). The lost generation left the country with an aging, increasingly outdated force and a deep modernization debt that now must be repaid if we hope to remain a superpower.

Modernization Debt and the Cost of Repaying It

The cost of repaying the nation's modernization debt would be daunting if we could sequence investments and pay it out in tranches. We have no such luxury. The modernization bills of the army, air force, navy, marine corps, and nuclear enterprise are coming due at the same time.

In 2018, the bipartisan National Defense Strategy Commission summarized the recapitalization needs well. For the army, "more armor, long-range fires, engineering, and air-defense units are required to meet the ground-heavy challenges posed by Russia in Eastern Europe," and "additional air-defense and logistical forces" are necessary in the Pacific. The navy must "expand its submarine fleet" and "dramatically recapitalize and expand its military sea-lift forces" to project power into the Pacific. The air force "will need more stealthy long-range fighters and bombers . . . as well as more tankers to refuel them," and it must supplement with additional lift and intelligence, surveillance, and reconnaissance capabilities. The entire nuclear triad of bombers, ICBMs, and submarines needs modernizing, as does the supporting infrastructure, and the list goes on to include cyber capabilities, missile defenses, space, munitions, and more.[11]

The intervening years have only increased the urgency and cost. In 2017, for example, the Congressional Budget Office estimated that the nuclear triad would cost $34.1 billion annually by 2021. But, by 2021, that estimate rose to $42.1 billion. Modernizing the triad's delivery systems alone will likely cost the Pentagon over $150 billion in this decade—and that number does not include other nuclear costs, such as modernizing warheads or operating and sustaining the nuclear enterprise.[12]

Moreover, the list of long-term modernization needs is concerning. The navy has repeatedly delayed three high-priority development projects: the DDG(X) program to replace its Arleigh Burke–class destroyers, the SSN(X) program to replace its Virginia-class attack submarines, and the next-generation air dominance program to replace its F/A-18 Super Hornets. The army needs to replace its soon-to-be-obsolete fleet of ground combat vehicles, including the Bradley fighting vehicle and the Abrams tank. The air force must develop the next-generation air superiority fighter, which will replace its rapidly aging F-15s and address the small F-22 inventory while maintaining its new bomber program.

The combined force of these investments creates what some have called the modernization bow wave. In a 2019 study of the same name, Mackenzie Eaglen dubbed it the "2020s Tri-Service Modernization Crunch."[13] That study documented what each service planned for this decade's first and second halves and provided a comprehensive assessment of their modernization requirements and associated costs. It does little good to restate her work. Suffice it to say that the modernization debt far exceeds the Pentagon's current procurement budget plans.

However, the debt goes beyond money. Thirty years of deferred modernization created two inescapable realities.

First, as seen in the air force's attempt to reverse a three-decade decline, we've lost the luxury of time. The services must all invest in near-term recapitalization efforts and longer-term modernization projects. They must do so immediately and over the course of the coming decade. And they must do so simultaneously. But can they act quickly enough to preserve the nation's ability to defend itself?

Second, as exemplified by the navy's shipbuilding woes, the defense industrial base is not up to the task. The cumulative effect of past choices has left it shrunken and hollow, with fundamental deficiencies that will hinder any effort to modernize the force.

Time versus Reality in the Air Force's Modernization Plans

Arguably, the air force took the largest hit during the lost generation of modernization. Its aircraft inventory is getting older, smaller, and less ready, and plans to reverse these trends by fielding upgraded and new aircraft have been slow to manifest. As such, a graveyard spiral that began three decades ago continues, and the ground is fast approaching.

The air force's procurement budget was cut in half through the 1990s, and it has consistently retired or lost more aircraft than it has acquired. At the end of the last fiscal year, the air force had 47 percent as many fighters, 42 percent as many bombers, 69 percent as many tankers, and 75 percent as many airlift platforms as it did in the late 1980s.[14] The administration planned to shrink those numbers further, but the recently passed National Defense Authorization Act restored purchases of some assets.

Not only is the inventory shrinking, but it is also aging. John Venable of the Heritage Foundation places the average age of the air force's aircraft at over twenty-nine years. Some prominent platforms, such as the B-52 bomber and the KC-135, exceed sixty years. The F-15 fighter fleet averages over thirty years—beyond the planned lifecycle of the aircraft—as do the F-16s. Correspondingly, the availability rates for air force fighters have declined for fifteen years, as have training opportunities. Low availability rates mean fewer aircraft ready to deploy in defense of the country's interests. For example, just 121 of the 304 F-15Cs in the air force's possession would qualify.[15] Diminished training means less proficient pilots, but it also leads to problems in retaining and recruiting airmen. Both harm the strategic readiness of the nation's air force.

A 2018 US Air Force study warned of the need to reverse these trends. It called for the service to grow from 312 to 386 squadrons, arm those squadrons with the most advanced aircraft, and provide pilots with more training time to prepare for high-end flights.[16] But the money never materialized, and the air force's procurement budget has not even kept pace with inflation. The problems persist, as a recent study from the Mitchell Institute warned:

> The air force lacks the force capacity, lethality, and survivability needed to fight a major war with China, plus deter nuclear threats and meet its other national defense requirements. This is the result of decades of inadequate budgets that forced the service to cut its forces and forgo modernizing aircraft designed fifty to seventy years ago for environments that were far more permissive than what exists today in the Indo-Pacific.[17]

The list of investment priorities required to reverse this trend is long and wide, including upgrading its command-and-control capabilities, surveillance and reconnaissance platforms, and munitions. But three programs warrant particular attention: the F-35A Joint Strike Fighter and the B-21 Raider, and the KC-46A tanker.

The F-35A is the top priority. The air force intends to acquire more than 1,700 to replace its ground attack and multirole aircraft. So far, it has 376 (356 in the active component) and plans to buy roughly 200 through FY2027 for more than $22 billion. However, the service cut its procurement rate to just 33 this year. Congress raised that to 38 in the NDAA, but it's still short of the 60 bought in 2021, much less the 100 that can be produced annually.

The F-35A now competes for procurement dollars with the F-15EX Eagle II, an upgraded F-15 intended for immediate entry into service. Air force leaders say the Eagle II is needed to relieve aging fighters, so it requested 24 of these aircraft in addition to the 33 F-35s. But even the two together are short of the 72 new fighters the air force needs to acquire each year to replace aging and retiring aircraft. Moreover, it drives down the buy rate of F-35s, making the production line more inefficient and putting off the eventual fielding of a full inventory of stealthy multirole fighters. In the effort to make up for lost time and ease the wear and tear on their aircraft, the air force is losing capacity and further delaying modernization, all while driving up the price tag.

After the F-35A, the B-21 Raider tops the list of air force interests. The B-21 long-range bomber, which was rolled out in dramatic fashion in December 2022, will replace the B-1 and B-2 and join the B-52 as the backbone of the nation's bomber fleet. Current plans call for acquiring at least one hundred at a little over $700 million each. Through 2027, that will come to roughly $32 billion—$20 billion in procurement and $13 billion in R&D.[18]

So far, it is the model acquisition program in many ways, but there is cause for concern. The bomber's first flight has already been delayed, and even if the bomber stays on schedule from here, it will not enter service until the late 2020s at best—at the tail end of the "decisive decade." History also gives cause for concern. Recent high-profile air force programs have either been severely truncated, as in the cases of the F-22 and the KC-46A tanker, which ran into problems, or been drawn out (see the previous paragraph).

Finally, there is the KC-46A Pegasus tanker. Intended as a replacement for the legacy tanker fleet of KC-135s and KC-10s, the tanker program has run into persistent technical and political hurdles, including a problem with the boom that connects the tanker to the refueling plane, which rendered it mission incapable. Despite these delays, the air force expects to have 95 in the fleet by the end of this fiscal year and 179 total by the decade's end.[19] Yet again, this isn't enough. The planned purchase would replace less than half of the country's tanker fleet, leaving most of it needing additional recapitalization.

These three programs—the F-35A, B-21A, and KC-46A—are intended to replace core platforms, and each is vital for the air force to preserve a combat-credible force, to help deter our adversaries over the coming decisive decade and to ensure the United States maintains airpower dominance well into the future. However, they all face questions of whether sufficient numbers will be delivered in time. Will the current pace of F-35A purchases be enough, particularly as the service fighter fleet shrinks? Will the B-21 Raider enter service in time to strengthen the nation's conventional deterrence during the window of maximum risk? Will fewer than two hundred KC-46As suffice as the legacy tanker fleet reaches old age? If the window of opportunity to deter China is closing, as national security officials have warned, will the air force be ready?

Industrial Limitations and the Navy

The navy faces a similar set of challenges. Like the air force, the navy has undergone a long-term contraction. Once claiming nearly six hundred ships in the waning days of the Cold War, the navy fleet has numbered less than three hundred since 2003. Then, the navy deployed 15 percent of its fleet at a time. Today, it deploys 35 percent.[20] That usage rate contributed directly to the exhausting deployments and tragic accidents previously referenced.

Successive administrations and secretaries of the navy bemoaned the situation, warned of a closing window of opportunity to deter China, and put forward grand plans for a navy with 355 ships. The Biden administration rolled out a new vision to grow it to 373 manned ships and 150 unmanned ships. But talk has not translated to action.[21]

The most recent administration budget proposed decommissioning twenty-four ships, nearly half of which are not even ten years old. The plan would put the navy on a path to 280 battle-force ships in 2027 and push the dream of a larger, more capable navy further into the future.[22] Meanwhile, the PLA navy already surpasses our fleet size, and the Pentagon expects it to grow to 400 ships by 2025 and 440 ships by 2030.[23]

Even if the United States wanted to build ships at that rate, we would be hard pressed due to a lack of shipbuilding and repair capacity. Indeed, the unique features of shipbuilding highlight a second component of the modernization debt: the inescapable limitations of America's industrial base.

The navalist Alexander Wooley sums up the problem well: "For decades, the number of public and private yards has been shrinking, resulting in little competition and reduced capacity. Yards won't invest in infrastructure without orders on the books, and without a steady flow of orders, builders lose skilled workers, know-how, and subcontractors. Unlike in China, there's little commercial shipping to fall back on to keep the US shipbuilding base afloat."[24] Wooley's diagnosis is backed by a 2018 Pentagon assessment of the defense industrial base, which warned that the subtiers of the defense supply chain have been hollowed out, the workforce weakened, and critical capabilities offshored.[25]

Today, the United States is home to just seven large-scale shipyards, compared to dozens operating in China. That disparity severely limits our ability to keep pace. In addition, once ships are built and commissioned, they still face problems created by insufficient infrastructure. Small numbers of old facilities have led to massive maintenance delays, effectively diminishing the fleet's size. In 2021, for example, the submarine fleet lost 1,500 days' worth of operational capacity due to backlogs in dry docks. Some surface combatants have sat in port waiting for maintenance for over a year.

To be clear, supply chain weaknesses, labor and equipment shortages, and shipyard limitations are not the principal source of the navy's modernization problem, nor are they the only obstacle to growing the navy. A lack of strategic clarity and insufficient and unpredictable budgets bear far more blame for the current situation.

Industrial shortages, however, exemplify how a generation of deferred modernization weakened the fighting force and decayed the infrastructure required to modernize, build, and maintain a modern military. To quote a recent bipartisan task force of the Reagan Institute, the slow erosion of our defense industrial base, hastened by underfunding and neglect, has "resulted in America being ill-prepared to act in a time of crisis, with insufficient shipyard capabilities, lack of surge capacity, and uncompetitive pricing."[26]

Moreover, while the navy may be the clearest example, the shortcomings of the defense industrial base reach across the military, as the war in Ukraine has made plain. Decades of "efficiencies" in producing precision-guided munitions have strained supply chains and led to critical dependencies, including on Chinese-made propellants. And unpredictable weapons purchases have whiplashed domestic producers, driving out small and medium-sized contractors.[27] A similar story has played out across the industrial base. Even if America were to commit the resources necessary to procure large numbers of advanced weapons, we would struggle to do so quickly.

America's modernization debt may give policy makers sticker shock, but it should also inspire some introspection. A fundamental truth of defense planning is that today's modernization is tomorrow's readiness. Every year that Washington defers necessary investments, it puts the military deeper in debt in the future and, therefore, in jeopardy.

The readiness crisis of the late 2010s should have taught us this lesson. In the wake of BCA-inflicted budget cuts, the military ran aground. The airframes of old aircraft began to fail, leading to tragic training accidents. Aircrews couldn't keep planes flying, so pilots didn't get the needed training. Scores left the service as a result. Army brigades preparing to deploy regularly couldn't find spare parts, so they would cannibalize them from other units' tanks and vehicles. Navy ships ran rust, and crews suffered long, brutal tours. The nation violated its sacred oath and sent men and women into harm's way without the training or equipment they needed.

The modernization crunch and industrial decay today tell the same story. Due to choices made ten, twenty, and even thirty years ago, the air force will face stealth fighter, bomber, and tanker shortages right at the moment that a peer adversary is making them most vital. The navy will likely be unable to keep pace with China's rapid ascension. America's modernization debt will have a lasting, deleterious effect on America's national security.

What Comes Next?

The case of the defense industrial base should also be a reminder of another, more worrying truth: even in a time of relative peace, America is struggling to build and maintain an undersize military. Yes, threats loom on the horizon, but the long wars have ended. American troops are as out of harm's way as they have been in years. Yet severe, systemic pressures remain and show few signs of abating.

There are many explanations, but the simplest is that defense spending has been deprioritized. Once making up half the federal budget, national defense

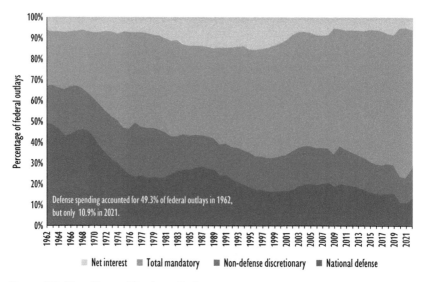

Figure 8.2 Sixty Years of Declining Defense

Source: Office of Management and Budget, Historical Tables, Table 8.1, "Outlays by Budget Enforcement Act Category: 1962–2028," accessed December 2022.

accounted for less than 11 percent of it in 2021 (see fig. 8.2). And as a percentage of GDP—a useful measure of the burden of defense spending on the economy—it has declined from 9 percent in 1962 to 5.7 percent in 1988 to just over 3 percent today. In place of the common defense, social security, Medicaid, Medicare, and other mandatory programs have become the government's principal business, consuming over 70 percent of every dollar Washington spends.

A similar dynamic has occurred within the defense budget. Fixed costs—such as personnel pay, health care, and other operation and maintenance accounts—consume an increasingly large portion of the Pentagon's finances. Operations and maintenance (O&M) and personnel costs account for almost two-thirds, as opposed to just over one-third for modernization accounts.

This balance is a far cry from the last time we faced an existential threat. During the last major modernization era—the Reagan buildup—the balance reached roughly 51 percent O&M and personnel to 45 percent modernization.

Moreover, not every "modernization" dollar is made equal. During that buildup, procurement was the largest account in the defense budget, and the Pentagon spent more than $3 buying equipment for every $1 spent developing it. Now, procurement is the third-largest account, and the modernization ratio has fallen to just $1.33 in equipment bought for each $1 spent on R&D.[28] While R&D spending is the foundation for future technological supremacy, it does not solve the immediate modernization or recapitalization needs of the military. Nor does it position America to win the "decisive decade."

In sum, the United States stands at a perilous moment. More than thirty years of deferred modernization has left the military with a shrinking, antique force and widespread structural deficiencies, including a brittle industrial base. And the future promises heightened competition with an increasingly aggressive Communist China and a widening gap between the nation's strategic goals and what it's willing to spend to accomplish them. No relief appears on the horizon. Instead, we're left with questions about the long-term solvency of America's strategic position and how to preserve it.

First, what would it take for the United States to pay down its modernization debt and restore itself to strategic solvency?

Congress took admirable steps in that direction with the 2022 National Defense Authorization Act, increasing the topline by 8 percent (in nominal terms). However, compare that to the Reagan buildup again, which saw *real* annual growth of upwards of 10 percent and a 49 percent *real* increase in defense spending from 1979 to 1985.[29]

That level of investment may not be necessary now, but it is emblematic of the kind of societal commitment required to recapitalize the force in the past. Is it possible to approach that level again?

The external budgetary pressures of unencumbered entitlement growth will likely not abate. Higher interest rates will drive up the cost of servicing the national debt, and a persistently weak economy would place additional pressure on Washington to prioritize domestic concerns. The internal pressures of pay, health care, and operating costs will also likely grow, spurred in part by inflation and the costs of transitioning away from fossil fuels.

Against those forces, will Congress and the administration get together to raise the level of investment in the common defense, accelerate the recapitalization of the military, and sustain the effort beyond one or two good years?

Second, given the realities of resource constraints, can the United States innovate its way to solvency?

Some have argued that the defense establishment should focus more on developing cutting-edge, revolutionary weapons and pay for them by scrapping legacy systems and shifting money toward these future-oriented programs.

This "divest to invest" concept has its merits, including that it's foolhardy to bet on higher budgets and that there is a military value to smaller, cheaper, dispersible, and survivable capabilities.

It also has its faults. For one, lawmakers and Pentagon leaders seem to forget about the second half of the divest-to-invest equation. That is, they decommission equipment and spend more on R&D, but they have yet to buy actual weapons or platforms at scale.

There is also the danger of trading away useful equipment before the replacement arrives. Much of the promised game-changing technology remains years away from maturity. Even if these research programs succeed fabulously, what is the solution to the shortages that would be produced in the next five years, which happen to coincide with the window of maximum danger from China, if America were to mothball its existing capabilities?

Finally, the argument that America must choose between legacy systems and advanced capabilities sets up a false choice. For one, it presupposes a definition of legacy systems that is hard to match with the reality of military power. The United States operates fleets of aircraft, ships, and vehicles acquired, upgraded, and upgraded again over decades. Some of the most advanced capabilities in the military's arsenal are found on so-called legacy systems. What is the proper definitional line here?

Moreover, the value of a weapons system depends on its intended use. For example, the promise of advanced capabilities largely hinges on their lethality and operational utility in combat. However, the armed services must also perform a long list of duties short of war, including assuring allies and signaling American intent, preserving free lanes of commerce in the commons, and the host of missions and postures that translate to conventional deterrence. These missions often require different tools.

The heated rhetoric of old versus new often skips over these basic considerations and therefore loses the necessary nuance.

THIRD, EVEN IF FUNDING IS SECURED, MODERNIZATION TAKES TIME. WHAT STEPS CAN THE UNITED STATES TAKE TO STRENGTHEN ITS POSITION IN THE INTERIM?

Congressman Mike Gallagher recently warned that "the reality is we won't be able to build the navy the nation needs within the next five years." Therefore, he suggested, the United States should assemble an "anti-navy—asymmetric forces and weapons designed to target the Chinese Navy, deny control of the seas surrounding Taiwan, and prevent the PLA's amphibious forces from gaining a lodgment on the island."[30]

What are the other opportunities, along these lines, to field asymmetric capabilities rapidly and maximize the value of those systems in which the Pentagon is already invested? For example, can upgraded munitions, radars, communications, or other technologies augment the survivability and lethality of American airpower? Or could loyal wingman concepts, wherein unmanned systems support manned systems, prove a force multiplier?[31] What about the potential to improve command and control through advanced battlefield management systems or other enabling tools? Though not revolutionary, these are the types of solutions that could yield tremendous near-term value—and help ease the burden of the modernization debt.

More simply, why not buy more of what's available? The commercial sector offers promising off-the-shelf technologies that could ease the burden on command staffs and operators alike, and the Pentagon has copious authorities to acquire more of it. The solution presents itself. The defense industry can deliver more as well. It just needs stable contracts. Does the military need more firepower? Sign munitions manufacturers to more long-term contracts. Need more airpower? Buy the F-35 at the full rate of production. Cost savings would follow.

Washington must also address two other deficiencies: the decay of the defense industrial base and the slow pace of technological innovation. The aforementioned Reagan Institute Task Force identified four critical steps for rebuilding the nation's industrial competitiveness: first, invest in the American worker by significantly expanding workforce development programs; second, increase access to patient capital through innovative public-private financing vehicles; third, modernize and invoke the Defense Production Act to help rebuild the ecosystem of downstream suppliers; and fourth, facilitate multination innovation and manufacturing by, for example, waiving technology-sharing restrictions.[32] The number of shipyards will not double overnight, but these steps, taken together, could point us in the right direction.

Similarly, if the cutting-edge capabilities of the future will depend upon technologies developed in the commercial sector, then Washington must leverage private capital markets to accelerate innovation. Put simply, hardware innovators need patient capital to get to a scaled product, but private capital is rarely patient. How can Washington help close the gap effectively? The first step is to buy more—make bets on proven technologies and use the Pentagon's buying power to its full extent. Some waste would be inevitable, but could it exceed what already exists in defense contracting? Another idea is to create a trusted "fund of funds," seeded with taxpayer money on a first-loss basis and used as a market-driven vehicle to incentivize greater private capital investment in strategic technologies.[33]

FINALLY, WHAT HAPPENS IF THE MODERNIZATION DEBT IS DEFERRED AGAIN?

The United States stands at a uniquely perilous moment. Vladimir Putin has threatened nuclear war, and his unjust war continues to rage in Ukraine. Xi Jinping recently reaffirmed the Chinese Communist Party's global ambitions, predicting "stormy seas" ahead for the world. Secretary of State Antony Blinken warned that Xi could soon go after Taiwan, and the US Navy brass echoed the alarm. Meanwhile, the administration and Pentagon leaders continue to make strong rhetorical commitments about standing up to China and strengthening America's strategic position.

Small comfort. The United States has a large and growing disconnect between its stated security and defense strategies and the resources it has committed to accomplishing them. Munitions stockpiles are running low, and the modernization debt accumulated over a generation is coming due. It seems the United States faces a stark choice: either match our resources to our strategy or change the strategy.

Notes

1. The White House, *National Security Strategy*, October 2022.

2. US Department of Defense (DoD), Office of the Under Secretary of Defense (Comptroller), *National Defense Budget Estimates for FY 2023 (Green Book)*, July 2022, Table 6-8.

3. Congressional Budget Office (CBO), *An Analysis of the President's Budgetary Proposals for Fiscal Year 2000*, April 1999, 43.

4. Sydney J. Freedberg Jr., "Military Personnel Struggle with Spare Parts," *Government Executive*, December 15, 1999.

5. Jonathan P. Wong, "Balancing Immediate and Long-Term Defense Investments" (PhD diss., Pardee RAND Graduate School, 2016).

6. Mackenzie Eaglen with Hallie Coyne, "The 2020s Tri-Service Modernization Crunch," American Enterprise Institute Report, March 2021.

7. Sandra Erwin, "Five Key Questions about the Defense Budget," *National Defense*, August 1, 2010.

8. Author calculations using data from the Office of Management and Budget and from the Office of the Under Secretary of Defense (Comptroller).

9. James M. Cunningham, "Readiness Tracker, Volume 2: On an Unsustainable Path," American Enterprise Institute Report, May 4, 2016; "Secretary of the Navy US Strategic Readiness Review," *USNI News*, December 14, 2017; Rachel S. Cohen, "Here's All the Military Planes That Keep Falling Short on Readiness," *Air Force Times*, November 16, 2022.

10. US Government Accountability Office, "Defense Acquisitions Annual Assessment: Drive to Deliver Capabilities Faster Increases Importance of Program Knowledge and Consistent Data for Oversight," GAO 20-439, June 2020, 23.

11. Eric Edelman and Gary Roughead, *Providing for the Common Defense: The Assessment and Recommendations of the National Defense Strategy Commission* (Washington, DC: US Institute of Peace, 2018), 36–43.

12. CBO, *Projected Costs of US Nuclear Forces, 2021 to 2030*, May 2021.

13. Eaglen and Coyne, "2020s Tri-Service Modernization Crunch."

14. Heritage Foundation, *2023 Index of Military Strength*, October 2022, https://www.heritage.org/sites/default/files/2022-10/2023_IndexOfUSMilitaryStrength.pdf; Philip Breedlove, John D. W. Corley, William R. Looney III, and T. Michael Moseley, "White House Cuts to F-35 Program Amid Increased Deployments Baffling," *RealClear Defense*, March 26, 2022; Abraham Mahshie, "Air Force to Retire Half Its AWACS Fleet, Most JSTARS, Leaving 'Small Gap' in ISR," *Air & Space Forces Magazine*, March 28, 2022.

15. CBO, *Availability and Use of Aircraft in the Air Force and Navy*, January 5, 2022.

16. Secretary of Air Force Public Affairs, "The Air Force We Need: 386 Operational Squadrons," September 17, 2018.

17. David A. Deptula and Mark A. Gunzinger, "Decades of Air Force Underfunding Threaten America's Ability to Win," Mitchell Institute Policy Paper vol. 37, September 2022.

18. Doug G. Ware, "B-21 Raider: US Military Ready to Unveil First New Bomber of 21st Century," *Stars and Stripes*, December 1, 2022.

19. Heritage Foundation, *2023 Index of Military Strength*.

20. Claude Berube, "Is America Still Born to Rule the Seas?" *War on the Rocks*, December 7, 2021.

21. "Navy Force Structure and Shipbuilding Plans: Background and Issues for Congress," Congressional Research Service RL32665, January 12, 2022.

22. Editorial Board, "The Shrinking US Navy," *Wall Street Journal*, April 4, 2022.

23. DoD, *Military and Security Developments Involving the People's Republic of China 2022: Annual Report to Congress*, November 29, 2022.

24. Alexander Wooley, "Float, Move, and Fight: How the US Navy Lost the Shipbuilding Race," *Foreign Policy*, October 10, 2021.

25. DoD, *Assessing and Strengthening the Manufacturing and Defense Industrial Base and Supply Chain Resiliency of the United States*, Report to President Donald J. Trump by the Interagency Task Force in Fulfillment of Executive Order 13806, September 2018.

26. Ronald Reagan Institute, *A Manufacturing Renaissance: Bolstering US Production for National Security and Economic Prosperity*, Report of the Task Force on National Security and US Manufacturing Competitiveness, November 2021.

27. DoD, *Manufacturing and Defense Industrial Base*; Stacie Pettyjohn and Hannah Dennis, "Precision and Posture: Defense Spending Trends and the FY23 Budget Request," Center for a New American Security, November 17, 2022, 18.

28. Author calculations using data from the Office of Management and Budget.

29. DoD, *National Defense Budget Estimates for FY 2023*.

30. Mike Gallagher, "The 'Anti-Navy' the US Needs against the Chinese Military," *Wall Street Journal*, October 25, 2022.

31. Gary Schmitt and James Cunningham, "Pilotless Fighters: Getting Numbers and Capabilities," *RealClear Defense*, June 16, 2021.

32. Ronald Reagan Institute, *A Manufacturing Renaissance*.

33. David H. McCormick with James M. Cunningham, *Superpower in Peril: A Battle Plan to Renew America* (Nashville, TN: Center Street, 2023).

9

A Requiem for Defense Innovation?

Ukraine, the Pentagon's Innovator's Dilemma, and Why the United States Risks Strategic Surprise

Christopher Kirchhoff

In 1989, Apple CEO John Sculley had a vision of the future. He foresaw a convergence of consumer electronics and telecommunications and started a secret group within Apple to explore what this would make possible. It was called the "Paradigm Project," and its mission was to build "a tiny computer, a phone, a very personal object. . . . It must be beautiful. Once you use it, you won't be able to live without it."[1]

When the small team's attempts to bring together the component technologies of the smartphone struggled for resources within a corporate culture at Apple that was pursuing other priorities, Sculley spun the company out, realizing it could only thrive if set apart. The spinout, General Magic, quickly grew to one hundred employees. Working feverishly in the early 1990s and eventually in partnership with Sony, Motorola, Philips, and AT&T, it developed precursors to USB, software modems, touchscreens, multimedia email, networked games, streaming TV, voice recognition–based personal assistants, and e-commerce applications.[2]

General Magic came tantalizingly close to realizing the vision for a tiny computer phone. Ultimately, its technology fell short of the advances needed for a consumer device. It would be another decade before Apple productized General Magic's innovations in the 2007 release of the iPhone, which brought the power of computing and the reach of the internet into the palms of our hands. Apple's iPhone became the fastest proliferating device in human history, revolutionizing how we live and work and laying the foundation for future industries, including today's "Internet of Things," which comprises 31 billion devices worldwide.

What does this story tell us about our world? The interplay between radical visions, motivated teams working outside of corporate strictures, and the struggle to bring innovation back into settled organizations is a common motif in the history of technology. The very structure of market capitalism and large institutions makes for a dynamic in which stunning advances often occur outside places where they can easily be scaled. This gives innovation its "fits and starts" character, with surprising gaps frequently emerging between the invention of technology and when it becomes widely available. Looking at the same phenomenon through a business lens, the late Harvard Business School professor Clayton Christensen described "the innovator's dilemma" faced by successful corporations that fail to pivot to the technologies that will prevail tomorrow.[3]

Seven years after Secretary of Defense Ash Carter spun out Defense Innovation Unit Experimental (DIUx) and launched the Defense Innovation Board (DIB) and the Defense Digital Service (DDS), it's time to ask whether this motif is playing out inside the Pentagon as well. These initiatives and other innovation cells inspired by them in each military service, like the Algorithmic Warfare Cross-Functional Team that launched Project Maven, have achieved stunning successes in both deployable technology and the methods used to develop and procure it. Yet despite notable progress in specific areas and on small scales, they have not meaningfully transformed how the Pentagon adopts emerging technologies or procures large systems for the future of war.

Like their fellow travelers at General Magic, who watched as Apple remained unmoved by the promise of an integrated smartphone, the innovators Carter unleashed in 2015 see the kind of war they imagined in 2016 and 2017 playing out today on the European steppe. Ukrainian command and control are substantially enabled by modern digital technology like smartphones, secure messaging apps, and Starlink. Significant intelligence, surveillance, and reconnaissance come from commercial satellites and social media apps that enable real-time citizen reporting of Russian positions. Commanders direct strikes using commercial drones. Perhaps most strikingly, commercial technologies are being deployed by both Russia and Ukraine in tandem with exquisite weapons systems to enhance their effectiveness and better enable their defeat. One of the most significant lessons to emerge from Ukraine may be the difference commercial technology makes in a great-power conflict, especially its ability to attrit superior enemy weapons systems, supplant legacy command, control, intelligence, and reconnaissance, and multiply the combat effectiveness of stock armaments from Ukraine, Russia, NATO, and the United States.

Yet eight months into a real-life demonstration of the hypothesis that led Ash Carter to launch his innovation initiatives, Pentagon acquisition chief Bill LaPlante—the man most responsible for future US armaments—said this:

> We're not fighting in Ukraine with Silicon Valley right now, even though they're going to try to take credit for it. The tech bros aren't helping us too much in Ukraine. . . . It's hardcore production of really serious weaponry. . . . That's what matters. . . . If somebody gives you a really cool liquored-up story about a DIU project or OTA contract, ask them when it's going into production. Ask them how many numbers, ask them what the unit cost is going to be, ask them how it will work against China. . . . Ask them all those questions because that's what matters. And don't tell me it's got AI and quantum in it. I don't care.[4]

LaPlante's sentiment that commercial technology is not a significant driver of battlefield outcomes in Ukraine and has few use cases against the Department of Defense (DoD) keeping pace with adversaries, while met with fierce criticism, is to a significant degree reflected in where dollars and leadership attention are spent.[5] Despite having the highest conversion rate to the production of any DoD entity, including the Defense Advanced Research Projects Agency (DARPA), DIUx's budget has flatlined after two successive under secretaries of research and engineering, the first of whom served under Trump and the other under Biden. Both chose not to support its growth. The sitting secretary of the air force just scaled back AFWERX, the service's commercial technology incubator, influencing the retirement of its director. Even as the commercial sector leads in eleven of the fourteen critical technology areas identified by the Pentagon's under secretary of defense for research and engineering, Heidi Shyu, her own office, which administers a new fund to transition emerging technologies expeditiously, recently made only one of ten awards to a venture-backed business.[6] While these outcomes are not the full story, they are certainly not what was hoped for by Ash Carter when he nudged the department toward embracing the fruits of the $25 trillion commercial technology market.

This paper traces efforts at defense innovation across three presidential administrations—those of Barack Obama, Donald Trump, and Joe Biden. It highlights significant successes but notes substantial stasis across existing initiatives. It explores whether, in light of Ukraine and parallel developments in other battlespaces, especially China, the stalling of the innovation agenda may spell a future strategic surprise for the United States.[7] The Pentagon's innovator's dilemma in this way may be an ordinary and expected outcome in the struggle for disruptive change in one of the world's largest institutions, while at the same time—because of the rapidly changing landscape—a strategic crisis for the United States.

Defense Innovation's First Wave: The Obama Years

Ash Carter's great insight into the future came in 2001. America's twenty-fifth secretary of defense, then a Harvard professor, wrote of a looming challenge to the military's technological edge. This challenge emerged not from an external threat but from "trends in the industrial and technology base." A decade after the end of the Cold War, advanced technology, "once largely the creation of the Department of Defense," he noted, is "increasingly becoming commercialized and globalized. Tomorrow's defense innovations will largely be derivatives of technology developed and marketed by commercial companies for commercial motives." To keep its edge, Carter concluded, the military "must be the world's fastest adapter and adopter of commercial technology into defense systems."[8]

Carter was sworn in as secretary at a time when the world was awash in the newly powerful technology he foresaw. The global consumer market was by now orders of magnitude larger than the Pentagon's acquisition and R&D budgets (see fig. 9.1). In less than a generation, the locus of innovation moved from defense labs to tech companies, many of them global, with some of the most important located in China. By 2015, Google and Apple were each larger by market capitalization than the US defense industry. Apple had, then, and has today, enough cash to buy all prime defense contractors outright. The result of this shift is seen in the hardware the military uses today. All but 4 percent of the components in one of the US military's most advanced electronic warfare systems—the Aegis-class destroyer—are commercially available.

This diffusion of military power, unprecedented in speed and scale, touched off an innovation race among advanced militaries. Carter moved to better position the United States for it by launching three initiatives, creating (1) an innovation board of luminaries to provide a vision for the department;

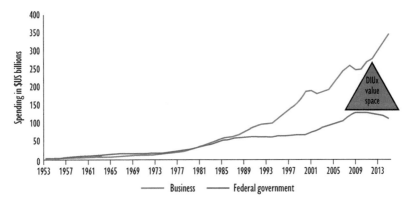

Figure 9.1 Commercial versus Federal Government R&D Expenditures, 1953–2013

The private sector outspends the federal government in R&D spending by a ratio of more than three to one.

Source: Defense Innovation Unit Experimental (DIUx), 2016.

(2) DDS, a software factory; and (3) DIUx, a new embassy of sorts in Silicon Valley. Specifically, DIUx was created to pilot commercial technologies in military missions and went on to open offices in the tech hubs of Boston, Austin, and later Chicago.

Momentum for using off-the-shelf technology and hardware and software from start-ups had been building. Special Operations Command's SOFWERX, the US Navy, US Cyber Command, and the National Geospatial-Intelligence Agency were already engaging the Valley differently in the 2010s. Small delegations from each arrived to find In-Q-Tel already there. Since its inception in 1999, the intelligence community's strategic investment firm has made three hundred twenty-five investments to advance the intel mission.[9] Multiple DARPA offices also had long sought R&D breakthroughs from start-ups and continued to engage them. Importantly, though, DARPA's mission to prevent and create strategic surprises through bold technical leaps was distinct from what Carter envisioned for DIUx, which focuses on adapting fully developed commercial technology for use on the battlefield.[10]

To a significant degree, Carter launched these initiatives out of desperation. In the view of Chris Brose, former staff director of the Senate Armed Services Committee, the second decade of the twenty-first century was one of colossal missed opportunities for the US military. DoD, on the whole, had missed the advent of modern software development, the move to cloud computing, the commercial space revolution, the centrality of data, and the rise of artificial intelligence (AI) and machine learning. This was the case despite having funded the fundamental research that led to many of these advances.[11] DIUx and DDS were to change this by placing DoD personnel directly in the commercial technology ecosystem.

DIUx was announced at Stanford University by Carter during the first visit to Silicon Valley by a secretary of defense in a generation.[12] When its first iteration failed to take root, Carter doubled down, announcing what he called "DIUx 2.0." With its additional features, the new release included a direct report to him and the capability to rapidly contract, which version 1.0 lacked.

DIUx 2.0 proved the validity of its model almost immediately. It funded $250 million in pilot technology projects in its first eighteen months. DIUx also pioneered a novel use of Other Transaction Authority (OTA), a little-used acquisition pathway developed in 1958 to meet NASA's need to contract quickly with small businesses during the space race. The specific OTA contract DIUx developed in 2016, called a Commercial Solutions Opening (CSO), could be closed in under a month and allowed for the immediate conversion of successful pilots into production—available to be bought by any customer across the DoD—without further negotiation. This contracting superpower was enabled by new authorities granted by Congress that no one in the department had bothered to use. DIUx exported this contracting innovation via a "how-to" manual so other entities across the department could run the same play. It also got Carter, in four weeks' time, to bless it as a DoD-wide policy. By 2022, this small revolution in procurement was used to acquire $39 billion of commercial technology for the DoD.[13]

DIUx's early projects mirrored General Magic's experimentation with the component technologies of the future. They included microsatellites using low-cost synthetic aperture radar (SAR) sensors to pinpoint enemy weapons, AI-powered drones, robotic boats that provide surface effects at fractions of the cost of a destroyer, cloud computing infrastructure with native machine-learning capabilities, and even flying cars and autonomous undersea vehicles.[14]

While not every project was a success, and not every company DIUx worked with is still in business today, its early track record was promising. Among DIUx's initial wins: finding a low-cost way to deliver on-orbit SAR capability against a top-five military intelligence priority and developing an app that optimized mission planning for fifteen-hundred daily tanker refuelings during the air war against ISIS. With its tanker refueling app, DIUx did for the air force in one hundred thirty-two days and for $1.5 million what a ten-year, $750 million program of record had not. The chief of staff of the air force was sufficiently impressed by DIUx's handiwork that he moved to create Kessel Run, the air force's software factory, which now employs 1,200 people, and named the project manager of the tanker app to lead it.[15]

Crucially, early rounds of DIUx contracts helped catalyze a new trend of venture funding for start-ups that explicitly target the defense market, with the round Andreessen Horowitz led for Capella Space at DIUx's instigation being something of a shot heard 'round the Valley. Traditional defense contractors also shifted into innovation gear, with Boeing's HorizonX, Lockheed Martin Ventures, and Airbus Ventures becoming investors in the Valley ecosystem.

The DIB and DDS bolted out of the starting blocks as well. Filled with technology luminaries, the DIB's members traveled with the leaders of DDS and DIUx to dozens of installations in the United States and overseas, meeting with commanders and rank-and-file operators.[16] They transformed insights from hundreds of hours of observation into landmark reports that established a framework for the software revolution that swept the department, the adoption of AI, how to grapple with 5G, and how to manage talent more effectively. They also established a set of principles for the ethical use of AI in war.[17] DDS quickly created the federal government's first-ever bug bounty program, memorably titled "Hack the Pentagon," which was open to coders in all countries except Iran, North Korea, and China. DDS also created a new compliance framework to more rapidly get new software up and running and dispatched its "SWAT team" of coders and data scientists to all corners of the department.[18]

By the time Ash Carter left office on January 20, 2017, his three vehicles for commercial innovation—DIB, DDS, and DIUx—were not even two years into their operational missions. Yet each made its mark, producing local success with global lessons for how DoD could import powerful technologies honed in commercial markets. By themselves, these vehicles were not designed to be of the scale or heft to foundationally alter department practices. The three entities had little more than a hundred people and a combined budget of less than $100 million. Yet they succeeded on the terms Ash Carter set by proving the model of innovation they were predicated on and by inspiring others to follow in their wake. To borrow a phrase from Mao Zedong that Carter would chuckle at were he still with us, his actions let a thousand flowers bloom, particularly as commands in each service set up their own miniature DIUxs and DDSs (see fig. 9.2). It would be up to his successors to build on this momentum.

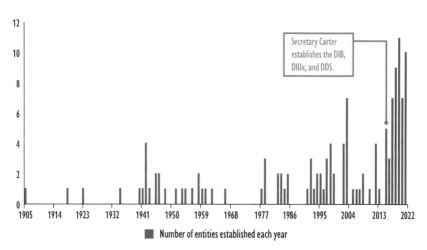

Figure 9.2 Historical Pace of Innovation in the US Armed Forces

Sources: Eric Schmidt, "Remembering Ash Carter: The Innovative Secretary of Defense Who Changed the Pentagon, Silicon Valley, and the Trajectory of Our Nation," Special Competitive Studies Project, January 26, 2023; data drawn in part from Under Secretary of Defense for Research and Engineering, "Innovation Organizations."

Innovation under the Trump Administration

The election of Donald J. Trump as the forty-fifth president was a pivotal point for so many things, including commercial approaches in the department, which changed due to the absence of political leadership and the new directions from that leadership once it finally arrived. In an alternate universe where Hillary Clinton would have been elected president, continuity at the political level would almost certainly have ensured Carter's initiatives scaled dramatically, even if he had not remained secretary. Under Trump, the road was more uncertain.

While the Senate quickly confirmed James Mattis as secretary of defense, the rest of the political leadership was slow to arrive, leaving vacancies that persisted throughout the entire Trump administration but were especially severe in its first two years. Continuity was initially provided by the hold-over deputy secretary of defense, Robert O. Work, who worked closely with the vice chairman of the Joint Chiefs, Paul Selva, for the first six months of the Trump administration to push forward the innovation efforts begun by Carter.

Mattis, who had concurrently helmed the United States Joint Forces Command and served as NATO's Supreme Allied Commander Transformation, and went on to live in Silicon Valley and teach at Stanford after retiring from active duty, immediately grasped the value of DIUx. He declared loudly and repeatedly during his first visit to Silicon Valley as secretary in August of 2017 that DIUx was here to stay (see fig. 9.3).[19] He even affixed a decal of DIUx's logo to the leather notebook he carried everywhere as a deliberate symbol of support.[20] In the weeks after his visit, DIUx staff enjoyed seeing their logo appear in photos when Mattis met with the Crown Prince of Saudi Arabia and other world leaders.

Even as the political leadership of the Trump Pentagon was slow to coalesce around a new strategy and budget, innovation continued to bloom. Secretary of the Air Force Heather Wilson announced the creation of AFWERX in August 2017. She described it as an island of misfit toys for entrepreneurs in the air force who, by embracing commercial approaches, would increase "lethality at a lower cost."[21] In June 2018, the Joint Artificial Intelligence Center (JAIC), pronounced "jake," became the latest special purpose office

Figure 9.3 DIUx in Silicon Valley

Secretary of Defense James Mattis with the DIUx team in front of a Saildrone autonomous ship (August 10, 2017)

Source: Office of the Secretary of Defense, Public Affairs.

within the Office of the Secretary of Defense (OSD) to join the innovation ranks, with a remit to accelerate the delivery and adoption of AI. In August 2018, the army announced the stand-up of Army Futures Command, whose entire premise was that new technological approaches were needed to compete with near-peer adversaries and that accessing them would require new kinds of acquisition processes and partnerships with the private sector.

Inspired by DIUx, partners and allies sent liaison officers to reside in Mountain View, delegations to visit, and started innovation cells of their own. The UK launched a Defence and Security Accelerator in late 2016. Conversations begun inside NATO in 2016 and 2017 ultimately matured, at the alliance's usual pace of working, into the announcement of the NATO Innovation Fund in 2022. The militaries of Australia, India, Singapore, and France launched innovation initiatives for themselves. Mattis went one step further by announcing that DIUx would become a permanent part of the department, to be known simply as Defense Innovation Unit, without the "X." The experiment had succeeded. Deputy Secretary Patrick Shanahan, who provided day-to-day support for DIUx in the initial months of his tenure, codified this change in a memo signed on August 3, 2018.[22]

At the same time, Mattis's embrace of DIU and other innovation initiatives was not fully shared by several appointees who came to serve him in key positions. Michael Griffin, the new under secretary of defense for research and engineering, placed the innovation agenda low on his priority list and generally viewed Silicon Valley with skepticism, seeing its technology as second class to "real science and engineering" that took place in defense labs by "real scientists and engineers." This despite having once been the chief operating officer of In-Q-Tel. In private conversations with the DIB and the director of DIU, he was even dismissive and, at times, outright condescending. This was especially unfortunate from DIU's perspective because, administratively, DIU had come to report to Griffin rather than the secretary or deputy. Griffin abruptly fired long-standing members of the DIB, including its chair, Eric Schmidt. The momentum the DIB gained through four years of work met a sudden end. A two-year hiatus ensued until the DIB was ultimately reconstituted in the next administration with Michael Bloomberg as its chair, but only after a lengthy "zero-based review" of boards and commissions further delayed its relaunch.

Griffin and his deputy Lisa Porter were ultimately let go after less than eighteen months on the job. Their departure was at once a relief to advocates of innovation and a worry, as the chief technology officer position at the Pentagon was again vacant in a building already riddled with vacancies. That position was eventually filled for the last six months of the administration when President Trump's chief technology officer, thirty-three-year-old Michael Kratsios, was tapped to perform the additional role of the Pentagon's chief technology officer.[23]

Even though the vehicles Ash Carter created for innovation in 2015 had hoped for a different future in the Trump years, important progress was still made in the department's thinking about technology as a whole. The language around large system design and procurement used particularly by the air force for its Advanced Battle Management System displayed nuanced attention to how digital technologies and cloud computing will layer with the systems and installations that command and control military assets. A subsequent air force vice chief of staff, musing about the new approach to systems design, asked and answered his rhetorical question in the way a Silicon Valley programmer would have: "What exactly is ABMS?" he asked. "Is it software? Hardware? Infrastructure? Policy? The answer is yes to all."[24] This same approach to design informs the ambitious and beleaguered Joint All-Domain Command and Control (JADC2), a reimagining of cross-service command and control on an even grander scale.[25] The scale of JADC2 is so grand that many wonder how so many component systems will be tied together when the department is only at the earliest stages of moving to a cloud-based architecture and continues to define JADC2's scope.[26]

Whatever historians and defense analysts ultimately assess about the Trump Pentagon, it seems safe to conclude now that something of a paradox was at work. On the one hand, Trump secured astonishing budget increases for the Pentagon in his first two years in office, upping its budget by $65 billion in FY2018 and a further $17 billion in FY2019. During his presidency, DoD spending grew $98 billion, or 16 percent.[27] The infusion of new resources on a level not seen since 9/11 provided a remarkable moment of opportunity in a system so captured by its own inertia and strictures imposed by congressional line items that new money was often the only way to set off in new directions. But in the absence of a detailed strategy pushing significant changes upon the military services, led personally by the secretary and a fully seated political leadership, the infusion of new money was largely put toward existing programs of record and the incremental modernization they sought.

Even had a muscular strategy of commercial technology adoption been at the ready, the devolution by Congress of many acquisition authorities to the services as part of a package of reforms that split Acquisition, Technology, and Logistics (AT&L) into two offices by now made a centralized strategy, developed by the secretary, more difficult to achieve. Trump, at this point, made matters even worse by rapidly cycling through defense secretaries. The abrupt resignation of Mattis in December 2019 in protest of the withdrawal from Syria was the first domino to fall. Trump left Mattis's deputy Patrick Shanahan in acting status for six months before nominating Secretary of the Army Mark Esper to the post, who he later fired by tweet. Acting secretary Christopher Miller's seventy-two days of service in the chaotic last months of the administration were marred by the events of January 6th and no notable policy accomplishments produced.[28]

Looking through the civil-military tumult that defined the Trump years, three moments from his stewardship of innovation at the Pentagon stand out. The first is his insistence on creating a space force over the wishes of the civilian and military leadership of the air force. The new miniature service has come to carve out an esprit de corps that unapologetically embraces the culture and modalities of innovation. A short walk down the new space force hallway in the Pentagon reveals displays filled with levity, pop-culture references, and *Star Trek* memorabilia, which stand in delightful, even subversive, contrast to the solemn, severe oil paintings of marine corps commandants on the opposite wall.[29] (US Space Force's motto, *Semper supra*, Latin for "always above," even plays homage to or perhaps is a playful twist on the US Marines' *Semper fidelis*, for "always faithful.")

The second was the sudden downscoping of DIU's largest contract after an incumbent firm, Oracle, which had not even competed for it, filed a protest with the Government Accountability Office (GAO). The chain of events is as follows. US Transportation Command (TRANSCOM), via DIU, awarded a production OTA contract to a firm named REAN Cloud after it successfully demonstrated a prototype that automated the movement of insecure legacy TRANSCOM applications to the cloud. The production contract was the largest DIU had awarded to that point, with a $950 million ceiling, though with far less funds initially obligated.[30] Two weeks after the award, the legacy cloud provider, Oracle, filed a protest with the GAO questioning REAN's partnership with Amazon Cloud Services as well as the use of the OTA contract vehicle for the award. Several days later, and more than two months before the GAO ruled on the protest, the Pentagon press secretary announced from the podium that the DoD was downscoping the original DIU contract by 90 percent to $65 million and narrowing its scope to use only by TRANSCOM and not across the DoD as enabled by the production OTA.[31] While the exact reasons behind the downscoping remain contested, the collapse of this contract reverberates in Silicon Valley to this day as yet another reason why it's not worth it for new entrants to compete for department business.[32]

The third and perhaps most symbolic moment vis-à-vis innovation came earlier in Trump's presidency, in March 2017, when he christened the $13 billion USS *Gerald Ford*. On the deck of this new class of carriers, Trump vowed to expand the number of carriers from ten to twelve.[33] The whole episode, in the zero-sum game of weapons procurement, reinforced a preference for legacy platforms at the expense of experimentation with new ones and came at a time when the advent of Chinese "carrier-killer" missiles so clearly signaled the end of the carrier era. Instead of confronting the crisis of commissioning a ship that is unlikely to survive the opening salvos of war in the Pacific, Trump developed a peculiar obsession with the *Ford*'s electromagnetic catapult system and spent much of his remarks wondering aloud whether the navy should return to proven steam technology to launch planes.

Biden Takes the Helm

The Biden administration arrived in Washington to find the city ringed by barricades put in place after the events of January 6. It was also filled with a new consensus that China's aggregation of military capability needed to be urgently countered. The Chinese had been busy enacting their own ambitious military innovation strategy, termed "military-civilian fusion," in which every commercial innovation by industry will be made available to the People's Liberation Army. Xi Jinping announced this strategy almost in parallel to Carter's initiatives in 2015. By 2022, it was beginning to bear fruit of the kind that kept making US forces lose in war games. When coupled with well-funded Chinese national initiatives in multiple technology sectors, new energy existed in Washington for substantial change to US forces, statecraft, and industrial policy.

At the White House, the Biden National Security Council (NSC) established a deputy national security advisor for cyber and emerging technology and enlarged the NSC's technology directorate. President Biden went on to inhibit China's access to advanced microprocessors, curtail foreign investments in sensitive US technology, and implement the CHIPS Act, which underwrote the onshoring of microprocessor production and government-sponsored research for future chip generations. It was a stunning acceleration of the decoupling with China that began under Trump and the first major act of industrial policy in decades. The moves garnered bipartisan support and deepened a kind of US-China cold war while making the geopolitical dimensions of commercial technology more visible.

At the Pentagon, DIU director Mike Brown, the former CEO of Symantec, was put forward to serve as under secretary for acquisition and sustainment. It was a historic nomination—the first person since David Packard with a software and Silicon Valley background to oversee the Pentagon's $200 billion procurement spend. Secretary Lloyd Austin, too, was initially vocal about commercial technology even as he disregarded the advice of venture capitalists and the heads of his own innovation initiatives on what policies to pursue. At his first major speech addressing the topic at the Reagan National Defense Forum in December 2021, Austin outlined a plan to double the Small Business Innovation Research (SBIR) program, open innovation hubs in Chicago and Seattle, and establish a Rapid Defense Experimentation Reserve to test new technologies.[34] The Biden team also announced an Emerging Capabilities Policy Office within the Office of the Secretary of Defense for Policy, created a Chief Digital and Artificial Intelligence Office, named the former head of machine intelligence at Lyft to lead it, and in late 2022 established the Office of Strategic Capital to liaise with private capital markets.[35] Space command also launched a commercial incubator named— you guessed it—SpaceWERX.

Even bigger pieces on the DoD chessboard were already in motion when the Biden team arrived. In his July 2019 guidance to the force, the newly installed commandment of the marine corps proposed sweeping changes to optimize the corps' ability to operate within denied areas in a fight in the Western Pacific.[36] Rocket artillery, drones, loitering munitions, electronic warfare, and littoral combat capabilities were in, while tanks were out, and artillery batteries, infantry, and helicopter lift were reduced. It was a rare example of a leader willing to remove the existing capability to make room for new ones. All hell broke loose in defense circles when this imaginative, thought-through plan surfaced.[37] As shocking as the idea of a marine corps without tanks and with three fewer infantry battalions was to retired marine generals and one former secretary of the navy, even more shocking to most was a sitting four-star general radically reshaping a military service to face down a new threat. It was as if force structure had become so immutable and unchanging that when someone altered it, no one initially believed it. With the support of Secretary Austin, the commandant presented detailed guidance affirming his initial judgments in March 2020.[38]

Change was thus in the air in the early Biden Pentagon. Encouragingly, a review by the Innovation Steering Group created by the deputy secretary surfaced a large and diverse ecosystem of DoD entities that had taken up the innovation mission. To illustrate their reporting relationship, the department printed one of its "horse-blanket" charts—Pentagon vernacular for a large diagram that could keep a horse warm. (See fig. 9.4 for a miniaturized version of this chart, published in May 2022.) The under secretary for research and engineering likewise compiled an online database of innovation entities, including a list and map view with eleven different categories of innovation institutions.[39]

DIU, meanwhile, kept chugging. With $892.7 million in contracts signed between June 2016 and the end of 2021, it began to approach its own kind of unicorn status in the Valley, that mythical billion-dollar valuation mark that denotes monumental success in the hypercompetitive world of entrepreneurship.[40] Companies funded by DIU had raised $11.7 billion from venture capitalists, with one of them, Anduril, joining Palantir and SpaceX as defense unicorns. The ecosystem Ash Carter wanted DIUx to seed was starting to take shape, with $20 of equity invested on average by the venture community for every $1 of prototype contracts that DIU awarded to a company.

By now, software factories were also beginning to deliver real capability. Five years after DIUx hacked its way to a new a tanker planning tool at the Combined Air Operations Center in Qatar, Kessel Run completed a total overhaul of that same center's entire command-and-control system, a significant milestone in the air force's in-house development of software.[41] The talent exchanges Carter called for in 2015 were also beginning, with Apple and other name-brand companies participating. AFWERX even launched a fellowship enabling midcareer officers, enlisted personnel, and civilians from all military branches to apply for short immersion experiences in venture capital firms, technology incubators, and start-ups.[42]

While there were many visible successes on the innovation front and many more nontraditional companies getting contracts from the services, there were early signs that the Biden DoD would ultimately not prioritize the innovation portfolio as much as Ash Carter did or spend political capital ensuring its success. Mike Brown's nomination was withdrawn after a whistleblower resurfaced complaints about whether DIU had misused hiring authority that DIU's general counsel had already adjudicated as spurious.[43] Rather than insist upon an expedited review by the inspector general, the secretary,

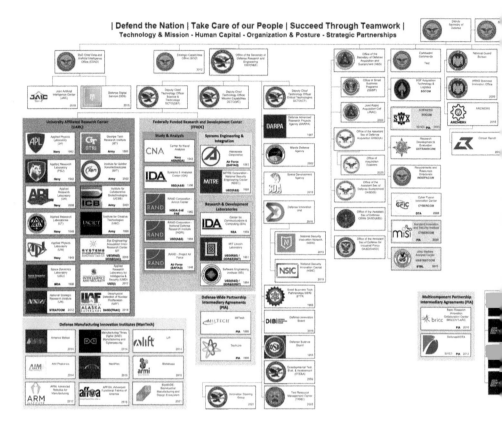

Figure 9.4 The Department of Defense Reporting Relationship Diagram

Source: Office of the Secretary of Defense, Innovation Steering Group: Michael Murray, Analyst, May 2022.

deputy secretary, and the White House took no steps at all. Brown's nomination collapsed, only to have the inspector general fully exonerate him one week after he stepped down as DIU director in September 2022.[44] It was a huge blow to advocates of innovation, who know the adage that "personnel is policy" is especially true in an administration's opening months and wished the department's leadership had gone to greater lengths to see Brown's nomination through.

The DIU budget was another sore spot. The political leadership of the Biden Pentagon kept suggesting lower levels than Congress was willing to fund, with DIU's expenditures at their high mark, reaching 0.01 percent of the DoD budget and less than 0.05 percent of the procurement budget. Rather

Innovation Ecosystem 2022

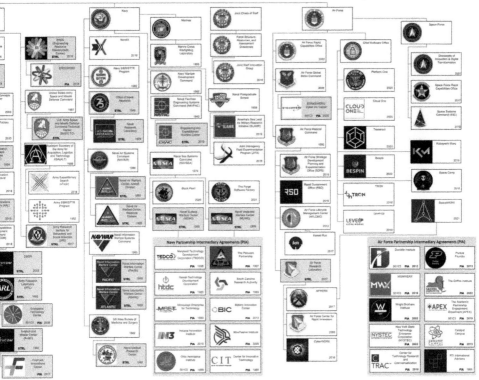

than growing into something on par with the size of DARPA and leading the adoption of commercial technology for the joint force, DIU's comparatively modest budget never gave it the heft many hoped for. Cuts at AFWERX, directed by the secretary of the air force, came the year after.

Other worrying signs continued to mount even before LaPlante, who was nominated in Brown's place, made his "tech bros" comments. Deputy Secretary Kathleen Hicks did not visit DIU on her first trip to Silicon Valley.[45] When asked by a group of entrepreneurs how their technology could most quickly enter the department, she suggested they explore SBIRs—a type of grant venture-backed companies are mostly ineligible to receive because of congressional small business set-asides prioritizing sole-owner enterprises.

In Silicon Valley, a series of SBIR awards with no further investment signals that you couldn't hack it—that venture investors looked at your technology and business model and declined to invest. As one former staff member on the Senate Armed Services Committee noted, "the just-under $2 billion that DoD spends on SBIR in minuscule, thinly spread tranches is a trifling amount compared to the $400 billion that venture capitalists have recently spent on innovation . . . or the $1.8 trillion private equity industry that is a barely tapped resource for DoD."[46]

McKinsey & Company similarly found that, despite all the innovation initiatives, the portion of the DoD budget dedicated to early-stage technology had not changed over time. By McKinsey's methodology, early-stage innovation accounted for only $34 billion of the $857 billion earmarked for US national security spending for 2022—approximately 4 percent of the total. The analysis further noted that this share had not changed significantly from prior years, nor was it programmed to change across the five-year future budget.[47]

Today in Ukraine, Tomorrow in Taiwan

As the Pentagon's policy agenda took greater shape toward the midpoint of Biden's term, any assessment of defense innovation would necessarily reach mixed conclusions. Individual services and the Office of the Secretary of Defense have more innovation entities than ever before, and more of them have connectivity with the Valley. Larger amounts are being spent on more CSOs year after year. But a composite military vision or approach that fully leverages commercial technology into a new construct for joint warfighting and an associated plan for force design and development is proving elusive. Nor are resources flowing to innovation at the scale needed for the department to realize Ash Carter's "fast-follower" vision. To the extent present military and civilian leadership is articulating a strategy, it is one built, for the most part, on a continuation of previous programmatic and budgetary trendlines with marginally greater inclusion of emerging technologies and only a few significant departures from historical baselines—with the marine corps being one of the more commendable. If there is a strategy for losing a future war with China, this is it. And yet, developments in international security so mirrored the world foreseen in 2015–16 by the original cast of defense innovators that the intellectual constructs they built their enterprises around now appear prophetic.

The first surprise of Biden's presidency occurred in May of 2021 when cyberattacks launched by a ransomware group likely based in Russia caused a shutdown of the 5,500-mile Colonial Pipeline, the single most important energy artery in the United States. Gas prices surged in the Southeast. Only quick action by authorities and the company averted a further cascade of effects in the lower forty-eight states.

The second surprise happened on July 27, 2021, when China launched the world's first nuclear-capable hypersonic weapon—an arrowhead-shaped sheath of titanium that flies at ten times the speed of sound, can't be seen by early warning radars, and can evade all known defenses. The chairman of the Joint Chiefs called this China's "Sputnik moment."[48] The USS *Ford*'s malfunction-prone electromagnetic catapult was suddenly less of an issue for the navy than the ship's radar signature.

The third surprise occurred two months later when unsophisticated commercial drones with loitering munitions decimated Armenian troops in the September–October 2021 conflict with Azerbaijan. Together with Russia's earlier, if unsuccessful, deployment of autonomous tanks in the Syrian civil war, these developments signaled that autonomous weapons of all kinds, some expensive and sophisticated, others cheap and attritable, would be persistent features on future battlefields.

The fourth and most significant surprise occurred when Putin ordered his forces into Ukraine. The conflict immediately had a kind of *Ghost Fleet: A Novel of the Next World War*–meets–MacGyver quality, with the most sophisticated weapons platforms fielded by the West and Russia, enmeshed together on the battlefield alongside lower-tech innovations that were lethal on their own and even more lethal when used in conjunction with major weapons systems.[49] To list just a few of the battlefield developments beyond those already mentioned in this paper's introduction: uncrewed small boats attacking Russian navy warships; Soviet-era surveillance drones modified by Ukraine being used to strike targets deep in Russian territory; $20,000 Iranian-made kamikaze drones built with 82 percent American technology shutting off the power in Kyiv in winter; Ukraine launching missiles costing between $140,000 and $500,000 to down them; DJI drones used by infantry units on both sides of the conflict; and spotter teams driving pickup trucks streaming video for targeting via a Starlink terminal connected to a generator in the back.[50] This is a war where the most lethal weapons system on the ground, the US-provided high-mobility artillery rocket system (HIMARS), is being directed where to fire by something that can be bought on Amazon.

Lieutenant General Jack Shanahan (Ret.), the former director of Project Maven and the JAIC, notes that "we are in a critical 'bridge period' where the most creative and innovative warfighters will figure out how to mate legacy equipment with emerging technologies, and along the way come up with novel operating concepts."[51] Commercial technology in Ukraine thus made for a deus ex machina moment, where god (and Elon Musk) reversed a seemingly hopeless situation to stop an invading Russian army and force it far into retreat.

Contrary to LaPlante's assertion, the tech "bros" and their tech are in Ukraine and matter to the fight. Microsoft and US Cyber Command repelled Russian cyberattacks long enough to keep Ukraine's internet running and allow the Ukrainian government to convert essential IT infrastructure and citizen services to cloud enclaves.[52] Elon Musk rushed in with Starlink terminals and repositioned his constellations of satellites. Amazon ferried in civilian supplies and ferried out 10 million gigabytes of tax, property records, banking, and other critical data in suitcase-sized "Snowball Edge" solid-state storage devices.[53] Capella Space supplies both the Ukrainian military and CNN with real-time imagery. Palantir is driving a new digital kill chain fueled by open-source intelligence.[54] Anduril has "hardware, software, and people in Ukraine," with Palmer Luckey and teams of engineers even traveling to the front to improve the software powering Anduril drones.[55] Counter-drone systems, including those fielded by firms that worked with DIU, are also on the battlefield, alongside half a dozen other companies in the DIU portfolio.[56] As Eric Schmidt's trip report from Kyiv makes clear, so too has Ukraine's own tech sector mobilized, creating apps for prosecuting the war and providing a digital backbone to the operation of the Ukrainian government that Russian state cyberspace operators have not yet succeeded in taking down. "For me," Schmidt writes, "the war answers a central question: what can technology people do to help their government, and the answer is a lot."[57]

Indeed, the conflict in Ukraine has affirmed the importance of major weapons platforms and the companies that make them. In fact, we all stand in debt to the heroic leadership LaPlante and his colleagues in Acquisition and Sustainment have provided—for getting platforms and munitions to the battlespace, mobilizing the defense industrial base when it became apparent our stores of advanced munitions were woefully inadequate, restarting production of key armaments whose factory lines had idled for fifteen years or more, and establishing a new command to funnel US and other armaments to Ukraine.

But it would be wrong and even tragic to read the platform-on-platform dynamics in Ukraine as a reassertion of warfighting paradigms they were built for or as justification for preserving the industrial base in the form it exists in today. To do this would be to miss the beguiling hybridity and asymmetry of the battlefield that has evolved over the last nine months, as well as parallel developments in other battlespaces, such as Armenia-Azerbaijan, North Korean drone incursions into Seoul, and the dramatic experimentation with commercial technologies by the People's Liberation Army. These developments suggest that much of our future can be glimpsed today.[58]

Shortly after Bill LaPlante made his remarks about Silicon Valley tech, Northrop Grumman publicly revealed the new B-21 strategic bomber, which LaPlante oversaw as head of acquisition for the air force.[59] With a reported unit cost of $692 million, the total program to develop, purchase, and operate 100 B-21s will exceed $200 billion.[60] In response, *Duffel Blog*, a satirical publication focusing on the military, published an article titled "B-21 nukes DoD budget."[61] Its key faux quote came in the third graph. "When we talk about low observability, it is incredibly low observability," said Kathy Warden, chief executive of Northrop Grumman. "You'll hear it, but you really won't see it eat into the defense budget until it's too late."

What makes the article's satire biting is the dilemma it highlights about how exquisite platforms impose tremendous future opportunity costs. This is not to say that the United States does not need some exquisite platforms but rather to question what adjacent possibilities exist if even a fraction of the resources dedicated to large programs were used to experiment and scale other technological approaches.

For the cost of a single aircraft carrier, the navy could purchase 21,702,838 Starlink terminals—or more than 400,000 for each of the United States' more than fifty treaty allies we are obligated to defend if attacked.[62] The cost of providing over 20,000 Starlink terminals and continuing service in Ukraine is on par with a couple of F-35s, whose internal processor is 800 times slower than commercially available NVIDIA chips.[63] If LaPlante admitted to the tech "bros" that their gaming consoles have higher specs than all deployed US military hardware, they might ask who was really the one getting "liquored up."

The Risks of Strategic Surprise

We are left, then, at an uncomfortable juncture, with radically different assessments of the Ukraine conflict and what affirmative policy agenda the Pentagon should pursue in the still-evolving war's wake. The debate, to some degree, boils down to Clayton Christensen's innovator's dilemma—to what extent should we discard the old in favor of the new as our adversaries threaten to displace our dominant position? The Pentagon, much like Apple's spinning out of General Magic in 1990, must now decide how much of the radical future it wants to import back in. Stasis and paradigm shifts each have risks. The question after Ukraine is what new balance to strike.[64]

As we strike this balance by recapitalizing older systems with new technology and building new systems around new operational concepts, it's worth enumerating the lessons that emerge from our exploration of defense innovation across three presidential administrations.

The first lesson is that the Pentagon will not win a future war without embracing commercial and emerging technology in equal or greater measure than its adversaries. China's strategy of civil-military fusion is thus a pacing threat of its own. Second, technology is only a part of how modern militaries field greater capability. As the head of OSD-Policy's new Emerging Capabilities Policy Office has powerfully argued in prior scholarship, human capital, institutional structures, and culture are crucial to adopting and spreading innovation.[65] In this way, enumerating organizations flying the banner of innovation is far easier than pursuing a strategy to bring innovation into the department at scale. Third, a massive flow of private capital and talent toward start-ups focused on developing technology for the Pentagon creates new and better options than existed even two years ago.[66]

Figure 9.5 visually illustrates this investment trend, which is fueled by Thomas Tull's US Innovative Technology Fund, America's Frontier Fund, a16z American Dynamism Fund, Embedded Ventures, Shield Capital, Razor's Edge Ventures, Irongate Capital Advisors, and Lux Capital. When taken in aggregate, this mobilization of new markets, together with defense primes increasingly working with new entrants, offers a path for the US to outcompete China with existing strengths and institutions.

A full articulation of what policy agenda to pursue is beyond the scope of this paper. But here is a sketch. Elevate DIU back to reporting to the secretary of defense and add to its mission the development of joint operational concepts powered by new technological approaches. Recruit a new director of standing in the commercial technology world. Change the metric by which DIU is judged from the number and size of OTA contracts let—a still important measure of technology adoption—to driving change in key operation plans, especially in the Indo-Pacific, and ultimately changing what gets bought across DoD's Future Years Defense Program. Build new linkages between DIU, the COCOMs (Combatant Commands), OSD-Policy, Forces & Plans, and Emerging Technologies Policy. With so many approaches pioneered by DIU at a "tipping point" just short of viable scale, work with Congress to

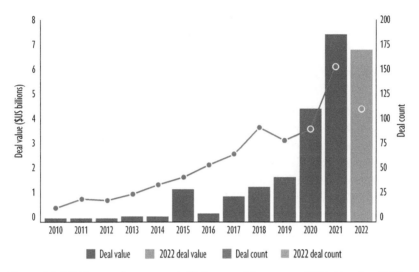

Figure 9.5 US Venture Investment in Defense and Aerospace, 2010–October 2022

Note: 2022 data as of October 13, 2022.
Source: Marina Temkin, "VCs Go outside Their Comfort Zone with Bets on Defense Tech," *PitchBook*, October 26, 2022 (data through October 13, 2022).

quickly ramp up DIU's budget to a trial period of $1 billion annually for three years and keep it there if results merit it. Do the same for other organizations driving commercial technology adoption in OSD and the services.

Give the innovation organizations on that horse-blanket chart marching orders. Have the deputy secretary of defense develop a top-down strategy for joint commercial technology adoption that meets "the thousand flowers blooming" from the bottom up. Hire more tech "bros" all across the department, especially in the outer E Ring of the Pentagon, where top leadership have offices so that the next leaders of Acquisition & Sustainment and Research & Engineering can aggressively exploit advances in commercial technology rather than view it as a boutique part of their responsibilities. Congress, too, must do its part. If DIU and other innovation entities are to equip DoD for a post-Ukraine battlefield, they must be funded aggressively. Congress must also raise reprogramming thresholds, especially if continuing resolutions will remain the norm and continue growing pools of flexible multiyear funding for technology. Senators and representatives must show real leadership, given the shifts that must be made to meet a rising China, by taking votes that will ultimately keep their constituents safer, even if this sometimes means giving up legacy defense jobs in their districts.

The last lesson to draw from fourteen years of defense innovation at this critical moment of resetting and relaunching the innovation agenda is that, like others innovating in large organizations, innovators rarely win. Scholars of security policy have long noted the preeminence of politics and organizational interests in shaping what capacities defense institutions develop. The literature on this point is voluminous and depressing, with self-interest and established ways of warfighting almost always trumping new notions of prevailing threats, objectives derived from planning processes, or technocratic visions of the possible.[67] Stasis is even more likely in the present political environment, with its stark divides across and within the parties.

Yet all hope is not lost. General Magic ceased operations in 2002 and was liquidated in 2004. But the magic it made lives on. Apple brought the iPhone to market in 2007, a product that made it the most valuable company in the world. While its competitors have tried mightily to unseat Apple's dominance in the ensuing fifteen years, it is simply too far ahead today to be beaten. The question now is whether the Pentagon will follow suit and architect at scale the battlefield innovations it has incubated within. Advocates of innovation must keep pressing. Leadership must back them to the hilt. The sound of glass breaking is the melody of progress.

Notes

The author dedicates this paper to the memory and immense legacy of Ash Carter. Thanks to Richard Danzig, Michael Brown, Raj Shah, Josh Marcuse, Jack Shanahan, Matt Cordova, Jared Dunnmon, Jonathan Reiber, Michael J. Boskin, and Kiran Sridhar for reviewing earlier drafts.

1. Mark Sullivan, "'General Magic' Captures the Legendary Apple Offshoot That Foresaw the Mobile Revolution," *Fast Company*, July 26, 2018.

2. Wikipedia entry, "General Magic" (accessed December 28, 2022).

3. Clayton M. Christensen, *The Innovator's Dilemma: When New Technologies Cause Great Firms to Fail* (Boston: Harvard Business School Press, 1997).

4. Valerie Insinna, "LaPlante Pokes Silicon Valley 'Tech Bros,' Calls for Increased Munitions Production for Ukraine," *Breaking Defense*, November 8, 2022; Eric Lofgren, "Getting Weapons into Production with USD A&S Bill LaPlante," *Acquisition Talk Podcast*, November 10, 2022.

5. Nick Siani, "Forging the Defense Industrial Base for the Digital Age" (rebuttal to LaPlante), *Defense Scoop*, December 1, 2022.

6. Office of the Under Secretary of Defense for Research and Engineering, "Critical Technology Areas," CTO.mil (accessed December 28, 2022); "Technology Vision for an Era of Competition," memorandum by Under Secretary of Defense

Heidi Shyu, February 1, 2022; Office of the Under Secretary of Defense for Research and Engineering, "DoD Announces First Set of Projects to Receive Funding from the Pilot Program to Accelerate the Procurement and Fielding of Innovative Technologies (APFIT)," US Department of Defense press release, July 19, 2022.

7. US Department of Defense (DoD), *Military and Security Developments Involving the People's Republic of China 2022: Annual Report to Congress*, November 29, 2022; Office of the Director of National Intelligence, *Annual Threat Assessment of the US Intelligence Community*, February 2022; US-China Economic and Security Review Commission, *2022 Report to Congress*, 117th Cong., 2d sess., November 2022.

8. Ashton B. Carter, Marcel Lettre, and Shane Smith, "Keeping the Technological Edge," in *Keeping the Edge: Managing Defense for the Future*, ed. Ashton B. Carter and John P. White (Cambridge, MA: MIT Press, 2001), 129–64, available at the Belfer Center for Science and International Affairs, https://www.belfercenter.org/sites/default/files/legacy/files/kte_ch6.pdf.

9. Christopher Kirchhoff, "Reshaping National Security Institutions for Emerging Technology," chap. 5 in *America's National Security Architecture: Rebuilding the Foundation*, ed. Nicholas Burns and Jonathon Price (Washington, DC: Aspen Institute, 2016), 86–96; Christopher Kirchhoff, "An Even Flatter World: How Technology Is Remaking the World Order," chap. 5 in *The World Turned Upside Down: Maintaining American Leadership in a Dangerous Age*, ed. Nicholas Burns, Leah Bitounis, and Jonathon Price (Washington, DC: Aspen Institute, 2017), 93–99; Christopher Kirchhoff, "Looking Back to Go Forward: Strategic Mismanagement of Platform Technologies and the Race for the Future," Alliance for Securing Democracy, July 23, 2020.

10. Sharon Weinberger, *The Imagineers of War: The Untold Story of DARPA, the Pentagon Agency That Changed the World* (New York: Penguin Random House, 2018); Regina E. Dugan and Kaigham J. Gabriel, "'Special Forces' Innovation: How DARPA Attacks Problems," *Harvard Business Review* (October 2013).

11. Christian Brose, *The Kill Chain: Defending America in the Future of High-Tech Warfare* (New York: Hachette Books, April 2020).

12. Beth Duff-Brown, "Secretary of Defense Ashton Carter Unveils Cyber Strategy, Calls for Renewed Partnership with Silicon Valley," *CISAC News*, Stanford University Center for International Security and Cooperation, April 23, 2015.

13. Jon Harper, "Special Report: 2021 Brought Another 'Banner Year' for OTAs," *National Defense Magazine*, February 3, 2022.

14. Fred Kaplan, "The Pentagon's Innovation Experiment," *MIT Tech Review*, December 19, 2016.

15. Kessel Run website, https://kesselrun.af.mil.

16. DoD, "Secretary Carter Names Additional Members of Defense Innovation Advisory Board," Department of Defense press release, July 26, 2016.

17. See Eric Schmidt, "Remembering Ash Carter: The Innovative Secretary of Defense Who Changed the Pentagon, Silicon Valley, and the Trajectory of Our Nation," Special Competitive Studies Project, January 26, 2023; Defense Innovation

Board, "Software Acquisition and Practices (SWAP) Study," May 2019; Milo Medin and Gilman Louie, "The 5G Ecosystem: Risks and Opportunity for DoD," Defense Innovation Board, April 3, 2019; C. Todd Lopez, "DoD Adopts 5 Principles of Artificial Intelligence Ethics," Department of Defense News, February 25, 2020.

18. See Directorate for Digital Services, https://www.dds.mil/work.

19. "Media Availability with Secretary Mattis at DIUx," Department of Defense (transcript), August 10, 2017; Tom Simonite, "Defense Secretary James Mattis Envies Silicon Valley's AI Ascent," *Wired*, August 10, 2017.

20. This was no accident—Mattis did it as a deliberate signal to the rest of DoD. James Mattis, personal communication to author, January 19, 2023.

21. Office of the Secretary of the Air Force, "Air Force Opens Doors to Universities, Small Businesses and Entrepreneurs to Boost Innovation," Public Affairs press release, July 21, 2017.

22. Deputy Secretary of Defense Patrick Shanahan, "Redesignation of the Defense Innovation Unit," memorandum, August 3, 2018, available at *FedScoop*, https://www.fedscoop.com.

23. DoD, "Michael Kratsios, DoD Biography." The thirty-three-year-old Kratsios, who had gained exposure to technology investing as chief of staff to Peter Thiel, had earlier come under criticism for serving as Trump's acting science advisor with only an undergraduate degree in politics and certificate in Hellenic studies. Scott Waldman, "Trump's Science Advisor, Age 31, Has a Political Science Degree," *Scientific American*, February 14, 2018.

24. "Advanced Battle Management System (ABMS)," *In Focus*, Congressional Research Service IF11866, February 15, 2022.

25. "Joint All-Domain Command and Control (JADC2)," *In Focus*, Congressional Research Service IF11493, January 21, 2022.

26. Nand Mulchandani and Lt. General (Ret.) John N. T. "Jack" Shanahan, "Software-Defined Warfare: Architecting the DoD's Transition to the Digital Age," Center for Strategic and International Studies, September 6, 2022.

27. Andrew Lautz, "Meet the Biden War Budget, Same as the Trump War Budget," *Responsible Statecraft*, Quincy Institute, January 5, 2023.

28. Beatrice Peterson and Morgan Winsor, "Former Acting Defense Secretary Testifies He Was Trying to Avoid Another Kent State on Jan. 6," ABC News, May 12, 2021.

29. Office of the Secretary of the Air Force, "USSF Hallway Unveiling," Air Force News Photo, released December 18, 2020.

30. Billy Mitchell, "Pentagon Awards Nearly $1B Contract for Cloud Migration to REAN Cloud," *FedScoop*, February 7, 2018.

31. Billy Mitchell, "Pentagon Scales Back Massive Cloud Contract by More Than 90 Percent," *FedScoop*, March 6, 2018.

32. Billy Mitchell, "REAN Cloud Claims It Got No Explanation for DoD Cloud Contract Scaleback," *FedScoop*, March 9, 2018; Luke Stangel, "Report: Oracle CEO

Privately Complained to Trump about Amazon's Odds to Win $10B Pentagon Cloud Contract," *Silicon Valley Business Journal*, April 5, 2018.

33. Scot Paltrow, "Special Report: Aircraft Carriers, Championed by Trump, Are Vulnerable to Attack," Reuters, March 9, 2017.

34. Lloyd J. Austin III, "Remarks by Secretary of Defense Lloyd J. Austin III at the Reagan National Defense Forum (as delivered)," US Department of Defense, December 4, 2021.

35. Chief Digital and Artificial Intelligence Office website, https://www.ai.mil; US Department of Defense, "Secretary of Defense Establishes Office of Strategic Capital," press release, December 1, 2022.

36. 38th Commandant of the Marine Corps, *Commandant's Planning Guidance*, July 16, 2019.

37. Paul McLeary and Lee Hudson, "How Two Dozen Retired Generals Are Trying to Stop an Overhaul of the Marines," *Politico*, April 1, 2022; Mark F. Cancian, "The Marine Corps' Radical Shift toward China," Center for Strategic and International Studies, March 25, 2020; Dov S. Zakheim, "Gen. Berger's Radical Plan to Reshape the Marines Needs Work—but Quickly," *The Hill*, April 22, 2022.

38. US Department of the Navy, *Force Design 2030*, US Marine Corps, March 2020.

39. Office of the Under Secretary of Defense for Research & Engineering, "Innovation Organizations," https://www.ctoinnovation.mil/innovation-organizations (accessed January 3, 2022).

40. DoD, *DIU Annual Report 2021*, Defense Innovation Unit News, January 25, 2022.

41. Kessel Run and Ninth Air Force, "AFCENT's 609th AOC Shifts to User-Focused Software Suite," US Air Forces Central press release, December 7, 2022.

42. Defense Ventures website, https://www.shift.org/dv (accessed January 3, 2022).

43. The complaint against Brown was authored by a single individual. The primary allegation was that Brown had too aggressively used personnel authorities to attract and pay Silicon Valley talent—which was, and is, the chartered mission of DIU. The complaint enumerated a number of other subsidiary allegations as well, including that junior officers overseeing the office snack fund, Snack-O, used an insufficiently robust system of cash accounting to buy Cheetos and coffee cups for the office Keurig. The inspector general, who had initially declined to investigate the complaint, suddenly said it would investigate the complaint and that it needed a year or more to do so.

44. Courtney Albon, "Inspector General Clears Former DIU Chief of Ethics Allegations," *Defense News*, September 13, 2022.

45. Valerie Insinna, "After Hearing Silicon Valley Complaints, Hicks Says No 'Magical' Fix to Acquisition," *Breaking Defense*, April 11, 2022.

46. Bill Greenwalt, "DIU's Director Tried to Overcome a Calcified Defense Innovation System. It Beat Him. Now What?" *Breaking Defense*, August 29, 2022.

47. Eric Chewning, Will Gangware, Jess Harrington, and Dale Swartz, "How Will US Funding for Defense Technology Innovation Evolve?" McKinsey & Company, November 4, 2022. The authors conclude their report with a double caution: "With such relatively low funding for defense technology innovation, it is unclear whether there will be enough capital to support the high-tech priorities embedded in the DoD's future architecture designs. Similarly, defense start-ups and commercial technology firms (as well as investors across public and private markets) may question whether the demand for defense tech innovation is sufficient to justify a focus on these offerings."

48. Sara Sorcher and Karoun Demirjian, "Top US General Calls China's Hypersonic Weapon Test Very Close to a 'Sputnik Moment,'" *Washington Post*, October 27, 2021.

49. P. W. Singer and August Cole, *Ghost Fleet: A Novel of the Next World War* (New York: Eamon Dolan/Houghton Mifflin Harcourt, 2015).

50. Paul McCleary and Erin Banco, "Ukraine Used Home-Modified Drones to Strike Russian Bases," *Politico*, December 7, 2022; "Ukraine Defends against Russia's Inexpensive Drones with Far Costlier Missiles," *New York Times*, January 3, 2023.

51. Lieutenant General John N. T. "Jack" Shanahan, correspondence with the author, January 5, 2022.

52. Brad Smith, "Defending Ukraine: Early Lessons from the Cyber War," *Microsoft on the Issues* (blog), June 22, 2022; Lauren Naniche, Jafer Ahmad, and Joe Wang, "Lessons Learned from Ukraine: Protecting Nations' Digital Freedom from External Aggression," Special Competitive Studies Project, December 16, 2022.

53. Russ Mitchell, "How Amazon Put Ukraine's 'Government in a Box'—and Saved Its Economy from Russia," *Los Angeles Times*, December 15, 2022.

54. David Ignatius, "How the Algorithm Tipped the Balance in Ukraine," *Washington Post*, December 19, 2022.

55. Kevin Costelloe, "Anduril Founder Confirms Involvement in Ukraine," *Orange County Business Journal*, July 13, 2022.

56. Ukrainian Ministry of Defense, "Ukraine Will Receive Titan Counter-UAV Systems from the USA," press release, September 29, 2022.

57. Eric Schmidt, "The First Networked War: Eric Schmidt's Ukraine Trip Report," Special Competitive Studies Project, September 13, 2022.

58. In the last week of 2022, five drones from North Korea crossed the border into South Korea largely undetected, with one penetrating the airspace of Seoul, prompting a public apology from the South Korean president.

59. Coined by the political journalist Michael Kinsley, a *Kinsley gaffe* occurs when a politician reveals a truth they hold that they did not intend to admit. See Wikipedia entry "Political Gaffe" (accessed December 29, 2022).

60. W. J. Hennigan, "Exclusive: The Making of the US Military's New Stealth Bomber," *Time*, December 3, 2022.

61. "B-21 Nukes DoD Budget," *Duffel Blog*, December 9, 2022.

62. Ben Watson, "Mapped: America's Collective Defense Agreements," *Defense One*, February 3, 2017.

63. Brose, *Kill Chain*, 56–57.

64. Special Competitive Studies Project, "Defense Panel Interim Panel Report: The Future of Conflict and the New Requirements of Defense," October 5, 2022.

65. Recent scholarship has called this "adoption-capacity theory." See Michael C. Horowitz, *The Diffusion of Military Power: Causes and Consequences for International Politics* (Princeton, NJ: Princeton University Press, 2010). See also Steven Rosen, *Winning the Next War: Innovation and the Modern Military* (Ithaca, NY: Cornell University Press, 1994).

66. Mark Sullivan, "Silicon Valley Wants to Power the US War Machine," *Fast Company*, November 1, 2021.

67. Harvey M. Sapolsky, Eugene Gholz, and Caitlin Talmadge, *US Defense Politics: The Origins of Security Policy*, 4th ed. (London: Routledge, 2020).

10

Department of Defense Budgeting
The Unrecognized National Security Threat

Michael Brown

Perhaps the most unrecognized national security threat is the slowness and lack of agility of our defense budgeting process, which may be the last vestige of the Cold War and unchanged from a half century ago. Many of the national security risks we recognize today are a result of renewed great-power competition combined with our ongoing counterterrorism needs. However, the threat environment is even more complex today when we include transnational risks like climate change and two new threat domains: space and cyberspace. Still, another national security concern is the internal divisiveness within our own country, which undermines our government and might make external enemies question our resolve. One extant threat that is all but forgotten today is the record size of our national debt—now 100 percent of our GDP—a level that likely inhibits us from spending more on defense in a time of higher interest rates. These are difficult challenges without easy answers *except* for the first one—the self-inflicted wounds of a lethargic and rigid defense budgeting process designed in large part by Defense Secretary Robert McNamara during the Kennedy administration.

It is little surprise that a process designed in the early 1960s—when the United States had a single and fairly predictable adversary, the Soviet Union—does not serve us well in a world of more and increasingly complex threats and when the future is anything but predictable. The current basis for defense budgeting—the programming, planning, budgeting, and execution

The views expressed in this chapter are solely those of the individual author and do not necessarily reflect the views of any organization with which they are, or have been, affiliated.

process—assumes that if we take longer to plan and think of defense as a large systems-engineering problem, we achieve better outcomes. While no one believes this logic today, we continue to budget this same way year in and year out because we have not focused on improving the process that affects both *what* we buy and *how rapidly* we buy new technologies and capabilities. Authoritarian regimes stand ready to exploit weaknesses in our democratic system, which is slow and lacks agility in how we modernize our forces. It is a monumental weakness.

The fundamental problems with our defense budgeting process are that we take two and a half years (thirty months) to program each dollar we spend, and once constructed, there is too little flexibility in the budget to adapt to changing circumstances. Today's defense budget contains approximately three thousand line-item appropriations (or silos) where money must be spent and where money may not be moved.[1] Worse, the feedback from Congress through such a cumbersome and disjointed budgeting process means there is very little strategic direction given to Department of Defense (DoD) leaders, who are left to guess intentions. We should, therefore, change this process to focus first on the strategic outcomes Congress would like the DoD to achieve, make these outcomes the focus of hearings on the Hill, and construct a new process that is only a year long and allows for flexibility across all portfolios of DoD programs. Such a reformed process would

- enable Congress to collaborate with the DoD in developing strategic direction and desired outcomes;
- speed up the DoD's responses to emerging threats and its ability to leverage new technologies (which are not possible when money must be programmed two to three years in advance); and
- improve the DoD's agility to allocate resources where they are needed most.

Three Recommendations for Defense Budgeting Reform
1. Congress Develops Strategic Direction and Outcomes with DoD

Today's National Defense Authorization Act (NDAA) contains one thousand sections, calls for 720 reports, and contains three thousand line items, or silos, of accompanying appropriations money, which are not necessarily rationalized holistically.[2] The NDAA provides direction in a piecemeal fashion with too little explanation of Congress's intentions and with very little discretion left to senior defense leadership (both civilian and military) to achieve desired outcomes. Unelected staffers to Congress's appropriations committees in the House and Senate are making the major trade-offs in program budgets and determining what our commanders go to war with in a manner that balances national security with preserving jobs in congressional districts. This resulting complexity ensures that the DoD has neither speed nor agility relative to adversaries.

Instead, Congress could adopt the model of a corporate board of directors to set direction and outcomes rather than micromanaging budget line items. Far more beneficial for national security would be a set of outcomes that Congress would like the Pentagon to achieve, such as the ability to defend Taiwan rather than directing how many F-35s should be built. The Pentagon should be tasked with executing a strategy that matches the outcomes specified and the budget appropriated. To accomplish this, Congress would have to reimagine its own processes to focus on a shorter NDAA with consensus on the strategic outcomes for our military rather than so many congressional members' individual priorities.

2. Speed: Budget in One Year without a Continuing Resolution

Congress should ensure that the budget process does not take longer than a year from the time the Pentagon planning process begins until the Office of Management and Budget (OMB) approves the budget. This would include the hearings and discussions on the Hill. No corporation, no matter its size and complexity, takes more than a year for a budgeting process, because companies know that the future is unpredictable and more time planning does not result in a better outcome. A one-year budget cycle is not possible today due to the complexity of thousands of fragmented line items in the budget. To move at speed, the process must be reimagined with reduced complexity at a higher level of abstraction that allows for agreement on strategic outcomes. Congress could focus on one hundred line items for *portfolios of capabilities* in the budget rather than thousands of highly granular line items. For example, in the 1960s, there was a single line item for tactical aircraft in the budget, and the US Air Force could decide how to best allocate that budget among various aircraft models.[3] Today, Congress decides the budget for each aircraft type and specifies procurement of aircraft that the US Air Force explicitly does not want or need. A portfolio approach would let the DoD make the trade-offs regarding how many of which type of aircraft would be best and how soon to retire older models and replace them with newer models.

Congress must also trim the half year that occurred in nine of the past ten years of a "continuing resolution." This is both wasteful of taxpayer dollars and difficult to manage for those within the DoD and its vendors. In a nutshell, the "continuing resolution" means that the DoD has the authority to spend a fraction (say, 80 percent) of what it spent the previous year and is unable to begin any new programs. This delays programs that incorporate new vendors and new technologies and creates additional pressure within the DoD to spend most of the year's budget in the second half of the fiscal year after the appropriations bill passes. If there is a new program or a budget increase to an existing program, all of that must be executed in the remaining half of the fiscal year, which leads to inefficiencies and waste. From FY1977 to FY2023 (almost fifty years), Congress passed the defense budget on time for the start of the fiscal year only five times. During three of those years, there was a lapse in funding, precipitating a full government shutdown.[4] In testifying to Congress about this year's continuing resolution, Air Force chief of staff General C. Q. Brown summed it up well: "All the money in the world cannot buy more time; time is irrecoverable, and when you are working to keep pace against well-resourced and focused competitors, time matters."[5]

3. Flexibility to Allocate Funds across Boundaries of Fiscal Year, Color, and Program Elements

The reduction in line items and consideration of portfolios of capabilities would enable more flexibility in spending and an improved ability to respond to urgent threats and leverage new technologies. The current lack of flexibility stems from several long-standing practices that should be changed or eliminated.

- *Five-Year Defense Budget Plan* These plans, called Future Years Defense Program (FYDP), anchor budgets with input created four years earlier and heavily favor the status quo. Their use ensures some stability for long-term programs but significantly hinders new programs or dynamic allocations of funds to more urgent priorities. Instead, FYDP should be eliminated, and the DoD should move to two-year budgets (current year and next year).
- *Budget Appropriations* Appropriations currently do not cross fiscal year boundaries and just result in the "use it or lose it" wasteful spending that occurs throughout the federal government.

- *Colors of Money* Specifying various categories of appropriations (so-called "colors of money," of which there are five) attempts to match appropriations precisely with uses. This approach discourages leadership initiative and judgment, eliminating the ability to reallocate funds to a more urgent need today relative to what was planned three years ago when the budget planning cycle began. In practice, the colors of money approach creates artificial boundaries, leading to wasted management time due to operating within these constraints. Instead, money should come in a single color and have no expiration date.
- *Program Elements* Over time, managed "program elements" within the defense budget have become so granular that there is little flexibility to move money to more urgent needs. With thousands of line items, senior leadership has so little discretion that trade-offs are managed by congressional staffers rather than those responsible for executing the military strategy. Program elements should be managed as much higher-level portfolios, such as all fighter aircraft or all hypersonic research. This was how we appropriated funds in the 1960s for aircraft. In the FY2022 budget, Congress instructed the DoD to buy major weapons platforms it did not want or need, such as A-10 Warthogs, B-1 bombers, RQ-4 Global Hawks, KC-135 and KC-10 refueling tankers, C-130Hs, E-8s, and some F-15s and F-16s.[6]
- *Reprogramming as a Solution* Reprogramming can take up to a year for the required congressional approvals. It is almost as cumbersome and time-consuming as the budgeting process itself and is therefore rarely used. The amount of management time for reprogramming discourages flexibility and initiative. The dollar threshold should be raised for reprogramming (allowing for the DoD to do more reprogramming without congressional approval), and the reprogramming process should be streamlined to enable faster decisions with fewer approvals. DoD senior leadership should have some flexibility to move funds across portfolios, e.g., up to 10 percent of the budget, to respond to urgent threats and eliminate the need for reprogramming.

Of course, it is Congress's job to oversee the DoD and how well the department spends the money appropriated. However, the question is whether this oversight is handled better by managing macro-level goals or micromanaging thousands of budget line items. The experience of the corporate world makes clear that using metrics to understand progress on a fewer number of high-level goals is not only more effective but more pragmatic than managing thousands of items. When Congress attempts to micromanage DoD programs, there is conformity to the law but tremendous inefficiencies result. Former deputy secretary of defense Bob Work said recently, "Over the last ten years, Congress has moved beyond measured oversight and into micromanagement, as indicated by the length of the NDAA and the amount of directives—we want you to split AT&L [Acquisition, Technology, and Logistics], we want you to stand up a CMO [Chief Management Office]. . . . Oops, we fooled you, we don't really want you to stand up a CMO."[7]

Peter Levine, who recently wrote the book *Defense Management Reform*, added, "The way that you show that you're an effective member of Congress or an effective staffer is you draft legislation. So you identify a problem and you draft legislation. . . . The fact that the NDAA is one of the few pieces of legislation that's still passed puts much more weight on the NDAA. Everybody wants to get a provision in it, and if everybody has to have a provision in it with 535 members of Congress, that's a lot of provisions."[8]

The three recommendations outlined above for defense budget reform are revolutionary given how we develop the budget today and will not be easy to implement against a backdrop of the two-party system, institutionalized processes, and entrenched interests, but they are critical for our national security. As John F. Kennedy reminded us in his call to send a man to the moon, if the goal is important, we should not be any less resolute just because the task is hard. Naturally, revolutionary changes would require those in the DoD and Congress to bring a different mindset to a reimagined process. However, this simplified process would also be easier to manage, require less manpower, and save taxpayer dollars because much of the analysis to develop three thousand line items today is done by hand by staff at the DoD and in Congress. When the NDAA and appropriations bills are passed, hundreds of people across the DoD (not to mention the suppliers, press, and think tanks) are reading through thousands of pages of text to find the relevant direction and budget items that affect them.

Why Is It Important to Create a Budget with More Speed and More Agility?

In a single word, the answer is China. With what the National Defense Strategy calls our "pacing threat," how can we live with a thirty-month process that creates an automatic eighteen-month delay relative to China? If China can budget for the People's Liberation Army (PLA) in a year, then our process ensures we remain eighteen months behind in implementing our best strategy, acquiring our best capabilities, and getting those capabilities to our warfighters. As a society, China has prioritized technology development and uses all instruments of its national power to acquire or steal foreign technology while developing technology indigenously. As an example, Made in China 2025 is a massive import substitution plan to ensure that China develops its own design and manufacturing capabilities for the industries of the future, such as semiconductors, satellites, advanced computing, synthetic biology, and artificial intelligence (AI). China is now at work on China Standards 2035, seeking to set global standards for its national champion firms, such as Huawei, in advanced telecommunications.

Further, civil-military fusion ensures that each commercial innovation in China is available to the PLA for exploitation. Finally, the Belt and Road Initiative expands global markets for Chinese goods, services, and technology standards. This global network includes physical ports, roads, and pipelines, among other assets, all of which can be exploited for military advantage. While China has its own bureaucracy to manage, the government's intent is quite clear through its well-articulated industrial strategy and policies focused on technological progress and the development of national capabilities.

In contrast, not only is the US government's intent quite muddled, but the impact of the slow and nonagile budgeting process has real national security implications, lengthening the time to adopt leading-edge technology for our military. Our defense budget cycle is longer than the average commercial technology product cycle, so our current process ensures we never buy the latest technology for warfighters. For example, the US Army program of record to buy small drones is the Short Range Reconnaissance program. This program took ten years to field a drone from an American vendor and imposed additional costs to customize the drone for military missions. During this time, the Chinese competitor with leading global market share, Da Jiang Innovations (better known as DJI), introduced new models every twelve to eighteen months at less than 10 percent of the cost of the Army drone. The budget cycle is partially responsible for the long cycle times to field this new technology. This is one example of a trend occurring throughout the DoD where the commercial sector is innovating rapidly.

The length of the budget cycle also discourages new vendors from competing to support the DoD because of the long and sustained investment required to sell to the US government. The leading-edge technology for eleven of the fourteen technologies that the Pentagon's chief technology officer says are important for national security, including AI and cyber tools, are developed by the private sector—not the defense establishment.[9] As a result, we need more leading technology providers to want to supply and successfully sell to the US government. Without improving the speed of our budgeting process, the DoD continues to discourage the very vendors we need in leading-edge technology areas from doing business with us.

Hedge Strategy: Lots of Small Things

These budget reforms are even more important when we consider that to modernize our forces today, we need to complement what we buy with different capabilities in the future. Our post–Cold War defense strategy has relied more on traditional platforms such as planes, tanks, and aircraft, complemented by counterterrorism capabilities. Our current budget process, with its multiyear planning and focus on large-weapons platforms—because these are the most expensive and create the most jobs—will naturally favor large platforms and those companies who can afford lobbying efforts for these programs. The resulting budget crowds out newer capabilities, especially those that are smaller, less expensive, and likely more resilient: the defense budget greatly prioritizes building new aircraft carriers over fielding swarms of small drones. The Ukraine conflict shows the importance of new technologies on the battlefield, such as drones, missiles, and capabilities based in space (Starlink and sensors in low Earth orbit), when fighting a large, industrialized force. Traditional large-weapons platforms take decades to field and provide stable targets for adversaries to understand, copy, and develop strategies against. In a technology environment that is changing more rapidly and is more global than ever before, the United States must consider that such rapid, distributed technological change presents an opportunity for adversaries and a heightened risk from asymmetric advantage or strategic surprise. By contrast, the US mastery of new technologies provides that advantage to our forces.

The director of naval research, Rear Admiral Lorin Selby, and I have described this as a *hedge strategy*, since new capabilities provide a hedge to our current traditional platforms, which are now more vulnerable than in previous eras due to peer or near-peer adversary capabilities.[10] We do not want to find ourselves in the next conflict with the equivalent of relying on battleships during a Pearl Harbor–style attack. The US Navy was better prepared after Pearl Harbor because it had invested in its own hedge at the time—the aircraft carrier, which proved decisive just a year later at Midway. Much of what we need in the future will be "lots of small things" in addition to the few big things.[11] Additionally, the resilience of "lots of small things" allows for the geographical dispersal of capabilities, which is also called for in the US Marine Corps's Force Redesign 2030. The Marines recognize that with peer adversaries, the United States may not have air superiority; therefore, the concentration of manpower and large platforms makes our forces vulnerable, just as it did at Pearl Harbor in 1941. Finally, lots of small things rely more heavily on the commercial market, which can deliver new capabilities much faster—in two to three years rather than the current seventeen-year average it takes to bring larger capabilities to the Pentagon.[12] Of course, developing next-generation fighter aircraft and buying small drones are not equivalent capabilities, but the critical point is that we need both. However, the only short-term means to augment the capability of our military is to complement the large weapons platforms with new technologies from the commercial sector.

This hedge strategy encompasses three ideas. The first involves maintaining and enhancing relationships across the private sector to leverage emerging commercial technologies to field alternative concepts and capabilities at scale to both complement and provide a hedge to our existing, exquisite (meaning costly, dominant, massive, and few) weapons system platforms. The hedge addresses the inevitable vulnerabilities to these exquisite platforms from new, often inexpensive emerging capabilities such as AI-powered antiballistic missiles.

The second idea combines existing commercial solutions with a sense of urgency and places a premium on speed. This enables the fielding of these capabilities at scale within the next few years (not decades). Moving rapidly provides additional deterrence and an element of unpredictability for adversaries who, for years, have focused on US platforms and how we use them.

The third idea is that hedge-strategy architecture should encompass small and low-cost, unmanned, many, and smarter capabilities. These are referred to as SUMS:

- *Small and low-cost* ensures we can field many resilient, attritable systems with diverse capabilities at an affordable cost that can overwhelm and confuse our adversaries.

- *Unmanned* extends the operational reach and efficacy of warfighters, which also mitigates the need for larger manned forces and potentially saves lives.
- *Many*, because the quantity will be an important deterrent and provide an asymmetric advantage relative to exquisite platforms, especially in survivability.
- *Smarter*, because software is the key to enhanced functionality of all hardware and because AI, machine learning, and cyber can provide new capabilities as teams of smaller systems are combined. Additionally, software capabilities can be updated in real time.

These capabilities can be combined in new ways, evolving over time more agilely than the large platforms that are still in use and have been mostly unchanged for decades.[13] Agility today means platforms that can be agile in function, of course, but also agile in mission adjustment and software upgrades on short timelines.

Note that such a strategy is incompatible with today's defense budgeting process, since it will be impossible to specify the relevant commercial technologies thirty months before they are in use, as they may not have been invented yet. Further, the lack of flexibility in the budget will not allow for substitutions of more desirable capabilities than what was specified in an appropriations bill. The current system of setting requirements, acquisition, and budgeting was more appropriate to a time when the United States was the dominant military superpower and technology leader than it is to the present, when commercial technology is both software led and far outpaces the US military in both investment and the speed of product cycles. Over the past half century, codified processes at the DoD often resist change and optimize for procuring more of "what we have" instead of developing "what we need" for the next conflict. Buying what we have is what the Pentagon does well. It ensures predictable revenue streams to predictable locations across the existing industrial base.

Current incentives for those in program offices at the DoD, and even those in Congress, are aligned with the status quo, which, unfortunately, may be the equivalent of buying many more battleships on the eve of Pearl Harbor. The defense budgeting process, in particular, will continue to commit trillions of dollars to more tanks, ships, planes, and nuclear weapons at the expense of fielding alternative concepts and capabilities, investing at the right level in new domains like space and cyber, or investing to support an industrial base in new technologies like small drones or commercial satellites. The result is a less flexible and hardware-centric force focused on our large platforms. What we need is a faster and more flexible budgeting process to complement our large weapons platforms with new capabilities that may be just now available and can scale quickly because they are commercially based. While there are a great many advantages to a hedge strategy in terms of saving taxpayer dollars and the ability to scale quickly with a broader vendor base, the primary advantage is a better military capability made possible through the elements of surprise and resiliency. Accompanying our major platforms with complementary hedge capabilities means we are fielding concepts that our enemies may not have seen before and with the resilience that comes from higher volumes of attritable assets.

How Can We Buy More Commercial Solutions Better?

Not having an effective approach to rapidly adopting commercial technology is a glaring weakness in modernizing the DoD. Technologies such as advanced communications, AI software, small drones, synthetic aperture radar (SAR) satellite imagery, and many others can be rapidly purchased from credible commercial vendors to deliver novel capabilities at a fraction of the cost of dedicated defense technologies. Thus, we need a better way to buy lots of small things.

To modernize faster, the DoD requires an order-of-magnitude increase in its adoption of commercial technologies, which are the new technologies the Pentagon's chief technology officer has called for—AI, cyber, space-based sensors, autonomous systems, etc. However, the DoD is not leveraging the commercial sector broadly enough or fast enough in its modernization efforts because it lacks a process to buy commercial technologies that address the differences between commercial and purpose-built defense solutions. Commercial technologies have nontrivial differences when compared to strictly defense technologies. First, commercial technologies are supplied in massive unit volumes—sometimes in the millions—often led by the consumer, as is the case with small drones. Second, in addition to larger volumes, commercial technologies evolve much faster than defense technologies, with products refreshed on twelve-to-eighteen-month cycles instead of decades. As a result, the DoD needs to move much faster in assessing and fielding these technologies. Third, commercial technologies such as AI software or commercial satellite imagery are not service specific. We do not need special versions for the navy or the air force (even though at the DoD, we often try to create these). Creating special versions by service makes it more difficult and costly for commercial suppliers to do business with the DoD. Fourth, since the DoD does not control the global diffusion of these technologies, slowly adopting these creates an asymmetric disadvantage if our adversaries adopt them more rapidly.

These differences are extremely relevant for conflicts we may face in the next decade where our adversaries effectively employ commercial technologies. For example, when US troops were stationed in Iraq, the Islamic State of Iraq and Syria (ISIS) sent small drones, like those that can be purchased on e-commerce platforms like Amazon, with grenades to kill American soldiers in Mosul, Iraq. Countries such as Azerbaijan and Ukraine are quickly adapting commercial technology in new ways to gain an edge on the battlefield. Azerbaijan decisively won the Nagorno-Karabakh conflict against Armenia due to its use of commercial drones, and more recently, the Ukrainians are effectively employing small drones called Switchblades to destroy Russian trucks and tanks. The DoD must add new capabilities like these in the next two years rather than the next two decades. The DoD must reform its sequential requirements, acquisition, and budgeting methods for these commercial technologies to adapt to an environment where the commercial industry leads technology development and prioritizes speed. The current sequential process lags commercial product cycles and delivers technology that is several generations behind and overpriced, which would be the equivalent of supplying flip phones and fax machines to our warfighters.

In other words, the DoD must become a "fast follower" to gain rapid access to these technologies to maintain at least technological parity with adversaries. This requires rethinking three interrelated Pentagon processes: requirements, acquisition, and budgeting. When it comes to buying commercial technology, we don't need to tell the commercial market what is required for them to build solutions they have already created. Similarly, some new adaptive acquisition frameworks (for urgent capability or middle tier) can be easily adapted for commercial technology to simplify the buying process. The cycle time for budgeting needs to be realigned to match the rate of introducing commercial solutions.

There has been much reform of acquisition practices in the past few decades, but almost no reform of either the requirements or the budgeting processes. These processes now hinder commercial technology from modernizing the DoD. Therefore, key tenets of a *fast-follower strategy* include the following:[14]

1. **Designate organizations for commercial capabilities with a consistent budget.** DoD needs to establish designated organizations for each of the commercial technologies (e.g., drones and counterdrones, digital wearables, and satellite imagery), which are not and do not need to be service specific. Today, it is not clear where in the DoD these non-service-specific technologies, like small drones, should be assessed and procured. Along with clarity for where this technology can be assessed and purchased, these designated organizations also need a stable budget for that capability. This is different from a "program of record," which reflects a rigid requirement and often a single vendor. This is a "capability of record," where the need for the capability and budget is ongoing, such as for small drones. With that ongoing budget, the DoD can continuously assess capability, choose the best vendor at a point in time, and refresh that capability with a frequency that matches commercial product cycles. Assigning an ongoing capability budget to these organizations also signals demand to private industry and avoids duplication across the DoD. This allows the DoD to adapt to rapidly evolving threats and procure solutions that were not even available when the DoD's budget was created more than two years earlier.
2. **Eliminate the requirements process** for these commercial technologies and replace this with a much more rapid validation of needs. Again, we do not need to develop detailed specifications for products the commercial market already builds; these specifications will limit both creative problem solving and the number of competitors.
3. **Apply the best practices of commercial procurement** by applying nonconsortia Other Transaction Authority through Commercial Solutions Openings more widely, which will help maximize competition while minimizing the opportunity costs of participating vendors. If a vendor successfully prototypes a solution, a re-compete should not be required at the end of the prototyping period, and the DoD should immediately scale the solution. If Congress budgets for "capabilities of record," then we avoid asking successful vendors to wait for the budget cycle to catch up, which can take up to two years and cause the death of a small company reliant on cash flow for survival.
4. **Coordinate with allies** by sourcing commercial technology from allies and selling proven solutions to allied militaries. For the United States to prevail in the competition with China, it must collaborate

more with allies and partners. The easiest form is with commercial technologies, which are unclassified and therefore more easily shareable, and which present excellent export opportunities for vendors.

This fast-follower strategy has several key benefits: maximizing competition through open assessments of solutions from multiple vendors; reducing costs by leveraging higher volumes of the commercial market; increasing speed and transparency of the acquisition process; and minimizing the opportunity cost for vendors to encourage participation in future competitions. The fast-follower strategy is simply a common-sense adaptation of how technology is adopted in the commercial world.

The Defense Innovation Unit, which I led for four years, successfully employed the fast-follower strategy to execute rapid competitions among multiple vendors for capabilities as varied as small drones, unmanned maritime vehicles supporting the US Navy's Task Force 59, digital wearable technologies as an early warning detection for COVID-19, and algorithms to predict aircraft parts failures to improve air squadron readiness.

The importance of applying a fast-follower strategy can be seen in Ukraine and as a possible deterrent to China for a conflict over Taiwan. An example would be commercial space-based sensors using different modalities such as electro-optical, synthetic aperture radar, infrared, and radio frequencies. Combining what we see in multiple modalities ensures that adversaries can be more closely watched in near-real time and are unable to surprise us. These capabilities provided the US intelligence community with unprecedented information about what Putin was doing on the Ukrainian border. Because it was commercial technology (rather than from classified sources), this information could be shared with Ukraine, allies, partners, and the media.

Another example would be commercial communications capability, such as the Starlink terminals provided by SpaceX, which enabled communications by the military, the government, and Ukrainian citizens in the face of Russian attacks on cellular infrastructure. The more current and resilient technologies we can employ, the better capabilities we have for deterrence or warfighting. A fast-follower strategy enables the fielding of more current and resilient capabilities.

Conclusion

We must reform our defense budgeting process now because the long and nonagile process we perpetuate is more suited to the Cold War than to the complex threat environment we face today. The United States needs to develop a hedge strategy to complement our large traditional platforms and execute a better means for buying commercial solutions for the military. China will exploit the weakness inherent in our slow process with the aim of a more agile PLA adopting more commercial technology more quickly as part of its civil-military fusion strategy. Moreover, as the US industrial base for defense continues to shrink, we will need to invest both in traditional defense-only products like energetics (propellants and explosives that power missiles) and those that have dual use, such as space-based sensors, small drones, air taxis, alternative fuels, and the like. The commercial, dual-use vendors we want to attract will be motivated to support the DoD if we can change the budget cycle to twelve months and procure more commercial capabilities through hedge and fast-follower strategies. Additionally, the DoD's support for emerging commercial technologies will create whole new industries in areas such as biotechnology, resilient and greener energy, and the construction of a space superhighway of satellites, space logistics, manufacturing, and multiorbit transportation. Otherwise, we cede to China not only a military advantage but the economic prosperity that comes with these new industries.

To address the only national security threat that is truly self-inflicted—our defense budgeting process—we need decisive change to field the right capabilities for our warfighters rather than prepare for the last war. The question is whether we can act before we are in wartime; we are not on the wrong end of a Pearl Harbor–style attack—*yet*.

If we act with urgency—to develop a hedge strategy, reimagine how we buy commercial solutions through a fast-follower strategy, and reform our defense budgeting process to be rapid (one year from plan to appropriation) and agile (allowing for the flexibility to adapt to changing conditions)—we deter our adversaries and ensure we can maintain peace through increased strength. As President Ronald Reagan reminded us, "We know only too well that war comes not when the forces of freedom are strong, but when they are weak. It is then that tyrants are tempted."[15]

Notes

1. Senate Armed Services Committee Funding Tables for the FY23 National Defense Authorization Act (NDAA), https://www.armed-services.senate.gov/imo/media/doc/fy23_ndaa_funding_tables.pdf.

2. National Defense Authorization Act (NDAA) for FY2023, House of Representatives Bill 7900—117th Congress (2021–22), https://www.congress.gov/bill/117th-congress/house-bill/7900.

3. William C. Greenwalt and Dan Patt, "Competing in Time: Ensuring Capability Advantage and Mission Success through Adaptable Resource Allocation," Hudson Institute, February 2021.

4. Jeff Arkin, "What Is a Continuing Resolution and How Does It Affect Government Operations?" Government Accountability Office, November 3, 2022.

5. Quoted in Elaine McCusker, "Another Round of Continuing Resolutions— Who Loses?" *The Hill*, September 8, 2022.

6. Stephen Losey, "Air Force Would Cut 150 Aircraft, Including A-10s, Buy Fewer F-35s in 2023 Budget," *Defense News*, March 28, 2022.

7. Eric Lofgren, "Has Congress Descended from Oversight to Micromanagement?" *Acquisition Talk* (blog), August 2, 2022.

8. Lofgren, "Has Congress Descended."

9. "Department of Defense Technology Vision for an Era of Competition," US Department of Defense, press release, February 3, 2022, https://www.defense.gov /News/Releases/Release/Article/2921482/department-of-defense-technology -vision-for-an-era-of-competition.

10. Heather Wishart-Smith, "A Strategic Hedge for National Security with the Small, the Agile, and the Many," *Forbes*, October 11, 2022.

11. James Timbie and Admiral James O. Ellis Jr., "A Large Number of Small Things: A Porcupine Strategy for Taiwan," *Texas National Security Review* 5, no. 1 (Winter 2021–22): 83–93.

12. There are two cycle times referred to in this paper: (1) the cycle time to prepare the defense budget, which is 30 months (2.5 years) with a recommendation of 12 months; and (2) the cycle time to adopt new weapons technologies, which is 9 to 26 years (17 on average); with commercial vendors and technology available today, this cycle can be shortened to 1–2 years for capabilities we buy commercially. See Greenwalt and Patt, "Competing in Time."

13. Of course, there are upgrades in both hardware and software that occur in major weapons platforms such as the F-35, but because these platforms are designed as integrated hardware-software platforms from a single vendor, the upgrades in hardware and software do not happen independently and these upgrades occur on a much longer cycle of time than those of commercial products, especially the software upgrades.

14. Michael Brown and Pavneet Singh, "Fast Follower Strategy," white paper written for the Defense Innovation Unit, US Department of Defense, 2022. Presented at the Aspen Security Forum in Washington in November 2021 and available to view at https://acquisitiontalk.com/2021/12/commercial-tech-fast-follower-strategies-and-a -framework-for-rapid-acquisition.

15. Ronald Reagan, speech at the Republican National Convention, July 17, 1980.

Technology, Innovation, Procurement

With Michèle Flournoy, Eric Fanning, and Raj Shah,
Moderated by Kiran Sridhar

KIRAN SRIDHAR: Let's begin with Secretary Michèle Flournoy.

MICHÈLE FLOURNOY: I wanted to focus my brief comments on realistic changes we can make in the near term to accelerate and expand the adoption of innovative technologies and concepts. I think many of the longer-term reforms, from increasing investment in recapitalization to fundamentally reforming the budget process, are really important and need to be pursued. But I want to focus on the fact that we, as Americans and the DoD, have a very time-urgent problem that demands that we focus on urgent steps that can be taken now to produce better operational outcomes in the next five years. And that is focused on ensuring that the United States, with its allies, can actually deter Chinese aggression against Taiwan or in the South or East China seas.

In this context, it's really not about choosing between legacy systems or new innovative capabilities but rather figuring out how to marry the best of the two to get new outcomes. There are three key elements in my view here. The first is to identify the most critical operational problems we have to solve to strengthen deterrence, whether it's increasing the resilience of our own command, control, communications, computers, intelligence, surveillance, and reconnaissance [C4ISR] systems and degrading China's. Or whether it's a matter of enhancing the speed and quality of our decision making relative to Beijing or increasing mass through human-machine teaming or teaming manned and unmanned platforms and so forth. But we also need to look at new ways of combining capabilities that we already have on hand or readily available in new ways to support new operational concepts. Think of the example that [former deputy secretary of defense] Bob Work has written about [regarding] putting navy munitions on air force long-range bombers that can hold Chinese naval assets at risk from outside harm's way. So it's an Apollo 13 problem. Shake everything out from our kit bag, look at what we have, and be creative about combining them in new ways to create different outcomes.

At the same time, we need to, as Mike [Brown] has talked about, identify commercial technologies that can meaningfully enhance the performance of our existing platforms and weapons systems and disrupt that of our enemies. And then, we need to fast-track their procurement and integration into the force at scale. All of this requires a different approach than we're seeing in the Pentagon, and it's very consistent with the hedge and fast-follower strategies that Mike just described.

But first and foremost, this has to be the highest priority for the secretary and the deputy secretary of defense, not just in strategy documents but in how they actually spend their time and in what they hold other senior leaders accountable for. I recently had a meeting with a very senior military leader in the Pentagon who told me he's spending four to five hours a day on Ukraine. My question is, who is spending that kind of time driving the train on the problem of deterring China as an urgent near-term problem? We need a similar wartime sense of urgency to actually deter and prevent conflict between two nuclear-armed powers in Asia. And so, what would that look like? It would mean bringing together INDOPACOM, PACFLT, and so forth to identify what are those critical operational needs that we absolutely need to address to be able to deter successfully. We need to bring service leaders in to propose creative solutions using existing or fast-emerging capabilities, rebuilding and pre-positioning stocks of critical munitions, and leveraging our unique innovation ecosystem to really offer up mature commercial capabilities and solutions that can complement these other capabilities. We also need to structure competitions within the department to develop new operational concepts to solve those hard problems and then fold those concepts and capabilities into experiments and exercises.

I applaud the department's creation of the RDER [Rapid Defense Experimentation Reserve] program, but it's on a twenty-four-month cycle, meaning if I get an exercise approved or an experiment approved today, I have to wait as much as two years, maybe, until it happens. That's not fast enough. And all of this needs to be done by a strategy-informed reveal or conceal policy to get the maximum deterrent effect.

Of course, we need to build congressional support for urgent efforts to shore up deterrence. And we do need to draw lessons from prior efforts, and I thought Jackie [Schneider]'s paper was excellent. The notion of identifying and empowering champions and policy entrepreneurs to drive the change, developing compelling narratives that win over support within the services and on the Hill, and then, most importantly, from my experience in business, is realigning incentive structures to change behavior. We've got to train, incentivize, and reward a new cadre or subcadre of acquisition professionals who are truly experts in rapid commercial technology procurement. We also need to train and reward service PEOs [program executive offices] to actually embrace disruption and be rewarded for embracing disruption of their own programs if it gets us to the ultimate operational outcome we're seeking faster.

SRIDHAR: Next is former secretary of the army Eric Fanning.

ERIC FANNING: I'm going to try and distill my remarks into three buckets: Congress, the industrial base, and the Pentagon.

First, and it was mentioned earlier, Congress is an integral part of whether we're going to succeed or fail on this. And I recognize we have a very highly regarded former HASC [House Armed Services Committee] chair [Mac Thornberry] with us. This isn't directed at anybody. [Former secretary of defense] Bob Gates used to say that nobody suffers in a bureaucracy more than a bureaucrat. And you could probably say that about Congress and members of Congress, particularly defense authorizers, so thank you for everything you've done.

We've already talked about how long the PPBE process is—the budgeting process and the planning process—but then the disruptions of not getting a budget on time are hugely disruptive to the Department of Defense. We all know that. They're disruptive to industry, but more importantly, over time, and this is a theme James [Cunningham] has in his paper about how cumulative effects over time just grow. It has distorted the contours of the industrial base as well. Years and years and years of this type of budgeting and inconsistency make it hard for industry to plan. That's one of the questions here: How do we rebuild the industrial base? Congress participating in regular order to get clear, consistent, dependable demand signals out there to the industrial base would be a big step in getting there. They also need to be a part of this "divest to invest" strategy. One of the questions—I think we have all landed on the same page here—is that it's not either-or in terms of what we have now and what's in the future. It's not even just a combination of those things. It's figuring out how to modernize what we have, how to combine it with new things that we've got and in the best order, as Michèle said. And Congress has to be a part of that and makes it very hard for the department to make trade-offs to succeed in that way.

As for industry, I don't really call it the "defense industrial base" anymore, and I think this room probably understands how it's changed better than most. But we really have to address that the industrial base supporting the Pentagon is different from [how] it was when the PPBE program process was set up.

There is the traditional defense industrial base. I can say that those companies don't like being called traditional. They think that they're very cutting edge in a lot that they do. And, in fact, they are. They build exquisite things that, for the most part, nobody else is going to build. Elon Musk isn't going to launch companies to build aircraft carriers and other types of things. So that's a part of the industrial base supporting the Pentagon that we need to support and maintain and find ways to move faster.

But as this panel has addressed, there are new parts to the industrial base. And the word "commercial" gets bandied about. It's like any other word the Pentagon uses—we kill it very quickly. But commercial for me means two things: it means off-the-shelf technology, [or] technology developed for something that's not defensive but has a defense application if we think creatively about it, or it can be modified in some way for a defense application. We talk a lot about that. We have to recognize that part of the industrial base supports the Pentagon. But there's another aspect to commercial as well, and those are companies that want to do business to support defense specifically but are set up on a commercial model—not a traditional defense model where R&D expenses are government funded or largely government funded—but are really using private capital from start to finish to figure out something. And that's something that I don't think the building understands and increasingly is not prepared to deal with as it becomes more of a force in the industrial base that's supporting the Department of Defense. There is so much money out there that wants to support our national security. But the investment cycle is shorter than the return cycle that we see with the process that we have now. So we've got to get at that because the department— and I was guilty of this, as many of us probably were—thinks that if they want $700 million or something, they get $700 million, and they give it to someone, and they build it. They don't think about the fact that a successful program of that size just brings a bigger round of investment behind it that we should be leveraging for our nation's security.

And then, finally, in the industrial base part, I don't think it's just enough to try and get new entrants and find ways for them to work their way into the Department of Defense. We want to get as many of these traditional companies and new companies involved in answering this question about old versus new and modernization. Bring them in earlier on requirements, and in fact, call it something prerequirement and get them involved in helping us figure out the disruption. Is there something we can do differently with something we have? Or to answer one of the questions in our section, will new technology replace something because we find a new way to do something? We want all of that expertise at hand on these problems, and that means bringing people in earlier to a process that is faster.

And then, finally, the Pentagon. But I'm going to offer some thoughts that are a little bit contradictory. First, on the planning process, I think that we should be exploring ideas where one size doesn't fit all. There are plenty of things that fit through a PPBE [planning, programming, budgeting, and execution] process that could be improved that give some confidence to Congress and taxpayers that the Pentagon has thought through how much something is going to cost over the long run to build and maintain. But there are plenty of things, as Mike [Brown] has pointed out, that we can't take advantage of if we don't move in a much faster and more iterative cycle. And that may require a different process for whatever part of the Pentagon acquisition procurement budget is iterating faster, where we now are not. When I say we, I mean the Department of Defense that is generating the technology that we're using, but is not finding ways to incorporate that with what's coming from outside. Keith [Alexander] said earlier that 90 percent of the internet is outside of the government. The same is true of technology. And so we have to think differently and it may require a different process, particularly when you think about the political dysfunction that we're facing in the United States right now, to take advantage of that and at speed.

And then secondly, this is where the contradiction is. You saw two organizational maps earlier today. Chris [Kirchhoff] put one up, the innovation map. And then there was one earlier that was the OSD [Office of the Secretary of Defense] organizational chart. The DoD organizational chart's an enormously elaborate, bureaucratic enterprise. We all know that. And of the leaders, particularly when they don't have a whole lot of time to create band-aids. And we need to do an assessment of these organizations we've set up, which of them are band-aids, which of them fixed the problem, or which of them are just continuing to be a bridge past the problem, figure out what the root cause of the problem was, and try and consolidate a little bit more. Because, and this has come up earlier, there are always more authorities available to us, to those in the Department of Defense, those outside, than we avail ourselves of. It's easier for a bureaucracy to create a new organization and then just repeat on a smaller scale what they were trying to fix by not recognizing the authorities. So the contradictory part is I say that we should look for ways to streamline. And with that, Michèle mentioned it is training people to use the authorities that they have to take risks to train leaders on how to understand risk and reward it in the right ways. But I do agree with Mike's idea that we should have an organization or a separate entity that is specifically focused on these types of things that are moving at a faster pace or some way to pull those things together and give them more lift. Because to Jackie's paper, culture, personality, and all of that can become a huge impediment. And the flip side of that is you've got to find a place to park something where it can scale and get larger entity echelon buy-in in order for it to move forward.

SRIDHAR: Next is former Defense Innovation Unit director Raj Shah.

RAJ SHAH: A wise DC leader once said budget is policy and strategy is budget. So, I think focusing on budget is really, really important. I want to talk about three things. One is the need for scale in areas that we can get leverage. Two, ideas on how we might organize to get after many of the problems that were described today. And thirdly, I wanted to end with a couple of things that give me some hope and encouragement in where we are today.

So from a scale standpoint, I think James's paper showed us quite clearly: we just need more stuff. We need more mass to deter China and to do a "four-plus-one" strategy. And to me, there are three ways we can get after that. One is topline growth, so we can acquire more hardware and platforms. We've seen how difficult that is in the current political climate. So maybe that'll happen, maybe not. I don't think we can bet our strategy on that. Two is a better mix of buying traditional industrial base–type of equipment versus more commercially oriented types of technologies. A lot of the work that Mike [Brown] did at DIU is relevant here. Additionally I would argue that the DoD should not build its own software programs that are commercially available, like the Defense Travel System [DTS]. We should just buy that capability commercially. That approach would save a lot of money. There are certainly challenges around scaling that approach, but I think most people would agree that it would result in better outcomes.

The third area, which I hear less about and I wanted to spend a little bit of time on, is how do we make our current defense systems more efficient and effective by leveraging commercial techniques and capabilities? Let me give one specific example. The F-35 has eight million lines of code in the jet and about twenty-four million lines of code in its ground systems. Anybody that's an engineer will tell you measuring lines of code is actually a terrible way to measure things. But I tried to figure out what percentage of the total cost of the F-35 program is somewhat software oriented. And it's not really broken out, but based on some analysis, I think 25 to 35 percent of that total cost is software. And I would argue that the best software engineers and the talent in our nation are not at the offices and companies that build that capability.

So if we want to do more with less money, buy more F-35s, have better ships, more ships, we need to find ways to improve the software component of our core weapons systems. Instead of saying, "I'm going to have hardware and then bolt on some really great software," have a software-first sort of development. And I think the way to do that, which I'll talk about in a minute, is we really need to deepen some of this partnership between the commercial organizations that know how to build that. And that's not going to, say, Google, and saying, "Build me a fighter jet," but how do we get those engineers working on this problem set?

So how do we organize around this? And how do we address this national security issue, our dependency on commercial technology?

Allow me to take one small detour in my comments, because I wanted to address some things that Admiral [Mike] Mullen and Ambassador [Michael] McFaul, and Michael O'Hanlon said, which is talking a lot about China and deterring China. One of the things that I think we need to recognize is that China's still our largest trading partner and growing. And it represents huge technology dependencies between the two countries. TSMC [Taiwan Semiconductor Manufacturing Company] is of course the most visible dependency, but it goes far deeper than that to include whole classes of chips made in mainland China. And so we need to think about how our strategy is going to be different in relation to China from what we did in the Cold War and even what we would do with Russia today from a deterrence standpoint.

So what else can we do about this from an organization standpoint, with $600 billion in private capital going to technology every year? In Chris [Kirchhoff]'s paper, he outlines it: Apple has enough cash on its book today to buy the entire traditional industrial base.

The centers of gravity have changed. The Department of Defense is no longer the monopsony buyer. And so, it needs to have a different approach to encouraging our best engineers and talent to work on it. So I think many of the ideas that Mike [Brown] had talked about: buying fast and reforming the budget process are part of it. The other parts to think about as we are replenishing our more traditional stocks of weapons, are there new or lower-cost manufacturing techniques? If you go to the Ford factory today, they don't build cars the way they built them in the seventies. There is automation. There is software. And my understanding is that our current approach to building more of core weapons stocks like Javelins and HIMARs will use the same processes we did in the seventies. I think there's a modernization opportunity for us here.

Finally, in my last section, what is the good news and progress to date?

I think the Ukraine situation has completely changed the attitude in the technology world, particularly in places like in Silicon Valley. I've never seen, in the ten years I've been working on this problem set, as many young entrepreneurs and brilliant technologists that want to solve these problems and who believe in the defense of democracy as a real calling. They are mission oriented, and yes, while they want to make some money, they are driven to work on things that are really important, and photo sharing doesn't meet that mark anymore. So I believe there's a really unique opportunity. Congress, DoD, and the policy ecosystem are slow to recognize this important trend—in fact, this whole conference is emblematic of that. We have an incredible range of leaders here around the table. I think folks really do want reform. The PPBE [Planning, Programming, Budgeting, and Execution] Reform Commission is another great example of focus on improving our processes.

My final point is that private capital is starting to move into area. The statistic more relevant is that about ten years ago, around a hundred million [dollars] was going into real defense-oriented types of companies. Last year it was $8 billion. Yet there's still a lot more available—there was $600 billion in total VC investment last year. There is a true and growing belief among investors that there's a real market in defense. I'll close with my observation that there is real, positive momentum, and now's the time to seize and act. Thank you.

SRIDHAR: Comments? Questions?

JOSEPH H. FELTER: Thank you. Amazing papers. This question is directed to Mike Brown. I think your paper was more of a manifesto, and it was an awesome one. I just want to get after one question. Let's say, just hypothetically, that you were currently serving the Pentagon, maybe in Ellen Lord's former role [as the under secretary of defense for acquisition and sustainment]. What might be some specific reforms you would look to implement— whether they're organizational or structural? What would be on your agenda in that role to help operationalize this robust strategy that you laid out?

MIKE BROWN: Well, I think it's already clear from some of the discussion here, applying some of the lessons that we have in Ukraine. So we need to be able to improve the munitions. We don't have a credible deterrence for China because we can't back up our talk. So we're getting after that. Ukraine's showing some of that. We have to clearly invest in the industrial base. We've got to improve the munitions' capability. Nadia [Schadlow] did some great work at the Hudson Institute to talk about that specifically. And then Eric's idea, we have to figure out how to go faster. If we can't change the whole system at the Pentagon, which you probably couldn't do in one person's term, we need an alternative system to get the hedge strategy in place and the fast-follower strategy in place. I think that's doable with leadership.

NADIA SCHADLOW: I just have a really quick comment on Raj's point about software. An interesting construct, which I wish I had come up with, is the DoD as a "creator" of software or a "consumer." DoD seems to think that it's fundamentally ambivalent, right? I think it should mainly be a consumer but it thinks of itself as a creator. That differentiation was coined by my colleagues Bryan Clark and Dan Patt.

BROWN: I think it's not that simple. I think we have to actually be doing both because there's a way to be a producer of software where you're going in and making small changes to existing systems, so you don't have to rely on a third party to do it. But the idea of creating software factories, so we don't need to rely on outside software is ridiculous. And Raj made that point effectively.

SHAH: My view is this, I don't actually care who does it. They just need to value software. Right now, the department knows how to buy physical things, but they don't value software and the energy that goes into it.

ROGER ZAKHEIM: I want to go back to the discussion about Congress, and I think Jackie hit on this in the beginning. And yes, CRs [continuing resolutions] and that is a problem of strategic importance, and that rests with Congress. But much of the other discussion around Congress, I think, needs to be revisited or at least balanced out by what good Congress does. And here, as a former staffer on an authorizing committee, you know where I stand. But let me just make a couple of points. I haven't heard anybody refute this, nor do people make this point. If you look at the authorization appropriations bill, 95 percent of what's in there, the Department of Defense requested. The biggest earmark is the Department of Defense coming in and putting it at the foot of the authorizers and appropriators. On top of that, whatever they don't get into that budget request, the unfunded requests come in from those same elements in the Department of Defense. So just as we're thinking about this reform to the four [PPBE] commissioners here and everybody else, recognize that much of the violence is coming from that five-sided building.

And then, when Congress does weigh in, it's not all bridges to nowhere. Let's give a few examples. Chairman [Mac] Thornberry is too modest to probably talk about the things he championed and got in there. But here are a couple that are top of mind. We mentioned the Cyber[space] Solarium Commission and counter-IEDs [improvised explosive devices] in the wars in Iraq and Afghanistan, and the MRAPs [mine-resistant ambush protected vehicles], that was Congress pushing them through. Talk about autonomy, the UAVs [unmanned aerial vehicles] that came from Congress, much to the chagrin of the leaders of the air force at the time. The European Deterrence Initiative, the Pacific Deterrence Initiative, and the list goes on and on. So the Department of Defense and the military benefit from annual authorizations and appropriations because it gives an opportunity to get stuff in. Remember the unelected problem here, perhaps, is not the appropriations staffer, but the bigger problem is the unelected bureaucracy of the Department of Defense.

Featured Discussion

With Secretary Jim Mattis and Secretary Leon Panetta,
Moderated by Secretary Condoleezza Rice

SECRETARY CONDOLEEZZA RICE: Well, I am delighted, first of all, to welcome all of you to this wonderful conference. I hear it's been going great. I want to thank Mike Boskin for the insight to bring us all together, and I also just want to welcome the many who have come from other places to be a part of this. Probably to my mind right now, this is a really important question: How do we think about the defense budget? How do we think about the relationship between the defense budget and what we need to do geostrategically as the most powerful country in the world with many different obligations?

Today, we've got two gentlemen here who have spent their time on the "Death Star," which is what, at the State Department, we used to call the Pentagon. And so, I'm going to have a chance to ask them a few questions and have them respond.

I'd then like to open it up for the last ten to fifteen minutes or so and have you ask questions. I'm a professor—I'll call on somebody if nobody asks the questions. So please get your questions ready. So let me just start with the following. You know Jim Mattis, secretary of defense. Leon Panetta, secretary of defense, and every other important job in government. And so, let me just start with the following. When you're in the jobs in the cabinet, you come out, and people say, "Well, did you enjoy that?" And you say, "That's not exactly the word that I would use, but it was fulfilling in the following ways." So I'm going to ask each of you to reflect a little bit on your time as Secretary of Defense. What was fulfilling? What was frustrating, and what does it say

The views expressed in this discussion are solely those of the individual participants and do not necessarily reflect the views of any organization with which they are, or have been, affiliated.

about the situation in which we find ourselves today? I'm going to start with you, Jim, a distinguished fellow here at the Hoover Institution.

Secretary Jim Mattis: Well, I may be pausing for a minute about what I enjoyed most because it was an unusual president I served. I think we all recognize that. I'm making progress in my twelve-step recovery process, but there are things about serving at the Department of Defense that are always satisfying. One is who you get to serve with. Most of the people you serve with can go out of the Department of Defense and make a lot more money somewhere else. And a number of them are here whom I owe a great deal to for choosing to serve at a time when as one of my senior appointees put it, "General, we all know we're not coming into this administration to burnish our personal credentials." They were motivated by a sense of service, a sense of purpose. You're also serving alongside just some of the finest human beings our country develops in terms of a sense of commitment, devotion, and a real love of country.

Even if they were too modest to use those words, you know that sense of purpose was their underlying motivation. I think that sense of purpose permeated almost everything. Things on the Hill could be frustrating at times, as my friend Chairman Thornberry can attest. But the House and Senate Armed Service Committees, as well as the Senate Intelligence Committee, were very nonpartisan. The defense of our country is not partisan. You can go back to a very conservative Republican senator named Arthur Vandenberg from Michigan, who was once asked in a town hall meeting, "Why are you supporting this socialist Truman?" And he said, "Stop right there." He said, "Politics stops at the water's edge" in a time when many people in our country feel a partisan pull to one extreme or the other. That is not the case with the Congress. So, generally speaking, it was not frustrating to go up in front of the Senate or the House. They were rough on me at times, with good reason, sometimes not for a good reason, but it didn't bother me. And afterward, we'd always shake hands and remain civil.

And I think that that is a reason for optimism as we gather here today, thanks to you, Michael. What might appear to be a fallow field can actually become a fertile field where we can work together to find common ground. There's a gentleman who's mentored a number of us in this room, General Colin Powell; rest in peace. And he used to say, "Show me your budget, and I'll show you your strategy." General Powell was a genius at tying together a budget and a strategy. But I also found that the opposite could be true. If you put a coherent strategy together and explain it carefully, it will help you win support for the budget you need. At the Pentagon, I put together the National Defense Strategy, which was informed by the broader National Security Strategy, which Nadia Schadlow was working on at the White House. I met with every key House and Senate member in both parties to explain what I was thinking and to get their input as well.

As a result, our National Defense Strategy was supported by 90 percent of congressmen and senators. That helped us immeasurably when the tough issues came along, as they always do. So there were frustrating moments, but as Churchill memorably said, "Democracy is the worst form of government, except for all the others." It was a true honor to serve as the secretary of defense. It certainly wasn't a job I was looking for. As a colonel, I'd been the executive secretary to Secretary Bill Perry and Secretary William Cohen back in the late-nineties, which truly helped prepare me for this assignment. We saw many of the problems coming with the centralization of the industrial base we've discussed today. And I'll throw that same question over to the great secretary of defense sitting here.

Secretary Leon Panetta: Thanks, Jim. Thank you very much. Thanks to Michael for putting this together, and thanks to all of you for participating in this effort to really try to look at the defense budget and look at the challenges that are out there and try to figure out how the United States can maintain the strongest military force on the face of the earth and address the crises that we're facing in the world. I've been in public life in one way or another for over fifty years, and I've often said that I've seen Washington at its best and Washington at its worst. The good news is that I've also seen Washington work. When I first went back to Washington, I went to work for a senator from California named Tom Kuchel, a moderate Republican. And he was the minority whip under Senator Everett Dirksen.

There were a lot of moderate Republicans at that time. But more importantly, their role was to reach out and work across the aisle with Democrats. A lot of statesmen who were Democrats at the time as well on the issues that were important, still worked together. Did they have their political differences? Of course, but they worked together. And when I got elected to Congress, it was the same thing. Tip O'Neill was a Democrat's Democrat from Boston, but he had a great relationship with Bob Michel, who was the minority leader. And again, they had their politics, but when it came to big issues, they worked together. They thought it was important for both parties to work together on principal issues, whether it was a Democratic president or a Republican president. When Ronald Reagan was president, it's hard to believe we passed social security reform on a bipartisan basis. We passed immigration reform on a bipartisan basis. We passed tax reform on a bipartisan basis.

And so it was from my own experience, whether it was working on defense issues or other issues, a great part of it was the ability to work across the aisle and to work with those that obviously shared common concerns for the country. Obviously the last twenty or more years, Washington has become much more partisan and much more divided. There's a lot more polarization. When I became director of the CIA, I recognized that the most important thing I could do was to reach out to Congress to try to build a relationship because of the partisanship on so many other issues. I thought it was very important to build a strong bipartisan partnership on the Hill, so I spent a lot of time with the House Intelligence Committee and the Senate Intelligence Committee.

And I felt the same way when I became secretary of defense, that despite the polarization, despite the politics, despite everything that made Washington in many ways an ugly place to work, if you could reach out to the bipartisan leadership of both the House and Senate Armed Services Committees and the Appropriations Committees, that you could build a partnership and try to get some things done. Because there is no question that Washington works best when you can develop those kinds of relationships. My biggest task when I became secretary of defense was to figure out how I was supposed to cut $500 billion from the defense budget. That's what I was handed because of the Budget [Control] Act that was passed by Congress. So I'm trying to figure out how to do $500 billion in deficit reduction. And what I didn't want to do was simply make it a budget exercise where I said, "We're going to cut everything back by a certain percentage." I really wanted to use it as a positive experience to try to develop a defense strategy for the future.

And so, it was a great opportunity to sit down. I took the staff at the top level and basically said, "We are going to work our way through this with the military leadership and with the civilian leadership and basically work through the entire budget." And we looked at the strategies we wanted to emphasize to try to build the defense force for the twenty-first century. That was an important process within the Pentagon. The ability to be able to have the relationship to work on strategies, to have the military there and then to bring the President of the United States into that process so that the President would be part of that process. And that, for me, was probably the most rewarding part of being secretary of defense. It was the ability to kind of reach out to the key players. And frankly, that's how democracy works best. Democracy is not a process where you can simply slam-dunk whatever you want. It doesn't work that way. You've got to reach out, you've got to build partnerships and you've got to make others understand why it's important to work together.

RICE: Thanks. I have a specific question, and then I want to come back to this question of strategy because, very often, the hardest thing to do is to align what you're going to spend with your strategy, particularly when you get unpleasant surprises in geopolitics. And so I'll come back to that, but let me just ask you a specific question, Jim. So, you took off your uniform and did this, and we've now done that again. Are there special challenges for someone who has been in uniform for that long, whose identity perhaps is as a military officer, and now our system is set up for the secretary of defense to really be the civilian representative of the defense within the National Security Council? Talk a little bit about that transition for you and maybe a little bit about [the current secretary of defense] Lloyd Austin since he's gone through the same transition.

MATTIS: Well, there are some military officers who probably should never be the secretary of defense, but perhaps there's some who could. It's also true that there are some civilians who shouldn't be the secretary of defense and some who could. So I don't think a president should be told, "You cannot pick a military officer." My time in the military helped me a lot to do that job. As I said, it also helped me having been the executive secretary to two secretaries of defense and sitting behind them at every one of their meetings, taking notes. I could even walk into the office on the first day and spin the combination on the safe, where you have to stick your classified gear at the end of the day. And they hadn't changed a thing since 1996 that I know of. But more seriously, I think that what I realized the first time they brought in the book of deployment orders is that I'd always been the one asking for forces, not deciding whether to approve the request.

I'd been leading troops in warfare, and whenever I needed this or that and I would make the request, and it would go to the secretary of defense. And when I was the person in the job and receiving the deployment orders to approve, I realized you get no real supervision as a cabinet officer other than congressional oversight, but that's not a day-to-day type of supervision. And I sat there looking at that book of deployment orders and was struck by the fact that not one air force squadron, not one army brigade, not one ship sails or goes overseas without the secretary of defense, the civilian leader of the military, signing off. The book comes in about once or twice a week, and most of the time you're exchanging this unit for that unit, or a ship is going on patrol or for an exercise, or it's another routine movements of troops. And sometimes it is not at all routine. But in any case, I handwrote on a big five-by-eight card and put it on my desk. And it said, "Does this deployment contribute sufficiently to the well-being of the American people to justify their deaths?"

I didn't just mean sending them in harm's way, or that they might get hurt. In any deployment, however routine it might seem, troops could die. Can I look the mother and father, the young widow, in the eye and say, "This was worth it"? So I kept that card on my desk every day. This was something I'd never had to confront before as a military officer. I had a mission as a military officer, and I tried to do it. And of course we always tried to bring all the young troops home alive. As secretary of defense, I had to look at this through a new lens. I'd sign off on most of them, but once in a while I'd circle one and say, "Chairman of the Joint Chiefs, come see me on this one." And we would talk, and sometimes I'd sign, and sometimes he'd take the order back and say, "Let me go back and look at this one." This was the big change in going from my military jobs to becoming the civilian secretary of defense—now I was putting America's word on the line. We were putting their soldiers, sailors, airmen, coast guardsmen, and marines on the line. That was a shift; that was the biggest one.

RICE: That's great. So it's been said that planning is something that you're doing until life intrudes. And one could say strategy is something that you're doing until life intrudes. So, talk a little bit about how one builds a strategy, given that most of our military procurement is sort of long tail, but then you get those unpleasant surprises. Our unpleasant surprise was obviously 9/11, and you had to sort of remake the military on the fly. And that's a more dramatic example, but you get those all the time. So talk a little bit about strategy and flexibility, how you think about building a force given that the United States has worldwide responsibilities, and I'm sure it was the same for the secretaries. Is this the 9/11 of the world? Can you fix this? How do you think about strategy, defense, and flexibility?

PANETTA: Well, obviously, the ability to be able to have the Defense Department and our military respond to challenges that are out there in order to protect our national security is the fundamental mission of what you do at the Department of Defense. And for that matter, my fundamental mission was to protect the American people. And for both positions at the time, 9/11 defined the period that we were in because there was no question that as a result of what happened in the attack on 9/11, this country essentially declared war against terrorism, especially those who were involved in the attack. So everything in the intelligence community was aimed at trying to determine just exactly where that enemy was, where they were located, and what they were up to. Our fear was that al-Qaeda was continuing to develop plans for another attack on the United States. And so the intelligence responsibility was to make sure that we were getting the intelligence we needed in order to make sure that that didn't happen again. And secondly, something I found out when I became director of the CIA was that I was, in essence, a combat commander. Because it was not just gathering intelligence, I was running operations against al-Qaeda's leadership, particularly in Pakistan.

And so intelligence was not only providing the information that policy makers needed, but we were also conducting operations against our enemy. And when I went to the Department of Defense, essentially, we were occupied in a war in Iraq, and we were occupied in a war in Afghanistan. And the reality is we went to war in order to make sure, number one, that we were going after those responsible for 9/11. And so I always felt our mission was very clear, that we had to go after terrorists who could attack the United States of America again. Number two, we wanted to make sure that they would never be able to find a safe haven again. And that's what brought us into Afghanistan: to try to make sure that Afghanistan would never again become a safe haven for terrorism.

So those were the missions, and that's what we were involved with. And I have to tell you, I'm very proud, and I think Jim is as well. I'm very proud of the capabilities that developed during that period. Not easy, but what we developed was an intelligence capability that worked with special forces, in particular, with the military, to create a real team approach to dealing with the mission we were involved with. And so intelligence identified targets, special forces went after those targets very effectively. I mean, essentially, we couldn't have done the Bin Laden raid, very frankly, with the SEALs if they had not done eight or nine raids a night in Afghanistan going after enemies. So the ability to work with the military and with intelligence was a very rewarding experience for me because it was protecting our national security. And the ability to make sure we were adjusting to the enemy we had to confront, that's, essentially, what happened with counterterrorism operations.

RICE: And in fact, it was a kind of fusion that I think people don't fully understand because it was military, it was intelligence, and it was also diplomatic. When we would go after a target in Pakistan, say in the North-West Frontier in Pakistan, you had the chief of station, the commander on the field, and the ambassador in the same room to assess all of the possibilities, so we got this incredible fusion. It seems to be, not forgetting that we may have to do that again, but it seems to be that we now have more traditional, let me call them that, military tasks when you think about China and the rise of China, or you think about what we're doing to support Ukraine. I don't know that any of us ever thought we were going to be in a ground war in Europe again. So, Jim, you were handed more of that world, it wasn't that counterterrorism was over, but talk about where you see us now in what is more of a great-power rivalry.

MATTIS: Right, and again, none of us are blank slates. We come into high office with our formative experiences. And we rightly, at this conference, we're looking at the problems—the warts—what can we do about them? How do we fix them? I will tell you I had six years as a four-star, including as the supreme allied commander in NATO, US Joint Forces Command, and US Central Command. And then I've had two years as secretary of defense. I don't know if there's anyone who's been in those positions for as long as I have who can say, "On not one strategic issue was I ever surprised thanks to our intelligence community. Not once." I know we've heard there are problems there too. And so, as I came back in the war against terrorism was becoming more moderated, but it was still going on.

You can declare a war over, as we heard earlier today, but the enemy gets a vote. They're still out there. It's an ambient threat. And the special forces and the CIA are very much committed to that fight. But on the great-power competition, I think nothing has been more heartening in this tragedy of Ukraine and the savage war that Putin has unleashed, than the use of intelligence by this administration.

Thanks to the most adroit use of intelligence I've seen in my forty-seven years of service, I think we are in a much stronger position to hold the Western democracies together.

PANETTA: I think we are living in a very dangerous world right now, and I know there's sometimes a tendency to focus on the problems we're having here at home, but the reality is we are in a dangerous world. There are probably more flash points out there today than we've seen since World War II. Just look at the threats. We're confronting Russia, which is now wide open in terms of our confrontation with Putin in Ukraine. But clearly, Russia represents a threat to the United States and the world. China, obviously, we're dealing with Xi Jinping and his approach to confronting the United States and the rest of the world and trying to promote China at a difficult time within China itself, which makes Xi a little bit unpredictable, just as we've seen Putin is unpredictable. And then to have Kim Jong-un in North Korea, this crazy man who's got nuclear weapons and begging for attention from the rest of the world, and threatening to essentially launch a missile with perhaps a nuclear weapon on top of that missile. He represents a real threat to the United States and the rest of the world.

Add to that the threat from Iran and the reality that Iran could have a nuclear weapon pretty soon, based on what we know has gone on with enrichment and the instability that they would promote. And then, look at the Middle East and the failed states in the Middle East with Yemen, Syria, and Libya, which are now breeding grounds for terrorism. Terrorism remains, from my point of view, a continuing threat to this country. And then add cyber, the world of cyberattacks, and the reality that you can use cyber to basically paralyze our country. Almost every country now builds cyber into its military plans.

So you're looking at a lot of threats out there, and to the extent that we've now engaged with Russia by providing support to Ukraine, I don't think we can kid ourselves. This is a major war in the twenty-first century. Because what happens in Ukraine is going to define for the twenty-first century what's going to happen with democracies. I don't think we can afford to just sit back and somehow hope that things turn out right. We have got to make sure they turn out right. This is a critical moment right now. There's a stalemate that's developed in Ukraine. My view, from a military point of view, is there's no such thing as a stalemate. You're either winning or losing. And when you have a stalemate, it gives Russia the opportunity to dig in, reinforce, and develop a new offensive. This is a moment when we have to make sure that doesn't happen.

So, I think the ability to build our alliances. I mean, obviously, the NATO alliance is very critical to our ability to confront Russia in Ukraine. Our ability to deal with Xi requires that we build alliances in the Pacific and have that capability there. The same thing is true, I think, in the Middle East. So I think the challenge today is how do we take our military strategies and our military capabilities and then combine them with our allies to make damn sure that our adversaries, wherever they are, cannot be successful. That's a big challenge. And I don't think, frankly, we've thought enough about the strategic approach for that kind of world.

RICE: Following up on that and bringing us back to the defense budget, that's the subject of this conference. Before I do that, though, I do want to just ask another question. As secretaries of defense, you also worked with allies. And I'd just like to have maybe just a minute on what's it like working with allies, and it is going to be a kind of different NATO now in some ways. Somebody said that Vladimir Putin had managed to end German pacifism and Swedish neutrality within a matter of months. We will see. But, comment on working with allies, and then we'll get back to the defense budget for our last few comments.

PANETTA: From my perspective, both as director of the CIA and also as secretary of defense, I have to tell you, working with our allies is incredibly important to our ability to get the job done. And look, I've gone to NATO conferences. Everybody in the old days sat down, you did talking points, and everybody went out and did their own thing. But I do think that's changed. I found it was really important to be able to build strong relationships with our strongest allies. Why? Not only because they worked with us if we were engaged militarily. Going back to Afghanistan, I have to tell you, our allies really did work with us in incredibly important ways to try to deal with the challenge there. And our ability to be able not only to work together, to fight together, but to share critical information. That's probably the most important thing I used to get out of those meetings, finding out what they knew that we did not know.

And understanding the world through their eyes, which by the way, from a diplomatic point of view, that's the most important thing we can do. It's not just going there and telling them what we want them to do. It's to go there and understand the world through their eyes and how they view their own security. And if you can do that, then you can really build a stronger relationship with our allies. Look, it's not easy to deal with all of our allies. They have their own interests, they have their own countries, they have their own security, and they have their own view of the world. And yet, the ability to reach out to them and be able to provide them the assistance and the training and the support systems that the United States can provide, I think, is incredibly important to our ability to build that set of alliances that we're going to need in the twenty-first century.

MATTIS: I'd say it's the only way we're going to build that set of alliances. Winston Churchill had it right. He said, "The only thing harder than fighting with allies is fighting without them." It is hard. It's the trigonometry level of diplomacy and warfare. But at the same time, having fought many times, I've never fought in an all-American formation, not once. And there was a young national security advisor that talked to my class of brigadier generals and rear admirals, and I never realized Dr. Rice's finger was seventy-two inches long. She looked at us and said, "Remember, young generals, we do things with and through our allies, not to them." And she made the point very, very clearly, and it was something that we carried forward.

I had three major lines of effort as secretary of defense. One was to make the military more lethal so our diplomats were heard and respected. We wanted our adversaries to know that they did not want to get on the wrong side of the Department of Defense—we wanted them to listen to our diplomats. The second one was to reform the business practices so we could gain the trust of Congress and the American people. And I brought in people like Ellen Lord here, who knew what she was doing, having been a leader from industry. And the third major priority where I spent 80 percent of my time was building the number of allies and deepening their trust. Those were the only priorities I set for myself during the twenty-four months, three days, twelve hours, and fourteen minutes I was secretary.

RICE: But who's counting, right? So Leon described a world that I think we all see, but that means staying power for the United States. And I want to ask you about three aspects of the defense budget, the defense apparatus, just to get your comments: the recruitment of people, the all-volunteer force, and the procurement process. One of the issues that we have here in the valley is these small companies will tell you, "I don't have time for the Defense Department RFPs [request for proposals]. My company will have gone out of business by the time you've hired me." And the third is something we don't talk enough about, the defense industrial base, which is showing some cracks as we have been running through equipment pretty quickly in Ukraine. So just briefly, those three aspects: people you have to have, the procurement process, and the defense industrial base if, in fact, we're getting ready for a long engagement, not one that's ephemeral.

PANETTA: I'm concerned about the people that we need to have in the military. And look, I know we've had a strong volunteer force. And frankly, we had some great men and women in uniform who were out there fighting in Iraq, Afghanistan, and elsewhere around the world. Really first-rate people. I've been there, just like Jim's been there. Looked into their eyes, and I can't tell you how important it was to see young men and women who were committed to protecting the country, putting their lives on the line in order to protect the country. Duty to country. I'm worried about that aspect today, and I teach young people at the Panetta Institute, just as Condi teaches, and Jim teaches young people here. And I sense that their sense of duty to their country isn't where it needs to be.

I believe that, ultimately, we need a national service system in this country. I think, frankly, every young person ought to spend two years giving some kind of service back to this country, whether it's in the military, whether it's in education, whether it's in health care, I don't care. But I think we've got to restore that sense of duty to country. Now, I think that the army, the navy, the marine corps, and others are going to have to reach out. They're going to have to really be able to attract those that want to serve this country because we are living at a time when I think people have second thoughts about whether they want to have to commit themselves to that kind of service. We will not have a strong military unless there is a commitment of young people to duty to country, so we've got to resurrect that sense of duty in order to make sure that we do have the men and women that are willing to fight and die for our country.

Secondly, let me just talk a little bit about the budget process and Washington. I'm a former chairman of the House Budget Committee, and I was OMB director in the Clinton administration. The budget process is badly broken. Badly broken. I mean, you've been talking about budgets and how we try to advance better technology and better innovation for the future. You're talking about a budget process that is broken. Congress hasn't passed a budget resolution in over twenty years. They don't pass budget resolutions anymore. And when I was chair of the committee, the purpose of a budget resolution was to identify priorities and then to have Congress basically follow those priorities. It's a discipline, fiscal discipline. It doesn't exist.

We're doing it by the seat of our pants. Everything comes down to a continuing resolution (a CR). And if you're lucky, you get a CR done. If you're not, you extend with another CR. Let me tell you, CRs are damaging to the

Defense Department. If you have to operate by a CR, you don't even know what you can do because it's total confusion. So somehow, we have got to get back to restoring that discipline. And I know I'm asking a lot, but if the Republicans are serious about wanting to do something about it, and they were when I was chairman of the committee, and if the reality of our economy is that we've got to do something about that, we have got to begin to develop budgets for the next five or ten years that begin to restore some discipline. Because if you do that, then I can build a defense budget, then I know where I'm going and not just operating by the seat of my pants. We have got to restore that process. And frankly, in order to do that, the Defense Department has got to be able to find ways to basically improve the way it operates.

And on procurement, it is a maze. I mean, Jim and I know, you build a weapons system, and the overruns on a weapons system are outrageous, but you keep building it even though sometimes it doesn't even make sense any-more. We have got to do procurement reform, serious procurement reform, that is able to not only expedite the process, but gives companies the feeling like they want to participate and be innovative and be creative. We don't do enough to reach out into the industries that are here and pick their brains about what we can do in order to improve our defense.

MATTIS: On the people, Dr. Rice, I'm not sure how we're going to answer Secretary Panetta's point about getting young people to want to join. I'm not sure that the way our history is taught today breeds an affection for this great big experiment. As imperfect as our democracy is, it's still the best thing going. And so here we are with the all-volunteer force facing the worst cri-sis since its founding this year. And yet, not the current president, not the last president, not his predecessor—I've never heard anyone say, "Uncle Sam needs you, young gal, young guy." I haven't seen the elected commander in chief do anything to help that army recruiter in Illinois go out and try and sell some parents on why their son or daughter ought to go into the US Army.

And so if we don't ask, "What is going on here? Why do we have a bro-ken budget process? Why do companies have no predictability?" They're not going to open more lines of production for artillery shells or for submarines or anything else. They have no predictability. I mean, we've met the enemy, and it is us. And it all seems to be symptomatic of something deeper, and that's a breakdown of trust in the country. There was a time when the US Army, what was it? Mark [Wilson], I think you wrote about it. Nineteen fifty-four didn't even have a budget because they just used the leftover money from the Korean War, and they could take care of all their needs. In other words, they were given that flexibility. Can you imagine today where you can't even get 1 percent of the budget to be reassigned to some other line that you need when you have a budget as big as it is?

What I'm seeing are all these symptoms of the breakdown of trust between Congress and the Department, between young people coming out of school and the country, and between educators on college campuses or high schools. It all seems to go back to how can we rebuild trust. Strategy will help you. Strategy will actually be an appetite suppressant on military adventure. It can put diplomacy first. Strategy can do a lot of things that would help free people from these myths of why they should distrust their fellow Americans, and we can get back to making things work better. I know I've kind of broadened the question, pulled it back out.

RICE: No, that's helpful.

MATTIS: But I think a lot of things we're talking about here are symptoms. And by the way, you all have done great work in these papers. But what I was able to hear this morning was a very good, to a Jesuit's level of satisfaction, definition of the problems. And you will never get everyone on board to the solution until you get them all on board on what the problems are. And this could be the biggest benefit coming out of this conference, that you all know how to define problems better than I've seen anywhere. And once we get everyone in agreement on that—remember how [Albert] Einstein answered when asked how he would save the world if he only had one hour? For fifty-five minutes he'd define the problem and get everyone to agree on that. Then save the world in five minutes. And so I really admire what you all are doing here.

RICE: Great. We have time for a couple questions. Mike, please.

MICHAEL BROWN: I appreciated kind of that broad perspective on budgeting. We're fortunate to have four commissioners here on the PPBE Commission, which really gets to the brass tacks of what we need to change about the budgeting process. So love to get your comments about what you would say we need to change. Pick the top two or three things you'd like to see the commission come out with?

MATTIS: Congressman Duncan Hunter, the senior, once identified six hundred laws in Congress that have some effect on how the Department of Defense is managed. There's got to be a scrub of all of those rules because many are contradictory. They complicate things, and they're additive. And that comes right from Congress. They need to cut these back.

PANETTA: I'm going to take a broader approach because, frankly, I think a broader approach is necessary. I mean, I think for Congress to be arguing, "Well, let's see, we've got to cut defense," or, "We really ought to cut Medicare or Social Security or whatever." I mean, that's not going anywhere. It's not going to happen. When I was chair of the Budget Committee, I remember meeting with President [George H. W.] Bush who said, "Read my lips: no new taxes." But we talked about the budget, and we were concerned. And I said, "Look, the deficit is in the wrong direction." In those days, we were worried about deficits going from $300 to $400 to $500 billion and $600 billion. That's what we were worried about at that point. And he said, "Look, we're going to have to sit down. We're going to have to put everything on the table. I can't do it right now," because he'd just gotten elected, but he said, "We have to do it." And we did that.

I mean, we went to Andrews Air Force Base and spent three months negotiating with everything on the table. And that's what you've got to do. I mean, if we're talking about the debt limit and cutting some kind of deal on the debt limit, let me tell you, the most important thing that could happen is if Congress and the president said, "We need to have another commission that looks at all things in the budget and makes a recommendation as to the approach we have to take." That would do wonders just to be able to get us back to talking about all the pieces you need to do.

You've got to look at discretionary spending. We had caps that grew both on defense and on discretionary spending. You've got to look at entitlements. My God, it's two-thirds of the federal budget. You're not going to do anything in the budget without dealing with entitlements. You can deal with it because frankly, you can find savings in the way Medicare is being applied, in the way veterans' programs are being applied. There are savings that can be achieved. The same thing is true in Social Security. And frankly, there are revenues that can be raised. Unless you've put all of that into a package, I mean, you're not going to get Republicans and Democrats to support anything unless everything is part of that deal. Because what you have to say to the American people is, "Everybody has to sacrifice for the sake of the country."

I remember with the Clinton budget, I met with a group of people who said, "How can you raise revenues?" And I said, "Well, wait a minute. We're doing a budget that cuts veterans' programs, that cuts agricultural programs, that deals with Medicare savings, that deals with all the areas of the budget. And you're telling me that somehow you don't have to be part of that process? Baloney. You've got to share the sacrifice that everybody has to share in order to be able to get this crazy deficit in the right direction." So unless you're looking at that big picture and everybody is willing to put everything on the table to get there, we're not going to get there by small bites. It's just not going to work very well.

I mean, although I could tell you, like Jim, there are areas of the defense budget where you can get savings. Duplication, they've got a bureaucracy at the Pentagon that's grown 40 percent both in headquarters as well as personnel. I mean, my God. Part of that is some of the problems that we're confronting. Same thing on procurement, same thing on BRAC [Base Realignment and Closure]. Very frankly, we need another BRAC process to go through in order to find the savings on that. These are all tough areas, but you're never going to get there with the defense budget unless everybody is participating in that bigger effort. That's the problem.

RICE: I've got two last questions, and then I'll come back to the two of you to close out.

MACKENZIE EAGLEN: Thank you all so much. I agree with the approach. We all have to hold hands and jump off the cliff together is how I would characterize Secretary Panetta's comments. This question is for all three of you, if you don't mind. Secretary Panetta, when you had the job in the Pentagon, you said we were within an inch of war with North Korea almost every day. At some point, if you're writing future memos to the next secretaries of State and Defense, are we thinking enough about how this ends, when it ends, and what happens?

ORIANA SKYLAR MASTRO: My question is about personnel recruitment and retention. I'm more optimistic about the sense of duty that the average young American has. And as a service member myself, I'm more optimistic about that. The thing that I saw at the Pentagon, and I'd like your views having been at the Pentagon, though I think it's less of a problem at the State Department, but I'd love to hear your views on it: The experience is outdated. The military system is set up for a 1950s system of men that are followed by their wives. And I guess I'm curious, what do we need to do to change that experience? I know, at least in the air force, the problem with dual military families, how long it took us to get maternity leave is insane, but even then, the maternity leave policy is that women are allowed to take it if they delay their promotions by a couple of years.

So how do we get back on track with some of those things? So I guess I'm curious about what do we need to do to change the system to be more flexible. I think military members should be able to easily leave for a year or two if they want to get graduate degrees and come back in much more easily than we do now. And if you have some ideas about how to update the military experience, what are some of the obstacles within the defense budgeting and procurement processes that make it so difficult for us to adjust the organization?

RICE: Let's take that question first and then we'll return to North Korea. So Leon or Jim? Jim?

MATTIS: It seems to me that the military is a somewhat unique type of employment because the missions that come to the military do not take into account the kind of flexibility you can sometimes give others. In the civilian world, people can quit their jobs. The last thing you want when a ship's getting ready to sail into harm's way and a conflict breaks out with China is for the sailors to say, "Well, I don't have to go. I can just say I'm going to quit now." So it is different. It's called service for a reason. You're not there for yourself.

Now, that's not to say we don't want to draw people in, but there is a certain degree of sacrifice associated with being in the military. But I think a lot of these things can be addressed simply by telling the service chiefs, "I want you to do everything you can to keep the right people in, and you come to me and tell me what you need in terms of legislative authority, in terms of internal departmental regulations and that sort of thing."

Right now, I don't think we're doing enough along those lines. But I also think that we're starting to get into a position where we forget that military imperatives are not always the same as civilian imperatives, and that is one of the reasons why, getting on the airplane to come down here, the airline says military members get on first because they recognize there's something special about the sacrifices that those families make.

RICE: I think the question is, if I can rephrase this, do we think enough about the North Korean problem, and what would you tell your successors to do about it? I'll tell you on the State Department side, but yes.

PANETTA: If I could quickly address this issue. I think we've got to think about service in the twenty-first century, and we've got to be able to adapt more to what's out there. I mean, I obviously thought it was very important to open up opportunities for women, for gays, for the people that were coming in who are immigrants to be able to serve. I think the most important thing for this country is to be able to have everyone who wants to serve this country have that opportunity. And very frankly, it's working. I mean, I've seen women now in special forces. I've seen women who are advancing in terms of military rank. I think we're getting there, but I also think we need to adjust to the times.

What we don't do enough is build careers in the military. Give them the opportunity to go back to school, give them the opportunity to be able to take some time off, be able to come back, and then advance. We have these arbitrary lines where, oh, you serve for two years or you serve for four years and you get the hell out. Baloney. You're now experienced. You ought to be able to build a career in the military. We're not providing enough incentives to do that, so we really do need to rethink this and provide a little more flexibility that gives people a little more opportunity to be able to adjust to the times and yet be able to serve their country.

On North Korea, the most important thing with dealing with Kim Jong-un is to show that the alliances between South Korea, Japan, and the United States are holding. Also that we maintain a military presence in South Korea with our troops and that we build even further additional allies with Australia, India, and others in order to be able to confront North Korea and make it clear that if North Korea does anything stupid, they're going to pay a high price. Kim Jong-un only understands force right now. I wish that there would be an opportunity to reach out and be able to look at opportunities to try to do something on a negotiated basis. And I would say if the State Department or others see that opportunity, we ought to pursue it, but we have to negotiate and deal with this guy from strength. And in order to show him that strength, you have to show that the alliance, particularly in that region, is firm, together, and we are not questioning one another but working together to confront North Korea.

MATTIS: It was four years ago when I was dealing with my counterpart in Beijing. We had a private walk in the woods at Mount Vernon one night, and

I said to him, "This is what great nations do. They solve problems. What are you going to do about North Korea? You keep saying you don't want all these American troops in the Korean Peninsula." I said, "You're going to see more American troops in the Korean Peninusla if you don't help us solve this problem." On a separate occasion, I had a conversation with a drunken communist Chinese officer. When I confronted her about the same issue at the National War College, she said, "We have fifty years of Communist solidarity. We have three thousand years of hatred. What do you think we think about them?"

But I think there is a reason why we need to try to find a way to manage our differences with China so we can deal with some of these problems. It may be we've gone beyond that point, at least for right now. Although I notice Secretary of State Antony Blinken is doing what he can to try to get some kind of talks going, I think there is some hope that we could work with China on this, especially if it's seen as we're not eager to have that number of troops on the Korean peninsula if this problem went away. That's one way I would look at it.

RICE: I'll just add, look, we had China in this chair of the six-party talks, and the idea was to align Japan, South Korea, China, Russia, and the United States so that North Korea couldn't play one off against the other. And I would just say three things. The first is to make sure that you're deterring China or Russia from making trouble in North Korea because the atmosphere is very different now, and I know that Vladimir Putin seems to be preoccupied, but I wouldn't put it past him to try to make trouble someplace else. So deter them from that.

Secondly, I think this is not a problem you're going to solve. It's a problem you have to manage. Sometimes in international politics, it's not time to solve something. And there are two management strategies from my point of view. One is, if I could get inspectors on the ground, I would do it, and I'd pay whatever price that took, and I'll tell you why in just one moment.

The third is I do believe that if you can keep them from testing, you're buying time because nuclear tests are not a matter of you get a little bit better, and you get a little bit better, and you get a little better. They're pretty binary. You succeed, you fail, you succeed, you fail. And so if you can keep them from testing, you may be able to retard that program. But back to the inspectors on the ground. So we had quite a knockdown, drag-out about this in the National Security Council about whether or not to pay a small price to get inspectors on the ground in North Korea. And I remember Vice President Dick Cheney, with whom I had a great relationship, by the way, but he said at this point,

"Mr. President, the Bush administration has to maintain its credibility on the use of force."

I said, "Mr. President, the one problem we don't have is credibility on the use of force. People think if they look at us the wrong way, we might use force. So that's not our problem. Our problem is to figure out how to get there." We did get inspectors on the ground, and the intelligence agencies told us that the North Koreans had ceased their uranium enrichment program and were only pursuing a plutonium program. And as you know, a plutonium reactor is above ground. It has to vent, and you can see it, but enrichment can be done underground.

And so, one of the deals that we've struck with the North Koreans was they had to give us the logs for every time they turned on the plutonium reactor. They gave us twelve thousand pages of logs. If you can get people on the ground, you learn things that you cannot learn through other means. And so that's my management strategy with the North Korean problem.

I want to thank our two secretaries of defense for their great insights, and I want to thank each and every one of you. And I just want to add my agreement here regarding rethinking the defense budgeting. Defense budgeting is really a critically important issue as we move forward. So thank you for participating in it. Thank you again, Michael [Boskin], for getting us all together, and enjoy the rest of the conference.

Part 4

Personnel and Talent Recruitment and Retention

11

The Challenges of the People Portfolio

David S. C. Chu

People, of course, are the central element of any military force. American policy statements highlight their importance:

> The Department of Defense workforce: military—active, reserve, and National Guard—and civilian personnel are the foundation of the department and constitute its most valued asset.[1]

While the people discussion typically focuses on active-duty military, it's actually a much broader portfolio, as the above quote emphasizes. Indeed, from a numerical perspective, the reserve components and federal civilian employees significantly outnumber active military. At the end of the last fiscal year, for example, 1.3 million people were serving on active duty with the five military services of the Department of Defense (DoD) versus 800,000 in the National Guard and selected reserve (i.e., those in units), 200,000 in the individual ready reserve, and 800,000 as appropriated-fund federal civilians, for a total of 1.8 million combined. Quite apart from those employed by firms manufacturing weapons for the DoD, additional civilians serve the department in a variety of arrangements, ranging from those working for nonappropriated funds to those engaged via service contracts.

The DoD personnel portfolio involves a rich variety of issues—and represents a considerable expense. Those employed directly by the DoD require nearly half of its budgetary resources, which makes controlling personnel costs essential to preserving the budget margin needed for investment. This paper focuses on several of the personnel issues most likely to affect the budget and where changes to current management paradigms might reduce explicit

The views expressed in this chapter are solely those of the individual author and do not necessarily reflect the views of any organization with which they are, or have been, affiliated.

costs or do so through improved performance. This includes choosing the best mix of people and managing the incentives necessary to recruit, retain, and motivate them. The paper concludes with lessons from past attempts at change—those that succeeded and, equally important, those that failed.

The People Mix

It's remarkable how little of the discussion on the US defense budget involves trade-offs among the different types of personnel that might staff the enterprise. Their pay scales and fringe benefits differ, as do their potential contributions to the capabilities the country needs. Presumably, this implies there's an "optimal" combination, but you won't usually find defense budget justifications discussing personnel numbers from that perspective.

The "Trade Space"

Active military personnel are the most expensive per capita but are continuously on duty and available to protect the nation's interests. Reserve component personnel are substantially less expensive until called up but may require additional training investment upon mobilization. While active personnel are assumed to embody a higher level of readiness, reserve component personnel sometimes bring higher proficiency levels for certain skills than can easily be sustained for the active military, based on their civilian experience (e.g., civil affairs). The DoD acknowledges this in defending the decision to build these capacities in the reserves. Civilians provide a depth of experience and sustained effort that may be particularly effective in supporting operations. Unlike the military recruiting model (which assumes skills will be taught after joining, an important cost to the enterprise), it's generally assumed civilians will acquire the professional skills they need, at least in part, before their government appointment. Ignoring the "law of war" question and whether their appointment allows deployment and exposure to combat risks, civilians may be better suited to certain tasks than uniformed personnel. Staffing with federal civilians, however, may be more or less expensive (or more or less effective) than using contractor personnel. The several "outsourcing" competitions the DoD has run illuminate some of the situations where federal civilians are more expensive and others where they are less.

Whom Do We Want from Each Personnel Community?

Beyond the issue of personnel mix by type, there is also the question of the characteristics desired from the members of these personnel communities, which likewise will affect cost and performance. In contrast to the relative silence about the broad mix issue, both Congress and the executive branch have been explicit in the quality standards they wish to set for military personnel, establishing minima and goals, especially for the enlisted ranks. The military services also specify the experience mix they desire in uniformed personnel, essentially a pyramid with a relatively large base. Rather than reflecting a choice based on analysis, some of this specificity may just be searching for a solution that is compatible with the constraints of a closed personnel system, in which virtually all personnel start at a junior level, progressing through a career via an up-or-out promotion mechanism, facing the incentive of what was until recently a cliff-vested annuity. Even with the recent annuity reform offering some retirement reward after two years of service, the retirement package retains a strong incentive to serve twenty years once the individual has completed ten years or so in uniform.

For federal civilians, a quite different paradigm governs the specification of personnel characteristics—a combination of what's considered "normal" for each particular job series, an experience profile importantly influenced by the promotion practices associated with civil service grade schedules (i.e., often encouraging long tenure), and a decentralized approach to both deciding "requirements" and administering the "rules of the game." In contrast to the uniformed military, for which the norms are quite clear, the civilian profile is thus a collage created by the decisions of lower-level executives. One important exception to this generalization is that the statutory requirement requires federal civilians to (usually) be US citizens. This is ironic, given that citizenship is not required for all uniformed personnel. They may enlist with a green card and sometimes less.

In contrast to federal civilians, the characteristics of contractor personnel are generally left to the contractor's discretion, except for those characteristics that might be explicitly or implicitly defined by the nature of the contract. That's as it should be since the contractor is asked to serve as an agent in making these decisions.

Could Civilians Play a Larger Role?

Besides the exception generated by any outsourcing competitions, the other exception to ignoring so much of the mix issue is the inclination of several secretaries of defense to propose greater use of federal civilians instead of uniformed personnel to reduce operating costs. These initiatives seem to stall short of what might be attempted and often encounter substantial congressional opposition (for example, the statutory bar imposed in 2007 on converting military medical billets to civilian status).

One limit on civilianization is the view that the law of war will require uniformed personnel for tasks that civilians might perform in peacetime. However, if one explored the British concept of sponsored reserves, there is a potential opportunity to consider some trade-offs. On a small scale, the United Kingdom allowed contracts for the provision of specialized services (such as trucking), in which the contractor was required to have all personnel become reserve force members who could be mobilized as uniformed personnel should the government decide it was warranted by developing circumstances. At one point, the UK also considered securing aerial tanker capacity in this manner, although it did not implement that option.

For the United States, perhaps the most serious impediment to considering additional civilians instead of military personnel lies in the differential manner in which the political process treats military and civilian slots. While the National Defense Authorization Act specifies military strength (thereby driving the funding level), civilian numbers are not usually specified. Their pay is funded from the operations and maintenance appropriation—an account that often suffers cuts relative to what's actually needed to run the department. Thus, within the department, a decision maker who proposes giving up military billets in favor of civilian staffing runs the risk of winding up with neither.

Blended Units

Of course, more than one type of personnel can serve in the same unit. The Pentagon staff is a mix of military, federal civilian, and contractor personnel. Mixing personnel types in line (versus staff) units is much less frequent, although not unknown. One extreme example: at the height of the Cold War, contractor tech reps served aboard deployed aircraft carriers to provide high-end repair expertise for sophisticated equipment.

A Way Ahead

Would substantial changes in the mix of personnel and their characteristics substantially reduce DoD costs or improve performance? Decisively answering that question would require significant investment in empirical analysis and perhaps some experimentation to test alternative staffing approaches. Raising new options requires reliable evidence that they would be better than what currently characterizes the largely successful DoD enterprise. Some of that evidence could come from our history of past practices; some might also come from the experience of other militaries. However, such a review could not be reasonably concluded in just a year or so. Committing to such a multiyear debate might be one of the most important reforms we could consider.

What Incentives Do We Need to Recruit, Retain, and Motivate the People We Want?
The Constraints on Departmental Action

Whatever mix of personnel might be desired, the ability of the department to attract and manage the people it wants is constrained by statutory constructs specific to each personnel type and policies that often have deep cultural roots, especially for direct compensation. Unlike the US private sector, where decision makers enjoy considerable latitude in designing compensation packages, basic pay for military and most federal civilian personnel is governed by pay tables, with annual adjustments that ultimately require congressional assent. In most years, the adjustment arrives as a uniform across-the-board change. Worse, reflecting political reality, the proposed and enacted adjustment is often the same for military and civilian personnel, even though there's no particular economic reason these should always be equal or even the same for active-duty and reserve component personnel.

Likewise, the important fringe benefits are effectively specified in the law, making it politically challenging to adapt them to changing circumstances, especially if change implies losers as well as winners.

Change Is Possible Nonetheless

However, when a serious problem arises, the political process can be willing to consider alternatives. With the DoD suffering significant midcareer military retention shortfalls in the late 1990s, above-average (targeted) pay raises were enacted for these personnel. Increases for military personnel equal to a half percentage point greater than those for civilians continued for much of the early 2000s, helping to sustain the all-volunteer force despite its engagement in a difficult and increasingly unpopular set of conflicts.

Similarly, when the George W. Bush administration persuaded Congress that the DoD's future success required a modernized civil service, it secured authority to reimagine the pay construct. It used that authority to establish a small number of pay bands for white-collar civilians (versus the fifteen grades of the general schedule), with managers allowed to set and adjust salaries within pay bands as necessary. This regime offered better latitude to meet market conditions in setting pay, especially since the DoD could exceed the usual ceiling on civilian pay, which is tied to the pay of Congress. The congressional pay ceiling (currently $174,000) makes it difficult to compete for highly compensated professionals, whether they are clinicians or among the technically adroit, whose alternative opportunities might offer several hundred thousand dollars per year. And in the hierarchical structure of civil service grades, a ceiling at the top translates into constraints on those at lower levels, with similar adverse effects on competitiveness.

Pay bands also offered the prospect of some savings in those situations where government positions were more generously compensated than might be necessary. But pay bands largely vanished with the revocation of the National Security Personnel System (NSPS), a victim of union opposition to the very flexibility that might otherwise recommend it (as well as the antici-pated difficulties of transition and the system's origin in a largely partisan pro-cess). With NSPS's demise, the authority to exceed the politically imposed ceiling on pay for federal civilians similarly lapsed.

Perhaps the lesson of this history is that it requires consensus regarding the solution to a significant problem to change the basic constructs under which DoD leaders must operate for federal personnel, military or civilian. Recommendations based on empirical analysis alone, such as efficiency, will not be sufficient to drive change. The response to the recent Quadrennial Review of Military Compensation (QRMC), which concluded that a time-in-grade versus time-in-service pay table produces better results for the military, is consistent with that hypothesis. Without a burning platform con-sensus that better results were needed, the department and Congress ignored the potential improved retention of high-quality personnel the QRMC sug-gested could result. Likewise, in the absence of a consensus that the complex set of allowances that constitute so much of military pay is a potential source of considerable inefficiency, the cultural opposition to a salary system ana-lyzed by the same QRMC that would replace the current pay and allowances construct doomed any attempt to consider such a shift seriously.

Rethinking Compensation

The Congressional Budget Office repeatedly points out that the US construct for military compensation is unusual compared to the practices of our larger society (most recently in its *Approaches to Changing Military Compensation*, January 2020).[2] The significant use of tax-sheltered allowances, for example, obscures the pay total, with military personnel typically underestimating the actual value of regular military compensation (RMC), which is the construct that estimates the average value of pay and major allowances, including the tax advantage the allowances enjoy. Particular difficulties arise from the housing allowance, which constitutes an important fraction of RMC for junior personnel. Those who live in government-furnished quarters surrender the housing allowance. For single personnel (about half the force), those quarters are barracks, and it's doubtful that most personnel value the barracks at the value of the allowance. Even for those with families, the economist's observation may pertain that in-kind compensation may not be valued as highly as the cash equivalent.

It's certainly the case that those who analyze military personnel issues believe the skew of fringe benefits toward families helps explain the earlier marriage rates for uniformed personnel relative to our society as a whole and earlier family formation. Put differently, giving single military personnel the housing allowance in cash, and exiting the barracks business, might markedly improve recruiting while relieving the DoD of part of its housing management challenge.

To overcome the limitations of the military pay system, the department uses bonuses extensively, as is well known, both to encourage entry into particular career fields and to meet retention goals. Some special pays the department employs serve these same purposes. In contrast to the relative rigidity of basic pay, the DoD enjoys wide latitude from Congress for these bonuses and special pays, both in size and how they are administered. Cultural norms may still occasionally limit their application, as in the recent reluctance of air force leaders to seek bonuses large enough, as estimated by their analysts, to solve the pilot retention problem.

Given the aggressive use of bonuses, it's interesting that the department is much less energetic in exploiting the potential of Assignment Incentive Pay (an auction to staff difficult-to-fill postings) and the continuation pay feature of the revised military retirement system to shape the experience profile. One hypothesis is that Assignment Incentive Pay contradicts the cultural expectation that you accept what the assignment system directs, even though, in practice, the reality is somewhat different. Disinterest in using the new continuation pay may reflect an unwillingness to rethink the desired experience profile now that it need not be so closely tied to the cliff-vesting of the annuity at twenty years of service and need not be the same for every career field.

In contrast to the aggressive use of bonuses and special payments to ensure that military compensation produces the recruiting and retention results desired, the DoD makes much less use of these instruments for civilian personnel. The DoD is not alone among federal agencies in its reluctance to do so. The result is chronic difficulty competing with the private sector for talent in selected skills, with the limited adjustment of grade levels in many cases being the only way to meet marketplace realities, and given the pay constraints related to the ceiling on congressional salaries. That competitive disadvantage is exacerbated by the careful nature of civil service hiring, such that often, the federal manager cannot make a prompt offer, even at the constrained salary. It should not be surprising that managers often prefer to use contractor personnel since the contractor is free to set salary and benefits as needed and can perhaps offer prompter staffing once the underlying contract mechanism is in place.

Further, the managerial challenge of dealing with subpar performers is the service contractor's responsibility. Contractors are generally viewed as being more responsive when performance problems occur versus the almost legendary difficulty of dismissing those with civil service status when they fail to perform or when they transgress.

These rigidities of the classic civil service system lead to a bias in the mix of the department's personnel, with managers desiring military personnel in situations where civilians might be more appropriate and contractor personnel taking the place of federal civil servants where the latter might be better from a governance perspective—i.e., with contractor personnel edging into inherently governmental responsibilities.

Beyond the Pecuniary

While pecuniary compensation directly affects the DoD budget, and while the DoD must compensate its people competitively lest they make other choices, it would be unwise to view salary and benefits as the only source of motivation for joining the national security team. Whether it's patriotism or a chance to contribute to a larger cause, the intangible notion of service is obviously a critical factor in staffing the department with both uniformed and civilian personnel. That's a standard observation about military service, but it is also true for civilians. Paul Light, the longtime observer of the US civil service, remarked years ago on the strong sense of mission he sensed among DoD civilians—stronger than he observed across the federal government as a whole.[3]

For the uniformed force especially, the military's reputation with the American public is crucial to recruiting success. With the success of the all-volunteer force, the military became one of the most respected institutions in American society. The recent erosion in that reputation—although it is still higher than for most of our institutions—is a cause for concern. Whatever is causing that drop may help explain the recent recruiting difficulties the armed services are facing, with the army missing its recruiting goal by fifteen thousand in FY2022—an extraordinary shortfall. Some of that shortfall may be the result of the wrenching effects of the COVID-19 pandemic coupled with the prevailing low unemployment rate.

Other likely factors, however, include the lower labor force participation rate for young men and perhaps mismanagement of recruiting resources. As some are fond of observing, it's really an all-recruited force and the skillful management of recruiting is necessary to sustain success. The marine corps recruiting model is often held up as the standard, starting with its emphasis on assigning the best personnel to recruiting responsibilities, continuing through the incentives facing its recruiters—they only receive credit after the recruit finishes basic training—and including its use of the period before recruits enter service for some basic acculturation and physical training. Practices like these merit consideration by the other services.

There is a concern that one of the classic incentives for military service—the GI Bill—is now less effective as other educational assistance programs have expanded. Given the importance of college aspiration for young Americans, the military has tried hard to make military service compatible with seeking a college degree, not only through the GI Bill but also by offering substantial tuition assistance to those in uniform and promoting college credit for selected military experiences. To the extent that college is less desired by our youth, the draw of the GI Bill is also commensurately reduced.

The military's attention to the career prospects of its members presumably improves its attractiveness. In that regard, the recent interest in "talent management" could be helpful. By giving individuals a chance to express their preferences regarding assignments in part by allowing them to describe their qualifications more fully than standard personnel records have allowed, military personnel gain agency in charting their respective career courses. Unfortunately, the systems for doing so still leave much to be desired, and there is an inevitable tension between such systems and the demands of an institution that must often ask its people to fulfill unexpected and potentially unpleasant requirements. Even apart from actual combat, the nation's need to employ its military power may require sudden moves to unfamiliar locales, either imposing an unwelcome geographic change on a family or a separation from the family that likewise makes a military career less attractive. Easing family burdens, especially spousal employment difficulties, is a crucial component of managing the people portfolio—through a mix of pecuniary benefits (e.g., subsidies to spousal careers) and nonpecuniary ones (e.g., the quality of the schools military family children attend).

Whether it's the design of talent management systems or family support programs, perhaps the most important issue is managing expectations. Creating expectations that cannot be fulfilled is a guaranteed route to failure. Some of the air force's retention difficulties during the Global War on Terror can be ascribed to disappointment among those assigned to duties distinctly out of their chosen career fields. Conversely, experience suggests that setting expectations in line with what the institution can deliver, even if disappointing to the aspirations of some, will more likely promote institutional success.

Can We Improve DoD's People Results? If So, How?

Among the many issues that might be addressed, two are particularly critical: reversing the recent recruiting weakness and attacking the high personnel costs that consume so much of the DoD budget. Without recruiting success, we cannot field the force we desire. And if costs cannot be better controlled, we cannot sustain that force over time.

Recruiting

The recruiting challenge is more urgent. At least four steps are worth considering. First, adapt the most successful elements of the marine corps recruiting model as appropriate to the needs of the other services. Next, sustain and, as necessary, enlarge efforts to ameliorate destructive behaviors (e.g., sexual assault, suicide) and the problematic effects of service (e.g., post-traumatic stress), which some fear contribute to the erosion of public respect for the military.

Third, equalize compensation for junior enlisted personnel who are single by paying some or all of their housing allowance in cash and pricing barracks at market-clearing rates, perhaps even limiting how much of a barracks business the DoD operates over the longer run. And last, offer military service as a route to citizenship for those who immigrated to the United States without authorization as children (the "Dreamers").

Increasing cash compensation for junior and single enlisted personnel imposes an explicit upfront cost, but it's an empirical question of whether it's more efficient than offering yet larger signing bonuses. It's certainly less costly than an across-the-board pay raise and avoids the additional family support costs that might otherwise accrue, which should be included in the net cost of a change.

The Personnel Mix

Determining the best mix of personnel communities—active, reserve, federal civilian, and contractor—to provide the capabilities needed is the most important way to curb personnel costs. If such an optimization reduces the demand for active-duty personnel, it would also relieve some of the recruiting burden. Moreover, for active-duty personnel especially, we should tailor the experience mix in each skill area to that skill area's needs. This would lead to the best organizational structure and offer a more viable approach than the one-size-fits-all experience pyramid in use today. The present practice is driven by the current closed personnel system (in which virtually everyone starts as a recruit or officer trainee) and the just-reformed cliff-vested pension, not necessarily by explicit empirical examination of what's best. To the extent that a skill needs more midcareer than junior personnel, lateral entry and midcareer retraining can be considered. Lateral entry also allows the military to benefit from talent developed in civil life—i.e., we begin to emulate the civilian practice of recruiting from the ranks of those who already possess a skill rather than assuming everyone will be trained from scratch, as is largely the case for the military today.

Three Other Ways to Confront Costs

Beyond explicitly choosing an optimal personnel mix, three other issues deserve attention in any serious effort to curb costs:

1. Relax the rigidity of the civil service regime for the DoD by replacing the fifteen-grade general schedule with a small number of pay bands (relieved of the congressional pay constraint at the top end) and adopting a hiring system that allows the department to compete successfully for talent (e.g., by granting direct hire authority for all DoD positions). The purpose, of course, is to make federal civilians an attractive option for managers to choose versus overrelying on both uniformed personnel and contractors.
2. Aim to increase the share of military compensation paid in cash over the long run versus allowances and income paid in kind. Because such a change presents a deep sociological challenge, it will likely

require a generation or more to accomplish and a gradual approach to addressing the specific issues involved.

3. Rethink the nature and delivery of health-care benefits. The DoD spends over 7 percent of its budget on the Military Health System. Nonetheless, many beneficiaries are dissatisfied with what they receive. That is especially true of younger households—the very community we're currently worried about from a recruiting perspective. One potential start is the proposal from the Military Compensation and Retirement Modernization Commission to offer a military-specific Federal Employee Health Benefit in lieu of the present system. The option developed by the commission was estimated to save $3 billion annually in steady-state DoD outlays.[4]

Public policy analysts would likely applaud changes of this sort, for which significant empirical support can be marshaled.[5] The political record, however, suggests that this alone would be insufficient to secure adoption. The reception to various quadrennial reviews of military compensation underscores this reality—as does Congress's ignoring the health-care recommendation from the Military Compensation Commission.

Nor is endorsement by prestigious leaders necessarily sufficient. In the George W. Bush administration, the secretary of defense and the Joint Chiefs of Staff endorsed a relatively modest change to the health-care benefit; the congressional response was to pile up in a hearing the mountain of adverse correspondence generated by advocates for the status quo.[6] The sad fate of the recommendations from the Dole-Shalala Commission, reforming Veterans Affairs disability (a much more significant issue), reinforces this reality.

Developing a Strategy for Change

What, then, might be the elements of a change strategy? First, as others would likely agree, the president's voice can be decisive. Experience from the last fifty years provides three examples of significant DoD personnel policy changes in which the president's leadership was arguably critical. These include the return to an all-volunteer force under President Richard Nixon, civil service reform for the DoD during President George W. Bush's administration, and the creation of the space force under President Donald Trump. Yes, others and other factors contributed, and success might require old-fashioned political horse-trading (e.g., Secretary Melvin Laird securing President Nixon's support for a military medical school, the "trade" in return for Chairman F. Edward Hébert allowing the volunteer force bill to emerge from his Armed Services Committee). And a subsequent president might reverse course, as happened when President Barack Obama decided to disestablish the National Security Personnel System. But that only underscores how important presidential support is to accomplishing difficult changes.

A second element in a change strategy may be less obvious: rethinking the motivation for action. The ideas presented here derive basically from principles with which economists and public policy analysts are comfortable. Military retirement reform was advocated based on similar arguments over a generation or more, never gaining political traction. But when the unfairness of the system became the basis for action, a degree of change became possible. Admiral Don Pilling, a vice chief of naval operations, pointed out to Secretary Donald Rumsfeld in an internal review that most military personnel would never collect an annuity. The Military Compensation Commission later took up this refrain, proposing reform to address this unfairness, which Congress adopted.[7]

It's worth noting in both these examples the critical contribution two experienced hands made to the change process. Thanks to Laird's and Pilling's deep understanding of the mechanisms and issues involved, they could identify what might be needed to move change proposals forward—elements that might not be evident to those approaching the challenge from a largely analytic perspective.

Two final thoughts are worth offering as one thinks about improving DoD's "people results." First, for all its shortcomings, the present system succeeds in creating a first-class military. The medical adage comes to mind as one contemplates change: "First, do no harm"—or at least ensure the benefits will importantly exceed the adverse effects that change may create. Second, while it is crucial to curb personnel costs to the extent we can, first-rate people will always be expensive to recruit and retain, be they military or civilian. And as history and current experience demonstrate, it's first-rate people you want when the nation's interests are at stake.

Notes

1. US Department of Defense, "DoD Strategic Management Plan: Fiscal Years 2022–2026," October 28, 2022, 27.

2. Congressional Budget Office, "Approaches to Changing Military Compensation," (publication 55648), January 2020.

3. Personal communication to author in 2005 (confirmed in an email, March 6, 2023).

4. Alphonso Maldon Jr., Larry L. Pressler, Stephen E. Buyer, Dov S. Zakheim, Michael R. Higgins, Peter W. Chiarelli, Edmund P. Giambastiani, J. R. Kerry, and Christopher P. Carney, "Report of the Military Compensation and Retirement Modernization Commission: Final Report," Defense Technical Information Center (ADA625626), January 2015, 262.

5. Beth J. Asch, "Setting Military Compensation to Support Recruitment, Retention, and Performance," RAND Corporation, 2019.

6. Author's recollection of his testimony to the House Armed Services Committee hearing on the Military Health System, March 29, 2006.

7. Briefing of the Defense Advisory Committee on Military Compensation to Secretary of Defense Donald Rumsfeld, September 30, 2005, Admiral Donald L. Pilling, Chairman (attended by author).

12

Cyber
From Bleeding Talent to Bleeding Edge

Vishaal "V8" Hariprasad and Casey "Waldo" Miller

Introduction

Russia has perpetrated software supply chain and ransomware attacks disrupting thousands of US businesses.[1] China has sponsored targeted attacks on research and academic organizations to steal intellectual property beneficial to its economy.[2] Cyber is a critical element of national power.[3] Yet, amid a rapid rise in digital crime and conflict over the last five years, the United States faces a critical shortfall of over seven hundred thousand cyber workers.[4]

Due in part to industrial-age thinking within hardware-centric services, the military is acutely affected by this technical cyber talent gap in areas that include (1) cyber roles and responsibilities; (2) technical talent management; and (3) acquisition risk avoidance.[5]

Companies across the nation are paying top dollar for cybersecurity and development talent. Near-peer and adversarial nations continuously demonstrate their maturation and are conducting cyberattacks of increased sophistication. The United States must field and rely upon a highly skilled and technical cadre of cyber talent to compete. How can the future US military force attract, train, and retain high-quality cyber talent?

This paper examines the various cyber roles with the Department of Defense (DoD), how leading companies manage equivalent talent, and how the current DoD budgeting and acquisition mentality detracts from retaining high-quality cyber talent. Ultimately, the DoD can improve the retention of critical cyber talent by empowering military workforce management at the unit level, getting compensation right, investing in and empowering continuity of expertise, and inverting the military cyber acquisition calculus.

The views expressed in this chapter are solely those of the individual authors and do not necessarily reflect the views of any organization with which they are, or have been, affiliated.

Military Cyber Roles

The DoD employs military, civilian, and contractor personnel in various cyber-related roles. Every role is vital in the cyber ecosystem, but cyber talent cannot be managed with a singular approach. Understanding how the DoD approaches cyberspace is essential to identifying and categorizing cyber talent management categories. Recommendations for talent management should be tailored to each category.

Military services today organize, train, and equip their respective cyber career fields. US Cyber Command is tasked with executing cyber operations.[6] Each service has occupational specialty codes for cyber operation career fields. When considering relevant cyber talent management, there are four general categories of focus for cyber talent in the military services:

1. *Information Technology Operations.* Corporate enterprises rely on information technology (IT) and communication networks. The Department of Defense Information Network (DODIN) is the world's largest enterprise data network, connecting all aspects of the DoD over cyber transport systems. The Defense Information Systems Agency is responsible for maintaining the DODIN. These tasks include the design, implementation, and upkeep of communications and information networks and infrastructure. These are traditional IT services that have the highest overlap with civilian equivalents.

2. *Defense.* Defending the DODIN requires teams that monitor, hunt, assess, and analyze adversary activity on or against the DODIN. This is known as defensive cyber operations (DCO) and is traditionally seen in the civilian sector as blue team, threat intel, and cybersecurity analysts.

3. *Offense.* Utilizing cyber capabilities to disrupt, degrade, or deny adversaries is known as offensive cyber operations (OCO).[7] Legally, offensive operations are not allowed by civilians. However, the skill sets required to conduct offensive operations share similarities with proactive cybersecurity services, such as penetration testing and red teaming, where companies hire security teams to simulate cyber-attacks and find vulnerabilities.

4. *Development.* The tools utilized for IT, DCO, and OCO are acquired from civilian companies and defense contractors or are developed organically by government and military members. This organic cyber capability development (CCD), which is similar to the

development work of senior software engineers and exploitation and vulnerability analysts in the commercial sector, is critical to providing the adaptability required to meet the challenges inherent in cyberspace. The pace of daily operations requires new and updated capabilities, which must keep pace with commercial patching—and move much faster than government contracting. The DoD is adopting modern coding practices and improving delivery speeds via software factories. Like manufacturing factories, software factories are assembly plants for development and integration, which contain multiple pipelines equipped with tools, process workflows, scripts, and environments, to produce software deployable artifacts with minimal human intervention.[8]

Table 12.1 compares each service's relevant career field and cyber skill category. Regardless of the service title for the roles, these cyber functional areas

Table 12.1. Summary of US Military Cyber Career Categories

Service	Officer Career Fields
Army*	17A Cyber Warfare (DCO / OCO)
	170D Cyber Tool Developer (CCD)
	25A Signals (IT)
Navy[†]	1800 Cryptologic Warfare (DCO / OCO)[‡]
	1820 Information Professional (IT)
	1840 Cyber Warfare Engineer (CCD)
Marines[§]	0602 Communications (IT)
	1702 Cyberspace Warfare (DCO / OCO)
	1705 Cyberspace Warfare Development (CCD)
Air Force & Space Force[ll]	17D Warfighter Communications Operations (IT)
	17S Cyber Effects Operations (DCO / OCO / CCD)

*See US Department of the Army, "CY Branch DA PAM 600-3," January 17, 2018.
[†] See US Department of the Navy, "Special Duty Officer—Cyber Warfare Engineer Information Sheet," US Naval Academy, February 2020.
[‡] See House Committee on Armed Services Bill, James M. Inhofe National Defense Authorization Act for Fiscal Year 2023. H.R. 7776 (2022).
[§] See US Department of the Navy, "Update to FY22 MOS Manual for the 17XX Occupational Field," US Marine Corps, MARADMINS 399/21, August 2021.
[ll] See US Department of the Air Force, "Air Force Officer Classification Directory," Air Force Personnel Command, October 31, 2021.

have the same general job descriptions for both military and civilian industries. The 2023 National Defense Authorization Act (NDAA), Section 1533 A.2.N, directs the study of "Whether the Department of Defense should create a separate service to perform the functions and missions currently performed by Cyber Mission Force units generated by multiple military services."[9]

Given the identical core technologies that underpin the cyber domain, nearly all work roles and missions can be filled and executed by civilians.[10] An additional RAND study went so far as to state: "There are tens of thousands of 'citizen soldiers' . . . who have the potential to support the Army's cyber mission needs or the propensity to learn cyber skills."[11] So why do we need military cyber talent?

Figure 12.1 displays the United States Cyber Command (USCYBERCOM) Force concept. On the right, routine (IT) uses for business operations are depicted in blue. In red, at the opposite end of the spectrum, are offensive (OCO) operations, with defensive (DCO) operations between them. The aspect of building the tools necessary to support the entire range is known as capability development (CCD). The offensive use case for cyber operations is unique to the military, while IT and defensive use cases are the same in the

Legend
DCO-RA is defensive cyberspace operations — response actions
ISR is intelligence, surveillance, and reconnaissance
OPE is operational preparation of the environment
DCO-IDM is defensive cyberspace operations — internal defensive measures

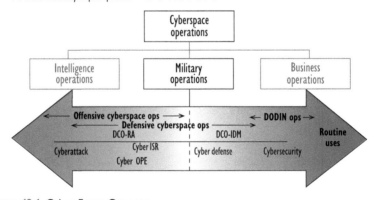

Figure 12.1 Cyber Force Concept

Source: Redrawn from Department of Defense Office of Inspector General, "DODIG-2016-026: (U) Combat Mission Teams and Cyber Protection Teams Lacked Adequate Capabilities and Facilities to Perform Missions (Redacted)," FOIA document, November 24, 2015, 33.

civilian sector. Therefore, when it comes to cyber talent retention, the military should focus its efforts on OCO and CCD in support of OCO.

Recruiting and retaining high-quality technical talent is not a new problem. Silicon Valley and large tech companies like Meta (Facebook), Microsoft, Amazon, Apple, and Google have dealt with technical talent management for three decades.[12] A common theme among large tech companies and successful start-ups is identifying and retaining employees who provide outsize returns. In his book *Game Changer: How to Be 10x in the Talent Economy*, serial entrepreneur Michael Solomon studied the highest-impact employees and coined the term "10x talent" to describe those who produced outsize returns to their organizations compared to the average worker.[13] Solomon's examination of high-performing and high-return technical talent identified three standard cultural norms. First, high performers enjoy solving complex problems. Second, they enjoy learning new skills while improving and mastering their current skills. Third, high performers appreciate feedback and results. They want to know that their work has had an impact, whether delivering revenue, executing on a mission, or providing personal fulfillment.[14]

Military cyber problem sets are challenging, require training and continuous improvement, and have outsize mission impacts. Moreover, the civilian sector cannot engage in offensive operations legally.[15] Therefore, individuals who find fulfillment and excitement in offensive and national defense missions will naturally gravitate toward a career in military cyber operations. The challenge, however, has been in how the department approaches managing, incentivizing, and retaining technical talent.[16] A RAND study focused on US Air Force cyber officer retention identified the desire to remain in technical roles for longer durations and frequencies throughout the officers' careers.[17] Assignments to nontechnical positions or away from the cyber mission led many midlevel technical officers to separate.

Cyber talent that separates does not have to wait long to find a job. Given the skill set overlap with the civilian sector, military cyber talent can find significantly higher salaries and equivalent or better benefits in the civilian sector. The civilian sector recruits and retains sought-after talent through competitive salaries. Jobs that require creativity, solving complex problems, and dealing with ambiguity tend to be higher paying than jobs that require adherence to checklists.[18] To the maximum extent possible, successful technology companies find ways to automate simple and repetitive tasks while freeing up talent to focus on hard-to-solve complex problems.[19]

The army has succeeded in early efforts to utilize Assignment Incentive Pay and the Selective Retention Bonus to compensate highly skilled cyber soldiers.[20] In addition, the 2016 NDAA established the Cyber Excepted Service (CES) program for Defense Department civilians. The CES system provides various tools to compensate civilian members based on technical skills and capabilities, allowing the department to be competitive with civilian compensation.[21] However, the focus of the CES program is only to enable flexibility within the current government service pay and promotion system. The maximum annual compensation for any member of the CES program is limited to $176,300.[22] By comparison, senior engineers at companies like Google, Facebook, Microsoft, and Apple earn $225,000 to $350,000 in total annual cash compensation.[23] Including stock options, senior engineers can earn $650,000 a year or more in total compensation.

Prioritizing high-quality talent who focus on the cutting edge of military cyber operations will require an appreciation for the work environment and values these individuals seek. Additionally, to remain competitive with the civilian sector, the military must ensure that top-tier talent continuously have compelling and challenging problems to solve, a growth path that incentivizes technological development, and pay and benefits commensurate with their skills.

Acquisition and Budgeting for Cyber Relevance

Speed is everything in cyber operations. To keep the best technical talent engaged, incentivized, and armed with the tools for success, acquisition and budgeting processes must evolve. With cyber operations, the operator is truly the defining factor. Whether an airman in an aircraft, a soldier in a tank, or a sailor on a ship, the expertise, training, and decision making of the individual matter as much as the platform they utilize. In cyber, the same is true. However, the platform can and will change based on the adversary, the timing, and the technologies involved.[24]

A recent congressional blue-ribbon panel, Section 809, identified that the Department of Defense acquisition process needs to evolve from "an outdated, industrial-era bureaucracy to a more streamlined, agile system able to evolve in sync with the speed of technology innovation."[25] With a focus on hardware, industrial-era weapons, and large-scale systems over individuals, the current acquisition and budgeting process cannot react to cutting-edge cyber technology evolution.

In addition to a systems-level approach, acquisitions lack clarity in the cyber operations domain.[26] With the traditional domains of war, success metrics were easier to visualize, understand, and implement. When it comes to cyber development, however, there can be ambiguity in what is needed to solve a pressing problem. The modern, agile approach to software and cyber problems requires the iterative flexibility to fail and learn fast.[27] Iterative problem solving requires comfort with a continuum of risk versus black-or-white metrics. Traditional acquisitions are de-risked through an exhaustive and time-consuming requirement-gathering and validation process to minimize the chance of program failure. This distorted focus on a perfect acquisition process over operational speed is a crucial concern for cyber operators.[28]

A study on navy cyber acquisitions recommended that acquisition governance for cyber be done at the lowest levels possible with appropriate accountability mechanisms.[29] Doing so allows for rapid integration and iteration in an agile manner. Agility and speed in the acquisition process for cyber-related systems and operations are just the starting point. There must also be a culture of risk-adjusted decision making that allows for failing fast while increasing the chances of success. One of the Air Force's best-known test pilots, General Chuck Yeager, said it best: "You don't concentrate on risks. You concentrate on results."[30]

Acquisitions and budgeting fall into two key categories for cyber: personnel and systems. Regarding personnel, there needs to be flexibility in payment and benefits tied to appropriate skills. Additionally, an investment must be made in continued technical educational growth and the retention of expertise through a thoughtful blend of active, reserve, and civilian force management. At the same time, systems acquisitions must adopt a fail-fast mentality where experimentation is part of the calculus, and fear is for lack of speed and innovation versus not attaining the perfect metrics.[31]

Recommendations
Empower Military Manpower Management at the Unit Level
Today, commanders are extremely limited in authority and time when hiring personnel. Except for highly classified (i.e., "green door") or specially coded units, air force squadrons receive the manpower assigned to them via the Air Force Personnel Center (AFPC). Commanders can advertise open, major command-approved positions through a "talent marketplace" web application for most officer career fields and a few enlisted fields. Subsequently,

military members slated to move to a new assignment can review open positions and place bids for the positions that interest them. This is a great start to increasing transparency and awareness, but ultimately the decision is left to AFPC—meaning there are instances where a commander and applicant can confirm a perfect match, and AFPC can (and does) overrule.

Unfortunately, hiring is not much easier or faster on the civilian side. On average, a new hire already working in the government should expect to wait two to four months after being selected to begin a position. That time balloons for hires outside of government—often taking well over a year. Furthermore, because commanders are not the final authority, it is not uncommon for an individual to have satisfactorily completed a technical interview by a board of their peers only to be informed much later by headquarters that they are, in fact, not qualified for a position.

Removing individuals provides similar challenges and outcomes—requiring commanders and leadership teams to devote a significant amount of time and energy to rehabilitate underperforming or toxic individuals before being allowed to remove them.

Improve Compensation

Although other services have already transitioned many of their civilian cyber billets to the DoD's CES, the air force is woefully behind. CES is an enterprise-wide approach for managing civilian cyber professionals across the department. The CES is aligned with Title 10 and Title 5 provisions, offering flexibilities for recruiting, retaining, and developing cyber professionals across departments. In addition to receiving increased pay, thanks to the targeted local market supplement, civilian employees can also be promoted based on qualification instead of time—encouraging employees to continue improving. However, until the compensation cap is removed, the most promising senior talent will always have enticing options in the civilian sector.

Congress authorized temporary promotions for military officers in Section 503 of the FY2019 NDAA to account for those who "have a skill in which the armed force concerned has a critical shortage of personnel (as determined by the secretary of the military department concerned)." The army is the only service to have leveraged this authority, yet even it only used a fraction of the nearly eight hundred authorized. This authority could be better leveraged to ensure the right folks are eligible for the right positions, regardless of rank—and tied to time in service.

However, more than pay and rank, what typically brings people to work for the government is the mission and purpose—and this is certainly true in cyberspace. Controlled tours and assignments that do not have a time limit are important for military members working in cyber because they allow for a structured and organized approach to the growth and development of technical expertise. This is particularly important in the field of cybersecurity, where the nature of the work can be complex and constantly evolving. By implementing controlled tours, military leaders can ensure that personnel are appropriately educated, have time and experience in threat-representative environments, and are ultimately prepared for operations. Additionally, controlled tours allow for more stability and effective resource management, as personnel can be scheduled and tasked in a way that maximizes their impact and minimizes disruptions to ongoing operations. Overall, controlled tours help ensure the safety and success of military members working in cyber jobs and are vital to effective military operations in the digital age.

Invest in and Empower Continuity of Expertise

The cyber domain is constantly evolving and advancing, and the military needs to keep pace with our adversaries to counter cyber threats effectively. By investing in and empowering continuity of expertise, the military can ensure it has a knowledgeable and skilled workforce that can adapt to new technologies and tactics.

For our active-duty military, this is only possible by defining, building, and investing in a technical track. To remain relevant in cyber, the military requires a strong foundation of technical knowledge and experience, which is crucial for the long-term success of cyber operations. By investing in training and development programs and committing to growing and promoting technical talent, the military can cultivate a competent and capable cyber workforce able to meet the challenges of the future.

There are few work roles in cyber today that only military members can fill. This fact provides an opportunity to consider more holistic courses of action regarding structuring and blending operations squadron manning—especially when taking into account the additional compensation tools available for the civilian workforce.

Finally, cyber is the ideal domain to fully exploit the resources available through the reserve total force initiative. Cyber operations require diverse skills, including information technology, communication, and intelligence, making it easy to integrate and utilize the expertise of National Guard and reserve members already working in these fields in their civilian lives. Operations are often conducted by small, highly skilled teams, allowing members with specialized cyber skills to significantly contribute to operations.

From nearly every angle, the military is trailing industry in cyber expertise. It should consider new, improved, and innovative ways to maximize its experience.

Invert Acquisition Calculus

It is possible that the fastest and most effective way for the military to recruit and retain incredible cyber talent is to change how it is structured and what it values. The military could start by automating and contracting out basic functions and tasks. This would help improve efficiency and reduce costs. Automation allows for the performance of repetitive tasks with a high degree of accuracy and speed—eliminating the need for a highly qualified and motivated force to complete them. Additionally, automating and contracting basic functions and roles can help to free up resources and allow the military's cyber experts to focus on more complex and value-added tasks. By outsourcing certain functions, the military can focus its time, money, and personnel on activities more directly aligned with its mission and goals. Overall, automating and contracting basic functions and roles would allow the military to operate more efficiently and effectively and better achieve its strategic objectives.

With the easy stuff automated, the military can focus on recruiting, hiring, and retaining the highest-quality ("10x talent") military and civilian force to focus on the most wicked problems. An added benefit of this approach is that a workforce with an increased talent density often requires less personnel overall. A decrease in the size of the force, so long as the talent density remains high, would ensure plenty of worthy work to keep the workforce challenged and feeling valued.

The last step is removing distractions or barriers to accountability, and modifying how the military is organized is a big part of that. Acquisitions and operations are two critical functions to the success of the military. Unfortunately, these two functions are deliberately siloed and operate independently, leading to inefficiencies and conflicts. Today, the military often chooses not to execute cyber operations at all rather than risk a mistake in acquisitions or contracting. To overcome these challenges and maximize the effectiveness of these functions, it is essential that acquisitions and operations work for the same operational commander.

One of the main benefits of having acquisitions and operations in the same chain of command is that it helps to align these two functions around a common set of goals and mission objectives. When acquisitions and operations work toward the same outcomes, it is easier for them to coordinate their efforts and collaborate to achieve their objectives. This helps to eliminate unnecessary duplication of effort and ensures that resources are used in the most effective way possible. And when things do go wrong, the team can quickly and effectively conduct a root-cause analysis to determine the issue and immediately implement a fix.

With acquisitions and operations under the same commander, the organization can begin fostering a culture of accountability and transparency. With these two functions combined, managers can more easily drive performance and ensure they meet operational needs. Additionally, having a single point of contact for acquisitions and operations makes it easier for combatant commanders to seek guidance and support when needed, which can help to improve operational outcomes while improving morale and fostering a sense of teamwork and collaboration within the organization. By aligning these functions around common operational goals and objectives, fostering a culture of accountability, and improving communication and collaboration, organizations can respond more quickly to better serve the needs of their stakeholders.

Notes

1. The White House, "Fact Sheet: Imposing Costs for Harmful Foreign Activities by the Russian Government," April 15, 2021.

2. US Department of Justice, "Four Chinese Nationals Working with the Ministry of State Security Charged with Global Computer Intrusion Campaign Targeting Intellectual Property and Confidential Business Information, including Infectious Disease Research," Office of Public Affairs, July 19, 2021.

3. US Cyberspace Solarium Commission, Report, March 2020, https://www.solarium.gov/report.

4. The White House, "Requests Your Insight and Expertise on Cyber Workforce, Training, and Education," Office of the National Cyber Director, October 3, 2022.

5. Catherine A. Theohary, "Defense Primer: Cyberspace Operations," Congressional Research Service Report IF10537, updated December 9, 2022; Chaitra M. Hardison, Leslie Adrienne Payne, John A. Hamm, Angela Clague, Jacqueline Torres, David Schulker, and John S. Crown, "Attracting, Recruiting, and Retaining Successful Cyberspace Operations Officers," RAND Corporation, 2019; Department of Defense Office of Inspector General, "DODIG-2016-026: (U) Combat Mission Teams and Cyber Protection Teams Lacked Adequate Capabilities and Facilities to Perform Missions (Redacted)," FOIA document, November 24, 2015.

6. Theohary, "Defense Primer."

7. Theohary, "Defense Primer."

8. US Department of Defense (DoD), "Memorandum: Department of Defense Software Modernization," Office of the Deputy Secretary, February 2, 2022.

9. James M. Inhofe National Defense Authorization Act for Fiscal Year 2023. H.R. 7776, 117th Congress (2022).

10. Albert A. Robbert, James H. Bigelow, John E. Boon Jr., Lisa M. Harrington, Michael McGee, Craig Moore, Daniel M. Norton, and William W. Taylor, "Suitability of Missions for the Air Force Reserve Components," RAND Corporation, 2014.

11. Jennie W. Wenger, Caolionn O'Connell, and Maria C. Lytell, "Retaining the Army's Cyber Expertise," RAND Corporation, 2017.

12. Marcel Schwantes, "What Smart Companies Like Facebook and Amazon Are Doing to Attract, Retain, and Manage Top Talent," *Inc.*, October 9, 2020.

13. Michael Solomon, Rishon Blumberg, and Daniel Weizmann, *Game Changer: How to Be 10x in the Talent Economy* (New York: HarperCollins Leadership, 2020).

14. Solomon, Blumberg, and Weizmann, *Game Changer*.

15. Catherine A. Theohary and Anne I. Harrington, "Cyber Operations in DOD Policy and Plans: Issues for Congress," Congressional Research Service Report R43848, January 5, 2015.

16. Hardison et al., "Attracting, Recruiting, and Retaining."

17. Hardison et al., "Attracting, Recruiting, and Retaining."

18. "Cybersecurity Supply/Demand Heat Map," *Cyber Seek* (accessed December 20, 2022).

19. Michael Chui, James Manyika, and Mehdi Miremadi, "Four Fundamentals of Workplace Automation," *McKinsey Quarterly* 29, no. 3 (November 2015): 1–9.

20. Wenger, O'Connell, and Lytell, "Retaining the Army's Cyber Expertise."

21. DoD, "Cyber Excepted Service: Frequently Asked Questions," *DoD Cyber Exchange*, Defense Civilian Personnel Advisory Service, January 2018, https://dl .dod.cyber.mil/wp-content/uploads/dces/pdf/GeneralCESFAQs.pdf.

22. DoD, "2022 Department of Defense Cyber Excepted Service Pay Rates," *DoD Cyber Exchange*, Defense Civilian Personnel Advisory Service, March 2022, https:// dl.dod.cyber.mil/wp-content/uploads/dces/pdf/2022_CES_Pay_Rates.pdf.

23. "Big Tech Salaries Revealed: How Much Engineers, Developers, and Product Managers Make at Companies including Apple, Amazon, Facebook, Google, Microsoft, Intel, Uber, IBM, and Salesforce," *Business Insider*, April 28, 2022.

24. Vasu Jakkal, "Cybersecurity Threats Are Always Changing—Staying on Top of Them Is Vital, Getting Ahead of Them Is Paramount," *Microsoft Security Blog*, February 9, 2022.

25. US Congress Section 809 Panel, *Report of the Advisory Panel on Streamlining and Codifying Acquisition Regulations, Volume 3 of 3*, January 2019.

26. US Government Accountability Office, "Defense Acquisitions: Cyber Command Needs to Develop Metrics to Assess Warfighting Capabilities," GAO-22 -104695, March 2022.

27. Bryan Casey, "Failing Fast, Traditional Strategy, and How They Work Together," *IBM Cloud*, October 4, 2019.

28. Thomas Klemas, Rebecca K. Lively, and Nazli Choucri, "Cyber Acquisition: Policy Changes to Drive Innovation in Response to Accelerating Threats in Cyberspace," *Cyber Defense Review* Special Edition: International Conference on Cyber Conflict (CYCON US) (2019): 103–20.

29. Isaac R. Porche III, Shawn McKay, Megan McKernan, Robert W. Button, Bob Murphy, Katheryn Giglio, and Elliot Axelband, "Rapid Acquisition and Fielding for Information Assurance and Cyber Security in the Navy," RAND Corporation, 2012.

30. Tim Stelloh and The Associated Press, "Chuck Yeager, Air Force Officer Who Broke Speed of Sound, Dies at 97," *NBC News*, December 7, 2020.

31. Charles W. Mahoney, "Corporate Hackers: Outsourcing US Cyber Capabilities," *Strategic Studies Quarterly* 15, no. 1 (Spring 2021): 61–89.

13

The All-Volunteer Force at Fifty
Productivity, Peace, and (Unmet) Potential

Tim Kane

American military manpower is remarkably successful as we mark the fifty-year anniversary of the all-volunteer force (AVF). American troops have been notably productive in waging warfare and securing peace, meaning the results on both fronts are impressive despite the bottom-line personnel costs growing increasingly expensive. Although the motivation to end conscription in 1973—properly understood as coerced labor by Milton Friedman, Martin Anderson, and other economists who were affiliated with the Hoover Institution at Stanford University—was driven more by social and political considerations of justice than budgets or strategy, the timing was fortuitous for the advent of the technological revolution in military affairs. An example of the relentless technological arms race is Ukrainian vice prime minister Mykhailo Fedorov's recent remark, "In the last two weeks, we have been convinced once again the wars of the future will be about maximum drones and minimal humans."[1] An overstatement, to be sure, but today even infantry soldiers are required to handle sophisticated technology, forcing Pentagon leaders to optimize military talent in what promises to be a new era of budget deficits and budget constraints.

This chapter explores the cost of military personnel and challenges us to rethink policy and strategy in light of a broader perspective that considers benefits. My focus is on the active force, not the millions of Americans serving in the National Guard and reserves, nor Department of Defense (DoD) civilians and military contractors, although they are shaped by similar

The views expressed in this chapter are solely those of the individual author and do not necessarily reflect the views of any organization with which they are, or have been, affiliated.

regulations. The increasing use of contractors should be kept in mind as a response to rigid employment regulations that bind the utilization of active and reserve personnel.

A cost-benefit analysis of the volunteer force should consider the economic perspective, not just accounting budgets in dollars and cents. Marines, airmen, sailors, and soldiers are not interchangeable parts with fixed costs and identical utility; rather, each is a uniquely talented individual. Quality matters. Utilization matters, too.[2]

The readiness goal for any talent management system should be to optimize talent quality. That principle seems obvious but is surprisingly at odds with much of the design of personnel policies in large organizations everywhere. Large organizations routinely build their personnel operations, as the saying goes, fighting the last war. That seems doubly true for the Pentagon, which still uses pay tables and an "up-or-out mentality" that were cutting edge with General Dwight Eisenhower's recommendations in the 1940s.

As of October 31, 2022, 1.3 million Americans were serving on active duty in the five branches of the US military.[3] That compares to 3.5 million service members in the early 1950s and late 1960s, or roughly one-third of the troop strength at the peak of the Cold War. When considered as a percentage of the US population over time, the military is currently one-sixth of that size, having decreased from 2.2 percent of the national population during the Korean War to 0.4 percent now (see fig. 13.1). Yet many would argue that the force is more lethal now than ever before. This partly explains why even though the headcount has declined by more than half since the 1950s, the total budgetary cost of personnel in inflation-adjusted dollars has more than doubled.[4]

In addition to providing an overview of the issue, I will put forward three main arguments in this paper:

1. Recurring problems with recruitment and retention are real but sensationalized challenges whose deep causes are structural. Laws and rules that shape military compensation hamstring the ability of military leaders to manage talent.

2. Core personnel operations were not reformed when the draft expired, so the transition away from a citizen (draft) army to a professional (volunteer) army was never fully implemented. Policy makers should reconsider the full set of Gates Commission recommendations, particularly professional compensation structures.[5]

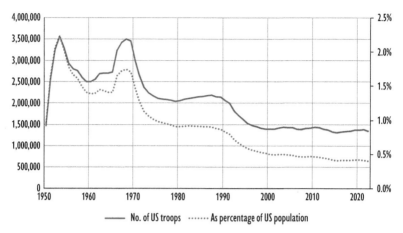

Figure 13.1 US Active-Duty Troops, 1950–2022

Source: DoD data compiled by the author. See Tim Kane, "The Decline of American Engagement: Patterns in US Troop Deployments," Hoover Institution Economics Working Paper 16101, January 11, 2016.

3. Experience has proved the volunteer force to be ready, resilient, extraordinarily lethal in war, and (perhaps most beneficially) an overwhelming deterrent to war.

Structural Roots of the Recruiting "Crisis"

Recruiting for all military branches in FY2022 was difficult, arguably the worst year since 1973 and only the fourth that the military has missed its recruiting goals. The bottom line is that the army fell short by fifteen thousand recruits in 2022—25 percent of its annual goal—then subsequently cut its projection for the overall force size by ten thousand soldiers.

These difficulties are similar to those of past cycles, with a strong correlation to the civilian unemployment rate. The AVF competes against other employers in the private sector, so recruiting is always more challenging when the labor market is tight. As I write, the current (December 2022) US unemployment rate is at a fifty-year low of 3.5 percent. To emphasize that point, the *only* time during the AVF era that the US unemployment rate fell below 4 percent was in the past four years, and it was below 4 percent during eleven of twelve months of 2022.[6]

The lingering, unpredictable social effects of the COVID-19 pandemic are another headwind. Until a recent policy shift by Congress, the DoD was required to impose a vaccine mandate that purportedly suppressed recruiting in some regions.[7] The policy change means that recruiting should get somewhat easier, but risk aversion among the young could be deeper and longer-lasting than the mandate.

Although the FY2022 recruiting shortfall has been heavily covered in the mainstream press, a unique and somewhat ironic factor is that it was the first year of peace after two full decades of fighting in the Middle East, specifically large and lengthy troop deployments to Iraq and Afghanistan. The increased interest in military service, and the increased quality of recruits, after the 9/11 attacks is a remarkable and underreported phenomenon. A popular critique is that the army and marines rely on recruits from poorer neighborhoods. In truth, multiple reviews of Pentagon enlistee data in the darkest years of the Iraq War found that the percentage of recruits from the poorest neighborhoods (representing one-fifth of the US population) declined from 18 percent in 1999 to 15 percent in 2003 and 14 percent in 2004 and 2005. However, recruit quality improved, a powerful vindication of the volunteer force and a generation of young Americans.[8]

The challenge of AVF recruiting is that the DoD maintains high-quality standards for enlistees. Before framing this as a problem to be solved, consider the benefits of having high-quality standards. As Army Secretary Christine Wormuth recently said, "We can develop all of the most high-tech new weapons systems like we are working on right now, but if we don't have the kinds of talented, motivated individuals to use those weapons systems, we won't be able to do what we need to do."[9]

In terms of literacy, raw intelligence, strength, physical resilience, and more, young enlistees in the American military do not "look like America" because they are measurably better. In terms of racial and religious demographics, both enlistees and officers are a healthy reflection of the national population, but the goal should be to have a military workforce that is not just average but measurably as smart, strong, and honorable as possible.

If anything, the problem is that measurements of troop quality are sparse. All branches require new recruits to score above certain thresholds on the Armed Forces Qualification Test (AFQT). It must be noted that AFQT scores are relative to the current crop of applicants, not absolute, resulting in lower relative scores for all during years when the applicant pool is thin. Moving to absolute metrics for cognitive skills and aptitudes would be useful for assessing recruit quality and longitudinal assessments of retention quality over time.

High standards mean that 70 percent of the thirty-three million Americans between the ages of seventeen and twenty-four cannot meet the minimum enlistment standards, implying a pool of 9.9 million potential recruits. Yet according to Stefan Borg, writing in *Parameters*, only 136,000 of that pool express a willingness to serve—a mere 1.5 percent of the eligible pool.[10] Fitness in terms of education, obesity, general health, and criminal background is a strong constraint but not nearly as strong as willingness. That challenge is routinely overcome with personal outreach and bold advertising campaigns. Aversion to the unknown can only be overcome by exposure of young men and women to American service members, especially when surveys show that 50 percent of potential recruits "know little" about military service, and few have any personal or familial contact. Credit goes to the US Army for experimenting with new pre–basic training pilot programs. Much more needs to be done.

Overview of Personnel Budget Costs

Personnel costs account for one of every five defense dollars and even more when accounting for deferred costs associated with veterans' health care. According to the Congressional Budget Office (CBO), military pay represents 55 percent of total compensation for the average officer and 53 percent for the average enlisted service member. Here, I use the definition of "pay" as regular military compensation that includes base/basic pay, allowances for housing and food, and the tax advantage of various allowances. Health care for the active force represents another 9 to 14 percent of costs. The remainder is deferred costs, with Veterans Affairs (VA) benefits, retiree health care, and retirement pensions. The efficiency of VA and health-care expenditures is beyond the scope of this paper, and I will leave it there because they have negligible impact on personnel incentives for the active force.[11]

In contrast, basic pay is disbursed using a rigid formula based on two factors: the number of years in service and rank. However, an individual's rank is based almost entirely on years in service (following rigid promotion timetables). The net effect is that 99 percent of military pay is based on seniority and less than 1 percent on skill, merit, or performance. Special pays exist for hazardous duty and some sixty other categories, though none are based on performance. This stands in sharp contrast to billions of dollars allocated to bonuses for retention each year, which are universal rather than individually targeted. In a 2015 survey I conducted with *Military Times*, which involved a forty-point assessment of leadership and talent practices, the lowest mark by far was on the metric "Bonuses are used to reward good work."[12]

Paying for performance remains a major area for improvement, given that the law allows great leeway in the use of assignment incentive pay and other channels to compensate talent directly. One option would involve legislators decoupling military pay raises from the basic pay tables or going further by requiring the services to disburse pay raises as bonuses for merit, performance, and (applied) skills.

Pay Premium

In 2002, the Ninth Quadrennial Review of Military Compensation (QRMC) concluded, "Pay at around the 70th percentile of comparably educated civilians has been necessary to enable the military to recruit and retain the quantity and quality of personnel it requires." What does it mean that pay was around the 70th percentile? Higher than average pay represents a premium, which labor economists explain as compensation for harder, hazardous work. A similar premium is paid to comparably educated workforces in law enforcement and deep-sea fishing, as just two examples. Other explanatory factors for the military pay premium include the higher levels of health and fitness demanded of uniformed service members.

The military pay premium weighs heavily on the Pentagon budget, especially if it increases. At the time of the 2012 QRMC report, pay rose to the 90th percentile (education controlled) for enlisted members and the 83rd percentile for officers. The most recent QRMC, published in 2020, found that the high premium had continued: "For the first twenty years of service, [pay] was at the 85th percentile of the civilian wage distribution for enlisted personnel and at the 77th percentile for officers."[13]

The pay premium for military labor could be reduced if the quality of life of service members were better. Surveys routinely find that troops do not value many military fringe benefits, whereas they report frustration with rigid personnel policies such as frequent job rotations (especially the impact of cross-state moves on spouses and children). The bottom line is that the unit budgetary cost for labor has risen in recent decades, which could be alleviated by personnel reforms such as fewer permanent-change-of-station (PCS) moves and more personal control over careers (including more fluidity to exit and reenter the ranks).

Reinstating a coercive draft could handily help the services upsize or downsize quantitatively, but this would come with a degradation of quality. The draft is probably a nonstarter in the context of potential conflicts involving advanced weapons systems. Future DoD leaders need to consider the options to refine policies governing the volunteer force that will *optimize* talent.

Citizen to Professional

On January 27, 1973, Secretary of Defense Melvin Laird declared, "I wish to inform you that the armed forces henceforth will depend exclusively on volunteer soldiers, sailors, airmen, and marines. The use of the draft has ended."[14] Legal authorization for the draft was already set to expire later that summer.

While the all-volunteer force deserves praise and celebration on its fiftieth anniversary, it must be remembered that the transition from a citizen army to a professional army was instituted by letting the clock run out on the draft law, not by design. A dozen reforms, large and small, were recommended by the Gates Commission in 1970, but none were implemented other than ending the draft. The transition to a fully volunteer force remains incomplete as a consequence.

To be sure, there have been significant reforms since. The Defense Officer Personnel Management Act (DOPMA) in 1980 created uniform regulations governing promotions with years-of-service zones for each rank. The Goldwater-Nichols Act in 1986 required joint duty assignments and joint military education for senior officer promotions. More recently, the National Defense Authorization Act (NDAA) of 2016 created a blended retirement system—a small but significant revision to the defined benefit pension. That was followed a year later by numerous personnel reforms in the 2017 NDAA, including service autonomy over promotions, even allowing for lateral entry of junior officers (e.g., commissioning an individual as a captain or major).

A summary of recommendations made by the Gates Commission includes the following:[15]

- End conscription and establish an all-volunteer force.
- Increase overall base pay.
- Add supplemental pay and compensation flexibility.
- Transition to a salary system to replace in-kind allowances.
- Eliminate enlistment terms with open-term employment.
- Offer a choice of occupation upon enlistment and during a career.
- Pursue lateral hiring of civilian personnel into higher ranks.
- Reform military retirement (e.g., lower vesting from twenty years to five).

The budgetary costs of failing to implement some of these reforms (e.g., widespread lateral entry) are negligible, but the economic costs can be high. As the late George Shultz noted, "The ironic thing about the all-volunteer force is that those who enter the armed services volunteer only once—when they join. After joining the armed forces, their careers become subject to a variety of regulations, regardless of their own preferences."[16] In a nutshell, the DoD's current system spends millions training individuals to reach peak productivity at twenty years in uniform, then another $1 million (net present value retirement pension) incentivizing them to leave immediately. Recent secretaries of defense have expressed frustration with the "bureaucratic concrete" in the personnel system as one of the greatest challenges the military must overcome to win wars of the future. The 2017 NDAA reforms were animated by Senator John McCain's argument in 2015 that "too often, our military is losing and misusing talent because of an archaic military personnel system. Promotions are handed out according to predictable schedules with only secondary consideration of merit."[17]

Recall that talent management aims to increase the numerator of talent over the denominator of expense, i.e., to maximize productivity. In that light, policies that lead to a marginal reduction of talent—bleeding talent through external loss or internal misallocation—reduce the numerator and, therefore, net productivity. Let's call this "less lethality for the buck."

Lateral entry has been authorized as of the 2017 NDAA but remains very sparsely implemented. Choice of occupation has been more widely applied among the services in the past five years, with the creation of job assignment marketplaces online that hold tremendous promise (more career control is the top desire for service members who consider leaving the ranks). Yet a serious impediment to all this is the rigid retirement structure. Consider the puzzle of trying to attract a world-class cyber expert with ten years of civilian experience to an assignment as a US Air Force major—how does her military retirement work? It doesn't. Or how does the retirement system handle a sailor who leaves for multiple opportunities, gains invaluable logistics expertise, and then wants to reenlist?

The Pentagon's defined benefit (DB) pension, with its 100 percent vesting after twenty full years, is coercive to such an extreme that it would be illegal in the private sector. Federal law governing all public and private pensions falls under US Code Title 26, section 411, which mandates that DB pensions partially vest one-fifth of the funds after three years or less; all funds at seven years or less.[18] These rules were codified because longer vesting schedules are coercive. The US military pension, easily five times more coercive than allowable by law, is not worthy of a professional force.

As a budgetary matter, the Pentagon pension is growing exponentially more expensive. Annual outlays for military pensions represent one of every ten defense dollars. The liabilities of the program are nearly $2 trillion (roughly one-tenth the size of the US GDP).[19]

As the Gates Commission noted in 1970, all-or-nothing vesting at twenty years has "a number of undesirable effects," one being that it has little to no value in recruiting. The commission noted two other perverse incentives in the retirement structure, the first being that soldiers "cannot afford to separate from the service" beyond their tenth year, and second that it "induces many individuals to retire as soon as they are eligible." Payments from the pension begin immediately upon retirement, instead of some fixed age. In short, too many personnel stay in uniform before the twenty-year cliff, and too few stay after.

The distortion is visible in continuation rates, with data showing a plateau of continuation from the twelfth year of service and a mass exodus immediately after the twentieth year (see fig. 13.2).[20]

My analysis of retirement data showed that all branches of the US military lost more than half of active service members at the twenty-year point.[21] The destructive impact on productivity is difficult to overstate. Consider the prospect of any other organization losing half of its employees with twenty years of experience—age thirty-eight for noncommissioned officers, age forty-two for officers—every year, and how daunting that would be.

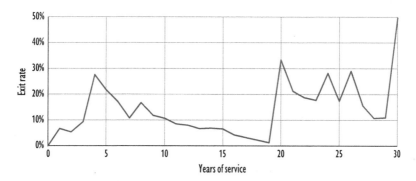

Figure 13.2 **Exit Rate for US Military Enlisted, by Years of Service**

Source: "Approaches to Changing Military Compensation," Congressional Budget Office publication no. 55648, January 2020.

There are few, if any, defenders of the military retirement structure. In 1978, the US Government Accountability Office was calling for an end to the twenty-year cliff in a clearly titled report, "The 20-Year Military Retirement System Needs Reform":

> Twenty-year retirement, in conjunction with present personnel management policies, is an inefficient means of attracting new members, causes the services to retain more members than are needed up to the 20-year point, provides too strong an incentive for experienced personnel to leave after serving 20 years, and makes it impossible for the vast majority of members to serve full careers.[22]

In 2006, the Defense Advisory Committee on Military Compensation took aim at the status quo pension system as inefficient, inflexible, and inequitable. In 2011, the Defense Business Board issued a report that proposed replacing the defined benefit entirely with a savings plan.

The introduction of the Blended Retirement System (BRS) in 2018 was heralded as a major reform because it added a Thrift Savings Plan (TSP) with optional matching, like a private-sector 401(k) plan. The reality is that BRS did not fundamentally change the twenty-year cliff pension, which still involves 80 percent of the dollars (i.e., the pension payment now has a base-pay-times-years-of-service multiplier of 0.20 instead of 0.25) but *no modification in the timing of payments*. Unless the perverse incentives of the pension's cliff vesting at twenty years are reformed, it will be difficult to manage talent.

The introduction of the BRS did open the door for future reform options. One option is to allow opting out of the defined benefit entirely in exchange for a TSP that is larger than the current maximum match of 5 percent of base pay. A second option is to reform when and how DB vesting happens. A third option is to revise the DB payout timing to a fixed age. Until these retirement reforms are made, lateral entry and service term fluidity will be barely usable tools for talent managers.

Global US Troop Deployments

In this section, we turn to the issue of benefits that flow from US military manpower, of which two are fundamental. The mission of military personnel is to win wars, and lethality is the measure of productivity in this unique realm. Perhaps just as important as war making is peacemaking, with lethality as critical a factor for its maintenance. Potential enemies become deterred enemies when US troops are maximally lethal. President George Washington said in his fifth annual address to Congress in 1793, "If we desire to secure peace . . . it must be known, that we are at all times ready for War."[23]

In this final section of the paper, I will make the case that the deployment of American troops abroad has been a singularly unique factor in keeping the peace. It has been widely noted that ISIS emerged in Iraq only after US forces were completely removed in 2011, that Russia attacked Kyiv only after the United States closed its embassy and withdrew the last marines in 2022, and that North Korea began significant attacks across the 38th parallel only weeks after all US combat forces were withdrawn in June 1949 (and invaded less than a year later).

After World War II, the United States stationed combat troops in permanent bases throughout Japan and Germany during the immediate postwar occupation period. US forces were also hosted by dozens of allied countries, including the United Kingdom, France, the Philippines, South Korea, and even China. Large drawdowns were swiftly reversed in the early 1950s, when the Cold War intensified. I've maintained a dataset of global deployments of US troops, using annual Pentagon reports, that shows permanent deployments across 206 countries and territories since 1950.

The level of deployed troops stationed permanently on European soil tripled during the 1950s as a deterrent to a Soviet invasion. Any attack on allied hosts would be a de facto attack on America. In West Germany alone, there were 250,000 permanent US "boots on the ground" until 1990. And the distribution of troops among NATO allies was wide, covering some twenty-three countries in Western Europe. There were 5,000 US troops in Iceland and 2,000 apiece in Denmark and Finland. Now the question is whether to add new bases in Eastern Europe beyond Poland. But during the 1990s, the number of US forces in Europe was reduced by more than half. Today, with fewer than 70,000 boots on European ground, American engagement is closer to one-fifth of its Cold War presence.

Did this drawdown yield a peace dividend that helped lower national deficits and allow greater investments in new weapons systems? Too much of the defense budget conversation frames personnel as a trade-off for modernization, as per a recent Congressional Research Service report: "Some have raised concerns about the impact of personnel costs on the overall defense budget, arguing that they decrease the amount of funds available for modernizing equipment and sustaining readiness."[24] This might be a false choice.

Today, there are fewer deployed US troops based overseas relative to the world population than at any time since 1950.[25] Yet annual US budget deficits have risen so high that the baseline deficit now exceeds $1 trillion (or

5 percent of GDP). History will note that the peace dividend was not so much a cost saving thanks to retrenchment. Rather, it was (and is) decades of prosperity under the American security umbrella. Since 1945, no allied country hosting a significant number of American military personnel has been invaded.

The presence of US troops should not be regarded as an "imperial act"—far from it. A recent study of public opinion in fourteen countries hosting US military personnel found another surprising benefit: "In non-combat settings, US personnel may, in fact, facilitate more supportive attitudes among the host population" by, among other things, increasing US soft power.[26] Deploying a fifty-question survey of more than one thousand local citizens, the authors found significant, robust, and large positive relationships in countries including Australia, Belgium, Japan, Kuwait, the Philippines, and Turkey. Foreigners who experienced personal contact with US troops were 5–7 percentage points more favorable in their "attitudes toward the US military presence in their country" and "attitudes toward the US people."

South Korea provides a case study of the challenges of drawing down. President Donald Trump repeatedly signaled his frustration at maintaining US troops in South Korea, mirroring another president's instinct for total withdrawal. During his 1976 campaign for the presidency, Jimmy Carter was telling editorial boards and voters that he favored withdrawing all US forces from South Korea. Once the Carter presidency began, White House press secretary Jody Powell said that the president had a "basic inclination to question the stationing of American troops overseas."[27] His efforts were rebuffed by American generals but also by steadfast South Korean leaders.

The economic strength of South Korea today dwarfs the failed communist regime of Pyongyang, a fact that motivates many critics who argue that the US presence is no longer necessary. However, the budgetary cost of basing troops is lower abroad than domestically, thanks to host country subsidies.[28] The government in Seoul was paying $830 million annually to support the costs of 28,500 US troops, which increased to $924 million in 2019.[29] Meanwhile, the status quo of peace on the peninsula has been a seventy-year triumph for the United States and South Korea.

The policy recommendations one should draw begin with recognizing that the benefits of a US troop presence in foreign countries are a mix of depth (number of troops) and duration. The data indicates that the raw number of American forces matters less than duration and some trip-wire threshold indicating genuine commitment. Perhaps no more than a few hundred American soldiers are needed, but more study is required. The policy rule seems to be that to avoid conflict, the United States should deploy between one hundred and one thousand troops to any allied countries willing to host them. A policy of wider deployments would likely be more effective than increasing force strength at current overseas bases, implying that a new policy of basing alliances throughout Eastern Europe (e.g., Lithuania, Estonia, Slovakia) and Asia (e.g., Thailand, Taiwan, Philippines) would be wise investments in preventing open warfare with Russia and China. The cumulative cost of all US bases abroad is an estimated $55 billion, roughly the same as the $50 billion in aid sent to Ukraine by the United States after Russia's invasion last year.[30] An ounce of prevention would have been worth a pound of war.

In conclusion, the all-volunteer force remains a vibrant multiplier of American hard and soft power fifty years after its start. While there is ample room for improved productivity and reform, it should be remembered that near-peer rivals in China and Russia depend on conscripted armies with all of their myriad dysfunctions that the Pentagon left behind a half century ago. Pushing for more advanced drones, cyber, intelligence, and other modernizations in capital equipment is vital, but defense leaders should never forget that maintaining the talent edge requires constant innovation as well.

Notes

1. Mark Bowden, "The Tiny and Nightmarishly Efficient Future of Drone Warfare," *The Atlantic*, November 22, 2022.

2. Consider the waste of paying a $35,000 annual skill bonus for pilots and requiring these individuals to remain qualified in that skill to receive the bonus, all while employing them in nonflying jobs for a decade or more.

3. Figures come from the DoD's Defense Manpower Data Center online reports at https://dwp.dmdc.osd.mil/dwp/app/dod-data-reports/workforce-reports, accessed December 10, 2022.

4. Seamus P. Daniels, "Assessing Trends in Military Personnel Costs," Center for Strategic and International Studies, September 2021.

5. Formally known as the President's Commission on an All-Volunteer Armed Force.

6. For historical data, see US Bureau of Labor Statistics, "Data on the Unemployment Rate," https://data.bls.gov/pdq/SurveyOutputServlet, accessed January 6, 2023.

7. Catie Edmondson, "Congress Clears Military Bill Repealing Vaccine Mandate for Troops," *New York Times*, December 15, 2022.

8. Tim Kane, "Who Are the Recruits? The Demographic Characteristics of US Military Enlistment, 2003–2005," Heritage Foundation, October 26, 2006.

9. Ian Thomas, "The US Army Is Struggling to Find the Recruits It Needs to Win the Fight over the Future," CNBC.com, October 26, 2022.

10. Stefan Borg, "Meeting the US Military's Manpower Challenges," *Parameters* 52, no. 3 (Autumn 2022): 99.

11. Todd Harrison's 2012 study found, for example, "More than 80 percent of service members in each age group would be willing to have the retirement collection age raised to 50 in exchange for a 1 percent increase in basic pay."

12. Tim Kane, *Total Volunteer Force: Lessons from the US Military on Leadership Culture and Talent Management* (Stanford, CA: Hoover Institution Press, 2017).

13. See the Thirteenth QRMC report (2020) at https://militarypay.defense.gov /Portals/3/QRMC-Vol_1_final_web.pdf.

14. David E. Rosenbaum, "Nation Ends Draft, Turns to Volunteers," *New York Times,* January 28, 1973.

15. *The Report of the President's Commission on an All-Volunteer Armed Force* (New York: Collier Books, 1970): 56–66.

16. George Shultz, from the Introduction to Kane, *Total Volunteer Force.*

17. John McCain, opening statement, "Department of Defense Personnel Reform and Strengthening the All-Volunteer Force," US Senate, Committee on Armed Services, December 2, 2015, https://www.govinfo.gov/content/pkg/CHRG-114shrg 20957/html/CHRG-114shrg20957.htm.

18. 26 USC § 411 Minimum Vesting Standards. See Cornell Law School Legal Information Institute, https://www.law.cornell.edu/uscode/text/26/411.

19. The Military Retirement Fund Audited Financial Report for FY2021 (November 2021) reports a balance sheet tally of $1,933,646,716.

20. "Approaches to Changing Military Compensation," Congressional Budget Office publication no. 55648, January 2020.

21. Kane, *Total Volunteer Force,* ch. 6.

22. Elmer B. Staats, "The 20-Year Military Retirement System Needs Reform," US Government Accountability Office (report to Congress), March 13, 1978.

23. George Washington's fifth annual address to Congress, December 13, 1793, https://www.mountvernon.org/library/digitalhistory/past-projects/quotes.

24. Lawrence Kapp and Barbara Salazar Torreon, "Military Pay: Key Questions and Answers," Congressional Research Service Report RL33446, accessed November 12, 2022.

25. Timothy Kane, "The Decline of American Engagement: Patterns in US Troop Deployments," Hoover Institution Economics Working Paper 16101, January 11, 2016.

26. Michael A. Allen, Michael E. Flynn, Carla Martinez Machain, and Andrew Stravers, "Outside the Wire: US Military Deployments and Public Opinion in Host States," *American Political Science Review,* last revised February 13, 2020. Available on SSRN, doi:10.1017/S0003055419000868.

27. Allen et al., "Outside the Wire."

28. This shouldn't be a controversial claim but it is clouded by the costs of 750 bases, pre-positioned equipment, and construction, rather than just personnel. The Pentagon estimated that total overseas basing in 2019 cost $21 billion, with $4 billion paid by the governments of Japan, Germany, and South Korea, according to a summary of the issues by Rick Berger: "'Cost Plus 50' and Bringing US Troops Home: A Look at the Numbers," *War on the Rocks*, March 15, 2019. Jonathan Stevenson provides a cumulative annual cost of $55 billion in "Chapter One: Overseas Bases and US Strategic Posture," International Institute for Strategic Studies, September 28, 2022.

29. Hyung-Jin Kim, "S. Korea, US Sign Deal on Seoul Paying More for US Military," Associated Press, March 8, 2019.

30. Stevenson, "Chapter One." For spending in Ukraine, see Jonathan Masters and Will Merrow, "How Much Aid Has the US Sent Ukraine? Here Are Six Charts," Council on Foreign Relations, last updated February 22, 2023.

Personnel and Talent Recruitment and Retention

With David S. C. Chu and Mackenzie Eaglen
Moderated by Captain Corey Braddock

CAPTAIN COREY BRADDOCK: I'm excited to kick off a discussion on personnel force strength, workforce efficiency, and the budget implications associated with defense staffing. Our first panelist will be Dr. David Chu. David has served the nation in many roles. Most notably as it relates to today's panel, he previously served as the under secretary of defense for personnel and readiness.

DAVID S. C. CHU: Thank you. And I thank you for the invitation to participate in this dialogue and specifically to address what I've characterized as the "people portfolio" of the department.

When you speak of people in the department, I think most Americans immediately have in mind the uniformed force, especially the active-duty force. But as members of this audience appreciate, that's only really part of the answer. In fact, if you look at the civilians employed by the federal government, the reserve components, and the civilians who might be working through service contractors, they together substantially outnumber the active-duty force. These other elements are, therefore, part of the answer on how best to staff the needs to develop the capabilities we require to defend America and advance American interests.

The department does emphasize, as we all know, with its declaratory statements, how important people are. The department characterizes people as its

The views expressed in these presentations and discussion are solely those of the individual participants and do not necessarily reflect the views of any organization with which they are, or have been, affiliated.

most significant asset. It's also the most costly single expense of the department. So cost control is an issue of considerable importance to think about when discussing how best to proceed.

But as my characterization of the portfolio might suggest, we really have three different silos here, three different communities. They have different performance attributes. We have different expectations of the skills that they'll bring to bear in helping the department succeed, and they cost differently in various dimensions. What's notable to me as an economist is that the department doesn't really have an organized, well-founded process for deciding what's the best mix of people to use, which might include, in fact, mixing people in units. (The air force experimented with mixed units using both guard and active personnel. But that's not a widespread phenomenon.)

Yes, we do have exceptions to the generalization that the department lacks a process for considering the mix of personnel types. Occasionally, the secretary of defense will push the organization to consider the trade between military and civilian personnel. That was true in the 1960s, true in the 1970s, and true in the 2000s. Congress is generally not enthused about that trade and often has put up statutory barriers to such changes. And yes, we do have competitions from time to time between providing a service with federal personnel versus hiring a contractor to do it for us, the so-called outsourcing competitions; we even recently had an insourcing competition when one secretary thought we'd gone too far in terms of using contracts. He wanted to bring certain services back inside the department, inside the Department of Defense.

The fact of the matter, as you all appreciate, is that these three silos rest on different statutory foundations. And so, we have various differences in terms of what you can or cannot do, including certain anomalies. For example, as you appreciate, most federal jobs require you to be a US citizen. But the irony is you do not have to be a US citizen to enlist in the military! In practice, we only require a green card, and the department does enjoy some limited latitude even to hire those who are here without green cards (although as a matter of policy, only those who are here legally, I might emphasize). It could actually have anybody join the military service, and that is an old tradition. The Filipino stewards of navy ships in the 1930s and 1940s are an example of that phenomenon.

So the central thesis of my paper is we would benefit over the long term from a better process, a more cohesive process, and an ongoing process, which really is multiyear in character, to think about what's the best combination of personnel to carry out the functions of the department. At the same time, we need to think about what set of incentives we need to recruit, retain, and motivate these different types of personnel over time. This is something Tim [Kane] and Casey Miller have touched on.

If you come down from this fifty-thousand-foot level to some specific issues, you might think in terms of creating better outcomes. There are three issues I would identify that might produice better outcomes. First, there probably is a role for more civilians, although I think Mackenzie [Eaglen] will argue the opposite—and if I heard Secretary [Leon] Panetta correctly, he might also endorse that view. But that only illustrates how important it is to have that debate and have an organized process. What's the right mix of people to bring to bear? I think our commander here would take more civilians if he could get them or be allowed to hire them.

Second, I think we need to think about the standards that we impose as a matter of policy on each personnel community. Those standards reflect our underlying philosophy of how we do business. On the one hand, for the uniformed military, we basically try to bring raw talent into the service at a junior level, and we'll provide all the training you need to succeed in the service. (The exceptions are the professions: law, medicine, and the clergy. We do take people directly from civilian life and give them a commission.) Civilians, on the other hand, we think of as coming to the government with most of the skills and preparation they need to succeed at their entry-level job. They already have the degree, and they already have the skill. Why is there this dichotomy in how we do business?

Could we, for example, not take more individuals in the military who already have that credential that we need, that skill? Cyber is a classic example of that sort of thing, i.e., giving those with the credentials and skills a direct appointment to the military. That's talked about mostly for officers. Congress—thanks, really, to the energy of a young staff member who convinced Senator [Thom] Tillis to advance this idea—has given the Department of Defense greater authority to do so. It's not really being very aggressive, in my judgment, in using that authority.

But in another cabinet department, Admiral Linda L. Fagan, the new coast guard commandant, just this last week gave an interview that I think signals an interesting potential opportunity. She talked about bringing enlisted personnel into the coast guard who already have a skill and skipping most of the usual A-School preparation they would need. Her examples were cooks and medical technicians. Her view is, if you're a graduate of the Culinary Institute of America, I do not need to teach you how to cook. I may need to teach you about coast guard procedures, but you know how to cook already. And similarly for medical technicians. Could we not think of more of that sort of thing?

On standards more broadly, I think revisiting the experience profile we desire, consistent with the chart that Tim showed earlier, would have great merit. Our current model for the military is that there's a big base at the bottom, and the desired experience profile is pyramid shaped, so it comes to a small apex at the top. That might be true for organized line units in classic conventional forces designed for conflict. It's not necessarily true of our colonel's cyber unit. There may be more demand for what you could call a Michelin man profile—in other words, it's very fat in the middle ranks—people with great experience and great depth, who might be civilians.

Civilians could be used in a military fashion if they are given reserve appointments. The UK has a very interesting small experiment that it tried some years ago, called Sponsored Reserves. The contractor would be hired to provide a service with the stipulation that every person on that contract would have to hold a reserve appointment in Her Majesty's forces—now His Majesty's forces. And if the government so decided, the contractor force could be mobilized on short notice. For trucking in peacetime, civilians would be just fine; in a theater with combat going on, maybe we want them in a uniform and we can mobilize them. The British even talked about—but they didn't do much about it, I should add—providing aerial tanker services on this basis. In other words, a "wet lease." The contractor provides the tanker and the crews to fly the tanker. Could we do something like that? Well, maybe, maybe not. But we should be thinking about those kinds of things in the future.

And finally, we should debate what kind of incentives we need. Tim Kane provides a good guide from the Gates Commission fifty years ago as to the issues that should be considered. We're not limited to just pecuniary incentives. They're important, but quasi-pecuniary and nonpecuniary incentives are also important. I might particularly highlight the importance of dealing with spousal careers that are injured by the frequent moves that military service requires. If we don't deal with that, we will have a continuing drag in terms of retention—the attractiveness of military service.

Is change possible? If you think about the really big changes, the president's voice is critical. There have been four big changes in my lifetime on military personnel matters: one, Richard Nixon ends the draft; two, George W. Bush brings civil service modernization to the department; three, Barack Obama takes it back in his term of office; and then four, Donald Trump insists on a space force over considerable skepticism by various parties in and outside the Department of Defense. That was a big change. You need the president, in my estimation, for any big change.

In motivating any change, I think you need to think a lot about the rationale. I think Tim implied this with his chart. The kinds of arguments that appeal to me as an economist, to policy analysts, do not work in the political space for the most part. That it's cost effective will not be a good reason to do it. The retirement reform issue is the case in point that I would cite. The retirement reform idea, as Tim showed, has been there for fifty years. Same arguments over and over again. When did it gain traction (modest traction, because we have now had some modest reform, a diminished annuity at twenty years of service but giving everybody some degree of IRA-type account if they have at least two years of service)? It happened when the argument became, "The current system is unfair"—that most people who start, especially enlisted personnel, will never collect. So we have this big pot of money, and it's going to a small number of people. Shouldn't everybody share in some fashion? And that argument actually helped, I think, change the answer.

A final thought and conclusion. I might sound negative but I don't intend to. This is, in many ways, a very successful department. You have only to contrast it with other federal departments. I won't name names here, but you all have your favorite candidates, I would expect. And so, a first caution is the medical adage "First, do no harm." Or at least to amend this, first, make sure the benefits of the change will substantially exceed the costs that you'll have to impose, because there'll inevitably be losers as well as gainers from any change that might happen.

With that, I thank you.

BRADDOCK: Our final presenter will be Mackenzie Eaglen.

MACKENZIE EAGLEN: I'll be super brief, and I'll try to focus on the topics of this panel from my paper for this panel. I love Dr. Chu's point that we have to look at the Defense Department as essentially having three workforces. He calls it silos. I call it workforces—military, obviously active and reserve components, federal defense civilians, and the defense contracting workforce that builds and services software and IT support the same Defense Department. And when you look at it that way, it's bigger than three million people. Three million people are on the direct payroll. The indirect payroll is probably closer to four million. And in a perfect world, I would love to do exactly that. Or have someone smart, a commission or a presidential commission, think about the totality of these workforces and putting people in the right place.

I'll borrow from my AEI [American Enterprise Institute] colleague and former employee of many people around the table, Elaine McCusker's paper here. Well, for starters, the emotion has to be taken out of it. Your point on when it became unfair, although the system is designed—for the pyramid, you serve one or two tours and get out, and that's exactly what we want it to do. But it was unfair. And that is the argument that ultimately worked to Elaine's bigger point in her paper, which we'll also get into.

Which is just the sheer cost of these two. The first of the two workforces. Can we put that aside? Sure. Can we talk about ways to arrest the rate of growth? Absolutely. Are there reforms therein that are possible? Sure. But even doing what she asks, you have to think about how she characterizes it in her paper: non-core defense functions. So meaning, what are things that the Defense Department can do that only it's expected to do? And, of course, that's to kill and use violence in the name of the state when needed, period.

So when it comes beyond that to the cook, for example, the scrub would be, does the cook need to fire the rifle too? I don't know. Maybe, maybe not. Maybe on the ship. My point is, an unemotional look across the workforce is to say, and when the Defense Business Board did this and it made the front page of the *Washington Post*, which one of you was in government? You remember what I'm talking about. It basically said there's $25 to $40 billion, I think it was, in overlap and duplicity.

Duplication in the Defense Department workforces, and basically, all of these military people could just become civilians, and Washington just freaked out, a scientific term. But to look at these three workforces, which needs to be done for that scrub that Dr. Chu is describing and, I think, was echoed in the other panel. It has to be rational and probably objectively outside of the department's purview, then we receive buy-in at the presidential level and by Congress. Some sort of up or down vote on whatever the results are. And with the Secretary of Defense's agreement. So I'll say that point, and then secondly, I wanted to get at the commander [Casey Miller]'s point from the cyber squadron. When we're talking specifically in my paper, I talk about not that the civilians can or can't grow—federal defense civilians. I talk about linking the workforces to what happens in the active-duty force. They should grow or shrink in tandem but defense civilians don't get to bulge when active duties get squeezed.

That's exactly what happens almost every four years. DoD civilians go up, active duty goes down, and there's no linkage there, there's no rationale—there's no purpose behind it. It's just the way that things are getting done for whatever reason. Putting that point aside, though, again, I get back to the need for an unemotional examination of the facts. Today as it stands, over half of all DoD civilians are veterans. You kind of made that point. They take off the uniform, they put on the suit, and they come back.

There is a need for a discussion about all of the preferential hiring that was put in place after 9/11 for good reasons that now needs to be reexamined. Because are we now losing true core civilians? Of course, all veterans are civilians. Yes. But I'm talking about never-served civilians who bring a special and unique viewpoint to service. That's going to be different than what Secretary Jim Mattis brings, or what Mackenzie Eaglen brings, or Tim Kane, or whomever. Increasingly it's all a defense viewpoint whether you're in uniform or in the suit working for the department.

And that's something that fundamentally has to be grappled with and talked about and wrestled with.

MICHAEL J. BOSKIN: I have three quick points I want to make in my question that I don't know the answer to, and I'm sure almost everybody else in the room does. At least have a general overview of this. I failed to mention one point about the move to the all-volunteer force, which I think Tim accurately described was heavily driven by the unpopular draft. Two Hoover fellows played a very large role in that. Milton Friedman was the intellectual voice arguing for that for some period of time, and the late Martin Anderson, my Hoover colleague, was President Nixon's domestic policy advisor.

And that linkage was very important in forming Nixon's views on these things. But obviously, the unpopularity of the draft was a big deal. I want to just emphasize that the dual career earning issue is a huge issue everywhere. If you're lucky and you're hiring in a very large labor market like the Bay Area or something, it's usually solvable. But that's a minority of the total United States, and it becomes a very, very difficult problem. And I think that more flexibility and more attention to that is undoubtedly worthwhile.

I want to emphasize the point that Mike Mullen made to me at a dinner this summer that a huge fraction of our enlistees have relatives, parents, grandparents, aunts, and uncles who have served. I've forgotten. Somebody mentioned a number earlier, I forgot what it was, but it's vastly disproportionate. But people were talking about the pyramid. This is an inverted funnel because, in every generation, there are fewer and fewer of those people. So that's something that's really not sustainable at some point. Maybe, for a while, it is with the uptick in Iraq and Afghanistan.

But these go through cycles like those acquisition cycles. We had World War II, and that worked for a couple of generations, then Vietnam, etc. But that's really something, looking at it arithmetically, that is very important to personnel policy. I have a question and an analogue that may or may not be usable or may not be used. A lot of discussion has been about service identities and so on and so forth, and we all know there are often conflicts about priorities.

Here is an example that was given about relaxing these standards. There are about twenty-six states that now have reciprocal minimum licensing requirements for professions, where as long as you pass these minimum standards, if you're okay in state X, you don't have to go through recertification in state Y. I'm just wondering if anything like that goes across the services or could be done? And more generally, a best practice that might work in an experiment like this could spread beyond the siloed services.

So does anybody have any views on that or knowledge about that? I'd love to learn a bit about it.

CHU: The department has actually worked hard to promote compacts of exactly that sort to benefit spouses. So there's a compact for nurses, there's a compact for teachers. And it's also worked on a related issue. This all occurs over the course of time. The military requires you to move frequently, and that's hard on the household in various ways. And so it also goes down to the children. In the early 2000s, the states working with the National Governors Association tried to get all states signed up for a compact covering how children's access to school would be governed when they changed states.

So each state has different ideas about how to teach math, for example. So a kid who starts out in stage A goes to stage B, and they do things in different sequences. They are now disadvantaged. A different issue is sports qualifications. Tryouts occur in a certain season that may not accord with when the military household shows up. They probably got a fair amount of traction on this issue. You have to have a campaign, is what we've discovered. There the prestige of the military is very helpful.

The military is still one of the most respected institutions in the United States, even though it has come down somewhat in the last few years, which is troublesome. And so, the department was able to get a lot of mileage out of how legislators wanted to be seen as being helpful. And this is a nonpecuniary solution. The famous red, yellow, green kind of chart. We had a chart for every state when the governors came to visit the secretary. He would like to take out the chart. He'd like to have a governor who had all green with the governor who had all red. It worked.

I would get the states to change their policy since the one policy change that was achieved was to ensure that states would all let children of military personnel enroll in the state college university system at the in-state rates regardless of the parent's state of residence. And the further achievement after considerable work was they would also get to continue at the in-state rate once the household had moved, but the child wanted to finish their degree.

These all get down in the weeds and work the problem, find solutions. But they are, I think, essential to making military life—I don't want to say bearable, makes it sound too hard. But to accept the burdens Secretary Mattis pointed to in his comments. I think they're essential to success. But yes, the compacts are very helpful in that regard.

NADIA SCHADLOW: I have a question, Casey. Really, to anyone. When DoD created a new cyber branch or created the new space corps, did we try to inject more flexibility? It seemed that with space command, there were opportunities to do things differently, but we have inserted it right back into the existing set of dysfunctionalities. It's my understanding, as I learn more about its creation, that we took the air force acquisition corps and just made them the space command acquisition corps for the most part. We did not address the underlying problems! Am I being too harsh, or was there a way to treat this new corps in a different way, or were they just put back into the dysfunctional family?

CASEY "WALDO" MILLER: So my fear is, if we do go down the path of standing up a cyber force, that it would end up looking very similar to what you just described on the space force side. I told Roger [Zakheim] he has my favorite quote of the event so far when he said—Roger, can you say it again? I'm going to butcher it.

ROGER ZAKHEIM: The nonelected bureaucrats of the DoD, something along those lines.

MILLER: Right now, because cyber is joint, we have the same requirements across all services in regards to what training looks like for OCO [offensive cyberspace operations] and DCO [defensive cyberspace operations] forces in support of US CYBERCOM. So that is very clean, and for each one of the specific work roles, there is a service responsible for building out what that curriculum needs to look like, what those requirements are that need to be met, and how we verify those. And so, from that perspective across services, it's pretty darn clean.

What I've loved in terms of thinking outside of the box and what I would love to see is if there is some—no kidding—progress being made, especially given some of the verbiage in the most recent NDAA in terms of asking the services. And I can't specifically remember who it was that was asked to consider what a cyber force would look like by looking at what's done in industry, with the idea being, can I put the best person in the right job regardless of the amount of time they've spent in the service?

So, one of my favorite stories, a very good friend of mine separated from the air force right before he pinned on major. He was set to go be the DO [director of operations] of a cyber operations squadron. The reason why he left was that he got picked to go be the CISO [chief information security officer] for Pokémon. So you have this person with unbelievable talent who can just go and just crush whatever challenge is handed to him. The growth plan the air force had him was simply that he'll go be the DO.

Whereas from a strictly talent-based perspective in this space, he was way beyond that. Really way beyond anything that we even have within the air force. And so, how can we look at the unique value that each of our folks brings, and how do we build a structure that, at the end of the day, allows us to put the right people in those right positions at the right time regardless of how much time they've spent in uniform?

Tim Kane: I just wanted to add to what Casey and I were speaking about earlier, regarding the situation his unit faces. We all should have this number ringing in our ears: 80 percent attrition rate. Why is that? Correct me if I'm wrong, Casey, but is this not a situation where the typical young cyber officer or NCO [noncommissioned officer] simply wants to continue in their current job? They want longevity, but there is no systemic flexibility. We tend to hear "flexibility" as a cry for a system to allow faster movement, but in this case it is a vast majority of workers begging for flexibility to move slower. They want to stay at that location doing that job, and they're told, "No, you have to move to something completely unrelated to your cyber mission where you have all these amazing skills." That's one problem.

The second problem is the lack of differential pay in the ranks. Today, if you're an E-7, you get paid as an E-7. There are essentially no performance, merit, or skill bonuses in any military branch. Two exceptions are combat pay and flight pay (which ironically is not for serving as a pilot, rather it's for being qualified to fly). The Pentagon actually could really make a dent in keeping people on a mission if it had those two kinds of flexibility. Is that fair to say, Casey?

MILLER: It is. And it kind of brings those two things together. What I think is unique is I don't have folks leaving before their commitment is up. So they leave when the air force tells them it's time for them to leave.

KANE: Time to rotate.

MILLER: Correct. So they're getting job offers, and they could be leaving. They get to my unit. They owe two years because of the move. But they're getting job offers. So they could leave in two years. They're staying, and they're continuing to do the mission until the air force is physically telling them we're going to move you, at which point they're dropping their paperwork.

And then the other phenomenon that's been very interesting for me to research and then look to apply within the air force is my best folks were going to be incredible regardless of whether they joined the air force or not. There is nothing that we are providing them in the service in terms of training or education that is making them amazing. And I think that changes the inherent relationship between the service and the individual.

BRADDOCK: I'm going to take the last three questions. Mike [Brown], if you'll go, then Admiral Mullen, and then Jackie [Schneider].

MICHAEL BROWN: I want to pick up on Casey's last point where we're trying to bring in people who have unique skills, subject matter experts, such as Raj [Shah] and me. [As leaders within government,] we're trying to bring in people who have some expertise in some of these different emerging technologies. Think about AI, cyber autonomy, etc. And this is a question about this mismatch of our view of how we're going to use our same old process with people who have lots of choices. So, for example, we were trying to bring in an AI expert. He was a PhD in computer science at Stanford and a Rhodes Scholar.

And we went through the selection process [and told the candidate,] "Fantastic, we'd love to have you." He was ready to come. It took us *seven months* for the Pentagon to generate the offer letter. So we've already been through the selection process, [then] seven months at Washington Headquarters Services [to do] the paperwork [to generate the offer letter]. And we can't operate this way where the candidate has so many choices, and we ask them to wait seven months to come on [board]. Not to get a security clearance, just the offer letter to start work.

So this is a huge opportunity if we think about needing to bring digital skills into the military, which we vastly need. I would argue that we don't have nearly the skill set we need with digital-age talent, and yet we are really still in a mode where you should be lucky to get the government paycheck and please wait for us to generate the paperwork to get it. I can't even express my frustration. How do we change that? So maybe some input for the PPBE [Planning, Programming, Budgeting, and Execution] commission. If someone has any suggestions, I'd love to hear them. But it's the most frustrating thing I encountered in my government service.

H.R. MCMASTER: I just want to make a quick point that those are probably long-term civil servants who are unfireable who are responsible for that personnel process. So I think civil service reform is necessary.

ADMIRAL MIKE MULLEN: Just, actually, a couple comments as opposed to a question. One is, and this is from a service chief perspective, from a chairman's perspective, and from a uniform perspective. Don't give any more civilians to DoD. They're up 40 percent or 50 percent, whatever the number is. I don't need them, quite frankly. Give me the right ones. Whatever the combination is, I'm fine with that. We have way too many, and that is a huge part of the bureaucracy. Secondly, the recruiting problem at its base right now is the influencers are not telling the kids to go join.

So the parents, the coaches, the teachers, the people that influence the potential recruits. Even post 9/11. We're out of the 9/11 window. It's been twenty years, whatever it is, where we had them lined up ten deep across government, not just in the military. And so, we've got to change how we're doing this.

So what I like about your paper, David, is within all services, we all need to adopt the marine corps model. With the marine corps model, basically, 80 percent of the battalion commanders—which is the key command level in all the services—80 percent of them were recruiters. What [marine corps commandant Charles] Krulak did in the 1990s was he took all of his best majors and put them in recruiting. They then screened for battalion command, and 20 percent of the flag officers in the marine corps were recruiters.

You need to have that throughout, and I don't think the marine corps has missed a shipment of recruits since that time. That's the model all services need, something like that. If you want to fix recruiting, you've got to get your best people in it. It's where we start. If we aren't recruiting well, we don't have much of a future. And the other services, none of the other services, including my own, do it that way.

The retirement piece is interesting, David, because we did go to this blended system, and Tim, you mentioned it. But I hope we haven't forgotten the fervor when the law actually changed to, I think it was 38 percent. And that lasted one year because the fervor was this: It's this twenty-year thing, it's been 50 percent, it's been locked in forever, and there's a psychological barrier there that you almost can't get over. Maybe we can now, but historically we were unable to get over it. And I'm also reminded, the number may have changed, but 17 percent of our force get to twenty years, or some number like that, and we do pay a huge price for that. But changing that is a monumental task, and the best way to do it, I think, would be grandfathered as opposed to anybody who's actually serving. So it's a long time to put into place.

And then Michael [Boskin], just to pick up a little bit on what you said—and I thought you were going to make a related point—back in the day when I was a service chief—a joint chief, actually—I worried, and still worry, about our military becoming further and further disconnected from America. That gets me to the draft piece. We're smaller and smaller. We come from fewer and fewer places, and we don't broadly represent America at large, the democracy that we need to be so careful about.

Back in the day, President George W. Bush was hosting sixteen four-stars for an hour in the Cabinet Room at a dinner. This was with Secretary [Donald] Rumsfeld, and the Bushes were great. They did this every year, and we'd have dinner over there with our spouses. Before that, we'd meet with the president. There was a break in the discussion with sixteen four-stars, and Rumsfeld said to President Bush, "I don't know, Mr. President, if you know this, but fifteen of the sixteen four-stars sitting here have kids in the military." That got my attention. From then on—this was in 2005 or 2006—I started to pulse that as I went around the forces over the next five or six years. The number of troops who were there because their parents were in or were more senior NCOs who had kids serving both enlisted and officer ranks. What I worry about is, we become a class unto ourselves, and that creates more disconnection from the American people. We have to be very, very careful about that. That's another family piece that's very relevant in the current force that we have.

BOSKIN: Absolutely. The separation from the broader population issue is as important as the numbers, perhaps more so.

JACQUELYN SCHNEIDER: As someone who has served as active-duty, reservist, civilian, and for a brief second a contractor, I really appreciate this conversation, because I've been on all sides of the panel on this one. I want to get back to a previous brief discussion. Tim, in your PowerPoint about qualifications, you said, "I don't want to decrease the qualifications. We want the best and the brightest." I think that's true. There are, however, some things that we've done to ourselves that have nothing to do with the best and the brightest. There is a litany of medical reasons why individuals are summarily not allowed to serve, and that has not been reviewed.

Now, because of the digitization of records, they're finding that it's really, really difficult to bring forces in because we used to just lie. "Oh, I never had childhood asthma. Are you kidding?" Now they can see, "Oh, right. Yeah." Now they can see. That's something we're doing to ourselves. There is a larger question about the force that we're building today versus the force that we might need if the Taiwan scenario or some other major commitment of our forces occurs. I'm not confident that we can keep up the quality and the quantity required for that type of conflict. It brings up a whole question about the draft but I think something that we haven't talked about here at all is what the role of the reserves should be as we think about pivoting toward China.

The reserves as they are right now, it's partly the beginning of the total force, which is the all-volunteer force, which is fifty years old this year. It's also a product of twenty to thirty years of the reserves being a one-for-one substitute for active-duty units, which was extremely helpful for decreasing the public pain of sustaining two decades of conflict without having to go to a draft. The problem is, because of that, we haven't invested at all in the strategic reserve. We have billets for strategic reserve, IRR [individual ready reserve], PIRR [participating individual ready reserve], and nonparticipating and participating ready reserves. None of the services actively maintain this. There's almost no roster of talent within this specialized reserve force. Even in the very few circumstances where IRR is actively being used, the air force has a few of these programs, none of the services actually fund the administration for these types of reservists.

I am a flexible reservist. It's called an IMA [Individual Mobilization Augmentee] program: I am alone. Currently, I can't be paid because the IT system is on Internet Explorer, and it went down seven days ago, and they don't know when it'll be back up. That's kind of funny and anecdotal but it's a theme because there hasn't been an investment in a flexible reserve force. I would say I hope in the future, as we think about the future of personnel, we lean more heavily on the reserves and think about how we can build a flexible strategic reserve force so we can maintain the quality and the quantity.

CHU: I think you made a great point about the power that reserve appointments can give to solving problems in the department. It's an opportunity to have our cake and eat it too, if we're willing to ingest it. That's really the challenge, is to be sure that the enterprise, especially active force, is willing to accept people, for example, who go in and out of service. That's not a general pattern that's applauded, unfortunately. There's a cultural change, I think, that's needed to exploit the full benefit of using that appointing authority, back to Michael [Brown]'s problem getting his expert on board.

On the civilian side, the answer to your problem is what's called direct hire authority. I'm disappointed they didn't have that. My solution would be just give DoD so-called direct hire authority. And that goes back to one of the flexibilities I think we need in terms of the future. The white-collar civil service system is really a heritage from the late nineteenth century when the principal function of the US government was paying civil war pensions. That's a clerical task. It invites, again, this hierarchical system. It's where we get the general schedule from. And, of course, there's this issue of fairness that everybody has to be considered, which is what gets in the way, basically. It's typically, maybe not in that particular case but particularly what leads to the inability at a job fair to say, "You're hired," which others can do in their hiring.

There's no reason DoD can't do that except for certain statutory constraints. That's why I think civil service reform is one of the most important avenues to further progress in federal government performance in the United States. Whether we ever get back to that, given the opposition, which is very strong from the union perspective. They do not like the direct hire approach. They're the strongest defenders of the lists of three, or seven, or whatever it might be, that you have to consider and go through. Again, back to one of my main theses, it will take the president backing civil service reform in a big way to get us from here to there.

BOSKIN: And David, maybe given the politics of it all, it will take a Democrat president. It took Nixon to go to China. A Democrat couldn't have done that.

CHU: I think it's in everyone's interest to get civil service reform. The question is how we get everybody together. Back to Secretary Panetta's challenge, how do we get everybody on the same page?

BOSKIN: I totally agree with that. I think the lift will be extra hard for a Republican president. It would be easier for the unions to totally oppose.

CHU: Yes. There's a book by one of my colleagues, Peter Levine, that goes into the history of the failed national security personnel system or the failure to sustain the national security personnel system. Peter's main point is that we did not have bipartisan backing for it, so it became a partisan issue. You can get it. What history demonstrates is that you can get it to happen on a partisan basis. For the better part of four years, five years, we did have a different system for DoD, including, most importantly, back to your compensation issue, a different pay system. We were successful in removing the ceiling on civil service pay. We could pay up to several hundred thousand dollars a year if we chose to do so. We got pay bands, which are the source of flexibility.

In other words, instead of having fifteen grades for white-collar workers, we had four pay bands. You, the manager, could name any number within the pay band associated with that particular job—wonderful flexibility. Despite the fact there was some bipartisan support [for the reform], despite the fact that Senator [Carl] Levin [was a supporter], and despite the fact that when President Obama revoked the system, the statute allowed the secretary to repropose that feature. Unfortunately, the administration decided not to do so.

Part 5

Reform Recommendations and Budget Implications

14

Keeping the Pentagon Running

Commonsense Changes to Defense Budgeting

Mackenzie Eaglen

A near-constant reform effort has been underway at the world's largest bureaucracy for the past two decades. The Department of Defense (DoD) is under the microscope constantly. Its four-thousand-page annual policy and oversight bill has been enacted into law every year for over a half century, unique among all federal agencies. Beyond the defense authorization act, however, have been numerous other internal and external change efforts— ranging from "Better Buying Power" and the Levin-McCain Weapons Systems Acquisition Reform Act of 2009 to "Night Court" and the efficiency drills run by former secretary of defense Robert Gates. There is no shortage of constant churn to improve how the Pentagon does business. What there is a shortage of, however, is lasting results.

Updates and improvements are important for the transparency of taxpayer investments, accountability of officials, staying relevant in a rapidly changing world, and meeting varied threats over differing time frames. But change for change's sake, or change intended to bolster political arguments to sustain needed defense spending levels, is unhelpful. Indeed, it is time for reformers to focus more on what policies can be sunsetted, what laws must expire, what rules and regulations should go away, and what specific work and tasks of lesser or outdated importance can be stopped.[1] Reform that removes barriers is more important than efforts to add layers of new rules, organizations, or manpower to the Defense Department.

While threats are evolving, as is America's response to them, the base defense budget mostly stays the same year after year as if in a constant

The views expressed in this chapter are solely those of the individual author and do not necessarily reflect the views of any organization with which they are, or have been, affiliated.

peacetime posture.[2] Defense planning, programming, and budgeting are rife with flaws and overdue for updates. This is why Congress established a commission to review and reform these internal processes to help prioritize and allocate nearly three-quarters of a trillion dollars annually.

While the commission investigates at a detailed level over many months, some practical and quickly implementable reforms at a macro level are outlined in this paper. In the meantime, Congress and the executive branch should begin the earnest process of scrubbing the books, and axe procedures, headquarters, and regulations where necessary. By undertaking this necessary but difficult job of slashing and burning the barnacles of bureaucracy that have piled up and calcified over time, policy makers will demonstrate their seriousness about needed defense rehabilitation while skipping the defense reform theater that has plagued the military for too long.

Strike a Two-Year Budget Deal for Defense and Nondefense Discretionary Spending Now

Of the more than 1,200 days of operating under a continuing resolution or spending freeze over the past decade, one fiscal year stands apart: 2019.[3] This year saw defense appropriations enacted on time, a virtual miracle in modern times. The single biggest reason for this outcome of true efficiency was the two-year budget deal struck the previous year between the two political parties, both chambers, and the White House ahead of time. Signed in an attempt to raise the defense and nondefense discretionary spending caps under the Budget Control Act of 2011, this deal set overall federal spending levels for two years, offering much-needed clarity and certainty to keep the government functioning.[4] And, in doing so, it made FY2019 the only fiscal year in the last decade when the Pentagon was not under a continuing resolution (see fig. 14.1).[5] Compare that to the passage of FY2022 appropriations, when there was no two-year deal. At that time, it took four short-term freezes for appropriations to be passed, and they were enacted nearly half a year after the start of the fiscal year.[6]

Predictability of finances for a federal agency that buys more goods, services, and IT/software than all other agencies combined per year is as important as a new, additional defense dollar to the topline when needed. Removing the guesswork and endless stop-start negotiations allowed Pentagon planners and program managers to allocate resources in the most cost-effective manner possible in 2019. It also enabled the industry to manage workforces,

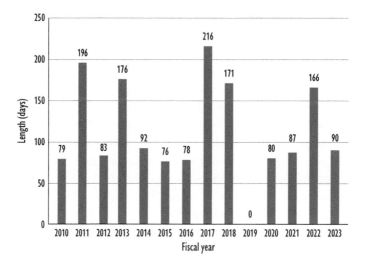

Figure 14.1 Department of Defense under Continuing Resolutions

Sources: US Government Accountability Office, "Defense Budget: DOD Has Adopted Practices to Manage within the Constraints of Continuing Resolutions," GAO-21-541, September 13, 2021; Consolidated Appropriations Act, 2022, Pub. L. No. 117-103; Consolidated Appropriations Act, 2023, Pub. L. No. 117-328.

suppliers, and investments to support the warfighter. Moreover, it untethered funding the government from raising the debt ceiling.[7]

Further, two-year budget deals help prevent government shutdowns and spending freezes, both of which lead to a serious loss of buying power for the Defense Department. This wasteful effort of forcing feds to live in stasis at last year's levels causes hundreds of misaligned programs, millions of wasted dollars, training time that cannot be recovered, and further self-imposed technology delays vis-à-vis China across the military. Continuing resolutions add entirely avoidable burdens to stressed systems across the defense enterprise. Plus, no one can buy back time. The longer a continuing resolution drags on, the higher the likelihood of inadvertent staff reductions, insufficient operating budgets, and the underfunding of existing programs that the military needs to remain on schedule.

Looking ahead to 2024, the Office of Management and Budget should use the national defense topline number of $858 billion in FY2023 appropriations as a floor and adequately adjust for inflation-accounted real growth.[8] Assuming a 6 percent inflation rate, according to a recent estimate provided to the Senate Appropriations Committee by Secretary of the Navy Carlos Del Toro, a national defense budget (Function 050) for 2024 would need to be roughly $909 billion.[9] A 6 percent inflation rate may seem to be an overestimation but with the start of the next fiscal year only twenty-three weeks away (as of this writing), that high level of inflation appears increasingly likely. After inflation is accounted for, 3 percent real growth should be added to better and more speedily enact the National Defense Strategy, resulting in an overall defense topline (Function 050) of about $936 billion for 2024.

While the Budget Control Act offered an impetus for a two-year spending deal in 2018, Congress should pursue such a deal now because of the certainty and flexibility that it provides.[10] Lawmakers would then be able to complete their work on time, and defense officials and industry leaders would benefit from the deal's fiscal stability.

Sequester Paychecks until Delayed Appropriations Are Enacted past the Start of the Fiscal Year

To avoid spending freezes, bold moves are needed to break the logjam and attractiveness of holding the defense budget hostage in nondefense negotiations. In an attempt to incentivize the passing of appropriations bills on time and punish lawmakers for failing to do so, members of Congress should have their paychecks sequestered until appropriations are passed starting October 1 of each year. This automatic action would be designed to avoid the scores of problems that continuing resolutions cause for the military and industry, chief among these being misaligned funding. As continuing resolutions pause spending increases (or decreases) and lock in last year's funding levels, appropriations accounts become misaligned, work stalls, readiness takes a hit, and time is wasted waiting on the system to work as intended and, often, for funding increases to arrive for strategic priorities.[11] Continuing resolutions also prevent the start of any new acquisition programs, wreaking havoc on the armed forces' modernization plans.[12] For instance, the latest continuing resolution delayed procurement funds for the Air Force's Long Range Stand-Off Weapon, a new procurement program in Fiscal Year 2023.[13]

More than just the start of new programs, continuing resolutions delay the progression of established programs. The Pentagon depends on a steady flow of funding for production increases that keep its many weapons, services, and technical programs on track for development and delivery to the warfighter. By willfully injecting uncertainty into that funding profile, continuing resolutions create inefficiencies and cost overruns, rendering industry leaders unable to plan appropriately.[14] Workforces and vendors cannot adequately staff up when funds do not arrive on time.[15] Finally, continuing resolutions are simply wasteful. The most recent one in FY2023 forced the military to miss out on over $200 million per day in funding. By the time regular appropriations became law on December 29, 2022, the Defense Department had lost $18 billion in buying power in those previous three months.[16]

While this reform would certainly be difficult to implement, no less for the reason that members of Congress may not willfully withhold their own pay, there have been similar proposals introduced in recent years. For instance, multiple bills have been introduced in previous Congresses that would prohibit members from being paid during a government shutdown. And, as a sign of Congress's ability to resist the urge to increase its members' own pay, the body has not received a salary increase since January 2009.[17] Lastly, the mere floating of this reform would be helpful, as it could draw more stakeholders into policy debates, thereby putting more pressure on politicians to do their core job on time each year.

For all these reasons, garnishing politicians' pay until they do the basic job of keeping the government functioning through on-time funding would help ensure that continuing resolutions are a worst-case solution instead of a tool for Congress to routinely rely on.

No More "Use It or Lose It" Penalty on the Defense Department for Expired Appropriations

As a result of continuing resolutions, federal agencies often have less than a year to obligate a year's worth of appropriations in key accounts. That means there may be a rush at the end of the fiscal year to obligate funds, leading to an end-of-year spending bulge if politicians do not do their job and provide on-time funds.[18] In 2016, for example, the Congressional Research Service found that obligations jumped to over $43 billion in September, the last month of the fiscal year, well above the year's $25 billion monthly average.[19]

In the Pentagon's case, that bulge may be exacerbated due to the time limits on each appropriations account for when funds must be obligated.[20] On the shorter end, operation and maintenance and military personnel funds must be obligated within one year of being appropriated, while on the longer end, research, development, test, and evaluation funds must be obligated within two years and procurement funds, three.[21]

Thanks to these limits due to the so-called "color of money," the Pentagon experiences a "use it or lose it" phenomenon, where program managers worry that unspent funds will expire permanently and be returned to the Treasury, and that the lack of full spend will send the wrong signal—that there is a decreased funding need.[22] This has a number of negative effects, ranging from reduced negotiating leverage in government contracts to misplaced or wasteful uses of funds.[23]

To fix this phenomenon, Congress must allow for greater carryover authority, letting funds meant to expire in one fiscal year to be used in the next.[24] That's all the more urgent given just how much money has been returned, or gone unobligated, in recent years (in large part because of Capitol Hill's delayed work). A Government Accountability Office analysis found that between $8.9 billion and $16.3 billion went unobligated between FY2013 and FY2018 at the Pentagon—most of which were one-year operation and maintenance dollars.[25]

Prior to 1990, expired budget authority remained available indefinitely in certain appropriations accounts. According to the Government Accountability Office, these balances "could be used to pay valid obligations incurred before the budget authority had expired, including certain upward adjustments."[26] This same report noted how the flexible authority allowed the military to "pay routine bills as they became due and to fund valid but previously unrecorded obligations or increases in amounts originally obligated for a particular activity when circumstances warranted." As a reasonable limit, the authority could not be used to incur new obligations.

Given how much larger the defense budget is today, perhaps Congress could grant a carryover authority in the one-year military personnel and operation and maintenance accounts of 20 percent, allowing the department to retain significant amounts of money that are often provided late. With rampant inflation affecting defense spending in many ways, this type of benefit would seem desirable and necessary.[27]

Some may be concerned that allowing the services to keep more money would lead to a lapse in oversight and, ultimately, abuse. While valid, safeguard measures can be put in place to prevent this, including midyear budget reviews provided to Congress where information on anticipated expenditures and surpluses for the remaining part of the fiscal year may be provided. Congress could also institute a limit on when carryover funds expire.[28] If Congress cannot and will not give the military on-time funds every year, there is no reasonable case for Capitol Hill to simultaneously punish the armed forces for being unable to spend money in a timely fashion once it finally arrives. Providing carryover authority would allow the Pentagon to increase flexibility in its finances and avoid the negative and wasteful effects of rushed spending.

Increase Defense Reprogramming Thresholds

Once Congress allocates funding, albeit often late given the frequency of continuing resolutions, it often does not provide the Pentagon with enough flexibility to match investments to changing needs against a great-power competitor in China. One of the prime reasons for this is the inadequacy of reprogramming thresholds, which prevent dollars from being shifted without consulting layers of bureaucracy within the Pentagon and on Capitol Hill. For the current fiscal year, reprogramming thresholds for prior approval, otherwise known as above threshold reprogramming, are set at $10 million for military personnel and operation and maintenance, while for research, development, test, evaluation, and procurement, that threshold is $10 million or 20 percent of the budget line item, whichever is less.[29]

If a reprogramming request exceeds those limits, it is subjected to a battery of reviews. The process may consist of up to twelve rounds of review within the Defense Department before being sent to the White House budget office for review and eventually on to the House and Senate Armed Services and Appropriations Committees for their stamps of approval.[30] One study found that this whole process can take an average of ninety-six days, all while the often-urgent need necessitating a reprogramming request is still present and languishing.[31] Prior approval reprogramming thresholds are, in the words of former Pentagon comptroller Dov Zakheim, "much too low, and too constrained, and prevent the timely adjustment of accounts for a host of programs."[32]

If the US military is to truly operate at the "speed of relevance," as stated by then secretary of defense Jim Mattis, then bureaucracy must catch up to the times—and the sheer size of the massive defense budget. Thresholds from an era when toplines were less than $215 billion are irrelevant today and only help our competitors and enemies go faster while Washington continues its Soviet-style central management approach to defense investments.[33] To circumvent the lengthy approval process and provide the armed forces with the flexibility to shift funds as needed, reprogramming thresholds must increase.

At a minimum, allowable reprogramming amounts should keep pace with inflation, which has generally not been the case despite adjustments to the thresholds over time. Following the advice of the Section 809 Panel, reprogramming thresholds should rise to compensate for the loss in buying power due to inflation and the steady growth of the overall topline. Raising these limits will not just benefit the military by providing flexibility in terms of budget execution, but it will also shift congressional committees' limited time and bandwidth away from exercising oversight over small programs (and their relatively small amounts of money). Their oversight is better focused on larger, more expensive, technical, and complicated programs.[34] Raising reprogramming thresholds for prior approval will provide a number of benefits to both branches of government while increasing agility and necessary flexibility.

Reorganize the Major Appropriations Accounts for a More Realistic Summary of Priorities

Accountability in budgeting should not be limited to just accountants, auditors, and comptrollers. All defense stakeholders spanning the service chiefs, combatant commanders, and civilian officials able to pull on the Pentagon's purse strings, should have so-called skin in the game. The more transparent funds are to each stakeholder, the more awareness there will be across viewpoints about the costs of doing business—costs that outpace inflation every year and for each appropriations account at the Defense Department.[35]

One area ripe for more transparency is the organization and public presentation of major defense appropriations accounts. Within the division of these accounts are the true and varied labor costs of the three defense workforces, which are deeply buried and marbled throughout the budget documents. Because civilian pay and benefits and the bulk of funding for the Defense Health Program are included in the operation and maintenance account, service chiefs may assume people cost less than they do by solely evaluating spending through the military personnel account.[36] Even more complicated is that military health-care costs are spread across the procurement, research, development, test and evaluation, and military construction accounts.[37] To resolve this obfuscated dataset that totals more than half of all defense spending, and provide more clarity as to the true costs of professionals, the simple composition of these accounts should be changed.

No longer should there be a spending account for just military personnel. Rather, federal defense civilian salaries should move out of operation and maintenance, along with the bulk of the Defense Health Program, into the military personnel account. Costs of the Defense Health Program and Military Health System spread across other appropriations accounts should also move into military personnel. In addition, given that they provide benefits to service members, funding for dependents' education and family housing should be reallocated to the military personnel account.

If such changes were implemented using defense appropriations for enacted 2022 levels, the military personnel account would grow from over $167 billion to $276 billion—nearly a 65 percent increase. On the other hand, operation and maintenance's size would fall by about 35 percent, from $307 billion to $200 billion. This is only a partial accounting of the true costs of personnel spread across the appropriations accounts, and should other personnel costs be included, such as those contained within base operations support, this total would certainly grow even more. The restructured appropriations accounts can be seen in figures 14.2 and 14.3, with military personnel being renamed defense personnel to reflect the inclusion of civilian pay and benefits, as well as health care and other personnel costs across the enterprise.

This analysis takes into account the costs of compensation and benefits for direct hire and direct-funded personnel. Given the difficulties in determining

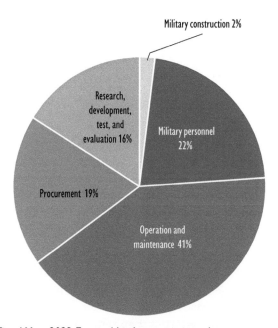

Figure 14.2 Fiscal Year 2022 Enacted by Appropriations Account

Source: US Department of Defense, Office of the Under Secretary of Defense, (Comptroller)/ Chief Financial Officer, *Defense Budget Overview: Fiscal Year 2023 Budget Request*, April 2022, Table A-1.

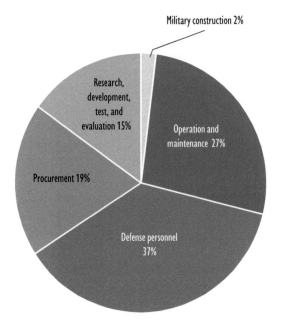

Figure 14.3 Fiscal Year 2022 Enacted with Defense Personnel Account

Sources: Bryce H. P. Mendez, "FY2023 Budget Request for the Military Health System," Congressional Research Service Report IF12087, April 29, 2022; US Department of Defense, Office of the Under Secretary of Defense, (Comptroller)/Chief Financial Officer (DoD CFO), *Defense Budget Overview: Fiscal Year 2023 Budget Request,* April 2022, Table A-1; DoD CFO, *Defense Operation & Maintenance Overview Book: Fiscal Year 2023 Budget Request,* May 2022; DoD CFO, *Fiscal Year 2023 Budget Estimates: DoD Dependents Education,* April 2022.

where reimbursable funded personnel receive compensation, whether from the Department of Defense or other federal agencies, they were excluded from this analysis.[38] But, should the over $31 billion worth of compensation and benefits for direct hire, reimbursable funded personnel be included, operation and maintenance would decrease by close to 45 percent, from $307 billion to $169 billion. As for military personnel, the account would grow from $167 billion to $307 billion, an 83 percent increase.

Restructuring the appropriations accounts is a simple act of accounting that will strike a disproportionate and fierce resistance to implementing it for a variety of parochial interests. These will come from stakeholders such as the appropriators themselves. But the alternative to not doing so is worse. Service leaders, the Office of the Secretary of Defense, Congress, and taxpayers are not receiving an accurate picture of the costs of labor, typically the largest balance sheet item of any big organization, of which the military is no different. Creating a defense personnel account would immediately improve transparency at a time when Capitol Hill is set to review enlisted pay tables in the 118th Congress and increase the salaries of those in uniform.

Link Total Federal Defense Civilians to the Size of the Active-Duty Force

More sunshine about the actual labor cost across the sprawling defense bureaucracy is only a net positive. Another reason for this overdue step is that because of obscurity and obfuscation, too often in modern times, active-duty military rolls have shrunk while their supporting workforces grew. This makes little sense, given that federal defense civilians and defense contracting workforces exist to support the uniformed services. To keep these three defense workforces in balance, they should be linked explicitly.

Federal defense civilian head count should grow or shrink only in tandem with the overall size of the active-duty military. Under the broadest definition of a civilian employee at the Defense Department, 815,000 full-time equivalent civilians were permitted to be employed in FY2022 per enacted levels.[39] Using a narrower definition of a civilian employee, 785,000 full-time equivalents worked for the department in FY2022.[40]

As the most recent *Green Book* notes, the military fell below two service members per civilian in 2010 and has not improved since. The president's proposed force mix for 2023 offers a 1.68:1 ratio of active-duty military personnel to civilian employees, the lowest ratio since World War II. For perspective, the Pentagon maintained an approximately 2.2:1 ratio of uniforms-to-civilians throughout the height of the Iraq War and a staggering 5.11:1 ratio in 1944.[41]

As shown in figures 14.4 and 14.5, between 2010 and 2022, there was a nearly 6 percent drop in active-duty personnel, while Pentagon civilians grew by largely the same amount (5.65 percent) in that period. This discrepancy between the trends in active-duty personnel and the defense civilian workforce is largely a result of the Pentagon's failure to undertake a thorough "rightsizing" of its workforce, adequately matching personnel to workforce requirements.[42]

This growth in the civilian workforce comes with a cost. The Congressional Budget Office has projected that compensation for civilian defense employees will consume 33 percent of operation and maintenance dollars between 2022 and 2031.[43] Biasing one workforce over another is unsound and mismatched to global requirements. While there is no doubt that the feds do

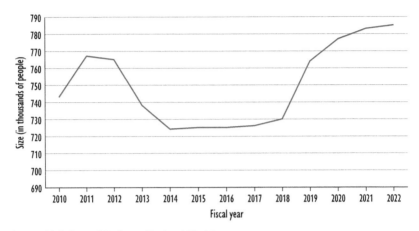

Figure 14.4 Size of Defense Civilian Workforce

Note: Civilians are composed of US and foreign national direct hires. The civilian workforce is counted in full-time equivalents.
Source: US Department of Defense, Office of the Under Secretary of Defense, *National Defense Budget Estimates for FY 2023*, July 2022, Table 7-6.

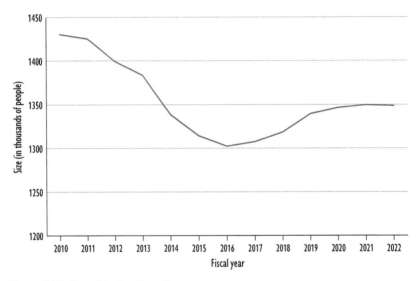

Figure 14.5 Size of Active-Duty Force

Note: Figures for 2022 reflect enacted amounts for military personnel.
Source: US Department of Defense, Office of the Under Secretary of Defense, *National Defense Budget Estimates for FY 2023*, July 2022, Table 7-5.

important and valuable work, there is still not enough clarity for senior leaders as to what labor is unique versus duplicative to what the services or Joint Staff may already be doing.[44]

One of the prime drivers of overhead bloat has been a continuous increase in the various headquarters' staffing. As retired major general Arnold Punaro notes in his book *The Ever-Shrinking Fighting Force*, the staffs of the Office of the Secretary of Defense, Joint Chiefs, combatant commands, and defense field activities alone employ more than 240,000 defense civilians and contractors. From the 1950s on, the growth of these staffs has helped push the defense-wide spending category from 5 percent of the defense budget to nearly 20 percent.[45]

Rightsizing defense workforces is challenging; to do it smartly will take time and require careful leadership. No small reason for this is that nearly half of all federal defense civilians are veterans.[46] Understanding the need for certain hiring preferences and programs and whether those goals have been met must also be balanced with keeping civilians involved in US national security structures. Although veterans are civilians, they retain a military ethos, training, and sometimes a mindset not shared by their colleagues who have not served in the armed forces or deployed in conflict.

In 2018, the congressionally mandated National Defense Strategy Commission cautioned that "civilian voices have been relatively muted on issues at the center of US defense and national security policy, undermining the concept of civilian control."[47] Due to the potential for increased interest relative to nonserving peers or preferential hiring practices and other factors, many considerations must be deliberated before taking action.

Even if defense civilians were to shrink only due to attrition or a hiring freeze, the 1990s track record bears dismal results. Blue-collar positions were disproportionately reduced while white-collar civilian supervisor billets were repeatedly filled—resulting in a misshapen workforce with imbalanced skill sets.[48] And in the 1980s, increases in the civilian workforce followed the trend line in military personnel, just as a shrinking civilian workforce in the 1990s followed troop strength cutbacks.[49] Congress should take note and ensure that the growth of the federal defense civilian workforce is tied to the active-duty military's growth (or decline).

Reforming the Pentagon Bureaucracy by Subtraction

Addition is not the only way to bring greater flexibility, stability, and accountability to the Defense Department. Subtraction of rules, regulations, and bureaucracy is another path and one that Congress should consider embarking on as it looks to reform the Pentagon. The below reforms aim to do just that.

First, when it comes to updating and modernizing bureaucracy, reformers should look no further than the Office of the Under Secretary of Defense for Personnel and Readiness. This office is a bureaucratic add-on that has lacked the innovation and creativity it needs to be effective.[50] And even when the office has attempted bold and creative change, such as in its attempt to overhaul the military in what was dubbed the "Force of the Future" initiative, it was swatted down by Congress and labeled by the late chairman of the Senate Armed Services Committee John McCain (R-AZ) as "an outrageous waste of official time and resources."[51]

Duplication of work and general dysfunction call for the division of this secretariat's portfolio of statutorily mandated responsibilities among existing organizations within the Defense Department and the sunsetting of the superfluous. For instance, housing, compensation and benefits, health care, education, and training all fall under the purview of the office. Oversight of these areas should be doled out elsewhere in the Pentagon to offices such as the Office of Cost Assessment and Program Evaluation, the Joint Staff, and the Comptroller.[52] Additionally, closing the organization would free up civilian and military personnel to work on these issues in existing organizations or stop missions altogether. Budget documents put the total number of civilians working in personnel and readiness at 146 full-time equivalents in 2022, though this is undoubtedly an undercount when military billets and contractors are considered.[53]

Similarly, Congress should review whether or not the US Space Command is duplicative or redundant now that the US Space Force has fully stood up. For instance, while space is a warfighting domain (in a narrow sense today), we are not yet at the stage where there are full-on battles and combat operations executed in space. That may obviate the need for an entire command dedicated, like the other geographic combatant commands, to planning and executing combat operations.[54] Moreover, given the multiple space-focused organizations spread across the services and the intelligence community, space command is worth a relook to see if it is truly needed.[55]

Another way to trim the Pentagon bureaucracy is a relatively simple one in that it cuts down on the fuel of bureaucracy everywhere: paperwork. Congress should consider reducing the plethora of reports that it mandates the Pentagon produce for the institution. According to the Government

Accountability Office, Pentagon reporting requirements grew 178 percent between 2000 and 2020, from just over 500 in 2000 to over 1,400 two decades later.[56] While there's no doubt that many of the reports produced by the department are useful, such as the Selected Acquisition Reports, which lay out details of the most expensive acquisition programs, others are far from needed.[57] Take, for example, the readiness reports issued by the Office of Personnel and Readiness to Congress each quarter. To compile these, the organization simply collects readiness reports issued by each individual service and then makes a few changes, failing to offer valuable insight into the data that is contained within them.[58] Each report also comes with a price tag for the labor and expenses used to produce them, such as the Section 718 report on restructuring military treatment facilities, which costs $46,000 in labor.[59] Individually, the cost of a report may not seem like much, but given their varied costs and their explosion in number since 2000, eliminating some of the requirements for them would be a useful step to both rolling back bureaucracy and saving taxpayer dollars. While Congress has moved to ensure all recurring reports have a sunset date certain, there is much more work to be done in minimizing the sheer number of reporting requirements on the executive branch.

Another way that Congress can practice subtraction rather than addition when it comes to reforming the Defense Department is by reducing contracting requirements. Here again, as with the reporting requirements mandated by Congress, bureaucracy has reared its ugly head. Nowhere is this more evident than in commercial item procurement, covered under Federal Acquisition Regulation Part 12, as my colleague Bill Greenwalt has noted. According to the Section 809 Panel, government-specific contracting clauses for commercial items, as well as commercial off-the-shelf (COTS) contracts, increased 189 percent between 1995 and 2018, jumping from 57 to 165.[60] As a matter of principle, these clauses in and of themselves aren't harmful. Contracting regulations, such as those in the Truthful Cost or Pricing Data Act, help ensure the American taxpayer receives a fair shake in the Pentagon's dealings.[61]

But, the growth in government-specific contracting clauses means that companies have to spend more to comply with government regulations. In turn, those costs act as a barrier to doing business with the Defense Department—especially for new entrants and innovative small businesses and technology start-ups.[62] This is all the more concerning given the Pentagon's increasing reliance on commercial sector solutions for its hardware, software, and services. Congress should carefully consider which contracting clauses are absolutely necessary and which are simply a barrier to entry for businesses that want to work with the Pentagon.[63]

Bite-Sized Changes with Outsize Immediate Impact

The kinds of defense budget reforms needed today to meet the moment fall into two categories: (1) change that aims at a reduction—whether of rules, head count, regulations, laws, provisions, and more; and (2) change that aims to increase accountability for passing appropriations on time and realizing the true costs of running the Department of Defense.

These recommendations are mostly simple, but they're not easy. Yet there is too much admiring of defense budget problems and far too little action and change for bold new ideas. Political will and leadership are required across the various stakeholders in both branches of government but that is a small price to pay, given that the status quo is not working. The challenge of China is too great and too urgent to continue business as usual. Allowing Pentagon leaders to be better able to respond to shifting priorities and threats should not wait.

Notes

1. Mackenzie Eaglen, "Just Say No: The Pentagon Needs to Drop the Distractions and Move Great Power Competition beyond Lip Service," *War on the Rocks*, October 28, 2019.

2. Mackenzie Eaglen, "The Paradox of Scarcity in a Defense Budget of Largesse," American Enterprise Institute, July 18, 2022.

3. US Government Accountability Office (GAO), "Defense Budget: DOD Has Adopted Practices to Manage within the Constraints of Continuing Resolutions," GAO-21-541, September 13, 2021; Consolidated Appropriations Act, 2022, Pub. L. No. 117-103; and Consolidated Appropriations Act, 2023, Pub. L. No. 117-328.

4. Grant A. Driessen and Megan S. Lynch, "The Budget Control Act: Frequently Asked Questions," Congressional Research Service Report R44039, October 1, 2019.

5. Bipartisan Budget Act of 2018 (Pub. L. 115-123) (June 2018); Susan Davis, Jessica Taylor, Kelsey Snell, and Scott Neuman, "Trump Signs 2-Year Spending Pact," National Public Radio, February 9, 2018; GAO, "Defense Budget: DoD Has Adopted Practices."

6. GAO, "Federal Budget: Selected Agencies and Programs Used Strategies to Manage Constraints of Continuing Resolutions," GAO-22-104701, June 2022.

7. Mackenzie Eaglen, "Congress, It's Time for Two-Year Budget Deal: Eaglen at AEI," *Breaking Defense*, American Enterprise Institute, January 10, 2021.

8. Patrick Leahy, "Fiscal Year 2023 Omnibus Appropriations Bill: Highlights," a summary report from the US Senate Committee on Appropriations, December 20, 2022.

9. US Senate, Committee on Appropriations, Subcommittee on Defense, "Review of the President's Fiscal Year 2024 Budget Request for the Navy and the Marine Corps" (testimony by Carlos Del Toro, March 28, 2023).

10. Grant A. Driessen and Megan S. Lynch, "The Budget Control Act: Frequently Asked Questions," Congressional Research Service Report R44874, October 1, 2019.

11. Mackenzie Eaglen and Rick Berger, "1,000 Days of Continuing Resolutions in 10 Years," American Enterprise Institute, June 10, 2019.

12. Mackenzie Eaglen, "These Key Programs Face Real Delays from Continuing Resolution," *Breaking Defense*, American Enterprise Institute, October 27, 2021.

13. US Department of the Air Force, *Department of Defense Fiscal Year (FY) 2023 Budget Estimates: Justification Book Volume 1 of 1, Missile Procurement*, April 2022, vols. 1-15, 1-16, https://www.saffm.hq.af.mil/FM-Resources/Budget.

14. Eaglen and Berger, "1,000 Days."

15. Eaglen, "These Key Programs."

16. US Senate Committee on Appropriations, *FY23 Omnibus Appropriations Package, Topline Summary*; John Ferrari and Elaine McCusker, "4 Initial Highlights from the 2022 Omnibus Appropriations Bill," American Enterprise Institute, March 11, 2022; Elaine McCusker, "Another Round of Continuing Resolutions—Who Loses?" *The Hill*, September 8, 2022.

17. Ida A. Brudnick, "Salaries of Members of Congress: Recent Actions and Historical Tables," Congressional Research Service Report 97-1011, January 25, 2022.

18. *Prudent Planning or Wasteful Binge? Another Look at End of the Year Spending, Hearing before the US Senate, Subcommittee on Federal Spending, Oversight and Emergency Management, Committee on Homeland Security and Governmental Affairs*, 115th Cong., 1st sess. (2017), testimony by Heather Krause, Director, Strategic Issues, US Government Accountability Office.

19. Frederico Bartels, "Changing Current 'Use It or Lose It' Policy Would Result in More Effective Use of Defense Dollars," Heritage Foundation, June 23, 2021; Moshe Schwartz, "End-Year DOD Contract Spending," Congressional Research Service Report IF10365, November 17, 2017.

20. Bartels, "'Use It or Lose It.'"

21. Defense Acquisition University, "Appropriation Lifecycle," https://www.dau.edu/acquipedia/pages/ArticleContent.aspx?itemid=613.

22. Robert F. Hale, "Bad Idea: The "Use-It-or-Lose-It" Law for DoD Spending," Center for Strategic and International Studies, December 15, 2020.

23. Allan Burman and Gabriel Nelson, "Reforming the 'Use It or Lose It' Problem in Defense Acquisition," *War on the Rocks*, January 18, 2018.

24. Bartels, "'Use it or Lose It.'"

25. Bartels, "'Use It or Lose It'"; Tony Bertuca, "DoD Draws Fire from Sanders for Returning $80B in Funding," *Inside Defense*, March 6, 2019.

26. GAO, "Expired Appropriations: New Limitations on Availability Make Improved Management by DoD Essential," GAO/NSIAD-91-225, July 1991.

27. US Department of Defense (DoD), Office of the Under Secretary of Defense, Acquisition and Sustainment, "Managing the Effects of Inflation with Existing Contracts," memorandum, September 9, 2022, https://www.acq.osd.mil/dpap /policy/policyvault/USA001773-22-DPC.pdf.

28. Jason Fichtner and Adam N. Michel, "Curbing the Surge in Year-End Federal Government Spending: Reforming 'Use It or Lose It' Rules—2016 Update," Mercatus Center, September 2016.

29. US Senate Committee on Appropriations, *Explanatory Statement for the Department of Defense Appropriations Bill, 2023,* June 2022; Brendan McGarry, "DoD Transfer and Reprogramming Authorities: Background, Status, and Issues for Congress," Congressional Research Service Report R46421, June 17, 2020; DoD, Office of the Under Secretary of Defense (Comptroller), *Budget Execution Flexibilities and the Reprogramming Process,* January 13, 2021.

30. Eric Lofgren, "Pathways to Defense Budget Reform," paper presented at the Nineteenth Annual Acquisition Research Symposium, Naval Postgraduate School, Monterey, CA, May 11–12, 2022.

31. Robert A. Fritsch, Jacob J. McMurtrey, and Joseph F. Sullivan, *The Nature of DoD Reprogramming and Associated Trend Analysis,* Naval Postgraduate School, Monterey, CA (June 2020).

32. *Goldwater-Nichols Reform: The Way Ahead, Hearing before the House Armed Services Committee,* 114th Cong. (2016) (testimony by Dov S. Zakheim, Senior Fellow, Center for Naval Analyses, Senior Adviser, Center for Strategic and International Studies).

33. Section 809 Panel, *Report of the Advisory Panel on Streamlining and Codifying Acquisition Regulations,* "Recommendation 47: Restore Programming Dollar Thresholds to Match Their Previous Levels Relative to Inflation and the Budget," January 2019, https://discover.dtic.mil/wp-content/uploads/809-Panel-2019/Volume3 /Recommendation_47.pdf; Office of Management and Budget, Historical Tables, Table 5.1, "Budget Authority by Function and Subfunction: 1976–2027," https:// www.whitehouse.gov/omb/budget/historical-tables.

34. Section 809 Panel, "Recommendation 47."

35. Eaglen, "Paradox of Scarcity."

36. Bryce H. P. Mendez, "FY2023 Budget Request for the Military Health System," Congressional Research Service Report IF12087, April 29, 2022; DoD, Office of the Under Secretary of Defense (Comptroller)/Chief Financial Officer, *Defense Operation & Maintenance Overview Book: Fiscal Year 2023 Budget Request,* May 2022, https://comptroller.defense.gov/Portals/45/Documents/defbudget/FY2023 /FY023_OM_Overview.pdf.

37. Mendez, "FY2023 Budget Request."

38. Elaine McCusker, "Defense Budget Transparency and the Cost of Military Capability," American Enterprise Institute, November 9, 2022.

39. DoD, Office of the Under Secretary of Defense (Comptroller), *National Defense Budget Estimates for (Green Book) FY 2023,* July 2022, Table 7-5, https://

comptroller.defense.gov/Portals/45/Documents/defbudget/FY2023/FY23 _Green_Book.pdf; Seamus Daniels, "Assessing Trends in Military Personnel Costs," Center for Strategic and International Studies, September 9, 2021.

40. DoD, *National Defense Budget Estimates for FY 2023*, Table 7-6.

41. DoD, *National Defense Budget Estimates for FY 2023*, Tables 7-6 and 7-5.

42. Mackenzie Eaglen, "Cut the Pentagon's Civilian Workforce," *Breaking Defense*, April 30, 2014.

43. US Congressional Budget Office, "Long-Term Costs of the Administration's 2022 Defense Budget," January 2022.

44. Mackenzie Eaglen and Todd Harrison, "To Better Serve Personnel and Readiness, the Pentagon Should Shutter Its Personnel and Readiness Shop," *War on the Rocks*, November 3, 2017.

45. Mackenzie Eaglen, "A US Defense Budget That Makes China Smile," *1945*, July 27, 2021.

46. Frances Tilney Burke and Mackenzie Eaglen, "Is Veterans' Preference Bad for the National Security Workforce?" *War on the Rocks*, June 16, 2020; US Office of Personnel Management, *Employment of Veterans in the Federal Executive Branch: Fiscal Year 2020*, May 2022.

47. National Defense Strategy Commission, *Providing for the Common Defense: The Assessment and Recommendations of the National Defense Strategy Commission*, November 13, 2018.

48. Mackenzie Eaglen, "Shrinking Bureaucracy, Overhead, and Infrastructure: Why This Defense Drawdown Must Be Different for the Pentagon," American Enterprise Institute, March 2013.

49. Eaglen, "Shrinking Bureaucracy."

50. Eaglen and Harrison, "To Better Serve."

51. *Hearing before the Committee on Armed Services, US Senate, to Consider the Nominations of: Honorable Brad R. Carson to Be the Under Secretary of Defense for Personnel and Readiness; Jennifer M. O'Connor to Be the General Counsel of the Department of Defense; and Todd A. Weiler to Be an Assistant Secretary of Defense for Manpower and Reserve Affairs*, 114th Cong. (2016) (testimony by Brad Carson, to be Under Secretary of Defense for Personnel and Readiness).

52. Eaglen and Harrison, "To Better Serve."

53. DoD, *Fiscal Year (FY) 2023 Budget Estimates, Volume 1, Part 1 of 2, Justification for FY 2023 Operation and Maintenance, Defense-Wide*, April 2022, https:// comptroller.defense.gov/Portals/45/Documents/defbudget/fy2023/budget_jus tification/pdfs/01_Operation_and_Maintenance/O_M_VOL_1_PART_1/OM _Volume1_Part_1.pdf.

54. Brian Weeden, "Space Force Is More Important than Space Command," *War on the Rocks*, July 8, 2019.

55. Spencer Kaplan, "National Security Space Organizations 101," Center for Strategic and International Studies, July 14, 2022.

56. GAO, "Defense Management: DOD Should Collect More Stakeholder Input and Performance Data on Its Congressional Reporting Process," GAO-22-105183, February 10, 2022.

57. AcqNotes, "Acquisition Process: Selected Acquisition Report (SAR)," https://acqnotes.com/acqnote/acquisitions/selected-acquisition-report-sar.

58. Eaglen and Harrison, "To Better Serve."

59. Under Secretary of Defense for Personnel and Readiness, "Section 718 Report," Department of Defense, July 1, 2022, https://www.health.mil/Reference-Center/Reports/2022/07/01/Section-718.

60. Section 809 Panel, *Report of the Advisory Panel*, "Recommendation 2: Minimize Government-Unique Terms Applicable to Commercial Buying."

61. 41 USC Ch. 35, Truthful Cost or Pricing Data.

62. Section 809 Panel, *Report of the Advisory Panel*, "Recommendation 2."

63. Peter Levine and Bill Greenwalt, "What the 809 Panel Didn't Quite Get Right," *Breaking Defense*, April 4, 2019.

15

Reforming Defense Budgeting

Elaine McCusker

The defense budget is burdened with a significant and increasing number of programs and activities that do not produce military capability. Absent intervention, this trend is likely to continue. In addition, the defense budget is not structured to answer today's important management and oversight questions or to meet requirements at a speed of relevance for a modern ready force. The current budget structure does not easily tell us what we are spending on military capability and does not enable quickly producing and fielding the force we require.

As we rethink defense budgeting, it is useful to examine three key challenges. First, the Department of Defense (DoD) budget contains nearly $109 billion in spending that does not directly produce military capability. For context, even a fraction of this amount—$30 billion—could buy weapons and platforms that are critical for countering the pacing challenge of China and supporting the nation's deterrence and response missions, including one Virginia-class submarine, two Columbia-class submarines, 2,000 ground artillery rockets, 100 high-end fighters, and 500 armored multipurpose vehicles. Defense resources and attention are diffused among programs and spending that should be separated from defense spending or managed by domestic departments and agencies, including the Departments of State, Energy, Health and Human Services, Homeland Security, and Education and the Environmental Protection Agency.

Second, the definition of national security continues to expand such that the trend of adding noncore missions, programs, and activities to the defense budget is likely to grow. Along with the increasing costs of health care,

The views expressed in this chapter are solely those of the individual author and do not necessarily reflect the views of any organization with which they are, or have been, affiliated.

benefits, and compensation, the true cost of military capability is disguised and squeezed out by these other priorities.

Third, key characteristics of the defense budget need improvement. It should be transparent, responsive, and supportive of management and oversight functions. It should be flexible and agile in quickly adapting to and taking advantage of technological advances. Yet it currently struggles to do any of these things.

Evidence of these problems, which are not new, abounds. A closer examination of these challenges, all of which point to a need for change in the development, content, justification, and execution of the defense budget, is useful in illuminating key elements of potential solutions. What follows is a summary of each challenge and why it matters, followed by a section on potential solutions.

Diffusion of Defense Resourcing

Today's federal government does many things. Defense, as the federal government's only mandatory and exclusive job, should not be *a* priority; it should be *the* priority. Americans should understand what this priority costs. As we rethink defense budgeting, we should know how much of the budget is spent on compensation, benefits, and related activities necessary to support an all-volunteer force. We should be aware of the parts of the defense budget where nondefense spending resides and where DoD is diverted from its core function.

The notion of a "core function" is crucial. It means the things that DoD is expected to do and that only it can do, such as building a navy, army, air force, space force, and cyber proficiency capable of competing with China; sustaining and modernizing air, marine, ground, and special operations forces with power projection competence; and maintaining America's nuclear capabilities.

The definition of national security, and thereby defense, has expanded to include numerous other federal functions and missions. As a result, DoD and its budget have become an "easy button" to address problems that are not part of the DoD core mission and function. Some of these activities may seem small in the scheme of the overall budget, and many are worthy efforts. However, they artificially inflate the defense budget and distract from true defense priorities.

To get a clearer look at core defense spending, the recent report "Defense Budget Transparency and the Cost of Military Capability" divides the defense

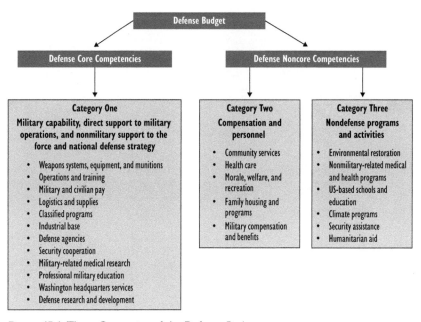

Figure 15.1 Three Categories of the Defense Budget

Source: Author's analysis of data from Department of Defense FY2023 budget documents.

budget into three categories.[1] Simply put, the categories are (1) core military competencies and the infrastructure necessary to manage the business; (2) indirect costs of supporting and retaining the all-volunteer force; and (3) nondefense programs and activities and extraneous missions assigned to DoD (see fig. 15.1).

Detailed analysis of budget justification documents submitted to Congress reveals that close to $109 billion in programs and activities are in the second two categories (see table 15.1). Though they support the force and may be important, they do not directly contribute to military capability and could be moved in favor of a reimagined defense budget that better meets national security needs.

For example, spending for must-pay expenses, including health care and compensation and benefits, could be treated as entitlement funding and moved to a separate budget. Then, programs that support the core mission of other federal departments and agencies could move to their appropriate organizations.

The remaining defense budget would contain programs and activities supporting the core mission and could then be updated to better reflect key

Table 15.1 Appropriation Title Breakdown

By Title	Budget Transparency (in $US millions)
Operations and maintenence (O&M)	$52,867
Military personnel	$38,649
Military construction	$2,683
Research, development, test, and evaluation (RDTE)	$1,057
Procurement	$572
Other (FTEs and revolving funds)	$12,733
Total Budget Transparency	$108,561

Source: Author's analysis of the Department of Defense budget, fiscal year 2023.

characteristics we need, including transparency, responsiveness, and reliable performance information for management and oversight. With the updated budget, we would finally, and with finality, attack long-term problems associated with the technology "valley of death" (where innovative technologies funded by DoD fail to make the transition from prototype to real capability), joint program integration, byzantine acquisition and financial processes, and other systems.

The Diffusion Trend Continues

Recent strategic documents confirm that the trend of increasing noncore spending in the defense budget described above is likely to continue. The National Security Strategy bluntly declares what had previously been strongly implied and directed through the budget submissions: everything is national security.[2] Domestic issues are national security. Environmental issues are national security. Social issues are national security. Once dividing lines are broken down between foreign and domestic policy, the strategy points to far-reaching investments here at home in our industrial and innovation base that will increase our competitiveness and better position us to deal with everything from climate to global health, to food security, to energy.[3]

This expanding definition is driven by three fundamental purposes. It justifies continuing to load the must-pass defense policy and appropriations bills with domestic programs that may not otherwise receive support. It sanctions applying the expert, can-do military planning and management culture to complex domestic challenges that require such a disciplined approach but that should be managed by domestic agencies. And, it waters down a core defense mission that does not appear to have the interest, understanding, or support of liberal Democrats. For example, the House Defense Appropriations Subcommittee chairwoman called defense appropriations a "jobs bill" during the 117th Congress, essentially blurting out the truth of what she thought would prompt her conference to support the bill.

Though the federal government, including domestic departments and agencies, should focus on the nation's security, each should contribute through their assigned missions in education, energy, the environment, and health. Those missions should not be assigned to the Pentagon. Doing so further blurs the lines and budgets between defense and nondefense programs and activities, increasing the diversion of defense spending from military capabilities to domestic concerns.

The nation's security—and economic competitiveness—require an educated and skilled workforce in critical areas such as cyber, data analytics, artificial intelligence, microelectronics, engineering, and languages. We should focus the Department of Education on producing a workforce with the national security skills we need, not add this task to the DoD mission. Doing so not only distracts DoD from its core mission, it forces DoD to assume the mission of another department, and it inflates the defense budget, which is particularly damaging if budget agreements continue to require parity between defense and nondefense spending.

The tendency to rely on defense capabilities and funding is increasingly widespread. The same strain noted on education occurs with energy, environmental, and medical priorities.

Other federal agencies with more technical expertise in these respective areas should take the lead on these efforts and ensure that their management systems are effective. Assigning these responsibilities to DoD results in an overinflated sense of what the nation is spending for its security and diffuses attention from military capabilities.

For example, the federal government has an agency—the Environmental Protection Agency (EPA)—assigned to "protect[ing] human health and the environment."[4] With its specific mission, designated expertise, and accountability for performance in that area, EPA should receive the funding it needs, which is now included in the defense budget for environmental cleanup and restoration, climate change, and related research.

The National Institutes of Health, under the Department of Health and Human Services, has the mission to "seek fundamental knowledge about the nature and behavior of living systems and the application of that knowledge to enhance health, lengthen life, and reduce illness and disability."[5] As such, it is conducting basic and applied medical research on cancer and autism, among other things. DoD should not be duplicating this important work.

There is also a second-order corrosive effect of the habit of deferring to defense planning, management, and response expertise. Assigning non-defense missions to the Pentagon has ramifications for civilian-military relations. As the military is asked to perform nonmilitary activities, the lines between military and civilian roles and responsibilities get blurred, which risks damaging the military's historical, appropriate place in society.

The Further Case for Defense Budget Reform

In addition to the problem of defense resources and attention being diffused to programs and activities that do not produce military capability, as described above, the defense budget is not structured to adapt to strategic priorities or answer today's key management and oversight questions. It is not responsive in supporting modernization timelines and the innovation and industrial base resilience necessary to produce the military capacity and capability we need.

Strategy and Resourcing

Budgets that truly reflect new stated strategic priorities are notably difficult to achieve. A large percentage of the budget in any given year is committed by decisions made in past years to proceed with planned procurements, conduct directed operations and tasks, operate and sustain existing capabilities, and provide pay and benefits to the current force.[6] The rest is often rebranded or recategorized into new stated priorities rather than actually shifted to new things, making it difficult to achieve or demonstrate real change.

The inflexibility innate in the requirements, budgeting, and acquisition processes produces programs of record with a priority of sticking to planned execution rather than adapting to better alternatives to achieve intended outcomes.

For example, the current structure can tell you if you are spending money the way you said you would, and it incentivizes doing so, but it can't quickly tell you if that spending is producing the outcome you intended. Nor can the structure tell you how closely that spending is really aligned to your strategic objectives or if your budget is even sufficient to support those objectives. And if funding is insufficient to meet strategic requirements, the budget structure is not helpful in describing the nature and timing of the risk incurred due to the strategy-resourcing mismatch.

Transparency, Agility, and Responsiveness

Evidenced by perpetual management challenges and reorganization, manual data calls that gather information in an unreliable and nonrepeatable way, program and process workarounds, and detailed congressional direction and reporting requirements, the budget is also not as transparent and responsive as it needs to be in supporting program management or in answering key oversight questions.[7]

Congress is routinely dissatisfied with the level of transparency provided by the reams of data the Pentagon produces to justify its budget, so it continues to pile on new exhibits and reporting requirements in the hopes of getting what it needs to conduct its important oversight functions.

The fiscal year 2023 defense authorization and appropriations bills contain more than five thousand pages of statute and committee report direction. Despite the fact that some of the legislative sections have nothing to do with defense (the authorization bill contains an entire division entitled "Non-Department of Defense Matters"), the frustration coming from Congress is clear and leads to legislating something as basic as a briefing request.

There is also plenty of evidence that the current budget structure and process are not serving the needs of today's military.[8] Numerous reports, papers, conferences, webinars, DoD pilot programs and special funds, and congressional language and direction tell us about the challenges we face.[9] We have opportunities to address defense industrial base issues, lag times in modernization, missed opportunities that create a technology transition "valley of death," lost buying power due to expiring and canceling funds caught up in a labyrinth of different appropriations ("colors of money"), budget line items, activities, and program elements with varying periods of availability (life of funds).[10] All of these challenges connect to a lack of responsiveness and agility in the current planning, programming, budgeting, and execution (PPBE) process.

In an attempt to understand the overall effectiveness of the Pentagon PPBE process and why what seem to be fundamental questions about program cost and performance are so difficult to answer, Congress established a commission, which is currently underway and which one commissioner noted has an "incredible opportunity to scale and tailor the PPBE process to match the pace and innovation in order to accelerate capability to the warfighter."[11]

Further emphasizing the central importance of the defense PPBE process to our national security, the often-quoted National Security Commission on Artificial Intelligence said: "Unless the requirements, budgeting, and acquisition processes are aligned to permit faster and more targeted execution, the US will fail to stay ahead of potential adversaries."[12] This blunt recommendation to the Defense Department makes clear the urgency for cultural and structural updates to the way the department currently does business.

The department recognizes it is often slow to take advantage of innovative opportunities and has created, often with congressional support, numerous funds and offices over the years to work around its own systems. The latest attempts—Rapid Defense Experimentation Reserve (RDER) and the Office of Strategic Capital—are just getting started but are likely to struggle to institute substantive lasting change without a fundamental shift in the culture of how requirements, resourcing, and acquisition decisions are made.[13] Once process workarounds are institutionalized into the system, they become part of the system and fall victim to the same cultural, governance, and process delays that prompted their creation in the first place.

The challenges are well documented. The level of focus and understanding on them may be reaching levels required to produce actionable solutions and actual action to achieve them.

Characteristics of a Reformed Budget

Despite all the challenges noted here, the planning, programming, budgeting, and execution processes developed over decades served a fundamental purpose—obtaining the resources necessary to provide for the common defense. What worked to bring us here won't work well to take us further.

We can't stop time and start over with a blank piece of paper, but we can do something similar and just as powerful. We can harvest what has worked and what we have learned to build a reimagined budget that is also capable of further reform.

We should first consider principles for what we expect from the defense budget. What should be in it? What characteristics should it exhibit? How should it be structured, assessed, and conveyed?

The budget for defense in a constitutionally based federal democratic republic should adhere to the fundamental intent described at the start of this chapter, with national defense as the priority. It should be transparent (with necessary classification exceptions) to the nation's people and their elected representatives. It must be accountable to the laws governing its structure and the activities it supports without adding undue restrictions to those laws. It should enable definition and acceptance of well-defined risk in decision making—specifically, what risk, to whom, for how long? It should be agile, resilient, and responsive. It must reflect and support the way the military will evolve and operate—digital, jointly, and in coalitions. It should be developed, analyzed, presented, and assessed with outcomes at the forefront.

How do we get to this budget structure utopia? Incrementally, boldly, relentlessly, and in partnership with Congress.

First, we need to clear out the non-core-mission programs and activities that have complicated the budget structure and diffused resources and attention from core programs. I recommend a direct approach to doing this:

- Align current defense programs that are the primary mission of other organizations to those organizations. Programs found to be of lesser priority should be ended, at least at the federal level.
- Move entitlement-like spending embedded in the defense budget (health care, compensation, and benefits) that do not produce military capability to a separate budget for management and execution.

Once non-core-mission funding is removed from the defense budget, we should also prioritize federal domestic spending to support the nation's security. For example, the Department of Education should focus resources on vibrant, interactive primary, secondary, and workforce education and training in skill sets the nation needs for long-term security and economic vitality.

Second, we need to modify and update the budget to support the way programs should be developed, tested, and procured today and to easily—and automatically—answer key management and oversight questions. These updates must fix the key problems noted above related to speed, transparency, responsiveness, and alignment to strategy.

Ultimately, the new budget structure would remove or reduce artificial barriers like shares of the budget between the Military Departments, "color of money," life of funds, budget activities, program elements, and programs of record. These would be replaced with capability management and real-time, dynamic tools that provide visibility on program performance, status, and progress in producing outcomes. Elements of this new budget structure would include the following key characteristics.

Joint Capability-Focused Budgets

Joint development of capability-oriented budgets—not service-specific plat-forms—that include the Combatant Commands (COCOMs) and Joint Staff are a broad and necessary reform. This approach would reduce and combine program elements and budgets under outcome-focused management and mitigate the friction between capability providers and COCOM demand signals. If budgets are unable to support requirements, then defined risk would be accepted or strategies would need to be adjusted—as would COCOM-directed tasks—to avoid the current and perpetual strategy-resource mismatch as well as the cognitive dissonance that takes place during program/budget review when we try to pretend such a mismatch does not exist.

The reduction of budget divisions and the resulting flexibility would release program managers from sticking to old plans and instead incentivize exploration.[14] Programs not dedicated to a specific program or weapons system would support the integration of existing systems, the insertion of new technologies, and the creation of new operational concepts that would allow the department to competitively improve warfighting outcomes now rather than waiting years for new weapons systems, thereby possibly also eliminating the technology valley of death.

As programmers and program managers are the center of gravity in rescuing innovations from the valley of death, we need to alter the expectation that they can predict the future and instead allow them to adapt to it *and* take advantage of it. The concept would also better mirror a modular rather than program-of-record approach pursued by industry partners.

Biennial Budget

We should take another shot at a biennial budget process to fully incorporate program performance and strategic direction into budget development. Strategic direction would need to be clear and actionable. Substantial funds would be held back from programming for a program/budget review that is not crammed into the end of the calendar year. Combining this change with reforms to the budget itself that allow for—and actually encourage—changes to proposed plans to incorporate innovative solutions that could not have been known during plan development would contribute to a cultural change in favor of outcomes management, not just budget execution.

Each year's Program Objective Memorandum (POM) development process should have past performance as the first question, bullet, assessment, and fact on every decision brief. What changed? What are the lifetime operations and sustainment cost projections with key drivers and unknowns? Where and when will technology refresh occur? The "planned vs. actual" facts and figures should be easily generated from a budget and financial system supporting management and decision making. They should not be tough questions to answer, requiring mostly manual, nonrepeatable data calls as they do now.

Data is power. Efforts to create a single data analytics system (Advana) to harness the power of the financial, budget, personnel, contracts, logistics, information, readiness, and property data now available in the myriad of systems should be expanded and accelerated.

The new structure and the accompanying generation of timely, reliable, and responsive program data would support congressional oversight responsibilities. It could also potentially create some useful temporary new friction related to committee jurisdictional divisions. Noting the plan in the 118th Congress for a China-focused forum to cross committee lines, policy makers are already aware that improvements to the oversight structure are necessary as well.[15]

The proposed changes are not easy or straightforward, or we would have made them by now. There are reasons for how things currently are and numerous stakeholders who must participate in creating the necessary changes.

The first set of changes—moving noncore or entitlement-like efforts out of the defense budget—should be achievable relatively quickly, in one to two budget cycles. The second set of changes—reforming how the budget is developed, managed, assessed, and conveyed—will take more time (three to four budget cycles), as well as concentrated leadership and focused partnership with Congress.

Concluding Thoughts

Ultimately, we would never want budget or funding solutions to consume a large quantity of time or attention. Funding should be a positive background enabler to the military mission, not a time-consuming hurdle to capability or program outcomes.

That said, our form of government also requires a strong emphasis on stewardship. The money being spent belongs to the American taxpayer. As such, we always need to keep in mind three basic things: First, funds must be used consistent with the strategy. Second, we should get a dollar's worth of value for every dollar spent, and investments should produce the outcomes the nation needs. Third is transparency and accountability. The defense budget structure must enable each element of stewardship, which is foundational to trust in the use of taxpayer funds.

Finally, I could not conclude this chapter without also mentioning the critical requirement that the budget structure support budget agreements that avoid the damages of continuing resolutions, which carry last year's funding and priorities into the next year when Congress fails to act on annual appropriations bills.[16] Implementation of the most productive and successful defense budgeting modernization effort for speed, agility, responsiveness, and transparency won't matter without budget agreements that enable on-time enactment of annual appropriations. The Defense Department has operated under continuing resolutions for sixteen hundred days since fiscal year 2010. The latest iteration, from October 1 to December 23, 2022, cost the department $17 billion in buying power plus time that can't be bought back.

The defense budget is not just about dollars and cents. It is at the core of our nation's security and the safety of those who provide it. We know that reform is needed. We should agree on fundamental desired characteristics of the ultimate outcome, some of which are outlined here. Then, we must simply begin.

Notes

1. Elaine McCusker, "Defense Budget Transparency and the Cost of Military Capability," American Enterprise Institute Report, November 9, 2022.

2. The White House, "National Security Strategy," October 2022.

3. Jake Sullivan quoted in Aamer Madhani, "Biden Global Strategy Tackles China, Russia, Domestic Needs," *The Independent* (US Edition), October 13, 2022.

4. US Environmental Protection Agency, "Our Mission and What We Do," June 13, 2022.

5. US National Institutes of Health, "Mission and Goals," July 27, 2017.

6. Mackenzie Eaglen, "The Paradox of Scarcity in a Defense Budget of Largesse," American Enterprise Institute Report, July 18, 2022.

7. Jaspreet Gill, "Pentagon Seeks More 'Jointness' for JADC2 as OSD Stands Up New Office," *Breaking Defense*, October 27, 2022; US Department of Defense (DoD), "Department of Defense Disestablishes Chief Management Office," press release, September 3, 2021; DoD, "Executive Summary: DoD Data Strategy," September 30, 2020; DoD, Office of the Under Secretary of Defense for Acquisition and Sustainment, "DoD Instruction 5000.81: Urgent Capability Acquisition," December 31, 2019; National Defense Authorization Act for Fiscal Year 2023, H.R. 7900, 117th Cong. (2022), see Subtitle C—Plans, Reports, and Other Matters.

8. Day One Project, "Relevant Literature," https://www.dayoneproject.org/defense-budget/relevant-literature.

9. Eric Lofgren, Jerry McGinn, and Lloyd Everhart, "Execution Flexibility and Bridging the Valley of Death: An Acquisition Next Report," George Mason University Center for Government Contracting, October 26, 2022.

10. National Defense Authorization Act for 2023 (H.R. 7900), Subtitle E, "Industrial Base Matters"; William C. Greenwalt and Dan Patt, "Competing in Time: Ensuring Capability Advantage and Mission Success through Adaptable Resource Allocation," Hudson Institute, February 25, 2021; Elaine McCusker and Emily Coletta, "What We Can Learn from the Government Accountability Office's Unused Funds Report," American Enterprise Institute, *AEIdeas*, May 26, 2021; Matt MacGregor, Greg Grant, and Peter Modigliani, "Five First Steps to a Modern Defense Budgeting System," MITRE Center for Data-Driven Policy, August 1, 2022, https://www.mitre.org.

11. Commission on PPBE Reform, https://ppbereform.senate.gov; Commission on PPBE Reform, "A Status Report from the Commission on Planning, Programming, Budgeting, and Execution (PPBE) Reform," undated, accessed March 15, 2023.

12. National Security Commission on Artificial Intelligence, "Final Report," March 2021.

13. DoD, Office of the Under Secretary of Defense for Research and Engineering, "Rapid Defense Experimentation Reserve," undated, accessed March 15, 2023; DoD, "Memorandum for Senior Pentagon Leadership, Commanders of the Combatant Commands, Defense Agency and DoD Field Activity Directors: Establishment of the Office of Strategic Capital," December 1, 2022, https://media.defense.gov/2022/Dec/01/2003123982/-1/-1/1/ESTABLISHMENT-OF-THE-OFFICE-OF-STRATEGIC-CAPITAL.PDF.

14. Elaine McCusker and Dan Patt, "Faster Weapon Buys: Try Evolutionary Innovation," American Enterprise Institute, op-ed, July 2, 2021.

15. Congressman Mike Gallagher, "Gallagher Announced as Chairman of Select Committee on China," press release, December 8, 2022.

16. Elaine McCusker, "Another Continuing Resolution? The Enemy Is Us," *Breaking Defense*, December 8, 2022.

16

US Defense Budget Reform
Historical Perspectives (1940s–2020s)

Mark R. Wilson

Introduction

In recent months, politicians and other policy makers have stepped up their criticisms of the US defense budgeting system. Many commentators have suggested that just when US strategy is turning to a long-run competition with China, the entire national security enterprise, including the defense budget process, is insufficiently agile. Some of these critics, who include business leaders, elected officials, and defense acquisition specialists, have further suggested that the defense budget system is a lumbering relic of the Cold War "industrial era" wedded to Stalinist "central planning," totally unsuitable for translating today's post-industrial technologies into military capabilities.[1] Summing up this critique, one recent study concluded that the current system is unacceptable. "Given the accelerated modernization of advanced peer rival militaries, rapid technology refresh, and other critical factors," a MITRE study team declared in 2022, "[the Department of Defense] cannot afford to continue the current budgeting processes."[2]

Some of today's reformers focus on the limitations of the Pentagon's decades-old planning, programming, budgeting, and execution sequence, now known as PPBES, which was launched in 1961.[3] Informed by the recent critiques of the Pentagon's lack of agility, Congress used the FY2022 defense authorization act to establish a new legislative commission dedicated to PPBE reform. In theory, the work of this body could lead to major changes in the workings of the annual ritual of defense budgeting, at least on the side of the Department of Defense (DoD), which in recent years has employed an estimated twenty-five thousand people on budgeting work.[4]

The views expressed in this chapter are solely those of the individual author and do not necessarily reflect the views of any organization with which they are, or have been, affiliated.

Other reformers insist that much of the blame for slow acquisitions and other dysfunctions rests with Congress. Indeed, recent Pentagon leaders have been blunt about their contempt for legislators when it comes to the work of the defense budget. Robert Gates (secretary of defense from 2006 to 2011) regarded Congress's repeated failures to pass defense budgets on time as an "outrageous dereliction of duty" by a legislative body that has become overwhelmingly "uncivil, incompetent, . . . micromanagerial, hypocritical, [and] egotistical."[5] One of Gates's successors, the late Ash Carter (secretary of defense from 2015 to 2017), expressed similar disgust, calling Congress's annual defense authorization bills as "mostly meaningless" gestures, failing to provide the military with prompt appropriations while creating "a preposterous level of micromanagement."[6]

Given the widespread worries that today's US defense budgeting system is inadequate for twenty-first-century needs and has become more dysfunctional over time, it is worth reviewing some relevant history. This paper surveys the history of successful and failed efforts to reform the US defense budget since World War II. It is organized chronologically, as it reviews a series of episodes or moments from the beginning of the Cold War through the 2010s and early 2020s. These individual episodes may serve as reminders of the origins of key elements of today's systems—such as the Pentagon's PPBES or Congress's current practice of having the line-item details of each budget scrutinized annually by both authorizers and appropriators. Understanding when and why these specific institutions were born and in what context may be helpful to today's would-be reformers.

At the same time, the historical episodes covered in this paper may also be read as cases of certain varieties of reform efforts, which have echoed across time. In most of these episodes, reformers pursued one or more of four broad goals: coherence, adequacy, stability, and agility. Most would-be reformers today prioritize agility, as they worry about equipping the US military and its allies with fast-changing technologies in the context of a great-power competition with China. Some of today's reformers are also concerned about sheer adequacy—whether the budget's size may be significantly too small (or too big). Such concerns about agility and adequacy also troubled reformers in the past, starting with the early Cold War years of the late 1940s and early 1950s.

Past policy makers have also often been concerned with budget stability, which frequently proved elusive, not only because of waves of higher and lower defense spending but also because of Congress's annual line-item interventions, hard budget caps and sequestrations, and failure to provide timely appropriations. Finally, past reformers have repeatedly been concerned with the budget's coherence, especially whether it was organized rationally in a way that could overcome parochial concerns and promote the national interest, along with a good understanding of actual costs.

An overview of the relevant history calls attention to important past cases and can also illuminate longer-run structural transformations. A long-run perspective on modern US defense budget reform seems to offer plenty of support for those who contend that the current system is overdue for a major overhaul. Indeed, most of the elements of today's system were developed during the 1950s–1970s period. Many of the weaknesses of the system being decried now, and many of the proposed solutions being suggested today, were already widely discussed by the 1980s. It is certainly possible to imagine that the time has finally come for a major reconstruction of the half-century-old budgeting system as the United States moves ahead with what would appear to be an expensive new long-run great-power competition.

On the other hand, the impressive endurance of the old defense budgeting system, now several decades beyond the Cold War, may suggest that the most likely outcome in the coming years will not be a radical revision but additional minor modifications. Since the 1980s, we have witnessed the end of the Cold War; the September 11 attacks; wars in Afghanistan and Iraq; a supposed revolution in military technologies; and the recent strategic pivot to focus on Russia and China. All or any of these developments might be considered disruptive enough to inspire a major restructuring of the defense budgeting enterprise, such as the one realized during the early Cold War. But that never occurred. Instead, Congress and the Pentagon have made do with a variety of more modest shifts in acquisition and budgeting practices, which, together with world-beating levels of defense expenditures, might be understood as having delivered good-enough levels of security. It seems quite possible that in the absence of a truly large new global security shock or unanticipated shift in domestic politics, the US defense budgeting system may continue to stumble forward for many years to come, using supplements and workarounds, as it has done since the end of the Cold War, rather than achieving comprehensive reform.

Regardless of the specific lessons it might appear to offer about the best or most likely paths forward, a review of the relevant history may inspire today's reformers in the direction of more open-minded curiosity as well as humility. Time and again, past reformers on various sides have described existing defense budgets as woefully inadequate or tragically excessive; some have insisted that the budgeting and acquisition system needed to become far more agile and decentralized, while others demanded that it was more important for the system to become more coordinated and stable. In retrospect, a sizable fraction of the calls for major reform over the past seven decades looks to have been based on overestimates of external threats or exaggerations of the budgeting system's flaws. Even if today's reformers fail in the coming months to correct what they understand as the most serious weaknesses of our Cold War–vintage budgeting system, we may take some solace in knowing that in the face of so many profound uncertainties about the future security environment, a radically overhauled system might not end up being preferable to one that continued business as usual, with minor adjustments.

Foundational Reforms, the Late 1940s–Early 1980s

Policy makers in the 2020s are working with a US defense budget process developed during the Cold War. The period between the late 1940s and the early 1980s saw a series of fundamental reforms, encompassing huge changes in the size and organization of the defense budget and the budget process for the Pentagon and Congress. Most major elements of the current systems, and awareness of the weaknesses of those systems and ideas for reform, were already in place by the 1980s, about four decades ago.

Dawn of the Cold War: Redefining Budget Categories and Reassessing Adequacy, 1948–60

At the start of the 1950s, the US defense budget was overhauled from two directions. On the one hand, the Defense Department, established in 1947, worked to consolidate the budget and make it more coherent by replacing a decades-old system of hundreds of legacy appropriation line items with a smaller number of functional categories. At the same time, the sheer size of the base defense budget was seeing a massive expansion in response to the intensification of the Cold War, including the start of the Korean War in 1950. By the end of President Dwight Eisenhower's first year in office (1953–54), the US defense budget radically differed from just five years earlier. Although there were powerful pressures to increase the budget further during the second half of the 1950s, Eisenhower mostly resisted those new attacks on adequacy. The size and shape of the budget, and the budget process, would not see major changes until the new administration's arrival in 1961.

One part of this story, the near-tripling of the base defense budget in the early years of the Cold War, has long been familiar to historians, political scientists, and policy makers. In the late 1940s, the Truman administration and most members of Congress agreed that the nation, which was starting to pay down its giant World War II debt, could afford an annual DoD budget of only around $12 to $15 billion, or about 5 to 6 percent of GDP. By the mid-1950s, after the United States had demobilized from the Korean War emergency, and despite President Eisenhower's fiscal conservatism and his embrace of a relatively cheap "New Look" strategy relying heavily on nuclear weapons, the new base DoD budget was settling in at $35 to $40 billion, or roughly 10 percent of GDP. Remarkably, the United States had embraced the near-tripling of the defense budget that had been called for by Cold War hawks such as Paul Nitze in the United States Objectives and Programs for National Security (better known as NSC-68) report, completed before the start of the Korean War. This larger defense budget, which allowed for a global military superpower, has persisted in real dollar terms over the long run, even as defense spending as a fraction of GDP has declined (see figs. 16.1 and 16.2).

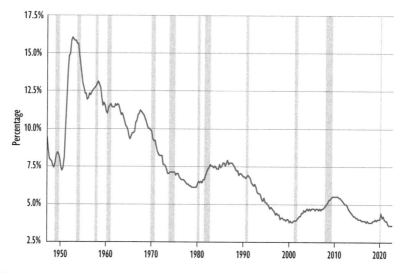

Figure 16.1 National Defense Spending as a Percentage of GDP, 1947–2022

Notes: Shaded areas indicate US recessions. Includes defense-related spending by non-DoD agencies.
Source: US Bureau of Economic Analysis, via Federal Reserve Economic Data, Federal Reserve Bank of St. Louis (FRED), http://fred.stlouisfed.org.

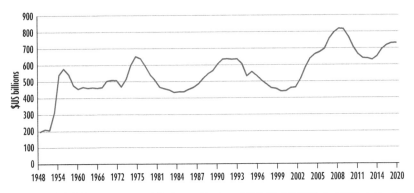

Figure 16.2 US Department of Defense Outlays, FY1948–FY2022 (in 2022 dollars)

Source: US Department of Defense, Office of the Under Secretary of Defense (Comptroller), *National Defense Budget Estimates for FY 2022 (Green Book)*, August 2021, Table 6-12, pages 151–57.

The story of NSC-68 and the jump in the US defense budget in the early Cold War has been described at length by countless scholars, so it need not be reviewed in detail here. For our purposes, it may be enough to briefly address what caused such a remarkable change in consensus about the adequacy of the size of the base defense budget. After all, the 2020s' equivalent of an NSC-68 would be recommending that the US defense budget be hiked to $2 trillion. The short answer is that policy makers and voters had their sensibilities altered by a remarkable series of global events between 1948 and 1950, including the coup in Czechoslovakia, the first Soviet atomic bomb test, the birth of the People's Republic of China, Kim Il-Sung's invasion of southern Korea, and—perhaps most important of all—developments in the opening weeks of the Korean War, including President Harry Truman's decision to take the US and its allies to war, and China's intervention in the conflict.[7]

The record of the Truman years seemed to suggest that evidence of growing external threats caused fundamental reassessments of the adequacy of the US defense budget. However, the Eisenhower years showed that warnings of dire inadequacies were sometimes overblown and could be resisted. As countless scholars have noted, the President's fiscal conservatism informed the Eisenhower administration's New Look strategy, which relied on nuclear weapons rather than expensive large conventional sources. Soon after taking office, Eisenhower told his National Security Council they would seek "more security for less dollars." In Eisenhower's mind, as Secretary of Defense Robert S. McNamara would later explain, "fiscal security was the true foundation of military security." Using the New Look, the Eisenhower administration lowered the defense budget to about $36 billion.[8]

From 1956 through the end of his second term, Eisenhower resisted intense pressures, from the Joint Chiefs of Staff, expert commissions, and leading members of Congress, for another big jump in the size of the defense budget. Before and after the news of Sputnik (October 1957), congressional investigations claimed that the US was falling behind the Soviet Union in the quality and quantity of bomber aircraft and missiles. In 1958, Senator John F. Kennedy blamed President Eisenhower for putting "fiscal security ahead of national security."[9] From 1958 to 1960, a Democratic Party–controlled Congress did force the Eisenhower administration to spend a few more billion dollars on these systems, including the Atlas and Titan ICBMs, Polaris submarines and missiles, and the B-70 bomber. But Eisenhower (whose deficit hawk instincts were supplemented with knowledge from intelligence reports that the alleged "bomber gap" and "missile gap" were myths) refused to condone large budget increases. He refused to implement the recommendations of new NSC-68-style calls for large new expenditures, including those of the Gaither Report and Rockefeller Brothers Fund report of 1958, which called for the defense budget to be raised immediately by around 20 or 25 percent.[10]

These struggles over adequacy in the post–World War II defense budget, which ended with large increases in the Korean War years but no second big jump in the late 1950s, were inseparable from tax policy. In 1948, Congress overrode President Truman's veto to provide a substantial tax cut. During the Korean War, taxes were hiked back up, close to the levels of World War II. During the Eisenhower years, the new defense budget level of $35 billion or more meant that Congress could not restore tax rates to where they had been in the late 1940s. Instead, high World War II–style rates prevailed for over a decade until the Kennedy-Johnson cuts of the early 1960s (see fig. 16.3). When his critics called for higher defense spending in the late 1950s, Eisenhower, in effect, challenged them to raise taxes even higher, to pay for a new buildup. Congress proved unwilling to go that far.[11]

Although the unprecedented jump in the size of the base defense budget stands as the most remarkable budget "reform" of the early Cold War years, it is also worth remembering that this same period saw an overhaul of the composition of the defense budget, as it was formulated by the DoD and presented to Congress. This was the transition away from the huge number of decades-old appropriations lines largely tied to the military services' technical bureaus in favor of using a smaller number of broader "functional" categories. This radical

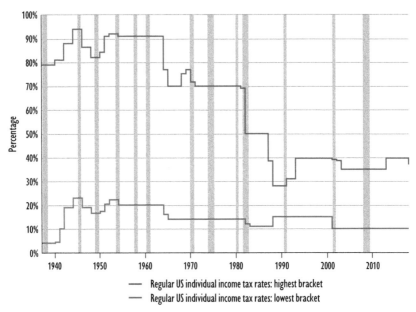

Figure 16.3 Rates of Highest and Lowest Individual Income Tax Brackets, 1937–2018

Note: Shaded areas indicate US recessions.

Source: US Department of the Treasury and Internal Revenue Service, via Federal Reserve Economic Data, Federal Reserve Bank of St. Louis (FRED), http://fred.stlouisfed.org.

reform, in favor of consolidation and greater DoD discretion, was undertaken in 1949–51, concurrent with the massive increase in the budget's size.

The consolidation of defense budget lines of the early 1950s was demanded by Section 4 of the National Security Act of 1949, which called for "performance budgeting" while providing the Pentagon with a comptroller. This reform followed the recent recommendations of the Hoover Commission, which concluded that the Pentagon should create "a budget based upon functions, activities, and projects." In the late 1940s, there were still hundreds of separate appropriations lines, including small ones for newspapers and water coolers or individual claims, as well as giant ones such as those covering pay and subsistence for entire services. Individual installations, such as the National Naval Medical Center in Bethesda, Maryland, relied on dozens of budget lines from a dozen major appropriation titles. As the Pentagon's first comptroller recalled, it took "269 pots of money" to run a single hospital. The Hoover Commission recommended that all these could be consolidated under a single appropriation, perhaps labeled medical care.[12]

Embracing the Hoover Commission report, and empowered by the 1949 legislation, Pentagon comptroller Wilfred McNeil crafted a new kind of defense budget, emphasizing broad "functional" categories. By the eve of the Korean War, in May 1950, McNeil and his team had already drafted a budget comprising major appropriations titles, including personnel, military construction, research and development, procurement, and operation and maintenance. It was a historical shift, which has endured to the present day, in how the budget was organized and understood by the Pentagon and Congress. It was part of a broader reorganization of power in the military services, away from the old technical bureaus, in favor of the general staff. Although this consolidation of budget categories took years to accomplish and never achieved true "performance" budgeting (in which results and costs could be visualized), it was nonetheless a major, lasting reform.[13]

The 1950 move to a more "functional" defense budget with consolidated appropriations lines meant that Congress further delegated authority to the DoD. The change to the new functional categories confused some legislators, who already felt incapable of matching the expertise of military officers and executive branch officials.[14] McNeil, the Pentagon comptroller, would recall that the use of large functional categories only worked because he had a strong relationship with congressional appropriations committees, which were willing to trust his active management of the budget.[15]

Congress was relatively deferential and generous to the Pentagon in the 1950s, a decade that saw some spectacularly successful development and production of weapons systems, such as the F-100 fighter and Polaris submarines and missiles. However, we should be wary of imagining the 1950s—an era before the rise of PPBS and congressional micromanagement—as a time when defense budgeting and acquisition were fantastically agile. Defense policy makers of the 1950s still faced the annual appropriations cycle; they dealt with massive uncertainties about future external threats and technological change and struggled to balance the benefits and costs of sequential and concurrent acquisition methods.[16] As McNeil recalled, "With the Middle East blowing up, with the vacuum in Greece, and the British pulling out of Lebanon and Palestine, and so forth—with changes like that occurring, I was bothered very much by the time it took between developing a force plan and actually getting the money to implement it. It was just impossible."[17] As one careful study of 1950s defense acquisition noted, "the units administering weapons programs must submit their financial requirements some three to five years in advance of expected expenditure dates, despite all the technological and strategic uncertainties to which they are subject."[18] Ultra-rapid major weapons development stories such as the F-100 and Polaris, which saw the systems fielded three years after the start of design work, are cited by some would-be reformers in our day as models for twenty-first-century acquisition but even in the 1950s, they were the exception, not the rule.[19] Average acquisition cycles were closer to a full decade long, which caused widespread fears in the 1950s that the United States and its allies would fall behind the Soviet Union, which allegedly could field new weapons in half the time.[20]

Overhauling DoD Processes: The Creation and Modification of PPBS, 1961–70

The US defense budget was overhauled again in 1961 by a new Pentagon team led by the forty-four-year-old secretary of defense, Robert S. McNamara. The Pentagon's new way of budgeting was organized around PPBS, which took a step toward functional-performance budgeting by grouping expenditures by entire cross-service military missions. It also used five-year plans as part of an effort to measure the long-run costs of defense investments better. Under McNamara, PPBS involved a major shift in power away from the individual military services and toward civilian analysts. In 1969–70, the PPBS system was modified by Secretary of Defense Melvin Laird and his deputy, David Packard, in ways that restored some budgeting power to the military services. Although there have been various efforts since 1970 to reform the PPBS (now called PPBE), today's system is not much different from the one in place a half century ago.

McNamara entered office in 1961 intent on making major disruptions to routine Pentagon practices, using quantitative analysis to challenge existing routines, just as he and his fellow "whiz kids" had done at the Ford Motor Co. in the years after World War II. When he looked at the existing defense budget, McNamara saw a system in which the air force, navy, and army had been awarded slices of the expenditure pie and allowed to develop their own budget requests without much concern for the broader military mission and the national interest. "The results," McNamara recalled, "could be described fairly as chaotic. . . . Our new form of budget for the first time grouped together for planning purposes units which must fight together in the event of war."[21] Parochial budgeting by the services caused overlapping and potentially redundant programs in areas such as ballistic missiles and also systematic underinvestment in some important areas, such as antisubmarine warfare, ammunition, spare parts, and tactical air support. To help him create a more rational budget, McNamara recruited a new comptroller, Charles Hitch. As chief of the economics division at the RAND Corporation, Hitch had already been working for years on ways to have the defense budget better comprehend long-term "total system costs" and become organized more by military "outputs," or missions.[22]

In 1961–62, McNamara and Hitch and their team installed PPBS, which set up new budgeting processes and categories in the Pentagon without doing much to alter the structure of the defense budget used by Congress. The newest element in PPBS was the "programming" phase, which was needed in part because McNamara and Hitch decided it would be too difficult to present Congress with a budget that abandoned the five large functional categories (such as personnel or procurement), organized by service, that had been established by McNeil just one decade earlier. As Hitch explained it, with regard to the document the administration sent to Congress at the beginning of the calendar year, "We decided to leave the budget structure undisturbed."[23] However, within the Pentagon, the "programming" phase of PPBS saw the military's various activities grouped under "major programs" (originally nine in number), including strategic systems, general purpose forces, airlift and sealift, and research and development. The broad programs comprised nearly one thousand smaller "program elements," such as individual tactical air wings.[24] The size, cost, and personnel requirements of the programs and program elements were estimated for five to eight years into the future to create a Five-Year Defense Plan. According to the McNamara-Hitch team, PPBS and the Five-Year Defense Plan allowed them to make rational decisions about the best use of defense dollars by examining strategic priorities and long-range cost-effectiveness simultaneously.[25]

The PPBS clearly created more work for the services and the Office of the Secretary of Defense but did not radically increase the length of the budget cycle. As noted above, in the 1950s, observers were already complaining that expenditures lagged original plans by a matter of years. Under PPBS, the major planning documents, such as the Joint Strategic Objectives Plan created by the Joint Chiefs of Staff and the secretary of defense's "tentative force guidance" sent to the services, needed to be completed early in the calendar year—meaning that they were already starting to be compiled during the previous year. This allowed the programming phase to unfold from spring to fall. Under McNamara, much of the programming was crafted in "Draft Presidential Memorandums" composed by the civilian analysts, which circulated among the services and the Joint Chiefs of Staff for comment and

revision. The preparation of the budget being sent to Congress was done at
the end of the calendar year so the White House could send the whole proposed budget to the Hill in January. If Congress passed an appropriations bill
on time, by the start of the fiscal year on July 1, the lag between the start of
planning and the start of spending was around two years—or even close to
three, if one considered the earliest planning stages.[26]

The PPBS installed by McNamara's team in 1961 has endured to the
present day. But it was revised meaningfully in 1969–70, under the leadership of Secretary of Defense Melvin Laird and his deputy, David Packard.
They changed PPBS to give more power back to the military services, in a
decentralization of budget-making authority that reduced the power of civilian analysts in the secretary's office. In fact, by the mid-1960s, the services
had already begun to challenge the "McNamara Monarchy" by ramping up
their own capacities to provide the kind of quantitative analysis needed to
prevail in budget debates.[27] Laird and Packard gave the services more formal
responsibility by restoring the 1950s practice of providing them in advance
with guidance about dollar limits and allowing them to make their own
choices about allocating resources. Now the key programming documents
became Program Objective Memorandums (POMs) generated by the services instead of the draft presidential memorandums that McNamara's civilian
analysts had crafted.[28] Since 1970, the balance of power between the services
and civilians has altered slightly, back and forth.[29] In the 1980s, the Pentagon's
budgeting effort was modified by Secretary of Defense Caspar Weinberger
and his deputy, Frank Carlucci. They increased the influence of combatant
commanders, as well as that of the Defense Resources Board, which included
service secretaries and other top civilian officials, along with the chairman
of the Joint Chiefs.[30] Despite these developments, however, today's PPBES
looks very similar to its 1970 antecedent.[31]

The PPBE Reform Commission working today (in 2023) has the difficult
task of trying to alter a complex, entrenched system that has already survived
a couple of generations of critics. In the era of the Carter administration, military reform proponent Franklin C. Spinney was already describing the system
as ossified and unacceptable. "The PPBS has become so cumbersome and
infected by bureaucratic gaming," Spinney declared in a 1980 briefing, "that as
we get nearer to the January budget deadline, we are responding more to the
bureaucratic constraints imposed by the system rather than using the system
as a tool to adjust to changing circumstances."[32] When Spinney composed

those words, the PPBS had been in place for less than two decades. Now we are nearly forty-five years further down the road.

Empowering Congress: Increased Legislative Power and Its Consequences, 1959–85

Whereas the transformation of the DoD budget process occurred mostly in the 1950s and 1960s, Congress's handling of the defense budget was reshaped somewhat later, with many new procedures inaugurated in the 1970s. By that decade, it became clear that Congress was asserting more power over the defense budget than it had during the early Cold War. This shift occurred in the context of the failure of the US war in Vietnam and postwar defense budget cuts, along with economic distress and a broader rethinking of national priorities, the US role in the world, and the balance of power between the executive and legislative branches. By the early 1980s, when the defense budget was increasing again, legislative oversight had become so seemingly strong that Congress was routinely accused of "micromanagement."

As political scientists and historians have documented at length, the 1970s marked the end of a half-century era during which the White House took most of the initiative in the budget process and during which a handful of congressional committees and committee chairs dominated the legislative side of defense policy. Following the Budget and Accounting Act of 1921, which set up the Bureau of the Budget as an executive agency, there was a fifty-year period of "presidential dominance" in the budget process.[33] The same years are remembered as the "Committee Era" in the legislative branch, when a few committee chairs and senior members, who enjoyed great deference from their colleagues, controlled congressional oversight of defense budgeting and other defense policies.[34] The powerful committee chairs generally made few changes to the defense budgets submitted by the White House, and if executive branch officials did run into an obstacle or anticipated a problem, interfacing with Congress was simple and quick. As one former junior member of McNamara's Pentagon recalled, as late as the mid-1960s, "if you wanted to see if Congress was with you on an issue, you could go over and talk to four people."[35]

One key shift toward more congressional oversight—arguably reducing both agility and stability—was expanding the armed services committees' work on annual authorizations. In the 1950s, most defense spending other than military construction was done under broad, semipermanent authorizations such as those allowing the navy to procure fifteen thousand aircraft and 2.5 million tons' worth of shipbuilding. This changed at the end of the decade, with Congress's concerns about competing with the Soviet Union in the missile age. Responding to his colleagues' complaints about inadequate information provided by the DoD and evidence of redundancies in the military services' missile and air defense programs, Senator Richard Russell crafted an amendment to the Military Construction Authorization Act of 1959, which stated that starting in 1961, the armed services commit-tees would need to authorize the procurement of missiles, aircraft, and ships. The Eisenhower and Kennedy administrations, the DoD, and the appropria-tions committees in Congress all opposed this new policy, warning that it would cause duplication of effort between authorizers and appropriators and would constrain the Pentagon's legitimate needs for agility.[36] As one observer claimed at the dawn of the new authorization regime, "it is clear that any attempt to authorize procurement in detail, which might simultaneously hin-der reprogramming, carries heavy disadvantages in an era of exploding mili-tary technology."[37] Despite these concerns, the scope of the armed services committees' annual authorizations expanded steadily from the 1960s into the 1980s until they covered every corner of the defense budget, including research and development, operations and maintenance, personnel, and pro-curement and construction.[38]

Although the expansion of annual authorizations was well underway when McNamara left the Pentagon in 1968, the development of what critics would call congressional micromanagement of the defense budget did not occur until the 1970s. As late as 1968–70, the annual defense authorization bill was only about ten pages; it was normally passed on voice votes after less than a single day of debate.[39] Just one decade later, by the late 1970s and early 1980s, the annual defense authorization and appropriations bills were both hundreds of pages long; each year, both authorizers and appropriators were altering hundreds of individual line items—more than half of all line items in the budget submitted by the White House. From the Pentagon's perspective, the number of members of Congress and their staffers who had a hand in the defense budget had expanded dramatically in just a few years to dozens and dozens of people.[40]

The remarkable 1970s expansion of congressional management of defense budgets was part of what has been called a broader "congressionalization of defense policy," involving a new willingness to challenge the executive branch and new budget processes, as well as a decentralization of power in the legislative branch.[41] At the end of the 1960s and into the early 1970s, in the context of growing public discontent with the war in Vietnam, Congress started to hold lengthy debates on defense policy and imposed significantly larger cuts to the president's budget requests than it had done during the early Cold War. Meanwhile, a younger cohort of new members pushed Congress out of the "Committee Era" with new rules that gave more power to subcommittees and individual members.[42] After clashing with President Richard Nixon over defense and domestic spending, Congress passed the 1974 Congressional Budget Impoundment and Control Act, the foundation of the current legislative budget process. The 1974 act created the budget committees responsible for crafting a budget resolution on spending and revenue, as well as the Congressional Budget Office. The start of the fiscal year shifted from July 1 to October 1 to allow more time for what was, in theory, a three-stage sequential process requiring action from the budget committees, the authorizers, and the appropriators. The act expanded Congress's capacity to manage the budget, as did the rise in the number of staffers in the offices of individual members and the committees. Congressional staff doubled between the late 1960s and the end of the 1970s.[43]

The new US defense budget regime created in the early 1970s operated for only a few years before encountering major criticisms from two different directions. First, hawks sounded loud alarms about the inadequacy of US defense spending in light of the threat of expanding Soviet nuclear and conventional forces. Starting in 1976, the CIA determined that Soviet defense outlays had been considerably higher in recent years than it had previously estimated. (A decade later, the CIA would determine that it overestimated Soviet defense spending in the late 1970s and early 1980s.)[44] Meanwhile, US defense budgets, now managed closely by a more dovish Congress in the context of a global economic recession and high inflation, had declined in real dollar terms by about a third from their 1968 wartime peak (see figs. 16.1 and 16.2).[45] In short order, the growing unease about US defense budget inadequacy caused major reforms in the realm of dollar quantity. The big defense budget increases that allowed the Reagan buildup of the early 1980s, popular with Congress and the public, were the most obvious manifestations of the shift. But the change in sensibilities about adequacy was underway much earlier, as suggested by President Jimmy Carter's abandonment of his 1976 campaign promise to cut the defense budget as early as his first year in office.[46]

A second set of criticisms about the US defense budget in the late 1970s pointed to the dysfunctional aspects of the more heavily congressionally managed budget process established just a few years earlier. Unlike the warnings about the inadequacy of the budget's size, these alarms about the problems with the budget process were never addressed with major reforms. Indeed, the same complaints about the high costs of congressional overmanagement of the defense budget have continued to echo into the 2010s and 2020s.

By the time of the Reagan buildup of the 1980s, it was widely observed—by scholars, journalists, executive branch officials, and legislators themselves—that Congress was overmanaging the defense budget. In theory, the 1974 budget act and other increases in congressional capacity had provided a salutary dose of democratic accountability to the White House and the Pentagon, which had demonstrated in the 1960s that they could not be trusted to carry out wise, economical defense policies. But "in practice," as one expert observer put it, Congress's new process, involving the close scrutiny of the budget by multiple committees in each house over the better part of a year, "has proved to be a nightmare."[47] By the early 1980s, when every major defense budget category was subject to annual authorizations, it was clear that the armed services and appropriations committees largely duplicated one another's work, as they both manipulated hundreds of line items. "Three different committees in each house," lamented Senator Sam Nunn in the 1980s, "should not be doing essentially the same thing."[48] Perhaps worse still, they were increasingly disregarding one another's actions, forcing the Pentagon to tiptoe around problems of unauthorized appropriations or unappropriated authorizations.[49] Meanwhile, the new legislative process launched in 1974 had failed to deliver the on-time passage of appropriations bills, despite the three-month extension of the start of the fiscal year.[50] These regular delays, combined with the annual interventions by authorizers and appropriators, caused what the Pentagon and its contractors regarded as excessive, wasteful instability.

By the time of the Carter-Reagan defense buildup in the late 1970s and early 1980s, a three-decade period of major reforms to the US defense budget system was coming to an end. In 1950, there was a major shift in the national consensus about budget adequacy. Policy makers created a much larger baseline defense budget to provide a global military superpower, a condition that persists. Meanwhile, in a two-step consolidation process, the DoD reorganized the budget. In the early 1950s, hundreds of decades-old accounts were consolidated into new broad appropriations titles, and in the early 1960s, the McNamara team grouped programs and their costs into major military missions as part of the new PPBS. Finally, in the 1970s, Congress began to assert more power over defense budgeting by doing more to challenge the president's budget, expanding authorizations, and decentralizing authority in ways that allowed ordinary members more power to influence defense spending. The system in place by the early 1980s, with its many evident problems, is not much different from today's. Since the 1980s, there have been several efforts at defense budget reform but most have either failed or had modest effects.

Business as Usual, Modified by Supplements and Workarounds, the 1980s–2010s

Since the 1980s, the US defense budgeting system has proven resistant to major reforms. Even reform efforts that were tried repeatedly and enjoyed wide support, such as multiyear budgeting, have floundered. Other proposed reforms suggested repeatedly since the 1980s, such as the consolidation of congressional authorization and appropriations committees, have proven to be nonstarters. Nevertheless, even if no foundational overhauls occurred, there were a few areas in which reformers could point to some success. The endless drive for defense acquisition reform created more agility in the system, starting in the 1990s, by moving a larger part of the defense budget into a more commercial orientation. During the post–9/11 wars in Afghanistan and Iraq, some of the inflexibilities of the normal budget system were reduced by huge supplemental appropriations and special acquisition authorities. And since the 2010s, further acquisition reform efforts have provided a few new tools that can serve as workarounds to provide more agility in at least a few small pockets of the defense enterprise. Would these various band-aids and workarounds, applied atop a foundational US defense budgeting system that had not changed much since the 1970s, continue to suffice, given that the sheer size of the US defense budget continued to dwarf its rivals? This is a key question for US policy makers looking ahead to the mid-twenty-first century.

The Failure of Multiyear Defense Budgeting and Related Reforms, the 1980s–2000s

Over the last half century, perhaps the single most energetic, widely endorsed plan to reform US defense budgeting was the effort to create a biennial or multiyear budget. Multiyear defense budgeting promised to reduce work for Congress and the DoD while adding stability to acquisition programs and other expenditures, which would reduce costs. This reform effort was partially tried in the 1980s and 2000s but never took hold. Its failure was partly attributable to Congress's obvious reluctance to reduce its power over budgeting. But the history of its failure also suggested that the benefits of adding long-run stability to defense budgets may be smaller than advertised because of the many uncertainties and unpredictable events that inevitably impinge on the work of security policy makers.

In the 1980s, would-be reformers frequently called for a shift to multiyear budgeting to cut down on the many thousands of person-hours of work for Congress and the DoD, reducing congressional overmanagement and adding cost-saving stabilities to the budget execution phase. "The time has come to simplify the budget process," former Congressional Budget Office director Alice Rivlin argued in the mid-1980s, as she made a case for multiyear budgeting (as well as consolidating budget line items and the authorizing and appropriations processes).[51] Rivlin's call for multiyear defense budgeting was echoed by many other major would-be reformers in the 1980s, including the Grace Commission members, who suggested ways to reduce costs across the federal government. Jacques Gansler, a defense acquisition guru, argued strongly for multiyear budgeting, pointing out that the United States was exceptional in its use of annual bills.[52] This then amplified the US legislative branch's uniquely large powers, relative to its counterparts in other nations, over budgeting and defense policy.[53] Biennial budgeting was also endorsed by the Packard Commission, which criticized Congress's elaborate, annual budget interventions as "excessive and harmful to the long-term defense of the country."[54]

In the 1980s, Congress took steps toward multiyear budgeting but refused to implement it. By the time of the Reagan buildup, the idea of multiyear budgeting enjoyed some support in Congress, where Rep. Leon Panetta (D-CA) had been sponsoring biennial budgeting bills since the late 1970s.[55] Congress held hearings on the issue in the early 1980s; some committees endorsed the idea, even as opponents complained that the legislature would give up too much oversight. Then, in the National Defense Authorization Act (NDAA) for FY1986, Congress required the executive branch to submit two-year budgets.[56] The Pentagon duly submitted biennial defense budgets starting in the late 1980s. But Congress—particularly the appropriations committees—never abandoned its traditional practice of crafting annual bills. By the 1990s, even as the Clinton administration's National Performance Review called for multiyear budgeting, the Pentagon was asking to be relieved of the task of drafting biennial budgets because legislators ignored them.[57]

The idea of biennial budgeting was revived at the Pentagon in the early 2000s under Secretary of Defense Donald Rumsfeld. Calling the defense budget system "broken," Rumsfeld criticized the existing PPBS as "a relic of the Cold War." Rumsfeld and his team gave the system an updated label: the Planning, Programming, Budgeting, and Execution System (PPBES). They also attempted to make it more efficient and stable by having the secretary's main planning guidance document, along with the POMs prepared by the services, be prepared just once every two years instead of annually. But this new process failed. In practice, the services and the secretary's office made so many changes in the off-year that the process never managed to break away from de facto annual budgeting. By 2006, efforts to use biennial budgeting were already fading; the Pentagon formally announced a return to annual budgeting in 2010.[58]

The failure of Congress and the Pentagon to adopt multiyear budgeting was not caused by a falling away of concerns about the inefficiencies and instabilities created by the annual process. Indeed, top policy makers and experts complained about those problems into the early twenty-first century, as they continued to voice support for multiyear budgeting. As the former Lockheed Martin chairman and CEO Norm Augustine observed in 2001, the "constant turmoil" of the annual defense budgeting process, unique to the United States, created huge increases in costs of major programs, such as the F-22, by forcing contractors to repeatedly reorganize their production plans, "due to budget changes."[59] According to Secretary of Defense Gates, Congress's continuing failures to pass defense bills on time, year after year, "played havoc with acquisition programs."[60] In the 2010s, many experts, including former DoD comptroller Dov Zakheim, were still recommending that the United States move to a biennial defense budgeting system.[61]

Given the strong support for multiyear defense budgeting voiced over the last half century, how can we explain the failure of this proposed reform? One obvious answer is that self-interested parties, especially on the key congressional committees, have little interest in losing influence. As Alice Rivlin noted in her mid-1980s call for reform, a shift away from annual authorizations and appropriations "threatens the existing power structure."[62] Political scientist James Lindsay suggested that there seemed to be a lot of explanatory power in a quip attributed to then speaker of the house Tip O'Neill: "The name of the game is power, and the boys don't want to give it up."[63] Perhaps this was too crude of an explanation, given that Congress did sometimes act to give up its powers over the details of budgeting and defense policy. It arguably did so in the form of automatic budget caps and sequesters from the 1980s through the 2010s; its 1996 endorsement of the line-item veto (ruled unconstitutional in 1998); its creation of the Base Realignment and Closure (BRAC) commissions at the end of the Cold War; and earmark reform in the 2010s. Nevertheless, there is no getting around the conclusion that Congress's unwillingness to lose power is one important cause of both insta-bility and lack of agility in defense. This has been the case not just with regard to proposals for multiyear budgeting but even more so for the suggestions by Rivlin and others that the work of the authorizers and appropriators should be consolidated.

Although the proposals for multiyear defense budgeting were surely sty-mied by Congress's reflexive reluctance to cede authority, they were also chal-lenged by critics who raised sensible questions about a loss of agility. These critics pointed out that given the many uncertainties about future defense needs and economic conditions, under a multiyear budgeting system, Congress and the DoD might well find themselves making so many midcourse adjustments to out-year budgets that there would not end up being much less work or intervention than what was already being done in the formal annual process.[64] Given this problem and the apparent political reality that Congress was unlikely to embrace major reforms, some experts suggested that it made more sense to try more modest proposals, such as moving the beginning of the fiscal year to January 1.[65] In theory, such a change might at least increase the chances that Congress could pass on-time appropriations bills, reducing the costs faced by the DoD from operating for several weeks or months most years under continuing resolutions (or government shutdowns).

A half century after would-be reformers such as Alice Rivlin and Leon Panetta first suggested that Congress, the DoD, and other agencies would benefit from multiyear budgeting and consolidating duplicative efforts by authorizers and appropriators, the defense budgeting system of the 1970s still has not been changed in those directions. Rather, in many ways, the problems those proposed reforms aimed to cure, such as budget instability, overmanagement, waste, and lack of agility, seem to have worsened. In the early twenty-first century, the length of defense authorization and appropria-tions bills, associated reports, and numerous floor amendments continued to grow.[66] Between the 1980s and the late 2000s, there was also a dramatic rise in earmarks, which by the mid-2000s numbered more than two thou-sand items worth nearly $10 billion in the annual defense appropriations bill alone.[67] In the early 2010s, Congress's failure to close a budget deal caused across-the-board sequestration, which Secretary of Defense Leon Panetta decried as a "stunning" development, returning to the misguided crude cap and sequestration schemes of the 1980s, "guaranteed to damage America's military readiness."[68] Although sequestration was avoided after the mid-2010s, the DoD continued struggling with continuing resolutions at the start of each fiscal year. From the 1970s through the 2000s, the average time working under continuing resolutions had been about one month; in the 2010s, it was closer to four months.[69] All in all, the pathologies of the US defense budgeting system in the early twenty-first century closely resembled those decried in the 1980s; in the eyes of some veteran observers, it had become even worse, thanks to rising parochialism and polarization.[70]

Defense Budget Reform via Supplements, Workarounds, and Acquisition Reform: From the Packard Commission to McCain-Thornberry, the 1980s–2010s

Thanks to the failure of multiyear budgeting and related efforts to alter the PPBS or curtail congressional overmanagement, the US defense budget system created in the early Cold War era has endured. However, over the past three decades, there have been meaningful changes in defense budgeting, defined broadly, in the form of direct or indirect effects of defense acquisition reform. Although cynics assert, with some reason, that defense acquisition reform is a never-ending process with much bark and little bite, there have been at least a few shifts in acquisition policy that have provided additional tools to those working under the traditional constraints imposed by Congress, the PPBES, and the defense bureaucracy. Meanwhile, in the 2000s and 2010s, the large supplemental appropriations for war and reconstruction in Afghanistan and Iraq provided the military establishment not just with historically large overall budgets but also some substantial funding not fully covered by normal processes and oversight. Those add-ons, together with acquisition reform, provided policy makers with band-aids and workarounds, offering additional stability or flexibility beyond what the traditional budget system provided.

The history of US defense acquisition and efforts to reform it is a complex, much-discussed subject.[71] For this paper, it may suffice to review the multiple acquisition reforms aimed at promoting commercialization and speed in the 1990s and the 2010s. These reforms clearly affected how parts of the defense budget were executed, and so at least indirectly served as defense budget reform. In particular, the procommercialization reforms addressed widespread concerns about the traditional budgeting system's slowness and lack of flexibility by moving some defense spending into areas less constrained by the standard processes and regulations. In this sense, policy makers found partial workarounds to overcome some of the weaknesses of the budgeting system that had taken shape during the early Cold War.

One significant push in the direction of commercialization occurred in the 1990s, during the years of the Clinton administration, at the dawn of the post–Cold War era. In the 1980s, the Packard Commission and other would-be reformers had called for the Pentagon to buy more off-the-shelf products, using simpler, faster transactions. But the Pentagon was slow to take up the Packard Commission recommendations in the late 1980s; to some extent, the acquisition was becoming slower rather than faster, partly because of new regulations imposed by Congress in the wake of the recent scandals involving alleged fraud, waste, and abuse.[72] Some steps toward commercialization were taken during the tenure of Secretary of Defense Dick Cheney (in office 1989–93), as the DoD revised its 5000-series acquisition guidance documents and pushed back against what Cheney regarded as congressional micromanagement.[73] But the most substantial procommercial reforms came during the Clinton years, during the post–Cold War drawdown when there was remarkable coordination of efforts by the White House, the Pentagon, and Congress. As the Clinton administration promoted "reinventing government" in ways that promised to reduce bureaucracy, Secretary of Defense Bill Perry—embracing recommendations of the Section 800 panel report issued in 1993—announced that the default approach to acquisition would be flipped to favor off-the-shelf items, rather than bespoke goods and services subject to elaborate and unique military specifications. At the same time, Congress passed the 1994 Federal Acquisition Streamlining Act (FASA) and, two years later, the Federal Acquisition Reform Act (FARA), as well as the Clinger-Cohen Act. Together, these laws and policies exempted more purchases from traditional acquisition rules, making it easier for the US military to buy things faster, particularly items not unique to defense, like paper or furniture, or dual-use technologies and items like computers and communications equipment.[74]

The acquisition initiatives of the 1990s and early 2000s, which emphasized commercialization and speed, served as a kind of de facto defense budget reform by offering workarounds to a traditional system that was viewed as too sclerotic. The net effects of this reform were mixed. On the one hand, there was no question that the Pentagon saved billions of dollars by using simpler transactions and specifications for many goods and services. (By the early beginning of the 2010s, commercial acquisition methods were used for around 20 percent of the dollar value of all DoD contracts.)[75] But the push for speed in acquiring complex major weapons systems, championed by Under Secretary of Defense Jacques Gansler in the late 1990s and Secretary Rumsfeld's team in the early 2000s, seems to have backfired.[76] At first glance, the effort to shorten the frustratingly long weapon acquisition cycles by decentralizing authority to the military services and the contractors seemed sensible enough. But in practice, the push for quick development and production was associated with major cost overruns (as with the F-35 and the Littoral Combat Ship) and total failures (as in the case of the army's Future Combat Systems). By the late 2000s, these troubles caused defense policy makers to reverse course. In Congress, Senator Carl Levin championed the 2009 Weapon Systems Acquisition Reform Act, which called for more methodical acquisitions with more thorough cost estimates by Pentagon civilian analysts.[77]

The wars in Afghanistan and Iraq caused some de facto defense budget reform, in the 2000s and 2010s, mainly by providing the Pentagon with more generous and flexible funding. As one former top policy maker recalled, starting in the early 2000s, "the normal discipline of five-year plans and budget control totals for budgeting purposes was thrown out the window."[78] Wartime supplemental appropriations approved by Congress for the fiscal years 2003 to 2007 were 20 to 40 percent above the base defense budget, which was increasing. These supplementals were not subject to the same level of review that Congress devoted to the base budget. Over time, it became clear that the Pentagon was using some of the supplemental funding—which came to use the label Overseas Contingency Operations (OCO)—to pay for items not associated directly with actions in Afghanistan and Iraq, such as the V-22 and F-35 programs. (Congress also used the supplementals as an opportunity to insert even more earmarks—a practice Secretary Gates denounced as "political bullshit.")[79] The OCO appropriations blunted the impact of the spending caps imposed by the 2011 Budget Control Act (and the sequestration crisis of 2013) because OCO was exempt from the caps. Thanks in part to a total of $2 trillion in supplementals, the Bush, Obama, and Trump administrations all enjoyed relatively generous defense budgets, larger in real dollar terms than those that Congress had provided at the height of the Reagan buildup (see fig. 16.2).[80]

The last decade has seen another wave of defense acquisition reform, emphasizing commercial solutions and agility, comparable to the 1990s and early 2000s. This new effort appeared to offer some de facto budget reform, via new acquisition vehicles and workarounds, at least in some small pockets of the defense enterprise. The latest push for speed occurred in the context of growing concerns about the rise of China and a refocus in US defense policy on the competition with near-peer great powers. The Pentagon's "Third Offset Strategy," announced in 2014, aimed at maintaining US military superiority over its rivals via investment in cutting-edge technologies such as cyber warfare, robotics, and artificial intelligence. To tap these technologies, most defense policy makers of the 2010s believed, the DoD would need to do more with commercial firms, including some that had not previously filled defense contracts. Since the election of President Donald Trump in 2016 and continuing into the Joe Biden presidency, the national conversation about great-power competition has become more hawkish. By 2018, for example, the National Defense Strategy Commission warned of a "grave crisis of national security and national defense," the most serious crisis in decades, which demanded that the United States and its allies move with "extraordinary urgency" to improve their military capabilities.[81]

Informed by this new concern for quick action in the face of a rising China and more belligerent Russia, Congress and the DoD moved in the late 2010s toward acquisition reforms intended to provide new ways of getting around the traditional slow-moving budgeting and purchasing system. Secretary of Defense Ash Carter created the Defense Innovation Unit, Experimental (DIUx), which aimed to get funds into the hands of promising companies within one or two months. To pay for research and prototypes, the DIUx and other defense entities increasingly used "other transaction authority" (OTA) mechanisms, which Congress encouraged by providing permanent authorization, starting with the NDAA for FY2016. By the end of the 2010s, OTA awards were starting to be used more heavily, especially by the army, to the tune of several billion dollars per year.[82] The same NDAA for FY2016, which reflected the acquisition reform efforts of armed services committee chairs Senator John McCain and Representative Mac Thornberry, also funded "middle tier of acquisition" (MTA) pathways. The MTA mechanisms, which avoided some of the constraints of the traditional contracting system, were intended to allow program managers to field new equipment within just two to five years—a speedier acquisition cycle that some proponents believed had not been achieved since the 1950s.[83] By 2020, the MTA pathways were increasingly used, including by the Special Operations Command.[84] Meanwhile, McCain and Thornberry used the NDAA for FY2017 to push for additional acquisition reform by giving the military services more authority and separating the under-secretary-level oversight of acquisition and research into two jobs that had previously been joined.[85]

As of 2022, it was still too soon to tell whether these various reforms by the DoD and Congress, including the increasing use of MTA and OTA pathways and heightened efforts to engage with commercial firms, would deliver on their promise.[86] However, it was clear that an accumulation of acquisition reforms, supplementals, and workarounds had provided at least some partial relief from the burdens of the much-derided Cold War–era defense budgeting system. Various new rapid acquisition mechanisms provided more flexibility and agility in small but significant parts of the defense enterprise. So too, probably, did the substantial growth in the size of the classified portion of the budget since the end of the Cold War, which had been under 5 percent of defense spending in the early 1980s but more recently has been closer to 10 percent. Additional workarounds and pockets of higher agility were provided by the rise of "fourth estate" agencies, such as the Special Operations Command, smaller and ostensibly nimbler than the traditional services.[87]

Conclusions

The post–World War II history of US defense budget reform shows that there have been remarkably few major changes to basic processes over the last four decades. Between the late 1940s and the mid-1970s, reformers truly transformed how the Pentagon and Congress handled the work of defense budgeting. Since the 1980s, there have not been comparable foundational changes, although some parts of the defense budget and its execution were partially liberated from the constraints of the slow-moving basic system via acquisition reforms, war appropriations, and other workarounds. The paucity of dramatic changes in recent decades would seem to lend credence to the claims of today's would-be reformers, who contend that the defense budget system requires a massive overhaul to meet the new challenges of the current century. However, it is not easy to imagine Congress or the Pentagon upending their long-standing foundational practices, even in the current environment of heightened interest in reform. Institutional inertia and self-interest obviously work against the possibility of revolutionary change. But beyond this, some policy makers may legitimately conclude from the historical record that the Cold War–vintage system continues to serve adequately to balance the many concerns and needs of Congress and the defense establishment. Furthermore, they may conclude that today's geopolitical threats and patterns of technological change are not so radically different or more challenging than those of the early Cold War era when the current budgeting system took shape. Moreover, a closer look at the specific proposals of today's would-be reformers suggests that many would amount to relatively modest adjustments to business as usual.

What would a truly radical US defense budget overhaul look like in the 2020s and 2030s? The historical record since World War II suggests some possibilities. For example, a massive reassessment of the adequacy of the sheer size of the base budget, such as the one that occurred in the late 1940s and early 1950s, might call for a doubling of expenditure. To pay for this giant increase, Congress would likely need to approve a major hike in income tax rates in a partial return to the early Cold War tax regime. For the moment, such action seems out of the realm of possibility but perhaps a series of major security shocks, such as those in 1949–50, could radically alter the consensus about budget adequacy.

The historical record also offers a guide to what radical reform might involve in the realm of defense budget stability and agility. On the Pentagon side, a much quicker PPBES, or its equivalent, would need to compress planning and budgeting into just a few weeks instead of many months. This would require the DoD to work with truly unprecedented speed; it might require a far more centralized process, with less input from the services, than the one that has prevailed since 1969. On the legislative side, transformative reform might involve embracing several of the proposals recommended widely in the 1980s (and still echoing today), such as comprehensive multiyear budgeting and the consolidation of Congress's defense authorization and appropriation committees.[88] In theory, Congress could return to very broad permanent defense authorizations, which it used until the 1960s. As the history of the last four decades suggests, Congress does not seem to be eager to enact such changes, which would require levels of trust or deference to the executive branch and centralization of power in Congress itself, which were abandoned in the era of the US Vietnam War and the Watergate crisis. Bowing to these realities, some of today's would-be reformers of congressional practice have fallen back on far more modest suggestions, such as proposals to have the federal fiscal year start on January 1, which might add some budget stability by making it easier for legislators to pass bills on time.[89]

Another less-than-radical set of changes proposed recently involves the areas of budget line-item consolidation and reprogramming flexibility. As we have seen, in the 1950s and 1960s, there were major consolidations and reassessments of budget titles and categories. In recent years, some would-be reformers—including the Section 809 Panel that worked from 2016 to 2019—have suggested that the DoD move toward "capability portfolio management." The Packard Commission also suggested such a reform in the 1980s.[90] Doing so might involve consolidating multiple programs into broader mission areas, requiring that Congress's budgeting become more closely aligned to the kind of mission-oriented budgeting launched by McNamara's team in the early 1960s. A move to more "portfolio management" would ideally create a smaller number of budget elements and, therefore, larger pots of money that could be administered more flexibly by the Pentagon and the services, akin to those created by the consolidation reforms of the early Cold War era.[91] A related proposal voiced by the Section 809 Panel and others, which would require less significant structural change, calls for reforms in budget reprogramming—i.e., midyear actions by the defense establishment to move money between individual budget areas, ideally to reduce waste and enhance effectiveness. In recent years, reprogramming has become slower and more difficult, with multiple congressional committee staffs able to veto or delay requests from the DoD. The ceilings on the total dollars that can be reprogrammed are now only about 1 percent of the total budget. Some of today's reformers, including former Pentagon comptroller Dov Zakheim, suggest that this figure might be increased to a level closer to 5 percent to provide much-needed flexibility and agility.[92]

As the details of these specific proposals suggest, despite the stridency of today's rhetoric about the need for radical changes to meet current global security challenges, it would seem unwise to predict that the 2020s and 2030s will likely bring a fundamental overhaul of US defense budgeting of the kind that occurred during the early Cold War. Those reforms of the 1950s–1970s occurred in the context of the emergence of an unprecedented existential threat in the form of a nuclear-armed Soviet Union; the infancy of the DoD and Office of the Secretary of Defense; and a disastrous US war in Vietnam, which, along with the Nixon administration's downfall, inspired Congress to reorganize itself and become more assertive over defense policy and budgets. Meanwhile, other major developments, including the abrupt jumps in the late 1950s and 1970s in worries about the US-Soviet military balance, as well as the end of the Cold War and the 9/11 attacks and ensuing wars, caused some significant adjustments to the size of defense budgets but not much change to fundamental budget processes and systems. As we have seen, over the past half century, the flaws of those aging processes and systems have largely been dealt with by an array of supplements and workarounds rather than radical reform.

The unpredictability of domestic and global developments in the coming months and years, always the bane of defense policy makers and budgeters, means we cannot rule out the possibility of massive new reforms. In any case, whether the next few years see a big overhaul akin to that of the early Cold War or more modest adjustments like those that accumulated since the 1980s, reformers will benefit from reviewing the relevant history. If policy makers attempt to return to the practices of the 1950s, they will do well to remember the origins of those practices and the stories of why and how they were altered over time to establish the foundations of our current system.

Notes

1. William C. Greenwalt and Dan Patt, "Competing in Time: Ensuring Capability Advantage and Mission Success through Adaptable Resource Allocation," Hudson Institute, February 25, 2021; US Senator Jack Reed, speech and Q&A at Ronald Reagan Institute, May 11, 2021, https://www.reed.senate.gov/news/releases/defense-priorities-with-senator-jack-reed; Eric M. Lofgren, "Pathways to Defense Budget Reform," *Proceedings of the Nineteenth Annual Acquisition Research Symposium*, Naval Postgraduate School (May 2022): 336–55.

2. Matt MacGregor, Greg Grant, and Peter Modigliani, "Five First Steps to a Modern Defense Budgeting System," MITRE Center for Data-Driven Policy, August 2022.

3. This body is currently at work and is scheduled to issue interim and final reports in 2023–24.

4. Chris Higginbotham, "Procuring the Cross of Iron: The Effect of Congressional Approval on the US Defense Budget" (PhD diss., University of Kansas, 2017), 51.

5. Robert M. Gates, *Duty: Memoirs of a Secretary at War* (New York: Alfred A. Knopf, 2014), 580–81; also see 453–54.

6. Ash Carter, *Inside the Five-Sided Box: Lessons from a Lifetime of Leadership in the Pentagon* (New York: Dutton, 2020), 130, 136.

7. Melvyn P. Leffler, *A Preponderance of Power: National Security, the Truman Administration, and the Cold War* (Stanford, CA: Stanford University Press, 1993), 373, 451; Michael J. Hogan, *A Cross of Iron: Harry S. Truman and the Origins of the National Security State* (New York: Cambridge University Press, 1998), 311.

8. Douglas Kinnard, "President Eisenhower and the Defense Budget," *Journal of Politics* 39, no. 3 (August 1977): 596–623; Iwan W. Morgan, *Eisenhower versus "The Spenders": The Eisenhower Administration, the Democrats and the Budget, 1953–60* (London: Pinter Publishers, 1990), 51.

9. Morgan, *Eisenhower versus "The Spenders,"* 35.

10. Samuel P. Huntington, *The Common Defense: Strategic Programs in National Politics* (New York: Columbia University Press, 1961), 107–12; Edward A. Kolodziej, *The Uncommon Defense and Congress, 1945–1963* (Columbus: Ohio State University Press, 1966), 215–88; Arnold Kanter, "Congress and the Defense Budget: 1960–1970," *American Political Science Review* 66, no. 1 (March 1972): 129–43; Kinnard, "President Eisenhower and the Defense Budget," 611–17; Melvin R. Laird interview, August 18, 1986, Office of the Secretary of Defense, 3–12, https://history.defense.gov/Historical-Sources/Oral-History-Transcript-3; Aaron L. Friedberg, *In the Shadow of the Garrison State: America's Anti-Statism and Its Cold War Grand Strategy* (Princeton, NJ: Princeton University Press, 2000), 134–39; David L. Snead, *The Gaither Committee, Eisenhower, and the Cold War* (Columbus: Ohio State University Press, 1999). The Rockefeller Brothers Fund report is held up as a model by some of today's champions of more agile defense acquisitions, including former Google CEO Eric Schmidt. See Special Competitive Studies Project, *Mid-Decade Challenges to National Competitiveness*, September 2022. For an account of the original report, see John Andrew III, "Cracks in the Consensus: The Rockefeller Brothers Fund Special Studies Project and Eisenhower's America," *Presidential Studies Quarterly* 28, no. 3 (Summer 1998): 535–52.

11. Rebecca Lissner, *Wars of Revelation: The Transformative Effects of Military Intervention on Grand Strategy* (New York: Oxford University Press, 2021), 44–45.

12. *The Hoover Commission Report on the Organization of the Executive Branch of the Government* (New York: McGraw Hill, 1949), 36–37; Oral history interview with Wilfred J. McNeil, September 19, 1972, 19, Truman Library, Independence, MO, https://www.trumanlibrary.gov/library/oral-histories/mcneilwj.

13. Charles J. Hitch, *Decision-Making for Defense* (Berkeley: University of California Press, 1965), 69; Kolodziej, *Uncommon Defense and Congress*, 472; James E. Hewes Jr., *From Root to McNamara: Army Organization and Administration, 1900–1963* (Washington, DC: Center of Military History, United States Army, 1975), 271–84.

14. Kolodziej, *Uncommon Defense and Congress*, 147–49.

15. McNeil interview, Truman Library, 21–22. McNeil was reportedly a powerful player in 1950s defense budget making, who often made last-minute adjustments to the Eisenhower administration's requests, usually by trimming items to meet ceilings, not necessarily in ways that followed a broad set of strategic priorities. See Harold Brown with Joyce Winslow, *Star-Spangled Security: Applying Lessons Learned over Six Decades Safeguarding America* (Washington, DC: Brookings Institution, 2012), 18; Elliott V. Converse III, *History of Acquisition in the Department of Defense, Volume I: Rearming for the Cold War, 1945-1960* (Washington, DC: Office of the Secretary of Defense Historical Office, 2012), 86–87.

16. Huntington, *Common Defense*, 128–38, 225; Christian E. Jarchow, "Task Force on Budgeting and Accounting—Hoover Commission," *Woman C.P.A.* 19, no. 3 (1957): 5–10.

17. McNeil interview, Truman Library, 47.

18. Merton J. Peck and Frederic M. Scherer, *The Weapons Acquisition Process: An Economic Analysis* (Boston: Harvard University Graduate School of Business Administration, 1962), 51.

19. Christian Brose, *The Kill Chain: Defending America in the Future of High-Tech Warfare* (New York: Hachette, 2020), 43–46, 75.

20. Peck and Scherer, *Weapons Acquisition Process*, 4, 53–54; Michael E. Brown, *Flying Blind: The Politics of the US Strategic Bomber Program* (Ithaca, NY: Cornell University Press, 1992). One recent study has argued that the average length of the development and acquisition process for major programs has not actually changed much since the early Cold War era. See Morgan Dwyer, "Understanding Acquisition Speed for the Defense Department's Costliest and Most Complex Programs," Center for Strategic and International Studies, Report CSIS-AM-20-159, September 2020.

21. Robert S. McNamara, *The Essence of Security: Reflections in Office* (New York: Harper & Row, 1968), 90; Robert S. McNamara with Brian VanDeMark, *In Retrospect: The Tragedy and Lessons of Vietnam* (New York: Times Books, 1995), 23–25; Alain Enthoven interview, December 27, 1968, 19, LBJ Presidential Library, Austin, TX.

22. Hitch, *Decision-Making for Defense*, 18, 23–25, 33–34; Alain C. Enthoven and K. Wayne Smith, *How Much Is Enough? Shaping the Defense Program, 1961–1969* [originally published 1971], new edition (Santa Monica, CA: RAND, 2005), 36; Alain Enthoven interview, February 3, 1986, Office of the Secretary of Defense, 2–3, https://history.defense.gov/Historical-Sources/Oral-History-Transcript-3; Stephanie Caroline Young, "Power and the Purse: Defense Budgeting and American Politics, 1947–1972" (PhD diss., University of California, Berkeley, 2009), 54–65.

23. Hitch, *Decision-Making for Defense*, 30; This did not change over the course of McNamara's tenure, and remains true to this day. US Department of Defense, *Report to the President and the Secretary of Defense on the Department of Defense, by the Blue Ribbon Defense Panel*, July 1, 1970, 117; Lawrence J. Korb, "The Budget Process in the Department of Defense, 1947–77: The Strengths and Weaknesses of Three Systems," *Public Administration Review* 37, no. 4 (July–August 1977): 343; Robert F. Hale, "Financing the Fight: A History and Assessment of Department of Defense Budget Formulation Processes," Brookings Institution, April 2021, 11–12.

24. Hitch, *Decision-Making for Defense*, 35–38.

25. Some critics of PPBS from the time of its introduction in the 1960s through the present day have charged that five-year planning constrains policy makers' ability to alter defense budgets quickly in response to new conditions. This commonsensical proposition surely contains at least a grain of truth, but it was dismissed from the beginning by the architects of PPBS. According to Alain Enthoven, who led the systems analysis team in McNamara's office, the Five-Year Defense Plan was simply a "road map" that did not require any long-run commitments by the president or Congress. Enthoven claimed that the Five-Year Defense Plan actually provided more "flexibility to move in a new direction," by allowing policy makers to comprehend existing practices and the likely costs and benefits of a change. Enthoven and Smith, *How Much Is Enough?*, 31–72, 50.

26. Hitch, *Decision-Making for Defense*, 25, 31, 63; Korb, "Budget Process," 337; The United States does not appear to be exceptional, in this regard; many nations see a similar lag of approximately two years. Richard C. Eichenberg and Richard Stoll, "Representing Defense: Democratic Control of the Defense Budget in the United States and Western Europe," *Journal of Conflict Resolution* 47, no. 4 (August 2003): 411.

27. Korb, "Budget Process," 340.

28. Korb, "Budget Process," 341; David Packard interview, November 9, 1987, Office of the Secretary of Defense, 5, https://history.defense.gov/Historical-Sources /Oral-History-Transcript-3; William F. West, *Program Budgeting and the Performance Movement: The Elusive Quest for Efficiency in Government* (Washington, DC: Georgetown University Press, 2011), 41; Hale, "Financing the Fight," 13–14.

29. For example, Secretary of Defense Harold Brown tried in 1977 to allow more input from his office and from President Carter, before the services drafted their POMs—a move that was resisted by the services and their allies in Congress. See Russell Murray II memo on PPBS, September 26, 1977; Brown to JCS and service secretaries, October 25, 1977; Bob Sikes et al. to John C. Stennis et al., January 5, 1978, all in folder "Punaro: Military Budget (Fiscal Year 1979)," 1978, box 544, Sam Nunn Papers, Emory University.

30. Jerry Y. Draper, "Role of the Defense Resources Board in the Planning Phase of the Planning, Programming, and Budgeting System" (US Army War College, 1985); author correspondence with David Chu, February 7, 2023.

31. For descriptions of the process in recent years, see Higginbotham, "Procuring the Cross of Iron," 55–61; L. R. Jones, Philip J. Candreva, and Marc R. DeVore, *Financing National Defense: Policy and Process* (Charlotte, NC: Information Age Publishing, 2011).

32. Franklin C. Spinney, "Defense Facts of Life" slide presentation, December 5, 1980, 7, copy in folder "Military Affairs: Defense Technology, General File, 1981–1989," box 447, Nunn Papers.

33. Allen Schick, *The Federal Budget: Politics, Policy, Process*, 3rd ed. (Washington, DC: Brookings Institution Press, 2008), 14.

34. Julian E. Zelizer, ed., *The American Congress: The Building of Democracy* (Boston: Houghton Mifflin, 2004), 311.

35. Norman Augustine interview, December 14, 2001, Office of the Secretary of Defense, 22–24, https://history.defense.gov/Historical-Sources/Oral-History -Transcript-3.

36. Kolodziej, *Uncommon Defense and Congress*, 365–81; Herbert W. Stephens, "The Role of the Legislative Committees in the Appropriations Process: A Study Focused on the Armed Services Committees," *Western Political Quarterly* 24, no. 1 (March 1971): 146–62.

37. Bernard K. Gordon, "The Military Budget: Congressional Phase," *Journal of Politics* 23, no. 4 (November 1961): 710.

38. Robert J. Art, "Congress and the Defense Budget: Enhancing Policy Oversight," *Political Science Quarterly* 100, no. 2 (Summer 1985): 227–48; James M.

Lindsay, "Congress and the Defense Budget," *Washington Quarterly* 11, no. 1 (1988): 59–60; Aaron Wildavsky and Naomi Caiden, *The New Politics of the Budgetary Process*, 4th ed. (New York: Pearson, 2000), 250.

39. Wildavsky and Caiden, *New Politics of the Budgetary Process*, 251; Jamie M. Morin, "Squaring the Pentagon: The Politics of Post–Cold War Defense Retrenchment" (PhD diss., Yale University, 2003), 156–57.

40. James M. Lindsay, "Congress and Defense Policy: 1961 to 1986," *Armed Forces & Society* 13, no. 3 (Spring 1987): 371–400; Harold Brown interview, March 4, 1994, Office of the Secretary of Defense, 8, https://history.defense.gov/Historical-Sources/Oral-History-Transcript-3; Augustine interview, December 14, 2001, 22–24.

41. Morin, "Squaring the Pentagon," 39, 130.

42. Lawrence J. Korb, "Congressional Impact on Defense Spending, 1962–1973: The Programmatic and Fiscal Hypotheses," *Naval War College Review* 26, no. 3 (November–December 1973): 49; Lindsay, "Congress and Defense Policy"; Linda Sinclair, *The Transformation of the US Senate* (Baltimore: Johns Hopkins University Press, 1989); Morin, "Squaring the Pentagon," 85–86.

43. Wildavsky and Caiden, *New Politics of the Budgetary Process*, 74.

44. Charles W. Ostrom Jr. and Robin F. Marra, "US Defense Spending and the Soviet Estimate," *American Political Science Review* 80, no. 3 (September 1986): 819–42; Noel E. Firth and James H. Noren, *Soviet Defense Spending: A History of CIA Estimates, 1950–1990* (College Station: Texas A&M University Press, 1998).

45. Morin, "Squaring the Pentagon," 55.

46. Daniel Sargent, *A Superpower Transformed: The Remaking of American Foreign Relations in the 1970s* (New York: Oxford University Press, 2015), 266.

47. Lindsay, "Congress and the Defense Budget," 58.

48. Lindsay, "Congress and the Defense Budget," 66.

49. Art, "Congress and the Defense Budget," 227–48; Lindsay, "Congress and the Defense Budget," 59–60; Wildavsky and Caiden, *New Politics of the Budgetary Process*, 250; Paul Stockton, "Beyond Micromanagement: Congressional Budgeting for a Post–Cold War Military," *Political Science Quarterly* 110, no. 2 (Summer 1995): 254; Arnold Punaro, *The Ever-Shrinking Fighting Force* (McLean, VA: Punaro Press, 2021), 442–43.

50. Jacques S. Gansler, "Reforming the Defense Budget Process," *Public Interest* 75 (Spring 1984): 71.

51. Alice M. Rivlin, "The Need for a Better Budget Process," *Brookings Review* 4, no. 3 (Summer 1986): 3–10.

52. Gansler, "Reforming the Defense Budget Process," 65–68.

53. Robert Hanberg and Robert Bledsoe, "Shifting Patterns in the American Military Budget Process: An Overview," *Journal of Strategic Studies* 2, no. 3 (1979): 348; Eichenberg and Stoll, "Representing Defense," 411. This point is also made by those who would like to see non-US legislatures have a greater role. See, for example, Allen Schick, "Can National Legislatures Regain an Effective Voice in Budget Policy?," *OECD Journal on Budgeting* 1, no. 3 (2002): 15–42; Michael D. Hobkirk, *The*

Politics of Defence Budgeting: A Study of Organisation and Resource Allocation in the United Kingdom and the United States (Washington, DC: National Defense University Press, 1983), 39–42, 76–79; Aaron Wildavsky, *Budgeting: A Comparative Theory of Budgetary Processes* (Boston: Little, Brown & Co., 1975), 91, 225–27; Wildavsky and Caiden, *New Politics of the Budgetary Process*, 262.

54. President's Blue Ribbon Commission on Defense Management, *A Quest for Excellence: Final Report to the President* (Washington, DC, 1986), xix–xx, 21–30.

55. Defense policy makers had discussed the advantages of multiyear budgeting during the early McNamara years as well, but Pentagon officials believed Congress would never allow it. Hitch, *Decision-Making for Defense*, 63.

56. Jasmine Farrier, *Passing the Buck: Congress, the President, and Deficits* (Lexington: University Press of Kentucky, 2004), 42–45; Robert G. Boatright, "Biennial Budgeting Debates in Congress: 1977–2000," *Journal of Public Budgeting, Accounting & Financial Management* 15, no. 2 (Summer 2003): 275–308.

57. Robert J. Art, "The Pentagon: The Case for Biennial Budgeting," *Political Science Quarterly* 104, no. 2 (Summer 1989): 193–214; Wildavsky and Caiden, *New Politics of the Budgetary Process*, 238, 273.

58. Jones, Candreva, and DeVore, *Financing National Defense*, 108; Hale, "Financing the Fight," 19.

59. Augustine interview, December 14, 2001, 40.

60. Gates, *Duty*, 453.

61. US Senate Permanent Subcommittee on Investigations, Committee on Homeland Security and Governmental Affairs, *Defense Acquisition Reform: Where Do We Go from Here? A Compendium of Views by Leading Experts* (Washington, DC: GPO, 2014), 196, https://www.hsgac.senate.gov/subcommittees/investigations/library/files/defense-acquisition-reform-where-do-we-go-from-here_a-compendium-of-views-by-leading-experts; Jones, Candreva, and DeVore, *Financing National Defense*, 370–72; Punaro, *Ever-Shrinking Fighting Force*, 75–77, 453–57.

62. Rivlin, "Need for a Better Budget Process," 3–10.

63. Lindsay, "Congress and the Defense Budget," 66.

64. Lindsay, "Congress and the Defense Budget," 69–71; Louis Fisher, "Biennial Budgeting in the Federal Government," *Public Budgeting & Finance* 17, no. 3 (Fall 1997): 87–97; US House of Representatives, *The Broken Budget Process: Perspectives from Former CBO Directors: Hearing before the Committee on the Budget*, September 21, 2011, 112th Cong., 1st sess. (Washington, DC: GPO, 2012); Jessica Tollestrup, *Biennial Budgeting: Options, Issues, and Previous Congressional Action*, Congressional Research Service Report R41764, February 2, 2015, 9–11.

65. Lindsay, "Congress and the Defense Budget," 72–73; Punaro, *Ever-Shrinking Fighting Force*, 75–77, 453–57; Hale, "Financing the Fight," 15–21.

66. Punaro, *Ever-Shrinking Fighting Force*, 184–91.

67. Richard B. Doyle, "The Rise and (Relative) Fall of Earmarks: Congress and Reform, 2006–2010," *Public Budgeting & Finance* 31, no. 1 (Spring 2011): 1–22; Jones, Candreva, and DeVore, *Financing National Defense*, 189–90; Schick, *Federal*

Budget, 246; Iwan Morgan, *The Age of Deficits: Presidents and Unbalanced Budgets from Jimmy Carter to George W. Bush* (Lawrence: University Press of Kansas, 2009), 237; Scott A. Frisch and Sean Q. Kelly, *Cheese Factories on the Moon: Why Earmarks Are Good for American Democracy* (New York: Routledge, 2010), 132.

68. Leon Panetta with Jim Newton, *Worthy Fights: A Memoir of Leadership in War and Peace* (New York: Penguin, 2014), 371–72.

69. Punaro, *Ever-Shrinking Fighting Force*, 449.

70. Winslow Wheeler, *The Wastrels of Defense: How Congress Sabotages US Security* (Annapolis, MD: Naval Institute Press, 2004).

71. J. Ronald Fox, *Defense Acquisition Reform, 1960–2009: An Elusive Goal* (Washington, DC: US Army Center of Military History, 2012).

72. Morin, "Squaring the Pentagon," 181; Peter Levine, *Defense Management Reform: How to Make the Pentagon Work Better and Cost Less* (Stanford, CA: Stanford University Press, 2020), 104.

73. Philip L. Shiman, Elliott V. Converse III, and Joseph A. Arena, *History of Acquisition in the Department of Defense, Volume V: Reform and Experimentation after the Cold War* (Washington, DC: Historical Office, Office of the Secretary of Defense, 2022), 23–51.

74. Shiman, Converse, and Arena, *Reform and Experimentation after the Cold War*, 155–78; Levine, *Defense Management Reform*, 116–20; Michael Joshua Stricof, "The Peace Dividend and Defense Conversion in the United States after the Cold War, 1989–2001" (PhD diss., Université d'Aix-Marseille, 2019), 345–67.

75. Levine, *Defense Management Reform*, 118.

76. Shiman, Converse, and Arena, *Reform and Experimentation after the Cold War*, 299–343.

77. Jamie Morin testimony, in *Defense Acquisition Reform: Where Do We Go From Here?* (2014), 135–36; Levine, *Defense Management Reform*, 120–37; author interview with former SASC staffer, March 2018.

78. Author email exchange with former SASC staffer and DoD official, March 2018.

79. Morgan, *Age of Deficits*, 234–35; Jones, Candreva, and DeVore, *Financing National Defense*, 149–50, 219–22; Daniel Wirls, *Irrational Security: The Politics of Defense from Reagan to Obama* (Baltimore: Johns Hopkins University Press, 2010), 154–57; Gates, *Duty*, 312–13; Brendan W. McGarry and Emily M. Morgenstern, *Overseas Contingency Operations Funding: Background and Status*, Congressional Research Service Report IN11839, September 6, 2019; Hale, "Financing the Fight," 24–25.

80. Punaro, *Ever-Shrinking Fighting Force*, 325–28, 343.

81. *Providing for the Common Defense: The Assessment and Recommendations of the National Defense Strategy Commission* (2018), https://www.usip.org/publications/2018/11/providing-common-defense.

82. William J. Weinig, "Other Transaction Authority: Saint or Sinner for Defense Acquisition?," *Defense Acquisition Research Journal* 26, no. 2 (2019): 106–27; Douglas Steinberg, "Leveraging the Department of Defense's Other Transaction Authority to

Foster a Twenty-First Century Acquisition Ecosystem," *Public Contract Law Journal* 49, no. 3 (Spring 2020): 537–65; Rhys McCormick, "Department of Defense Other Transaction Authority Trends: A New R&D Funding Paradigm?," Center for Strategic and International Studies Brief (December 2020); Dolores Kuchina-Musina, "Other Transaction Authorities: Evaluating Innovation Policy Impact of Alternative Contract Vehicles in the Department of Defense" (PhD diss., Old Dominion University, 2022), 41–50.

83. William Greenwalt and John Lehman comments, in *Defense Acquisition Reform: Where Do We Go from Here?*, 92–95, 121.

84. Gregory J. Ingram, "Bridging the Innovation Gap at SOCOM" (DBA diss., University of South Florida, 2021), 36.

85. Levine, *Defense Management Reform*, 144–46.

86. William A. LaPlante comments at George Mason/NDU "Acquisition Next" Conference, November 4, 2022, https://acquisitiontalk.com/2022/11/podcast-getting-weapons-into-production-with-usd-as-bill-laplante.

87. Wildavsky and Caiden, *New Politics of the Budgetary Process*, 257; Morin, "Squaring the Pentagon," 470; Jones, Candreva, and DeVore, *Financing National Defense*, 78; Moshe Schwartz and Jason A. Purdy, *United States Special Operations Command Acquisition Authorities*, Congressional Research Service Report R45252, July 9, 2018; Russell Rumbaugh, "The Fragmentation of DoD: Changing Role of the Services and What It Means for the Space Force," Aerospace Corporation Center for Space Policy and Strategy (October 15, 2020), 5, 11.

88. Punaro, *Ever-Shrinking Fighting Force*, 75–77, 453–57. Compare to Lindsay, "Congress and Defense Policy," 394–95.

89. Hale, "Financing the Fight," 15–21.

90. President's Blue Ribbon Commission, *A Quest for Excellence*, xix–xx, 21–30.

91. *Report of the Advisory Panel on Streamlining and Codifying Acquisition Regulations: Volume 3 of 3* (Arlington, VA, 2019), 49–131; Eric Lofgren, "Pathways to Defense Budget Reform," George Mason University Center for Government Contracting White Paper Series 13 (November 1, 2022), 1–16.

92. Dov Zakheim, *A Vulcan's Tale: How the Bush Administration Mismanaged the Reconstruction of Afghanistan* (Washington, DC: Brookings Institution Press, 2013), 86, 289; *Report of the Advisory Panel on Streamlining and Codifying Acquisition Regulations: Volume 3 of 3*, 173–92; Richard E. Hagner, "Defense Appropriations: The Process, Politics, and National Security Implications" (PhD diss., Vanderbilt University, 2020), 63–69; Gates, *Duty*, 453; author interview with former HASC and OSD staff member, September 21, 2022; Lofgren, "Pathways to Defense Budget Reform."

17

Go Big or Go Home

Roger Zakheim

Not since the Reagan era has our country committed itself to a sustained, multiyear rebuilding of our military. At that time, the impact was transformative: it proved pivotal in winning the Cold War and continued to deliver capabilities decades after President Ronald Reagan left office. Today, we are at another pivotal moment; unless we go big on defense, any effort to sustain US military preeminence and realize the lofty goals of our National Defense Strategy (NDS) will be futile regardless of how much reform we try to squeeze out of the Pentagon.

Some may ask why arguing in favor of a peacetime buildup is relevant to a discussion centered around defense reform. It is true, all too often, in my view, that when experts discuss reform, they tend to refer to measures that might result in "efficiencies" or "more bang for the buck."[1] No doubt, participants in this conference will devote their energy toward highlighting fiscal inefficiencies, bureaucratic acquisition processes, antiquated accounting practices, and bloated management structures as areas ripe for reform. This well-trodden path, though laudable and essential, would play only "small ball" when our country needs to make some big moves.

Traditional defense reform will not deliver a force that can execute the NDS or alter spending so drastically that the Pentagon could miraculously afford what it needs without additional funding. Defense reform, therefore, is no longer an epochal effort that catalyzes strategic change. Rather, it is something perennially sought that rarely delivers strategic effects.[2]

The defense reform I will advance in this paper begins with making a strategic choice our country has not made in over four decades: committing

The views expressed in this chapter are solely those of the individual author and do not necessarily reflect the views of any organization with which they are, or have been, affiliated.

to a peacetime buildup of our national defense guided by the twin strategic objectives of building a military force that can win today AND tomorrow. Delivering such a go-big force, however, will require a significant boost in defense spending to around Reagan-era levels.[3]

Going Big Is a Choice

Reformers regularly critique the Pentagon for failing to make tough choices. Strategy, the argument goes, requires some form of sacrifice or the discipline to make do with less and ensure resources are spent judiciously on core areas of national interest.[4] A true strategist, therefore, lives in a world of trade-offs, choosing between sustaining conventional platforms or modernization, prioritizing unmanned systems over manned platforms, or focusing on the Indo-Pacific instead of Europe, to name a few of the most commonly referenced choices.[5] Those advocating the necessity of choice either believe the military should do less and therefore needs less, or they assume the military will have insufficient resources to complete all of its missions and must do less by necessity.[6] Though not necessarily ideologically opposed to robust American power, the latter camp adopts a pessimistic view of American economic strength or political will—twin essential ingredients for sustaining a robust military. Though for different reasons, both camps arrive at the same conclusion: that we ought to reduce our ambitions for the military.[7]

While choosing to do less is a reasonable choice, it is by no means the only choice available to the defense strategist. Choosing to go big and grow the military is legitimate, and I think the superior choice for the strategist and the nation given the state of the military and the global security environment.[8]

Foremost, we should choose to go big because that is precisely what the strategic moment requires. Our force must be capable of deterring adventurism in the present competition with China and others while also ensuring that we can prevail in any future twenty-first-century conflict. Robust investments in revolutionary technologies like quantum computing, artificial intelligence, and autonomy are critical. However, China's military expansion and Russia's invasion of Ukraine have demonstrated that conventional forces still matter: ships, submarines, tanks, fighters, bombers, munitions, and end-strength cannot be sacrificed in favor of a future capability that merely exists in a PowerPoint slide. We need to sustain our conventional capability to prevail in the current competition.[9]

To an outsider, it may seem curious to argue in favor of sustaining and growing today's force, given the US military's preeminence over the last four decades. But today's force, in many respects, is yesterday's force with plat-forms that are often older than the troops who operate them.[10] Of the five administrations that followed President Reagan, all deployed the force in armed conflict or sought a peace dividend by reducing the size of an invest-ment in the military. In other words, it has been over four decades since the military has seen sustained investment and growth outside the context of armed conflict.[11]

Moreover, we should choose to go big because that is what our defense strategy has called for since 2017. In an era with few points of agreement between our political parties, there is remarkable continuity across the Trump and Biden administrations' defense strategies.[12] Each would have the United States lead in three primary regions: the Indo-Pacific, Europe, and the Middle East. Each would seek to win—not simply manage—the competition against China and Russia. Each would also seek to deter Iran, North Korea, and ter-rorist groups. Climate change, of course, is the singular outlier reinforcing the overall continuity thrust across the two administrations. Delving into the details of each defense strategy, such as the force planning construct and global posture priorities, reveals that both the Trump and Biden administra-tions would have a US military postured globally and capable of deterring and, if necessary, defeating China while also deterring other adversaries.

In other words, the defense strategy presidents Donald Trump and Joe Biden advanced is a go-big strategy. Yet, each administration has failed to resource its strategy. The Trump administration's so-called "military rebuild" turned out to be a one-year defense bump that rightfully prioritized improv-ing the readiness of the force following years of combat operations in Iraq and Afghanistan but never made the sustained investments in growth and modernization.[13] By the end of the Trump administration, the defense budget barely kept pace with inflation, and the gap between the strategy and reality widened.[14]

It has been a similar story during the first two years of the Biden adminis-tration: an ambitious strategy accompanied by an insufficient defense budget request. Making matters worse, spiraling inflation has effectively eliminated any real growth in the budget request. This has placed Biden's defense offi-cials in the impossible position of trying to build an under-resourced force in service to a broad and expansive strategy.[15] This inevitably has forced dif-ficult choices, though not the sort of choices that lead to growth or strategic outcomes. The results are swiss cheese concepts like "integrated deterrence" and "divest to invest," which justify retiring so-called legacy platforms, many of which are strategically relevant and operationally viable. Combined with insufficient stockpiles of weapons and munitions, we are missing many of the basic elements critical to meeting the strategy outlined in the NDS.[16]

This glaring gap between strategy and resources was so apparent that Congress—notably a Congress with Democratic majorities in both chambers—felt it necessary to increase the defense budget over and above Biden's request in each of the past two years.[17] Congress did not allow the force to hollow out and instead authorized and appropriated increases that gave the Department of Defense (DoD) 3 percent real growth in fiscal year (FY) 2022 and 5 percent real growth in 2023, a total additional investment of around $70 billion.[18]

Funding the Strategy: 3 to 5 Percent Real Growth Is Not Enough

Even with congressional attempts to bridge the gap between strategy and resources, there is reason to doubt whether these funding efforts alone will be enough to see the defense strategy sufficiently resourced and executed. The Trump NDS stated that the DoD's goals are to defend the homeland, to remain the world's preeminent military power with a favorable balance of power, and to uphold an international order conducive to our security. The Biden NDS establishes similar lofty goals. It assumes global responsibilities to deter China and Russia simultaneously while tackling other state actors, terrorism, and transnational challenges.

Both strategies identify the ends but leave out the means. Both strategies correctly identify the problems but lack the resources to address them.[19] The back-of-the-envelope budget that the 2017 bipartisan National Defense Strategy Commission endorsed called for 3 to 5 percent growth annually. According to the commission, the 3 to 5 percent benchmark was "indicative of the level of investment needed to meet the ends" established in the 2017 NDS.[20] In the seven years following the 2017 NDS, this threshold was achieved four times—FY2017, FY2020, FY2022, and FY2023 (only when Congress stepped in to appropriate above the threshold in FY2022 and FY2023). The remaining years saw effectively flat or declining budgets.[21] Had Congress sustained 5 percent growth annually from FY2018–23, the Pentagon would have had an additional $375 billion to help place the military in a substantially more favorable position than it is in today.[22]

Ironically, this baseline, first advanced by former secretary of defense Jim Mattis and chairman of the Joint Chiefs of Staff Joe Dunford, was tied to a defense program that preceded the 2017 NDS and had not fully absorbed the breadth and reach of the new strategy.[23]

How much funding does the go-big NDS require? Reagan's peacetime military buildup averaged 6 percent of GDP.[24] This is the correct historical analogy and slightly higher than the 4.5–5 percent required for today's force.[25] Here's why: The fulcrum of the go-big strategy is sustaining, and in some cases building up, today's force and making the investments required to modernize the force for tomorrow. The current defense program falls short on both fronts.

Winning Today

While a full inventory of capability shortfalls is beyond the scope of this paper, listed below is a high-level summary of six deficiencies in today's force critical to executing the NDS. Each presents a significant strategic vulnerability requiring urgent attention and resources if we are to prevail today.

- *Size of the Navy* With under 300 ships in its current battle force, the navy is significantly below its stated goal of 355 ships, with no plan to fill the void for decades. The Biden administration's April 2022 thirty-year shipbuilding plan would not reach the 355-ship threshold until after 2040.[26] Meanwhile, the navy's so-called 2045 plan would not deliver 375 ships until 2045. At the same time, the Chinese navy has 340 ships and is expected to grow to 400 by 2025 and 440 by 2030.[27] Both plans reveal significant vulnerability to the NDS goals in the two-decade interregnum as China races ahead in deploying a world-class navy. Accelerating shipbuilding will require increasing shipbuilding accounts and demand capital investments in shipbuilding capacity. Several years of focused congressional oversight concluded that squeezing more shipbuilding out of the current industrial base is nearly impossible.

  A prime example is attack submarines, or SSNs. Few experts would contest the argument that the navy should increase its output of attack submarines, yet industrial capacity constraints and retirements will result in fewer total SSNs in the coming years than we have today.[28] As the NDS Commission concluded, "to project and sustain combat power into the Western Pacific and other theaters, the Navy must dramatically recapitalize and expand its military sealift forces."[29]

- *Fighters and Bombers*   A similar tension of balancing near- and long-term needs applies to fighter aircraft, with the total combat aircraft inventory scheduled to decline from 1,970 to 1,800 beginning in FY2023.[30] Amidst this reduction in airpower, Congress has prohibited retirements of capable aircraft, like the F-22 Raptor and the F-18, on the grounds that the platforms remain relevant to today's fight and new capabilities—be they manned or unmanned—are not yet ripe for production.

  The B-21 Raider's extended range and large payload, coupled with next-generation stealth technology, is a game changer in the expansive Indo-Pacific theater.[31] Yet, we are years away from the B-21 coming online and unlikely to have enough capacity to defeat our adversaries' increasingly sophisticated defenses. Like shipbuilding, the math continues to work against the size and capability of the force: we are retiring more capability than we are bringing online.

- *Weapons and Air Defense Shortfalls*   Though the war in Ukraine has recently put US weapon shortfalls into the public discourse, this was a central focus of defense strategists going back to at least the 2017 NDS.[32] As the NDS Commission noted, "nearly any conflict between the United States and its most capable competitors would entail significant demand for long-range, high-precision munitions so that US forces can remain outside the range of advanced air defense systems and other anti-access/area denial capabilities."[33] The war in Ukraine has only reinforced the urgency and scale of the problem. Capacity limitations within existing production lines are not limited to now well-known weapons like HIMARs, Stingers, and Javelins but plague production lines across the spectrum. In the first three months of the war, the United States provided over a third of its stockpiled Javelins and a quarter of its stockpiled Stingers.[34] Again, Congress has taken initial steps to make capital investments in production lines but the effort is not comprehensive and will require sustained support.[35]

  Similarly, air and missile defense systems remain a high demand/low availability capability. In December, the United States shifted two surface-to-air missile batteries from the Middle East to Ukraine to fend off Russia's brutal missile campaign against its cities, leaving the Middle East with a capability gap that will not be backfilled for two years.[36] It's a similar story for Taiwan, which also seeks US air and missile defense systems and long-range precision weapons as it postures against Chinese aggression.[37] Last year, Boeing was forced to delay the Harpoon Coastal Defense System's delivery to Taiwan by one to two years.[38] The limiting factor to supporting both partners is insufficient capacity.[39]

- *Overseas Basing*   Basing is an area that receives little attention but is no less critical to posturing the military in accordance with the NDS. It is perhaps the most significant component of what the 2022 NDS refers to as "campaigning." This focuses "on the access and warfighting requirements that enable our efforts to deter potential [Chinese] and Russian aggression against vital US national interests, and to prevail in conflict if deterrence fails."[40] Specifically, distributing forces and hardening bases are critical steps toward implementing "campaigning" in the Indo-Pacific. To meet this goal, Congress authorized over $6 billion of the Pacific Deterrence Initiative (PDI) to improve posture and presence, accounting for over half of PDI's total authorization.

  Yet, PDI has received only tepid support from the Pentagon. In FY2023, Congress nearly doubled the Biden request for PDI.[41] As one analyst noted, "the Pentagon's request left US Indo-Pacific Command with $1.5 billion in unfunded requirements."[42] Moreover, the Pentagon plan would shrink PDI by more than a quarter to $4.4 billion by FY2027. Notably, that is the date by which China aims to accelerate its military modernization with an eye on seizing Taiwan.[43] There remains much more to be done in the years ahead: "Despite the Pentagon's focus on a more distributed posture, over three-quarters of posture funding in the initiative is concentrated in Japan and Guam . . . projects in the Second Island Chain, Oceania, and Southeast Asia account for a small portion of investment."[44]

- *Nuclear Weapons*   Though Vladimir Putin's nuclear saber-rattling in Ukraine, and China's rapid nuclear modernization, have elevated public awareness of nuclear weapons, the necessity of a credible nuclear deterrent has long been the cornerstone of the NDS. Absent modernized strategic forces, the United States will not be able to deter a second adversary in the event we find ourselves in a conflict with a major power. Fortunately, nuclear modernization is one area where the words of the NDS have consistently been backed up by action. To date, efforts to recapitalize all three legs of the nuclear triad have received sufficient funding, and all three programs are approaching production. Yet, our current nuclear deterrence delivery systems are reaching the end-of-service life in the 2025 to 2035 time frame. The replacement programs can, therefore, ill afford funding interruptions or programmatic setbacks to ensure there are no gaps in capability when the legacy systems age out. This will require significant investment over the next twenty years.

Strategic weapons are not the full story, however. Tactical nuclear weapons have reemerged in military strategy as Russia and China have modernized and produced these weapons and integrated them into their military doctrine and operational concepts.[45] Though these developments were foreseeable, military planners and nuclear strategists have not adequately prepared a response to them. Plans to add nuclear-capable cruise missiles have been stymied within the Biden administration,[46] once again leaving it to Congress to fund continued research on the sea-launched cruise missile.[47]

- *Size of the Force*   While the navy and air force—the two services at the heart of the NDS—will see modest growth, the FY2023 National Defense Authorization Act lowered army end-strength to 452,000—the smallest active-duty force since the start of the all-volunteer force in 1973. While recruiting woes explain the dramatic drop, some argue that our shift to the Indo-Pacific justifies an army end-strength below 485,000 (the previous year's authorized army end-strength).[48] This would be ill-advised: less than eighteen months ago, the army's chief of staff said that a force of 485,000 soldiers was too small and that an ideal size would be closer to 540,000.[49] In other words, the army—even without its recruiting challenges—will be significantly below the end-strength levels required to meet the demands of the NDS, either for peacetime missions or preparing for contingency operations.[50]

These examples illustrate how the price of building and sustaining today's force significantly exceeds the current defense program. Moreover, as noted above, the procurement costs of filling these capability gaps carry substantial capital investment costs. Taken together, these items, in addition to other areas of the defense budget that require real growth annually, such as the personnel, readiness, and operation and maintenance accounts, lead one to begin to appreciate the true cost of winning today.[51]

Winning Tomorrow

The go-big strategy also demands sustained and increased investments in new technologies critical to winning tomorrow's conflicts. Both the 2017 and 2022 NDSs delineate the technologies and capabilities critical to the future force.[52] Integrating artificial intelligence and best-in-class software into current and future platforms, moving command and control to the edge of the battlefield, integrating space assets into military operations, and deploying cheaper (we hope) autonomous systems in the force are the sine qua non of tomorrow's force.[53] Here, the challenge resides not just with developing new technologies but also with transitioning these technologies from research, development, testing, and evaluation projects into programs of record and ready for production.[54] The double-digit real growth that DoD's space programs enjoyed in recent years serves as a template for what simultaneously investing in the capabilities of today and tomorrow looks like.

The go-big strategy necessitates that producing and fielding these technologies do not come at the expense of today's force while also ensuring efforts to strengthen today's force will not stymie modernization efforts. However, delaying the transition to tomorrow's force may be less an issue of budgetary trade-offs than an insufficient body of investment. A survey of the Pentagon's budget materials reveals the dearth of funding dedicated to critical technology areas, which according to the DoD, "will accelerate transitioning key capabilities to the Military Services and Combatant Commands."[55] Investment in the DoD's fourteen critical technologies combined with its funding of advanced component development and prototypes amounts to $45 billion in FY2023. This includes $10 billion toward hypersonics, a unique military capability that the United States has successfully tested only once and which the DoD cannot rely on the commercial sector to innovate and deliver.

Meanwhile, China has conducted numerous hypersonic missile tests, and Russia has used them in combat.[56] Put into context, this $45 billion investment is around 5 percent of the total Pentagon budget and about a third of the Pentagon's Research, Development, Test, and Evaluation budget.[57] These numbers do not fully capture all technology investments. For example, autonomy and space are covered elsewhere in the budget. This snapshot does suggest that we are a long way off from the scale of investment required to replace air, land, and sea platforms with AI-infused autonomous systems. As one report noted, "for defense startups seeking to raise funds or live up to lofty valuations, the relatively small portion of the DoD budget allocated to defense technology innovation may not be sufficient to attain scale unless they carefully consider their options."[58] In comparison, China is leveraging its civil-military fusion to rapidly incorporate the achievements of its commercial sector into its military modernization. This is allowing China to quickly integrate revolutionary technologies that will shape the future of warfare.[59]

In 1981, the defense budget jumped from 4.5 percent of GDP to 5.7 percent of GDP and 6.5 percent of GDP in 1982.[60] Going big requires a similar jump from today's spending levels of just over 3 percent to around 5 percent of GDP. This would enable the military departments to utilize today's assets in the day-to-day military competition with China and Russia while allowing technology investments to mature and integrate into the force without an intervening capability gap. At the strategic level, these funds would allow the military to focus on the Indo-Pacific while also sustaining our security commitments in Europe and the Middle East. This is the essence of the go-big strategy.

Will America Support Going Big?

Public opinion data demonstrates that Americans already support going big. The latest Reagan National Defense Survey, conducted in November 2022 after the midterm elections, found that about three-quarters (76 percent) favor increasing government spending on the military, including supermajorities across party lines with 68 percent favorability among Democrats, 72 percent among Independents, and 87 percent among Republicans. This support has been remarkably consistent across previous surveys, hovering at around three-quarters since the survey began asking the question in 2018. Not only do Americans support increasing defense spending, but 63 percent, including bipartisan majorities, also express concern that high inflation means the military cannot purchase as much equipment as it might need, leading to reduced military capabilities.[61]

Relatedly, Americans support US global engagement. According to the survey, a plurality (40 percent) believe it is better for the United States to be more engaged and take the lead regarding international events, while 32 percent believe we should be less engaged and react to events; 24 percent say it depends. Notably, support increases when the question becomes less abstract and more tangible. For example, regarding our forward-deployed military presence, 65 percent, including over 60 percent of both Democrats and Republicans, believe it is better for the United States to maintain military bases around the world to deter attacks and respond quickly if something happens, while 27 percent believe the United States should reduce its military presence overseas and only deploy troops in response to aggression. This, too, has been remarkably consistent across four previous surveys.[62]

Americans' preference for a go-big strategy complements their views on Russia and China. Regarding the war in Ukraine, not only are 77 percent concerned about a Russian victory in the war, but a majority of Americans want to continue providing tangible support to the Ukrainians, even though the war had, at that time, dragged on for almost a year. With regard to America sending military equipment and financial assistance to Ukraine, a majority (57 percent) believe the United States must continue to stand with the people of Ukraine and oppose Russian aggression in order to protect a friendly democracy and prevent future Russian aggression in Europe. Only a third (33 percent) believe America has enough problems at home and cannot afford to spend more on the conflict and risk further provoking Russia. The survey also found that 59 percent are concerned about US military aid to Ukraine causing the United States to deplete its own weapons stockpile, which mirrors the percentage that would like to continue supporting Ukraine. This suggests that Americans believe we can and should support Ukraine and invest in replenishing our weapons stockpile.[63]

Looking at American views through a strategic lens, Americans generally align with the NDS and want the United States to oppose China and Russia. When asked where we should focus our military forces, a plurality (31 percent) say, East Asia, while 18 percent say we should focus them in Europe. Additionally, Americans understand the connection between Ukraine and Taiwan, as 71 percent are concerned that Russian aggression will inspire other authoritarian countries to invade their democratic neighbors. In fact, bipartisan majorities support efforts to deter a Chinese invasion of Taiwan: 61 percent support increasing the US military presence near Taiwan, and 58 percent support increasing arms sales to Taiwan.[64]

Despite the go-big strategy's popularity, Americans recognize that our military is currently not prepared and requires further investment. Considerably less than half (40 percent) think the US military is the best in the world in terms of overall capabilities when compared to other countries' militaries. Around the same percentage (43 percent) think the United States' conventional weaponry, such as tanks, battleships, and airplanes, is the best, and 37 percent think our military's high-tech weaponry, such as artificial intelligence and missile technology, is the best. Only a quarter (25 percent) believe our military's cyber technology, cybersecurity, and cyber warfare are the best in the world.[65]

Contrary to the pronouncements from neo-isolationists and restrainers, the majority of Americans support the go-big strategy and support efforts to fund it.

The Role of the Reformer in a "Go-Big" Strategy

This paper argues that the essential choice in executing the NDS is making a sustained, robust financial investment in the military. It is only upon committing to this choice that one can delineate which sort of defense reform initiatives will contribute to building the force of today and tomorrow. In other words, reform qua reform initiatives will, at best, be NDS neutral or, at worst, distract from the business of going big. Below are a few reform efforts that would enhance the execution of the NDS:

- *Budget Process*   Much ink has been spilled on the antiquated defense budgeting process.[66] Budget reform of any kind will miss the mark if the Pentagon continues to submit budgets based on two-year-old assumptions and information. It is long overdue for the Pentagon to employ dynamic budgeting processes on par with the practices of Fortune 100 companies. It's foolhardy attempting to build tomorrow's force based on yesterday's old information.

  Any budget reform discussion cannot overlook the harm of continuing resolutions that have become ingrained due to political gridlock and their normalization in the political process. Eliminating continuing resolutions seems fanciful given our current politics, but taking steps to mitigate its harmful effects on budget execution,[67] such as flexibility for "new starts," would have a transformative effect on advancing DoD's strategic goals.[68]

- *Industrial Capacity*   Whether building more Virginia-class submarines, increasing munitions production, or scaling up procurement of autonomous systems, the go-big strategy will place demands on the industrial base it cannot currently meet. Significant investments are needed along the lines of the "defense infrastructure" amendment recently authored by Senators Richard Shelby, Jim Inhofe, and Roger Wicker.[69] However, money is necessary but insufficient to solve this problem as new manufacturing methods and processes will be required.[70]

- *Integrating New Technologies* The commercial technologies that will define the future force have yet to fully penetrate the walls of the Pentagon. Despite commitments from multiple secretaries of defense across Republican and Democratic administrations to help new, innovative companies overcome the so-called "valley of death," only a handful can claim the much-vaunted program of record.[71] The Reagan Institute Task Force on Technology and Workforce offered several specific recommendations for the Defense Department on this point, including some form of reform to Pentagon management practices and acquisition policies.[72] Others have correctly argued that current acquisition processes and management structures undermine "on-time-based innovation, experimentation, and operational prototyping," which are the coin of the realm for integrating private-sector innovation.[73] Absent these reforms, the military risks losing the attention and investment of America's commercial innovation base.[74]

Conclusion

The 2017 NDS Commission warned that anything short of its recommendation will require the Pentagon "to alter the expectations of US defense strategy and our global strategic objectives."[75] In other words, the choice is binary: we either need to resource or change the strategy. Seven years later, we have done the opposite: expanded the strategy without committing to resourcing it.

Advocates of a strong US national defense posture often invoke President Reagan's "Peace through Strength" philosophy, but it is worth reflecting on the meaning of that core principle. At the height of the 1980s military buildup, President Reagan argued, "Peace is not the absence of conflict, but the ability to cope with conflict by peaceful means."[76] To ensure we can address today's challenges, we need to commit to resourcing a strategy that prevails in the competition with China while holding off adversaries and spoilers in other regions. The alternative to the go-big strategy is to cede our military supremacy and go home resigned to becoming a regional power, an alternative we cannot accept. The peace President Reagan spoke of was not simply a campaign slogan but a policy mandate backed by an integrated budget and strategy leading to an end state where American interests, economic prosperity, and freedom were secured by the strength of a well-funded military capable of outcompeting those who might do us harm. It's time we go big again.

Notes

1. Peter Levine, "Can the Pentagon Save Its Way to Better Management?," *War on the Rocks*, August 6, 2019.

2. An example of epochal reform is Secretary Robert McNamara's creation of the Planning, Programming, and Budgeting System (PPBS), which centralized the entire DoD budget within OSD by creating a complete statement of costs over each platform throughout its life cycle. PPBS cemented the power of the Secretary of Defense over the service chiefs and permanently altered the Pentagon budgetary process. The PPBS (now PPBE, with "E" for execution) process has outlived its shelf life and is in need of major changes. See Commission on PPBE Reform, https://ppbereform.senate.gov.

3. Of course, there are strategies that go bigger. During the Cold War, the defense strategy called for a two-war construct. See Raphael S. Cohen, "Ukraine and the New Two War Construct," *War on the Rocks*, January 5, 2023. Cohen outlines how a go-big strategy could possibly be even larger. He proposes the Ukraine model, that the United States should be prepared for a major contingency and have the capacity to act as the "Arsenal of Democracy" by having the industrial base to allow our partners to win if they choose to fight.

4. Hal Brands, *What Good Is Grand Strategy?: Power and Purpose in American Statecraft from Harry S. Truman to George W. Bush* (Ithaca, NY: Cornell University Press, 2014), 7.

5. Brands, *What Good Is Grand Strategy?*, 4.

6. American power is being diluted and plummeting toward strategic insolvency. The United States can decrease commitments, live with risk, or build up, which Brands and Edelman argue is the correct strategic choice and not as fiscally daunting as it appears. See Hal Brands and Eric S. Edelman, "Avoiding a Strategy of Bluff: The Crisis of American Military Primacy," Center for Strategic and Budgetary Assessments, 2017, 2.

7. Roger Zakheim, "Restore Reagan's Military 'Margin of Safety,'" *Wall Street Journal*, August 28, 2022.

8. Critics point out that the United States is a bigger military spender than the rest of the world combined. This argument is deeply flawed. See Jim Talent, "US Defense Spending and False Comparisons," *National Review*, July 18, 2017.

9. US Senate, Armed Services Committee, *Hearing on Global Security Challenges and Strategy before the Senate Armed Services Committee*, 117th Cong. 3, 2022 (statement by Roger Zakheim, Director of the Ronald Reagan Institute).

10. Any budget growth went for readiness for counterinsurgency over combined arms training or loitering drones for stability operations instead of next-generation air superiority fighters. See Thomas G. Mahnken and Roger Zakheim, "Antiques Road Show: The Real State of the US Military," *The Atlantic*, July 27, 2019.

11. Mackenzie Eaglen, "Our Incredible Shrinking Military," American Enterprise Institute, July 29, 2016.

12. US Department of Defense (DoD), *Summary of the 2018 National Defense Strategy of the United States of America*, January 2018, 2; DoD, *2022 National Defense Strategy of the United States of America*, October 2022, 4–6.

13. US Senate, Armed Services Committee, *Hearing on Global Security Challenges* (Zakheim).

14. DoD, *Fiscal Year 2020 Budget Request*, March 2019, https://media.defense .gov/2019/Mar/12/2002099931/-1/-1/1/FY-2020-BUDGET-ROLLOUT-BRIEF .PDF.

15. Dov S. Zakheim, "Biden's National Security Strategy: A Vision More Aspirational than Realistic," *The Hill*, October 21, 2022.

16. Mike Gallagher, "Biden's 'Integrated Deterrence' Fails in Ukraine," *Wall Street Journal*, March 29, 2022; Elaine Luria, "Does the Pentagon Take China Seriously?," *Wall Street Journal*, July 7, 2021.

17. Bryant Harris, "Congress Authorizes 8% Defense Budget Increase," *Defense News*, December 15, 2022.

18. US Congress, *National Defense Authorization Act for Fiscal Year 2022*, 117th Cong. (2021–2022); US Senate Committee on Armed Services, *Summary of the Fiscal Year 2023 National Defense Authorization Act*, 117th Cong. 1 (2023).

19. DoD, *2018 National Defense Strategy*, January 2018, 4, 7. (The words "budget", "funding," or "dollar" do not appear in the 2022 NDS.)

20. National Defense Strategy Commission, *Providing for the Common Defense: The Assessment and Recommendations of the National Defense Strategy Commission*, November 2018, xii.

21. Office of Management and Budget (OMB), "Historical Tables," Table 5.1— Budget Authority by Function and Subfunction: 1976–2028, https://www.white house.gov/omb/budget/historical-tables.

22. These calculations assume a 5 percent inflation factor for FY2022–23.

23. National Defense Strategy Commission, *Providing for the Common Defense*, xii.

24. Assuming nominal GDP of $26.19 trillion, 4.5 percent GDP is around $1.18 trillion, roughly $321 billion above the FY2023 defense appropriation. International Monetary Fund, "GDP Current Prices 2023: United States," https://www.imf .org/external/datamapper/NGDPD@WEO/USA?zoom=USA&highlight=USA (accessed January 4, 2023); OMB, "Historical Tables," Table 5.1; and Table 10.1— Gross Domestic Product and Deflators Used in the Historical Tables: 1940–2028, https://www.whitehouse.gov/omb/budget/historical-tables. See the comparison of 050 account to overall GDP, for yearly average of 6.13 percent GDP allocated to defense 1981–89 after 4.5 percent allocated to defense in 1980.

25. Adam O'Neal, "Russia, China and the New Cold War," *Wall Street Journal: Weekend Interview*, March 18, 2022; Connor O'Brien, "Democrats' Dilemma: Back Biden's Pentagon Budget or Supersize it," *Politico*, April 5, 2022. Elaine Luria

advocates a trillion-dollar defense budget, citing the profound strategic challenge of China and Russia.

26. Sam LaGrone, "Navy's Force Design 2045 Plans for 373 Ship Fleet, 150 Unmanned Vessels," *USNI News*, July 26, 2022.

27. DoD, *2022 Report on Military and Security Developments Involving the People's Republic of China*, November 2022, 145.

28. "The United States must expand its submarine fleet": See National Defense Strategy Commission, *Providing for the Common Defense*, 36; Megan Eckstein, "Workforce Development, Process Improvements Will Make or Break the Virginia-Class Submarine Program," *Defense News*, January 6, 2022.

29. Eckstein, "Workforce Development."

30. John A. Tirpak, "Air Force Would Reduce Fleet by 250 Old Aircraft, Bring On 82-Plus New Ones," *Air & Space Forces Magazine*, March 28, 2022.

31. Stephen Losey, "'Deterrence the American Way': The New B-21 Bomber Debuts," *Defense News*, December 2, 2022.

32. DoD, *2018 National Defense Strategy*, 11.

33. National Defense Strategy Commission, *Providing for the Common Defense*, 41.

34. Ellen Mitchell, "Pentagon Moves $1.45 Billion to Restock Javelin, Stinger Missiles Sent to Ukraine," *The Hill*, May 6, 2022.

35. US Senate Committee on Armed Services, *Summary of the Fiscal Year 2023 National Defense Authorization Act* (December 2022). The go-big approach is criticized for throwing money at the problem but this is exactly what solving munitions shortfalls requires. The only way to increase production capacity and the workforce are providing promises of continued demand and investment. Edward N. Luttwak, "Why We Need More Waste, Fraud, and Mismanagement in the Pentagon," *Survival: Global Politics and Strategy* 24, no. 3 (1982): 117–30.

36. Lee Hudson, "US Looks to Shift Air Defense Systems from Middle East to Ukraine, Raytheon Chief Says," *Politico*, December 1, 2022.

37. Harry Halem and Eyck Freymann, "Ukraine Shows Why Taiwan Needs More Air Defense," *War on the Rocks*, April 7, 2022.

38. Ryan White, "The US Delays Delivery of Harpoon Coastal Defense System to Taiwan," *Naval Post*, March 9, 2021.

39. Patriot air defense systems are a scarce resource; the Pentagon must understand the cost to US modernization and training efforts. See Dan Lamothe, Karen DeYoung, and Alex Horton, "Pentagon Preparing to Send Patriot Missile System to Ukraine," *Washington Post*, December 13, 2022.

40. DoD, *2022 National Defense Strategy*, 13.

41. DoD, Office of the Under Secretary of Defense (Comptroller)/Chief Financial Officer, *Defense Budget Overview: Fiscal Year 2023 Budget Request*, April 2022, 3-3.

42. Dustin Walker, "Show Me the Money: Boost the Pacific Deterrence Initiative," *War on the Rocks*, June 29, 2022.

43. Walker, "Show Me the Money."

44. Walker, "Show Me the Money."

45. Michael Kofman and Anya Loukianova Fink, "Escalation Management and Nuclear Employment in Russian Military Strategy," *War on the Rocks*, September 19, 2022.

46. Rather than adopting a comprehensive nuclear posture and developing capabilities that could deter an adversary from escalating to a tactical nuclear strike, the Biden administration remains stuck in the immediate post–Cold War mindset that hesitated to develop new battlefield nuclear weapons.

47. Roger Zakheim, "Ukraine War Shows Us That Old Nuclear Strategies Won't Keep Us Safe and Biden Must Wake Up," *Fox News*, October 10, 2022. On congressional funding in the fiscal year 2023 NDAA, see US Senate Committee on Armed Services, *Summary of the Fiscal Year 2023 National Defense Authorization Act*. Both China and Russia are modernizing and introducing theater nuclear capabilities and we cannot rely on the threat of strategic nuclear forces and must utilize lower-yield theater nuclear capabilities of our own. See US Senate, Armed Services Committee, *United States Nuclear Strategy and Policy*, 117th Cong. 8 (2022) (statement by Eric S. Edelman, Counselor for Center for Strategic and Budgetary Assessments, and Franklin C. Miller, Principal of the Scowcroft Group).

48. Jon Harper, "Lawmakers Want to Shrink Army, Grow Navy," *National Defense Magazine*, February 28, 2022.

49. Ethan Sterenfeld, "Army End Strength Could Fall to 445,000 in FY-23," *Inside Defense*, July 19, 2022.

50. One need only look back to Operation Enduring Freedom and Operation Iraqi Freedom to see how an active-duty army force below 500,000 cannot sustain a sustained ground conflict.

51. Readiness and Operation & Maintenance spending accounts for roughly 60 percent of the Pentagon budget. DoD, Under Secretary of Defense, *2023 Budget Request*, 6-17. Additional funding would overcome the cannibalizing effect that personnel and operation and maintenance accounts tend to have on modernization accounts in a flat budget scenario. Ronald Reagan Institute and the Center for Strategic and Budgetary Assessments, *America's Strategic Choices: Defense Spending in a Post-COVID-19 World*, January 2021.

52. DoD, *2022 National Defense Strategy*, 6. "New applications of artificial intelligence, quantum science, autonomy, biotechnology, and space technologies have the potential not just to change kinetic conflict, but also to disrupt day-to-day US supply chain and logistics operations"; DoD, Under Secretary of Defense, *2023 Budget Request*, 4-5.

53. Doug Cameron and Micah Maidenburg, "Space Launches Should Withstand Chinese Challenge, Pentagon Mandate Says," *Wall Street Journal*, January 10, 2023. See new DoD requirements that new US spy satellites must be capable of fending off Chinese and Russian interference, a change from previous standards strictly concerned with cost and reliability.

54. Eric Lofgren, "Sources of Defense Tech Transition Funding," *Acquisition Talk,* October 27, 2022.

55. DoD, Under Secretary of Defense, *2023 Budget Request,* 4-2.

56. Oren Liebermann, "US Air Force Carries Out First Fully Successful Test of Air-Launched Hypersonic Missile," CNN, December 12, 2022.

57. Eric Chewning, Will Gangware, Jess Harrington, and Dale Swartz, "How Will US Funding for Defense Technology Innovation Evolve?," McKinsey & Company, November 4, 2022.

58. Chewning et al., "How Will US Funding for Defense Technology Innovation Evolve?"

59. DoD, *2021 Report on Military and Security Developments Involving the People's Republic of China,* November 2021, 145, 147.

60. OMB, "Historical Tables," Tables 5.1 and 10.1.

61. Ronald Reagan Institute, *Reagan National Defense Survey,* November 2022, distributed by Beacon Research and Shaw & Company Research.

62. Ronald Reagan Institute, *Reagan National Defense Survey.*

63. Ronald Reagan Institute, *Reagan National Defense Survey.*

64. Ronald Reagan Institute, *Reagan National Defense Survey.*

65. Ronald Reagan Institute, *Reagan National Defense Survey.*

66. Commission on PPBE Reform, "About Us," https://ppbereform.senate.gov /aboutus (accessed April 7, 2023).

67. US Government Accountability Office, *Defense Budget: DoD Has Adopted Practices to Manage within the Constraints of Continuing Resolutions,* highlights of GAO-21-541, a report to congressional committees, September 2021. DoD has insulated itself from the harmful effects of CRs by developing spending plans for various CR scenarios and adjusting contracts to reflect CR spending availability.

68. Defense Technical Information Center, *Report of the Advisory Panel on Streamlining and Codifying Acquisition Regulations,* January 2019, 2. See reforms including that Congress should allow one year validity of all funding appropriated under CRs to eliminate budget compression effect.

69. Connor O'Brien, "GOP Senators Look to Add $50B for Defense into Critical Infrastructure Bill," *Politico,* August 5, 2021. See $25.4 billion investment to upgrade Navy shipyards to support new ships and a larger fleet.

70. For a discussion on digitally enabled flexible and customizable manufacturing in the defense sector, see Ronald Reagan Institute, *A Manufacturing Renaissance: Bolstering US Production for National Security and Economic Prosperity,* Task Force on National Security and US Manufacturing Competitiveness, November 2021, 15.

71. Lloyd Austin, Luncheon Keynote Speech, and Panel 10 (Mark Esper), "Protecting Stength: A Discussion with Former National Security Leaders," at Reagan National Defense Forum 2022: Protecting Peace, Projecting Strength (Simi Valley, CA, December 2, 2022). During his address Secretary Austin announced the creation of the Office of Strategic Capital. "This is an example of how we're creating

the conditions for innovation for our innovators to succeed. You know this kind of change doesn't always move as smoothly or as quickly as I'd like, but we are determined to change the way that the Pentagon does business." Secretary Mark Esper expressed similar sentiments during Panel 10: "We have to accelerate the access of innovation from the private sector into DoD to capitalize on cutting edge technologies that are out there."

72. Ronald Reagan Institute, *The Contest for Innovation: Strengthening America's National Security Innovation Base in an Era of Strategic Competition*, Task Force on 21st Century National Security Technology and Workforce, December 2019. The task force's recommendations include (1) making use of its alternative acquisition pathways to award contracts as part of programs of record to companies to ensure a sustainable funding profile; (2) measuring progress in contracts awarded, total dollars awarded, and speed of procurement, focusing on writing fewer, larger checks both as a way to leverage key emerging technologies and as a signal to investors; and (3) overhauling software acquisitions to move away from requirements lists to iterative capabilities and maximize the use of commercial standards for interoperability.

73. Bill Greenwalt, "Competing in Time: How DoD Is Losing the Innovation Race to China," *Breaking Defense*, March 9, 2021; William C. Greenwalt and Dan Patt, "Competing in Time: Ensuring Capability Advantage and Mission Success through Adaptable Resource Allocation," Hudson Institute, February 25, 2021. Greenwalt and Patt find that the key to national security strategy success is managing the budgeting process, not the acquisitions process as conventional wisdom would indicate. Keeping the massive Pentagon bureaucracy churning is the critical engine for a long-term military competition. The budget process and PPBE is antiquated. The emerging technologies critical for tomorrow's battles are not resourced in the same fashion as the technology that won the Cold War. As the United States enters a new era of strategic competition, it must holistically reform PPBE to maintain a competitive advantage in long-term competition.

74. Shands Pickett, "Reboot the Defense Innovation Ecosystem," *War on the Rocks*, April 7, 2022.

75. National Defense Strategy Commission, *Providing for the Common Defense*, 52.

76. Ronald Reagan, "Address at Commencement Exercises at Eureka College," given in Eureka, IL, May 9, 1982.

Reform Recommendations and Budget Implications

With Admiral Gary Roughead, Ellen Lord, and David L. Norquist,
Moderated by Michael J. Boskin

MICHAEL J. BOSKIN: We've talked about lots of things. We have a remarkable military with great capabilities. Our adversaries and potential adversaries have been gearing up in a way that reduces our advantages. We have a lot of ideas about what the problems are and about what some solutions are. I think everybody wants us to have a stronger national defense and security system than we do. We've had many great ideas. But of course, none of this happens unless some reform happens. That is going to be the purpose of our next panel.

We've heard people complaining about the Pentagon, people complaining about Congress. The White House has sometimes been mentioned. Obviously, the American public has to be educated and brought along on a lot of this stuff. From my standpoint, we have a lot to improve, but we should be proud of many things we've done, and we should take those lessons and try to apply them.

MACKENZIE EAGLEN: I'm going to start with some potentially good news. There is a competition underway for a major contract at the Defense Department. I wasn't tracking it until recently, but it's a traditional defense company against a software company for a major defense acquisition program. Put it on your calendar the day that this happens. We don't know which one is going to win, but it's Palantir versus Raytheon. The construct of the contract is, build the

The views expressed in these presentations and discussion are solely those of the individual participants and do not necessarily reflect the views of any organization with which they are, or have been, affiliated.

software first, and then we're going to build a truck. At least on the Palantir side, that's how they're doing it. Anduril is going to then build the truck after Palantir builds the software. It's remarkable. Watching who wins will be very interesting to the future of many questions we've been talking about.

I raise that because the Defense Department spends most of the money that goes in when you put aside the cost of labor. It goes back out the door in terms of purchases of goods, labor, IT, technology, and software. The discussion and the reform are often on one part of that pie, the purchase of things. That's not what the Defense Department predominantly buys anymore. Ask David [L. Norquist] and Ellen [Lord]. It's services, labor, IT, and software. Everybody wants to reform the purchasing of things. In fact, we're at the point now, as James Cunningham highlighted, that the three-decade modernization squeeze is here.

We don't buy enough things is not the problem anymore. I'd argue it's been over-reformed. There's been too much reform about procurement and not enough on every other part of the defense budget. The bottom line of my paper is "you're only serious about reform" if you're talking about two things. Reforming Congress. I can't do that, so I'm not going to talk about it, but Congress needs reforming, particularly appropriations. You're only serious about reform if you're talking about taking something away. What rules, regulations, and laws are you going to sunset, expire, scrub, and get rid of or end? Anyone who says, I've got ten thousand pages of this acquisition reform act to give you, I say, there's the door.

We don't need more additive band-aids to the problems that plague the Defense Department. What are you going to take away? Everything needs to be scrubbed for what needs to go away, what needs to end, and what needs to be sunsetted. Laws, rules, regs, everything.

That's where we are in the reform space because this is a department that's under constant reform, internal and external, as you saw in my paper. I use the term a little pejoratively later in my paper, "Defense Reform Theater." Not all of these efforts were that, of course. I say it meaning, often reform is for reform's sake to justify defense toplines, and politicians understand that. I get the politics of it, or at least that part of the politics of it. I'm no Mac Thornberry.

We are now at the point where saying fraud, waste, and abuse are the problem. Or these efficiencies and night courts are going to get you the dollars to buy new and more defense strategy. Not true. Too much of the defense budget is on autopilot. It's calcified. It's essentially fenced and fixed, so anything you want to do has to be additive in dollars. You want more strategy? You need more money because that's just where we are. Too many constituencies, too many things that are immovable objects inside that budget, absent some sledgehammer, five-year effort where Kumbaya, all of Washington agrees—it just doesn't happen.

ROGER ZAKHEIM: I don't view myself as a reformer, and I wish reformers would not view themselves as reformers so much as they view themselves as builders. I think if the approach that reformers took was how we could build up the military, I think there would be far more alignment with the strategy, which of course, is the focus of my paper. This conference is rethinking defense budgeting. And I'll note that it's not rethinking the defense strategy. That's important because we ought to have a strategy-driven budget and not a budget-driven strategy. And I argue that if you analyze the current defense strategy and its predecessor, the one Secretary [Jim] Mattis put forward, that was a go-big strategy, there is no way to look at that strategy and come out with a conclusion that somehow we were not going to be a superpower, a major power that could operate in the three dominant regions of the world.

That is, you can't look at those strategies and come to the conclusion we're going to be something less. And if that's the case, we have a serious math problem. Now, one of the errors or elements that really is missing in each of the strategies, and not just the past two but as far back as I've been able to review since the NDS were [made] public, is that they never talk about budget. And so, what you have is a huge gap between the means and the ends. And so, throughout our discussion today, I have not heard anyone suggest somehow we should have a different strategy, a strategy that aims to do less. In which case, the focus on the budget should be how do we get more? Which, of course, is where I land. Now, we've done this before in terms of seriously resourcing a strategy and being committed to resourcing a strategy, building up a force. You have to go back forty years to the Reagan administration.

And James [Cunningham] hit on this in his presentation. Commanders in chief have done one of two things. They've either employed the force in armed conflict, or they've taken a peace dividend. In the intervening time between Reagan and where we are today, we have never consistently invested to build up the force to meet the strategy in peacetime. You can argue that we did invest in the force in Iraq and Afghanistan, but that was off-budget on the supplementals of the overseas contingency operations, and it wasn't lasting. And we've done away with much of it, and certainly, we didn't build a force to deal with the strategy we have today.

ADMIRAL GARY ROUGHEAD: Here are some thoughts from over the years around what I have been involved in. One of the issues we face is a perception problem. Yes, 76 percent [of the public] think we should spend more on defense. But you also have people that look at the topline and they can't believe you can't get done what you need to get done. It's really important to begin to pull away what I would call the investment account from the total budget, because I think that aligns with how people associate things to a budget. And right now, we have views skewed because of the cost of personnel and the cost of operations. So just changing how we talk about it would be important.

I would also say that because of the way we've evolved, the acquisition process has, in my view, become much more process and compliance driven than outcome driven. A program manager is going to get rewarded for checking the process boxes and will be forgiven for things that may not be delivered on time or may not deliver what they said they would. It's more, the reward is on that. I think it's also important, as we think about the budget and acquiring things, in particular, to keep in mind that it's really a bifurcated process. We have the need to determine what it is that we need, the budgeting that goes into deciding what we think we should spend on it. And then we have the acquisition process and have created an acquisition corps, and we've invested heavily in that acquisition corps with training, and they stay in that community. They have repetitive assignments, and maybe they move from program to program, but we have those who are on one half of the equation, who are there just in a haphazard way. And others may say no, there's more process to that. But I think we need to look at that. And I'm going to comment a bit on the budgeting and the requirements side.

I think Eric [Fanning], you mentioned it in different words, but the DoD still thinks of itself as the center of the universe, particularly as it comes to technology. And they'll be the techno tourists that come out to Silicon Valley and then go back, and they've been enlightened, and they can talk about technology, but it's no longer DoD that's in the driver's seat. Particularly in R&D if we want to do reforms there. One of the things that has to happen is there has to be a rationalization of the extensive laboratory enterprise that exists within the department. Tackling it is probably one of the hardest political things that you're going to do. But we acknowledge here that most of the R&D is occurring outside the department, yet we are spending a lot of money on DoD R&D infrastructure. We have a lot of human resources associated with that enterprise. It would be good to just rationalize and question how much we're getting out of it.

This is not on the uniform side. I agree with Mike [Admiral Mullen], there is huge overhead within the civilian force, but we've also made it very onerous for people in industry to be able to come in and out. And I would venture to say if you were to go into the acquisition appointees in the Department of Defense, very few would have had extensive P&L [profit and loss] experience in running businesses and enterprises. The inability for those types of people to come in, go out, and not relinquish a great deal of wealth is a problem. And we've got to figure out how to do that.

Now, going back a little bit on the uniform side, particularly on the budget and the requirements, I think one of the most damaging things to the competencies and the experience within those who play in the budget and requirement process has been the need to adhere to the incentives for promotion within the Goldwater-Nichols Act. If I'm a young officer and have repeated tours in budgeting in the Pentagon, that's a good thing for our acquisition system. It's not a good thing for your promotion, because if you don't get that joint box checked, you're not going to get promoted, plain and simple. So what are we rewarding? And I think we have to be able to reward both. Goldwater-Nichols has done wonderful things for joint warfighting. But it has turned into a personnel system that is corrupting what we're all talking about here today, which is how we can become better acquirers of things.

The other thing about the acquisition force is that it's driven on the basis of a promotion system. And if we were to look at a lot of the programs within the department, the program managers are going to be assigned in ways that do not hinder their opportunities for promotion. They're not being assigned to programs to stay there until certain milestones are achieved. The argument I would get was, if this person doesn't get one of the milestone tours, they're not going to be able to get promoted. Outcome be damned, we're going to get the individual promoted. I would ask anyone here in Silicon Valley, would you move someone who you had made responsible for a key product and pull them out halfway through its development?

On the industrial base, there's a lot more talk about what's needed to improve it. But I think we have to realize that the workforce in the industrial base is also bifurcated. There's what I would call the technical side and then the undervalued trade and skill side. And the country has not incentivized people to become welders and electricians and occupations like that. That's a very serious problem. And oh, by the way, a nuclear welder at Newport News is probably going to be knocking down around $200,000 a year. Not a bad profession.

The other thing that would be a healthy exercise is we are talking about how to improve ourselves, but China has become the manufacturing hub of the world. And as you look at their military equipment, it's starting to get pretty good. And I think it would be a good exercise for those in the acquisition communities to study how China is acquiring things and building things, and the quality processes they put in place. I look at their shipbuilding, both military and commercial, they're doing pretty good. So are we looking at them as a competitor in an industrial sense? That could incentivize and could stimulate some thinking on our part because they're not minor league anymore, in my mind.

Obviously, and we've talked about it here, it's far too hard to move new ideas and to allow the deployment of those new ideas. They get trapped in a very extensive and well-seasoned test and evaluation process. But it can inhibit getting those systems out to the school of hard knocks for people to try, for the young operators that we have to experiment with them, to bring it back so you can make improvements. It just takes far too long to do that.

And the other thing I would say, particularly as we think of what I would call the big breakthroughs, and this goes back to the process emphasis that we have: We're no longer betting on horses, we're betting on a process, we're betting on some technical specifications. But I just thought about what I consider to be the three really revolutionary changes that have taken place in military technology and how they transformed warfare in a significant way.

The first one was the Manhattan Project, which created nuclear warfare. The second one, being very parochial, was the nuclear submarine. And I would say the third, again, from a naval perspective, was integrated air and missile defense that's best manifested in the Aegis weapon system. What did those three things have in common? They had one person in charge of everything. [General Leslie] Groves for the Manhattan Project, [Admiral Hyman] Rickover for the nuclear submarine, and [Admiral] Wayne Meyer for Aegis. I was in a meeting, and Meyer said, "Never let people or money stand in the way of getting it done," because he could pull the threads on every single one. So on the big things, I really think that's the model to use, to bet on the horse. And that horse may not work out and gets fired, so put another horse in. But the idea that you can just move from program manager to program manager,

I think we're going to be wasting a lot of time. And oh, by the way, before Groves did the Manhattan Project, he also built the Pentagon in sixteen months. So if we can find another Groves, we may not have to have another conference, Michael [J. Boskin].

ELLEN LORD: So we were asked how do we achieve defense budgeting reform? I believe it takes fanatical focus and a bias for action. So what I'm going to do is talk about three areas that I believe deserve our focus. And then I challenge each and every one of you, as a call to action here, what can you do personally in the circles in which you travel, whether that be family, friends, and/or professional, to move this whole process along?

I want to address three things. One is overall communication. Two is adopting and buying commercial technology. And three is enabling allies and partners.

So to start with communication, I believe that we owe it to the US public to help them understand that we as a nation enjoy all of the economic benefits and security because of our national security efforts. Our economic security and our national security are very tightly interwoven. And it's hard to tell that story without relevant vignettes. I believe we all have the Ukraine theater as a fantastic example to talk about our near-peer threats, the way that commercial technology has been mobilized, and the art of the possible. However, you can't tell a story and have it be credible without the data behind it with a few facts and figures. And I think a lot of that has been provided here today.

Why is it important to tell this story? Because, frankly, it's a choice to get involved in national security. It's a choice for a student to study national security. It's a choice for a graduate to go and take a job in national security. It's a choice, once you've served in government or been in business, to come back and be part of the community trying to move things forward. And frankly, it takes reinforcing. It takes really having the feeling that you're part of something important. And I think all the people in this room can do that.

I think we also tend to communicate, we as a group writ large, to one another a lot. We think of Congress, and we typically think of [congressional committees]. We think of the executive branch. We might think a little bit about academia from time to time. We think a little bit about the investment community; venture capitalists, and private equity now. But we're not thinking as much about our neighbors and our friends who work in the telecommunications industry, or in the energy industry, or in a whole variety of others that have national security challenges. And I think it's up to us to distill a few stories to make it real to them.

And then what do you do with that? We cannot compel Congress to change, and we cannot compel the executive branch to change without all of our citizens speaking up and articulating what the problem is to those people that they're voting for to put in office. So we need to really activate the average American to have the lexicon to talk very simply about this in a three-minute conversation, in a 30-minute conversation, or for experts in a three-hour version. So what can each of you do to activate your communities and tell the stories with what we've heard here today to get the process going? Because I think only then will we have reform.

The second point I want to talk about is the fact that fifty, sixty years ago, most of the critical technology was developed by the government and rolled out. Well, now we've flipped that script. It's really the commercial sector that's developing most of our innovative technology, yet we have not adjusted our planning, programming, budgeting, and execution processes. Perfect example: our systems today, most of our large warfighting systems, I would say, are hardware enabled yet software defined. So hardware is becoming the commodity. We know how to buy hardware to a degree. But we are treating software like it's hardware, along with discounting the fact that it takes infrastructure to develop software.

So I think when you're in the executive branch, you like to point at Congress all the time and say, "Oh, Congress is constraining us." What I learned, being totally ignorant going into DoD in 2017 as to how government really works, is that Congress actually has put a lot of reforms out there. What has not happened is that statute has not been translated into policy and then again into what they call at DoD implementation guidance, which means the procedures to operationalize policy. And then, even if all of that is done, we have fallen down in terms of training the workforce on how to do this.

So there are a lot of things that can be done, but the DoD workforce is not trained to do them, and they're very risk averse because there are few incentives to assume risk. And one area where I think DoD as part of government could be a little bit more like industry—it's not a one-for-one translation, but in industry, when you run a business, you have lawyers that are smart about different aspects of your business. You seek their best legal advice, and then you use your business acumen to determine what you're going to do. You do not take their advice and implement it wholeheartedly with a few extra caveats to make sure you are not going to get in trouble. That is an issue in government, and we need to tell stories about how things are done in business and what are smart risks to take.

We talk about software being incredibly important in this age of digital engineering, with AI and machine learning, and how do we procure it? We have software pathfinder projects from Congress. The BA-8 authority addresses that we are constrained by colors of money: research, development, testing, and evaluation, procurement, or operation and maintenance [O&M], where you basically go to jail if you use the wrong color of money. And there's one-year money, two-year money, and three-year money, which causes you to do all sorts of unnatural acts at the end of the budget year. With the software color of money [BA-8], you can do the development, the production, and the sustainment with one budget line, one type of money. Why is this important? Because if you are doing contemporary coding, you are developing, producing, and maintaining on a daily basis and hopefully running your testing overnight. Yet we haven't caught up at DoD. And this is not all, "Yeah, Congress, bad DoD," but I think the issue is we're not talking about what we need to change in our procurement system to efficiently acquire software to quickly field capability to the warfighter. We're not effectively communicating examples of new authorities that allow practitioners to learn. We are not adequately developing the workforce to adopt new procurement practices.

I like to talk about creative compliance. We have generated a DoD program management and acquisition workforce that is motivated and rewarded to act like a pilot. And when you're a pilot, it's really important to go through that checklist, as everybody knows. But you know what? When you are a businessperson inside of DoD trying to work with technologists, you have to use what I call "creative compliance." You have to figure out how to do things legally, but utilizing the minimum number of steps, so you can get out of your own way and deliver capability downrange at the speed of relevance.

There is a lot we can do to tell stories to communicate about how we smartly adopt some commercial practices and how we can buy commercial services and goods. And there are authorities to do that. The dilemma is most of these are band-aids and workarounds. So our challenge is, how do we scale those authorities? We have the Defense Innovation Unit, we have the Strategic Capabilities Office, and we have the Rapid Capabilities Office.

You know what? Those groups have no special authorities. They just get a lot of senior leadership attention, they put the best and the brightest there, and they convene and get things done. We need to tell those stories to really spur everyone on to use these.

So finally, allies and partners. We know, and again, Ukraine is a great example of this, that we do not currently have the capability and capacity to manufacture everything we need. And the general public doesn't understand that a company just can't say, "Oh gee, I want to build a new plant. That's a good idea. We'll go ahead and do it." They have to go to their board of directors, and they have to have a business case analysis. They have to show there's going to be a return on that investment. Well, if there is not a demand signal that shows what's going to be purchased over a number of years, they can't make that business case.

So we're working through that, but we have allies and partners that want to develop manufacturing capability, and we are rather constipated in our system in terms of getting going with this. We have a lot of policies that require multiple agencies to approve exporting technical data critical to manufacturing weapons. Let's look at Australia. We have AUKUS [security partnership among Australia, the United Kingdom, and the United States]. Everybody thinks of nuclear-powered subs, as they should, but there's quantum capability, munitions, and other technologies and products called out in Pillar 2 of the policy. We have a little bit of an easy pass to get through some of the ITAR [International Traffic in Arms Regulations] regulations, get the technical data packages over there, and let the Australians use their capital to develop indigenous capability, not only to build weapons to help us against China, but also to help bolster what we have for our inventories and forward deploy and have all the distributed logistics that we need. Yet, we are not telling the story. We are not allowing lawmakers and those in the executive branch to understand what those authorities are and how to implement them, how to be actionable, and how to respond to the Australians and make this work.

So just a whole number of examples there. And I will finish with saying foreign military sales are a tortured process. But you know what? You can get in the fast lane if you know how to work it. Again, we're not telling the story. We're not getting it done. We can sell very complex weapons through direct commercial sales channels and perhaps have a little bit of a hybrid case with a little bit of FMS [Foreign Military Sales] or some of the critical technology.

We're not telling the story of how you can do that, and it's been done for decades, and it's been done very, very successfully.

So with that, I will just say I think if we ourselves individually take it upon ourselves to tell stories about what the art of the possible is, we can make a huge difference, not only for our communities, not only for our nation but for our allies and partners as well.

DAVID L. NORQUIST: First of all, I appreciate everyone's willingness to spend an entire day with me talking about the budget. The withdrawal symptoms are going away. I'm really feeling back in my element. So thank you for doing that for me.

A couple of quick comments on things people have already said; one about the importance of the defense industrial base and the importance of including that and its capacity as part of our plans for what we're looking for in the future because often that's not there. Roger [Zakheim] made a very effective point about funding to the strategy. You really put yourself at risk when you have a strategy that's in excess of your funding. You create some real vulnerabilities. Oriana [Skylar Mastro]'s comments about strike missiles. Long-range strike is one of the major things we emphasized when I was in the department. And of course, Elaine [McCusker]'s always wise comments about all the fun things that are funded in the defense budget that are not defense.

We've talked about a lot of reforms, so what I want to spend my time on here is, why do some reforms succeed, and why do others fail? And [as] I was trying to think how to go through this, Admiral Mullen gave me my perfect example, which is, for twenty years the Department of Defense said to Congress, "I have no interest in auditing the Department of Defense." And he was rightfully frustrated with the amount of money that the department spent in that time. But the only correction I'd make is they didn't spend that money on the audit. They spent that money to not have an audit. In fact, one year, they spent $770 million to avoid having the audit but to show Congress they were very, very, very serious. And they hired outside consultants to come in and advise. But the thing they didn't do was to actually have the audit.

So, then, when Secretary Mattis and I were confirmed in 2017, we started the audit. The audit itself is only $200 million a year. And here's what they found in the first couple of years: $2.7 billion in navy supplies that the navy did not know it had because people hadn't logged the parts into the supply system. So when you looked for the part, you couldn't find it. We had V-22s [Osprey tilt-rotor aircraft] that were grounded because they were waiting on the private sector to produce spare parts that the navy had but didn't know they had.

Just using the navy as an example, in 2017, 5 percent of the buildings on the navy's books did not exist. They had been knocked down and didn't come off the books. The navy uses those numbers to allocate budgets to bases. They also use it when they're answering BRAC [Base Realignment and Closure] questions about whether they have too much capacity. But 5 percent of those buildings had been gone for years. They also found an entire warehouse they didn't know existed. One had a UAV [unmanned aerial vehicle] inside. Others had parts for airplanes the navy had retired several years ago.

The other thing the audit did was cyber testing. People don't realize this is an important part of a financial statement audit. But they attempt to penetrate your business systems, your logistics systems, and your payroll systems. People in DoD are discovering vulnerabilities in their systems. They weren't being caught by our normal internal cyber controls, but the auditors found them, and the auditors would ding them for it.

And then, from all that, one of the things you have to do to have an audit is the auditors want your universe of transactions. "Give me all the transactions so I can pull a sample." Well, we didn't have that, so we had to create it. We had to politely go to different people and say, "Will you share your data with us?" As Bob Work [former deputy secretary] would say, this is an incredibly unnatural act in the Department of Defense. Now, we did it the right way, which is we didn't say, "Can I use your data to go beat you up in the POM [Program Objective Memorandum] process?" Since everyone would wisely say no. We sent sweet, innocent accountants who said, "I have this thing called the audit. Would you mind sharing your data with us?" They'd let us hook up the information, and then we'd extract a copy of the data on a regular basis and then make it available to the original owner but with training and advanced data analytical tools so they could better run their operations. So, these numbers are probably a year or two old, but 23 billion transactions pulled from 220 systems across the Department of Defense come into a system called Advana that only exists because of the financial statement audit.

So the question is, how did we go from nineteen years of what rightfully created frustration among senior leaders and was viewed as wasting money to a system that now is one of the key tools the deputy secretary pulled out of the comptroller's office and elevated to her because it was central to her vision of how to run the department? Well, there are a couple of things. First of all, under the previous approach, it clearly didn't have support in the Department of Defense. DoD had no clear vision that there was an upside to the audit. When people talked about the audit, they talked about the financial statement as if the stock was going to be bought or sold somehow. And the answer is, it won't. If anyone's curious, by the way, the largest asset on the financial statement of the Department of Defense is not ships, not planes, it's Treasury bills. The department owns over a trillion dollars in Treasury bills because it has a $2 trillion pension liability. Before 2017 there was no credible measure of progress, because they didn't hire auditors to come check. DoD hired consultants, and then they told the consultants how to write the reports, and the purpose of the reports was to be able to send them to the Hill. So there were metrics, right? And the Hill somehow didn't find that satisfactory, because it didn't seem to fix anything.

Part of the reason I believed we needed to start the audit is I had spent a period of time over at Homeland Security [DHS] as their CFO. There we didn't have a choice. They already had an annual financial statement audit. DHS consistently failed the audit. They didn't originally even have department-wide financial policies and procedures. But DHS now has a clean opinion. In fact, they have had a clean opinion for ten years running. And the only way they got there was they had an audit every year, whether they wanted it or not. And the auditors were frankly quite helpful. They'd come in and explain why you didn't have your property books right and what you were skipping in the inventory of your buildings. For example, if you want people to conduct a credible real property inventory annually, make it easy on them by including the GPS [Global Positioning System] location data in the property books.

So what I wanted to do today was to walk through the rules that I have used in my career for when you drive a change in a process, how do you make sure it goes well? Because a lot of folks here have tremendously good reform ideas. And the answer is the audit was a good reform idea that wasted money for nineteen years, despite individuals along the way trying to do the right thing.

The first thing to remember is that the bureaucracy is going to resist reform, because that's why you made it a bureaucracy. We don't ask the people who do payroll to innovate different ways of paying people in different amounts at different times of the year. We want it the same way every day, all the time. And that's what they do. And also, in the federal government many of our rules are in law. So even when you find the rule that's the problem, the time of fixing it has this extra cycle built in, and everyone gets to play. If you have experience trying to reform health care or the commissaries or the PXs [post exchanges], you'll discover there's a very large number of people who have an opinion on these topics.

In addition, in DoD's case, it is legitimately complex. Delta [Air Lines] has about eight hundred airplanes. It's a very large, very complex operation. DoD, just counting attack and fighter planes, has about 3,400. Never mind helicopters and everything else. So the audit task is extraordinarily complex.

So what are the key lessons? The first lesson is when you decide you're going to drive change, you need to ask a lot of questions. And people think, "I do that, so I get buy-in." No. It's lovely that you get buy-in. The reason you're doing it is you'll learn a lot. It's like a really cool murder mystery. The first suspect is not the guilty one, and the thing you think is broken is not the problem at all. And until you drill into that, you don't see it. It's what makes reforming a bureaucracy fun.

The second lesson is you have to scout out for obstacles. Nadia [Schadlow] brought this up in her topic. Just a couple examples. We have classified stuff. We have things that we can't even explain how to wrestle with unless you have a clearance. And the federal accounting standards advisory board was filled with uncleared people. So we had to go get them all clearances. Now, they very nicely all signed up. They all got clearances so they could help give us guidance on how to handle certain things in the Department of Defense that have that. We also know that in the private sector, the moment the auditor knows you've failed, they're going to stop auditing. Well, that's kind of pointless, because we knew we were going to fail when we started the audit. So we had to change the rules to say, "No, please go on. Find as many mistakes as you can. Find the cyber vulnerabilities, find the data problems so we can fix those."

Third, you've got to know the mechanics of the process, whether you're in the acquisition world or something else. It's technical. It's hard. You've got to have people who understand it. In addition to CPAs, we had to have people with direct experience with financial statement audits. So we brought people from outside DoD. The CFO of the navy was someone we brought from the coast guard who had helped get the coast guard to a clean opinion, because there weren't many people in the navy who had actually seen a clean opinion or been through a financial statement audit.

Fourth, you need schedules and plans. This is why people have earned PMPs [Project Management Professional certifications]. You need to know, "Who's going to do what, by when?" The biggest weakness before the audit was measuring progress. People couldn't show what they had accomplished in the previous three years. Now, they may have done something great, but you couldn't tell it to the Hill. You couldn't prove it to your own staff. You couldn't build support. So we put effort into documenting every time we found a savings. For example, the air force audit found uninstalled missile motors worth $53 million that were usable, that the air force had thought were unusable. We could show hundreds of millions of dollars worth of savings that dwarfed what we were spending on the financial statement audit.

Fifth, you will need a champion for change. Whatever you're taking on, there will come a point that it will not be solvable at your level, and you'll need to go up to the secretary and know that you've got backing, or you're going to need to go to the Hill or some other place. And those folks have to understand what you're doing and why you're doing it and be there to back you up as you do it. If you're lucky, you end up in a place where I did, where you end up moving up and being the champion. So then, when Elaine was carrying the torch on the audit, she could look at people and say, "Well, okay, I understand you don't want to do the audit, but let's go talk to the deputy secretary and see if he thinks the audit's important." So I got to play the heavy, and I didn't have to have too many meetings. But you can help move that forward.

Sixth, in our world, you also have to plan for the transition. It is going to outlast you. Whatever you are trying to do, if it's really worthwhile, it will only be obviously worthwhile when the next administration picks up the torch. They may rename it, or they may call it theirs. They may have thought it was theirs. It doesn't matter. If that idea dies every time there's an election, it's not going to be worth the investment. So I had the advantage when I was at Homeland Security, I recruited a very talented deputy that the Obama administration later nominated to be the CFO. So we had straight continuity with her carrying the torch. Much of what I did on the audit, I had picked up from what Mike McCord [under secretary comptroller/CFO] had started, and then I handed over to Kathleen Hicks [deputy secretary], who was very excited to pick up the data analytics and take it further.

Seventh, the last item on the list I have is you have to watch the incentives. Water doesn't roll uphill. So if you build a system where you need the water to roll uphill, you are going to spend tons of energy trying to force compliance. So with the audit, what we did was we made it incredibly easy for anyone who wanted to share data with us. And if you didn't, we just skipped you, and we went to the next person who wanted to. And we told that person, "You give us the data." We then added data analytics tools, such as Python, and the visualization ones, and we made it available to the office that had given us the data. And we trained their staff. And the Army started discovering they didn't need to wait for third-quarter or midyear financial reviews. They could see their unused funds earlier at a transaction level. So they started freeing up hundreds of millions of dollars for their leadership because of this tool. I'm told they ended up actually killing a commercial contract that was somewhat expensive because they were getting better analytics free from OSD [Office of the Secretary of Defense].

The whole point was to get people to want to join the train. And by making it easy and free and offering the training, all these groups in DoD who would never normally play came together, shared their data, and allowed us to do data analytics. One of my great joys with Ellen was I was hosting, as deputy, the DMAG [Deputy's Management Action Group], and there were no PowerPoint slides. Everything in this review of the department's metrics was coming straight from the underlying database: readiness data, personnel data, and maintenance data. So no one can say, "Well, Mr. Secretary, that's three-month-old readiness data, so we shouldn't look at it." The answer is, "No, this is what was in the system yesterday. And by the way, if it's inaccurate, your office is responsible for that data, so why don't you tell us what you're going to do to fix it?" It also freed up a whole bunch of weekends for majors who were no longer putting together PowerPoint slides for their boss.

But the main takeaway that I have here for you is there are reforms that could have succeeded and died in execution. And this is one that for years was hemorrhaging money, not making the type of progress it needed, and now has been the foundation not only of some of our biggest internal savings and process changes and cybersecurity improvements but the data analytics tool that it's created is the foundation for a whole series of reforms that are going to follow. And so, knowing how to do that and what the mechanics are for success is key to this. So I'm always happy to say what reforms I want, but I really thought, given all the conversations we had, it was worthwhile to spend some time on what makes them work and what makes them not and what the difference looks like.

SECRETARY JIM MATTIS: One caution. What happened with this audit and its genesis is I was sitting in 1996 behind a man named Bill Perry, the secretary of defense up on Capitol Hill, as he testified in the House and Senate Armed Service Committees. The staffers there have a very long corporate memory that sometimes drives us half nuts. And I remember Dr. Perry said, "We're going to have an audit. We're going to do the audit." Years later, I was nominated to come back as secretary of defense only to find that there had been no audit. And then during the confirmation process you have to meet privately with everybody before you have your formal confirmation hearing in front of the Senate committee. And Senator McCain told me he was going to ask me about this, and he said, "I'm hard over about it." I said, "Well, yes, I last heard about that almost twenty years ago that we were going to do it, so I guess we'd better do it."

But then, after the hearing, I saw immediately after my hearing, even before I was approved by the Senate, I pulled Senator McCain aside and said, "You can be very volatile, Senator." We had known each other many years. And I said, "We're going to find things wrong when we start the audit. What I don't need you to do is start punishing us when we find things wrong. We're going to find it, we're going to correct it, but this cannot become something you beat me up with in public." And he was true to his word. I said, "Now, if you find something just criminal and stupid, I know what you're going to do, so here's your hunting license. No sweat."

But my point is that if you try to do reforms, try to anticipate the first, second, and third order blowup, and at least craft a way to get through it. And it's best if you do it, as Dr. [Condoleezza] Rice said, with some friends and allies. Get allies on the Hill. And they're not unreasonable up there, at least not on DoD's two authorizing committees. But when you get the bulk of them on your side, you can really do a lot of good on reform if you can sustain it. If you can, pass it on.

And an administration now that wants to basically divorce itself from the previous one has basically embraced the whole Trump administration national security strategy. I think they added pandemic and climate change, which I'm against, shouldn't militarize it, but everything else is still there. So if a new administration carries through, whether it be a strategy or a reform, that's when you know you are successful. It's not when you get it through. It's when the next team carries it on through.

BOSKIN: I have a comment or two I want to make before we turn it over to Mac [Thornberry]. One is that a lot of our systems go through upgrades. So they may be thirty years old and they may be getting long in the tooth, but they're not quite the capability when they first came on. Apaches have been upgraded multiple times, for example.

It's a minor point, but when I was a young scholar at Stanford, I developed a bunch of capital accounts for the federal government, which was something very badly missing that's more been taken over by OMB [Office of Management and Budget]. They do an okay job of it. But during the Reagan administration, I was asked to brief the president about this, and President Reagan loved the idea because, of course, as you have a huge acquisition and defense buildup, you appreciate that that's the investment side of things. But [Secretary of Defense] Caspar Weinberger went ballistic when I said, "Well, we have to also realize it's going to depreciate and obsolesce, and we have to take that into account as well." And he proclaimed, "We're going to give the Russian secrets. We can't do it." And that killed the idea. Of course, we could have aggregated in a lot of other things. We tried to pick it up again with [Secretary Dick] Cheney and especially Don Atwood, who was deputy at the time. And we spent some time working on it, but it never took off. But I think the idea of what we're doing to build for our future is something that's worth separating out more clearly, for sure.

And Gary's comment about time and position and the importance of having a leader trying to do something for more than two years and rotating out, I think, is really essential. It was driven home to me by my father-in-law, a World War II submarine commander, who said that, in abbreviation, "Rickover was the biggest SOB in the navy, but he was the SOB the navy needed and needed for a long time."

ROUGHEAD: Maybe a little too long, Mike.

BOSKIN: Yes, that's true. You have to figure out how you transition the person out, not leave them there permanently. And then also, Ellen, I couldn't agree with you more about the public education, building public support, and we've all talked various ways about how that's waned at the younger generation and schools. Jim talked about duty to country, et cetera. That's a vital investment.

Many of us have talked about Congress, many have said some very nice things about it. Others have had complaints. Everybody has frustrations. Democracy is a very messy institution. But as I think many of our leaders have said, it's not a spectator sport. You need to be engaged. So we couldn't have anybody better to talk about the view from Congress than Mac Thornberry. So over to John Rader for our final panel.

Part 6

The View from Congress
National Security and the Budget

18

Can We Buy Like We Talk?

Mac Thornberry

For where your treasure is, there your heart will be also.

—Matthew 6:21

The Pentagon excels at producing strategy documents, reports, studies, and policy papers. They are just words on paper (or the monitor) without the funding to make them a reality. When and how the money is spent, and what the money is spent on, provide a more accurate reading of the United States national security strategy. But it can be difficult to see the connection if one compares the strategy documents written by various administrations with the actual spending.[1]

Why does military funding not follow the proclaimed US strategy? Part of the reason is that the strategy is produced solely by the executive branch, usually without seeking much input from the legislative branch. Funding, on the other hand, is primarily a legislative responsibility.

Many people assume that when it comes to national defense, the president and cabinet officials decide what is needed and send the request to Congress, which may quibble but eventually salutes smartly and writes the check. But that is not what the Constitution says. Article I, Section 8 provides, "The Congress shall have power . . . to raise and support armies . . . to provide and maintain a navy," among other duties. And Article I, Section 9 states, "No Money shall be drawn from the Treasury but in Consequence of Appropriations made by Law."

In reality, the executive branch submits a funding request, but it is up to Congress to decide how much to spend and on what, subject of course to

The views expressed in this chapter are solely those of the individual author and do not necessarily reflect the views of any organization with which they are, or have been, affiliated.

the president's veto of the relevant legislation. Congress does consider the individual items in the administration's request but also takes input from the members themselves based on their oversight, travel, and parochial interests, as well as proposals from outside groups.

Congress's decisions on defense spending occur primarily with two of the bills it enacts each year. The National Defense Authorization Act (NDAA) sets recommended funding levels for each program and establishes the policies under which the funds are spent. The annual appropriations bill actually provides the funds.

The different perspectives and responsibilities of the two branches of government make it difficult to have actual spending that reflects a single, coherent defense strategy. However, beyond the separation of powers, our system is challenged in four areas related to defense spending: the amount we spend, what we spend it on, how we spend it, and the time it takes to get results. Some brief observations on each from a congressional perspective may be useful in finding a better approach.

The Amount

Under the 1974 Budget Act, Congress is supposed to approve a budget establishing the amounts to be spent in various categories of federal spending, including defense. That topline number is then given to the authorization and appropriations committees to write the individual bills. In reality, Congress has not followed this road map in some time, and the topline spending number is generally decided well after the fiscal year has begun, in a negotiation among the House, Senate, and White House. Therefore, the total amount of defense spending is more the result of a political negotiation than a considered strategy. It is obviously challenging for planners and program managers to cope with these year-to-year topline fluctuations resulting from political forces and negotiations.

Defense spending as a percentage of the economy (measured by the gross domestic product) was around 9 percent during the Cold War years of the early 1960s and was between 6 and 7 percent during the Reagan years. It is now less than 4 percent. Similarly, as a percentage of total federal spending, defense has fallen from roughly 50 percent of total spending in the early 1960s to about 13 percent today.[2]

While the trend over the last sixty years is clear, world events, such as Russia's invasion of Ukraine, can affect the political dynamics and thus the topline amount for defense. At the same time, the year-to-year change in

US defense spending is followed closely by other countries looking for signs either of growing resolve and unity or of dissonance and unreliability in US defense commitments.

The What

As typically categorized, the largest component of defense spending is operation and maintenance, which includes upkeep and operation of existing equipment, training costs, expenses to run military bases, military health care, and a host of other items. The next largest category is personnel costs. Procurement of weapons and equipment comprises about 20 percent of defense spending, with research and development at about 15 percent.[3]

Perhaps surprisingly, with political fluctuations and yearly bills, what defense funding actually buys is largely consistent from one year to the next. The vast majority of the funding continues to fund the same kinds of operations, pay roughly the same number of people, and buy the same weapons and equipment as the year before. Changes are only on the margins.

Some of that makes sense. We need some stability in personnel. Large weapons purchases take years to buy, then to train personnel to use and maintain. But there is also a certain degree of inertia. Virtually any spending program has a constituency interested in maintaining or growing that funding and will resist efforts to cut it. Cuts can be made but only with a willingness to take on program supporters. With most of the money locked in, even marginal changes can have disproportional consequences for the warfighter. For example, defense spending cuts under sequestration and pursuant to the Budget Control Act of 2011 resulted in less money for maintenance and training, leading to alarming increases in accident rates.[4]

Over the years, defense procurement dollars have been geared toward purchases of hardware, often large, complex weapons. The entire system is oriented toward—and is more comfortable with—those kinds of buying decisions. It is much less comfortable with acquiring software, for example, which is increasingly essential in everything from weapons systems to decision making.[5] Without a significant push from within or from Congress, the Department of Defense (DoD) will continue to buy what it is comfortable buying, and that will exclude newer technologies, nontraditional suppliers, and different approaches to getting military capabilities to the troops.

Virtually all the spending on weapons and equipment results from decisions made by the military services. The rest of the department can issue lists of important technologies associated with the strategies it produces and make declarations about the changing nature of warfare, but they have limited tools to force compliance from the services.

For example, the DoD's under secretary for research and engineering has identified fourteen critical technologies that she considers vital to national security. But analysis of how much is spent on each area points to a discrepancy in what is said versus what is done. The business intelligence firm Govini looked not at budget requests or appropriations but at actual contracts that were issued. They found that increases in many areas of technology identified as a high priority were not commensurate with the guidance.[6]

The How

In addition to how much the government spends on defense and what those defense dollars are used to buy, the matter of how the money is spent—what process is followed—presents challenges for those responsible for safeguarding the country. The long, complex process usually begins with a five-year budget plan that attempts to meet a military need with a spending program that must find its way into a bill that becomes law. Even after a decision on what to buy is made, funds are approved, and a contract is awarded to a particular company, that is not the end of the story. Other bidders may appeal the awarding of the contract, leading to a protracted bid appeal process. And the many regulations that affect defense spending must be applied.

As with any endeavor pursued by human beings, mistakes are made in various stages, some intentionally and some not. Those mistakes often result in a new legal or regulatory requirement to reduce the chance of the mistake happening again. Over time, the laws and regulations, as well as the informal cultural caution they instill, add up to impose greater costs in dollars and time on the system. They also reduce the number of suppliers willing to enter the defense marketplace.

Congress and various Pentagon officials have regularly and recurringly pushed acquisition reform over the years with mixed results. Various mechanisms have been created to short-circuit these laborious requirements, to include streamlined acquisition authorities and even new offices and organizations. All of these, however, are workarounds to an increasingly clogged system through which most of the DoD spending is made.

A glimpse of what might be possible was provided by the COVID-19 pandemic. By utilizing the Defense Production Act and other authorities, the Trump and Biden administrations developed, produced, and delivered effective vaccines and protective equipment in a remarkably short time compared with the normal government process.

The Time

Time—it may be the most difficult and most significant challenge facing defense spending in the United States. By any standard, the time it takes to go from an identified need to getting something into the hands of the warfighters is excessive. And it is even worse when compared with the pace at which technology now develops and the speed at which successful commercial companies operate. It calls to mind the statement General Douglas MacArthur made in 1940: "The history of failure in war can almost be summed up in two words: 'Too late.'"[7]

Part of the reason for the sluggishness is an outdated process designed for a different time and for purchasing a large number of items usually made of metal. That process has been encumbered over the years by layer upon layer of additional mandates and regulations. Another factor is that competition over resources, whether within the executive branch or among Congress, and the decision-making process to sort it all out take time. The test and evaluation process at the Pentagon, which can have the effect of writing or amending the attributes required of the product, is often blamed for more delays. Of course, erratic funding usually means efficient production is compromised, and delivery is delayed even further.

Whatever the factors are creating the delays, the results speak for themselves. A study by Bill Greenwalt and Dan Patt of the Hudson Institute found:

> Historical analysis of innovation time cycles—the time measured from the origin of a new concept for military capability until its initial fielding—indicates the cycles were shorter prior to the implementation of the triad of McNamara-era processes, commonly with an average time around five years for both ships and aircraft, and have grown steadily since.[8]

Greenwalt and Patt compared the time to market for commercial aircraft and automobiles to DoD aircraft and found that as automobiles took less time to get to market over the last fifty years and commercial aircraft slightly more, DoD aircraft went from five years in 1975 to more than twenty-five currently.

While we have slowed down, China is speeding up.

China

US defense spending has to be placed in the context of the global geostrategic environment, which also shapes our domestic political environment. China "is the only competitor with both the intent to reshape the international order and, increasingly, the economic, diplomatic, military, and technological power to advance that objective," according to the Biden National Security Strategy.[9]

And that "competitor" has marshaled its resources to win the competition. As the annual DoD report on Chinese military developments reported in November 2022:

> The PRC [People's Republic of China] has mobilized vast resources in support of its defense modernization, including through its Military-Civil Fusion (MCF) Development Strategy, as well as espionage activities to acquire sensitive, dual-use, and military-grade equipment. The PRC has substantially reorganized its defense-industrial sector to improve weapon system research, development, acquisition, testing, evaluation, and production.[10]

While we will never emulate the Chinese, we have to make better use of the considerable strengths of the American system. We need all segments of our society to contribute to keeping the country safe. We need all of our players on the field.

How to Improve

Comprehensive solutions to all our challenges in defense spending are beyond the scope of this paper. Some achievable improvements, however, would make a considerable positive difference.

We can start with the recognition that we will not and should not upend the fundamentals of our system of government. Separation of powers is built into our system and is one of our great strengths. We will continue to have administrations draw up national security strategies, which will depend upon congressional funding decisions consistent with those strategies. Administrations that consult more closely with bipartisan leaders of the relevant congressional committees in writing their strategies will find a greater likelihood that their strategies are funded.

No category of defense spending can be exempt from reform. For example, accelerating the adoption of artificial intelligence (AI) can make equipment maintenance more efficient and improve availability rates, as some commercial companies are proving daily. It can also increase the efficiency of administrative functions and decision making, as well as a host of other operations.

Congress and the DoD must continually reexamine military pay and benefits to ensure that the proper recruitment and retention incentives are in place
to continue to attract the best and brightest of our nation. We will always pay
our service members more than our adversaries, and our personnel costs will
be higher.[11] But we should never automatically assume that the current benefits package continues to address the interests and concerns of those who
volunteer to serve and their families. The passage of the new military retirement system, discussed below, is a good model to follow when adjustments
seem appropriate.

When it comes to the acquisition of goods and services, those working in
the trenches of DoD acquisition seem to generally believe that the Pentagon
has the authorities it needs to deliver appropriate capability to the warfighter. No doubt, those authorities can be streamlined and made easier to
use, but too often, those responsible for various programs do not make full
use of the authorities Congress has provided. Beyond authorities, however,
there are two areas where improvements are clearly needed, funding—the
actual appropriations made available to the department—and culture.

Funding

On funding, there is little dispute that the process developed by the RAND
Corporation and brought into the Pentagon by Secretary Robert McNamara
in the early 1960s is out of date. Even with the modifications made over the
years, it does not fit an era of rapidly changing technology and innovations
developed largely in the commercial market. Congress has authorized a commission to examine and make recommendations about the current budgeting system. The Commission on Planning, Programming, Budgeting, and
Execution Reform is scheduled to publish its final report in March 2024.[12]
The commission is expected to recommend significant reforms that will
have to be debated and voted on by Congress and, at best, take some time to
implement.[13]

In the meantime, there are at least three important steps that can be taken to
improve the funding of military capability. One is to permit greater flexibility
and speed in making certain purchases. The National Security Commission
on Artificial Intelligence noted in its final report:

> The DoD's budget process requires that funds be requested two years
> in advance of their execution and focuses planning within the five-
> year Future Years Defense Plan. Resources are allocated to program

elements that are defined at the system level and based upon cost build-ups for pre-determined and highly specified system requirements. In addition, the life-cycle-phased appropriation categories that govern the DoD budget structure run counter to the iterative process inherent to AI and other software-based technologies.[14]

The commission recommended a portfolio management approach for certain purchases. The idea is that Congress would approve money for a particular portfolio of capabilities, such as AI applications. The DoD's program office would have the flexibility to spend out of that fund for capability within the portfolio without having to get Congress's approval for each expenditure. It would, however, be required to report each expenditure to Congress for full transparency. The DoD would also not be limited by "color of money" restrictions that separate research and development spending from procurement or operations, distinctions that do not make much sense for certain technologies.

This kind of funding flexibility does not fit many kinds of capabilities, but for others, it would not only speed up getting capabilities into the hands of the warfighters but also make it easier for more companies to work with the DoD. It requires that Congress loosen the control strings a bit on prior approvals. Fortunately, there are signs that key legislative leaders now recognize that changes are needed.

A second important step is to provide more stability in funding. Congress always will and should put its stamp on defense spending, but it must do its work on time. The actual cost to the American taxpayer in wasteful spending, lost productivity, and the inefficient purchasing that comes with every continuing resolution (CR) is massive.[15] According to the Government Accountability Office, the federal government has operated under a CR for all but three of the last forty-six years.[16] And, with one exception (FY2019), the DoD has begun the fiscal year under a CR for twenty-six straight years. While many in Congress would resist a two-year budget for both, the authorization and appropriations bills could provide some relief if this trend continues.

In addition to passing bills on time, multiyear procurement can be expanded. Large ships have been authorized and funded over several years because of the high costs of each ship. The FY2023 NDAA authorized multiyear contracts for certain kinds of missiles and ammunition to give suppliers the surety they need to expand factories and hire workers. Again, multiyear contracts do not fit all DoD purchases, but wider use would provide greater stability, certainty, and efficiency.

A third improvement that can be made in DoD funding is to make it easier for nontraditional suppliers, whether they are established commercial companies, new start-ups, or something in between, to do business with the DoD. Max Boot writes that "to the limited extent that we can generalize about five hundred years of history, it seems fair to say that the most radical innovations come from outside of formal military structures."[17] Certainly, most innovation today occurs in the private sector, and those companies have a choice of whether to do business with the DoD. If the difficulties in funding and regulatory burden are too great, they will focus only on the commercial market. Vital innovation, capability, and differing perspectives are lost.

Congress and the DoD have contributed to the mound of regulations, and both will have to participate in easing them. In the FY2016 NDAA, Congress established a commission to recommend specific ways to streamline the acquisition process. Known as the 809 Panel, it issued several volumes of reports with a number of recommendations.[18] Only a small percentage of its final recommendations were implemented, partly because some were so sweeping that they attracted considerable opposition and were viewed as beyond the Section 809 Panel's charge. Another focused attempt to identify and enact specific improvements, however, should be made.

The so-called "valley of death" occurs when a company receives DoD funding to develop a product but encounters a time gap, often in years, between initial funding and when production funding is included in the DoD's five-year budget request. Few companies can continue to pay their workforce or hold ready the capital improvements while they wait. The idea gaining traction in both the Pentagon and Congress is to have funds that can be used to help bridge that time gap for the company and also speed the time in which the capability gets to the warfighter.

It is also important to remember that taxpayers can never provide all the resources needed to research and develop all that our warfighters need. Companies, whether large, traditional prime contractors or new start-ups, need to be attractive to private investors and stockholders. They also must have the chance to make a profit. Making it too difficult or cumbersome for defense suppliers to be successful only increases the burden on taxpayers and denies the warfighters what they need to do their job.

Culture

In addition to funding, the other area in which improvements are a prerequisite for success is the culture surrounding the defense budget process. The culture of organizations has been the subject of many studies and countless books. It is influenced by the organization's mission, its power, its leadership, and especially by incentives—what sort of behavior is rewarded and what gets punished.

Within both the DoD and Congress, the culture must accept and encourage a willingness to experiment and fail quickly when developing new capabilities. It must also accept a willingness to field a 70 percent solution rather than the perfect answer years later.

Many of the needed changes are countercultural for the DoD. As an example, former Defense Innovation Board chair Eric Schmidt and former deputy secretary of defense Bob Work wrote an article recently arguing that the DoD should embrace a new offset strategy that uses a distributed, network-based force; fully integrates human-machine teaming; and integrates software into its decision aids, combat systems, and operations.[19] All of those changes make the DoD and most of its congressional overseers uncomfortable. Implementing them requires, if not a change in culture, an openness to doing things differently.

Congress plays a key role in determining the department's culture by its budget, its authorization and appropriations process, the hearings and oversight it conducts, and the laws it passes. It is always tempting for Congress to pass a new restriction or requirement when the department does not perform as it should, but the result is delay and caution. Over the years, congressional and media scrutiny have sent the message to the DoD that "you'd better not try something that you are not sure about." And that message has been received. Congress willingly adds oversight and control but rarely relaxes it. One key to changing the Pentagon's culture is congressional restraint, especially in new mandates.

At the same time, it is too easy for those in the department to blame Congress for being parochial and political while ignoring those same tendencies within the services themselves, as well as failing to acknowledge inconsistent decisions as military and civilian leaders rotate in and out of jobs. History has shown that in some cases, only Congress can mandate reforms that the department cannot or will not make on its own. In short, there is room for improvement, and both branches must participate.

Is Change Possible?

Is it even possible to make significant reforms in a system so well entrenched and in a time of such extreme partisanship? Recent history says that it is and offers some valuable lessons.

The FY2016 NDAA (Pub. L. 114-92) reformed the military retirement system, one of the most sensitive and politically volatile issues Congress or the Pentagon could tackle. The new law was based upon the recommendations of a commission that Congress had created three years before to study the all-volunteer force's health and sustainability. The plan provided a transition so that the rules would not change for those who had been in the system for a number of years but offered greater benefits for those just entering the system. Not only did the fully enacted plan reduce taxpayer costs by billions of dollars, but it also added flexible retirement benefits to service members.[20]

Congress enacted numerous provisions related to acquisition reform in the FY2016–18 NDAAs.[21] The ideas resulted from a concerted effort to solicit suggestions from sources inside and outside government that began two years prior.[22] Both chairs of the House and Senate Armed Services Committees placed the highest priority on seeing these reforms enacted into law. Some at the Pentagon have utilized these authorities effectively and made a real difference. But many others have not taken advantage of them and continued to follow the traditional path. Of course, it is always easier for Congress to add new authorities than to take some away. But one of the key lessons for recent years is that providing more authority does not mean it will be used. Culture and various incentives can work against the hoped-for benefits.

A crisis can lead to reform. The attacks on 9/11 led to the creation of the Department of Homeland Security and the director of national intelligence position. A spying scandal at a national laboratory led to the creation of the National Nuclear Security Administration. While there had been occasional calls for a separate military service devoted to space for some time, intelligence briefings given to a House Armed Services Committee subcommittee convinced its chairman and ranking member that we could afford to wait no longer. After initially failing to convince the Senate about the proposal, their bipartisan solidarity and presidential support overcame the many opposing arguments and created the US Space Force, the first new military service since the creation of the air force in 1947.[23] Of course, our goal should be to act ahead of the crisis and thus avert it.

There have also been attempts at reform that were not successful. The FY2004 NDAA, for example, established the National Security Personnel System to provide greater flexibility in managing the DoD civilian personnel than was allowed under the General Schedule that applies to all federal civilian employees. It was opposed by federal employee unions from the beginning and became a partisan issue. The new system was never fully implemented and was then repealed in 2009.[24]

One of the key lessons from the reform efforts of recent years is that the chances of success are greater when Congress and an administration work together in enacting and then implementing the changes. Another is that commission recommendations can help provide specific reforms but need advocates in both houses of Congress. A third is that the reform should have support from both political parties.

In many ways, the armed services committees have been the last vestige of bipartisan cooperation in Congress. It is a credit to the leaders of those committees, especially in the last two years, that they continued to focus on the men and women who serve our country and American national security in an increasingly contentious political environment. That must be encouraged and give us hope for needed reforms.

So far, the annual defense authorization bill has been one of the few pieces of legislation sure to become law, if need be, over a presidential veto, with a large majority from both parties voting for the final product. The NDAA process allows a large number of House and Senate members to contribute and thus gain a stake in the outcome.[25] Appropriations bills are also enacted yearly in some form but do not usually attract the same level of support and are often the product of each party holding hostage some spending valued by the other side.

Of course, no reform will occur without leadership, which is necessary to overcome inertia and outright resistance to change. Professor Williamson Murray writes in *America and the Future of War* that "[bureaucracies] are happiest with established wisdom and incremental change. . . . And in the absence of driving political leadership, even structured debate may produce only paralysis."[26] There are organizations with that kind of bureaucratic behavior not only in the DoD but in other parts of the executive branch, such as the Office of Management and Budget, and in Congress. "Driving political leadership" can come from a president or secretary of defense or, as it often has in the past, from within Congress, such as with the Goldwater-Nichols reforms in the 1980s.

In national security policy, the various interests and considerations involved are not what most Americans encounter in their daily lives. That makes communication about what is at stake and why it matters even more important than it is for other issues. Much of leadership is about reminding as much as educating. Especially in the United States, with our many differences, we need leadership that reminds us of our commonality. Some of those reminders need to be of what we have achieved—past accomplishments, not just past failings. And with those reminders, leaders can point us optimistically toward a safer, more prosperous future that we can build together.

One final thought: How can we ask America's finest young men and women to put their lives on the line for our country if we are not providing them with the very best training and equipment that our nation—our whole nation—can produce? Our ability to provide for them depends on our spending decisions. These men and women are our true treasure—the 1 percent of the population that defends the freedom and way of life of the other 99 percent. Our actions, not just words, must reflect our commitment to them and the vital mission they perform for us all.

Notes

1. It may be worth noting that some of the words used around defense spending have meanings that create some confusion to some audiences. For example, "defense budgeting" can mean the overall process, or it can mean the amount of money allocated for defense in a president's budget request or congressional budget resolution. Similarly, "authorize" is sometimes used for broad approval rather than a specific authorization in a defense authorization act. "Funding" also can sometimes mean the money approved for a purpose, but it can also reference an appropriation.

2. "FY2022 National Defense Authorization Act: Context and Selected Issues for Congress," Congressional Research Service Report R47110, updated May 20, 2022.

3. Peter G. Peterson Foundation, "Budget Basics: National Defense," June 1, 2022.

4. Tara Copp, "The Death Toll for Rising Aviation Accidents: 133 Troops Killed in Five Years," *Air Force Times*, April 8, 2018.

5. David Ignatius, "Opinion: How the Algorithm Tipped the Balance in Ukraine," *Washington Post*, December 19, 2022.

6. Robert O. Work and Tara Murphy Dougherty, "The National Security Scorecard," Critical Technologies Edition, Govini, June 2022, https://govini.com/wp-content/uploads/2022/06/Govini-National-Security-Scorecard-Critical-Technologies.pdf.

7. "The history of failure in war can almost be summed up in two words: 'Too late.' Too late in comprehending the deadly purpose of a potential enemy; too late in realizing the mortal danger; too late in preparedness; too late in uniting all possible forces for resistance; too late in standing with one's friends. Victory in war results from no mysterious alchemy or wizardry but depends entirely upon the concentration of superior force at the critical points of combat." Statement by General Douglas MacArthur in 1940, quoted by James B. Reston in *Prelude to Victory* (New York: Pocket Books, 1942), 64.

8. William C. Greenwalt and Dan Patt, "Competing in Time: Ensuring Capability Advantage and Mission Success through Adaptable Resource Allocation," Hudson Institute, February 2021.

9. The White House, "National Security Strategy," October 2022.

10. US Department of Defense, *Military and Security Developments Involving the People's Republic of China 2022: Annual Report to Congress*, November 2022.

11. Bret Stephens, "Are We Sleepwalking through a 'Decisive Decade?,'" *New York Times*, December 6, 2022.

12. "Commission on Planning, Programming, Budgeting, and Execution (PPBE) Reform Releases Status Update," US Senate, March 2, 2023.

13. For a discussion of the current planning, programming, budgeting, and execution process and potential issues that the commission may address, see "DoD Planning, Programming, Budgeting, and Execution (PPBE): Overview and Selected Issues for Congress," Congressional Research Service Report R47178, July 11, 2022.

14. Eric Schmidt and Bob Work, "Final Report: National Security Commission on Artificial Intelligence," March 2021, 308.

15. Stuart Roy Kasdin, "Continuing Costs: The Impact of Continuing Resolutions on Federal Contracting," *American Review of Public Administration* 51, no. 7 (September 2021): 542–59; Adam Mazmanian, "6 Hidden Costs of Continuing Resolutions," *FCW*, August 19, 2015.

16. US Government Accountability Office, "Federal Budget: Selected Agencies and Programs Used Strategies to Manage Constraints of Continuing Resolutions," Report to Congressional Requestors (GAO-22-104701), June 2022.

17. Max Boot, *War Made New: Technology, Warfare, and the Course of History: 1500 to Today* (New York: Avery, 2007), 457.

18. To review the panel's various reports, see Defense Technical Information Center, "Section 809 Panel" at https://discover.dtic.mil/section-809-panel. A summary of which recommendations were enacted can be found in a document issued by the Naval Postgraduate School, "List of Section 809 Panel Recommendations," https://discover.dtic.mil/wp-content/uploads/809-Panel-2019/Promo-Outreach/ImplementationTracker.pdf. An example of the bipartisan criticism of its final report can be found at Peter Levine and Bill Greenwalt, "What the 809 Panel Didn't Quite Get Right: Greenwalt & Levine," *Breaking Defense*, April 4, 2019; and the panel chair's response is at David Drabkin and Lt. Col. Sam Kidd, "War of the Acquisition Reformers: 809 Panel Defends New Commercial Approach," *Breaking Defense*, April 30, 2019.

19. Eric Schmidt and Robert O. Work, "How to Stop the Next World War," *The Atlantic*, December 5, 2022.

20. For a fuller description of the legislative path of retirement reform, see William McClellan Thornberry, "National Defense Authorization Act: The Sturdy Ox of Legislation," *Harvard Journal on Legislation* 58, no. 1 (Winter 2021): 1–22.

21. For more information about the reforms enacted, see "Acquisition Reform in the FY2016–FY2018 National Defense Authorization Acts (NDAAs)," Congressional Research Service Report R45068, updated January 19, 2018.

22. In addition, draft legislative proposals were released publicly approximately two to three months before the committee took action, with feedback and suggested

modifications encouraged. The amended provisions were then considered as part of the usual NDAA process.

23. National Defense Authorization Act for Fiscal Year 2020, Pub. L. 116-92 (2019).

24. Anthony R. Crain, "NSPS: The Brief, Eventful History of the National Security Personnel System," Office of the Secretary of Defense, Historical Office, *Occasional Papers*, no. 1 (February 2017).

25. Thornberry, "National Defense Authorization Act."

26. Williamson Murray, *America and the Future of War: The Past as Prologue* (Stanford, CA: Hoover Institution Press, 2017), 131.

The View from Congress
National Security and the Budget

With Mac Thornberry, Moderated by John N. Rader

JOHN N. RADER: We couldn't have anybody better than the Honorable Mac Thornberry to speak to us today about the opportunities and the risk related to Congress and its role in budget and national security. So with that, I turn it over to you.

MAC THORNBERRY: Well, thank y'all. I appreciate not only being a part of this conference today, but I think really y'all have been more restrained than I expected. At the end of the day, I expected Congress would have taken a lot of hits, and there have been a few, most of them fair, but y'all have been more restrained than I expected, so I appreciate that.

Actually, all day I've been thinking of something I didn't say in the paper, but I want to say at the beginning, and that's what Ellen Lord just touched on. In a democracy, you can't sustain anything without public support or at least public acquiescence. And so whatever we think ought to happen with the defense budget or what our strategy ought to be is not going to count for anything unless there's enough public support or public acquiescence to actually make it happen. And I think the point, Admiral [Mike] Mullen actually made this earlier, it is up to the national leadership to help inform and remind us why this is important, and frankly, I don't think the last few presidents have done that very well. But it's not just presidents, it's Congress's responsibility as well. I finally figured this out late in my tenure, and I decided I was going to get out of Washington and go to chambers of commerce and community groups around the country and just give a little presentation with photographs, no PowerPoint, to connect to the local economy. So I went to Memphis, Tennessee, where cotton shipping is a big deal, and I reminded them about how it's the United States Navy that guarantees the freedom of the seas that enables them to ship their cotton. I went to talk to the New York Chamber and reminded them that every transaction on the New York Stock Exchange is linked to our GPS [Global Positioning System], now operated by the US Space Force and, previously, by the air force.

If you want to mess with the US economy like that, just start messing with our GPS system. And so my theory was, not only is it important for DoD to keep you safe, but it's connected to how you earn a living. Your ability to provide for and raise your family traces back to what the military does for us all. And I think that narrative needs to come from presidents and congresses, and we haven't done that very well.

The last thing on this point, and nobody's mentioned it today, we should never underestimate the disinformation campaign that is coming from foreign adversaries to undermine our will to fight. I can tell you stories about my town hall meetings where people were literally in tears because they thought the military was going to come and confiscate their guns. And then it turns out the *New York Times* writes a story, it's a couple years later, that however this rumor started, the Russian bot farms were sending it out far and wide. And so it doesn't really matter how many tanks, or ships, or whatever we've got if they can systematically undermine our will to fight. At that point, weapons are not going to be much use, and adversaries are working on that.

In my paper, I really just try to start with a simple point that money is what counts. We can write all sorts of things, and we can make all sorts of pontifications, but it's where the money goes that makes the difference. And just as a reminder, in the US Constitution, Congress is the one that decides where it goes. Now, the president can veto what they do, but you're not going to be able to implement a strategy or do much of anything else in defense without Congress having a role, because Congress is the one that approves the money.

As I think about money in defense, there are four issues. One is how much we spend. Two is what we spend it on. Three is the process that we use to spend it. And by the way, the process does not end at the appropriation. It's all the way through the contracting process. And then fourth, it's the time that all of that takes, given the time frame our adversaries are moving at, given the time frame that technology is refreshing. And obviously, all of that ought to cause us a lot of concern.

I suggest some reforms that I think are doable while the PPBE Commission figures out how to fix the whole thing. I do think there is a growing interest on the Hill and elsewhere for greater budget flexibility. The interest that the new House Defense Appropriations chair, Ken Calvert, has shown in greater flexibility is incredibly encouraging. He's the one who put into the last appropriations bill a small warfighter innovation fund with a lot of flexibility in how to spend it, and his intention is to grow it. Mike Gallagher is talking about a capability of record versus a program of record. There are folks on the Hill who are recognizing we're going to have to move faster, and that's going to require greater flexibility.

And by the way, the other part of that is greater transparency coming back to the Hill on how that money was spent. There's got to be a quid pro quo to some extent here, but I think that's doable while we're waiting on the PPBE Commission to give us a broader reform.

Stability—most members on the appropriations and authorizing committees oppose a two-year budget. But the argument on the other side is, "If y'all can't get your act together and get this done on time, we're going to have to go to a two-year budget funding," or something like that. I agree that a two-year budget plan has to be married with the flexibility on how you spend the money. Because if it's thirty months in a one-year budget plan, I can't even do the math on what it would be for a two-year.

I also think simplicity is key. Fewer regulations are needed in order to do something about the valley of death. Y'all know those issues. I won't repeat them. We tried. One of the things [Senator John] McCain and I created was the [Section] 809 Panel. So we put a number of acquisition reforms into place, and then we said, "When you get down to exactly which regulations need to change, we need a commission to figure it out." When they came back in their interim report, we adopted a number of the things they put forth. Their final report might have been overly ambitious. But I do think we could use another commission willing to get down in the weeds and that nitpicky stuff and figure out, okay, get rid of this regulation, these laws need to go away or change or so forth. And I think that would be useful.

Sidenote: one of my nerdish pursuits was to simplify all of the acquisition statutes. We first passed the outline and then we passed the first tranche, enlisting a guy who used to work at Office of Legislative Counsel to put all of these acquisition statutes in one place under one title so that you could see how they fit together—not trying to change the law but just trying to have it in a digestible form and place as a step towards simplicity. And so I think there are some steps that hopefully set up for future reform.

I just want to emphasize the point that Eric [Fanning] made really well. There will never be enough taxpayer money to do everything that we need to do for defense. We have got to be able to attract investment into businesses, because private investment can multiply whatever the trillion dollars or whatever the taxpayers come up with tremendously. Now to do that, you've got to have the return on investment, the kinds of things that investors or shareholders are looking for. And I don't think that's a mindset at DoD. I didn't really focus on that when I was in Congress that much, and yet I think it is so crucially, crucially important.

Congress can help the culture get better or it can make the culture get worse, because of the hearings they hold and because of the laws they pass. I kept threatening my staff to hold a hearing with program managers who have programs that failed, and I wanted to pat them on the back and say, "Good, you learned what did not work." Now, we always got bumped by something else, some other topic for the hearing. So I never got to do it. But that's an example of where Congress can affect culture, in my opinion.

On the other hand, following David [Chu]'s lead, I know the blended retirement system didn't solve everything that needed to be solved, but I'll tell you from our end, we took a lot of incoming to get that done. Everybody who was invested in the system and their families and so forth didn't want any changes whatsoever. And so to say, "Okay, you can retire at six years and still get something for it. You're protected if you've been in it this long. You have a choice if you've been in it this long. If you're new, you're going to be in the new system." To me, that is a template for other pay and benefit reform and entitlement reform for the country as a whole. I know it didn't do everything, but in the face of the opposition we faced with all sorts of organizations, I think it's a fairly significant accomplishment.

On acquisition reform, I've got a quick list of fifteen things that we did to try to give more authorities. I think it is a fair point Mackenzie [Eaglen] made, that it's a lot easier to give authorities than to take them away. And we were giving authorities, sometimes they've been used—not always. Some services have used them more than others. But we tried to at least offer some more options. What people tell me is, "Okay, we've got the authority we need. It's the money and the culture that is yet to be changed." I focus on money and culture in my paper, because I think those are the two pillars that have yet to be done.

Sometimes it takes a crisis to get change done. I really think space force is an example of a crisis leading to change. Because a Republican and a Democrat, a chair and a ranking member of the Strategic Forces Subcommittee, had enough classified briefings that they got deeply concerned. And so we had it in the House bill, and it passed the House. We couldn't convince the Senate the first year. Then the House guys also got the president involved. And the second year, it got passed into law. And then on the other side, and Dr. [David] Chu has already talked about this, the National Security Personnel System is an example where reform didn't go well. I do think the government employee unions' strong opposition from the beginning made it a partisan issue. And frankly, they used a number of tactics to delay the implementation of it, so you didn't ever get to really see the benefits. And so when the administration changed, we lost it.

The last point I want to make—somebody I think said this earlier, I think—truly the last vestige of bipartisan cooperation on the Hill is with the Armed Services Committees. And I hope everybody will encourage, applaud, and pat those folks on the back, because it's harder and harder to work across the aisle, and they need to be appreciated. I think we're up to, what, the sixty-third straight year of having a National Defense Authorization Act become law, and I think they will be able to get it through again this year. There are always some differences, but not very many that are partisan. They mainly try to work their way through problems to find acceptable solutions. And I think that's encouraging, but it's got to be rewarded in some way.

In politics, you get more of whatever you reward, depending on what your currency is—if it's votes, if it's Twitter clicks, if it's whatever. There's got to be some way for people who are willing to put the country ahead of partisan interest to be rewarded. And I hope that they can be in whatever fashion makes sense because then you'll get more of it. And that's good for the country.

On the other hand, I hope I'm wrong, but I think we're in for a year-long CR [continuing resolution] because I don't see how they work out the appropriations deals this year. I hope that's not the case. But if we really have a yearlong CR, that's the time to really hit them with the budget flexibility arguments and say, "Okay, if we're going to have a yearlong CR, give us this authority to be more flexible in spending this money as a way to compensate for the damage that the CR does." As Rahm Emanuel said, "Never let a crisis go to waste." If we're going to have one, we need to be ready with some ideas about how to take advantage of it. Thanks.

RADER: Open for questions. Mike?

MICHAEL BROWN: You and I had a quick conversation before dinner last night about the power of appropriations committees and the staffers. What do you think would be the reform? Picking up on your last point about flexibility, which, of course, I completely agree with, what would be the best way to try and take a step there? Because I would imagine if I'm an appropriations committee staffer, everything is losing power and control, so I fight that like hell. What do you think could get done there, and how to do it?

THORNBERRY: Well, the first thing that comes to most people's minds is expanded reprogramming authority, and that's probably useful. Reprogramming can be painful, because if a relevant party says "no," then that usually stops it. So, there are lots of vetoes. I really think you probably can't do portfolio management at a broad level, but you might pick a few areas like software or something where it's so obvious that the technology is moving so fast, you've got to have a different way to do it. The National Commission on AI suggested this for AI applications and some areas like that. I think it really could be the nose under the tent to show it can be effective. But to repeat myself, I think they need to be ready to go.

RADER: David?

DAVID S. C. CHU: In terms of issues that were raised today, I'm curious for your reaction, especially your assessment of the Hill's acceptance of two older possibilities that have been pushed forward. First, on the budget front, could there be something that resembles what the VA [Department of Veterans Affairs] has had for medical care, a number of cycles, which is an advance appropriation for the next year? In other words, it's subject to change again when the budget year is executed, but it gives DoD the money and the flexibility at the start of October to act if Congress has not acted. It's done for the VA because the medical situation requires the money. So there's a precedent for it. It's in the national security space, and I think it has been reasonably successful.

The other is a much bigger idea, which the economists would push. I wonder if there is a way to reframe the defense budget debate by separating the capital needs of the department from the operating needs. Could DoD have a separate capital budget? Could we size that budget off the established

[Department of] Commerce estimates for the size of the defense capital stock? In other words, we would have to keep this stock replenished over time. We draw it down and use it every year, just like any corporation depreciates its assets. But that gets the investment account debate separated from the annual budget deficit focus. States do this with their budgets, as you know, and they have separate capital budgets. Those are debated separately, and they're not thought about in the same parlance that characterizes the main budget.

That would be a major change. Not trivial. It would probably take years to explain it, although economists have pushed this idea before without any success. But I wonder if such an idea could eventually gain traction.

THORNBERRY: I would say on advance appropriations for particular purposes that could be articulated, I think that's a possibility. We've already decided that we can't afford to fund aircraft carriers in a single year. We need to have multiyear procurement. They just did this for munitions, multiyear procurement for munitions is in this last bill. So if you can make the case that there is a particular need that will extend over more than one year, and we need to be able to have this authority, I think that is a doable thing within those categories, not widespread, but within those categories.

On the capital budget, I think that's too complicated and too hard to see the benefits. Economists might like it, but most members of Congress will see it as an effort to try to take part of defense spending off budget, in effect, and they don't want you to do that. They want to keep all of defense in the game because it's part of the political negotiation that happens every year, which is how we figure out domestic spending as well as defense spending. I think that's a bridge too far. The other one, I think, is a possibility.

RADER: Mackenzie?

MACKENZIE EAGLEN: I really enjoyed that a lot. I appreciate you being our closing speaker today. Two questions. Can you reflect on—Elaine [McCusker] and I both referenced it differently—the growth of the NDAA, which I think the first one was one page, and we're now, depending on how you count it, we're at somewhere between 4,000 and 5,500 pages for defense bills. Can you talk about the absurdity of that, when you, of course, were chairman? Are we going to be at 10,000 pages in three years, and when does that stop? When does it become too much paper, too many directives? As Elaine said, for every report you require, you have to take three away. I want to sort of turn the tele-scope on Congress for a minute and talk about the growth in the number and types of overseers to executors, basically is what I'm getting at.

And that could be through staffers or reports or whatever. So be a little hard on yourself because I think we've hit the absurd point. And then sec-ondly, correct me if I'm wrong on the point Eric made. But if this is true, nowhere in the PM/PEO [program manager/program executive officer] world, in my understanding, are they charged with caring about the defense industrial base. So they have to meet the compliance, they have to check the boxes, they have to follow the rules. But the concern around this, the theme from today is—well, there's a couple of things. We're really lousy at history. We're lousy at geography. And the third is no one has cared enough about the industrial base, and now there's no arsenal of democracy. But should that be part of the portfolio of people who are charged with contracting and oversee-ing that to actually care?

Wait a minute, flagging it for you, civilian overseer, whether that's the DoD or on the Hill, this is a permanent production line shut down. The bomber plant here in California is now a Walmart. I know Congress weighed in to save the army's last tank plant, but in the president's 2023 budget, permanent pro-duction line closures are littered throughout the budget that are going to shut down other lines forever. Congress thankfully said, "Um, not a great idea." But why should it have to get to that level? Should it sort of be a part of the defense acquisition processes ahead of time?

THORNBERRY: On the growth of the NDAA, yes. One of my greatest failures as chairman is when I went in there, I said, "We're going to reduce the number of reports, and the ones that are left are going to be ones we follow up on, that really count. We're going to say fewer things, but we're going to really mean what we say." And it completely fell apart, partly because if Roger [Zakheim] has an amendment that is a terrible idea, one way I buy him off is to give him a report in exchange. And so it just multiplies, in essence.

But the other thing is there are fewer and fewer opportunities to legislate in Congress. Fewer and fewer bills go through. So if you're a freshman who's just been elected and you've got to go home in less than two years and talk about what you've accomplished, you've got to figure out something that gets signed into law. And a lot of times, it's an amendment to the NDAA, even if it's added on the floor and if it's added by unanimous consent. "I did something.

I got it signed into law." There are so few opportunities to do that anymore that more and more stuff just gets added on to the defense authorization bill.

This happens to the extent that you have whole other bills that get clumped on because they can't pass on their own, but they figure, "Well, that'll pass." And so financial services, health care, it doesn't matter. They're coming out of the woodwork, and it's stuff that the Armed Services Committees don't know about it. It's basically up to the committee of jurisdiction and the leadership to say, "Yeah, y'all got to take that." And so as a result, the NDAA is this big. And so I think it is a reflection of the dysfunction of the institution as much as it is a considered judgment on managing DoD.

On the defense industrial base, you're right. If it's clear to Congress that shutting this down means we lose this capability, like in the case of the tanks, we'll give them some money and keep them open. I think your point is, or at least my opinion is, that the Department of Defense needs to have a business intelligence unit such as private industry has to know what the state of the defense industrial base is, writ large. It's not just tanks, planes, and ships; it's other things as well. And so that intelligence unit would include the willingness of Silicon Valley organizations to do business with the Department of Defense. I think that's a useful thing to feed back into the department. And then it's going to be a question of what you do about it. I've been impressed by some of the companies that have business intelligence units and the effort they put into understanding the business environment in their area, and what they learned from that.

ELLEN LORD: If I could just build on that. I think one of the largest challenges is there are so few people in DoD with business acumen, particularly in this administration. Even during the last one, if you were coming in from business, you were deemed a moneygrubbing, horrible person. [Senator] Elizabeth Warren thought it was going to be a huge payday for me to go to serve at DoD. So, you start with that bias, if you will. And then secondly, people don't understand business cycles and what it takes to invest, that there has to be a virtuous business cycle, and so forth. And that happens on the congressional side as well. It's just that Business 101 isn't there. And frankly, I think a lot of the contracting officers are extremely worried about showing any bias. They are not encouraged by leadership to take any risks. So, they tend to go with the tried-and-true because if the buddies on either side of them did it and didn't get into trouble, they're probably going to go that way as well.

Here again, this gets back to a huge educational issue, I think. And there's probably the only silver lining of COVID, which is the American public, and I think, therefore, DoD and Congress became more aware of the challenges of 100 percent offshoring and the resiliency of supply chains, cyber threats, and so forth. So I think we're a little bit smarter, but DoD is not set up to address recruiting, developing, and retaining a diverse and resilient defense industrial base. There's one small Industrial Policy group in OSD [Office of the Secretary of Defense] under A&S [acquisition and sustainment]. But it's understaffed, with a bunch of open billets. A number of billets were taken and given to CIO [chief information officer] this past year, which is very troubling.

RADER: Michael?

MICHAEL J. BOSKIN: I wanted to make two comments about Congress, and especially the second one is aimed at the Senate, Mac. The first is I think everybody would be thrilled if we could get back to some semblance of regular order and the expertise of people that's reflected not just in the Armed Services Committee but a lot of other committees. I was involved in much of the work of the Ways and Means and Senate Finance Committees, both when I was in the government and beforehand, with the 1986 tax reform. I spent weekends at Airlie House with the committee, et cetera. And there were people. I mean, yeah, they had their political speeches out in public, but people who do a lot of hard work. And increasingly, it looks to me like it's not getting rewarded because of these deals at the end of the year done by leadership and that creates the disincentives that you mentioned.

The second is one of the things that's been a theme, maybe not elevated, but Ellen just highlighted it, is getting good people, including people with business experience. But getting good people into the key roles, into many roles, including laterals, et cetera. But the damn confirmation process has gotten so broken. We're asking so many people to put their life on hold for a year and go through tortuous stuff that they need to go through to get confirmed. We need field checks by the FBI, and we need the committees to do their work. But I think that's a big problem. I don't know what the resolution of that is because that's one, as you mentioned. It's one thing senators get to do and to showboat about. I know many people in a variety of areas who didn't go into the government when they were approached because of this. And if I know ten cases of that in the last five or six years, there's got to be a large total number. It's no comfort that, as Mike Brown indicated, it can also take seven months to get a written offer out to recruits at job fairs. I do want to add one really important thing that we mentioned, just a sentence in our paper. I think one of the really most optimistic things is that we've seen a lot more veterans elected in recent budget cycles, and they've been extremely attractive to voters. And I think we have to understand that phenomenon. And that may be the beginning of something where we get a higher fraction of our Congress that has military experience, given the all-volunteer army, and who understand these issues in a way that they can carry and educate their colleagues on. It's not something easy to measure other than the numbers, but I think that it's been very, very evident, especially in more or less swing districts, that veterans have been very, very attractive to voters.

THORNBERRY: I will just mention on that last point, we started to see the beginning of Iraq and Afghanistan veterans come into Congress. When they get there, they really want to work across the aisle and get stuff done. This was encouraging to me, too. Over time, there are these partisan pressures to get back in your corner. Don't play with those guys. Now, some people resist that depending on their district. Others not so much, but I think generally, most of these people who come from a recent military background want to get things done. They are mission oriented. And I agree that that's an encouraging thing.

RADER: Tim?

TIM KANE: Mac, you mentioned the reform, and I know the pension reform had been recommended decade after decade after decade by multiple blue-ribbon commissions. But if you look back, those were often final reports with ten suggestions or four options. And I think it was the Military Compensation and Retirement Modernization Commission that recommended a single reform recommendation—the blended system that was ultimately adopted by Congress.

THORNBERRY: It was.

KANE: So I was amazed when the Blended Retirement System happened. And I think that initial reform had to happen before another one could before you could go to a full Thrift Savings Plan as an option. I just wanted to press you a little bit, would you agree that without that retirement reform, it's going to be really difficult to do lateral hiring of somebody at the major lieutenant or colonel level unless there is some retirement package for them? And is it possible then that what I'd like to think opened the door for reform will let future Congresses say, "Yeah, let's have this at least be an option"?

THORNBERRY: It is, as long as the services don't push back too much. How about that? So if you have all the service chiefs saying, "Nah, we don't want these other people coming in that are not qualified and diluting what we have built up over time," it'll be hard. Now, we could make that case with cyber because everybody knows people with green hair and so forth may have the capability to work with cyber command and do some things, and regardless of how many pull-ups they can do or whatnot. So you can make the case with certain specialties, but it depends on the reaction of the broader military population and leadership. And I guess, maybe it depends on how bad the recruiting problems get.

RADER: Kiran?

KIRAN SRIDHAR: Speaking of one of the veterans who's now a member of Congress, [US Representative] Mike Gallagher has a very radical proposal, which is to scrap the Appropriations Committee and create standing committees, for example, the Department of Defense, that are responsible for all budgeting for the department and also all oversight. I know the likelihood of such a reform is remote, and appropriators will fight it tooth and nail. My question is, does there come a point where the appropriations process becomes so dysfunctional, like you were saying, where we'll have a full year of CRs where such a reform like that might be on the table, might be a possibility? And then, a second more personal question, you're from a deep red district, you have a very conservative voting record, yet you were able to work across the aisle quite effectively, and win trust with deeply liberal people.

I'm wondering how you were able to do that? Because as we get to Congress where a lot of districts are deep red and deep blue, if we're going to want to effectuate any of these reforms, we're going to need to build trust from people who have dramatically different ideological positions.

THORNBERRY: I think if it gets so bad the Appropriations Committee gets abolished, then things are really bad, and we don't want to live in that world. It would mean the economy melted down or something like that. There has been a somewhat different version of that that's been talked about. You don't abolish the Appropriations Committee, and I'll just simplistically say you take defense appropriations and put them with the Armed Services Committee to do the budget, the funding levels for the Department of Defense or a subcommittee. Or take the Defense Appropriations Committee and a group from the Armed Services Committee, not the whole committee, because appropriators get outvoted, but an equal number from the authorizing committee and have one committee that decides the authorization and appropriation for funding levels. And then, you still have your normal oversight duties and so forth. So I don't know, is that any more doable? Not in the current circumstances, but I do think the longer the dysfunction goes on, the more creative juices flow about, "Okay, there's got to be a better way to do this."

However, just remember the fundamental issue when it comes to appropriations is that Democrats think Republicans care about it, and they hold it hostage to get what Democrats care about, and vice versa. So, it's a mutual hostage standoff. That's why it's up to the White House and the leadership to resolve. And that's the only time you get a breakthrough, unless you have a two-year budget deal like we had that one time. So, it's not the existence of the committee so much as it is the political dynamics that, I guess, gets to your second question.

I went to Congress to try to do things—not to become famous, not to raise a bunch of money. The incentives are different now, and social media is part of it. We could have a whole conference on the changes in our society that alter the reward calculus for people running for office. I really thought COVID would have more of a positive impact than it has. But I do think for people who want to do things, whether you come from a very Democratic district or a very Republican district, you will figure out that you may disagree about health care and taxes, but you can work together on regulating social media or whatever issue it is. So you'll find common ground in order to get something done. You will work with people that you don't normally work with.

But on the other hand, if it's, "Okay. These people are evil, they're the opponent, and I can't work with them because . . . ," then that's a different mindset, because it's going to interfere with your TV hit that day or your Twitter post. That's a different mindset, and that's got to really change. But Roger's point is exactly right. It's a really small, loud number who are that way. The media tends to focus on them and give them actually more influence than they have inside Congress itself. But still, if you've got a four-seat majority and you get five yahoos that are banding together, then they can stop things.

RAJ SHAH: We need more folks like you in Congress, hands down. I just wanted to highlight something you said at the beginning, which was, "At the end of the day, the power for reform and what we do comes from the people," right? The American populace. And earlier, I don't remember if someone made the comment that most of America probably can't find Taiwan on a map. And so, as you think about the education of the populace around why this is important, why we want to spend treasure and, God forbid, blood, what advice do you have? How can we send that message better? And are there things that others in this group might do that can help.

THORNBERRY: I think Secretary [Jim] Mattis made the point we don't teach history anymore. When I would go around talking to people about cotton in Memphis and all that stuff, I would start with a history lesson about something relevant to them. This has been ascribed to Oliver Wendell Holmes and a variety of other people: "It's more important to remind people what they already know than it is to educate them about what they don't know." And so, I would try to remind people we got into World War I, we became isolationist and weak, and because of that, we had the greatest calamity in the history of the human race if you judge by total deaths, which was World War II. And that shocked us so much that we said, "We're not doing that anymore." And so, we created NATO and the CIA and the Department of Defense and the World Bank and all of this stuff, and then I have the charts to show human life expectancy, economic prosperity, and the number of people living in democracies have gone up ever since.

With these things [smartphones] buzzing in our pockets all the time, what we lose as individuals is context, why it matters. And so to me, that's the key. People will listen to you about Taiwan once you remind them, "If you don't stand up to bullies, they're going to be at your doorstep next." And you need to have historical examples about that. H.R. [McMaster] talked about that. And so to me, it's reminding them what they already know, but they have to be reminded, because these things are distracting them all the time. So, that's at least my theory of the case.

RADER: Eric and then Admiral Mullen to close out.

ERIC FANNING: I just have a comment following up on Mackenzie's question about the industrial base. I agree with everything that Ellen said. There's just a basic lack of understanding of free-market economic principles in the

Department of Defense, like the importance of profits to spur economic development. But sometimes, because of these industrial base issues, we find ourselves in conscious budget trade-offs. Really, if I'm simplifying, two different things: One is what we're facing in Ukraine right now—munitions, for example, that there's granularity to the number of munitions. We can say, "Oh, in the endgame with the budget, we're going to cut 20 percent here as a bill payer for something else." You can't cut 20 percent of F-35s or an aircraft carrier, and we do that, year after year after year after year. And then simultaneously, we're telling our contractors to cut costs, be as efficient and lean as possible.

So the surge capability or the capability of the industrial base is a capability in and of itself, but it comes at an expense that doesn't necessarily get you something immediately that you can put in a warehouse. If you want to have eight of something and not have the company you're buying it from make it as efficiently as possible, keep the workforce and the infrastructure to double that overnight, it comes at an expense without something that's coming out the other end. And we've done that for years and years and years in some of these things. And we didn't start this in February of last year when our warehouses were full, and we are behind in deliveries to Taiwan. And now we're surging all this stuff to Ukraine and not having as much that is forcing us into directions in terms of what we're trying to give them now a year later.

That may not be what we would give them in other cases, but it may force us faster into the direction that some people want to go. But a lot of this, I think, is just the budget trade-off in the endgame, going back to this concept of, "What do we need in the future?" but we ask more of the department than we resource it for. And these are cumulative effects, as James [Cunningham]'s paper pointed out. Oftentimes, I think that the decision makers know this is happening, but they're going someplace for a trade-off in the endgame.

THORNBERRY: And Congress is partly responsible, pushing for efficiency, to be more efficient [you must] cut costs, and so forth. So you just have as many munitions as your war plans call for. And "Well, what happens if something unexpected occurs? Well then, we need some more." And that's not something we have paid for yet. Again, it follows the money.

RADER: Admiral Mullen.

ADMIRAL MIKE MULLEN: Thanks, Chairman. Very helpful. I actually don't object to a 7,500-page or 4,000-page NDAA and the 720 reports because I understand that's just part of doing business. I learned that over time, as frustrating as it is. I don't know how many reports I signed, hundreds, that I never saw have any impact. Part of the conversation has been about this midcareer or shift to bring civilians into the personnel world. Coincidentally, I did a study on women at the CIA and another on minorities at the CIA. And in both those studies, and because we're doing people stuff, I'd try to understand careers and who gets promoted and who doesn't.

We talked to a number of midcareer civilians who'd been very successful on the outside and came in to the CIA, and the tribes inside basically killed them. The culture's so strong in that agency the tribes killed them. We have tribes. So as we think about this and doing it in cyber right now, some of what I would call relevant and very timely help, interpreters in the Iraq and Afghanistan wars, as an example, could help cyber now. The system will tolerate some of that, but you have to bring them in and really make it fair for them. And that's far beyond just onboarding them.

We talked about a BRAC [Base Realignment and Closure]. I'm done with BRAC. Every time we do a BRAC, it's because we have 20 percent too much overhead. We take out 20 percent on Friday, and on Monday we still have 20 percent too much overhead. And nobody ever audits that, by the way. At least I haven't seen that that's been audited. But I do worry. It just moves us further and further away from the American people. We're in fewer and fewer places. We're not coaching kids in little league, we're not going to church, we're not teaching, we're not working in a place in far too communities in our country. And at some point in time, again, it just feeds this fact that our military gets further and further away from the American people. I'm willing to pay that overhead at this particular point, given the number of BRACs that we've been through. In the navy, we're virtually out of the Northeast. With one exception, we're gone. And so, that part of the country just finds out about us in the press, in the media, et cetera. And that's a very dangerous trend. David, I appreciate being caught up on the audit. I would only say that twenty years is about the normal pace in the place. I would hope that we could continue this. That we finally got here, because that was a long and very painful and expensive process.

And then lastly, Gary [Roughead] mentioned this. I'm a requirements guy, so I never thought I had a problem. We spend an extraordinary amount, I don't know what the number is, 25 percent, 30 percent on requirements growth in the acquisition process. The individual who signed the requirements document doesn't have anything to do with its growth, because the uniform leadership is out of it once you sign it back to Goldwater-Nichols. Cutting down requirements growth is a massive requirement in order for us to deliver the systems in a reasonably efficient and more effective way, from a financial standpoint.

BOSKIN: Well, first of all, we want to thank everybody for coming. It's been a very long day. We've covered a lot. Everyone in the room could have commented at length on every one of the sessions. So we appreciate your forbearance, letting other people speak on these topics, which are so interrelated. That's number one. Number two, we're just so appreciative of your service, past, present, and future, whether in uniform or out. We want to thank you for that.

About the Contributors

General Keith Alexander, founder and CEO of IronNet Cybersecurity, is one of the world's foremost authorities on cybersecurity. A four-star army general, he was previously the first commander and the highest-ranked military official of the US Cyber Command, the National Security Agency, and the Central Security Service. He led these Department of Defense agencies during the conflicts in Afghanistan and Iraq, when attempted cyberattacks against the United States began to increase.

Michael J. Boskin is the Hoover Institution's Wohlford Family Senior Fellow and Stanford University's Tully M. Friedman Professor of Economics, and a research associate at the National Bureau of Economic Research. As chair of the Council of Economic Advisers under President George H. W. Bush, he helped resolve the Third World debt and the savings and loan financial crises, expand regional and global trade, introduce emissions trading in environmental regulation, and control government spending while protecting the defense budget. On Ronald Reagan's Tax Policy Task Force during his presidential candidacy, Boskin helped develop the policies that, during Reagan's presidency, lowered tax rates, indexed tax brackets to inflation, accelerated depreciation, and created IRAs and 401(k)s. He also chaired the CPI Commission, whose report transformed the way government statistical agencies around the world measure inflation, GDP, and productivity.

Captain Corey Braddock is a twenty-seven-year veteran of the military, having served in the US Army and US Coast Guard leading troops, piloting aircraft, and overseeing a myriad of organizational constructs. Braddock has served at Coast Guard Air Stations in San Francisco, Detroit, and Savannah, Georgia; at the Helicopter Interdiction Tactical Squadron in Jacksonville,

Florida; and at coast guard headquarters. In the army, he commanded troops in the Second Infantry Division, the 101st Airborne Division, and the 337th Infantry Regiment (active component to reserve component). He has logged four thousand hours flying military helicopters as an instructor pilot and maintenance test pilot.

Michael Brown is a visiting scholar at the Hoover Institution of Stanford University and a partner at Shield Capital. He serves on the advisory boards of the Center for a New American Security and the US Innovative Technology Fund. Brown previously served as the director of the Defense Innovation Unit (DIU) at the US Department of Defense (2018–22). From 2016 to 2018, he was a White House Presidential Innovation Fellow. Prior to civil service, Brown was the CEO of Symantec Corporation (2014–16), the former chairman and CEO of Quantum Corporation (1995–2003), and the chairman of EqualLogic (2003–8). He received his BA degree in economics from Harvard and his MBA from Stanford University.

David S. C. Chu led the Institute for Defense Analyses as CEO for over ten years, retiring in 2020. His federal career included serving as under secretary of defense for personnel and readiness (2001–9); as director, then assistant secretary of defense, for program analysis and evaluation (1981–93); and as assistant director for national security and international affairs of the Congressional Budget Office (1978–81). Chu served a tour of duty with the US Army and worked for the RAND Corporation, where his responsibilities included directing the Arroyo Center and RAND's Washington, DC, office. He earned his PhD in economics from Yale University.

James M. Cunningham is the coauthor, with David H. McCormick, of *Superpower in Peril: A Battle Plan to Renew America* (Center Street, 2023). He previously served as senior policy advisor to McCormick on his US Senate campaign in Pennsylvania and as an associate in the office of the CEO at Bridgewater Associates. Before that, he was a national security analyst at the Hoover Institution and the American Enterprise Institute.

Commander Bart D'Angelo is a naval intelligence officer with over twenty-one years of active service. D'Angelo completed his undergraduate degree in maritime operations at the US Merchant Marine Academy in Kings Point,

New York, and holds master's degrees from the Naval Postgraduate School and the Naval War College. He has had many varied assignments in the navy, including service aboard two aircraft carriers and three tours of duty in Japan. He has also worked on the staffs of multiple admirals and generals, including the commanders of Task Force 72, Task Force 74, the Seventh Fleet, the Pacific Fleet, and US Northern Command.

Mackenzie Eaglen is a senior fellow at the American Enterprise Institute (AEI), where she works on defense strategy, defense budgets, and military readiness. She is also a regular guest lecturer at universities, a member of the US Army Science Board, and a member of the steering committee of the Leadership Council for Women in National Security. Before joining AEI, Eaglen worked on defense issues in the US House of Representatives, in the US Senate, and at the Pentagon in the Office of the Secretary of Defense and on the Joint Staff.

Eric Fanning is president and CEO of the Aerospace Industries Association, which Fanning joined after serving as the twenty-second secretary of the army, providing leadership and oversight of our nation's largest military service. He previously served as chief of staff to the secretary of defense, as acting secretary and under secretary of the air force, and as deputy under secretary/deputy chief management officer of the navy. He is the only person to hold senior appointments in all three military departments and the Office of the Secretary of Defense. Over more than thirty years of service, Fanning worked on the staff of the House Armed Services Committee, was senior vice president of strategic development for Business Executives for National Security, was deputy director of the Commission on the Prevention of Weapons of Mass Destruction Proliferation and Terrorism, and was associate director of political affairs at the White House.

Joseph H. Felter is a research fellow at the Hoover Institution and director of Stanford University's Gordian Knot Center for National Security Innovation. He has been published widely in top peer-reviewed academic journals and is the coauthor, with Eli Berman and Jacob N. Shapiro, of *Small Wars, Big Data: The Information Revolution in Modern Conflict* (Princeton University Press, 2018). From 2017 to 2019, Felter served as US deputy assistant secretary of defense for South and Southeast Asia. He is a former US Army Special

Forces officer with multiple combat tours and served as director of West Point's Combating Terrorism Center. He received a BS from the US Military Academy, an MPA from Harvard Kennedy School, and a PhD from Stanford.

Michèle Flournoy is cofounder and managing partner of WestExec Advisors, and cofounder, former CEO, and currently chair of Center for a New American Security (CNAS). Flournoy served as the under secretary of defense for policy from 2009 to 2012. She was the principal advisor to the secretary of defense in the formulation of national security and defense policy, oversight of military plans and operations, and National Security Council deliberations. Flournoy serves on numerous boards, including CNAS, Booz Allen Hamilton, Astra, Amida Technology Solutions, CARE, America's Frontier Fund, and the Special Competitive Studies Project.

Vishaal "V8" Hariprasad is the cofounder and CEO of Resilience, a Silicon Valley–based cyber risk management start-up. After graduating from the US Air Force Academy with a BA in mathematics, Hariprasad served as a cyber effects operations officer for the air force, with multiple assignments overseas as well as with the National Security Agency. He then went on to cofound Morta Security (acquired by Palo Alto Networks), serve as the architect for threat intelligence at Palo Alto Networks' Unit 42, and become a partner at the Pentagon's Defense Innovation Unit Experimental (DIUx) in Mountain View, California. Hariprasad is a major in the US Air Force Reserve and is currently the reserve director of operations for the active-duty 90th Cyber Operations Squadron in San Antonio, Texas, where he focuses on tool development for cyber operations.

Lieutenant Colonel James M. Harrington, representing the US Air Force, is a national security affairs fellow for the academic year 2022–23 at the Hoover Institution. Harrington is a cyberspace officer with a background in deployed communications, network engineering, information operations, cyberspace operations, and joint planning. He commanded two separate communications squadrons and served in US Central Command, NATO's Strategic Operational Headquarters, and on the Air Staff. He has deployed several times, supporting various named operations around the world. Most recently, he served as the cyber protection branch chief within the Office of the Air Force Chief Information Security Officer at the Pentagon. Harrington graduated from the US Air Force Academy with a bachelor of science in computer science. He also holds a master of science in management information systems from the University of Illinois, Springfield.

Tim Kane is president of the American Lyceum and a visiting fellow at the Hoover Institution. Before earning a PhD in economics, Kane cofounded two software firms and served as an intelligence officer in the US Air Force, with two tours of duty overseas. His latest book is *The Immigrant Superpower* (Oxford University Press, 2022). Kane also authored *Total Volunteer Force: Lessons from the US Military on Leadership Culture and Talent Management* (Hoover Institution Press, 2017), *Balance: The Economics of Great Powers from Ancient Rome to Modern America* (with Glenn Hubbard; Simon & Schuster, 2013), and *Bleeding Talent: How the US Military Mismanages Great Leaders and Why It's Time for a Revolution* (Palgrave Macmillan, 2012).

Christopher Kirchhoff, PhD, is an expert in emerging technology. He founded the Pentagon's Silicon Valley office, Defense Innovation Unit X, and helped scale $1 billion in philanthropic programs at Schmidt Futures. Under the Obama administration, he was director for strategic planning at the National Security Council and the senior civilian advisor to the chair of the Joint Chiefs of Staff. Kirchhoff has penned four landmark reports: the Obama administration's official lessons learned report from the US response to the Ebola crisis (2016); the White House's "Big Data: Seizing Opportunities, Preserving Values" (2014); the official US history of the Iraq reconstruction experience *Hard Lessons* (2009); and the space shuttle *Columbia* accident investigation report (2003).

Ellen Lord spent August 2017 until January 2021 as under secretary of defense for acquisition and sustainment, reporting to the secretary of defense with oversight of a $400 billion annual budget. Previously, she spent thirty-three years at Textron, a global multiple industry corporation, finishing as CEO of Textron Systems. During her time at DoD, her team rewrote the Pentagon's acquisition policy, with a focus on speed and simplicity while adding procedures for cybersecurity, intellectual property, and software development. Lord now serves on public, private, and nonprofit boards, as well as advising companies in the aerospace and defense sector.

Oriana Skylar Mastro, PhD, is a center fellow at the Freeman Spogli Institute for International Studies and courtesy assistant professor of political science at Stanford University, where her research focuses on Chinese military and security policy, Asia-Pacific security issues, war termination, and coercive diplomacy. She was previously an assistant professor of security studies at Georgetown University. She is also a nonresident senior fellow at the American Enterprise Institute and continues to serve in the US Air Force Reserve, for which she works as a strategic planner at US Indo-Pacific Command.

Secretary Jim Mattis was raised in southeastern Washington and graduated from Central Washington State College. He served over forty years in the US Marine Corps as an infantry officer, plus duty in the Office of the Secretary of Defense, as NATO supreme allied commander and as commander of US Central Command, formed of 250,000 US and allied troops in combat across the Middle East and South Asia. Retiring in 2013, he was named a Davies Family Distinguished Fellow at Stanford University's Hoover Institution, a position to which he returned after serving as the twenty-sixth secretary of defense (January 2017–December 2018).

Elaine McCusker is a senior executive with over thirty years of national security expertise developed through complex policy, strategy, budget, and leadership positions in the private sector, academic community, and government service, and on Capitol Hill. As acting under secretary of defense (comptroller), McCusker oversaw the development, justification, and execution of an average annual $700 billion defense budget supporting the National Defense Strategy. She drove the Pentagon to harness the power of its financial, contracting, personnel, and logistics data through an advancing analytics capability. She led complex engagement strategies with multiple stakeholders, including the US Congress, to explain difficult, sometimes contentious, issues.

Michael McFaul is the director and senior fellow at the Freeman Spogli Institute for International Studies and the Peter and Helen Bing Senior Fellow at the Hoover Institution at Stanford University. He served for five years in the Obama administration as special assistant to the president and senior director for Russian and Eurasian affairs at the White House National Security Council (2009–12), then as US ambassador to the Russian Federation (2012–14). He has authored several books, including the *New York Times* bestseller *From Cold War to Hot Peace: An American Ambassador in Putin's Russia* (Penguin Books Limited, 2018). He is also an analyst for NBC News and a contributing columnist to the *Washington Post*.

H.R. McMaster is the Fouad and Michelle Ajami Senior Fellow at the Hoover Institution, Stanford University, and a distinguished university fellow at Arizona State University. He is also the Bernard and Susan Liautaud Fellow at the Freeman Spogli Institute and lecturer at Stanford University's Graduate School of Business. Upon graduation from the US Military Academy in 1984, McMaster served as a commissioned officer in the US Army for thirty-four years. He retired as a lieutenant general in June 2018 after serving as the twenty-fifth assistant to the president for national security affairs. He holds a PhD in military history from the University of North Carolina at Chapel Hill. At the Hoover Institution, McMaster is the host of *Battlegrounds: International Perspectives on Crucial Challenges to Security and Prosperity* and is a regular on *GoodFellows*.

Casey "Waldo" Miller has been researching, experimenting with, and executing software development teaming and delivery methodologies for seventeen years. He is currently in the US Air Force and serves as the commander of the 90th Cyberspace Operations Squadron, where he leads more than 250 military, civilian, and contractor cyber professionals in developing exploits and malware to enable military objectives across warfighting domains. He entered the air force through the ROTC program at Miami University and began his career in acquisitions before crossflowing to cyberspace operations, and he has held key positions, from squadron to major command levels. He is married to the former Lisa Ingle of Beavercreek, Ohio, and has six sons.

Admiral Mike Mullen is president of MGM Consulting, which provides counsel to global clients on issues related to geopolitical developments, national security interests, and strategic leadership. He served as the twenty-eighth chief of naval operations from 2005 to 2007 and as the seventeenth chair of the US Joint Chiefs of Staff for presidents Bush and Obama from 2007 to 2011. He led the military during a critical time of change and transition. Admiral Mullen advanced the rapid fielding of innovative technologies, championed emerging and enduring global partnerships, and promoted new methods for countering terrorism. He spearheaded the elimination of the "Don't Ask, Don't Tell" policy, ushering in the open service of gay and lesbian men and women for the first time in US military history.

David L. Norquist is the president and CEO of the National Defense Industrial Association. Norquist has over thirty years of public- and private-sector experience in national security and federal financial management. He has served in three Senate-confirmed positions: as chief financial officer (CFO) of the Department of Homeland Security, as under secretary of defense comptroller/CFO, and most recently as the thirty-fourth deputy secretary of defense.

Michael O'Hanlon is senior fellow, director of research, and Phil Knight Chair in Defense and Strategy in the Foreign Policy program at the Brookings Institution, where he also directs the Strobe Talbott Center on Security, Strategy and Technology. He is also a member of the Defense Policy Board and adjunct professor at Georgetown and Columbia universities. Previously, he worked in the National Security Division at the Congressional Budget Office (1989–94). His latest book is *Military History for the Modern Strategist: America's Major Wars since 1861* (Brookings Institution Press, 2023). His degrees are in the physical sciences and from the School of Public and International Affairs at Princeton; earlier he worked on a dairy farm in upstate New York and was a Peace Corps volunteer in the Democratic Republic of the Congo.

Secretary Leon Panetta has had a fifty-year career in public service, from the US Army to the highest levels of government, including as the twenty-third secretary of defense. As director of the CIA, he successfully led the operation that brought Osama bin Laden to justice. In 1969–70, as director of the Office for Civil Rights, he was responsible for enforcing equal education laws. Panetta represented his California district in US Congress for sixteen years (1977–93) and created the Monterey Bay National Marine Sanctuary. Under President Clinton, he was named director of the Office of Management and Budget (1993–94) and chief of staff (1994–96). In 1997, Panetta established the Panetta Institute for Public Policy, a nonpartisan, nonprofit study center that seeks to inspire men and women to lives of public service. He chronicled his life in public service in his best-selling memoir *Worthy Fights* (Penguin Press, 2014).

John N. Rader is a visiting fellow at the Hoover Institution and the chief operating officer at Affinity Partners Global LLC. Rader previously served at the highest levels of the legislative and executive branches of both state and federal government, most recently as chief of staff to US senator Bill Hagerty. In the White House, Rader served on the National Security Council as a special assistant to the president and senior policy advisor to the assistant to the president for national security affairs, General H.R. McMaster; and as deputy assistant to the president and advisor for policy and strategy for senior advisor to the president Jared Kushner.

Secretary Condoleezza Rice is the Tad and Dianne Taube Director of the Hoover Institution and the Thomas and Barbara Stephenson Senior Fellow on Public Policy. In addition, she is a founding partner of Rice, Hadley, Gates & Manuel LLC, an international strategic consulting firm. From January 2005 to January 2009, Rice served as the sixty-sixth secretary of state for the United States. Rice previously served as President George W. Bush's national security advisor from January 2001 to January 2005. Rice served as Stanford University's provost from 1993 to 1999. Rice has been on the Stanford faculty since 1981 and has won two of the university's highest teaching honors.

Admiral Gary Roughead is a graduate of the US Naval Academy whose career culminated in serving as the US Navy chief of naval operations and a member of the US Joint Chiefs of Staff. He previously held six operational commands and is one of only two officers in the navy's history to have commanded both the Atlantic and Pacific fleets. Admiral Roughead is the Robert and Marion Oster Distinguished Military Fellow at the Hoover Institution at Stanford University and serves on several corporate, university, and financial-sector boards.

Nadia Schadlow, PhD, is a visiting fellow at the Hoover Institution and a senior fellow at the Hudson Institute. Previously, she served as a deputy national security advisor for strategy. Her book *War and the Art of Governance: Consolidating Combat Success into Political Victory* (Georgetown University Press, 2017) explored the challenges of undertaking postconflict operations and identified optimal practices. She writes frequently on defense, national security, and technology-related issues. Schadlow received a BA from Cornell University and an MA and PhD from the Johns Hopkins School of Advanced International Studies.

Jacquelyn Schneider, PhD, is a Hoover Fellow at the Hoover Institution and an affiliate with Stanford's Center for International Security and Cooperation. She was previously a senior policy advisor to the Cyberspace Solarium Commission and had previous positions at the Center for a New American Security and the RAND Corporation. Before beginning her academic career, she spent six years as an air force officer in South Korea and Japan and is currently a reservist assigned to US Space Systems Command. She has a BA from Columbia University, an MA from Arizona State University, and a PhD from George Washington University.

Raj Shah is the managing partner of Shield Capital, a venture capital firm focused on technologies at the nexus of the commercial and defense markets. He is also the chairman of Resilience, a start-up powering new approaches to cyber insurance. Previously he ran the Pentagon's Defense Innovation Unit Experimental (DIUx), reporting to the secretary of defense. Shah led DIUx in its efforts to strengthen US armed forces through contractual and cultural bridges between Silicon Valley and the Pentagon. Shah serves as a reserve F-16 pilot in the Air National Guard and has completed multiple combat deployments. He holds an AB from Princeton University and an MBA from the Wharton School at the University of Pennsylvania. He is a member of the Council on Foreign Relations and is an adjunct professor at Stanford University.

Kiran Sridhar is the head of strategic initiatives for Resilience, which provides cyber insurance and cyber risk management solutions to enterprises. He also is on the investment team of Shield Capital, which backs companies that solve both commercial and national security problem sets, and the chair of Waste No Food, a nonprofit that serves the food insecure. He received a BA in economics from Stanford University; a master's in global affairs from Tsinghua University, where he was a Schwarzman Scholar; and a master's in operations management from the University of Cambridge, where he was a Gates Cambridge Scholar.

Mac Thornberry served US Congress for twenty-six years and continues to work at the intersection of technology and national security. He serves various companies and nonprofit organizations as a board member and advisor. A former chair of the House Armed Services Committee, he was also a member of the House Intelligence Committee for more than a decade. Prior to his election to Congress, Thornberry served in the State Department during the Reagan administration and as staff on Capitol Hill, and practiced law. He graduated from Texas Tech University and received a law degree from the University of Texas.

Mark R. Wilson is a professor of history at the University of North Carolina–Charlotte. He is the author of the books *The Business of Civil War* (Johns Hopkins University Press, 2006) and *Destructive Creation: American Business and the Winning of World War II* (University of Pennsylvania Press, 2016). In 2022–24 he holds an Andrew Carnegie Fellowship from the Carnegie Corporation of New York, which is supporting his current work on a history of the US military-industrial complex since 1950.

Roger Zakheim serves as the Washington director of the Ronald Reagan Presidential Foundation and Institute. He previously practiced law at Covington & Burling LLP, where he led the firm's Public Policy and Government Affairs practice group. His government experience includes serving as general counsel and deputy staff director for the US House Armed Services Committee and deputy assistant secretary of defense for coalition affairs. Zakheim is on the board of directors for both the United States Institute of Peace and Marvell Government Solutions. He also serves on the Congressional Commission on the National Defense Strategy of the United States.

Amy Zegart is the Morris Arnold and Nona Jean Cox Senior Fellow at the Hoover Institution and professor of political science (by courtesy) at Stanford University. She is also a senior fellow at Stanford's Freeman Spogli Institute for International Studies, chair of Stanford's Artificial Intelligence and International Security Steering Committee, and a contributing writer at *The Atlantic*. She is an internationally recognized expert in US intelligence, emerging technologies, and global political risk management. Zegart is the author of five books, including the best-selling *Spies, Lies, and Algorithms: The History and Future of American Intelligence* (Princeton University Press, 2022). She has served on the National Security Council staff and as a presidential campaign foreign policy advisor. She received an AB in East Asian studies from Harvard and a PhD in political science from Stanford. She serves on the board of directors of the Council on Foreign Relations.

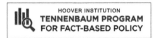

About the Tennenbaum Program for Fact-Based Policy

The Tennenbaum Program for Fact-Based Policy is a Hoover Institution initiative aimed at improving the quality of information that is shaping the nation's highly debated policy questions, through collecting and analyzing data and providing credible research in readable, nontechnical essays and other educational formats.

The unique program convenes scholars and experts with diverse policy perspectives to produce data-driven analyses intended to counter preconceived ideas and biases and to expose the strengths and weaknesses of untested interpretations, assumptions, and arguments. This work also provides bases for out-of-the-box thinking on and original solutions to today's most significant policy challenges.

Public opinion polling on subjects Americans want to know more about helped inform the selection of initial projects: national security and the defense budget; US deficits and debt and their effects on inflation, economic growth, and intergenerational equity; the integrity of democratic elections in America; and energy and environmental challenges.

The program is made possible by a generous endowment from Suzanne (Stanford '75) and Michael E. Tennenbaum and organized by Michael J. Boskin, Wohlford Family Senior Fellow at the Hoover Institution and Tully M. Friedman Professor of Economics at Stanford University.

Index

Note: The letter f following a page number denotes a figure; the letter t denotes a table.